Libraries and Information Services in the United Kingdom and the Republic of Ireland 2005–2006

Libraries and Information Services in the United Kingdom and the Republic of Ireland 2005–2006

ſ facet publishing

© CILIP: the Chartered Institute of Library and Information Professionals 2005

Published by Facet Publishing
7 Ridgmount Street
London
WC1E 7AE

Facet Publishing (formerly Library Association Publishing) is wholly owned by CILIP: the Chartered Institute of Library and Information Professionals.

First published as *Libraries in the United Kingdom and the Republic of Ireland* by The Library Association, 1960 and thereafter annually.

Twenty-ninth edition published as *Libraries and Information Services in the United Kingdom and the Republic of Ireland* by Facet Publishing, 2002.
This thirty-second edition 2005

ISBN 1-85604-532-3
ISSN 1741-7120 (*Libraries in the United Kingdom and the Republic of Ireland* 1369-9687)

Whilst every effort has been made to ensure accuracy, the publishers cannot be held responsible for any errors or omissions.

This thirty-second edition has been compiled by Lin Franklin and June York.

Typeset in 8/10pt Humanist 521 by Facet Publishing.
Printed and bound in Great Britain by MPG Books Ltd, Bodmin, Cornwall.

CONTENTS

CONTENTS

How this book is organized

Libraries and Information Services in the United Kingdom and the Republic of Ireland is published annually, and is a listing of organizations falling into the four categories below.

1 Public library authorities

- All public library authorities in the UK and the Republic of Ireland, arranged under home countries
  - Public Libraries in England, Northern Ireland, Scotland, Wales and Crown Dependencies
  - Public Libraries in the Republic of Ireland

  It is clearly impossible to list here all branch libraries, mobile bases and so on, so each entry includes headquarters/central library details, together with major branches and area/regional/group libraries, as supplied by each individual library. Libraries in this section are arranged by name of authority.
- Children's, Youth and Schools Library Services

  This section gives you more specific information about what services for children and young people are available within the public library authorities, and how you can contact them.

A listing of the nine Government regions in England, indicating which public library authorities fall in their areas, is given on page 501.

2 Academic libraries (arranged by name of institution)

- University libraries in the UK and the Republic of Ireland, together with major department and site/campus libraries
- College libraries at the universities of Oxford, Cambridge and London

  Please note: potential users of the Oxford and Cambridge libraries should be aware that their use is restricted to members of the college, and to bona fide scholars on application to the Librarian; any additional information about their use is given with each entry.
- Scottish central institutions
- The university-equivalent colleges in the Republic of Ireland
- Other degree-awarding institutions in the UK

  All colleges of higher education funded by HEFCE, SHEFC and HEFCW are included.

3 Selected government, national and special libraries in the UK and the Republic of Ireland

■ Entries for government departments include at least the main library for the department, together with any specialist libraries. For example, the entry for the Health and Safety Executive includes the Nuclear Safety Division.

■ Special libraries are included if they are one of the main libraries or organizations in their subject field. For example, the British Architectural Library at the Royal Institute of British Architects is included for architecture, the Institution of Civil Engineers for civil engineering.

Many of the libraries in this section require a prior appointment to be made before visiting.

4 Schools and departments of information and library studies

■ Each academic institution offering courses in information and library studies, with full contact details of the departments concerned.

5 Key library agencies and other relevant organizations

■ This section lists the **key national and regional agencies, professional organizations and other relevant bodies**. It provides contact details for each body together with a short description of its function within the library profession.

6 Index

■ Organizations are fully indexed by name and place.

Updating Libraries and Information Services in the UK

The directory is compiled by mailing questionnaires or entries for updating to libraries already listed in this book, and to others that have been suggested for inclusion. We would like to thank all the libraries for taking the time to reply to yet another mailing. With their assistance we received a 100% return rate. This means that every entry has been approved by the institution concerned.

We are dependent upon libraries to keep us informed of changes throughout the year. In this way we shall be able to ensure that our mailing label service is as current as possible. Libraries will, of course, be contacted afresh for the preparation of the next edition.

Mailing list

The directory is also available to rent in a variety of formats including .csv files via e-mail, on disk/CD or as laser-quality adhesive labels. Visit the Facet Publishing website at www.facetpublishing. co.uk for further information.

Full set
Named Chief Librarian	ISBN 1 85604 026 7
Acquisitions Librarian	ISBN 1 85604 198 0

Public libraries (main headquarters)
Named Chief Librarian	ISBN 0 85365 587 1
Acquisitions Librarian	ISBN 1 85604 199 9

Public libraries (main headquarters and branches)
Named Chief Librarian	ISBN 1 85604 025 9

Academic and special libraries
Named Chief Librarian	ISBN 0 85365 959 1
Acquisitions Librarian	ISBN 1 85604 201 4

Children's, youth and schools library services
Named Children's/Schools Officer	ISBN 1 85604 247 2

Key library agencies
Named Chief Officer	ISBN 1 85604 447 5

Please help us to improve this directory

Any comments about additions or other changes to *Libraries and Information Services in the United Kingdom and the Republic of Ireland* will be welcomed. Please address them to:

The Editor, Libraries and Information Services in the UK, Facet Publishing, 7 Ridgmount Street, London WC1E 7AE

Tel: 020 7255 0590
e-mail: info@facetpublishing.co.uk

Public Libraries in the United Kingdom, the Channel Islands and the Isle of Man

England
Northern Ireland
Scotland
Wales
Crown Dependencies

BARKING AND DAGENHAM

Authority: London Borough of Barking and Dagenham
HQ Central Library, Barking, Essex IG11 8DQ
☎020 8724 1312 (enquiries); 020 8724 1322 (administration)
Fax 020 8724 1316
e-mail: libraries@lbbd.gov.uk
url: www.lbbd.gov.uk/4-libraries/libraries-menu.html
Head of Library Services Trevor Brown MCLIP (e-mail: trevor.brown@lbbd.gov.uk)
Principal Librarian (Learning & Development) Mrs Susan Leighton MA MCLIP (e-mail: susan.leighton@lbbd.gov.uk)
Principal Librarian (Information & Resources) Tony Clifford BA MCLIP (e-mail: tony.clifford@lbbd.gov.uk)
Principal Librarian (Customer & Professional Services) Vacant
Principal Librarian (Quality & Standards) David Bailey BSc MCLIP (e-mail: david.bailey@lbbd.gov.uk)

Community libraries

▶ Fanshawe Library, Fanshawe Community Centre, Barnmead Road, Dagenham, Essex RM9 5DX
☎020 8270 4244
▶ Marks Gate Library, Rose Lane, Chadwell Heath, Essex RM6 5NJ
☎020 8270 4165
▶ Markyate Library, Markyate Road, Dagenham, Essex RM8 2LD
☎020 8270 4137
▶ Rectory Library, Rectory Road, Dagenham, Dagenham, Essex RM9 5DX
☎020 8270 6233
▶ Robert Jeyes Library, High Road, Chadwell Heath, Essex RM6 6AS
☎020 8270 4305
▶ Rush Green Library, Dagenham Road, Rush Green, Essex RM7 0TL
☎020 8270 4304
▶ Thames View Library, Bastable Avenue, Barking, Essex IG11 0LG
☎020 8270 4164
▶ Valence Library, Becontree Avenue, Dagenham, Essex RM8 3HS
☎020 8270 6864
▶ Wantz Library, Rainham Road North, Dagenham, Essex RM10 7DX
☎020 8270 4169
▶ Woodward Library, Woodward Road, Dagenham, Essex RM9 4SP
☎020 8270 4166

BARNET

Authority: London Borough of Barnet
HQ Cultural Services, Building 4, North London Business Park, Oakleigh Road South, London N11 1NP
☎020 8359 7770
Fax 0870 889 6804
url: www.barnet.gov.uk/cultural_services/index.php3

Head of Cultural Services Ms Pam Usher BA(Hons) DMS MCLIP (e-mail: pam.usher@barnet.gov.uk)
Library Services Manager/Deputy Head of Cultural Services Ms Tricia Little BA MCLIP (e-mail: tricia.little@barnet.gov.uk)
Business Performance and Library Resources Manager Ms Mary Ross BA(Hons) MCLIP (e-mail: mary.ross@barnet.gov.uk)
E-services Manager Richard Nurse BA(Hons) MA MCLIP (e-mail: richard.nurse@barnet.gov.uk)

Area libraries
▶ Chipping Barnet Library, 3 Stapylton Road, Barnet, Herts EN5 4QT
  ☎020 8359 4040
  e-mail: chipping.barnet.library@barnet.gov.uk
  Area Manager Ms Veronica Padwick BA MCLIP (e-mail: veronica.padwick@barnet.gov.uk)
▶ Hendon Library, The Burroughs, London NW4 4BQ
  ☎020 8359 2628
  e-mail: hendon.library@barnet.gov.uk
  Area Manager Mrs Gill Harvey MCLIP (e-mail: gill.harvey@barnet.gov.uk)

BARNSLEY

Authority: Barnsley Metropolitan Borough Council
HQ Central Library, Shambles Street, Barnsley S70 2JF
☎(01226) 773911/12/30 (enquiries), (01226) 773913 (administration)
Fax (01226) 773955
e-mail: barnsleylibraryenquiries@barnsley.gov.uk
url: www.barnsley.gov.uk/service/libraries/index.asp
Chief Libraries Officer Steven Bashforth BA MCLIP DMS

Central/largest library
Central Library, Shambles Street, Barnsley, Barnsley, South Yorks S70 2JF
☎(01226) 773940 (enquiries), (01226) 773927 (administration)
Fax (01226) 773955
e-mail: barnsleylibraryenquiries@barnsley.gov.uk
Lending Services Officer Mrs Kathryn Green BA MCLIP

Group headquarters
▶ Goldthorpe Branch Library, Barnsley Road, Goldthorpe, Rotherham, South Yorks S63 9NE
  ☎(01709) 893278
  Fax (01709) 893278
  Dearne Group Librarian John Coldwell BA MCLIP
▶ Penistone Branch Library, High Street, Penistone, Sheffield S36 6BR
  ☎(01226) 762313
  Penistone Group Librarian Ms Jill Craven MCLIP
▶ Priory Information & Resource Centre, Pontefract Road, Lundwood, Barnsley, South Yorks S71 5PN
  ☎(01226) 770616/7

Fax (01226) 771425
Library and Information Officer, Priory Ms Clara Crehan MSc BInf
▶ Royston Branch Library, Midland Road, Royston, Barnsley, South Yorks S71 4QP
☎(01226) 722870
Royston Group Librarian Roger Wilson BSc(Econ) MCLIP

BATH AND NORTH EAST SOMERSET

Authority: Bath and North East Somerset Council
HQ HQ Customer Service, Libraries and Information, PO Box 3403, Bath BA1 2ZG
☎(01225) 396424
url: www.bathnes.gov.uk/bathnes
Head of Customer Services, Libraries and Information Mrs Julia Fieldhouse
Customer Services Operational Mrs June Brassington MCLIP (e-mail:
june_brassington@bathnes.gov.uk)

Central/largest library
Bath Central Library, The Podium, Northgate Street, Bath BA1 5AN
☎(01225) 787400 (enquiries), (01225) 396082 (administration)
Fax (01225) 787426
e-mail: bath_library@bathnes.gov.uk
Libraries Development Manager Ms Julia Burton BLib MCLIP (01225 396078; e-mail:
julia_burton@bathnes.gov.uk)
Local Area Managers Mrs Victoria Flowers, Peter Moth

Group libraries
▶ Keynsham Library, The Centre, Keynsham, Bristol BS31 1ED
☎(01225) 394191
Fax (01225) 394195
e-mail: keynsham_library@bathnes.gov.uk
Local Area Manager Ms Susan Holmes
▶ Midsomer Norton Library, 119 High Street, Midsomer Norton, Bath BA3 2DA
☎(01761) 412024
Fax (01761) 417838
e-mail: midsomernorton_library@bathnes.gov.uk
Local Area Manager Ms Susan Holmes

BEDFORDSHIRE

Authority: Bedfordshire County Council
HQ Libraries, County Hall, Cauldwell Street, Bedford MK42 9AP
☎(01234) 228752
Fax (01234) 213006
url: www.bedfordshire.gov.uk
Head of Libraries Barry S George MCLIP (01234 228752; e-mail:
barry.george@bedscc.gov.uk)
Library Resources Manager Andy Baker MCLIP (01234 228785)
Library Services Manager Ms Jenny Poad BA DMS MCLIP (01234 350931)

Central/largest library

Bedford Central Library, Harpur Street, Bedford MK40 1PG
☎(01234) 350931 (enquiries/administration)
Fax (01234) 342163
e-mail: bedford-library@bedfordshire.gov.uk
Central Library Manager Ms Joanne Smith

Gateway libraries

▶ Dunstable Library, Vernon Place, Dunstable, Beds LU5 4HA
☎(01582) 608441
Fax (01582) 471290
e-mail: dunstable-library@bedfordshire.gov.uk
Library Manager Ms Ruth Lambert
▶ Leighton Buzzard Library, Lake Street, Leighton Buzzard, Beds LU7 1RX
☎(01525) 371788
Fax (01525) 815368
e-mail: lbuzzard-library@bedfordshire.gov.uk
Library Manager Ms Hazel Kerr

Area libraries

▶ Biggleswade Library, Chestnut Avenue, Biggleswade, Beds SG18 0LL
☎(01767) 312324
Fax (01767) 601802
e-mail: biggleswade-library@bedfordshire.gov.uk
Library Manager Ms Sue Townsend
▶ Flitwick Library, Conniston Road, Flitwick, Beds MK45 1QJ
☎(01525) 715268
Fax (01525) 713897
e-mail: flitwick-library@bedfordshire.gov.uk
Library Manager John Booth
▶ Shefford Library, High Street, Shefford, Beds SG17 5DD
☎(01462) 639070
Fax (01462) 639071
e-mail: shefford-library@bedfordshire.gov.uk
Library Manager Ms Carol Forse

Neighbourhood libraries

▶ Houghton Regis Library, Bedford Square, Houghton Regis, Beds LU5 5ES
☎(01582) 865473
Fax (01582) 868466
e-mail: houghton-regis-library@bedfordshire.gov.uk
Library Manager Ms Sue Bishop
▶ Kempston Library, Halsey Road, Kempston, Beds MK42 8AU
☎(01234) 853092
Fax (01234) 841476
e-mail: kempston-library@bedfordshire.gov.uk
Library Manager Ms Ros Willis

▶ Putnoe Library, Library Walk, Putnoe, Bedford MK41 8HQ
☎(01234) 353422
Fax (01234) 272833
e-mail: putnoe-library@bedfordshire.gov.uk
Library Manager Ms Coral Clarke

BEXLEY

Authority: London Borough of Bexley
HQ Directorate of Law and Administration, Libraries and Community Information, Ground
Floor, Footscray Offices, Maidstone Road, Sidcup, Kent DA14 5HS
☎020 8309 4100
Fax 020 8309 4142
url: www.bexley.gov.uk
Head of Libraries and Community Information F V Johnson LLB DMS MCLIP MILAM
(020 8309 4131; e-mail: fred.johnson@bexley.gov.uk)
Library Development Manager H C M Paton BA DipLib MCLIP (020 8309 4134; e-mail:
hugh.paton@bexley.gov.uk)
Technical Services Librarian Mrs J A Peacock MCLIP (020 8309 4175)
Principal Librarian Mrs Lynn Sawbridge BA MCLIP (020 8309 4155; e-mail:
lynn.sawbridge@bexley.gov.uk)
Principal Librarian Geoff Boulton BA MCLIP (020 8309 4135; e-mail:
geoff.boulton@bexley.gov.uk)

Central/largest library

Central Library, Townley Road, Bexleyheath, Kent DA6 7HJ
☎020 8301 1066 (reception), 020 8301 5151 (information line)
Fax 020 8303 7872

BIRMINGHAM

Authority: Birmingham City Council
HQ Learning and Culture Directorate, Council House Extension, Margaret Street,
Birmingham B3 3BU
☎0121 303 4511 (enquiries), 0121 303 2454 management
Fax 0121 303 4458 (enquiries), 0121 233 9702 (management)
e-mail: libraries@birmingham.gov.uk
url: www.birmingham.gov.uk
Strategic Director, Learning and Culture Tony Howell
Assistant Director, Community Learning and Libraries John Dolan OBE BA DipLib
MCLIP (e-mail: john.dolan@birmingham.gov.uk)
Head of Community Library Strategy Geoff Mills MSc BA DipLib MCLIP (e-mail:
geoff.mills@birmingham.gov.uk)
Head of Performance and Planning Mrs Linda Butler BA MCLIP (e-mail:
linda.butler@birmingham.gov.uk)
Head of Central Library Brian Gambles (e-mail: brian.gambles@birmingham.gov.uk)

BLACKBURN WITH DARWEN

Authority: Blackburn with Darwen Borough Council
HQ Central Library, Town Hall Street, Blackburn, Lancashire BB2 1AG
☎(01254) 661221 (enquiries), 01254 587902 (administration)
Fax (01254) 690539
url: http://library.blackburnworld.com
Head of Library and Information Services Mrs Susan Law MCLIP (01254 587906;
e-mail: susan.law@blackburn.gov.uk)
Information and Development Manager Ian Sutton MCLIP (01254 587901; e-mail:
ian.sutton@blackburn.gov.uk)
Operations Manager Mrs Kath Sutton MCLIP (01254 587907; e-mail:
kath.sutton@blackburn.gov.uk)
Reader Development and Resources Manager Miss Jean Gabbatt BLib MCLIP (01254
587937; e-mail: jean.gabbatt@blackburn.gov.uk)
Literacy Development Manager Mrs Geraldine Wilson MCLIP (01254 587236; e-mail:
geraldine.wilson@blackburn.gov.uk)
Performance and Quality Manager Miss Elizabeth Townson MCLIP (01254 587954;
e-mail: elizabeth.townson@blackburn.gov.uk)
Projects and Development Officer Vacant
Central Library Manager Miss Adele Karwat MCLIP (01254 587941; e-mail:
adele.karwat@blackburn.gov.uk)

BLACKPOOL

Authority: Blackpool Borough Council
HQ Leisure, Culture and Community Learning, Progress House, Clifton Road, Blackpool,
Lancashire FY4 4US
☎(01253) 478080 (enquiries), 01253 478105 (administration)
Fax (01253) 478071
url: www.blackpool.gov.uk
Assistant Director, Lifelong Learning and Cultural Services Mrs P Hansell MBA BA
MCLIP (e-mail: pat.hansell@blackpool.gov.uk)
Head of Libraries Mrs A Ellis BA MCLIP DMS (e-mail: anne.ellis@blackpool.gov.uk)
Principal Arts Officer John Sculley BA(Hons) (e-mail: john.sculley@blackpool.gov.uk)

Central/largest library
Central Library, Queen Street, Blackpool, Lancashire FY1 1PX
☎(01253) 478080
Fax (01253) 478082

BOLTON

Authority: Bolton Metropolitan Borough Council
HQ Central Library, Le Mans Crescent, Bolton, Lancashire BL1 1SE
☎(01204) 332169 (administration), (01204) 333173 (enquiries)
Fax (01204) 332225
e-mail: central.library@bolton.gov.uk

Assistant Director, Heritage, Information and Arts Mrs Stephanie Crossley BA(Hons) PGDipLIS MCLIP (e-mail: stephanie.crossley@bolton.gov.uk)
Lifelong Learning and Information Manager Ms Marguerite Gracey BA(Hons) DipLib DMS MCLIP (e-mail: marguerite.gracey@bolton.gov.uk)
Resources and E-Services Manager Ms Amanda Stevens BA(Hons) MCLIP (e-mail: amanda.stevens@bolton.gov.uk)
Customer Services Manager Mrs Julie Spencer MBE BA(Hons) MBA MCLIP (e-mail: julie.spencer@bolton.gov.uk)
Communities and Access Manager Ms Mary Keane BA(Hons) PGDipLib MCLIP (e-mail: mary.keane@bolton.gov.uk)

BOURNEMOUTH

Authority: Bournemouth Borough Council
HQ Bournemouth Libraries, Leisure and Tourism Directorate, Town Hall, Bournemouth BH2 6DY
☎(01202) 454848 (general enquiries)
Fax (01202) 454830
e-mail: bournemouth@bournemouthlibraries.org.uk
url: www.bournemouth.gov.uk/libraries
Head of Arts, Library and Museum Services Ms Shelagh Levett BA(Hons) CertEd MCLIP (01202 454615; fax: 01202 454620; e-mail: halms@bournemouthlibraries.org.uk)
Principal Area Services Manager Mrs Carolyn Date GradIPD MCLIP (01202 454826)
Principal Development and Support Services Manager Mrs Elaine Arthur BA(Hons) MCLIP DMS (01202 454825), Mrs Linda Constable BA(Hons) MCLIP PGDip(Res) (job share)

Central/largest library
The Bournemouth Library, 22 The Triangle, Bournemouth BH2 5RQ
☎(01202) 454848

BRACKNELL FOREST

Authority: Bracknell Forest Borough Council
HQ Education and Libraries Department, Seymour House, 38 Broadway, Bracknell, Berks RG12 1AU
☎(01344) 423149
Fax (01344) 411392
e-mail: bracknell.library@bracknell-forest.gov.uk
url: www.bracknell-forest.gov.uk/libraries
Head of Libraries and Information Ms Ruth Burgess BLib MCLIP (01344 353134; e-mail: ruth.burgess@bracknell-forest.gov.uk)

Central/largest library
Bracknell Library, Education and Libraries Department, Town Square, Bracknell, Berks RG12 1BH
☎(01344) 352400
Fax (01344) 352420

e-mail: bracknell.library@bracknell-forest.gov.uk
url: www.bracknell-forest.gov.uk/libraries
Library and Information Manager Vacant

BRADFORD

Authority: City of Bradford Metropolitan District Council
HQ Central Library, Prince's Way, Bradford BD1 1NN
☎(01274) 433600
Fax (01274) 395108
e-mail: public.libraries@bradford.gov.uk
url: www.bradford.gov.uk
Director, Arts, Heritage and Leisure Ms Jane Glaister BA FMA PGDipLib (01274
432647; e-mail: jane.glaister@bradford.gov.uk)
Head of Libraries, Archives and Information Service Ian Watson BA MCLIP (01274
433640; e-mail: ian.watson@bradford.gov.uk)

Group libraries

◗ North Group, c/o Shipley Library, 2 Wellcroft, Shipley, West Yorks BD18 3QH
☎(01274) 437150
Fax (01274) 530247
e-mail: shipley.library@bradford.gov.uk
Group Librarian Mrs Jackie Kitwood BA DipLib MCLIP (e-mail:
jackie.kitwood@bradford.gov.uk)
◗ South Group, c/o Central Library, Prince's Way, Bradford BD1 1NN
☎(01274) 433600
Fax (01274) 395108
e-mail: central.library@bradford.gov.uk
Group Librarian Miss Sally Williams BA MCLIP (e-mail:
sally.williams@bradford.gov.uk)

BRENT

Authority: London Borough of Brent
HQ Education, Arts and Libraries, 4th Floor, Chesterfield House, 9 Park Lane, Wembley,
Middlesex HA9 7RW
☎020 8937 3144
Fax 020 8937 3023
url: www.brent.gov.uk
Director of Education, Arts and Libraries John Christie
Assistant Director, Lifelong Learning and Cultural Services Ms Marianne Locke BA
MCLIP (020 8937 3146; e-mail: marianne.locke@brent.gov.uk)
Head of Library Services Ms Susan McKenzie BA DAA (020 8937 3142; e-mail:
susan.mckenzie@brent.gov.uk)

Area libraries

◗ Barham Park Library, Harrow Road, Sudbury, Middlesex HA0 2HB
☎020 8937 3550

Fax 020 8937 3553
Principal Librarian, North Kevin Batchelor MCLIP
▶ Cricklewood Library, 152 Olive Road, Cricklewood, London NW2 6UY
☎020 8937 3540
Fax 020 8450 5211
Principal Librarian, South Mike Perry BA(Hons) DMS
▶ Ealing Road Library, Coronet Parade, Wembley, Middlesex HA0 4BR
☎020 8937 3560
Fax 020 8795 3425
▶ Harlesden Library, Craven Park Road, Harlesden, London NW10 8SE
☎020 8965 7132
Fax 020 8838 2199
▶ Kensal Rise Library, Bathurst Gardens, Harlesden, London NW10 5JA
☎020 8969 0942
Fax 020 8960 8399
▶ Kilburn Library, Salusbury Road, Kilburn, London NW6 6NN
☎020 8937 3530
Fax 020 7625 6387
▶ Kingsbury Library, Stag Lane, Kingsbury, London NW9 9AE
☎020 8937 3520
Fax 020 8905 0264
▶ Neasden Library, 277 Neasden Lane, London NW10 1QJ
☎020 8937 3580
Fax 020 8208 3909
▶ Outreach Library Service, 2-12 Grange Road, Willesden, London NW10 2QY
☎020 8937 3460 (tel/fax)
▶ Preston Library, Carlton Avenue East, Wembley, Middlesex HA9 8PL
☎020 8937 3510
Fax 020 8908 6220
▶ Tokyngton Library, Monks Park, Wembley, Middlesex HA9 6JE
☎020 8937 3590
Fax 020 8795 3440
▶ Town Hall Library, Brent Town Hall, Forty Lane, Wembley, Middlesex HA9 9HV
☎020 8937 3500
Fax 020 8937 3504
▶ Willesden Green Library, 95 High Road, Willesden, London NW10 2ST
☎020 8937 3400
Fax 020 8937 3401
Principal Librarian, Willesden Green John Verstraete MLIS DLIS BA(Hons)

BRIGHTON AND HOVE

Authority: Brighton and Hove City Council
HQ Royal Pavilion Libraries and Museums Division, Cultural Services, Jubilee Library, Jubilee
Street, Brighton BN1 1GE
☎(01273) 290800
Fax (01273) 296976
url: www.citylibraries.info

Head of Libraries and ICT Ms Sally McMahon BA DipLib MCLIP (01273 296963)
Operational Resources Manager Ms Julia Hugall BA DipLib MCLIP (01273 296933)
Professional and Collections Manager Nigel Imi BA DipLib MCLIP
Community and Development Manager Alan Issler BA MCLIP

Central libraries

Jubilee Library, Jubilee Street, Brighton BN1 1GE
☎(01273) 290800

Hove Library, 182-186 Church Road, Hove, East Sussex BN3 2EG
☎(01273) 290700 (minicom)

BRISTOL

Authority: Bristol City Council
HQ Central Library, College Green, Bristol BS1 5TL
☎0117 903 7200 (all enquiries)
Fax 0117 922 1081
e-mail: bristol_library_service@bristol-city.gov.uk
url: www.bristol-city.gov.uk
Head of Libraries Ms Kate Davenport MA MCLIP DMS (e-mail:
kate_davenport@bristol-city.gov.uk)
Libraries Manager (North) Ms Ann Casey BA MCLIP
Libraries Manager (South) Vacant
Business Support Manager Ms Kate Cole BA MCLIP
Central Library Manager Ms Janet Bremner BA MCLIP, Ms Julie Bowie BA MCLIP
Special Projects Manager Ms Julie York BA MCLIP

BROMLEY

Authority: London Borough of Bromley
HQ Central Library, High Street, Bromley, Kent BR1 1EX
☎020 8460 9955 (enquiries and administration)
Fax 020 8313 9975
e-mail: reference.library@bromley.gov.uk
url: www.bromley.gov.uk
Assistant Director, Libraries and Lifelong Learning Ms Linda Simpson (e-mail:
linda.simpson@bromley.gov.uk)
Library Operations Manager Leo Favret BA MIMgt DipMgt MCLIP (e-mail:
leo.favret@bromley.gov.uk)
Library Development Manager David Brockhurst BA MCLIP (e-mail:
david.brockhurst@bromley.gov.uk)

Central/largest library

Central Library, High Street, Bromley, Kent BR1 1EX
☎Tel/fax etc. as HQ
Group Manager John Wilkins BSc MCLIP (e-mail: john.wilkins@bromley.gov.uk)

District libraries

▶ Beckenham Library, Beckenham Road, Beckenham, Kent BR3 4PE
☎020 8650 7292/3
Area Manager Miss Christina Alabaster BA MCLIP (e-mail:
tina.alabaster@bromley.gov.uk)

▶ Orpington Library, The Priory, Church Hill, Orpington, Kent BR6 0HH
☎(01689) 831551
Area Manager Tim Woolgar MCLIP (e-mail: tim.woolgar@bromley.gov.uk)

BUCKINGHAMSHIRE

Authority: Buckinghamshire County Council
HQ County Library, County Hall, Walton Street, Aylesbury, Buckinghamshire HP20 1UU
☎(01296) 382830
Fax (01296) 382405
e-mail: library@buckscc.gov.uk
url: www.buckscc.gov.uk/libraries
Head of Libraries and Heritage Bob Strong BA DipLib MCLIP (01296 382251; fax:
01296 382259; e-mail: rstrong@buckscc.gov.uk)
Libraries Resources Manager Mark Bryant BA DipLib MCLIP DM (01296 382252; fax:
01296 382259; e-mail: mbryant@buckscc.gov.uk)
Libraries Development Manager Peter Mussett MCLIP (01296 382254; fax: 01296
382259; e-mail: pmussett@buckscc.gov.uk)
District Manager, Aylesbury Vale/Chiltern Mrs Janet Sonpal BSc DipLIS MCLIP (01296
383071; fax: 01296 382259)
District Manager, Wycombe/South Bucks Mrs Elaine Collier BSc DipLib MCLIP (01494
672295; e-mail: ecollier@buckscc.gov.uk)

Main group libraries

▶ Amersham Library, Chiltern Avenue, Amersham, Bucks HP6 5AH
☎(01494) 586878
Fax (01494) 586870
Library Manager Ms Glenys Brown

▶ Aylesbury Central Library, Walton Street, Aylesbury, Buckinghamshire HP20 1UU
☎(01296) 382248
Fax (01296) 382641
Library Manager Derek Morris BA DipLib MCLIP

▶ Beaconsfield Library, Reynolds Road, Beaconsfield, Bucks HP9 2NJ
☎(01494) 672295
Fax (01494) 678772
Library Manager Ms Judy Williamson BA PGDipLib MC MCLIP

▶ Buckingham Library, Verney Close, Buckingham MK18 1JP
☎(01280) 813229
Fax (01280) 823597
Library Manager Ms Steph Gassor MCLIP

▶ Chesham Library, Elgiva Lane, Chesham, Bucks HP5 2JD
☎(01494) 772322
Fax (01494) 773074

Library Manager Ms Jenny Mainwaring MCLIP
▶ Hazlemere Library, 312 Amersham Road, Hazlemere, Bucks HP15 7PY
☎(01494) 815266
Fax (01494) 533086
Library Manager Ms Janet Webb
▶ High Wycombe Library, Queen Victoria Road, High Wycombe, Bucks HP11 1BD
☎(01494) 464004
Fax (01494) 533086
Library Manager Ms Helen Goreham BLib MCLIP
▶ Marlow Library, Institute Road, Marlow, Bucks SL7 1BL
☎(01628) 486163
Library Manager Ms Sarah Townsend PGDipIM MCLIP

BURY

Authority: Bury Metropolitan Borough Council
HQ Cultural Services, Athenaeum House, Market Street, Bury, Lancs BL9 0BN
☎0161 253 5863 (administration)
Fax 0161 253 5915
e-mail: information@bury.gov.uk
url: www.bury.gov.uk/culture.htm
Library Services Manager Mrs Diana Sorrigan BA MCLIP (0161 253 6077; e-mail:
d.sorrigan@bury.gov.uk)
Principal Librarians Mrs Lesley Kelly BA MA MCLIP (0161 253 7579; e-mail:
s.l.kelly@bury.gov.uk), Tony Jowett BA MA MCLIP (0161 253 5876; e-mail:
t.jowett@bury.gov.uk)

Central/largest library

Central Library, Manchester Road, Bury, Lancs BL9 0DG
☎0161 253 5873
Fax 0161 253 5857
e-mail: information@bury.gov.uk
Principal Librarian Tony Jowett BA MA MCLIP (e-mail: t.jowett@bury.gov.uk)

Branch libraries

▶ Prestwich Library, Longfield Centre, Prestwich, Manchester M25 1AY
☎0161 253 7214
Fax 0161 253 5372
e-mail: prestwich.lib@bury.gov.uk
Library Supervisors Ms Joan Watkiss BA DipLib (0161 253 7219), David Galloway BA
DipLib (0161 253 7219)
▶ Radcliffe Library, Stand Lane, Radcliffe, Manchester M26 1NW
☎0161 253 7161
Fax 0161 253 7165
e-mail: radcliffe.lib@bury.gov.uk
Library Supervisors Ms Barbara Walker NEBS (0161 253 7160), Ms Joanne Smillie
NEBS (0161 253 7160)
▶ Ramsbottom Library, Carr Street, Ramsbottom, Bury, Lancs BL0 9AE

☎0161 253 5352
Fax (01706) 824638
e-mail: ramsbottom.lib@bury.gov.uk
Library Supervisor Miss Deborah Smith NEBS
▶ Tottington Library, Market Street, Tottington, Bury, Lancs BL8 3LN
☎0161 253 6652
Fax (01204) 886517
e-mail: tottington.lib@bury.gov.uk
Library Supervisors Mrs Lynsay Snape NEBS, Mrs Stephanie Lamb NEBS
▶ Unsworth Library, Sunnybank Road, Unsworth, Bury, Lancs BL9 8ED
☎0161 253 7560
Fax 0161 253 7566
e-mail: unsworth.lib@bury.gov.uk
Library Supervisor Mrs Louise Guilboyle NEBS
▶ Whitefield Library, Pinfold Lane, Whitefield, Manchester M45 7NY
☎0161 253 7510
Fax 0161 253 7514
e-mail: whitefield.lib@bury.gov.uk
Library Supervisor Mrs Janet Moores

Outreach libraries
▶ Ainsworth Library, Church Street, Ainsworth, Lancs BL2 5RT
☎(01204) 523841
e-mail: ainsworth.lib@bury.gov.uk
▶ Brandlesholme Community Library, 375 Brandlesholme Road, Bury, Lancs BL8 1HS
☎0161 764 2731
▶ Castle Sport and Leisure Library, Castle Leisure Centre, Bolton Street, Bury, Lancs BL9 0EZ
▶ Moorside Community Library, St John's Church Hall, Parkinson Street, Bury, Lancs BL9 6NY
☎0161 253 5885
e-mail: moorside.lib@bury.gov.uk
▶ New Kershaw Centre, Deal Street, Bury, Lancs BL9 7PZ
☎0161 253 6400
e-mail: kershaw.lib@bury.gov.uk
▶ South Cross Street Community Library, 90 South Cross Street, Bury, Lancs BL9 0RS
☎0161 253 6079
▶ Topping Fold Library, Topping Fold Road, Bury, Lancs BL9 7NG
☎0161 253 6361
e-mail: topping.lib@bury.gov.uk

CALDERDALE

Authority: Calderdale Metropolitan Borough Council
HQ Central Library, Northgate, Halifax, Yorkshire HX1 1UN
☎(01422) 392605
Fax (01422) 392615
e-mail: libraries@calderdale.gov.uk

url: www.calderdale.gov.uk
Head of Libraries, Museums and Arts Gary Borrows MCLIP
Operations and Service Development Manager Vacant
Collections and Services Development Manager David Duffy BA MCLIP (01422 392630)

CAMBRIDGESHIRE

Authority: Cambridgeshire County Council
HQ Cambridgeshire Libraries and Information Services, Roger Ascham Site, Ascham Road, Cambridge CB4 2BD
☎(01223) 717023 (administration)
Fax (01223) 717079
e-mail: your.library@cambridgeshire.gov.uk
url: www.cambridgeshire.gov.uk/library
Head of Libraries and Information (Public Services) Mrs Lesley Noblett MA MCLIP (01223 717292; e-mail: lesley.noblett@cambridgeshire.gov.uk)
Head of Support Services for Lifelong Learning Chris Heaton MA MCLIP (01223 717061; e-mail: chris.heaton@cambridgeshire.gov.uk)
Service and Business Planning Manager Geoff Langridge MA MLS MCLIP (01223 717064; e-mail: geoff.langridge@cambridgeshire.gov.uk)

Central/largest library
Central Library, 7 Lion Yard, Cambridge CB2 3QD
☎0845 045 5225
Fax (01223) 712018

Hub libraries
▶ Ely Library, 6 The Cloisters, Ely, Cambs CB7 4ZH
 ☎0845 045 5225
 Fax (01353) 616164
▶ Huntingdon Library, Princes Street, Huntingdon, Cambs PE29 3PH
 ☎0845 045 5225
 Fax (01480) 459563
▶ March Library, City Road, March, Cambs PE15 9LT
 ☎0845 045 5225
 Fax (01354) 754760
▶ St Ives Library, Station Road, St Ives, Huntingdon, Cambs PE27 5BW
 ☎0845 045 5225
 Fax (01480) 386604
▶ St Neots Library, Priory Lane, St Neots, Huntingdon, Cambs PE19 2BH
 ☎0845 045 5225
 Fax (01480) 396006
▶ Wisbech Library, 1 Ely Place, Wisbech, Cambs PE13 1EU
 ☎0845 045 5225
 Fax (01945) 582784

CAMDEN

Authority: London Borough of Camden
HQ Leisure and Community Services Department, The Crowndale Centre, 218 Eversholt Street, London NWI IBD
☎020 7974 4001
Fax 020 7974 1615
url: www.camden.gov.uk
Head of Libraries and Information Services David Jones BA(Hons) DipLib (020 7974 4058; e-mail: david.jones@camden.gov.uk)

Central/largest library
Swiss Cottage Library, 88 Avenue Road, London NW3 3HA
☎020 7974 6522 (general enquiries)
Fax 020 7974 6532
e-mail: swisscottagelibrary@camden.gov.uk
Library Manager Bob Gryspeerdt BA MCLIP (020 7974 5411)

Other libraries
▶ Belsize Library, Antrim Road, London NW3 4XN
☎020 7974 6518
Fax 020 7974 6508
e-mail: belsizelibrary@camden.gov.uk
Library Manager Gary Fantie
▶ Camden Town Library, Crowndale Centre, 218 Eversholt Street, London NWI IBD
☎020 7974 1563
Fax 020 7974 1582
e-mail: camdentownlibrary@camden.gov.uk
Library Manager Mrs Gloria Keys (020 7974 1563/1531))
▶ Chalk Farm Library, Sharpleshall Street, London NWI 8YN
☎020 7974 6526
Fax 020 7974 6502
e-mail: chalkfarmlibrary@camden.gov.uk
Library Manager Mrs Gloria Keys
▶ Heath Library, Keats Grove, London NW3 2RR
☎020 7974 6520 (tel/fax)
e-mail: heathlibrary@camden.gov.uk
Library Manager Ms Katharine Chasey
▶ Highgate Library, Chester Road, London N19 5DH
☎020 7974 5752, 020 7281 2546 (home library service)
Fax 020 7974 5555
e-mail: highgatelibrary@camden.gov.uk
Library Manager Ms Katharine Chasey
▶ Holborn Library, 32-38 Theobalds Road, London WCIX 8PA
☎020 7974 6345/6, 020 7974 6342 (Local studies)
Fax 020 7974 6356
e-mail: holbornlibrary@camden.gov.uk
Library Manager Ms Shirley Jacobs (020 7974 6353)

▶ Kentish Town Library, 262-266 Kentish Town Road, London NW5 2AA
☎020 7974 6253
Fax 020 7842 5650
e-mail: kentishtownlibrary@camden.gov.uk
Library Manager Roberto Cioccari (020 7974 6261/6253)

▶ Kilburn Library, Cotleigh Road, London NW6 2NP
☎020 7974 1965
Fax 020 7974 6524
e-mail: kilburnlibrary@camden.gov.uk
Library Manager Gary Fantie

▶ Queen's Crescent Library, 165 Queen's Crescent, London NW5 4HH
☎020 7974 6243
Fax 020 7485 6252
e-mail: queenscrescentlibrary@camden.gov.uk
Library Manager Roberto Cioccari (020 7974 6243)

▶ Regent's Park Library, Compton Close, Robert Street, London NW1 3QT
☎020 7974 1530
Fax 020 7974 1531
e-mail: regentsparklibrary@camden.gov.uk
Library Manager Ms Shirley Jacobs

▶ St Pancras Library, Town Hall Extension, Argyle Street, London WC1H 8NN
☎020 7974 5833
Fax 020 7860 5963
e-mail: stpancraslibrary@camden.gov.uk
Library Manager Mrs Gloria Keys (020 7974 5865)

▶ West Hampstead Library, Dennington Park Road, London NW6 1AU
☎020 7974 6610
Fax 020 7974 6539
e-mail: westhampsteadlibrary@camden.gov.uk
Library Manager Gary Fantie (020 7974 6620)

CHESHIRE

Authority: Cheshire County Council
HQ Adult and Community Services Department, County Hall, Chester CH1 1SF
☎(01244) 602424 (County Hall switchboard)
Fax (01244) 602767
url: www.cheshire.gov.uk
County Librarian and Information Officer Ian Dunn BA DAA FSA (01244 606034; fax: 01244 602478; e-mail: dunni@cheshire.gov.uk)
Acting Manager of Public Library Operations Ms Barbara M West MCLIP (01270 505280; fax: 01270 256962; e-mail: barbara.west@cheshire.gov.uk)
Resources and Development Manager Hedley Skinner DipEdTech MCLIP (01244 606023; e-mail: skinnereh@cheshire.gov.uk)

Group HQs

▶ Business Information Service, Ellesmere Port Library, Civic Way, Ellesmere Port, Cheshire CH65 0BG

☎0151 357 4695
Fax 0151 355 6849
e-mail: bisep@cheshire.gov.uk
url: www.cheshire.gov.uk/bis
Community and Business Information Manager Ms Linda Morris
▶ Chester Library, Northgate Street, Chester CH1 2EF
☎(01244) 312935
Fax (01244) 315534
e-mail: ipchester@cheshire.gov.uk
Group Librarian Angus Madders MCLIP (e-mail: maddersab@cheshire.gov.uk)
▶ Congleton Library, Market Square, Congleton, Cheshire CW12 1BU
☎(01260) 271141
Fax (01260) 298774
e-mail: ipcongleton@cheshire.gov.uk
Group Librarian Miss Sheila M Kane MCLIP (e-mail: kanesm@cheshire.gov.uk)
▶ Crewe Library, Prince Albert Street, Crewe, Cheshire CW1 2DH
☎(01270) 211123
Fax (01270) 256952
e-mail: ipcrewe@cheshire.gov.uk
Group Librarian Mrs Jo Norton BA MCLIP (e-mail: nortonrowland@cheshire.gov.uk),
Mrs Caroline Balabil BA MA MCLIP (e-mail: nortonrowland@cheshire.gov.uk)
▶ Ellesmere Port Library, Civic Way, Ellesmere Port, Cheshire L65 0BG
☎0151 357 4684
Fax 0151 355 6849
e-mail: ipeport@cheshire.gov.uk
Group Librarian Roger D Booth BSc DipLib MCLIP (e-mail:
boothrd@cheshire.gov.uk)
▶ Macclesfield Library, 2 Jordangate, Macclesfield, Cheshire SK10 1EE
☎(01625) 422512
Fax (01625) 612818
e-mail: ipmacclesfield@cheshire.gov.uk
Group Librarian Miss Pat M Owen BA MCLIP (e-mail: owenpm@cheshire.gov.uk)
▶ Northwich Library, Witton Street, Northwich, Cheshire CW9 5DR
☎(01606) 44221
Fax (01606) 48396
e-mail: ipnorthwich@cheshire.gov.uk
Group Librarian Mrs Sheila Scragg BA MCLIP (e-mail: scraggs@cheshire.gov.uk)
▶ Wilmslow Library, South Drive, Wilmslow, Cheshire SK9 1NW
☎(01625) 415037
Fax (01625) 548401
Group Manager Paul Everitt (01625 415037; fax: 01625 548401; e-mail:
paul.everitt@cheshire.gov.uk)

CORNWALL

Authority: Cornwall County Council
HQ Education, Arts and Libraries, Unit 17, Threemilestone Industrial Estate,
Threemilestone, Truro, Cornwall TR4 9LD

☎(01872) 324316 (enquiries)
Fax (01872) 223509
e-mail: library@cornwall.gov.uk
url: www.cornwall.gov.uk
Assistant Director, Education, Arts and Libraries C Ramsey BSc(Hons) MA
AdvDipBFM(CIPFA)

Additional libraries

▶ Bodmin Library, Lower Bore Street, Bodmin, Cornwall PL31 2LX
   ☎(01208) 72286
▶ Bude Library, The Wharf, Bude, Cornwall EX23 8LG
   ☎(01288) 352527
▶ Callington Library, Launceston Road, Callington, Cornwall PL17 7DR
   ☎(01579) 383236
▶ Camborne Library, The Cross, Camborne, Cornwall TR14 8HA
   ☎(01209) 713544
▶ Camelford Library, Town Hall, Market Place, Camelford, Cornwall PL32 9PD
   ☎(01840) 212409
▶ Falmouth Library, The Moor, Falmouth, Cornwall TR11 3QA
   ☎(01326) 314901
▶ Fowey Library, Caffa Mill House, 2 Passage Lane, Fowey, Cornwall PL23 1JS
   ☎(01726) 832332
▶ Hayle Library, Commercial Road, Hayle, Cornwall TR27 4DE
   ☎(01736) 753196
▶ Helston Library, Trengrouse Way, Helston, Cornwall TR13 8AG
   ☎(01326) 572321
▶ Launceston Library, Bounsalls Lane, Launceston, Cornwall PL15 9AB
   ☎(01566) 773306
▶ Liskeard Library, Barras Street, Liskeard, Cornwall PL14 6AB
   ☎(01579) 343285
▶ Looe Library, Sea Front Court, Looe, Cornwall PL13 1AL
   ☎(01503) 262365
▶ Lostwithiel Library, Taprell House, North Street, Lostwithiel, Cornwall PL22 0BL
   ☎(01208) 872747
▶ Newquay Library, Marcus Hill, Newquay, Cornwall TR7 1BD
   ☎(01637) 873538
▶ Padstow Library, The Institute, Padstow, Cornwall PL28 8AL
   ☎(01841) 532387
▶ Par Library, Hamley's Corner, Eastcliffe Road, Par, Cornwall PL24 2AH
   ☎(01726) 814853
▶ Penryn Library, St Thomas Street, Penryn, Cornwall TR10 8JN
   ☎(01326) 372203
▶ Penzance Library, Morrab Road, Penzance, Cornwall TR18 4EY
   ☎(01736) 363954
▶ Perranporth Library, Oddfellows Hall, Ponsmere Road, Perranporth, Cornwall TR6 0BW
   ☎(01872) 572590
▶ Redruth Library, Clinton Road, Redruth, Cornwall TR15 2QE
   ☎(01209) 219111

▶ St Agnes Library, The Car Park, St Agnes, Cornwall TR5 0TP
☎(01872) 553245
▶ St Austell Library, 2 Carlyon Road, St Austell, Cornwall PL25 4LD
☎(01726) 73348
▶ St Columb Library, The Town Hall, St Columb, Cornwall TR9 6AN
☎(01637) 881480
▶ St Ives Library, Gabriel Street, St Ives, Cornwall TR26 2LU
☎(01736) 795377
▶ St Just Library, Market Street, St Just, Cornwall TR19 7HX
☎(01736) 788669
▶ Saltash Library, Callington Road, Saltash, Cornwall PL12 6DX
☎(01752) 842478
▶ Torpoint Library, Fore Street, Torpoint, Cornwall PL11 2AG
☎(01752) 812207
▶ Truro Library, Union Place, Truro, Cornwall TR1 1EP
☎(01872) 279205
▶ Upton Cross Library, Upton Cross School, Liskeard, Cornwall PL14 5AX
☎(01579) 363878 (tel/fax)
▶ Wadebridge Library, Southern Way, Wadebridge, Cornwall PL27 7BX
☎(01208) 812202

COVENTRY

Authority: Coventry City Council
HQ Coventry Libraries and Information Services, EL228, Civic Centre 1, Earl Street, Coventry CV1 5RS
☎024 7683 1579
Fax 024 7683 1584
Director of Education and Libraries Vacant
Head of Libraries and Information Services Andrew Green BA MLS DMS MCLIP
(e-mail: andrew.green@coventry.gov.uk)
Assistant Head of Libraries and Information Services: East Area, Media and Cultural Development Ms Sorrelle Clements (024 7683 2800; fax: 024 7683 1584; e-mail: sorrelle.clements@coventry.gov.uk)
Assistant Head of Libraries and Information Services: West Area, Equalities and Young People Bob Parsons (e-mail: bob.parsons@coventry.gov.uk)
Assistant Head of Libraries and Information Services: Central Library, Information and Learning Simon Rice (024 7683 1707; fax: 024 7683 1584; e-mail: simon.rice@coventry.gov.uk)
Business Manager Colin Scott (024 7683 2457; fax: 024 7683 1584; e-mail: colin.scott@coventry.gov.uk)

Central/largest library
Central Library, Smithford Way, Coventry CV1 1FY
☎024 7683 2314 (enquiries), 024 7683 2321 (administration)
Fax 024 7683 2440 (enquiries)
e-mail: library.office@coventry.gov.uk
url: www.coventry.org.uk

Assistant Head of Libraries and Information Services: Central Library, Information and Learning Simon Rice (024 7683 1707; fax: 024 7683 1584; e-mail: simon.rice@coventry.gov.uk) (Based at HQ address above)

East Area Libraries

▶ Aldermoor Farm Library, Aldermoor Farm School, Pinley Fields, Stoke Aldermoor, Coventry CV3 1DD
☎024 7644 2840
Fax 024 7644 2840
e-mail: aldermoorfarm.library@coventry.gov.uk

▶ Arena Park Library, Coventry Arena Shopping Park, Classic Drive, Rowley's Green, Coventry CV6 6AF
☎024 7678 5181
Fax 024 7670 0329
e-mail: arenapark.library@coventry.gov.uk

▶ Bell Green Library and Learning Centre, 17-23 Riley Square, Bell Green, Coventry CV2 1LS
☎024 7668 8986
Fax 024 7666 3468
e-mail: bellgreen.library@coventry.gov.uk

▶ Cheylesmore Community Library, Poitiers Road, Cheylesmore, Coventry CV3 5JX
☎024 7650 2106
Fax 024 7650 5287
e-mail: cheylesmore.library@coventry.gov.uk

▶ Foleshill Library, Broad Street, Foleshill, Coventry CV6 5BG
☎024 7668 9154
Fax 024 7666 7461
e-mail: foleshill.library@coventry.gov.uk

▶ Hillfields Community Library, St Peter's Centre, Charles Street, Coventry CV1 5NP
☎024 7663 3878
Fax 024 7623 1970
e-mail: library.hillfields@coventry.gov.uk

▶ Holbrook Library, Briscoe Road, Holbrook, Coventry CV6 4JP
☎024 7668 7561
Fax 024 7666 3082
e-mail: holbrook.library@coventry.gov.uk

▶ Stoke Library, Kingsway, Stoke, Coventry CV2 4EA
☎024 7645 2059
Fax 024 7645 2567
e-mail: stoke.library@coventry.gov.uk

▶ Willenhall Library, 106 Remembrance Road, Willenhall, Coventry CV3 3DN
☎024 7630 2383
Fax 024 7630 2151
e-mail: willenhall.library@coventry.gov.uk

▶ Wyken Community Library, Wyken Community Centre, Westmorland Road, Coventry CV2 5BY
☎024 7670 9348

Fax 024 7670 9348
e-mail: wyken.library@coventry.gov.uk

West Area Libraries
▶ Canley Library, Prior Deram Walk, Canley, Coventry CV4 8FT
☎024 7667 3041
Fax 024 7671 7361
e-mail: canley.library@coventry.gov.uk
▶ Coundon Library, Moseley Avenue, Radford, Coventry CV6 1HT
☎024 7659 3496
Fax 024 7659 8768
e-mail: coundon.library@coventry.gov.uk
▶ Earlsdon Library, Earlsdon Avenue North, Earlsdon, Coventry CV5 6FZ
☎024 7667 5359
Fax 024 7671 7958
e-mail: earlsdon.library@coventry.gov.uk
▶ Finham Library, Droylsdon Park Road, Finham, Coventry CV3 6EQ
☎024 7641 4050
Fax 024 7641 9524
e-mail: finham.library@coventry.gov.uk
▶ Jubilee Library, Jubilee Crescent, Radford, Coventry CV6 3EX
☎024 7659 6762
Fax 024 7659 5728
e-mail: jubileecrescent.library@coventry.gov.uk
▶ Tile Hill Library, Jardine Crescent, Tile Hill, Coventry CV4 9PL
☎024 7646 4994
Fax 024 7669 5774
e-mail: tilehill.library@coventry.gov.uk
▶ Whoberley Community Library, St John's School, Winsford Avenue, Allesley Park,
Coventry CV5 9HZ
☎(07903) 749521

CROYDON

Authority: London Borough of Croydon
HQ Central Library, Katharine Street, Croydon CR9 1ET
☎020 8760 5400
Fax 020 8253 1004
url: www.croydon.gov.uk
Assistant Director, Libraries Ms Adie Batt BA MCLIP (020 8253 1001; e-mail:
adie.batt@croydon.gov.uk)

CUMBRIA

Authority: Cumbria County Council
HQ Economy, Culture and Environment, Arroyo Block, The Castle, Carlisle CA3 8UR
☎(01228) 607295 (enquiries), (01228) 607296 (management)
Fax (01228) 607299

url: www.cumbria.gov.uk/libraries/
Corporate Director of Economy, Culture and Environment Ralph Howard
Head of Culture Jim Grisenthwaite (01228 607282; e-mail:
jim.grisenthwaite@cumbriacc.gov.uk)
Library Services Manager Alan Welton BA MCLIP (01228 607307; e-mail:
alan.welton@cumbriacc.gov.uk)
Library Operations Manager Mrs Liz Bowe MCLIP (01228 607338; e-mail:
liz.bowe@cumbriacc.gov.uk)
Principal Administrative Officer Paul Graham (01228 607294; e-mail:
paul.graham@cumbriacc.gov.uk)

Group libraries

▶ Barrow-in-Furness Library, Ramsden Square, Barrow-in-Furness, Cumbria LA14 1LL
☎(01229) 894370
Fax (01229) 894371
e-mail: barrow.library@cumbriacc.gov.uk
Area Library Manager Ms Bernadette Maine
▶ Carlisle Library, 11 Globe Lane, Carlisle CA3 8NX
☎(01228) 607310
Fax (01228) 607333
e-mail: carlisle.library@cumbriacc.gov.uk
Area Library Manager Mike Lister BA MCLIP
▶ Daniel Hay Library, Lowther Street, Whitehaven, Cumbria CA28 7QZ
☎(01946) 852900
Fax (01946) 852911
e-mail: whitehaven.library@cumbriacc.gov.uk
Area Library Manager Mrs Alayne Cowling
▶ Kendal Library, Stricklandgate, Kendal, Cumbria LA9 4PY
☎(01539) 773520
Fax (01539) 773544
e-mail: kendal.library@cumbriacc.gov.uk
Area Library Manager Tom Holliday
▶ Penrith Library, St Andrews Churchyard, Penrith, Cumbria CA11 7YA
☎(01768) 242100
Fax (01768) 242101
e-mail: penrith.library@cumbriacc.gov.uk
Area Library Manager Mike Lister BA MCLIP
▶ Workington Library, Vulcans Lane, Workington, Cumbria CA14 2ND
☎(01900) 325170
Fax (01900) 325181
e-mail: workington.library@cumbriacc.gov.uk
Area Library Manager Trevor Jones

DARLINGTON

Authority: Darlington Borough Council
HQ Central Library, Crown Street, Darlington DL1 1ND
☎(01325) 462034 (enquiries), 349610 (administration)

Fax (01325) 381556
e-mail: crown.street.library@darlington.gov.uk
url: www.darlington.gov.uk/library
Head of Libraries and Community Learning Mrs Ruth Bernstein
Library Manager Mrs Lynne Litchfield

Branch library

◗ Cockerton Library, Cockerton Green, Darlington DL3 9AA
☎(01325) 461320
Community Librarian Ms Carole Houghton

DERBY

Authority: Derby City Council
HQ Derby City Libraries, Department of Development and Cultural Services, Roman House, Friar Gate, Derby DE1 1XB
☎(01332) 716607
Fax (01332) 715549
e-mail: libraries@derby.gov.uk
url: www.derby.gov.uk/libraries
Head of Library Services David Potton MA DipLib MCLIP (01332 716602; e-mail: david.potton@derby.gov.uk)
Assistant Head of Library Services (ICT, Information and Lifelong Learning) Mark Elliott BLib(Hons) MCLIP PGC(Man) (01332 716609; e-mail: mark.elliott@derby.gov.uk)
Assistant Head of Library Services (Operations) Ms Fran Renwick MA MCLIP (01332 716610; e-mail: fran.renwick@derby.gov.uk)

Central/largest library

Central Library, The Wardwick, Derby DE1 1HS
☎(01332) 255398/9 (enquiries), 255400/1 (renewals), 255390 (administration)
Fax (01332) 369570
Assistant Head of Library Services (Central Libraries & Resources) Bernard Haigh MLS MCLIP (01332 255389; e-mail: bernard.haigh@derby.gov.uk)

DERBYSHIRE

Authority: Derbyshire County Council
HQ Cultural and Community Services Department, County Hall, Matlock, Derbyshire DE4 3AG
☎(01629) 580000 ext 6591 (enquiries), ext 6590 (administration)
Fax (01629) 585363
e-mail: derbyshire.libraries@derbyshire.gov.uk
url: www.derbyshire.gov.uk
Director of Cultural and Community Services Martin Molloy BA DipLib MCLIP (e-mail: martin.molloy@derbyshire.gov.uk)
Deputy Director of Cultural and Community Services and Head of Libraries and Heritage Division Miss Jaci Brumwell MCLIP (e-mail: jaci.brumwell@derbyshire.gov.uk)

Assistant Director, Policy, Information and Partnership Robert Gent BA DMS MIMgt MCLIP (e-mail: robert.gent@derbyshire.gov.uk)
Assistant Director of Libraries and Heritage Divison Don Gibbs BA MCLIP (e-mail: don.gibbs@derbyshire.gov.uk)

Central/largest library

Chesterfield Library, New Beetwell Street, Chesterfield, Derbyshire S40 1QN
☎(01246) 209292
Fax (01246) 209304
District Librarian Mrs Ann Ainsworth BA MCLIP (e-mail: ann.ainsworth@derbyshire.gov.uk)

Other main libraries - Amber Valley District

▶ Alfreton Library, Severn Square, Alfreton, Derbyshire DE55 7BQ
☎(01773) 833199
Fax (01773) 521020
District Librarian Mrs Julie Potton BA MCLIP (e-mail: julie.potton@derbyshire.gov.uk)

Bolsover District

▶ Bolsover Library, Church Street, Bolsover, Derbyshire S44 6HB
☎(01246) 823179
Fax (01246) 827237
District Librarian Vacant

Derbyshire Dales District

▶ Matlock Library, Steep Turnpike, Matlock, Derbyshire DE4 3DP
☎(01629) 582480
Fax (01629) 760749
District Librarian Ms Trisha Hill BA DipLib MCLIP (e-mail: trisha.hill@derbyshire.gov.uk)

Erewash District

▶ Ilkeston Library, Market Place, Ilkeston, Derbyshire DE7 5RN
☎0115 930 1104
Fax 0115 944 1226
District Librarian Mrs Jan Colombo BSc MCLIP (e-mail: jan.colombo@derbyshire.gov.uk)

High Peak District

▶ Buxton Library, Kents Bank Road, Buxton, Derbyshire SK17 9HJ
☎(01298) 25331
Fax (01298) 73744
District Librarian Ms Tessa Cozens BA MCLIP (e-mail: tessa.cozens@derbyshire.gov.uk)

North East Derbyshire District

▶ Dronfield Library, Manor House, Dronfield, Derbyshire S18 1PY

☎(01246) 414001
Fax (01246) 291489
District Librarian Mrs Sue Crabb MLS MCLIP (e-mail: sue.crabb@derbyshire.gov.uk)

South Derbyshire District
▶ Swadlincote Library, Civic Way, Swadlincote, Derbyshire DE11 0AD
☎(01283) 217701
Fax (01283) 216352
District Librarian Ms Ruth Jameson MCLIP (e-mail: ruth.jameson@derbyshire.gov.uk)

DEVON

Authority: Devon County Council
HQ Devon Library and Information Services, Great Moor House, Bittern Road, Sowton, Exeter, Devon EX2 7NL
☎(01392) 384315
Fax (01392) 384316
e-mail: devlibs@devon.gov.uk
url: www.devon.gov.uk/libraries
Head of Library and Information Services Mrs Lynn Osborne BA MCLIP (e-mail: lynn.osborne@devon.gov.uk)

Group libraries
▶ North and West Devon. North Devon Library and Record Office, Tuly Street, Barnstaple, Devon EX31 1EL
☎(01271) 388619 (tel/fax)
Group Librarian Ian Tansley MCLIP (e-mail: ian.tansley@devon.gov.uk)
▶ South and East Devon. Central Library, Castle Street, Exeter, Devon EX4 3PQ
☎(01392) 384222
Fax (01392) 384228
Group Librarian Mike Maguire MCLIP (e-mail: mike.maguire@devon.gov.uk)

Larger libraries
▶ Barnstaple Library, Tuly Street, Barnstaple, Devon EX31 1EL
☎(01271) 388619 (tel/fax)
Library Manager Geoff King
▶ Bideford Library, New Road, Bideford, Devon EX39 2HR
☎(01237) 476075 (tel/fax)
Librarian i/c Mrs Rose Wiseman
▶ Exeter Central Library, Castle Street, Exeter, Devon EX4 3PQ
☎(01392) 384222
Fax (01392) 384228
Library Manager Andrew Davey BSc MCLIP
▶ Exmouth Library, 40 Exeter Road, Exmouth, Devon EX8 1PS
☎(01395) 272677
Fax (01395) 271426
Public Services Librarian Kelvin Crook MCLIP

▶ Honiton Library, 48 New Street, Honiton, Devon EX14 1BS
☎(01404) 42818
Fax (01404) 45326
Librarian i/c Miss Jenny Wood
▶ Kingsbridge Library, Ilbert Road, Kingsbridge, Devon TQ7 1EB
☎(01548) 852315
Librarian i/c Mrs Wendy Bloomer
▶ Newton Abbot Library and Education Centre, Market Street, Newton Abbot, Devon TQ12 2RJ
☎(01626) 206420
Librarian i/c Mrs Linda Roland-Howe
▶ St Thomas Library, Cowick Street, Exeter, Devon EX4 1AF
☎(01392) 252783
Librarian i/c Mrs Jill Hughes
▶ Sidmouth Library, Blackmore Drive, Sidmouth, Devon EX10 8LA
☎(01395) 512192
Librarian i/c Mrs Gill Spence
▶ Tavistock Library, The Quay, Plymouth Road, Tavistock, Devon PL19 8AB
☎(01822) 612218
Fax (01822) 610690
Librarian i/c Mrs Moira Andrews
▶ Teignmouth Library, Fore Street, Teignmouth, Devon TQ14 8DY
☎(01626) 774646
Librarian i/c Mrs Pauline Anderson MCLIP
▶ Tiverton Library, Phoenix House, Phoenix Lane, Tiverton, Devon EX16 6SA
☎(01884) 244644
Librarian i/c Mrs Hazel Skinner
(Note: These do not represent the full list of branch libraries)

DONCASTER

Authority: Doncaster Metropolitan Borough Council
HQ Central Library, Waterdale, Doncaster DN1 3JE
☎(01302) 734305 (general enquiries), (01302) 734298 (Principal Librarians' Office)
Fax (01302) 369749
e-mail: reference.library@doncaster.gov.uk
url: www.doncaster.gov.uk
Head of Library and Information Services Keith Robinson MCLIP (01302 734298;
e-mail: keith.thomas.robinson@doncaster.gov.uk)
Manager: Service Development D John L Mellor BA MCLIP (01302 734311; e-mail:
john.mellor1@doncaster.gov.uk)
Manager: Community Services Dave Butler BA MCLIP (01709 582424; e-mail:
dave.butler@doncaster.gov.uk)
Manager: Services to Special Groups Ms Donna Peverley MCLIP (01302 734301;
e-mail: donna.peverley@doncaster.gov.uk)

DORSET

Authority: Dorset County Council
HQ County Library HQ, Colliton Park, Dorchester, Dorset DT1 1XJ
☎(01305) 225000 (enquiries)
Fax (01305) 224344 (administration)
e-mail: dorsetlibraries@dorsetcc.gov.uk
url: www.dorsetcc.gov.uk/libraries
Head of Cultural Services, Libraries and Arts Paul Leivers BA MBA MCLIP (e-mail:
p.leivers@dorsetcc.gov.uk)
Business Support Manager Nick Goddard MCLIP MCMI APMP FRGS (e-mail:
n.r.goddard@dorsetcc.gov.uk)
Senior Manager, Stock and Children's Ms Sharon Kirkpatrick BLS MCLIP (e-mail:
s.d.kirkpatrick@dorsetcc.gov.uk)

Divisional libraries

▶ Central Division. Dorchester Library, Colliton Park, Dorchester, Dorset DT1 1XJ
  ☎(01305) 224652 (Lending Library), (01305) 224448 (Reference Library)
  Fax (01305) 225160 (Lending Library), (01305) 266120 (Reference Library)
  Senior Manager, Central Division Norman L Shirley MCLIP (01305 224578; e-mail:
  n.l.shirley@dorsetcc.gov.uk)
▶ East Division. Ferndown Library, Penny's Walk, Ferndown, Dorset BH22 9TH
  ☎(01202) 874542
  Fax (01202) 896097
  Senior Manager, East Division Roger J Dale MCLIP (01202 896545; e-mail:
  r.j.dale@dorsetcc.gov.uk)
▶ West Division. Weymouth Library, Great George Street, Weymouth, Dorset DT4 8NN
  ☎(01305) 762410 (lending), (01305) 762418 (reference)
  Fax (01305) 762412 (lending), (01305) 780316 (reference)
  Senior Manager, West Division Ms Tracy Long BA(Hons) MCLIP (01305 762402;
  e-mail: t.long@dorsetcc.gov.uk)

DUDLEY

Authority: Dudley Metropolitan Borough Council
HQ Dudley Library, St James's Road, Dudley, West Midlands DY1 1HR
☎(01384) 815568 (administration)
Fax (01384) 815543
e-mail: dudlibref.ed@dudley.gov.uk
url: www.dudley.gov.uk/libraries
Assistant Director of Education – Head of Libraries Chris Wrigley BA MCLIP (01384
814746/814387; e-mail: chris.wrigley@dudley.gov.uk)
Assistant Head of Libraries (North) Mrs Elizabeth Woodcock BA (01384 815551;
e-mail: elizabeth.woodcock@dudley.gov.uk)
Assistant Head of Libraries (South) Mrs Kate Millin BLib MCLIP (01384 814745; e-mail:
kate.millin@dudley.gov.uk)
Management Support Officer Miss Sue Helm BA MCLIP DipMS (01384 815572; e-mail:
sue.helm@dudley.gov.uk)

Town libraries

▶ Brierley Hill Library, High Street, Brierley Hill, West Midlands DY5 3ET
☎(01384) 812865
Fax (01384) 812866
e-mail: bhilllib.ed@dudley.gov.uk
Town Librarian Stephen Masters MCLIP

▶ Dudley Library, St James's Road, West Midlands DY1 1HR
☎(01384) 815560
Fax (01384) 815543
e-mail: dudlibref.ed@dudley.gov.uk
Town Librarian Mrs Katherine Allcock BA MA MCLIP, Mrs Hilary Riley MCLIP (job-share)

▶ Halesowen Library, Queensway Mall, The Cornbow, Halesowen, West Midlands B63 4AJ
☎(01384) 812980
Fax (01384) 812981
e-mail: hallib.ed@dudley.gov.uk
Town Librarian Mrs Angela Horton MCLIP

▶ Stourbridge Library, Crown Centre, Crown Lane, Stourbridge, West Midlands DY8 1YE
☎(01384) 812945
Fax (01384) 812946
e-mail: stourlibref.ed@dudley.gov.uk
Town Librarian David Hickman MSc MCLIP

Group Libraries Headquarters (North)

▶ Sedgley Library, Ladies Walk Centre, Ladies Walk, Sedgley, West Midlands DY3 3UA
☎(01384) 812790
e-mail: sedglib.ed@dudley.gov.uk
Group Librarian Mrs Hazel Birt MCLIP, Mrs Linda Wattis BA (job-share)

Group Libraries Headquarters (South)

▶ Kingswinford Library, Market Street, Kingswinford, West Midlands DY6 9LG
☎(01384) 812740
e-mail: kfordlib.ed@dudley.gov.uk
Group Librarian Mrs Sharon Whitehouse BA

Archives and Local History Service

▶ Mount Pleasant Street, Coseley, Dudley, West Midlands WV14 9JR
☎(01384) 812770 (tel/fax)
e-mail: archives.ed@dudley.gov.uk
Borough Archivist Vacant

DURHAM

Authority: Durham County Council
HQ Culture and Leisure, County Hall, Durham DH1 5TY
☎0191 383 3595 (enquiries), 0191 383 3713 (administration)
Fax 0191 384 1336
e-mail: alm@durham.gov.uk
url: www.durham.gov.uk

Director, Culture and Leisure Patrick Conway BA FRSA FCLIP MIMgt MILAM
Assistant Director, Collections and Strategy Ms Rosemary Laxton MCLIP
Assistant Director, Delivery and Support Nigel Canaway MBA MCLIP

Divisional libraries
▶ Eastern Division. Peterlee Library, Burnhope Way, Peterlee, Co Durham SR8 1NT
☎0191 586 2279
Fax 0191 586 6664
Divisional Manager Ms Sheila Owens BA MCLIP
▶ Northern Division. Durham Clayport Library, Millennium Place, Durham DH1 1WA
☎0191 386 4003
Fax 0191 386 0379
Divisional Manager Ms Anne Davison BA MCLIP
▶ Western Division. Crook Library, Market Place, Crook, Co Durham DL15 8QH
☎(01388) 762269
Fax (01388) 766170
Divisional Manager Ms June Gowland BA(Hons) MCLIP DipMgt

EALING

Authority: London Borough of Ealing
HQ Library Administrative Office, 3rd Floor SE, Perceval House, 14–16 Uxbridge Road,
London W5 2HL
☎020 8825 5600
Fax 020 8579 5280
e-mail: libuser@ealing.gov.uk
url: www.ealing.gov.uk/libraries/index.htm
Head of Service Vacant
Community Services Manager Ms Heather Farrar (e-mail: hfarrar@ealing.gov.uk)

Central/largest library
Central Library, 103 Ealing Broadway Centre, London W5 5JY
☎020 8567 3670 (enquiries), 020 8567 3656 (reference)
Fax 020 8840 2351

Main libraries
▶ Acton Library, High Street, London W3 6NA
☎020 8752 0999
Fax 020 8992 6086
▶ Greenford Library, Oldfield Lane South, Greenford, Middlesex UB6 9LG
☎020 8578 1466
Fax 020 8575 7800
▶ Southall Library, Osterley Park Road, Southall, Middlesex UB2 4BL
☎020 8574 3412
Fax 020 8571 7629
▶ West Ealing Library, Melbourne Avenue, London W13 9BT
☎020 8567 2812
Fax 020 8567 1736

EAST RIDING OF YORKSHIRE

Authority: East Riding of Yorkshire Council
HQ Library and Information Services, Council Offices, Main Road, Skirlaugh, East Riding of Yorks HU11 5HN
☎(01482) 392702
Fax (01482) 392711
url: www.eastriding.gov.uk
Libraries, Arts and Heritage Group Manager Alan Moir (e-mail: alan.moir@eastriding.gov.uk)
Library Operations Manager Ms Margaret Slattery BA DMS (01482 392740; e-mail: margaret.slattery@eastriding.gov.uk)
Development and Central Services Manager Ms Libby Herbert (01482 392715; e-mail: libby.herbert@eastriding.gov.uk)

EAST SUSSEX

Authority: East Sussex County Council
HQ Library and Information Services, G-Floor, Centre Block, County Hall, St Anne's Crescent, Lewes, East Sussex BN7 1UE
☎(01273) 481870 (enquiries), (01273) 481538 (administration)
Fax (01273) 481716
url: www.eastsussex.gov.uk
Assistant Director, Education: Libraries and Community Learning Dr Irene Campbell MA DipLib MCLIP (01273 481347; e-mail: irene.campbell@eastsussex.gov.uk)
Assistant Head of Library and Information Services: Operations Mrs Helena Sykes MCLIP (01273 481872; e-mail: helena.sykes@eastsussex.gov.uk)
Assistant Head of Library and Information Services: Policy Ms Rhona Drever MA(Hons) DipLib MCLIP (01273 481329; e-mail: rhona.drever@eastsussex.gov.uk)

Central/largest library

Hastings Group Office, Hastings Library, Brassey Institute, 13 Claremont, Hastings, East Sussex TN34 1HE
☎(01424) 420501 (enquiries), (01424) 461955 (administration)
Fax (01424) 430261
Group Manager Mick Bacon MCLIP (01424 461955; e-mail: mick.bacon@eastsussex.co.uk)

Group area offices

▶ Bexhill Library (Rother), Western Road, Bexhill on Sea, East Sussex TN40 1DY
☎(01424) 212546
Fax (01424) 819138
Group Manager Ms Noreen Finn MCLIP (01424 819138; e-mail: noreen.finn@eastsussex.gov.uk)
▶ Eastbourne Library, Grove Road, Eastbourne, East Sussex BN21 4TL
☎(01323) 434206
Fax (01323) 649174
Group Manager Vacant

▶ Lewes Library, Albion Street, Lewes, East Sussex BN7 2ND
☎(01273) 474232
Fax (01273) 477881
Group Manager Barry Forster MCLIP (01273 479729; e-mail:
barry.forster@eastsussex.gov.uk)
▶ Uckfield Library (Wealden), High Street, Uckfield, Uckfield, East Sussex TN22 1AR
☎(01825) 763254
Fax (01825 769762
Group Manager Mrs Joss Makin MCLIP (01825 769761; e-mail:
joss.makin@eastsussex.gov.uk)

ENFIELD

Authority: London Borough of Enfield
HQ Leisure, Culture and Youth, PO Box 58, Civic Centre, Enfield, Middlesex EN1 3XJ
☎020 8366 2244 (enquiries), 020 8379 3752 (administration)
Fax 020 8379 3753
url: www.enfield.gov.uk
Assistant Director (Leisure, Culture and Youth) Ms Claire Lewis BA MSc MCLIP
(e-mail: claire.lewis@enfield.gov.uk)
Head of Libraries and Museums Ms Julie Gibson MA MCLIP (e-mail:
julie.gibson@enfield.gov.uk)

Central/largest library

Central Library, Cecil Road, Enfield, Middlesex EN2 6TW
☎020 8366 2244
Fax 020 8379 8400
Area Library Manager Mrs Sheila Barford MCLIP (020 8379 8301)

Area libraries

▶ Edmonton Green Library, 36/44 South Mall, London N9 0NX
☎020 8807 3618
Fax 020 8379 2615
Area Library Manager Peter Brown BA MCLIP (020 8379 2605)
▶ Palmers Green Library, Broomfield Lane, London N13 4EY
☎020 8886 3728
Fax 020 8379 2712
Area Library Manager Ms Pam Tuttiett BA MCLIP (020 8379 2694)

ESSEX

Authority: Essex County Council
HQ County Library HQ, County Hall, Markey Road, Chelmsford, Essex CM1 1QH
☎(01245) 438438 (all enquiries)
Fax (01245) 492780 (general), (01245) 436769 (Management Team)
e-mail: essexlib@essexcc.gov.uk
url: www.essexcc.gov.uk/libraries
Head of Libraries, Culture and Adult Learning Richard McKay (01245 436080)

Planning and Performance Manager Geoff Elgar DipLib BA(Hons) MCLIP (01245 436760)
Libraries Manager Ms Michele Jones MSc BA(Hons) DipLib MCLIP (01245 436761)

Central/largest library
Chelmsford Library, PO Box 882, Market Road, Chelmsford, Essex CM1 1LH
☎(01245) 492758
Fax (01245) 492536 (enquiries), (01245) 436769 (administration)
e-mail: cfdlib@essexcc.gov.uk

Area Headquarters
▶ East Area. Colchester Library, Trinity Square, Colchester, Essex CO1 1JB
  ☎(01206) 245900
  Fax (01206) 245901
  e-mail: colchester.library@essexcc.gov.uk
  Strategic Manager, Reading and Learning Mrs Moira Tarrant (e-mail:
  moira.tarrant@essexcc.gov.uk)
▶ Mid Area. Chelmsford Library, PO Pox 882, Market Road, Chelmsford, Essex CM1 1LH
  ☎(01245) 492758
  Fax (01245) 492536
  e-mail: cfdlib@essexcc.gov.uk
  Strategic Manager, Transformation and Resources Martin Palmer BA MBA MCLIP
  MCMI (e-mail: martin.palmer@essexcc.gov.uk)
▶ South Area. Basildon Central Library, St Martin's Square, Basildon, Essex SS14 1EE
  ☎(01268) 288533
  Fax (01268) 286326
  Strategic Manager, Digital Citizenship Ms Elaine Adams BA MCLIP DMS (e-mail:
  elaine.adams@essexcc.gov.uk)
▶ West Area. Harlow Library, The High, Harlow, Essex CM20 1HA
  ☎(01279) 413772
  Fax (01279) 424612
  Strategic Manager, Community and Civil Values Vacant

GATESHEAD

Authority: Gateshead Metropolitan Borough Council
HQ Libraries, Arts and Information Services, Central Library, Prince Consort Road,
Gateshead, Tyne and Wear NE8 4LN
☎0191 433 8400
Fax 0191 477 7454
e-mail: enquiries@gateshead.gov.uk
url: www.gateshead.gov.uk/libraries
Head of Cultural Services David Bunce (e-mail: davidbunce@gateshead.gov.uk)
Cultural Services Manager, Libraries, Arts and Tourism Ms Ann Borthwick BA MCLIP
(e-mail: annborthwick@gateshead.gov.uk)
Cultural Support Manager Matthew Watson BA MCLIP (e-mail:
matthewwatson@gateshead.gov.uk)

Cultural Development Manager Ms Mary Fleming BA MCLIP (e-mail:
maryfleming@gateshead.gov.uk)
Principal Libraries Manager Stephen Walters BSc MCLIP (e-mail:
stephenwalters@gateshead.gov.uk)
Libraries Operations Manager Ms Angela Parker MCLIP (e-mail:
angelaparker@gateshead.gov.uk)
Arts Development Manager Ms Ednie Wilson BA (e-mail:
edniewilson@gateshead.gov.uk)

Libraries, Arts and Information Services, Civic Centre, Regent Street, Gateshead, Tyne and
Wear NE8 1HH
☎0191 433 3000
Head of Cultural Services David Bunce (e-mail: davidbunce@gateshead.gov.uk)

GLOUCESTERSHIRE
Authority: Gloucestershire County Council
HQ Libraries and Information Services, Quayside House, Shire Hall, Gloucester GL1 2HY
☎0845 230 5420 (general enquiries), (01452) 425048 (management)
Fax (01452) 425042
e-mail: libraryhelp@gloucestershire.gov.uk
url: www.gloucestershire.gov.uk/libraries
Head of Libraries and Information David Paynter MCLIP (e-mail:
david.paynter@gloucestershire.gov.uk)
Assistant Head of Libraries and Information (Policy and Performance) Ms Sue
Laurence BA(Hons) DipLib MCLIP (e-mail: sue.laurence@gloucestershire.gov.uk)
Assistant Head of Libraries and Information (Direct Services) Ms Jo Hand BA DipLib
MCLIP (e-mail: jo.hand@gloucestershire.gov.uk)
**Assistant Head of Libraries and Information (Business Management and Special
Projects)** John Holland BA(Hons) DipLib MCLIP (e-mail:
john.holland@gloucestershire.gov.uk)
Policy Development Officer, Children and Young People Ms Helen Briggs BA DMS
MCMI MCLIP (e-mail: helen.briggs@gloucestershire.gov.uk)
Policy Development Officer, Access and Reader Development Ms Jill Barker BA
DipLib MCLIP, Ms Kay Franklin MCLIP (e-mail: pdoaccess&rd@gloucestershire.gov.uk)
Policy Development Officer, Information and Adult Learning Ms Sarah Arnold
BA(Hons) (e-mail: sarah.arnold@gloucestershire.gov.uk)
Stock Manager Ms Helen Dorricott BA DipLib MA MCLIP (e-mail:
helen.dorricott@gloucestershire.gov.uk)

Central/largest libraries
Cheltenham Library, Clarence Street, Cheltenham, Glos GL50 3JT
☎(01242) 532688/532685
Fax (01242) 532684
Library Manager Ms Jane Allen

Gloucester Library, Brunswick Road, Gloucester GL1 1HT
☎(01452) 426973

Fax (01452) 521468
Library Manager Ms Jenny Potter

Area libraries
▶ Cheltenham and Tewkesbury. Based at Cheltenham Library, Clarence Street, Cheltenham, Glos GL50 3JT
☎(01242) 532678
Fax (01242) 532673
Area Manager Ms Kathleen Sullivan BA MA (e-mail: kathleen.sullivan@gloucestershire.gov.uk)
▶ Gloucester and Forest. Based at Gloucester Library, Brunswick Road, Gloucester GL1 1HT
☎(01452) 426976
Fax (01452) 521468
Area Manager Ms Christiane Nicholson BA MCLIP (e-mail: christiane.nicholson@gloucestershire.gov.uk)
▶ Stroud and Cotswolds. Based at Stroud Library, Lansdown, Stroud, Glos GL5 1BB
☎(01453) 756842
Fax (01453) 757829
Area Manager Mrs Mary Tucker BA MLib MCLIP (e-mail: mary.tucker@gloucestershire.gov.uk)

Selected branch libraries
▶ Cirencester Bingham Library, The Waterloo, Cirencester, Glos GL7 2PZ
☎(01285) 659813
Fax (01285) 640449
Library Manager Ms Carole Summerell
▶ Tewkesbury Library, Sun Street, Tewkesbury, Glos GL20 5NX
☎(01684) 293086
Fax (01684) 290125
Library Manager Ms Janet Thomson

GREENWICH

Authority: London Borough of Greenwich
HQ Culture and Community Services, 13th Floor, Riverside House, Woolwich High Street, London SE18 6DN
☎020 8317 4466
Fax 020 8317 4868
e-mail: libraries@greenwich.gov.uk
url: www.greenwich.gov.uk
Head of Community Services Vacant

District libraries
▶ Blackheath Library, 17-23 Old Dover Road, London SE3 7BT
☎020 8858 1131
Fax 020 8853 3615
▶ Eltham Library, Eltham High Street, London SE9 1TS
☎020 8850 2268

Fax 020 8850 1368
▶ Woolwich Library, Calderwood Street, London SE18 6QZ
☎020 8921 5750
Fax 020 8316 1645

HACKNEY

Authority: London Borough of Hackney
HQ Strategic Leadership Team, Homerton Library, Homerton High Street, London E9 6AS
☎020 8356 1697
Fax 020 8356 1692
Head of Libraries, Archives and Information Services Ms Nicola Baker BA MCLIP
MBA (020 8356 2560; fax: 020 8356 7575; e-mail: nicola.baker@hackney.gov.uk)
(Based at First Floor, Maurice Bishop House, 17 Reading Lane, London E8 1HH)
Archives and Information Manager, Libraries Edward Rogers (e-mail:
edward.rogers@hackney.gov.uk)
Development Manager, Libraries Ms Anita Kane (020 8356 1696; fax: 020 8356 1693;
e-mail: anita.kane@hackney.gov.uk)
Operations Manager, Libraries John Holland (020 8356 1695; fax: 020 8356 1693;
e-mail: john.holland@hackney.gov.uk)

Central/largest library
Hackney Central Library, Technology and Learning Centre, 1 Reading Lane, London E8 1GQ
☎020 8356 2562
Library Manager Ms Sue Comitti (e-mail: sue.comitti@hackney.gov.uk)
Information Services Co-ordinator Cyprian Marah (020 8356 2568; e-mail:
cyprian.marah@hackney.gov.uk)

Town centre libraries
▶ C L R James Library, 24-30 Dalston Lane, London E8 3AZ
☎020 8356 1665
Fax 020 7254 4655
▶ Clapton Library, Northwold Road, London E5 8RA
☎020 8356 1620
Fax 020 8806 7849
▶ Community Services Team, Stoke Newington Library, Church Street, London N16 0JS
☎020 8356 5238
▶ Hackney Archives, 43 De Beauvoir Road, London N1 5SQ
☎020 7241 2886
Fax 020 7241 6688
e-mail: archives@hackney.gov.uk
url: www.hackney.gov.uk/archives
Principal Archivist Vacant
▶ Homerton Library, Homerton High Street, London E9 6AS
☎020 8356 1690
Fax 020 8525 7945
▶ Shoreditch Library, 80 Hoxton Street, London N1 6LP
☎020 8356 4350

❱ Stamford Hill Library, Portland Avenue, London N16 6SB
☎020 8356 1700
Fax 020 8809 5986

❱ Stoke Newington Library, Church Street, London N16 0JS
☎020 8356 5230
Fax 020 8356 5237
Library Manager Ms Jackie Obeney (020 8356 5238; e-mail:
jackie.obeney@hackney.gov.uk)

HALTON

Authority: Halton Borough Council
HQ Halton Lea Library, Halton Lea, Runcorn, Cheshire WA7 2PF
☎(01928) 715351
Fax (01928) 790221
url: www2.halton.gov.uk
Library Services Manager Mrs Paula Reilly-Cooper BSc DipLib MCLIP (0151 424 2061
ext 4096; e-mail: paula.reilly-cooper@halton-borough.gov.uk) (Based at Runcorn Town
Hall, Heath Road, Runcorn, Cheshire WA7 5TD)
Specialist Services Manager Mrs Julie Potter BA(Hons) MCLIP, Philip Cooke BA(Hons)
MA (e-mail: philip.cooke@halton-borough.gov.uk)
Stock Specialist Officer Miss Trudy Burr BA(Hons) MCLIP
Reference and Information Officer Mrs Jean Bradburn MCLIP
Systems Officer Philip Cooke BA(Hons) MA (e-mail:
philip.cooke@halton-borough.gov.uk), Miss Shauna Henry BA(Hons) DipLib MCLIP
Bibliographical Services Officer Mrs Geraldine Kane BA(Hons) MCLIP

Central/largest library
Halton Lea Library, Halton Lea, Runcorn, Cheshire WA7 2PF
☎Tel/fax etc. as HQ
Senior Librarian Miss Siobhan Kirk BA(Hons) MCLIP

Area libraries
❱ Ditton Library, Queens Avenue, Ditton, Widnes, Cheshire WA8 8HR
☎0151 424 2459
Senior Librarian Mrs Kay Marshall BA MCLIP (0151 907 8383)

❱ Runcorn Library, Egerton Street, Runcorn, Cheshire WA7 1JL
☎(01928) 574495
Senior Librarian Miss Siobhan Kirk BA(Hons) MCLIP (01928 715351)

❱ Widnes Library, Victoria Square, Widnes, Cheshire WA8 7QY
☎0151 907 8383
Fax 0151 907 8384
Senior Librarian Mrs Kay Marshall BA MCLIP (0151 907 8383)

HAMMERSMITH AND FULHAM

Authority: London Borough of Hammersmith and Fulham
HQ Hammersmith Library, Shepherds Bush Road, London W6 7AT

☎020 8753 2400 (24-hr information phoneline), 020 8753 3823 (enquiries), 020 8753 3813 (administration)
Fax 020 8753 3815
url: www.lbhf.gov.uk
Head of Libraries David Herbert BA MLS MCLIP (020 8753 3810; e-mail: david.herbert@lbhf.gov.uk)
Borough Archivist and Local History Manager Ms Jane Kimber BA(Hons) DAA MSc (020 8741 5159; e-mail: jane.kimber@lbhf.gov.uk)
Library Development Manager Ms Amanda Stirrup BA MCLIP (020 8753 3811; e-mail: amanda.stirrup@lbhf.gov.uk)
Library Operations Manager Steve Liddle BA(Hons) DipLib (020 8753 3811; e-mail: steven.liddle@lbhf.gov.uk)

Area libraries

▶ Fulham Library, 598 Fulham Road, London SW6 5NX
  ☎020 8753 3879
  Senior Librarian Ms Jenny Samuels MCLIP
▶ Hammersmith Library, Shepherds Bush Road, London W6 7AT
  ☎Tel/fax etc. as HQ
  Senior Librarian Ms Gaynor Lynch MCLIP, Ms Linda Hardman MSc MCLIP (job-share)

Branch libraries

▶ Askew Road Library, 87/91 Askew Road, London W12 9AS
  ☎020 8753 3863
▶ Barons Court Library, North End Crescent, London W14 8TG
  ☎020 8753 3888
▶ Sands End Library, The Community Centre, 59-61 Broughton Road, London SW6 2LA
  ☎020 8753 3885
▶ Shepherds Bush Library, 7 Uxbridge Road, London W12 8LJ
  ☎020 8753 3842
  Fax 020 8740 1712

Mobile Library Service and Housebound Readers Service
☎020 7610 4251

HAMPSHIRE

Authority: Hampshire County Council
HQ Library and Information Service, 81 North Walls, Winchester, Hants SO23 8BY
☎(01962) 826600
Fax (01962) 856615
url: www.hants.gov.uk/library
Head of Library and Information Service Richard Ward MLib MCLIP (01962 826621; fax: 01962 850667; e-mail: richard.ward@hants.gov.uk)
Head of County Services John Dunne BA MCLIP (01962 826616; e-mail: john.dunne@hants.gov.uk)
Head of Strategy and Performance Miss Sue Greenfield BA MIMgt MCLIP (01962 826684; e-mail: sue.greenfield@hants.gov.uk)

Head of Operations Mrs Marija Davies MCLIP (01962 826619; e-mail: marija.davies@hants.gov.uk)
Head of E-Government and ICT Ms Jan Jones BLib MCLIP (01962 826759; e-mail: jan.jones@hants.gov.uk)

HARINGEY

Authority: London Borough of Haringey
HQ Haringey Library Services, Central Library, High Road, Wood Green, London N22 6XD
☎020 8489 2754 (enquiries)
Fax 020 8489 2722
url: www.haringey.gov.uk
Head of Libraries, Archives and Museum Services Ms Diana Edmonds BA DipLib FCLIP
Principal Officer for Library Service Delivery Ms Maria Stephanou BSc(Hons) (020 8489 2736; e-mail: maria.stephanou@haringey.gov.uk)

Central/largest library
Wood Green Central Library, High Road, Wood Green, London N22 6XD
☎020 8489 2754
Fax 020 8489 2722
Principal Librarian Vacant

Area libraries
▶ Hornsey Library, Haringey Park, London N8 9JA
☎020 8489 1434
Principal Librarian Periyasamy Manoharan BSc(Hons) MSc
▶ Marcus Garvey Library, Tottenham Green Leisure Centre, 1 Philip Lane, London N15 4JA
☎020 8489 5353
Principal Librarian Kameljit Bedi

HARROW

Authority: London Borough of Harrow
HQ Civic Centre Library, PO Box 4, Civic Centre, Station Road, Harrow, Middlesex HA1 2UU
☎020 8424 1055/6 (enquiries), 020 8424 1059/1970 (administration)
Fax 020 8424 1971
e-mail: library@harrow.gov.uk
url: www.harrow.gov.uk
Group Manager Library Services Bob Mills BSc MCLIP DMS (e-mail: bob.mills@harrow.gov.uk)

Central/largest library
Gayton Library, Gayton Road, Harrow, Middlesex HA1 2HL
☎020 8427 6012/8986

Principal Librarian (Lending Services) John Pennells MCLIP DMS (e-mail: john.pennells@harrow.gov.uk)

HARTLEPOOL

Authority: Hartlepool Borough Council
HQ Central Library, 124 York Road, Hartlepool TS26 9DE
☎(01429) 272905
Fax (01429) 275685
e-mail: infodesk@hartlepool.gov.uk
url: www.hartlepool.gov.uk
Borough Librarian Mrs Susan Atkinson BA MCLIP DipRSA (e-mail: susan.atkinson@hartlepool.gov.uk)
Direct Services Officer Graham Jarritt BA(Hons) (e-mail: graham.jarritt@hartlepool.gov.uk)

Resources and Development
▶ Resources and Development Section, 2 Cromwell Street, Hartlepool TS24 7LR
☎(01429) 523644
Fax (01429) 275665
Resources and Development Officer Mrs Kay Tranter BA(Hons) (e-mail: kay.tranter@hartlepool.gov.uk)

HAVERING

Authority: London Borough of Havering
HQ Central Library, St Edwards Way, Romford, Essex RM1 3AR
☎(01708) 432389 (enquiries), (01708) 432379 (administration), (01708) 432393 (information services)
Fax (01708) 432391
e-mail: info@havering.gov.uk
url: www.havering.gov.uk
Borough Librarian Vacant

HEREFORDSHIRE

Authority: Herefordshire Council
HQ Herefordshire Libraries, Shirehall, Hereford HR1 2HY
☎(01432) 359830
Fax (01432) 260744
url: www.libraries.herefordshire.gov.uk
Library Policy and Development Manager Jeremy Alder BA(Hons) MCLIP (01432 260557; e-mail: jalder@herefordshire.gov.uk)
Stock Manager Mrs Carolyn Huckfield BA(Hons) MCLIP (01432 261570; e-mail: chuckfield@herefordshire.gov.uk)

Central library
Hereford Library, Broad Street, Hereford HR4 9AU

☎(01432) 383600
Fax (01432) 383607
Area Customer Services Manager (Central) Ms Kate Murray BA MCLIP

Largest libraries

▶ Leominster Library, 8 Buttercross, Leominster, Herefordshire HR6 8BN
☎(01432) 383290
Fax (01568) 616025
▶ Ross-on-Wye Library, Cantilupe Road, Ross-on-Wye, Herefordshire HR9 7AN
☎(01432) 383280
Fax (01432) 383282

HERTFORDSHIRE

Authority: Hertfordshire County Council
HQ Community Information: Libraries, New Barnfield, Travellers Lane, Hatfield, Herts AL10 8XG
☎(01438) 737333 (enquiries and administration)
Fax (01707) 281589
e-mail: firstname.lastname@hertscc.gov.uk
url: www.hertsdirect.org
Director of Community Information Andrew Robertson (01992 555609; fax: 01992 555614)
Head of Libraries, Heritage and Arts Ms Glenda Wood BA(Hons) DipLib MCLIP (01992 555610; e-mail: glenda.wood@hertscc.gov.uk)
Library Operational Development Manager Derek Knight MCLIP
Stock Manager Ms Sue Valentine MA(Hons) (01707 281584; e-mail: sue.valentine@hertscc.gov.uk)
Library Information Services Manager Andrew Bignell BA DipLib MCLIP (01707 281584; e-mail: andrew.bignell@hertscc.gov.uk)
Children, Families and Equalities Manager Ms Sue Jones MA MCLIP (01707 281630; e-mail: sue.jones@herts-sls.org.uk)

Central/largest library

Central Resources Library, New Barnfield, Travellers Lane, Hatfield, Herts AL10 8XG
☎(01438) 737333
Fax (01707) 281514
Central Resources Librarian Ms Myra Campbell MA MCLIP

District libraries

▶ Bishop's Stortford Library, The Causeway, Bishop's Stortford, Herts CM23 2EJ
☎(01438) 737333
Fax (01279) 307471
e-mail: bishopsstortford.library@hertscc.gov.uk
District Librarian Ms Jean Holmes BA MCLIP
▶ Borehamwood Library, Elstree Way, Borehamwood, Herts WD6 1JX
☎(01923) 471333
Fax (01923) 338414

e-mail: borehamwood.library@hertscc.gov.uk

District Librarian Ms Rachel Bilton

▶ Hemel Hempstead Library, Central Library, Combe Street, Hemel Hempstead, Hertfordshire HP1 1HJ
☎(01438) 737333
Fax (01442) 404660
e-mail: hemelhempstead.library@hertscc.gov.uk
District Librarian Ms Claire Barraclough BA MCLIP

▶ Hitchin Library, Paynes Park, Hitchin, Herts SG5 1EW
☎(01438) 737333
Fax (01462) 640529
e-mail: hitchin.library@hertscc.gov.uk
District Librarian Ms Iris Oakey BA DipLib MCLIP

▶ Hoddesdon Library, 98a High Street, Hoddesdon, Herts EN11 8HD
☎(01438) 737333
Fax (01992) 411039
e-mail: hoddesdon.library@hertscc.gov.uk
District Librarian Ms Carol Hill BA MCLIP

▶ Rickmansworth Library, High Street, Rickmansworth, Herts WD3 1EH
☎(01923) 471333
Fax (01923) 710384
District Librarian Ms Marie Staunton BA DipLib MCLIP

▶ St Albans Library, The Maltings, St Albans, Hertfordshire AL1 3JQ
☎(01438) 737333
Fax (01727) 848613
e-mail: stalbans.library@hertscc.gov.uk
District Librarian Russel Barrow BA(Hons)

▶ Stevenage Library, Southgate, Stevenage, Hertfordshire SG1 1HD
☎(01438) 737333
Fax (01438) 219026
e-mail: stevenage.library@hertscc.gov.uk
District Librarian Ms Iris Oakey BA DipLib MCLIP

▶ Watford Library, Hempstead Road, Watford, Hertfordshire WD1 3EU
☎(01923) 471333
Fax (01923) 334688
e-mail: watford.library@hertscc.gov.uk
District Librarian Ms Marie Staunton BA DipLib MCLIP

▶ Welwyn Garden City Library, Campus West, Welwyn Garden City, Herts AL8 6AE
☎(01438) 737333
Fax (01707) 897595
e-mail: wgc.library@hertscc.gov.uk
District Librarian Jim Macrae MA MCLIP

HILLINGDON

Authority: London Borough of Hillingdon
HQ Central Library, 14-15 High Street, Uxbridge, Middlesex UB8 1HD
☎(01895) 250600 (enquiries), (01895) 250700 (administration)

Fax (01895) 811164 administration)

e-mail: clibrary@hillingdon.gov.uk

url: www.hillingdon.gov.uk

Assistant Director, Cultural Services Trisha Grimshaw (01895 250625; fax: 01895 250831; e-mail: tgrimshaw@hillingdon.gov.uk)

Head of Public Service Josie Mitchell MCLIP (01895 250716; e-mail: jmitchell@hillingdongrid.org)

Head of Resources and Development Ms Eileen Smyth MCLIP (01895 250701; e-mail: esmyth@hillingdongrid.org)

Head of ICT Development Derrick Fernandes (01895 250701; e-mail: dfernandes@hillingdon.gov.uk)

Area libraries

▶ Central Library, 14-15 High Street, Uxbridge, Middlesex UB8 1HD
☎(01895) 250714
Fax (01895) 811164
e-mail: clibrary@hillingdon.gov.uk

▶ Hayes Library, Golden Crescent, Hayes, Middlesex UB3 1AQ
☎020 8573 2855
Fax 020 8848 0269

▶ Manor Farm Library, Bury Street, Ruislip, Middlesex HA4 7SU
☎(01895) 633651
Fax (01895) 677555

HOUNSLOW

Authority: London Borough of Hounslow

HQ Hounslow Library Network (CIP), Centrespace, Treaty Centre, High Street, Hounslow, Middlesex TW3 1ES

☎0845 456 2800 (enquiries), 0845 456 2921 (administration)

Fax 0845 456 2880

url: www.cip.com

Director of Culture and Heritage/Borough Librarian Vacant

Principal Librarian Ms Frances Stanbury MCLIP (e-mail: frances-stanbury@cip.org.uk)

Strategic Library Managers:

(IT and Electronic Resources) Ms Sarah Vass BA(Hons) MSc

(Staff and Learning Development) Ms Joy Harrison MCLIP

(Stock and Reader Development) Ms Elizabeth Lee BA MCLIP

Team Leaders (Adult Library Services) Michael Clift BA

(Bibliographical Services) Ms Elizabeth Cutts MCLIP, Ms Rosemary Jones (020 8894 2550)

(Community Services) Ms Gulshan Iqbal BA DipLib (e-mail: gulshan-iqbal@cip.org.uk)

(Customer Services) Ms Ann Greene

(Systems Team) Mike Fahey (0845 456 2964)

Central/largest library

Hounslow Library, Treaty Centre, High Street, Hounslow, Middlesex TW3 1ES

☎0845 456 2800

Fax 0845 456 2880
Principal Librarian Ms Frances Stanbury MCLIP (e-mail: frances-stanbury@cip.org.uk)

Branch libraries
▶ Bedfont Library, Staines Road, Bedfont, Middlesex TW14 8BD
☎020 8890 6173
▶ Brentford Library, Boston Manor Road, Brentford, Middlesex TW8 8DW
☎020 8560 8801
▶ Chiswick Library, Duke's Avenue, Chiswick, London W4 2AB
☎020 8994 1008
▶ Cranford Library, Bath Road, Cranford, Middlesex TW5 9TL
☎020 8759 0641
▶ Feltham Library, 210 The Centre, High Street, Feltham, Middlesex TW13 4BX
☎020 8890 3506
▶ Hanworth Library, 2-12 Hampton Road West, Hanworth, Middlesex TW13 6AW
☎020 8898 0256
▶ Heston Library, New Heston Road, Heston, Middlesex TW5 0LW
☎020 8570 1028
▶ Isleworth Library, Twickenham Road, Isleworth, Middlesex TW7 7EU
☎020 8560 2934
▶ Osterley Library, St Mary's Crescent, Osterley, Middlesex TW7 4NB
☎020 8560 4295

ISLE OF WIGHT

Authority: Isle of Wight Council
HQ Library Headquarters, 5 Mariners Way, Somerton Industrial Estate, Cowes, Isle of Wight PO31 8PD
☎(01983) 203880 (enquiries and administration)
Fax (01983) 203899
url: www.iwight.com/thelibrary
Libraries Officer Rob Jones BA MCLIP CertEd (e-mail: rob.jones@iow.gov.uk)
Community Services Librarian Bernie Hawkins BA MCLIP (e-mail: bernie.hawkins@iow.gov.uk)
Support Services Librarian Andrew Walker BA MCLIP (e-mail: andrew.walker@iow.gov.uk)
Stock Manager John English BLib DMS MCLIP (e-mail: john.english@iow.gov.uk)
Reader Development Librarian Ms Ruth Buckingham BA(Hons) MCLIP (e-mail: ruth.buckingham@iow.gov.uk)
Reference Librarian Mrs Sheila Caws BA(Hons) DipLib MCLIP (e-mail: sheila.caws@iow.gov.uk)
Prison Librarian Michael Margerison BA(Hons) PGDipILM (e-mail: michael.margerison@iow.gov.uk)

Central/largest library
Lord Louis Library, Orchard Street, Newport, Isle of Wight PO30 1LL
☎(01983) 527655 (enquiries and administration)
Fax (01983) 825972

Area libraries

▶ Bembridge Library, Church Road, Bembridge, Isle of Wight PO35 5NA
☎(01983) 873102 (tel/fax)

▶ Brighstone, New Road, Brighstone, Newport, Isle of Wight PO30 4BB
☎(01983) 740150 (tel/fax)

▶ Cowes Library, Beckford Road, Cowes, Isle of Wight PO31 7SG
☎(01983) 293341 (tel/fax)

▶ East Cowes Library, The York Centre, 11 York Avenue, East Cowes, Isle of Wight PO32 6QY
☎(01983) 293019 (tel/fax)

▶ Freshwater Library, School Green Road, Freshwater, Isle of Wight PO35 5NA
☎(01983) 752377 (tel/fax)

▶ Niton Library, High Street, Niton, Isle of Wight PO38 2AZ
☎(01983) 730863 (tel/fax)

▶ Ryde Library, George Street, Ryde, Isle of Wight PO33 2JE
☎(01983) 562170
Fax (01983) 615644

▶ Sandown Library, High Street, Sandown, Isle of Wight PO36 8AF
☎(01983) 402748 (tel/fax)

▶ Shanklin Library, Victoria Avenue, Shanklin, Isle of Wight PO37 6PG
☎(01983) 863126 (tel/fax)

▶ Ventnor Library, High Street, Ventnor, Isle of Wight PO38 1LZ
☎(01983) 852039 (tel/fax)

ISLINGTON

Authority: London Borough of Islington
HQ Library and Cultural Services, Central Library, 2 Fieldway Crescent, London N5 1PF
☎020 7527 6900 (enquiries), 020 7527 6905 (administration)
Fax 020 7527 6906
e-mail: library.informationunit@islington.gov.uk
url: www.islington.gov.uk/libraries
Head of Library and Cultural Services Ms Rosemary Doyle MCLIP MBA (020 7527 6903; e-mail: rosemary.doyle@islington.gov.uk)
Assistant Head of Service (Support) Ms Val Dawson MCLIP (020 7527 6907; e-mail: val.dawson@islington.gov.uk)
Assistant Head of Service (Public) Brendan Redmond MCLIP (020 7527 6909; e-mail: brendan.redmond@islington.gov.uk)

Central/largest library

Central Library, 2 Fieldway Crescent, London N5 1PF
☎020 7527 6900
Fax 020 7527 6902
Public Services Manager Ms Teresa Gibson (020 7527 6950; e-mail: teresa.gibson@islington.gov.uk)

Other libraries

▶ Archway Library, Hamlyn House, Highgate Hill, London N19 5PH

☎020 7527 7820
Fax 020 7527 7833
▶ Finsbury Library, 245 St John Street, London EC1V 4NB
☎020 7527 7960
Fax 020 7527 7998
▶ John Barnes Library, 275 Camden Road, London N7 0JN
☎020 7527 7900
Fax 020 7527 7907
▶ Lewis Carroll Library, 180 Copenhagen Street, London N1 0ST
☎020 7527 7936
Fax 020 7527 7935
▶ Mildmay Library, 21-23 Mildmay Park, London N1 4NA
☎020 7527 7880
Fax 020 7527 7898
▶ N4 Library, 26 Blackstock Road, London N4 2DW
☎020 7527 7800
▶ North Library, Manor Gardens, London N7 6JX
☎020 7527 7840
Fax 020 7527 7854
▶ South Library, 115-117 Essex Road, London N1 2SL
☎020 7527 7860
Fax 020 7527 7854
▶ West Library, Bridgeman Road, London N1 1BD
☎020 7527 7920
Fax 020 7527 7929

KENSINGTON AND CHELSEA

Authority: Royal Borough of Kensington and Chelsea
HQ Central Library, Phillimore Walk, London W8 7RX
☎020 7361 3010 (general enquiries), 020 7361 3058 (management)
Fax 020 7361 2976
e-mail: headoflibraryservice@rbkc.gov.uk
url: www.rbkc.gov.uk/libraries
Head of Library Service Ms J E Battye BA MCLIP
Interim Head of Library Operations Miss Elizabeth Hibbs BA DipLib MCLIP
Interim Support Services Manager Mrs Jo Alaimo

Main libraries
▶ Brompton Library, 210 Old Brompton Road, London SW5 0BS
☎020 7373 3111
▶ Central Library, Hornton Street, London W8 7RX
☎020 7361 3010
Fax 020 7361 2976
▶ Chelsea Library, The Old Town Hall, Kings Road, London SW3 5EZ
☎020 7352 6056
▶ North Kensington Library, 108 Ladbroke Grove, London W11 1PZ
☎020 7727 6583

KENT

Authority: Kent County Council
HQ Libraries and Archives, Springfield, Maidstone, Kent ME14 2LH
☎(01622) 696505
Fax (01622) 696450
url: www.kent.gov.uk
Head of Libraries and Archives Ms Cath Anley
Strategic Manager, East Kent Area Ms Lesley Spencer BA DipLib DMS MCLIP MCMI
Strategic Manager, West Kent Area Ms Gill Bromley MCLIP
Strategic Manager, Mid Kent Area Ms Susan Sparks MCLIP
Stock Services Manager Ken Jarvis MCLIP DCMS MIMgt
Area Manager, East Kent Gavin Wright
Area Manager, Mid Kent Ms Valerie Wright
Area Manager, West Kent Ms Jane Setterfield

Central/largest library

County Central Library, Springfield, Maidstone, Kent ME14 2LH
☎(01622) 696511
Fax (01622) 753338
Information Services Manager Ms Christel Pobgee
District Manager Ms Katy Hill

Main town centre libraries

▶ Ashford Library, Church Street, Ashford, Kent TN23 1QX
  ☎(01233) 620649
  Fax (01233) 620295
  District Manager Ms Joy Pritchard
▶ Canterbury Library, High Street, Canterbury, Kent CT1 2JF
  ☎(01227) 463608
  Fax (01227) 768338
  District Manager Ms Pat Tomlinson
▶ Dartford Library, Central Park, Dartford, Kent DA1 1EU
  ☎(01322) 221133
  Fax (01322) 278271
  District Manager Ms Jackie Taylor-Smith
▶ Dover Library, Dover Discovery Centre, Market Square, Dover, Kent CT16 1PB
  ☎(01304) 204241
  Fax (01304) 225914
  District Manager Ms Kelly Reekie
▶ Gravesend Library, Windmill Street, Gravesend, Kent DA12 1BE
  ☎(01474) 352758
  Fax (01474) 320284
  District Manager Christopher Bull
▶ Maidstone Library, St Faith's Street, Maidstone, Kent ME14 1LH
  ☎(01622) 752344
  Fax (01622) 754980
  District Manager Ms Katy Hill

▶ Sevenoaks Library, Buckhurst Lane, Sevenoaks, Kent TN13 1LQ
☎(01732) 453118
Fax (01732) 742682
District Manager Ms Fiona Dutton

▶ Shepway - Folkestone Library, 2 Grace Hill, Folkestone, Kent CT20 1HD
☎(01303) 850123
Fax (01303) 242907
District Manager Ms Jan Rudolph

▶ Sittingbourne Library, Central Avenue, Sittingbourne, Kent ME10 4AH
☎(01795) 476545
Fax (01795) 428376
District Manager Ms Lesley Rich

▶ Thanet - Margate Library, Cecil Square, Margate, Kent CT9 1RE
☎(01843) 223626
Fax (01843) 293015
District Manager Ms Lynn Catt

▶ Tonbridge Library, Avebury Avenue, Tonbridge, Kent TN9 1TG
☎(01732) 352754
Fax (01732) 358300
District Manager Ms Sue Wheeler BA DipLib MCLIP

▶ Tunbridge Wells Library, Mount Pleasant Road, Tunbridge Wells, Kent TN1 1NS
☎(01892) 522352
Fax (01892) 514657
District Manager Ms Clare Hamilton

Other town libraries

▶ Broadstairs Library, The Broadway, Broadstairs, Kent CT10 2BS
☎(01843) 862994

▶ Cranbrook Library, Carriers Road, Cranbrook, Kent TN17 3JT
☎(01580) 712463

▶ Deal Library, Broad Street, Deal, Kent CT14 6ER
☎(01304) 374726

▶ Faversham Library, Newton Road, Faversham, Kent ME13 8DY
☎(01795) 532448

▶ Herne Bay Library, 124 High Street, Herne Bay, Kent CT6 5JY
☎(01227) 374896

▶ Hythe Library, 1 Stade Street, Hythe, Kent CT21 6BQ
☎(01303) 267111

▶ Ramsgate Library, Cannon Road Car Park, Cannon Road, Ramsgate, Kent
☎(01843) 593532
Temporary premises due to fire – limited services only

▶ Sandwich Library, 13 Market Street, Sandwich, Kent CT13 9DA
☎(01304) 613819

▶ Sheerness Library, Russell Street, Sheerness, Kent ME12 1PL
☎(01795) 566100

▶ Swanley Library, London Road, Swanley, Kent BR8 7AE
☎(01322) 662570

▶ Tenterden Library, 55 High Street, Tenterden, Kent TN30 6BD
☎(01580) 762558

▶ Whitstable Library, 31-33 Oxford Street, Whitstable, Kent CT5 1DB
☎(01227) 273309

(Note: these do not represent the full list of branch libraries)

KINGSTON UPON HULL

Authority: Kingston upon Hull City Council
HQ Central Library, Albion Street, Kingston upon Hull HU1 3TF
☎(01482) 210000 (enquiries), (01482) 616822 (administration)
Fax (01482) 616827
url: www.hullcc.gov.uk
City Librarian Mrs Jo Edge BA DipLib (01482 616832; e-mail: jo.edge@hullcc.gov.uk)

Area libraries

▶ Anlaby Park Library, The Greenway, Anlaby High Road, Kingston upon Hull HU4 6TX
☎(01482) 505506

▶ Avenues Library, 76 Chanterlands Avenue, Kingston upon Hull HU5 3TS
☎(01482) 331280

▶ Bransholme Library, District Centre, Goodhart Road, Bransholme, Kingston upon Hull HU7 4EF
☎(01482) 331234

▶ Fred Moore Library, Wold Road, Derringham Bank, Kingston upon Hull HU5 5UN
☎(01482) 331239

▶ Garden Village Library, Shopping Centre, Garden Village, Kingston upon Hull HU8 8QE
☎(01482) 781723

▶ Gipsyville Library, 728-730 Hessle High Road, Kingston upon Hull HU4 6JA
☎(01482) 616973

▶ Greenwood Avenue Library, Greenwood Avenue, Kingston upon Hull HU6 9RU
☎(01482) 331257

▶ Harry Lewis Library, Annandale Road, Kingston upon Hull HU9 5HD
☎(01482) 331264

▶ Ings Library, Savoy Road, Kingston upon Hull HU8 0TY
☎(01482) 331250

▶ James Reckitt Library, Holderness Road, Kingston upon Hull HU9 1EA
☎(01482) 331551

▶ Kingswood Community Library, Wawne Road, Kingston upon Hull HU7 4WR
☎(01482) 331275

▶ Preston Road Library, Preston Road, Kingston upon Hull HU9 5UZ
☎(01482) 376266

▶ Stadium Library, The Learning Zone, KC Stadium, Walton Street, Kingston upon Hull HU3 6HU
☎(01482) 381947

▶ Western Library, The Boulevard, Hessle Road, Kingston upon Hull HU3 3ED
☎(01482) 320399

KINGSTON UPON THAMES

Authority: Royal Borough of Kingston upon Thames
HQ Kingston Library, Fairfield Road, Kingston upon Thames, Surrey KT1 2PS
☎020 8547 6413 (administration)
Fax 020 8547 6426
url: www.kingston.gov.uk
Head of Library Service Ms B Lee BA MCLIP (020 8547 6423; e-mail:
barbara.lee@rbk.kingston.gov.uk)
ICT Development Manager M O'Brien (020 8547 6420; e-mail:
mike.obrien@rbk.kingston.gov.uk)
Senior Team Librarian (Adult Services) Mrs E Ryder MCLIP (020 8547 6409; e-mail:
elizabeth.ryder@rbk.kingston.gov.uk)
Lifelong Learning Manager Dr A Rizzo BA MA (020 8547 6421; e-mail:
antonio.rizzo@rbk.kingston.gov.uk)

Branch libraries

▶ Community Library, Surbiton Library Annexe, Ewell Road, Surbiton, Surrey KT6 6AG
☎020 8339 7900
Fax 020 8339 9805
Library Manager Mrs E Burnside
▶ Hook and Chessington Library, Hook Road, Chessington, Surrey KT9 1EJ
☎020 8397 4931
Fax 020 8391 4410
Library Manager Ms M Newman (e-mail: michaela.newman@rbk.kingston.gov.uk)
▶ Kingston Library, Fairfield Road, Kingston upon Thames, Surrey KT1 2PS
☎020 8547 6400
Fax 020 8547 6401
Library Manager A Gale (e-mail: alan.gale@rbk.kingston.gov.uk)
▶ New Malden Library, Kingston Road, New Malden, Surrey KT3 3LY
☎020 8547 6540
Fax 020 8547 6545
Library Manager Adam Moore (e-mail: adam.moore@rbk.kingston.gov.uk)
▶ Old Malden Library, Church Road, Worcester Park, Surrey KT4 7RD
☎020 8337 6344
Fax 020 8330 3118
Library Manager J Plummer (e-mail: john.plummer@rbk.kingston.gov.uk)
▶ Surbiton Library, Ewell Road, Surbiton, Surrey KT6 6AG
☎020 8547 6444
Fax 020 8339 9805
Senior Library Manager Mrs J Allum (e-mail: janet.allum@rbk.kingston.gov.uk)
▶ Tolworth Community Library and IT Learning Centre, The Broadway, Tolworth,
Surbiton, Surrey KT6 7DJ
☎020 8547 6470
Fax 020 8339 6955
e-mail: tolworth.library@rbk.kingston.gov.uk
Library Manager Ms C Roberts
▶ Tudor Drive Library, Tudor Drive, Kingston upon Thames, Surrey KT2 5QH

☎020 8546 1198
Fax 020 8547 2295
Library Manager Ms S Montague (e-mail: sheila.montague@rbk.kingston.gov.uk)

KIRKLEES

Authority: Kirklees Metropolitan Council
HQ Kirklees Culture and Leisure Services, Red Doles Lane, Huddersfield, Yorkshire
HD2 1YF
☎(01484) 226300
Fax (01484) 226342
url: www.kirklees.gov.uk
Head of Culture and Leisure Services Ms Kimiyo Rickett (01484 234002; e-mail:
kimiyo.rickett@kirklees.gov.uk) (based at Stadium Business and Leisure Complex, Stadium
Way, Huddersfield HD1 6PG)
**Assistant Head of Culture and Leisure Services (Libraries, County History,
Galleries, Town Halls and Registration)** Rob Warburton BA MCLIP (01484 226340;
e-mail: rob.warburton@kirklees.gov.uk)
Assistant Head of Service (Library and Information Centres) Ms Catherine Morris
BA DLIS MCLIP DMS (01484 222401; e-mail: catherine.morris@kirklees.gov.uk)

Central/largest library
Central Library, Princess Alexandra Walk, Huddersfield, Yorkshire HD1 2SU
☎(01484) 226300
Fax (01484) 221952
Librarian i/c David Hatcher BSc DipLib MCLIP DMS (e-mail:
david.hatcher@kirklees.gov.uk)

Area libraries
▶ Batley/Cleckheaton Area. Batley Library, Market Place, Batley, West Yorks WF17 5DA
☎(01924) 326305
Librarian i/c Ms Ann Blakeley BA MCLIP DMS (e-mail: ann.blakeley@kirklees.gov.uk)
▶ Dewsbury/Mirfield Area. Dewsbury Library, Railway Street, Dewsbury, West Yorks
WF12 8EQ
☎(01924) 325085
Librarian i/c Ms Louise Hazell MSc BEd CertEd MCLIP (e-mail:
louise.hazell@kirklees.gov.uk)
▶ Mobiles and Home Service, Cultural Services HQ, Red Doles Lane, Huddersfield,
Yorkshire HD2 1YF
☎(01484) 226350
Librarian i/c Alison Peaden BA MCLIP (e-mail: alison.peaden@kirklees.gov.uk)
▶ West Kirklees Branches, Holmfirth Library, 47 Huddersfield Road, Holmfirth, West
Yorks HD9 3JH
☎(01484) 222432
Librarian i/c Ms Janet Pearson BSc(Hons) PGDipInfStud PGCentMgt (e-mail:
janet.pearson@kirklees.gov.uk)

KNOWSLEY

Authority: Knowsley Metropolitan Borough Council
HQ Knowsley Metropolitan Borough Council, Municipal Buildings, Archway Road, Huyton, Merseyside L36 9YX
☎0151 443 3680
Fax 0151 443 3492
url: www.knowsley.gov.uk/leisure/libraries
Head of Libraries Peter Marchant MA BH(Hons) DipLib DM MCLIP (e-mail: peter.marchant.dlcs@knowsley.gov.uk)

Central/largest library

Huyton Library, Civic Way, Huyton, Merseyside L36 9UN
☎0151 443 3734
Fax 0151 443 3739
e-mail: huyton.library.dlcs@knowsley.gov.uk
Library Managers Ms Angela Arden, Brian Lester

Branch libraries

▶ Central Services Unit, 599 Princess Drive, Huyton, Merseyside L14 9ND
☎0151 482 1302
Fax 0151 482 1309
e-mail: central.services.unit.dlcs@knowsley.gov.uk
Central Services Manager Frank Wilson
▶ Halewood Library, Leathers Lane, Halewood, Merseyside L26 0TS
☎0151 486 4442
Fax 0151 486 8101
e-mail: halewood.library.dlcs@knowsley.gov.uk
Library Manager Philip Perry
▶ Kirkby Library, Newtown Gardens, Kirkby, Merseyside L32 8RR
☎0151 443 4290
Fax 0151 546 1453
e-mail: kirkby.library.dlcs@knowsley.gov.uk
Library Manager Ms Phyl Carolan
▶ Page Moss Library, Stockbridge Lane, Huyton, Merseyside L36 3SA
☎0151 489 9814
Fax 0151 480 9284
e-mail: page.moss.library.dlcs@knowsley.gov.uk
Library Manager Ms Margaret Wiggins, Ms Michele Hayes
▶ Prescot Library, High Street, Prescot, Merseyside L34 3LD
☎0151 426 6449
Fax 0151 430 7548
e-mail: prescot.library.dlcs@knowsley.gov.uk
Library Manager Mrs Diane Lester, Mrs Erica Jones
▶ Stockbridge Village Library, The Withens, Stockbridge Village, Merseyside L28 1SU
☎0151 480 3925 (tel/fax)
e-mail: stockbridge.library.dlcs@knowsley.gov.uk
Library Manager David Birchall

▶ Whiston Library, Dragon Lane, Whiston, Merseyside L3 3QW
☎0151 426 4757
Fax 0151 493 0191
e-mail: whiston.library.dlcs@knowsley.gov.uk
Library Manager Ms Trish Fletcher

LAMBETH

Authority: London Borough of Lambeth
HQ Libraries, Archives and Arts Headquarters, 3rd Floor, International House, Canterbury Crescent, London SW9 7QE
☎020 7926 0750 (enquiries)
Fax 020 7926 0751
url: www.lambeth.gov.uk
Head of Libraries, Archives and Arts Ms Lesley Ray MCLIP (e-mail: lray@lambeth.gov.uk)
Deputy Head of Libraries, Archives and Arts Ms Sandra Goodwin BSc (e-mail: sgoodwin@lambeth.gov.uk)
Development Manager, Learning and Access Ms Susan Doyle MCLIP (e-mail: sdoyle@lambeth.gov.uk)
Development Manager, Information and ICT Vacant
Support Services Manager Ms Michele Watkins (e-mail: mwatkins@lambeth.gov.uk)

Minet Archives and Lending Library
▶ Minet Library, 52 Knatchbull Road, London SE5 9QY
☎020 7926 6076
Fax 020 7926 6080
e-mail: minetlibrary@lambeth.gov.uk/archives@lambeth.gov.uk
Manager Jon Newman MA DAA (e-mail: jnewman@lambeth.gov.uk), Len Reilly BA DipLib MCLIP (e-mail: ljreilly@lambeth.gov.uk)

North Area
▶ Clapham Library, 1 Northside, Clapham Common, London SW4 0QW
☎020 7926 0717
Fax 020 7926 4859
e-mail: claphamlibrary@lambeth.gov.uk
Area Library Manager Michel Merson (e-mail: mmerson@lambeth.gov.uk)
▶ Durning Library, 167 Kennington Lane, London SE11 4HF
☎020 7926 8682
Fax 020 7926 8685
e-mail: durninglibrary@lambeth.gov.uk
▶ South Lambeth Library, 180 South Lambeth Road, London SW8 1QP
☎020 7926 0705
Fax 020 7926 0708
e-mail: southlambethlibrary@lambeth.gov.uk
▶ Waterloo Library, 114–118 Lower Marsh, London SE1 7AG
☎020 7926 8750

Fax 020 7926 8749
e-mail: waterloolibrary@lambeth.gov.uk

Central Area
▶ Brixton Library, Brixton Oval, London SW2 1JQ
☎020 7926 1056
Fax 020 7926 1070
e-mail: brixtonlendinglibrary@lambeth.gov.uk
Area Library Manager Ms Laura Chrysostomou (e-mail:
lchrysostomou@lambeth.gov.uk)
▶ Carnegie Library, 188 Herne Hill Road, London SE24 0AG
☎020 7926 6050
Fax 020 7926 6072
e-mail: carnegielibrary@lambeth.gov.uk

South Area
▶ Streatham Library, 63 Streatham High Road, London SW16 1PL
☎020 7926 6768
Fax 020 7926 5804
e-mail: streathamlibrary@lambeth.gov.uk
Area Library Manager Ms Marcia Bogle-Mayne (e-mail:
mboglemayne@lambeth.gov.uk)
▶ West Norwood Library, Norwood High Street, London SE27 9JX
☎020 7926 8092
Fax 020 7926 8032
e-mail: westnorwoodlibrary@lambeth.gov.uk

Support Services
▶ Library Systems, 188 Herne Hill, London SE24 0AG
☎020 7926 6090
Fax 020 7926 6072
e-mail: librarysystems@lambeth.gov.uk
Systems Manager (ICT) Ms Michelle Thomas BSc (e-mail:
mthomas3@lambeth.gov.uk)
▶ Stock Services, 188 Herne Hill Road, London SE24 0AG
☎020 7926 6069
Fax 020 7926 6072
e-mail: stocksupportservices@lambeth.gov.uk
Stock Services Manager Ms Clare Stockbridge-Bland BA MCLIP (e-mail:
cstockbridgebland@lambeth.gov.uk)

LANCASHIRE

Authority: Lancashire County Council
HQ Education and Cultural Services Directorate, County Library and Information Service,
County Hall, PO Box 61, Preston, Lancashire PR1 8RJ
☎(01772) 524008
Fax (01772) 534880

e-mail: library@lcl.lancscc.gov.uk

url: www.lancashire.gov.uk/libraries

County Library Manager David G Lightfoot MA DMS MCLIP (01772 534010; e-mail: david.lightfoot@lcl.lancscc.gov.uk)

Assistant County Library Managers David Blackett BA MCLIP (01772 534091; e-mail: david.blackett@lcl.lancscc.gov.uk), Ms Judith Farrell MCLIP (01772 532440; e-mail: judith.farrell@lcl.lancscc.gov.uk)

Divisional libraries

▶ Central Lancashire Division. Harris Library, Market Square, Preston, Lancashire PR1 2PP
☎(01772) 532676, (01772) 532409 (administration)
Fax (01772) 534053
Divisional Librarian Vacant

▶ East Lancashire Division. Divisional Library, Grimshaw Street, Burnley, Lancs BB11 2BD
☎(01282) 437115
Fax (01282) 831682
Divisional Librarian John Hodgkinson BA MCLIP

▶ North Lancashire Division. Divisional Library, Telephone House, Fenton Street, Lancaster LA1 1AB
☎(01524) 585270
Fax (01524) 845125
Divisional Librarian Steve Eccles MCLIP

▶ South East Lancashire Division. Divisional Library, St James' Street, Accrington, Lancs BB5 1NQ
☎(01254) 872385
Fax (01254) 306912
Divisional Librarian Ms Julie Bell BA(Hons) MCLIP

▶ South Lancashire Division. Divisional Library, Union Street, Chorley, Lancs PR7 1EB
☎(01257) 277222
Fax (01257) 231730
Divisional Librarian Denis Whitham BSc MCLIP

LEEDS

Authority: Leeds City Council

HQ Learning and Leisure Department, 7th Floor (West), No 110 Merrion Centre, Merrion House, Leeds LS2 8DT
☎0113 247 8330 (management enquiries)
Fax 0113 247 8331
url: www.leeds.gov.uk
Chief Libraries, Arts and Heritage Officer Ms Catherine Blanshard BA MCLIP (e-mail: catherine.blanshard@leeds.gov.uk)

Library headquarters

Library Headquarters, 32 York Road, Leeds LS9 8TD
☎0113 214 3300 (general enquiries)
Fax 0113 214 3312

Libraries Development Manager Ms Patricia Carroll BA MCLIP (e-mail: patricia.carroll@leeds.gov.uk)

Central/largest library

Central Library, Municipal Buildings, Calverley Street, Leeds LS1 3AB
☎0113 247 8274
Fax 0113 247 8268
url: www.leeds.gov.uk
Library Service Delivery Manager Ms Bev Rice BA (e-mail: bev.rice@leeds.gov.uk)

LEICESTER

Authority: Leicester City Council
HQ Education and Lifelong Learning Department, 12th Floor, Block A, New Walk Centre, Welford Place, Leicester LE1 6ZG
☎0116 252 6762 (administration)
Fax 0116 255 6048
e-mail: libraries@leicester.gov.uk/libraries
url: www.leicester.gov.uk
Head of Libraries and Information Services Ms Patricia Flynn BA(Hons) DMS (e-mail: patricia.flynn@leicester.gov.uk)
Libraries Network Manager Adrian Wills BA DMS MCLIP (0116 252 7327; e-mail: adrian.wills@leicester.gov.uk)
Quality & Development Manager Michael Maxwell BA(Hons) DMS MCLIP (0116 252 7334; e-mail: michael.maxwell@leicester.gov.uk)
Inclusion and Diversity Manager Ms Penny Leahy BA(Hons) MCLIP (0116 252 7336; e-mail: penny.leahy@leicester.gov.uk)

Central/largest libraries

Central Lending Library, 54 Belvoir Street, Leicester LE1 6QL
☎0116 299 5402 (enquiries)
Fax 0116 299 5434
e-mail: central.lending@leicester.gov.uk
Adult Lending Services Manager Michael Lewis

Reference and Information Library, Bishop Street, Leicester LE1 6AA
☎0116 299 5401
Fax 0116 299 5444
e-mail: central.reference@leicester.gov.uk
Central Reference and Information Services Manager Ms Sally Mitchell

LEICESTERSHIRE

Authority: Leicestershire County Council
HQ Library Services, County Hall, Glenfield, Leicester LE3 8SS
☎0116 265 7377 (enquiries), 0116 265 7380 (administration)
Fax 0116 265 7370
e-mail: libraries@leics.gov.uk

url: www.leics.gov.uk/libraries
Head of Library Services Ms Margaret Bellamy DMS MBA MCLIP (e-mail: mbellamy@leics.gov.uk)
Service Delivery Manager Nigel Thomas BLib(Hons) MCLIP (e-mail: nthomas@leics.gov.uk)

Main library group HQs

▶ Loughborough Library, Granby Street, Loughborough, Leics LE11 3DZ
☎(01509) 212985/266436
Fax (01509) 610594
Area Manager Ms Gill Loveridge BA MBA MCLIP (e-mail: gloveridge@leics.gov.uk)
District Community Manager Ms Lesley Bowell BA MCLIP (e-mail: lbowell@leics.gov.uk)

▶ Wigston Library, Bull Head Street, Wigston, Leicester LE18 1PA
☎0116 288 7381/257 1891
Fax 0116 281 2985
Area Manager Mrs Lorraine Selby (e-mail: lselby@leics.gov.uk)
District Community Manager Mrs Jane Berry BA DipLib MCLIP (e-mail: jberry@leics.gov.uk)

Market town libraries

▶ Coalville Library, High Street, Coalville, Leics LE67 3EA
☎(01530) 835951
Fax (01530) 832019
District Community Manager Mrs Jude StC Flint MLS DMS MCLIP (e-mail: jflint@leics.gov.uk)

▶ Hinckley Library, Lancaster Road, Hinckley, Leics LE10 0AT
☎(01455) 635106
Fax (01455) 251385
District Community Manager Ms Caroline Drodge BA DipLib MCLIP (e-mail: cdrodge@leics.gov.uk)

▶ Melton Mowbray Library, Wilton Road, Melton Mowbray, Leics LE13 0UJ
☎(01664) 560161
Fax (01664) 410199
District Community Managers Ms Ruth Pointer BA MCLIP (e-mail: rpointer@leics.gov.uk), Mrs Janet Gilchrist BA MCLIP (e-mail: jgilchrist@leics.gov.uk)

▶ Pen Lloyd Library, Adam & Eve Street, Market Harborough, Leics LE16 7LT
☎(01858) 821272
Fax (01858) 821265
District Community Managers Ms Stephanie Robbins BA MCLIP (e-mail: srobbins@leics.gov.uk), Mrs Jackie Knight MCLIP (e-mail: jknight@leics.gov.uk)

LEWISHAM

Authority: London Borough of Lewisham
HQ Education and Culture, 1st Floor, Town Hall Chambers, Catford, London SE6 4RU
☎020 8314 8024 (enquiries)
Fax 020 8314 3229

url: www.lewisham.gov.uk
Head of Libraries and Information Ms Julia Newton MCLIP (e-mail: julia.newton@lewisham.gov.uk)

Central/largest library

Lewisham Library, 199-201 Lewisham High Street, London SE13 6LG
☎020 8297 9677
Fax 020 8297 1169
Central Librarian Ms Michelle Gannon (e-mail: michelle.gannon@lewisham.gov.uk)

Neighbourhood library

▶ Catford Library, Laurence House, Catford, London SE6 4RU
☎020 8314 6399
Fax 020 8314 1110
Neighbourhood Librarian Ms Monica Yarde
(e-mail: monica.yarde@lewisham.gov.uk)

District library

▶ Wavelengths Library, Giffin Street, Deptford, London SE8 4RJ
☎020 8694 2535
Fax 020 8694 9652
District Librarian Ms Glenys Englert

LINCOLNSHIRE

Authority: Lincolnshire County Council
HQ Education and Cultural Services Directorate, County Offices, Newland, Lincoln LN1 1YL
☎(01522) 553207
Fax (01522) 552811
url: www.lincolnshire.gov.uk
Head of Libraries, Sport and Support Services John Pateman BA DipLib MBA FCLIP
(e-mail: john.pateman@lincolnshire.gov.uk)

Central/largest library

Lincoln Central Library, Free School Lane, Lincoln LN2 1EZ
☎(01522) 510800 (general enquiries), (01522) 579200 (management)
Fax (01522) 575011
e-mail: lincoln.library@lincolnshire.gov.uk
Training and Development Manager Mrs Jan Mehmet BA DipLib MCLIP AMITD
(e-mail: jan.mehmet@lincolnshire.gov.uk)

Area libraries

▶ Mid-Lincolnshire (Sleaford). Sleaford Library, Eastgate Centre, 105 Eastgate, Sleaford, Lincs NG34 7EN
☎(01529) 414770
Fax (01529) 415329
Resources Manager Gary Porter (e-mail: gary.porter@lincolnshire.gov.uk)

▶ North (Louth). Louth Library, Northgate, Louth, Lincs LN11 0LY
☎(01507) 602218
Fax (01507) 608261
Community Services Manager Ms Gill Fraser MA MCLIP (e-mail:
gill.fraser@lincolnshire.gov.uk)

▶ South (Boston), County Hall, Boston, Lincs PE21 6DY
☎(01522) 552871
Fax (01522) 552882
Information Services Manager Ms Dianne Slapp (e-mail:
dianne.slapp@lincolnshire.gov.uk)

Other services

▶ Library Support Services, Lexicon House, Stephenson Road, Off Station Road, North
Hykeham, Lincoln LN6 3QU
☎(01522) 552866
Fax (01522) 552858
Operations Manager Ms Alison Peden (e-mail: alison.peden@lincolnshire.gov.uk)

▶ Special Services (Schools and Library Services to Centres), Lexicon House, Stephenson
Road, Off Station Road, North Hykeham, Lincoln LN6 3QU
☎(01522) 552804
Fax (01522) 552858
Special Services Manager Ms W Bond BA MCLIP, Ms Toni Franck (job share)

LIVERPOOL

Authority: Liverpool City Council
HQ Liverpool Libraries and Information Services, 2nd Floor, Millennium House, 60 Victoria
Street, Liverpool L1 6JD
☎0151 233 6346
Fax 0151 233 6399
url: www.liverpool.gov.uk
Head of Libraries and Information Services Miss Joyce Little BA(Hons) MBA MCLIP
(e-mail: joyce.little@liverpool.gov.uk)
Manager (Library Effectiveness) Alan Metcalf BSc DipLib MCLIP (0151 233 5808;
e-mail: alan.metcalf@liverpool.gov.uk)
Manager (Learner Support) John Keane BA(Hons) MCLIP (0151 233 5833; e-mail:
john.keane@liverpool.gov.uk)
Manager (Operational Services) Kenneth Kay BA(Hons) DipLib MCLIP (0151 233 5857;
e-mail: kenneth.kay@liverpool.gov.uk)
Manager (Community Libraries) Ron Travis BA(Hons) MA MCLIP (0151 233 5847;
e-mail: ron.travis@liverpool.gov.uk)

Central/largest library

Central Library, William Brown Street, Liverpool L3 8EW
☎0151 233 5835 (enquiries), 0151 233 5851 (administration)
Fax 0151 233 5886 (enquiries), 0151 233 5824 (administration)
e-mail: refbt.central.library@liverpool.gov.uk

Manager (Central Library) Ms Kathy Johnson BA DipLib (0151 233 5879; e-mail: kathy.johnson@liverpool.gov.uk)

Other large libraries
▶ Allerton Library, Liverpool L18 6HG
☎0151 724 2987
e-mail: allerton.library@liverpool.gov.uk
▶ Childwall Fiveways Library, Liverpool L15 6QR
☎0151 722 3214
e-mail: childwall.library@liverpool.gov.uk
▶ Norris Green Library, Townsend Avenue, Liverpool L11 5AF
☎0151 226 1714
e-mail: norrisgreen.library@liverpool.gov.uk

LONDON, CITY OF

Authority: Corporation of London
HQ Guildhall Library, Aldermanbury, London EC2P 2EJ
☎020 7332 1852
Fax 020 7600 3384
url: www.citylibraries.info
Director David Bradbury MA MCLIP (e-mail: david.bradbury@corpoflondon.gov.uk)
Assistant Director (Libraries and Archives) Ms Lesley Blundell BA MCLIP (e-mail: lesley.blundell@corpoflondon.gov.uk)
Assistant Director (Art Galleries and Support Services) Barry Cropper MA DipLib MCLIP MIMgt (e-mail: barry.cropper@corpoflondon.gov.uk)

Central/largest libraries
Barbican Library, Barbican Centre, Silk Street, London EC2Y 8DS
☎020 7638 0569
Fax 020 7638 2249
Librarian i/c John Lake BA MCLIP (e-mail: john.lake@corpoflondon.gov.uk)

Guildhall Library, Aldermanbury, London EC2P 2EJ
☎020 7332 1868
Fax 020 7600 3384
Librarian i/c Ms Irene Gilchrist BD DipLib (e-mail: irene.gilchrist@corpoflondon.gov.uk)

Regional/district libraries
▶ Camomile Street Library, 12-20 Camomile Street, London EC3A 7EX
☎020 7247 8895
Fax 020 7377 2972
Librarian i/c Malcolm Key BA MCLIP (e-mail: malcolm.key@corpoflondon.gov.uk)
▶ City Business Library, 1 Brewers' Hall Garden, London EC2V 5BX
☎020 7332 1812
Fax 020 7332 1847
Librarian i/c Ms Diana Moulding (e-mail: diana.moulding@corpoflondon.gov.uk)
▶ Shoe Lane Library, Hill House, Little New Street, London EC4A 3JR

☎020 7583 7178
Fax 020 7353 0884
Librarian i/c Leslie King BA MCLIP (e-mail: leslie.king@corpoflondon.gov.uk)

LUTON

Authority: Luton Borough Council
HQ Libraries Service, Central Library, St George's Square, Luton, Bedfordshire LU1 2NG
☎(01582) 547418/9 (enquiries), (01582) 547404 (administration)
Fax (01582) 547461
e-mail: referencelibrary@luton.gov.uk
url: www.luton.gov.uk/library; lutonlibrary.com
Libraries Manager Ms Jean George BA DMS MCLIP (01582 547422; e-mail:
georgej@luton.gov.uk)
Principal Librarian, Adult Services and Reader Development Ms Fiona Marriott BA
MCLIP (01582 547417; e-mail: marriottf@luton.gov.uk)
Principal Librarian, Information Services and Electronic Delivery Mrs Lucy Cross
BLib MCLIP (01582 547432)

Central/largest library

Central Library, St George's Square, Luton, Bedfordshire LU1 2NG
☎Tel/fax etc. as HQ
Library Manager Robert Evans BA MCLIP (01582 547424; e-mail: evansr@luton.gov.uk)

Branch libraries

▶ Leagrave Library, Marsh Road, Luton, Bedfordshire LU3 2NL
   ☎(01582) 597851
   Library Manager Mrs Dawn Boother
▶ Lewsey Library, Landrace Road, Luton, Bedfordshire LU4 0SW
   ☎(01582) 696094
   Library Manager Vacant
▶ Marsh Farm Library and Housebound Unit, Purley Centre, Luton, Bedfordshire
   LU3 3SR
   ☎(01582) 574803
   Library Manager Mrs Lynne Lindars
▶ Stopsley Library, Hitchin Road, Luton, Bedfordshire LU2 7UG
   ☎(01582) 722791
   Library Manager Mrs Claire Dimmock
▶ Sundon Park Library, Hill Rise, Luton, Bedfordshire LU3 3EE
   ☎(01582) 574573
   Library Manager Mrs Ann Soan
▶ Wigmore Library, Wigmore Lane, Luton, Bedfordshire LU3 8DJ
   ☎(01582) 455228
   Library Manager Mrs Jane Wigley

MANCHESTER

Authority: Manchester City Council
HQ Central Library, St Peter's Square, Manchester M2 5PD
☎0161 234 1900
Fax 0161 234 1963
e-mail: dlt@libraries.manchester.gov.uk
url: www.manchester.gov.uk
Director of Libraries and Theatres Ms Vicky Rosin
Assistant Director Library Services Ms Nicola Parker BA(Hons) MCLIP (e-mail:
nicolap@libraries.manchester.gov.uk)
Central Library Manager Steve Willis BA DipLib MCLIP (e-mail:
stevew@libraries.manchester.gov.uk)

Library Operations

▶ Chorlton Group, Chorlton Library, Manchester Road, Chorlton, Manchester M21 9PN
☎0161 881 3179
Fax 0161 860 0169
Group Manager David Green (e-mail: davidg@libraries.manchester.gov.uk)
▶ Crumpsall Group, Crumpsall Library, Abraham Moss Centre, Manchester M8 5UF
☎0161 908 1900
Fax 0161 908 1912
Group Manager Mrs Elizabeth Long
▶ Didsbury Group, Didsbury Library, 692 Wilmslow Road, Didsbury, Manchester M20 2DN
☎0161 445 3220
Group Manager Ms Gail Mallet (e-mail: gmallet@libraries.manchester.gov.uk)
▶ Forum Group, Forum Library, The Forum, Forum Square, Manchester M22 5RX
☎0161 935 4040/1 (lending); 0161 935 4043 (reference)
Group Manager Ms Fran Goddard (e-mail: frang@libraries.manchester.gov.uk)
▶ Longsight Group, Longsight Library, 519 Stockport Road, Manchester M12 4NE
☎0161 224 1411
Fax 0161 225 2119
Group Managers Ms Helen Blagborough BSc DipLib MCLIP (e-mail:
helenb@libraries.manchester.gov.uk), Ms Sue Moores (e-mail:
suem@libraries.manchester.gov.uk)
▶ Miles Platting Group, Miles Platting Library, Varley Street, Miles Platting, Manchester
M40 8EE
☎0161 254 7021
Group Manager Ms Maxine Goulding (e-mail: maxineg@libraries.manchester.gov.uk)
▶ Community Services Co-ordinator Mobiles Services, Hammerstone Road Depot,
Gorton, Manchester M18 8EQ
☎0161 957 5900
Fax 0161 957 5901
Group Manager Ms Hilary Pate (e-mail: hilaryp@libraries.manchester.gov.uk)

MEDWAY

Authority: Medway Council
HQ Education and Leisure Directorate, Civic Centre, Strood, Rochester, Kent ME2 4AU
☎(01634) 306000 (administration)
url: www.medway.gov.uk
Assistant Director, Leisure Mrs Mairi Jones (01634 331013)
Library, Information and Museums Service Manager Ms Gillian Woodhams BA(Hons) DipLib MCLIP (01634 332400)
Libraries Development Manager Mrs Lyn Rainbow BA(Hons) MCLIP (01634 338736)

Central/largest libraries

▶ Chatham Library, Gun Wharf, Dock Road, Chatham, Kent ME4 4TX
☎(01634) 337799
Fax (01634) 337800
e-mail: chatham.library@medway.gov.uk
▶ Gillingham Library, High Street, Gillingham, Kent ME7 1BG
☎(01634) 281066
Fax (01634) 855814
e-mail: gillingham.library@medway.gov.uk
▶ Medway Archives and Local Studies Centre, Civic Centre, Strood, Rochester, Kent ME2 4AU
☎(01634) 332714
Fax (01634) 297060
e-mail: local.studies@medway.gov.uk
▶ Strood Library, 32 Bryant Road, Strood, Rochester, Kent ME2 3EP
☎(01634) 718161
Fax (01634) 297919
e-mail: strood.library@medway.gov.uk

MERTON

Authority: London Borough of Merton
HQ Libraries and Heritage Services, Apollo House, 66a London Road, Morden, Surrey SM4 5BE
☎020 8545 3770
Fax 020 8545 3237
url: www.merton.gov.uk
Head of Libraries and Heritage Services Ms Ingrid Lackajis BA MCLIP (020 8545 3770; e-mail: ingrid.lackajis@merton.gov.uk)
Operations and Performance Manager Gordon Brewin MCLIP (020 8545 3773; e-mail: gordon.brewin@merton.gov.uk)
Libraries Performance Manager Ms Pam Rew BA DipLib MCLIP (020 8545 4089; fax: 020 8545 3237; e-mail: pam.rew@merton.gov.uk)
Libraries Operations Manager Mike Warwick DipEd (020 8545 4038; fax: 020 8545 4037; e-mail: mike.warwick@merton.gov.uk)

Main libraries

▶ Mitcham Library, London Road, Mitcham, Surrey CR4 7YR
☎020 8648 4070
Fax 020 8646 6360
e-mail: mitcham.library@merton.gov.uk
Library Manager Mrs Raihana Ahmad MA

▶ Morden Library, Civic Centre, London Road, Morden, Surrey SM4 5DX
☎020 8545 4040
Fax 020 8545 4037
e-mail: morden.library@merton.gov.uk
Library Manager Mrs Di Reynolds

▶ Wimbledon Library, Wimbledon Hill Road, London SW19 7NB
☎020 8946 7432/7979 (reference and information)
Fax 020 8944 6804
e-mail: wimbledon.library@merton.gov.uk
Library Manager Selladurai Gunasingham MA

Branch libraries

▶ Donald Hope Library (Colliers Wood), Cavendish House, High Street, London SW19 2HR
☎020 8542 1975
Fax 020 8543 9767
e-mail: donaldhope.library@merton.gov.uk
Library Manager Ms Chrysella Holder

▶ Pollards Hill Library, South Lodge Avenue, Mitcham, Surrey CR4 1LT
☎020 8764 5877
Fax 020 8765 0925
e-mail: pollardshill.library@merton.gov.uk
Library Manager Mrs Anne Hutchings

▶ West Barnes Library, Station Road, New Malden, Surrey KT3 6JF
☎020 8942 2635
Fax 020 8336 0554
e-mail: westbarnes.library@merton.gov.uk
Library Manager Mrs Verity Thomas

MIDDLESBROUGH

Authority: Middlesbrough Borough Council
HQ Libraries and Information, Central Library, Victoria Square, Middlesbrough TS1 2AY
☎(01642) 729416 (administration)
Fax (01642) 729953
url: www.middlesbrough.gov.uk
Libraries and Information Manager Ms Chrys Mellor BSc(Econ) DipLib MCLIP (01642 729048; fax: 01642 729978; e-mail: chrys_mellor@middlesbrough.gov.uk)
(based at PO Box 134, 1st Floor, Civic Centre, Middlesbrough TS1 2YB)

Central/largest library

Central Library, Victoria Square, Middlesbrough TS1 2AY

☎(01642) 729002 (enquiries), (01642) 729416 (administration)
Fax (01642) 729953
Library Manager (Operations) Mrs Jen Brittain BA (e-mail:
jen_brittain@middlesbrough.gov.uk)
Library Manager (ICT Development) Ms Julie Tweedy BA MCLIP (e-mail:
julie_tweedy@middlesbrough.gov.uk)

MILTON KEYNES

Authority: Milton Keynes Council
HQ Library Service, Central Library, 555 Silbury Boulevard, Saxon Gate East, Milton Keynes
MK9 3HL
☎(01908) 254050
Fax (01908) 254089
url: www.mkweb.co.uk/libraries
Coordinating Librarian (Central Library Services) Ms Judith Howells BA DipLib
MCLIP (e-mail: judith.howells@milton-keynes.gov.uk)

Branch libraries HQ

▶ Bletchley Library, Westfield Road, Bletchley, Milton Keynes MK2 2RA
☎(01908) 372797
Fax (01908) 645562
Coordinating Librarian (Community Libraries) Mrs Barbara Merrifield BA DipLib
MCLIP (e-mail: barbara.merrifield@milton-keynes.gov.uk)

NEWCASTLE UPON TYNE

Authority: Newcastle upon Tyne City Council
HQ City Library, Princess Square, Newcastle upon Tyne NE99 1DX
☎0191 277 4100
Fax 0191 277 4137
url: www.newcastle.gov.uk
Head of Libraries, Information and Lifelong Learning Tony Durcan (e-mail:
tony.durcan@newcastle.gov.uk)
Assistant Head of Service (Operations) Allan Wraight BA MCLIP DMS (0191 277
4151; e-mail: allan.wraight@newcastle.gov.uk)
Senior Library and Information Manager (Central Services) Ms Eileen Burt MCLIP
(0191 277 4153; e-mail: eileen.burt@newcastle.gov.uk)
Senior Library and Information Manager (Information & E-Libraries) Andrew
Fletcher BA MCLIP (0191 277 4154; e-mail: andrew.fletcher@newcastle.gov.uk)
Senior Library and Information Manager (Access & Learning) Mrs Janice Hall MCLIP
(0191 277 4203; e-mail: janice.hall@newcastle.gov.uk)
Library and Information Manager (Support Services) Alan Macfarlane (0191 277
4158; e-mail: alan.macfarlane@newcastle.gov.uk)
Library and Information Manager (Lending & Customer Services) Mrs Barbara
Heathcote (0191 277 4115; e-mail: barbara.heathcote@newcastle.gov.uk)
Library and Information Manager (Reference & Information) Ms Angela Forster
(0191 277 4148; e-mail: angela.forster@newcastle.gov.uk)

Library and Information Manager (Heritage) Mrs Dilys Harding (0191 277 4119; e-mail: dilys.harding@newcastle.gov.uk)
Library and Information Manager (Facilities & Marketing) Ms Gail Wright (0191 277 4146; e-mail: gail.wright@newcastle.gov.uk)
Libraries PFI Project Manager Stephen Darby (0191 277 4128; e-mail: stephen.darby@newcastle.gov.uk)

NEWHAM

Authority: London Borough of Newham
HQ Library Management, Leisure Services Department, 292 Barking Road, East Ham, London E6 3BA
☎020 8430 2000 (switchboard), 020 8430 3994 (general enquiries)
Fax 020 8430 3921
url: www.newham.gov.uk
Divisional Director John Wood
Head of Library Service Adrian Whittle BA(Hons) MCLIP (020 8430 2476; e-mail: adrian.whittle@newham.gov.uk)

Largest library
Stratford Library, 3 The Grove, Stratford, London E15 1EL
☎020 8430 6890
Library Manager Mark Blair

Branch libraries
▶ Beckton Globe Library, 1 Kingsford Way, London E6 5JQ
  ☎020 8430 4063
  Library Manager Ms Jackie Lee
▶ Canning Town Library, Barking Road, Canning Town, London E16 4HQ
  ☎020 7476 2696
  Fax 020 7511 8693
  Library Manager Ms Helen Allsop
▶ Custom House Library, Prince Regent Lane, London E16 3JJ
  ☎020 7476 1565
  Library Manager Ms Jo Udall
▶ East Ham Library, High Street South, London E6 4EL
  ☎020 8430 3648
  Library Manager Ms Angela Conder
▶ The Gate Library and Local Service Centre, 4–20 Woodgrange Road, Forest Gate, London E7 0QH
  ☎020 8430 3838
  Library Manager Ms Angelina McIntyre
▶ Green Street Library, 337–341 Green Street, Upton Park, London E13 9AR
  ☎020 8472 4101
  Library Manager Steve Waltho
▶ Manor Park Library, Romford Road, Manor Park, London E12 5JY
  ☎020 8478 1177
  Library Manager Ms Mandy Webb

▶ North Woolwich Library, Storey School, Woodman Street, North Woolwich, London
E16 2LS
☎020 7511 2387
Library Manager Ms Nita Patel
▶ Plaistow Library, North Street, Plaistow, London E13 9HL
☎020 8472 0420
Library Manager David Langham

NORFOLK

Authority: Norfolk County Council
HQ Library and Information Service, County Hall, Martineau Lane, Norwich NR1 2UA
☎(01603) 222049
Fax (01603) 222422
e-mail: libraries@norfolk.gov.uk
url: www.library.norfolk.gov.uk
Head of Libraries Mrs Jennifer Holland BA(Hons) MCLIP MCMI (01603 222272; e-mail:
jennifer.holland@norfolk.gov.uk)
Head of Finance and Administration John Perrott DMF (01603 222054; e-mail:
john.perrott@norfolk.gov.uk)

Central/largest libraries

▶ Dereham Library, Church Street, Dereham, Norfolk NR19 1DN
☎(01362) 693184
Fax (01362) 691891
e-mail: dereham.lib@norfolk.gov.uk
Area Librarian Ms Sarah Hassan BA(Hons) MA MCLIP
▶ Gorleston Library, Lowestoft Road, Gorleston, Norfolk NR31 6SG
☎(01493) 662156
Fax (01493) 446010
e-mail: gorleston.lib@norfolk.gov.uk
Area Librarian Neil Buxton MCLIP
▶ Great Yarmouth Library, Tolhouse Street, Great Yarmouth, Norfolk NR30 2SH
☎(01493) 844551
Fax (01493) 857628
e-mail: yarmouth.lib@norfolk.gov.uk
Area Librarian Neil Buxton MCLIP
▶ King's Lynn Library, London Road, King's Lynn, Norfolk PE30 5EZ
☎(01553) 772568
Fax (01553) 769832
e-mail: kings.lynn.lib@norfolk.gov.uk
Area Librarian Ms Sarah Hassan BA(Hons) MA MCLIP
▶ Norfolk and Norwich Millennium Library, The Forum, Millennium Plain, Norwich
NR2 1AW
☎(01603) 774774
Fax (01603) 774705
e-mail: millennium.lib@norfolk.gov.uk
Area Librarian Ms Jan Holden BA DipLib MA

▶ Thetford Library, Raymond Street, Thetford, Norfolk IP24 2EA
☎(01842) 752048
Fax (01842) 750125
e-mail: thetford.lib@norfolk.gov.uk
Area Librarian Ms Sarah Hassan BA(Hons) MA MCLIP

Area library HQs
▶ Northern and Eastern Area HQ, Wroxham Library, Norwich Road, Wroxham, Norfolk NR12 8RX
☎(01603) 783412 (tel/fax)
e-mail: wroxham.lib@norfolk.gov.uk
Area Librarian Neil Buxton MCLIP
▶ Norwich Area HQ, Norfolk and Norwich Millennium Library, The Forum, Millennium Plain, Norwich NR2 1AW
☎(01603) 774774
Fax (01603) 774705
e-mail: millennium.lib@norfolk.gov.uk
Area Librarian Ms Jan Holden BA DipLib MA
▶ Southern and Western Area HQ, Attleborough Library, 31 Connaught Road, Attleborough, Norfolk NR17 2BW
☎(01953) 455196 (tel/fax)
e-mail: attleborough.lib@norfolk.gov.uk
Area Librarian Ms Sarah Hassan BA(Hons) MA MCLIP

NORTH EAST LINCOLNSHIRE

Authority: North East Lincolnshire Council
HQ Central Library, Town Hall Square, Grimsby, North East Lincs DN31 1HG
☎(01472) 323600 (enquiries), (01472) 323617 (administration)
Fax (01472) 323618
e-mail: librariesandmuseums@nelincs.gov.uk
url: www.nelincs.gov.uk
Culture and Libraries Manager Steve Hipkins BA(Hons) MA DipLib MCLIP (01472 323611; e-mail: steve.hipkins@nelincs.gov.uk)
Principal Librarian (Strategy) David A H Bell MCLIP (01472 323612; e-mail: david.bell@nelincs.gov.uk)
Principal Librarian (Customer Services) Mrs Joan Sargent BA DipLib (01472 323614; e-mail: joan.sargent@nelincs.gov.uk)
Finance and Administration Manager Mrs Isola Blow (01472 323616; e-mail: isola.blow@nelincs.gov.uk)
E-Library Manager Mrs Fran Humphrey BSc DipLib MCLIP (01472 323615; e-mail: fran.humphrey@nelincs.gov.uk)

Branch libraries
▶ Cleethorpes Library, Alexandra Road, Cleethorpes, Lincs DN35 8LG
☎(01472) 323648/323650
Fax (01472) 323652
▶ Grant Thorold Library, Durban Road, Grimsby, North East Lincs DN32 8BX

☎(01472) 323631
Fax (01472) 323816
▶ Humberston Library, Church Lane, Humberston, Lincs DN36 4HZ
☎(01472) 323682
▶ Immingham Library, Civic Centre, Pelham Road, Immingham, Lincs DN40 1QF
☎(01469) 516050
Fax (01469) 516051
▶ Laceby Library, The Stanford Centre, Cooper Lane, Laceby, Lincs DN37 7AX
☎(01472) 323684
▶ Nunsthorpe Library, Sutcliffe Avenue, Grimsby, Lincs DN33 1HA
☎(01472) 323636
▶ Scartho Library, St Giles Avenue, Grimsby, North East Lincs DN33 2HB
☎(01472) 323638
▶ Waltham Library, High Street, Waltham, North East Lincs DN37 0LL
☎(01472) 323656
▶ Willows Library, Binbrook Way, Grimsby, North East Lincs DN37 9AS
☎(01472) 323679

NORTH LINCOLNSHIRE

Authority: North Lincolnshire Council
HQ Scunthorpe Central Library, Carlton Street, Scunthorpe, North Lincs DN15 6TX
☎(01724) 860161 (tel/fax)
e-mail: ref.library@northlincs.gov.uk
url: www.northlincs.gov.uk/library/
Principal Librarian Mrs Margaret Carr BA MCLIP (e-mail:
margaret.carr@northlincs.gov.uk)

NORTH SOMERSET

Authority: North Somerset Council
HQ Libraries Office, The Winter Gardens, Royal Parade, Weston-super-Mare, Somerset
BS23 1AQ
☎(01934) 634820
Fax (01934) 612182
url: www.n-somerset.gov.uk; www.foursite.somerset.gov.uk (online catalogue)
Library and Information Service Manager Andy Brisley BLib MCLIP (e-mail:
andy.brisley@n-somerset.gov.uk)

Area libraries
▶ Clevedon Library, 37 Old Church Road, Clevedon, Somerset BS21 6NN
☎(01275) 873498/874858
Fax (01275) 343630
e-mail: clevedon.library@n-somerset.gov.uk
North Area Library Manager Graham Tuckwell BA MCLIP (e-mail:
graham.tuckwell@n-somerset.gov.uk)
▶ Weston Library, The Boulevard, Weston-super-Mare, Somerset BS23 1PL
☎(01934) 636638 (enquiries), (01934) 620373 (administration)

Fax (01934) 413046

e-mail: weston.library@n-somerset.gov.uk

South Area Library Manager Nigel Kelly BA MCLIP DMS MIMgt (e-mail: nigel.kelly@n-somerset.gov.uk)

NORTH TYNESIDE

Authority: North Tyneside Council

HQ Central Library, Northumberland Square, North Shields, Tyne and Wear NE30 1QU

☎0191 200 5424

Fax 0191 200 6118

e-mail: central.library@northtyneside.gov.uk

url: www.northtyneside.gov.uk/libraries/index

Libraries, Information and Museums Manager Mrs Julia Stafford BA MCLIP (e-mail: julia.stafford@northtyneside.gov.uk)

Adult Services and Strategic Support Manager Mrs Gayle Taylor BSc(Hons) MCLIP (e-mail: gayle.taylor@northtyneside.gov.uk)

Children's Services and Reader Development Manager Ms Andrea Stephenson BA (e-mail: andrea.stephenson@northtyneside.gov.uk)

Resources and Finance Manager Mrs Lesley Bird (e-mail: lesley.bird@northtyneside.gov.uk)

Main libraries

▶ Wallsend Library, Ferndale Avenue, Wallsend, Tyne and Wear NE28 7NB

☎0191 200 6968

Fax 0191 200 6967

e-mail: wallsend.library@northtyneside.gov.uk

▶ Whitley Bay Library, Park Road, Whitley Bay, Tyne and Wear NE26 1EJ

☎0191 200 8500

Fax 0191 200 8536

e-mail: whitleybay.library@northtyneside.gov.uk

NORTH YORKSHIRE

Authority: North Yorkshire County Council

HQ BACS HQ, Business and Community Services Directorate, 21 Grammar School Lane, Northallerton, North Yorks DL6 1DF

☎(01609) 767800 (enquiries and administration)

Fax (01609) 780793

e-mail: libraries@northyorks.gov.uk

url: www.northyorks.gov.uk/libraries

Assistant Director (Information) Ms Julie Blaisdale BA(Hons) MCLIP (e-mail: julie.blaisdale@northyorks.gov.uk)

Service Head, Operations and Delivery David Fay BA MCLIP (e-mail: david.fay@northyorks.gov.uk)

Service Head, Commercial and Development Stephen Harrison (e-mail: stephen.harrison@northyorks.gov.uk)

Support Services Manager Chris Riley DMA ACIS MIPD (e-mail: chris.riley@northyorks.gov.uk)
Management Co-ordinators Ms Lesley Willetts (e-mail: lesley.willetts@northyorks.gov.uk), Ms Iris Maynard (e-mail: iris.maynard@northyorks.gov.uk)

Larger libraries

▶ Library and Information Centre Harrogate, Victoria Avenue, Harrogate, North Yorks HG1 1EG
☎(01423) 720300 (Lending), 720305 (Reference)
Fax (01423) 523158
e-mail: harrogate.library@northyorks.gov.uk
url: www.northyorks.gov.uk/libraries/branches/harrogate.shtm
Principal Officer Ms Caroline Johnston (01423 720305; e-mail: caroline.johnston@northyorks.gov.uk)

▶ Library and Information Centre Scarborough, Vernon Road, Scarborough, North Yorks YO11 2NN
☎(01723) 383400 (Lending), 383407 (Reference)
Fax (01723) 353893
e-mail: scarborough.library@northyorks.gov.uk
url: www.northyorks.gov.uk/libraries/branches/scarborough.shtm
Principal Officer Ms Sandra Turner (01723 383401; e-mail: sandra.turner@northyorks.gov.uk)

(Note: These do not represent the full list of Library and Information Centres. Please see website for more details: www.northyorks.gov.uk/libraries)

NORTHAMPTONSHIRE

Authority: Northamptonshire County Council
HQ Libraries and Information Service, PO Box 216, John Dryden House, 8-10 The Lakes, Northampton NN4 7DD
☎(01604) 236236
Fax (01604) 237937
e-mail: nlis@northamptonshire.gov.uk
url: www.northamptonshire.gov.uk
Head of Community Information and Access Eric W Wright MA BSocSci BPhil MCLIP (e-mail: ewright@northamptonshire.gov.uk)
Principal Libraries and Information Officer (Service Delivery) Nick L Matthews BA MCLIP DMS (e-mail: nmatthews@northamptonshire.gov.uk)
Principal Libraries and Information Officer (Service Development) Ms Evelyn L Jarvis BA MA DipLib DMS MCLIP (e-mail: ejarvis@northamptonshire.gov.uk)

Central/largest library

Central Library, Abington Street, Northampton NN1 2BA
☎(01604) 462040
Fax (01604) 462055
Central Library Manager Miss Gill Howe (e-mail: ghowe@northamptonshire.gov.uk)

Area libraries

▶ Daventry Library, North Street, Daventry, Northants NN11 5PN
☎(01327) 703130
Fax (01327) 300501
Principal Librarian Ian J Clarke BA BSc MCLIP (e-mail:
iclarke@northamptonshire.gov.uk)

▶ Kettering Library, Sheep Street, Kettering, Northants NN16 0AY
☎(01536) 512315
Fax (01536) 411349
Principal Librarian Ms Ingrid Mercer BLS MCLIP (e-mail:
imercer@northamptonshire.gov.uk)

▶ Wellingborough Library, Pebble Lane, Wellingborough, Northants NN8 1AS
☎(01933) 225365
Fax (01933) 442060
Principal Librarian Mrs Hilary Ward BA(Hons) MCLIP (e-mail:
rhward@northamptonshire.gov.uk)

▶ Weston Favell Library, Weston Favell Centre, Northampton NN3 8JZ
☎(01604) 403100
Fax (01604) 403112
Principal Librarian Miss Amanda Poulton BA(Hons) MA MCLIP (e-mail:
apoulton@northamptonshire.gov.uk)

NORTHUMBERLAND

Authority: Northumberland County Council
HQ County Library HQ, The Willows, Morpeth, Northumberland NE61 1TA
☎(01670) 534501
Fax (01670) 534521 administration)
e-mail: libraries@northumberland.gov.uk
url: www.northumberland.gov.uk
Divisional Director, Libraries, Arts and Archives D E Bonser BA MCLIP

Central/largest library

County Library, Gas House Lane, Morpeth, Northumberland NE61 1TA
☎(01670) 534518 (lending), (01670) 534514 (reference)
Fax (01670) 534513
e-mail: morpethlibrary@northumberland.gov.uk

NOTTINGHAM

Authority: City of Nottingham Council
HQ Department of Leisure and Community Services, Libraries and Communications
Division, Isabella Street, Nottingham NG1 6AT
☎0115 915 5555
Fax 0115 915 8680
e-mail: community_libraries.admin@nottinghamcity.gov.uk
url: www.nottinghamcity.gov.uk

Assistant Director, Libraries, Information and Communications Services Ms Christina Dyer BA MCLIP (0115 915 8673)
Service Manager, Children's and Community Libraries Vacant

Central/largest library

Nottingham City Library, Angel Row, Nottingham NG1 6HP
☎0115 915 2828
Fax 0115 915 2850
e-mail: central_admin.library@nottinghamcity.gov.uk
url: www.nottinghamcity.gov.uk/libraries
Service Manager John P Turner BA MCLIP

NOTTINGHAMSHIRE

Authority: Nottinghamshire County Council
HQ Culture and Community/Libraries, Archives and Information, 4th Floor, County Hall, West Bridgford, Nottingham NG2 7QP
☎0115 977 4401
Fax 0115 977 2807
url: www.nottinghamshire.gov.uk
Assistant Director (Libraries, Archives and Information) David Lathrope BSc DMS MCLIP (0115 977 4201; e-mail: david.lathrope@nottscc.gov.uk)
Principal Libraries Officer (Public Services, Operations and Quality) Tony Cook BA MCLIP ALCM (0115 977 4437; e-mail: tony.cook@nottscc.gov.uk)
Principal Libraries Officer (Resources and Commissioning) Philip Marshall BA MCLIP (0115 985 4201; e-mail: philip.marshall@nottscc.gov.uk) (based at Glaisdale Parkway)

Central/largest library

County Library, Four Seasons Centre, Westgate, Mansfield, Notts NG18 1NH
☎(01623) 627591 (enquiries), (01623) 653551 (administration)
Fax (01623) 629276
e-mail: mansfield.library@nottscc.gov.uk
Principal Librarian Mrs Kath Owen BA MCLIP (e-mail: kath.owen@nottscc.gov.uk)

Group libraries

▶ Central Nottinghamshire Group. County Library, Front Street, Arnold, Nottingham NG5 7EE
☎0115 920 2247
Fax 0115 967 3378
e-mail: arnold.library@nottscc.gov.uk
Principal Librarian Roger Jones BA MCLIP (e-mail: roger.jones@nottscc.gov.uk)
▶ East Nottinghamshire Group. County Library, Beaumond Gardens, Baldertongate, Newark-on-Trent, Notts NG24 1UW
☎(01636) 703966
Fax (01636) 610045
e-mail: newark.library@nottscc.gov.uk
Principal Librarian Rupert Vinnicombe MCLIP DMA (e-mail: rupert.vinnicombe@nottscc.gov.uk)

▶ North Nottinghamshire Group. County Library, Churchgate, Retford, Notts DN22 6PE
☎(01777) 708724
Fax (01777) 710020
e-mail: retford.library@nottscc.gov.uk
Principal Librarian Mrs Linda Turner BA MCLIP (e-mail: linda.turner@nottscc.gov.uk)

▶ South Nottinghamshire Group. County Library, Foster Avenue, Beeston, Nottingham NG9 1AE
☎0115 925 5168/925 5084
Fax 0115 922 0841
e-mail: beeston.library@nottscc.gov.uk
Principal Librarian Ms Carol Newman BA MCLIP (e-mail: carol.newman@nottscc.gov.uk)

▶ West Nottinghamshire Group. County Library, Four Seasons Centre, Westgate, Mansfield, Notts NG18 1NH
☎(01623) 627591
Fax (01623) 629276
e-mail: mansfield.library@nottscc.gov.uk
Principal Librarian Mrs Kath Owen BA MCLIP (e-mail: kath.owen@nottscc.gov.uk)

Other services
▶ Support Services, Units 4-6, Glaisdale Parkway, Bilborough, Nottingham NG8 4GP
☎0115 985 4242
Fax 0115 928 6400
Principal Bibliographical Officer, Support Services Ms Anne Corin BA MCLIP
(0115 985 4208; e-mail: anne.corin@nottscc.gov.uk)
Principal Systems Officer, Support Services Nick London MCLIP (0115 985 5172;
e-mail: nick.london@nottscc.gov.uk)

OLDHAM

Authority: Oldham Metropolitan District Council
HQ Oldham Library, Union Street, Oldham, Lancashire OL1 1DN
☎0161 911 4645 (general enquiries)
Fax 0161 911 4630
e-mail: ecs.reference.lib@oldham.gov.uk
url: www.oldham.gov.uk
Head of Heritage, Libraries and Arts Ms Sheena Macfarlane (0161 911 4664; fax: 0161 911 3222; e-mail: ecs.sheena.macfarlane@oldham.gov.uk)

OXFORDSHIRE

Authority: Oxfordshire County Council
HQ Cultural Services, Central Library, Westgate, Oxford OX1 1DJ
☎(01865) 810191
Fax (01865) 810187
url: www.oxfordshire.gov.uk
Head of Cultural Services Richard Munro BA DipLib MCLIP (e-mail: richard.munro@oxfordshire.gov.uk)

County Librarian Ms Caroline Taylor DipLib MCLIP
(based at Cultural Services, Holton, Oxford OX33 1QQ; 01865 810212; fax 01865 810205)

Central/largest library
Central Library, Westgate, Oxford OX1 1DJ
☎(01865) 815549
Fax (01865) 721694
e-mail: centlib.occdla@dial.pipex.com
Principal Librarian Mrs Liz Rooke BA DipLib MCLIP (e-mail:
liz.rooke@oxfordshire.gov.uk)

Additional services
Performance and Development, Cultural Services, Holton, Oxford OX33 1QQ
☎(01865) 810234
Fax (01865) 810205
Assistant County Librarian Rex Harris MA DipLib MCLIP (e-mail:
rex.harris@oxfordshire.gov.uk)

Operations, Cultural Services, Holton, Oxford OX33 1QQ
☎(01865) 810247
Fax (01865) 810205
Assistant County Librarian Mrs Yvonne McDonald BA DMS DipLib MCLIP (e-mail:
yvonne.mcdonald@oxfordshire.gov.uk)

Information Services and Lifelong Learning, Cultural Services, Holton, Oxford OX33 1QQ
☎(01865) 810221
Fax (01865) 810205
Assistant County Librarian Charles Pettit MA MA(Lib) MCLIP (e-mail:
charles.pettit@oxfordshire.gov.uk)

PETERBOROUGH

Authority: Peterborough City Council
HQ Community Services: Libraries, Central Library, Broadway, Peterborough PE1 1RX
☎(01733) 742700
Fax (01733) 319140
e-mail: libraries@peterborough.gov.uk
url: www.peterboroughheritage.org.uk
Interim Library and Heritage Services Manager Geoff Allen (01733 742702; e-mail:
geoff.allen@peterborough.gov.uk)
Central Library Manager Mrs Jane Brown (01733 742720; e-mail:
jane.brown@peterborough.gov.uk)
Reader Services Manager Ms Heather Walton BLS MCLIP (01733 742708; e-mail:
heather.walton@peterborough.gov.uk)
Enquiry Services Manager Mrs Helen Sherley BLib MCLIP (01733 742704; e-mail:
helen.sherley@peterborough.gov.uk)
Senior Operations Manager Mrs Varsha Hindocha (01733 742703; e-mail:
varsha.hindocha@peterborough.gov.uk)

Neighbourhood Library Managers
North: Mrs Angela Wells (01733 742700; e-mail: angela.wells@peterborough.gov.uk);
South: Mrs Sally Leitch (01733 742700; e-mail: sally.leitch@peterborough.gov.uk)

District libraries
▶ Bretton Library, Bretton Centre, Bretton, Peterborough PE3 8DS
☎(01733) 742700
▶ Orton Library, Orton Centre, Orton, Peterborough PE2 0RQ
☎(01733) 742700
Manager Mark Norman BA(Hons) MCLIP (e-mail:
mark.norman@peterborough.gov.uk)
▶ Werrington Library, Staniland Way, Werrington, Peterborough PE4 6JT
☎(01733) 742700
Manager Mrs Sukaina Jaffer (e-mail: sukaina.jaffer@peterborough.gov.uk)

PLYMOUTH

Authority: Plymouth City Council
HQ Library and Information Services, Central Library, Drake Circus, Plymouth PL4 8AL
☎(01752) 305923 (enquiries and administration)
Fax (01752) 305929
e-mail: library@plymouth.gov.uk
url: www.plymouthlibraries.info; www.cyberlibrary.org.uk
City Librarian Alasdair MacNaughtan BA MCLIP DMS MCMI (01752 305901; e-mail:
alasdair.macnaughtan@plymouth.gov.uk)
Support and Development Librarian Frank Lowry MCLIP (01752 305911; e-mail:
frank.lowry@plymouth.gov.uk)
Resources and Information Manager Chris Goddard BMus DipLib MCLIP (01752
305900; e-mail: chris.goddard@plymouth.gov.uk)
Public Services Librarian Brian Holgate (01752 306790; e-mail:
brian.holgate@plymouth.gov.uk)

POOLE

Authority: Borough of Poole
HQ Culture and Community Learning, Central Library, Dolphin Centre, Poole, Dorset
BH15 1QE
☎(01202) 262400
Fax (01202) 262431
url: www.poole.gov.uk
Head of Culture and Community Learning K McErlane BA(Hons) DipLib MBA (e-mail:
k.mcerlane@poole.gov.uk)
Head of Library Services Vacant

Central/largest library
Central Library, Dolphin Centre, Poole, Dorset BH15 1QE
☎(01202) 262424
e-mail: centrallibrary@poole.gov.uk

Healthpoint (health information centre also serving Dorset) e-mail:
healthpoint@poole.gov.ukLibrarian Mrs V Grier BA ALA (01202 262436)

PORTSMOUTH

Authority: Portsmouth City Council
HQ Library Service, Central Library, Guildhall Square, Portsmouth PO1 2DX
☎023 9281 9311
Fax 023 9283 9855
e-mail: library.admin@portsmouthcc.gov.uk
url: www.portsmouth.gov.uk/learning/29.html
Library Service Manager Colin Brown MCLIP

Group libraries
▶ North Group. Cosham Library, Spur Road, Portsmouth PO6 3EB
  ☎023 9237 6023
  Fax 023 9266 8151
  e-mail: cosham.library@portsmouthcc.gov.uk
▶ South Group. North End Library, Gladys Avenue, North End, Portsmouth PO2 9AX
  ☎023 9266 2651
  Fax 023 9237 1877
  e-mail: northend.library@portsmouthcc.gov.uk

Community library services
▶ Carnegie Library, Fratton Road, Fratton, Portsmouth PO1 5EZ
  ☎023 9275 1737
  Fax 023 9273 9244
  e-mail: community.library@portsmouth.gov.uk

READING

Authority: Reading Borough Council
HQ Reading Central Library, Abbey Square, Reading RG1 3BQ
☎0118 901 5950
Fax 0118 901 5954
e-mail: info@readinglibraries.org.uk
url: www.readinglibraries.org.uk
Head of Museums, Archives and Libraries Alec Kennedy BA(Hons) DMS MCLIP
Library Services Manager Rhodri Thomas BA(Hons) DipLib MCLIP (0118 901 5940)
Finance and Resources Manager Ms Alison England BA(Hons) DipLib MCLIP (0118 901 5962)
Central Services Manager Mrs Clare Hutchinson BEd(Hons) MA MCLIP (0118 901 5968)
Branch Services Manager Byron Holder (0118 901 5947)

Branch libraries
▶ Battle Library, 420 Oxford Road, Reading RG3 1EE
  ☎0118 901 5100
  Branch Manager Mrs Marjorie McClure

▶ Caversham Library, Church Street, Caversham, Reading RG4 8AU
☎0118 901 5103
Branch Manager Ms Virginia Hobbs

▶ Mobile Library Services, c/o Tilehurst Library, School Road, Tilehurst, Reading RG3 5AS
☎0118 901 5118
Service Manager Andrew Mitchell

▶ Palmer Park Library, St Bartholomew's Road, Reading RG1 3QB
☎0118 901 5106
Branch Manager Miss Christine Gosling

▶ Southcote Library, Southcote Lane, Reading RG3 3BA
☎0118 901 5109
Branch Manager Mrs Elizabeth Long

▶ Tilehurst Library, School Road, Tilehurst, Reading RG3 5AS
☎0118 901 5112
Branch Manager Mrs Jeny Brant

▶ Whitley Library, Northumberland Avenue, Reading RG2 7PX
☎0118 901 5115
Branch Manager Mrs Caroline Kelly, Mrs Collette Shine

REDBRIDGE

Authority: London Borough of Redbridge
HQ Central Library, Clements Road, Ilford, Essex IG1 1EA
☎020 8478 7145
Fax 020 8708 2431
url: www.redbridge.gov.uk/libraries
Head of Libraries Martin Timms BA MCLIP (020 8708 2436; e-mail:
martin.timms@redbridge.gov.uk)
Central Library Manager Bob Terry (020 8708 2415; e-mail:
bob.terry@redbridge.gov.uk)
Development Manager Mrs Madeline Barratt BA MCLIP DipLaw (020 8708 2425;
e-mail: madeline.barratt@redbridge.gov.uk)
Customer Services Manager Ms Carol Boswarthack BA MCLIP (020 8708 2737; e-mail:
carol.boswarthack@redbridge.gov.uk)

Branch libraries

▶ Aldersbrook Library, 2a Park Road, London E12 5HQ
☎020 8496 0006
Branch Librarian Ms Linda Hubbard BA DipLib MCLIP (e-mail:
linda.hubbard@redbridge.gov.uk)

▶ Fullwell Cross Library, 140 High Street, Barkingside, Ilford, Essex IG6 2EA
☎020 8708 9281
Branch Librarian Ms Geraldine Pote BA MA MCLIP (e-mail:
geraldine.pote@redbridge.gov.uk)

▶ Gants Hill Library, 490 Cranbrook Road, Gants Hill, Ilford, Essex IG2 6LA
☎020 8708 9275
Branch Librarian John Weeks MCLIP (e-mail: john.weeks@redbridge.gov.uk)

▶ Goodmayes Library, 76 Goodmayes Lane, Goodmayes, Ilford, Essex IG3 9QB

☎020 8708 7750
Branch Librarian Mrs Kathryn Brown BA DipLib MCLIP (e-mail: kathryn.brown@redbridge.gov.uk)
▶ Hainault Library, 100 Manford Way, Chigwell, Essex IG7 4DD
☎020 8708 9206
Branch Librarian Nick Dobson (e-mail: nick.dobson@redbridge.gov.uk)
▶ Keith Axon Centre, 160–170 Grove Road, Chadwell Heath, Essex RM6 4XB
☎020 8708 0790
Branch Librarian Mrs Kathryn Brown BA DipLib MCLIP (e-mail: kathryn.brown@redbridge.gov.uk)
▶ South Woodford Library, 116 High Road, London E18 2QS
☎020 8708 9067
Branch Librarian Mrs Evelyn Reid BA MCLIP (e-mail: evelyn.reid@redbridge.gov.uk)
▶ Wanstead Library, Spratt Hall Road, London E11 2RQ
☎020 8708 7400
Branch Librarian Ms Linda Hubbard BA DipLib MCLIP (e-mail: linda.hubbard@redbridge.gov.uk)
▶ Woodford Green Library, Snakes Lane, Woodford Green, Essex IG8 0DX
☎020 8708 9055
Branch Librarian Archie Black LLB DipLib MCLIP (e-mail: archie.black@redbridge.gov.uk)

REDCAR AND CLEVELAND

Authority: Redcar and Cleveland Borough Council
HQ Chief Executive's Department, Information and Communication Division, Redcar and Cleveland House, Kirkleatham Street, Redcar, Cleveland TS10 1YA
☎(01642) 444000
Fax (01642) 444341
url: www.redcar-cleveland.gov.uk
Chief Communication, Information and Engagement Officer Mrs Carol Barnes BA DipLib (01642 444357; e-mail: carol_barnes@redcar-cleveland.gov.uk)
Support Services Officer Mrs Jan Richardson (01642 444319; e-mail: jan_richardson@redcar-cleveland.gov.uk)
Stock Management Officer Vacant

Central/largest library

Central Library, Coatham Road, Redcar, Cleveland TS10 1RP
☎(01642) 472162
Fax (01642) 492253
e-mail: redcar_library@redcar-cleveland.gov.uk
Libraries Officer I L Wilson BA MCLIP (01642 444263)

RICHMOND UPON THAMES

Authority: London Borough of Richmond upon Thames
HQ Department of Education, Arts and Leisure, First Floor, Regal House, London Road, Twickenham, Middlesex TW1 3QB

☎020 8831 6136
Fax 020 8891 7904
e-mail: libraries@richmond.gov.uk
url: www.richmond.gov.uk/libraries
Head of Library and Information Services Vacant
Assistant Head of Service Ms Aileen T Cahill BSocSc DipLib MCLIP
Assistant Head of Service Ms Sheila Harden BA MCLIP (e-mail:
s.harden@richmond.gov.uk)

Central/largest library

Richmond Lending Library, Little Green, Richmond, Surrey TW9 1QL
☎020 8940 0981/6857
Fax 020 8940 7516
e-mail: richmond.library@richmond.gov.uk
Customer Services Manager Leslie Cranfield MCLIP (e-mail:
l.cranfield@richmond.gov.uk)

Branch libraries

▶ Central Reference Library, Old Town Hall, Whitaker Avenue, Richmond, Surrey
  TW9 1TP
  ☎020 8940 5529/9125
  Fax 020 8940 6899
  e-mail: reference.services@richmond.gov.uk
  Central Reference Librarian Vacant
▶ East Sheen Library, Sheen Lane, London SW14 8LP
  ☎020 8876 8801
  e-mail: eastsheen.library@richmond.gov.uk
▶ Teddington Library, Waldegrave Road, Teddington, Middlesex TW11 8LG
  ☎020 8977 1284
  e-mail: teddington.library@richmond.gov.uk
▶ Twickenham Library, Garfield Road, Twickenham, Middlesex TW1 3JT
  ☎020 8892 8091
  e-mail: twickenham.library@richmond.gov.uk

ROCHDALE

Authority: Rochdale Metropolitan Borough Council
HQ Wheatsheaf Library, Wheatsheaf Shopping Centre, Baillie Street, Rochdale, Greater
Manchester OL16 1JZ
☎(01706) 864900 (enquiries), (01706) 864911 (administration)
Fax (01706) 864992
url: www.rochdale.gov.uk/libraries
Principal Librarian Mrs Sheila Sfrijan MCLIP (01706 864929; e-mail:
sheila.sfrijan@rochdale.gov.uk)
Community Services Manager Mrs Freda Fletcher MCLIP (01706 864964; e-mail:
freda.fletcher@rochdale.gov.uk)
Area Librarian (Rochdale and Pennine) Mrs Janice Tod BSc(Hons) MCLIP (01706
864976; e-mail: janice.tod@rochdale.gov.uk) (based at Wheatsheaf Library)

Main libraries

▶ Heywood Library, Church Street, Heywood, Greater Manchester OL10 1LL
☎(01706) 360947
Fax (01706) 368683
Area Librarian Vacant

▶ Middleton Library, Long Street, Middleton, Greater Manchester M24 6DU
☎0161 643 5228
Fax 0161 654 0745
Area Librarian Vacant

ROTHERHAM

Authority: Rotherham Metropolitan Borough Council
HQ Central Library, Walker Place, Rotherham, South Yorks S65 1JH
☎(01709) 823611 (enquiries), (01709) 823623 (management)
Fax (01709) 823650 (enquiries), (01709) 837649 (management)
e-mail: central.library@rotherham.gov.uk
url: www.rotherham.gov.uk
Libraries, Museums and Arts Manager Guy Kilminster BA(Hons) FMA (e-mail:
guy.kilminster@rotherham.gov.uk)
Manager, Library and Information Service Ms Elenore Fisher BA(Hons) DipLib MCLIP
(e-mail: elenore.fisher@rotherham.gov.uk)

RUTLAND

Authority: Rutland County Council
HQ Rutland County Library, Catmose Street, Oakham, Rutland LE15 6HW
☎(01572) 722918 (enquiries), 01572 758434 (administration)
Fax (01572) 724906 (enquiries), 01572 758403 (administration)
e-mail: libraries@rutland.gov.uk
url: www.rutland.gov.uk
Head of Cultural Services Roy Knight BA MCLIP
Library Manager Robert Clayton BA MA MCLIP (e-mail: rclayton@rutland.gov.uk)

Community libraries

▶ Ketton Library, High Street, Ketton, Stamford, Lincs PE9 3TE
☎(01780) 720580

▶ Ryhall Library, Coppice Road, Ryhall, Stamford, Lincs PE9 4HY
☎(01780) 751726

▶ Uppingham Library, Queen Street, Uppingham, Rutland LE15 9QR
☎(01572) 823218

ST HELENS

Authority: Metropolitan Borough of St Helens
HQ Chief Executive's Department, Public Affairs Division, The Gamble Building, Victoria
Square, St Helens, Merseyside WA10 1DY
☎(01744) 456989 (enquiries and administration)

Fax (01744) 20836
e-mail: criu@sthelens.gov.uk
url: www.sthelens.gov.uk
Head of Cultural Development Mrs Dorothy Bradley BSc(Hons) MCLIP DMS (01744 455300; fax: 01744 455497; e-mail: dorothybradley@sthelens.gov.uk)

Central/largest library
Central Library, The Gamble Building, Victoria Square, St Helens, Merseyside WA10 1DY
☎(01744) 456950
Fax (01744) 20836
e-mail: criu@sthelens.gov.uk
Principal Libraries Development Manager, Social Inclusion Ms Kerry Corbett BD DipLib MCLIP (e-mail: kerrycorbett@sthelens.gov.uk)
Principal Libraries Development Manager, Reading and Learning Ms Sue Thomas (e-mail: suethomas@sthelens.gov.uk)
Principal Libraries Development Manager, Performance and Marketing Ms Jill Roughley (e-mail: jillroughley@sthelens.gov.uk)

SALFORD

Authority: Salford City Council
HQ Education and Leisure Directorate, Minerva House, Pendlebury Road, Swinton, Salford, Manchester M27 4EQ
☎0161 778 0141
Fax 0161 728 6234
e-mail: libraries@salford.gov.uk
url: www.salford.gov.uk/libraries
Libraries and Information Service Manager Ms Sarah Spence BA(Hons) MCLIP (0161 793 3573; fax: 0161 727 7071; e-mail: sarah.spence@salford.gov.uk)

Main libraries
▶ Broadwalk Library, Broadwalk, Salford, Manchester M6 5FX
☎0161 737 5802
Fax 0161 745 9157
Senior Librarian Mrs Julie Stonebanks BA(Hons) DMS (e-mail: julie.stonebanks@salford.gov.uk)
▶ Eccles Library, Church Street, Eccles, Salford, Manchester M30 0EP
☎0161 789 1430
Fax 0161 787 8430
Divisional Librarian Ms Rosemary Farnworth DBA MCLIP (e-mail: rosemary.farnworth@salford.gov.uk)
▶ Swinton Library, Chorley Road, Swinton, Salford, Manchester M27 4AE
☎0161 793 3560
Fax 0161 727 7071
Divisional Librarian Chris Farey BA(Hons) DipLIS DBA MCLIP (e-mail: chris.farey@salford.gov.uk)
▶ Walkden Library, Memorial Road, Walkden, Salford, Manchester M28 3AQ
☎0161 790 4579

Fax 0161 703 8971
Senior Librarian Chris Carson BA DMS MCLIP (e-mail: chris.carson@salford.gov.uk)

SANDWELL

Authority: Sandwell Metropolitan Borough Council
HQ Library Support Services, Town Hall, West Bromwich, West Midlands B70 8DX
☎0121 569 4924
Fax 0121 569 4907
e-mail: information.service@sandwell.gov.uk
url: www.lea.sandwell.gov.uk/libraries
Chief Librarian Ms Linda Saunders BA DipLib MCLIP

Central/largest library
Central Library, High Street, West Bromwich, West Midlands B70 8DZ
☎0121 569 4904
Fax 0121 525 9465
Principal Libraries Officer (Learning and Information) Ms Heather Vickerman (0121 569 4906; e-mail: heather.vickerman@sandwell.gov.uk)

Additional services
▶ Community History and Archives Service, Smethwick Library, High Street, Smethwick, West Midlands B66 1AB
  ☎0121 558 2561
  Fax 0121 555 6064
  e-mail: archives.service@sandwell.gov.uk
  Borough Archivist Ms Teresa Nixon (0121 558 2561; e-mail: teresa.nixon@sandwell.gov.uk)
▶ Community Libraries, c/o Central Library, High Street, West Bromwich, West Midlands B70 8DZ
  ☎0121 569 4922
  Fax 0121 525 9465
  Principal Libraries Officer (Community Libraries) Anthony Piorowski MCLIP (0121 569 4922; e-mail: tony.piorowski@sandwell.gov.uk)
▶ Library Support Services, Town Hall, High Street, West Bromwich, West Midlands B70 8DT
  ☎0121 569 4909
  Fax 0121 569 4907
  Principal Libraries Officer (Library Support Services) Barry Clark BLib MCLIP (e-mail: barry.clark@sandwell.gov.uk)

SEFTON

Authority: Sefton Council
HQ Leisure Services Department, Pavilion Buildings, 99-105 Lord Street, Southport PR8 1RH
☎0151 934 2376
Fax 0151 934 2370
e-mail: library.service@leisure.sefton.gov.uk

url: www.sefton.gov.uk

Head of Library and Information Services Ms Christine Hall BA MCLIP (e-mail: christine.hall@leisure.sefton.gov.uk)

Principal Library Services Officer Mrs Jenny Stanistreet MA MCLIP (0151 934 2351; e-mail: jenny.stanistreet@leisure.sefton.gov.uk)

Central/largest libraries

Crosby Library, Crosby Road North, Waterloo, Liverpool L22 0LQ
☎0151 257 6400
Fax 0151 330 5770

Southport Library, Lord Street, Southport PR8 1DJ
☎0151 934 2118
Fax 0151 934 2115

SHEFFIELD

Authority: Sheffield City Council

HQ Sheffield Libraries, Archives and Information Services, Central Library, Surrey Street, Sheffield S1 1XZ
☎0114 273 4712 (enquiries), 0114 273 5052 (library management)
Fax 0114 273 5009
e-mail: libraries@sheffield.gov.uk
url: www.sheffield.gov.uk

City Librarian Ms Janice Maskort BA(Hons) MCLIP DMS (e-mail: janice.maskort@sheffield.gov.uk)

Lifelong Learning Manager David Isaac BA(Hons) DipLib DMS MCLIP (0114 273 6959; e-mail: david.isaac@sheffield.gov.uk)

Operations Manager Ms Jo McCausland BLib MCLIP (0114 273 6642; e-mail: jo.mccausland@sheffield.gov.uk)

Policy and Development Manager Martin Dutch BA(Hons) DipLib MCLIP (0114 273 6642)

Archives and Local Studies Manager Peter Evans

Collections and Reader Development Manager Ms Alison Jobey BA MCLIP (0114 273 4721)

ICT Manager John Murphy BSc(Hons) MA (0114 273 6645)

Information Services Manager Ms Elizabeth Wright MA MCLIP (0114 273 6645)

Lending Services Manager Andrew Milroy BA DipLib (0114 273 4403)

Performance Manager Ms Judith Adam MA(Hons) DipLib MCLIP (0114 273 4254)

District libraries

▶ Broomhill Library, Taptonville Road, Sheffield S10 5BR
  ☎0114 273 4276
▶ Burngreave Library, 179 Spital Hill, Sheffield S4 7LF
  ☎0114 203 9002
▶ Chapeltown Library, Nether Ley Avenue, Sheffield S35 1AE
  ☎0114 203 7000/1

▶ Crystal Peaks Library, 1-3 Peak Square, Crystal Peaks Complex, Waterthorpe, Sheffield S20 7PH
☎0114 293 0612/3

▶ Darnall Library, Britannia Road, Sheffield S9 5JG
☎0114 203 7429

▶ Ecclesall Library, Weetwood Gardens, Ecclesall Road South, Sheffield S11 9PL
☎0114 203 7222
Fax 0114 203 7227

▶ Ecclesfield Library, High Street, Ecclesfield, Sheffield S35 9UA
☎0114 203 7013 (tel/fax)

▶ Firth Park Library, 443 Firth Park Road, Sheffield S5 6QQ
☎0114 203 7433

▶ Frecheville Library, Smalldale Road, Sheffield S12 4YD
☎0114 203 7817

▶ Gleadless Library, White Lane, Sheffield S12 3GH
☎0114 203 7804 (tel/fax)

▶ Greenhill Library, Hemper Lane, Sheffield S8 7FE
☎0114 203 7700
Fax 0114 293 0012

▶ Highfield Library, London Road, Sheffield S2 4NF
☎0114 203 7204

▶ Hillsborough Library, Middlewood Road, Sheffield S6 4HD
☎0114 203 9529

▶ Jordanthorpe Library, 15 Jordanthorpe Centre, Sheffield S8 8DX
☎0114 203 7701
Fax 0114 293 0388

▶ Limpsfield Library, Limpsfield Middle School, Jenkin Avenue, Sheffield S9 1AN
☎0114 203 7430
Fax 0114 242 3808

▶ Manor Library, Ridgeway Road, Sheffield S12 2SS
☎0114 203 7805

▶ Mobile Services, 443 Handsworth Road, Sheffield S13 9DD
☎0114 273 4277

▶ Newfield Green Library, Gleadless Road, Sheffield S2 2BT
☎0114 203 7818 (tel/fax)

▶ Park Library, Duke Street, Sheffield S2 5QP
☎0114 203 9000 (tel/fax)

▶ Parson Cross Library, Margetson Crescent, Sheffield S5 9ND
☎0114 203 9533
Fax 0114 203 9656

▶ Southey Library, Moonshine Lane, Sheffield S5 8RB
☎0114 203 9531
Fax 0114 293 0024

▶ Stannington Library, Uppergate Road, Sheffield S6 8RB
☎0114 293 0489
Fax 0114 293 0488

▶ Stocksbridge Library, Manchester Road, Stocksbridge, Sheffield S36 1DH
☎0114 273 4205

- Tinsley Library, Tinsley Shopping Centre, Bawtry Road, Sheffield S9 1UY
  ☎0114 203 7432
  Fax 0114 293 0029
- Totley Library, 205 Baslow Road, Sheffield S17 4DT
  ☎0114 293 0406
- Upperthorpe Library, Upperthorpe Healthy Living Centre, 18 Upperthorpe, Sheffield S6 3NA
  ☎0114 270 2048
  Fax 0114 276 2189
- Walkley Library, South Road, Sheffield S6 3TD
  ☎0114 203 9532 (tel/fax)
- Woodhouse Library, Tannery Street, Sheffield S13 7JU
  ☎0114 269 2607 (tel/fax)
- Woodseats Library, Chesterfield Road, Sheffield S8 0SH
  ☎0114 293 0411

SHROPSHIRE

Authority: Shropshire County Council
HQ Library and Information Services, Community and Environment Directorate, The Shirehall, Abbey Foregate, Shrewsbury, Shropshire SY2 6ND
☎(01743) 255000
Fax (01743) 255001
e-mail: libraries@shropshire-cc.gov.uk
url: www.shropshire-cc.gov.uk/library.nsf
Head of Library and Information Services Jim Roads BA MCLIP (e-mail: jim.roads@shropshire-cc.gov.uk)
Principal Librarian – Development and Support Don Yuile BA MCLIP (e-mail: don.yuile@shropshire-cc.gov.uk)
Principal Librarian – Young People and Access Gordon Dickins BA MCLIP (e-mail: gordon.dickins@shropshire-cc.gov.uk)

Central/largest libraries

Castle Gates Library, Shrewsbury, Shropshire SY1 2AS
☎(01743) 255300
Fax (01743) 255309
Principal Librarian – Shrewsbury Ms Elaine Moss MCLIP (e-mail: elaine.moss@shropshire-cc.gov.uk)

Reference and Information Service, 1a Castle Gates, Shrewsbury, Shropshire SY1 2AQ
☎(01743) 255380
Fax (01743) 255383
Principal Librarian – Shrewsbury Ms Elaine Moss MCLIP (e-mail: elaine.moss@shropshire-cc.gov.uk)

Area libraries

- North Area. Oswestry Library, Arthur Street, Oswestry, Shropshire SY11 1JN
  ☎(01691) 653211

Fax (01691) 656994
Principal Librarian – North Ms Claire Cartlidge MCLIP (e-mail:
claire.cartlidge@shropshire-cc.gov.uk)
▶ South Area. Bridgnorth Library, Listley Street, Bridgnorth, Shropshire WV16 4AW
☎(01746) 763257
Fax (01746) 766625
Principal Librarian – South Adrian Williams BA MCLIP (e-mail:
adrian.williams@shropshire-cc.gov.uk)

SLOUGH

Authority: Slough Borough Council
HQ Libraries, Arts, Heritage and Information, Learning and Cultural Services, Town Hall,
Bath Road, Slough SL1 3UQ
☎(01753) 875578
Fax (01753) 875419
url: www.slough.gov.uk
Head of Libraries, Arts, Heritage and Information Mrs Yvonne M Cope MIMgt
MCLIP (e-mail: yvonne.cope@slough.gov.uk)
Library Services Manager, Strategy & Improvement Ms Sue Jarvis (e-mail:
sue.jarvis@slough.gov.uk)

Central/largest library
Slough Library, High Street, Slough SL1 1EA
☎(01753) 535166
Fax (01753) 825050
Library Services Manager, Operations Mrs Jackie Menniss BA(Hons) DipIM MCLIP
(01753 787506; e-mail: jackie.menniss@slough.gov.uk)
Library IT Manager Damon Guy (e-mail: damon.guy@slough.gov.uk)

SOLIHULL

Authority: Solihull Metropolitan Borough Council
HQ Central Library, Homer Road, Solihull, West Midlands B91 3RG
☎0121 704 6965 (public enquiries), 0121 704 6941 (administration)
Fax 0121 704 6991
e-mail: libraryarts@solihull.gov.uk
url: www.solihull.gov.uk
Head of Community Services (Libraries, Arts and Lifelong Learning) Nigel Ward BA
MA DMS MCLIP (0121 704 6945; e-mail: nward@solihull.gov.uk)
Support Services Manager Ms Hilary Halliday BA MCLIP (0121 704 8227; e-mail:
hhalliday@solihull.gov.uk)

Main area libraries
▶ Central Library, Homer Road, Solihull, West Midlands B91 3RG
☎0121 704 6965
Fax 0121 704 6991

Central Area Manager Ms Tracey Juric BLS(Hons) MCLIP (e-mail: tjuric@solihull.gov.uk)
▶ Chelmsley Wood Library, Stephenson Drive, Chelmsley Wood, Solihull, West Midlands B37 5TA
☎0121 788 4380
Fax 0121 788 4391
▶ Knowle Library, Chester House, 1667-9 High Street, Knowle, Solihull, West Midlands B93 0LL
☎(01564) 775840
Fax (01564) 770953
Community Libraries Manager Ms Yvonne Negus BA MCLIP MISM (01564 776331; e-mail: ynegus@solihull.org.uk)

SOMERSET

Authority: Somerset County Council
HQ Libraries, Arts and Information Service, Library Administration Centre, Mount Street, Bridgwater, Somerset TA6 3ES
☎(01278) 451201
Fax (01278) 452787
e-mail: librec@somerset.gov.uk
url: www.somerset.gov.uk/libraries
Head of Cultural Service Rob N Froud BLib DMS MIMgt FCLIP (e-mail: rnfroud@somerset.gov.uk)
Acting Principal Assistant County Librarian: Information and Support Services Ms Sue Crowley BLib MCLIP (e-mail: sacrowley@somerset.gov.uk)
Assistant County Librarian: (Operations) Philip Nichols BA MCLIP (01935 429614; e-mail: penichols@somerset.gov.uk) (located at Yeovil Library)
Assistant County Librarian: Policy and Development Miss Rachel Boyd BA MCLIP (e-mail: rboyd@somerset.gov.uk)
Business, Quality and Support Services Manager Stephen G May (e-mail: sgmay@somerset.gov.uk)
County Arts Officer Ms Susan Isherwood BA (e-mail: sisherwood@somerset.gov.uk)
Manager, Foursite Bibliographic Services Section Miss Carol Gold (e-mail: cgold2@somerset.gov.uk)
Manager, Enquiry Centre Mrs Jane Gill BA MCLIP (e-mail: jgill@somerset.gov.uk)
Projects, Research and Marketing Officer Paul Smith BA(Hons) DipLib DMS MCLIP (e-mail: psmith@somerset.gov.uk)

Group libraries
▶ Mendip & Sedgemoor Group, Bridgwater Library, Binford Place, Bridgwater, Somerset TA6 3LF
☎(01278) 458373
Fax (01278) 451027
Group Librarian Mrs Susan Crowley BA MCLIP (e-mail: sacrowley@somerset.gov.uk)
▶ South Somerset Group, Yeovil Library, King George Street, Yeovil, Somerset BA20 1PY
☎(01935) 423144
Fax (01935) 431847

Group Librarian Nigel J Humphrey BLib MA (e-mail: nhumphrey@somerset.gov.uk)
▶ Taunton Deane & West Somerset Group, Taunton Library, Paul Street, Taunton,
Somerset TA1 3XZ
☎(01823) 336334
Fax (01823) 340302
Group Librarian David J Cawthorne BA MCLIP (e-mail:
dcawthorne@somerset.gov.uk)

SOUTH GLOUCESTERSHIRE

Authority: South Gloucestershire Council
HQ Library Service, Civic Centre, High Street, Kingswood, South Glos BS15 9TR
☎(01454) 865782
Fax (01454) 868535
e-mail: libraries@southglos.gov.uk
url: www.southglos.gov.uk/libraries
Head of Library and Information Service Martin Burton BA MCLIP
Team Manager (North) Ms Anne Hartridge MCLIP (01454 865664)
Team Manager (South) Michael Duffy MCLIP (01454 868450)

Central/largest library
Yate Library, 44 West Walk, Yate, South Glos BS37 4AX
☎(01454) 865661
Fax (01454) 865665
Group Librarian Neil Weston BA MCLIP

Group libraries
▶ Downend Library, Buckingham Gardens, Downend, South Glos BS16 5TW
☎(01454) 865666
Librarian Mrs Helen Egarr MCLIP
▶ Kingswood Library, High Street, Kingswood, South Glos BS15 4AR
☎(01454) 865650
Librarian Ms Julie Barker
▶ Thornbury Library, St Mary Street, Thornbury, South Glos BS35 2AA
☎(01454) 865655
Librarian Bob Filer BA MCLIP

SOUTH TYNESIDE

Authority: South Tyneside Metropolitan Borough Council
HQ South Tyneside Libraries, Central Library, Prince Georg Square, South Shields, Tyne and
Wear NE33 2PE
☎0191 427 1818
Fax 0191 455 8085
e-mail: reference.library@s-tyneside-mbc.gov.uk
url: www.s-tyneside-mbc.gov.uk
Libraries Manager Mark C E Freeman BA(Hons) MCLIP (e-mail:
mark.freeman@s-tyneside-mbc.gov.uk)

SOUTHAMPTON

Authority: Southampton City Council
HQ City Library, Archives and Information Service, Central Library, Civic Centre, Southampton SO14 7LW
☎023 8083 2459 (administration)
Fax 023 8033 6305
url: www.southampton.gov.uk
Libraries, Arts and Heritage Manager David Baldwin (e-mail: david.baldwin@southampton.gov.uk)
Acting Assistant City Librarians Ms Siobhan McGarrigle (e-mail: siobhan.macgarrigle@southampton.gov.uk), Mrs Elizabeth Whale (023 8083 2595; e-mail: elizabeth.whale@southampton.gov.uk) (job-share)
Principal Bibliographic Services Librarian Martin Ceresa (e-mail: martin.ceresa@southampton.gov.uk)

Central/largest library

Central Library, Civic Centre, Southampton SO14 7LW
☎023 8083 2597 (Lending Library renewals), 023 8083 2664 (enquiry desk), 023 8083 2462/3 (Reference Library)
e-mail: lending.library@southampton.gov.uk
Principal Lending Librarian Richard Ashman (e-mail: richard.ashman@southampton.gov.uk)
Principal Reference Librarian Mark Illingworth (e-mail: mark.illingworth@southampton.gov.uk)

Branch libraries

▶ Bitterne Library, Bitterne Road East, Southampton SO18 5EG
  ☎023 8044 9909
  e-mail: eastern.library@southampton.gov.uk
  Supervisor Ms Barbara McCaffrey (e-mail: barbara.mccaffrey@southampton.gov.uk)
▶ Burgess Road Library, Burgess Road, Southampton SO16 3HF
  ☎023 8067 8873
  e-mail: burgess.road.library@southampton.gov.uk
  Supervisor Ms Marion Hancock (e-mail: marion.hancock@southampton.gov.uk)
▶ Cobbett Road Library, Cobbett Road, Southampton SO18 1HL
  ☎023 8022 5555
  e-mail: cobbett.road.library@southampton.gov.uk
  Supervisor Ms Norma Belbin (e-mail: norma.belbin@southampton.gov.uk)
▶ Lord's Hill Library, Lord's Hill District Centre, Southampton SO16 8HY
  ☎023 8073 2845
  Librarian Mrs Pat Hallett (e-mail: pat.hallett@southampton.gov.uk), Mrs Sharon Moore (e-mail: sharon.moore@southampton.gov.uk)
▶ Millbrook Library, 67 Cumbrian Way, Southampton SO16 4AT
  ☎023 8078 1819
  Supervisor Mrs Angela Zabiela
▶ Portswood Library, Portswood Road, Southampton SO17 2NG
  ☎023 8055 4634

Area Librarian Martin Pavey (e-mail: martin.pavey@southampton.gov.uk)
▶ Shirley Library, Redcar Street, Southampton SO15 5LL
☎023 8077 2136
Area Librarian Mrs Janet Moore (e-mail: janet.moore@southampton.gov.uk)
▶ Thornhill Library, 380 Hinkler Road, Southampton SO19 6DF
☎023 8044 7245
Supervisor Ms Maxine Webb (e-mail: maxine.webb@southampton.gov.uk)
▶ Weston Library, 6 Wallace Road, Weston, Southampton SO19 9GX
☎023 8044 4363
Supervisor Mrs Carolyn Taplin
▶ Woolston Library, Portsmouth Road, Southampton SO19 9AF
☎023 8044 8481
Supervisor Ms Jo Harley

SOUTHEND ON SEA

Authority: Southend on Sea Borough Council
HQ Southend Library, Victoria Avenue, Southend on Sea, Essex SS2 6EX
☎(01702) 612621
Fax (01702) 469241
e-mail: library@southend.gov.uk
url: www.southend.gov.uk
Library Services Manager Simon May BSc MSc MCLIP
Head of Information and Resources Chris Hayes BA DipLib MCLIP
Head of Children's and Access Mark Thres BA MCLIP

SOUTHWARK

Authority: London Borough of Southwark
HQ Southwark Environment and Leisure, 15 Spa Road, London SE16 3QW
☎020 7525 3719
Fax 020 7525 1568
e-mail: southwark.libraries@southwark.gov.uk
url: www.southwark.gov.uk
Head of Libraries and Information Adrian Olsen BA MCLIP (020 7525 1577; e-mail: adrian.olsen@southwark.gov.uk)
Library Operations Manager Ms Christine Brown BA MCLIP MLib (020 7525 3445; e-mail: christine.brown@southwark.gov.uk)
Library Development and Support Manager Ms Claire Styles BA(Hons) MSc(Econ) MCLIP (020 7525 3920; e-mail: claire.styles@southwark.gov.uk)

Branch libraries
▶ Blue Anchor Library, Market Place, Southwark Park Road, London SE16 3UQ
☎020 7231 0475
Fax 020 7232 1842
▶ Brandon Library, Maddock Way, Cooks Road, London SE17 3NH
☎020 7735 3430 (tel/fax)
▶ Camberwell Library, 17-21 Camberwell Church Street, London SE5 8TR

☎020 7703 3763
Fax 020 7708 4597
▶ Dulwich Library, 368 Lordship Lane, London SE22 8NB
☎020 7525 6220
Fax 020 7525 6221
▶ East Street/Old Kent Road Library, 168-170 Old Kent Road, London SE1 5TY
☎020 7703 0395
Fax 020 7703 2224
▶ Education Library Service, Southwark Education Resource Centre, Cator Street,
London SE15 6AA
☎020 7525 2830
Fax 020 7525 2837
▶ Grove Vale Library, 25-27 Grove Vale, London SE22 8EQ
☎020 8693 5734 (tel/fax)
▶ John Harvard Library, 211 Borough High Street, London SE1 1JA
☎020 7407 0807 (tel/fax)
▶ Kingswood Library, Seeley Drive, London SE21 8QR
☎020 8670 4803
Fax 020 8671 5125
▶ Local Studies Library, 211 Borough High Street, London SE1 1JA
☎020 7403 3507
Fax 020 7403 8633
▶ Newington Library, 155-7 Walworth Road, London SE17 1RS
☎020 7525 2176
Fax 020 7252 6115
▶ Newington Reference Library, 155-7 Walworth Road, London SE17 1RS
☎020 7525 2159
Fax 020 7252 6115
▶ Nunhead Library, Gordon Road, London SE15 3RW
☎020 7639 0264
Fax 020 7277 5721
▶ Peckham Library, 122 Peckham Hill Street, London SE15 5JR
☎020 7525 0200
Fax 020 7525 0202
▶ Rotherhithe Library, Albion Street, London SE16 1JA
☎020 7237 2010
Fax 020 7394 0672
▶ Special Library Services, Rotherhithe Library, Albion Street, London SE16 1JA
☎020 7237 1487
Fax 020 7237 8417

STAFFORDSHIRE

Authority: Staffordshire County Council
HQ Library and Information Services, Education and Lifelong Learning, Peel Building, St
Chad's Place, Stafford ST16 2LH
☎(01785) 278311
Fax (01785) 278319

url: www.staffordshire.gov.uk

County Librarian Mrs Olivia Spencer MCLIP (01785 278422; e-mail: olivia.spencer@staffordshire.gov.uk)

Deputy Head of Library Services Ms Janene Cox BLib MCLIP (01785 278368; e-mail: janene.cox@staffordshire.gov.uk)

Principal Librarian: Performance, Standards, Funding and Support Mrs Morna Williams MA(Hons) DipLib MCLIP (01785 278587; e-mail: morna.williams@staffordshire.gov.uk)

Principal Librarian: Books, Reading and Promotion Mrs Judy Goodson MCLIP (01785 278320; e-mail: judy.goodson@staffordshire.gov.uk)

Principal Librarian: Community Development/Partnerships Mrs Elizabeth Rees-Jones BA(Hons) MCLIP (01785 278344; e-mail: elizabeth.rees-jones@staffordshire.gov.uk)

Principal Librarian: Knowledge Management/Digital Citizenship Mrs Hilary Jackson BLib MCLIP (01785 278591; e-mail: hilary.jackson@staffordshire.gov.uk)

Portal clusters

▶ Burton Library, Riverside, High Street, Burton-on-Trent, Staffs DE14 1AH
☎(01283) 239556
Fax (01283) 239571
e-mail: burton.library@staffordshire.gov.uk
Portal Librarian Mrs Pat Phelps MCLIP (01283 239559; e-mail: pat.phelps@staffordshire.gov.uk)

▶ Cannock Library, Manor Avenue, Cannock, Staffs WS11 1AA
☎(01543) 510365
Fax (01543) 510373
e-mail: cannock.library@staffordshire.gov.uk
Portal Librarian Mrs Sue Ball BA(Hons) MCLIP (01543 510366; e-mail: sue.ball@staffordshire.gov.uk)

▶ Newcastle Library, Ironmarket, Newcastle, Staffs ST5 1AT
☎(01782) 297300
Fax (01782) 297323
e-mail: newcastle.library@staffordshire.gov.uk
Portal Librarian Kevin Reynolds MCLIP (01782 297305; e-mail: kevin.reynolds@staffordshire.gov.uk)

▶ Shire Hall Library, Market Street, Stafford ST16 2LQ
☎(01785) 278585
Fax (01785) 278599
e-mail: stafford.library@staffordshire.gov.uk
Portal Librarian Mrs Alison Reynolds BA(Hons) MA MCLIP (01785 278573; e-mail: alison.reynolds@staffordshire.gov.uk)

▶ Tamworth Library, Corporation Street, Tamworth, Staffs B79 7DN
☎(01827) 475645
Fax (01827) 475658
e-mail: tamworth.library@staffordshire.gov.uk
Portal Librarian Alan Medway BLib MCLIP (01827 475651; e-mail: alan.medway@staffordshire.gov.uk)

STOCKPORT

Authority: Stockport Metropolitan Borough Council
HQ Community Services, Stopford House, Piccadilly, Stockport SK1 3XE
☎0161 474 4447 (enquiries and administration)
Fax 0161 429 0335
url: www.stockport.gov.uk
Head of Library and Information Services John Condon (e-mail:
john.condon@stockport.gov.uk)

Central/largest library

Central Library, Wellington Road South, Stockport SK1 3RS
☎0161 474 4530 (Local Heritage Library), 0845 644 4307 (all other library enquiries)
Fax 0161 474 7750
e-mail: lending.library@stockport.gov.uk; information.library@stockport.gov.uk;
localheritage.library@stockport.gov.uk

Bibliographical Services Unit, Phoenix House, Bird Hall Lane, Stockport SK3 0RA
☎0161 474 5605
Fax 0161 491 6516

STOCKTON-ON-TEES

Authority: Stockton-on-Tees Borough Council
HQ Children, Education and Social Care, Stockton Borough Libraries, Church Road,
Stockton-on-Tees TS18 1TU
☎(01642) 526522
Fax (01642) 528078
url: www.stockton.gov.uk
Head of Lifelong Learning Mrs Andrea Barker MCLIP (01642 527038; e-mail:
andrea.barker@stockton.gov.uk) (located at Municipal Buildings, Church Road, Stockton-
on-Tees TS18 1XE)
Reading, Learning and Community Engagement Manager Ms Sue Anderson (01642
526518; e-mail: sue.anderson@stockton.gov.uk)
Community Engagement Officer Ms Emma Shields MSc (01642 526250; e-mail:
emma.shields@stockton.gov.uk)
Priority Services Officer Mrs Pam Wilson MCLIP (01642 526519; e-mail:
pam.wilson@stockton.gov.uk)
Lending Services Officer Mrs Penny Slee (01642 526521; e-mail:
penny.slee@stockton.gov.uk)
Reference and Information Services Officer Vacant
Community Libraries Officer Ms Deb McDonagh (01642 526520; e-mail:
debbie.mcdonagh@stockton.gov.uk)
Performance, Promotion and People's Network Manager Ms Laurayne Featherstone
(01642 526463; e-mail: laurayne.featherstone@stockton.gov.uk)
Performance and Improvement Co-ordinator Ms Anne Tingle (01642 526520; e-mail:
anne.tingle@stockton.gov.uk)

Reader Development Officer Mrs Claire Pratt BA MCLIP (01642 528044; e-mail: claire.pratt@stockton.gov.uk)

Books, Reading and Learning Officer Ms Alison Lambert (01642 526997; e-mail: alison.lambert@stockton.gov.uk)

Access to Digital Services Co-ordinator Steve Wild (01642 526501; e-mail: steve.wild@stockton.gov.uk)

Branch libraries

▶ Billingham Branch Library, Bedale Avenue, Billingham, Stockton-on-Tees TS23 1AJ
☎(01642) 527895
e-mail: billingham.library@stockton.gov.uk
Branch Librarian Vacant

▶ Egglescliffe Branch Library, Butterfield Drive, Orchard Estate, Egglescliffe, Stockton-on-Tees TS16 0EL
☎(01642) 527958
e-mail: egglescliffe.library@stockton.gov.uk
Branch Librarian Miss Margaret Chapman MA(Lib)

▶ Fairfield Branch Library, Fairfield Road, Stockton-on-Tees TS19 7AJ
☎(01642) 577962
e-mail: fairfield.library@stockton.gov.uk
Branch Librarian Richard Lacey MCLIP

▶ Ingleby Barwick Library, Ingleby Barwick Community Campus, Blair Avenue, Ingleby Barwick, Stockton-on-Tees TS17 5BL
☎(01642) 750767
e-mail: inglebybarwick.library@stockton.gov.uk
Branch Librarian Vacant

▶ Norton Branch Library, 87 High Street, Norton, Stockton-on-Tees TS20 1AE
☎(01642) 528019
e-mail: norton.library@stockton.gov.uk
Branch Librarian Mrs Cath Maddison BSc DipLib

▶ Roseberry Billingham Branch Library, The Causeway, Billingham, Stockton-on-Tees TS23 2LB
☎(01642) 528084
e-mail: roseberry.library@stockton.gov.uk
Branch Librarian Miss Beryl Sandles MCLIP

▶ Roseworth Branch Library, Redhill Road, Stockton-on-Tees TS19 9BX
☎(01642) 528098
Branch Librarian Vacant

▶ Thornaby Central Branch Library, The Pavillion, New Town Centre, Thornaby, Stockton-on-Tees TS17 9EW
☎(01642) 528117
e-mail: thornaby.central.library@stockton.gov.uk
Branch Librarian Mrs Shelagh Freeman MCLIP

▶ Thornaby Westbury Street Branch Library, Westbury Street, Thornaby, Stockton-on-Tees TS17 6PG
☎(01642) 528150
e-mail: thornaby.library@stockton.gov.uk
Branch Librarian Vacant

▶ Yarm Branch Library, 41 High Street, Yarm, Stockton-on-Tees TS15 9BH
☎(01642) 528152
e-mail: yarm.library@stockton.gov.uk
Branch Librarian Mrs Wanda Sandham BA MCLIP

STOKE-ON-TRENT

Authority: Stoke-on-Trent City Council
HQ Libraries, Information and Archives, City Central Library, Bethesda Street, Hanley, Stoke-on-Trent ST1 3RS
☎(01782) 238455 (enquiries); (01782) 238405 (administration)
Fax (01782) 238499
e-mail: stoke.libraries@stoke.gov.uk
url: www.stoke.gov.uk/council/libraries
Head of Library Services Ms Margaret Green BA MLS MCLIP (e-mail: margaret.green@stoke.gov.uk)
Customer and Support Services Manager Mrs Anne Mackey BA MCLIP (e-mail: anne.mackey@stoke.gov.uk)
Strategy and Service Development Manager Ian Van Arkadie BA DipLib DipMgt (e-mail: ian.vanarkadie@stoke.gov.uk)
City Archivist Chris Latimer MA DAA (e-mail: chris.latimer@stoke.gov.uk)

SUFFOLK

Authority: Suffolk County Council
HQ Libraries and Heritage, Endeavour House, Russell Road, Ipswich IP1 2BX
☎(01473) 265086 (enquiries and administration)
Fax (01473) 218843
url: www.suffolkcc.gov.uk/libraries_and_heritage
Assistant Director (Libraries and Heritage) Ms Guenever J Pachent BA DLIS MCLIP MILAM (01473 264385; e-mail: guenever.pachent@libher.suffolkcc.gov.uk)
County Manager Roger McMaster BA MA MCLIP (e-mail: roger.mcmaster@libher.suffolkcc.gov.uk)

Central/largest library

County Library, Northgate Street, Ipswich IP1 3DE
☎(01473) 583705/10 (enquiries and administration)
Fax (01473) 583700
Ipswich Locality Manager Ms Amanda Hewitt (e-mail: amanda.hewitt@libher.suffolkcc.gov.uk)

Area libraries

▶ Central Library, Sergeant's Walk, Off St Andrew's Street North, Bury St Edmunds, Suffolk IP33 1TZ
☎(01284) 352542
Fax (01284) 352566
St Edmundsbury Locality Manager Brandon King (e-mail: brandon.king@libher.suffolkcc.gov.uk)

▶ Central Library, Clapham Road South, Lowestoft, Suffolk NR32 1DR
☎(01502) 405342
Fax (01502) 405350
Waveney Locality Manager Ms Gill Jenkins (e-mail:
gill.jenkins@libher.suffolkcc.gov.uk)

Selected branch libraries
▶ Beccles Library, Blyburgate, Beccles, Suffolk NR34 9TB
☎(01502) 714073/716471
Fax (01502) 714073
Library Manager Ms Mary Storey
▶ Felixstowe Library, Crescent Road, Felixstowe, Suffolk IP11 7BY
☎(01394) 625766
Fax (01394) 625770
Library Manager Mrs Lynne Gibbs
▶ Hadleigh Library, 29 High Street, Hadleigh, Ipswich IP7 5AG
☎(01473) 823778
Fax (01473) 822557
Library Manager Geoff Ross BA
▶ Haverhill Library, Camps Road, Haverhill, Suffolk CB9 8HB
☎(01440) 702638
Library Manager Ms Madeline Tuck
▶ Mildenhall Library, Chestnut Close, Mildenhall, Bury St Edmunds, Suffolk IP28 7HL
☎(01638) 713558
Fax (01638) 510108
Library Manager Ms Denise Gray
▶ Newmarket Library, 1a The Rookery, Newmarket, Suffolk CB8 8EQ
☎(01638) 661216
Library Manager Mrs Grace Myers-Crump
▶ Stowmarket Library, Milton Road North, Stowmarket, Suffolk IP14 1EX
☎(01449) 613143
Fax (01449) 672629
Library Manager Ms Frances Law
▶ Sudbury Library, Market Hill, Sudbury, Suffolk CO10 2EN
☎(01787) 296000
Fax (01787) 296004
Library Manager Ms Sandra Curtis
▶ Woodbridge Library, New Street, Woodbridge, Suffolk IP12 1DT
☎(01394) 625095
Fax (01394) 625091
Library Manager Ms Linda Firth

SUNDERLAND

Authority: City of Sunderland Metropolitan District Council
HQ City Library and Arts Centre, Fawcett Street, Sunderland SR1 1RE
☎0191 514 1235 (enquiries and administration)
Fax 0191 514 8444

e-mail: enquiry.desk@sunderland.gov.uk
url: www.sunderland.gov.uk
Assistant Head of Culture and Tourism (Libraries, Heritage and Information) Mrs
Jane F Hall BA(Hons) MCLIP (e-mail: jane.hall@sunderland.gov.uk)
City Librarian Ms Valerie Craggs MCLIP (e-mail: valerie.craggs@sunderland.gov.uk)
Principal Librarian (Library Operations) Mrs Ann Scott MCLIP (e-mail:
ann.scott@sunderland.gov.uk)
Principal Librarian (E-Resources and Information Services) Ms Julie McCann
BA(Hons) MCLIP (e-mail: julie.mccann@sunderland.gov.uk)
Principal Librarian (Reader Development) Mrs Joanne Parkinson BA(Hons) (e-mail:
joanne.parkinson@sunderland.gov.uk)
Principal Librarian (Library Development) Ms Vivienne Foster BA (e-mail:
vivienne.foster@sunderland.gov.uk)
Principal Librarian (Libraries, Heritage and Information Projects) Mrs Vicki
Medhurst BSc(Hons) (e-mail: vicki.medhurst@sunderland.gov.uk)

Area library

▶ Washington Town Centre Library, Independence Square, Washington, Tyne and Wear
NE38 7RZ
☎0191 219 3440

SURREY

Authority: Surrey County Council
HQ Community Services, Room 176, County Hall, Kingston upon Thames, Surrey KT1 2DN
☎020 8541 9071
Fax 020 8541 9003
url: www.surreycc.gov.uk/libraries
Head of Libraries Chris Norris BA MPhil MBA (e-mail: chris.norris@surreycc.gov.uk)

Area management teams and largest libraries

▶ East Area Office, Omnibus, Lesbourne Road, Reigate, Surrey RH2 7JA
☎(01737) 737692
Fax (01737) 737649
Library Area Manager Mrs Hilary Ely MA MCLIP (020 8541 7060)
▶ Redhill Library, Warwick Quadrant, Redhill, Surrey RH1 1NN
☎(01737) 763332
Senior Library Manager Mrs Marion Saberi
Library Manager Ms Marilyn Apsee
▶ Mid-Surrey Area Office, Opus 2, Bay Tree Avenue, Kingston Road, Leatherhead, Surrey
KT22 7SY
☎(01372) 363920
Fax (01372) 360169
Library Area Manager Ms Sally Parker BA MCLIP (01372 363920; e-mail:
sally.p@surreycc.gov.uk)
▶ Epsom Library, 6 The Derby Square, Epsom, Surrey KT19 8AG
☎(01372) 721707
Fax (01372) 744441

Senior Library Manager Mrs Pauline Fella
▶ North West Area Office, Runnymede Centre, Chertsey Road, Addlestone, Surrey KT15 2EP
☎(01932) 794179
Fax (01932) 794189
Library Area Manager Mrs Rose Wilson BA(Hons) (01932 794178; e-mail: r.wilson@surreycc.gov.uk)
▶ Woking Library, Gloucester Walk, Woking, Surrey GU21 6EP
☎(01483) 770591
Fax (01483) 756073
Library Manager Ms Crishna Simmons
▶ South West Area Office, AO3 London Square, Cross Lanes, Guildford, Surrey GU1 1FA
☎(01483) 517402
Fax (01483) 517401
Library Area Manager Chris Phillips (01483 517337)
▶ Guildford Library, 77 North Street, Guildford, Surrey GU1 4AL
☎(01483) 568496
Fax (01483) 579177
Library Manager Mrs Susanne Bray
Library Services Development Manager (Information Services) Ms Janet Thomas (020 8541 7766)

Selected branch libraries
▶ Ashford Library, Church Road, Ashford, Middlesex TW15 2XB
☎(01784) 253651
Fax (01784) 257603
Library Manager Chris Ganderton
▶ Banstead Library, The Horseshoe, Bolters Lane, Banstead, Surrey SM7 2AN
☎(01737) 531271
Fax (01737) 373693
Library Manager Ms Gill McCormick
▶ Camberley Library, Knoll Road, Camberley, Surrey GU15 3SY
☎(01276) 63184; 01276 27718 (administration)
Fax (01276) 65701
Library Manager Geoff Cox
▶ Dorking Library, Pippbrook House, Regiate Road, Dorking, Surrey RH4 1SL
☎(01306) 882948
Fax (01306) 875006
Library Manager Mrs L Wyatt
▶ Ewell Library, Bourne Hall, Spring Street, Ewell, Epsom, Surrey KT17 1UF
☎020 8394 0951
Fax 020 8873 1603
Library Manager Ms Brenda Kebbell
▶ Farnham Library, Vernon House, 28 West Street, Farnham, Surrey GU9 7DR
☎(01252) 716021
Fax (01252) 717377
Library Manager Steve Sansom (e-mail: steve.sansom@surreycc.gov.uk)
▶ Godalming Library, Bridge Street, Godalming, Surrey GU7 1HT

☎(01483) 422743
Fax (01483) 425480
Library Manager Mrs Anne Collins
▶ Horley Library, Victoria Road, Horley, Surrey RH6 7AG
☎(01293) 884141
Fax (01293) 820084
Library Manager Ms Terry Cox
▶ Oxted Library, 12 Gresham Road, Oxted, Surrey RH8 0BQ
☎(01883) 714225
Fax (01883) 722742
Library Manager Ms Lyn Ives
▶ Staines Library, Friends Walk, Staines, Middlesex TW18 4PG
☎(01784) 454430; (01784) 463279 (administration)
Fax (01784) 461780
Library Manager Miss W Broadfoot
▶ Weybridge Library, Church Street, Weybridge, Surrey KT13 8DE
☎(01932) 843812
Fax (01932) 850878
Library Manager Ms Judith White

SUTTON

Authority: London Borough of Sutton
HQ Sutton Central Library, St Nicholas Way, Sutton, Surrey SM1 1EA
☎020 8770 4700 (enquiries), 020 8770 4602 (administration)
Fax 020 8770 4777
e-mail: sutton.library@sutton.gov.uk
url: www.sutton.gov.uk
Executive Head of Library, Heritage and Registration Services Trevor Knight MLib
FCLIP (e-mail: trevor.knight@sutton.gov.uk)
Assistant Head of Library and Heritage Services Mrs Cathy McDonough BSc MCLIP
(e-mail: cathy.mcdonough@sutton.gov.uk), Mrs Angela Fletcher BA(Hons) PGCE (e-mail:
angela.fletcher@sutton.gov.uk) (job-share)
Quality Services Manager David Bundy BA MCLIP (e-mail: david.bundy@sutton.gov.uk)
Library Services Manager (Reading and Information) Ms Tola Dabiri (e-mail:
tola.dabiri@sutton.gov.uk)
Library Services Manager (Operations) Jon Ward (e-mail: jon.ward@sutton.gov.uk)

Main libraries
▶ Carshalton Library, The Square, Carshalton, Surrey SM5 3BN
☎020 8647 1151
▶ Cheam Library, Church Road, Cheam, Surrey SM3 8QH
☎020 8644 9377
▶ Wallington Library, Shotfield, Wallington, Surrey SM6 0HY
☎020 8770 4900
▶ Worcester Park Library, Windsor Road, Worcester Park, Surrey KT4 8ES
☎020 8337 1609

SWINDON

Authority: Swindon Borough Council
HQ Environment and Culture, Premier House, Station Road, Swindon SN1 1TZ
☎(01793) 466036
Fax (01793) 466484
url: www.swindon.gov.uk
Libraries and Heritage Manager David Allen MCLIP (e-mail: dallen@swindon.gov.uk)

Central/largest library

Swindon Central Library, Regent Circus, Swindon SN1 1QG
☎(01793) 463238
Fax (01793) 541319
e-mail: libraries@swindon.gov.uk

Group libraries

▶ Acquisitions Group. Library Support Unit, Liden Library, Barrington Close, Liden, Swindon SN3 6HF
☎(01793) 463510
Fax (01793) 463508
Stock Manager Miss Jenny Hayes MCLIP (01793 463512; e-mail: jhayes@swindon.gov.uk)
▶ Coate Group. Central Library, Regent Circus, Swindon SN1 1QG
☎(01793) 463238
Fax (01793) 541319
Group Library Manager Mark Jones MCLIP (01793 463232; e-mail: mjones@swindon.gov.uk)
▶ Lydiard Group. North Swindon Library, Orbital Shopping Park, Thamesdown Drive, Swindon SN25 4AN
☎(01793) 707120
Group Library Manager Shaun Smith MCLIP (01793 707122; e-mail: ssmith@swindon.gov.uk)

TAMESIDE

Authority: Tameside Metropolitan Borough Council
HQ Sustainable Communities Directorate, Council Offices, Wellington Road, Ashton-under-Lyne, Tameside OL6 6DL
☎0161 342 3673
url: www.tameside.gov.uk/libraries
Borough Librarian Mrs Catherine Simensky MCLIP (0161 342 3673; e-mail: catherine.simensky@tameside.gov.uk)
Service Delivery and Inclusion Manager Ms Judith Hall BLib MCLIP (e-mail: judith.hall@tameside.gov.uk)
Operations Manager Ms Denise Lockyer (0161 336 8234; e-mail: denise.lockyer@tameside.gov.uk)
Service Development Manager Philip Jones BA MCLIP (0161 342 2035; e-mail: philip.jones@tameside.gov.uk)

Central/largest library

Tameside Central Library, Old Street, Ashton-under-Lyne, Tameside OL6 7SG

☎0161 342 2029 (lending/enquiries), 0161 342 2035 (bibliographical enquiries), 0161 342 2031 (reference)

Fax 0161 330 4762

e-mail: reference.library@mail.tameside.gov.uk; central.library@mail.tameside.gov.uk

Reference and Information Librarian Ms Karen Heathcote BA DipLIS MCLIP

Other large library

▶ Hyde Library, Union Street, Hyde, Cheshire SK14 1ND

☎0161 368 2447

Fax 0161 368 0205

e-mail: hyde.library@mail.tameside.gov.uk

TELFORD AND WREKIN

Authority: Borough of Telford and Wrekin

HQ Education and Leisure, Telford Library, St Quentin Gate, Telford, Shropshire TF3 4JG

☎(01952) 292151 (switchboard), (01952) 292138 (enquiries)

Fax (01952) 292078

e-mail: telfordlibrary@hotmail.com

url: www.telford.gov.uk

Borough Librarian Ms Sharon Smith BA MCLIP

Lifelong Learning and Libraries Manager Ian Yarroll

Acquisitions Manager Mrs Pat Narey (01952 210077)

Senior Librarian, Information Services Mrs Helen Nahal BLib MCLIP

THURROCK

Authority: Thurrock Council

HQ Libraries and Cultural Services Department, Grays Library, Orsett Road, Grays, Essex RM17 5DX

☎(01375) 383611 (enquiries), (01375) 382555 ext 221 (administration)

Fax (01375) 385504

e-mail: grays.library@thurrock.gov.uk

url: www.thurrock.gov.uk

Head of Libraries and Cultural Services Simon Black (01375 398274)

Chief Librarian Mrs Ann Halliday BA(Hons) DipLIS MCLIP (01375 383611 ext 32)

Central/largest library

Grays Library, Orsett Road, Grays, Essex RM17 5DX

☎(01375) 383611 (enquiries), (01375) 383611 ext 29 (administration)

Fax (01375) 370806

e-mail: grays.library@thurrock.gov.uk

TORBAY

Authority: Torbay Council
HQ Torquay Library, Lymington Road, Torquay, Devon TQI 3DT
☎(01803) 208300 (enquiries), (01803) 208310 (administration)
Fax (01803) 208311
url: www.torbay.gov.uk/libraries
Head of Library Services Peter Bottrill BA MCLIP (01803 208310; e-mail:
peter.bottrill@torbay.gov.uk)
Professional Services Librarian Miss Katie Lusty BA MCLIP (01803 208286; e-mail:
katie.lusty@torbay.gov.uk)
Resources and Technical Services Librarian Miss Elizabeth Kent BSc MCLIP (01803
208287; e-mail: liz.kent@torbay.gov.uk)
Operational Services Librarian Nick Niles BA DipLib (01803 208288; e-mail:
nick.niles@torbay.gov.uk)

Branch libraries
▶ Brixham Library, Market Street, Brixham, Devon TQ5 8EU
☎(01803) 853870
Branch Librarian Mrs Glenys Downes
▶ Churston Library, Broadsands Road, Paignton, Devon TQ4 6LL
☎(01803) 843757
Branch Librarian Mrs Rosie Corby BA MCLIP
▶ Paignton Library, Courtland Road, Paignton, Devon TQ3 2AB
☎(01803) 208321
Branch Librarian Miss Christina Weeks MCLIP

TOWER HAMLETS

Authority: London Borough of Tower Hamlets
HQ Bancroft Library, 277 Bancroft Road, London EI 4DQ
☎020 7364 1291
Fax 020 7364 1292
e-mail: bancroftlibrary@towerhamlets.gov.uk
url: www.towerhamlets.gov.uk
Head of Libraries Ms Anne Cunningham (020 7364 1285; fax: 020 7364 1286)
Library Manager (Development) Ms Kate Pitman BA MCLIP (020 7364 1288; fax: 020
7364 1286; e-mail: kate.pitman@towerhamlets.gov.uk), Ms Sue Bridgwater BA MPhil
MCLIP (020 7364 1288; fax: 020 7364 1286; e-mail:
sue.bridgwater@towerhamlets.gov.uk)
Library Manager (Customer Services) Stephen Clarke BA MCLIP (020 7364 1297; fax:
020 7364 1286; e-mail: stevej.clarke@towerhamlets.gov.uk)
Library Manager (Operations) John Hagerty (020 7364 2517; fax: 020 7364 2518;
e-mail: john.hagerty@towerhamlets.gov.uk)
Senior Admin Officer (Libraries) Miss Kuljinder Kundi (020 7364 1287; fax: 020 7364
1286; e-mail: kuljinder.kundi@towerhamlets.gov.uk)

Central/largest library

Bancroft Library, 277 Bancroft Road, London E1 4DQ
☎020 7364 1291
Fax 020 7364 1292
e-mail: bancroftlibrary@towerhamlets.gov.uk
Community Librarian Robert Stuart BA(Hons)
Local History Librarian Christopher Lloyd BLib MCLIP (020 7364 1290; fax: 020 7364 1292; e-mail: localhistorylibrary@towerhamlets.gov.uk)
Borough Archivist Malcolm Barr-Hamilton BA DAS (020 7364 1290; fax: 020 7364 1292; e-mail: localhistorylibrary@towerhamlets.gov.uk)
Principal Librarian, Outreach Services Graham Pollard (020 7364 1281/1283; fax: 030 7364 1292; e-mail: outreachservices@towerhamlets.gov.uk)

Divisional libraries

▶ East Division. Cubitt Town Library, Strattondale Street, London E14 3HG
  ☎020 7987 3152
  Fax 020 7538 2795
  e-mail: cubitttownlibrary@towerhamlets.gov.uk
  Minicom 020 7987 3152
  Community Librarian Ms Sandra Murray BA MCLIP DMS
▶ Idea Store, Bow, 1 Gladstone Place, Roman Road, London E3 5ES
  ☎020 7364 4332
  Fax 020 7364 5773
  Idea Store Manager Sergio Dogliani (e-mail: sergio.dogliani@dial.pipex.com)
▶ Idea Store, Chrisp Street, 1 Vesey Path, London E14
  ☎020 8364 4332
  Idea Store Manager Zoinul Abidin (e-mail: zoinul.abidin@towerhamlets.gov.uk)
▶ Mid Division. Library Resources Department, Bancroft Library, 277 Bancroft Road, London E1 4DQ
  ☎020 7364 1276
  Fax 020 7364 1295
  e-mail: libraryresources@towerhamlets.gov.uk
  Library Manager (Customer Services) Stephen Clarke BA MCLIP (e-mail: stevej.clarke@towerhamlets.gov.uk)
▶ Mid Division. Watney Market Library, 30-32 Watney Market, London E1 2PR
  ☎020 7790 4039
  Fax 020 7265 9401
  e-mail: watneymarketlibrary@towerhamlets.gov.uk
  Minicom 020 7790 4039
  Community Librarian Mrs Lesley Harris MCLIP, Ms Sarah Paxton
▶ Mid Division. Whitechapel Library, 77 Whitechapel High Street, London E1 7QX
  ☎020 7247 5272
  Fax 020 7247 0396
  e-mail: whitechapellibrary@towerhamlets.gov.uk
  Minicom 020 7247 0265
  Community Librarian John Love
▶ West Division. Bancroft Library, 277 Bancroft Road, London E1 4DQ
  ☎020 7364 1291/1296

Fax 020 7364 1292
e-mail: bancroftlibrary@towerhamlets.gov.uk
Minicom 020 7364 1295
▶ West Division. Bethnal Green Reference Library, Cambridge Heath Road, London E2 0HL
☎020 8980 3902
Fax 020 8981 6129
e-mail: bethnalgreenlibrary@towerhamlets.gov.uk
Minicom 020 8980 3902
Community Librarian Ms Sheila Brown BA
Principal Information Librarian John Jasinski MCLIP (e-mail:
100633.624@compuserve.com; referencelibrary@towerhamlets.gov.uk)
▶ West Division. Dorset Library, Ravenscroft Street, London E2 7QX
☎020 7739 9489
Fax 020 7729 2548
e-mail: dorsetlibrary@towerhamlets.gov.uk
Minicom 020 7739 9489
Community Librarian Ms Sheila Brown BA
▶ West Division. Stepney Library, Lindley Street, London E1 3AX
☎020 7790 5616
Fax 020 7264 9873
e-mail: stepneylibrary@towerhamlets.gov.uk
Minicom 020 7790 5616
Community Librarian Robert Stuart BA(Hons)

TRAFFORD

Authority: Trafford Metropolitan Borough Council
HQ Community Rights, Learning and Libraries, Stretford Library, Kingsway, Stretford,
Manchester M32 8AP
☎0161 912 5152 (enquiries and administration)
Fax 0161 865 3835
e-mail: libraries@trafford.gov.uk
url: www.trafford.gov.uk/libraries
Principal Librarian (Community Rights, Learning and Libraries)
Mrs Gillian Fitzpatrick BA

Regional/district libraries
▶ Altrincham Library, 20 Stamford New Road, Altrincham, Cheshire WA14 1EJ
☎0161 912 5920
Fax 0161 912 5926
▶ Bibliographical Services, Davyhulme Library Site, Hayeswater Road, Davyhulme,
Manchester M41 7BL
☎0161 912 2882
Fax 0161 912 2895
▶ Sale Library, Sale Waterside, Sale, Cheshire M33 7ZF
☎0161 912 3008
Fax 0161 912 3019
▶ Stretford Library, Kingsway, Stretford, Manchester M32 8AP

☎0161 912 5150
Fax 0161 865 3835
▶ Urmston Library, Crofts Bank Road, Urmston, Manchester M41 0TZ
☎0161 912 2727
Fax 0161 912 2947

UPPER NORWOOD JOINT LIBRARY

Authority: Upper Norwood Joint Library
HQ Upper Norwood Joint Library, Westow Hill, Upper Norwood, London SE19 1TJ
☎020 8670 2551
Fax 020 8670 5468
e-mail: unjl@unisonfree.net
Chief Librarian Bradley Millington MCLIP

WAKEFIELD

Authority: Wakefield Metropolitan District Council
HQ Library Headquarters, Balne Lane, Wakefield, Yorkshire WF2 0DQ
☎(01924) 302210 (enquiries and administration)
Fax (01924) 302245
e-mail: lib.admin@wakefield.gov.uk
url: www.wakefield.gov.uk/libraries
Head of Cultural Services Colin J MacDonald BA MBA DipLib MCLIP
Principal Librarian (Community Services) Ms Catherine Threapleton MCLIP DMS
Principal Librarian (Information Services) Ms Anne Farrington BA(Hons) MCLIP
Principal Librarian (Resource Services) Neil Scarlett DMA

Major libraries

▶ Balne Lane Reference and Information Library, Balne Lane, Wakefield, Yorkshire WF2 0DQ
☎(01924) 302230
Senior Librarian Ms Kathryn Harrison BA(Hons) DipLib MCLIP
▶ Castleford Library, Carlton Street, Castleford, West Yorks WF10 1BB
☎(01977) 722085
Senior Librarian Mrs Judith Walker
▶ Drury Lane Library, Drury Lane, Wakefield, Yorkshire WF1 2TD
☎(01924) 305376
Senior Librarian Ms Kathryn Harrison BA(Hons) DipLib MCLIP
▶ Featherstone Library and Community Centre, Station Lane, Featherstone, West Yorks WF7 5BB
☎(01977) 722745
Senior Librarian Andrew Wright BMus(Hons) DipLib
▶ Normanton Library and Community Centre, Market Street, Normanton, West Yorks WF6 2AR
☎(01924) 302525
Senior Librarian Mrs Jayne Britton BA(Hons) DipLib MCLIP
▶ Ossett Library, Station Road, Ossett, West Yorks WF5 8AB

☎(01924) 303040
Senior Librarian Ms Christine Wadsworth MCLIP
▶ Pontefract Library, Shoemarket, Pontefract, West Yorks WF8 1BD
☎(01977) 727692
Senior Librarian Mrs Judith Walker

WALSALL

Authority: Walsall Metropolitan Borough Council
HQ Lifelong Learning and Community Division, Tameway Tower, 12 Floor, 48 Bridge Street, Walsall, West Midlands WS1 1JZ
☎(01922) 653130
Fax (01922) 721682
e-mail: thelibrarian@walsall.gov.uk
url: www.walsall.gov.uk/libraries
Head of Libraries and Heritage Mrs Sue Grainger MCLIP (e-mail: graingers@walsall.gov.uk)

Central/largest library

Central Library, Lichfield Street, Walsall, West Midlands WS1 1TR
☎(01922) 653121 (lending), (01922) 653110 (reference); (01922) 653109 (computer booking)
Fax (01922) 722687 (lending), (01922) 654013 (reference)
e-mail: reference@walsall.gov.uk
Central Library Manager Ms Barbara Wallace
Information Services Manager Ms Rita Kennedy

Area libraries

▶ Aldridge Library, Rookery Lane, Aldridge, Walsall, West Midlands WS9 8NN
☎(01922) 743601
e-mail: aldridgelibrary@walsall.gov.uk
▶ Beechdale Library, Beechdale Centre, Stephenson Square, Walsall, West Midlands WS2 7DX
☎(01922) 721431
e-mail: beechdalelibrary@walsall.gov.uk
▶ Bentley Library, Queen Elizabeth Avenue, Bentley, Walsall, West Midlands WS2 0HP
☎(01922) 721392
e-mail: bentleylibrary@walsall.gov.uk
▶ Bloxwich Library, Elmore Row, Bloxwich, Walsall, West Midlands WS3 2HR
☎(01922) 710059
e-mail: bloxwichlibrary@walsall.gov.uk
▶ Brownhills Library, Brickiln Street, Brownhills, Walsall, West Midlands WS8 6AU
☎(01543) 452017
Fax (01543) 371832
e-mail: brownhillslibrary@walsall.gov.uk
▶ Coalpool Library, Coalpool Lane, Walsall, West Midlands WS3 1RF
☎(01922) 721325
e-mail: coalpoollibrary@walsall.gov.uk

▶ Darlaston Library, 1 King Street, Darlaston, Walsall, West Midlands WS10 8DD
☎0121 526 4530
Fax 0121 526 2298
e-mail: darlastonlibrary@walsall.gov.uk

▶ Forest Gate Library, New Invention, Willenhall, Walsall, West Midlands WV12 5LF
☎(01922) 710208
e-mail: forestgatelibrary@walsall.gov.uk

▶ Furzebank Library, Willenhall Comprehensive School, Furzebank Way, Willenhall,
Walsall, West Midlands WV12 4BD
☎(01902) 630530
e-mail: furzebanklibrary@walsall.gov.uk

▶ Home Library Service and Public Mobile Library, Mobile Library Depot, Willenhall Lane,
Bloxwich, Walsall, West Midlands WS3 2XN
☎(01922) 710625
e-mail: mobilelibrary@walsall.gov.uk

▶ Local History Centre, Essex Street, Walsall, West Midlands WS2 7AS
☎(01922) 721305
Fax (01922) 634954
e-mail: localhistorycentre@walsall.gov.uk

▶ Pelsall Library, High Street, Pelsall, Walsall, West Midlands WS3 4LX
☎(01922) 682212
e-mail: pelsalllibrary@walsall.gov.uk

▶ Pheasey Library, Collingwood Centre, Collingwood Drive, Pheasey, Birmingham
B43 7NE
☎(01922) 654865
e-mail: pheaseylibrary@walsall.gov.uk

▶ Pleck Library, Darlaston Road, Pleck, Walsall, West Midlands WS2 9RE
☎(01922) 721307
e-mail: plecklibrary@walsall.gov.uk

▶ Rushall Library, Pelsall Lane, Walsall, West Midlands WS4 1NL
☎(01922) 721310
e-mail: rushalllibrary@walsall.gov.uk

▶ Shelfield Library, Birch Lane, Shelfield, Walsall, West Midlands WS4 1AS
☎(01922) 682760
e-mail: shelfieldlibrary@walsall.gov.uk

▶ Sneyd Community Library, Sneyd School, Sneyd Lane, Bloxwich, Walsall, West Midlands
WS3 2PA
☎(01922) 710728
e-mail: sneydlibrary@walsall.gov.uk

▶ South Walsall Library, West Bromwich Road, Walsall, West Midlands WS5 4NW
☎(01922) 721347
e-mail: southwalsalllibrary@walsall.gov.uk

▶ Streetly Library, Blackwood Road, Streetly, Birmingham B74 3PL
☎0121 353 4230
e-mail: streetlylibrary@walsall.gov.uk

▶ Walsall Wood Library, Lichfield Road, Walsall Wood, Walsall, West Midlands WS9 9NT
☎(01543) 452517 (tel/fax)
e-mail: walsallwoodlibrary@walsall.gov.uk

▶ Willenhall Library, Walsall Street, Willenhall, Walsall, West Midlands WV13 2EX
☎(01902) 366513
e-mail: willenhalllibrary@walsall.gov.uk

WALTHAM FOREST

Authority: London Borough of Waltham Forest
HQ Administrative Office, Walthamstow Library, High Street, London E17 7JN
☎020 8496 1100/1101 (enquiries and administration)
Fax 020 8509 9539
e-mail: central.lib@al.lbwf.gov.uk
url: www.lbwf.gov.uk
Head of Libraries and Cultural Services Ms Katherine Pedley
Information Services Manager David Watkins

Central Information Services, 6 Central Parade, Hoe Street, London E17 4RT
☎020 8496 1150
Fax 020 8509 9654
Information Services Manager David Watkins

WANDSWORTH

Authority: London Borough of Wandsworth
HQ Leisure and Amenity Services Department, Wandsworth High Street, London SW18 2PU
☎020 8871 6369 (enquiries and administration)
Fax 020 8871 7630
e-mail: libraries@wandsworth.gov.uk
url: www.wandsworth.gov.uk/libraries
Head of Libraries, Museum and Arts Ms Jane Allen BA(Hons) DMS DipLib MCLIP
Assistant Head of Libraries Ms Meryl Jones MCLIP

Largest libraries
▶ Balham Library, Ramsden Road, London SW12 8QY
☎020 8871 7195
Fax 020 8675 4015
▶ Battersea Library, Lavender Hill, London SW11 1JB
☎020 8871 7466
Fax 020 7978 4376
▶ Putney Library, Disraeli Road, London SW15 2DR
☎020 8871 7090
Fax 020 8789 6175
▶ Tooting Library, Mitcham Road, London SW17 9PD
☎020 8871 7175
Fax 020 8672 3099

WARRINGTON

Authority: Warrington Borough Council
HQ Central Library, Museum and Art Gallery, Museum Street, Cultural Quarter, Warrington, Cheshire WA1 1JB
☎(01925) 442889 (enquiries), (01925) 442733 (administration)
Fax (01925) 411395
e-mail: library@warrington.gov.uk
url: www.warrington.gov.uk
Head of Library, Museum and Archives Service Martin Gaw BA DipLib MCLIP (01925 442733)
Principal Libraries Manager Ms Fiona Barry BA MCLIP (01925 442892)

Branch libraries

▶ Birchwood Library, Brock Road, Warrington, Cheshire WA3 7PT
  ☎(01925) 827491 (tel/fax)
▶ Burtonwood Library, Chapel Lane, Burtonwood, Warrington, Cheshire WA5 4PS
  ☎(01925) 226563 (tel/fax)
▶ Culcheth Library, Warrington Road, Culcheth, Warrington, Cheshire WA3 5SL
  ☎(01925) 763293 (tel/fax)
▶ Grappenhall Library, Victoria Avenue, Grappenhall, Warrington, Cheshire WA4 2PE
  ☎(01925) 262861 (tel/fax)
▶ Great Sankey Library, Marina Avenue, Great Sankey, Warrington, Cheshire WA5 1JH
  ☎(01925) 231451 (tel/fax)
▶ Lymm Library, Davies Way, Off Brookfield Road, Lymm, Warrington, Cheshire WA13 0QW
  ☎(01925) 754367 (tel/fax)
▶ Orford Library, Poplars Avenue, Orford, Warrington, Cheshire WA2 9LW
  ☎(01925) 812821 (tel/fax)
▶ Padgate Library, Insall Road, Padgate, Warrington, Cheshire WA2 0HD
  ☎(01925) 818096 (tel/fax)
▶ Penketh Library, Honiton Way, Penketh, Warrington, Cheshire WA5 2EY
  ☎(01925) 723730
  Fax (01925) 791264
▶ Stockton Heath Library, Alexandra Park, Stockton Heath, Warrington, Cheshire WA4 2AN
  ☎(01925) 261148
  Fax (01925) 267787
▶ Westbrook Library, Westbrook Centre, Westbrook Crescent, Warrington, Cheshire WA5 5UG
  ☎(01925) 416561
  Fax (01925) 230462
▶ Woolston Library, Holes Lane, Woolston, Warrington, Cheshire WA1 3UJ
  ☎(01925) 816146 (tel/fax)

WARWICKSHIRE

Authority: Warwickshire County Council
HQ Department of Libraries, Heritage and Trading Standards, Barrack Street, Warwick
CV34 4TH
☎(01926) 418154 (enquiries and administration)
Fax (01926) 412471/412165
e-mail: librariesandheritage@warwickshire.gov.uk
url: www.warwickshire.gov.uk
Director Noel C Hunter OBE FITSA FRSA (01926 412166; e-mail:
noelhunter@warwickshire.gov.uk)
Head of Library and Information Service Ms Kushal Birla BA(Hons) Business Law DTS
MBA (01926 412862; e-mail: kushalbirla@warwickshire.gov.uk)
Core Services, Quality and Operations Manager Ayub Khan BA(Hons) FCLIP (01926
412657; e-mail: ayubkhan@warwickshire.gov.uk)

Divisional libraries

▶ Central Warwickshire Division. Leamington Library (Central Divisional Library), Royal
Pump Rooms, The Parade, Leamington Spa, Warwicks CV32 4AA
☎(01926) 742721/742722
Fax (01926) 742749
e-mail: leamingtonlibrary@warwickshire.gov.uk
Divisional Librarian Paul MacDermott BA DipLib MCLIP (e-mail:
paulmacdermott@warwickshire.gov.uk)
Area Manager, Central Warwickshire John Crossling BSc AMA (e-mail:
johncrossling@warwickshire.gov.uk)
▶ North Warwickshire Division. Atherstone Library (North Divisional Library), Long
Street, Atherstone, Warwicks CV9 1AX
☎(01827) 712395/712034
Fax (01827) 720285
e-mail: atherstonelibrary@warwickshire.gov.uk
Divisional Librarian Andrew Button BA MCLIP (e-mail:
andrewbutton@warwickshire.gov.uk)
▶ Nuneaton and Bedworth Division. Nuneaton Library, Church Street, Nuneaton,
Warwicks CV11 4DR
☎024 7638 4027/024 7634 7006
Fax 024 7635 0125
e-mail: nuneatonlibrary@warwickshire.gov.uk
Divisional Librarian David Reed BA(Hons) MCLIP (e-mail:
davidreed@warwickshire.gov.uk)
Area Manager, North Warwickshire and Nuneaton & Bedworth Adrian Litvinoff
MA FRSA (e-mail: adrianlitvinoff@warwickshire.gov.uk)
▶ South/East Division. Rugby Library (South Divisional Library), Little Elborow Street,
Rugby, Warwicks CV21 3BZ
☎(01788) 533250
Fax (01788) 533252
e-mail: rugbylibrary@warwickshire.gov.uk

Divisional Librarian Ms Sandra Barnsley MCLIP (01788 533270; e-mail: sandrabarnsley@warwickshire.gov.uk)
Area Manager, South and East Warwickshire Mrs Linda Kay BA MCLIP DMS (e-mail: lindakay@warwickshire.gov.uk)
▶ Stratford Library, Henley Street, Stratford-upon-Avon, Warwicks CV37 6PZ
☎(01789) 292209/296904
Fax (01789) 268554
e-mail: stratfordlibrary@warwickshire.gov.uk
Divisional Librarian Vacant

WEST BERKSHIRE

Authority: West Berkshire District Council
HQ Library, Information and Communication Service, Council Offices, Market Street, Newbury, Berks RG14 5LD
☎(01635) 519904
Fax (01635) 519392
e-mail: library@westberks.gov.uk
url: www.westberks.gov.uk
Strategic Development Manager Mrs Christine Owen BA(Hons) MCLIP (01635 519904; e-mail: cowen@westberks.gov.uk)
Libraries Operations Manager Ken Richardson BA(Hons) DipLib MCLIP (01635 519813; e-mail: krichardson@westberks.gov.uk)

Central/largest library
Newbury Central Library, The Wharf, Newbury, Berks RG14 5AU
☎(01635) 519900

WEST SUSSEX

Authority: West Sussex County Council
HQ Library Service Administration Centre, Tower Street, Chichester, West Sussex PO19 1QJ
☎(01243) 382540
Fax (01243) 382554
url: www.westsussex.gov.uk
BT Gold 74: SKK125
County Librarian Mrs Susan Hawker BA(Hons) MCLIP (e-mail: susan.hawker@westsussex.gov.uk)
(For management enquiries contact headquarters; for services contact one of the principal libraries)

Principal libraries
▶ Crawley Library, Northgate Avenue, Crawley, West Sussex RH10 1XG
☎(01293) 895130
Fax (01293) 895141
Group Librarian: Crawley Mrs Rita Lucas MCLIP (e-mail: rlucas@westsussex.gov.uk)
▶ Worthing Library, Richmond Road, Worthing, West Sussex BN11 1HD

☎(01903) 704824
Fax (01903) 821902
Group Librarian: Worthing Miss Robina Edser BA MCLIP (e-mail:
robina.edser@westsussex.gov.uk)

WESTMINSTER

Authority: Westminster City Council
HQ Customer Services Department, 4th Floor, Westminster City Hall, 64 Victoria Street,
London SW1E 6QP
☎020 7641 2496 (administration); 020 7641 1300 (library enquiries), 020 7641 1400
(renewals)
Fax 020 7641 2764
url: www.westminster.gov.uk/libraries/gateway
Minicom: 020 7641 4879
Director of Library Services David Ruse MCLIP MILAM (020 7641 5160; e-mail:
druse@westminster.gov.uk)
Head of Library Operations Ms Iona Cairns MCLIP (020 7641 8969; e-mail:
icairns@westminster.gov.uk)
Development Manager ICT/Staff Chris Lally (020 7641 8968/1176; e-mail:
clally@westminster.gov.uk)
Group Manager – Performance Tony Rice (020 7641 8970; e-mail:
trice@westminster.gov.uk)
Group Manager – Learning John Hughes (020 7641 1782; e-mail:
jhughes@westminster.gov.uk)

Largest libraries

▶ Charing Cross Library, 6 Charing Cross Road, London WC2H 0HF
☎020 7641 4628 (enquiries), 020 7641 4676 (renewals), 020 7641 4623 (Chinese
Community Librarian)
Fax 020 7641 4629
e-mail: charingcrosslibrary@westminster.gov.uk
Minicom: 020 7641 4879
Site Manager Miss Elizabeth Williams BA MCLIP (020 7641 6591; e-mail:
elizabeth.phmslib@cms-uk.org)
Duty Supervisor Ms Rebecca Tibbles (020 7641 6591; e-mail:
rtibbles@westminster.gov.uk)
▶ Church Street Library, Church Street, London NW8 8EU
☎020 7641 5479 (enquiries), 020 7641 5480 (renewals)
Fax 020 7641 5482
e-mail: churchstreetlibrary@westminster.gov.uk
Minicom: 020 7641 4879
Libraries Manager Daniel Waller (020 7641 5483; e-mail:
dwaller@westminster.gov.uk)
Duty Supervisor Ms Michaela Hope (020 7641 5483; e-mail:
mhope@westminster.gov.uk)
▶ Maida Vale Library, Sutherland Avenue, London W9 2QT
☎020 7641 3659 (enquiries), 020 7641 3666 (renewals)

Fax 020 7641 3660

e-mail: maidavalelibrary@westminster.gov.uk

Minicom: 020 7641 4879

Site Manager Vic Stewart (020 7641 4311; e-mail: vstewart@westminster.gov.uk)

Duty Supervisor Ms Andrea O'Connor (020 7641 3663; e-mail: aoconnor@westminster.gov.uk)

▶ Mayfair Library, 25 South Audley Street, London W1K 2PB

☎020 7641 4903 (enquiries/renewals)

Fax 020 7641 4901

e-mail: mayfairlibrary@westminster.gov.uk

Minicom: 020 7641 4879

Site Manager Hugh Thomas (020 7641 4095; e-mail: hthomas2@westminster.gov.uk)

Duty Supervisor Ms Margaret Chown (020 7641 4905; e-mail: mchown@westminster.gov.uk)

▶ Paddington Library, Porchester Road, London W2 5DU

☎020 7641 4475 (enquiries), 020 7641 4480 (renewals)

Fax 020 7641 4471

e-mail: paddingtonlibrary@westminster.gov.uk

Minicom: 020 7641 4879

Site Manager Ms Susanna Barnes (020 7641 4400; e-mail: sbarnes2@westminster.gov.uk)

Duty Supervisor Ms Vicky Hallam (020 7641 4490; e-mail: vhallam@westminster.gov.uk), Ms Jane Wood (e-mail: jwood@westminster.gov.uk)

▶ Pimlico Library, Rampayne Street, London SW1V 2PU

☎020 7641 2983 (enquiries/renewals)

Fax 020 7641 2980

e-mail: pimlicolibrary@westminster.gov.uk

Minicom: 020 7641 4879

Site Manager Ms Francesca Corragio (e-mail: fcorragio@westminster.gov.uk)

Duty Supervisor Ms Paula Campbell (020 7641 2984; e-mail: pcampbell@westminster.gov.uk)

▶ Queen's Park Library, 666 Harrow Road, London W10 4NE

☎020 7641 4575 (enquiries/renewals)

Fax 020 7641 4576

e-mail: queensparklibrary@westminster.gov.uk

Minicom: 020 7641 4879

Site Manager Mark Tiller (020 7641 4577; e-mail: mtiller@westminster.gov.uk)

Duty Supervisor Ms Carole McCabe (020 7614 4577; e-mail: cmccabe@westminster.gov.uk)

▶ St James' Library, 62 Victoria Street, London SW1E 6QP

☎020 7641 2989 (enquiries), 020 7641 2987 (renewals)

Fax 020 7641 2986

e-mail: stjameslibrary@westminster.gov.uk

Minicom: 020 7641 4879

Site Manager Ms Sarah Goward-Jones (020 7641 2988; e-mail: sgoward-jones@westminster.gov.uk)

Duty Supervisor Ron Laing (020 7641 2988; e-mail: rlaing@westminster.gov.uk)

▶ St John's Wood Library, 20 Circus Road, London NW8 6PD
☎020 7641 5087 (enquiries), 020 7641 5098 (renewals)
Fax 020 7641 5089
e-mail: stjohnswoodlibrary@westminster.gov.uk
Minicom: 020 7641 4879
Site Manager Ms Anabel Lopez (020 7641 5090; e-mail: alopez@westminster.gov.uk)
Duty Supervisor Ms Rachel Gibson (020 7641 5012; e-mail: rgibson@westminster.gov.uk)

▶ Victoria Library, 160 Buckingham Palace Road, London SW1W 9UD
☎020 7641 4287 (enquiries), 020 7641 4295 (renewals), 020 7641 4292 (Westminster Music Library)
Fax 020 7641 4281
e-mail: victorialibrary@westminster.gov.uk
Minicom: 020 7641 4879
Site Manager Ms Helen Rogers (020 7641 4290; e-mail: hrogers@westminster.gov.uk)
Library Manager Fred Jardin (020 7641 4290; e-mail: fjardin@westminster.gov.uk)

Other services

▶ City of Westminster Archives Centre, 10 St Ann's Street, London SW1P 2DE
☎020 7641 5180
Fax 020 7641 5179
e-mail: archives@westminster.gov.uk
Minicom: 020 7641 4879
Archives and Local Studies Manager John Sargent (020 7641 5160; e-mail: jsargent@westminster.gov.uk)

▶ Marylebone Library, 109-117 Marylebone Road, London NW1 5PS
☎020 7641 1037 (enquiries), 020 7641 6111 (renewals)
Fax 020 7641 1044
e-mail: marylebonelibrary@westminster.gov.uk
Minicom: 020 7641 4879
Site Manager Ms Ann Farrell (020 7641 1033; e-mail: afarrell@westminster.gov.uk)
Duty Supervisor Ms Helen Nottage (020 7641 1034; e-mail: hnottage@westminster.gov.uk)
Marylebone Information Service Manager Michael Lightowlers (e-mail: mlightowlers@westminster.gov.uk)
☎020 7641 1031

▶ Westminster Reference Library, 35 St Martin's Street, London WC2H 7HP
☎020 7641 4636
Fax 020 7641 4606
e-mail: referencelibrarywc2@westminster.gov.uk
Minicom: 020 7641 4879
Development Manager – Information Ms Susanna Barnes (020 7641 5252; e-mail: sbarnes2@westminster.gov.uk)
Admin Officer Ms Val Wethey (020 7641 5235; e-mail: vwethey@westminster.gov.uk)

WIGAN

Authority: Wigan Council
HQ Wigan Leisure and Culture Trust, Robin Park Headquarters, The Indoor Sports
Complex, Loire Drive, Robin Park, Wigan WN5 0UL
☎(01942) 828508
Fax (01942) 828542
e-mail: infounit@wlct.org.uk
url: www.wlct.gov.uk
Libraries Management Team:
Operational Services Manager Ms Rosanne Patterson MCLIP
Service Development Manager Stephen Ruffley BA(Hons) MCLIP DMS

Central/largest libraries
Leigh Library, Turnpike Centre, Civic Square, Leigh, Lancs WN7 1EB
☎(01942) 404556 (lending), (01942) 404557 (information)
Fax (01942) 404567

Wigan Library, College Avenue, Wigan WN1 1NN
☎(01942) 827621 (lending), (01942) 827619 (information)
Fax (01942) 827640

WILTSHIRE

Authority: Wiltshire County Council
HQ Libraries and Heritage, Bythesea Road, Trowbridge, Wilts BA14 8BS
☎(01225) 713700 (enquiries), (01225) 713727 (information)
Fax (01225) 713993
e-mail: libraryenquiries@wiltshire.gov.uk
url: www.wiltshire.gov.uk/libraries/
Assistant Director, Libraries and Heritage Mrs Pauline Palmer MSc MCLIP DMS
MIMgt (e-mail: paulinepalmer@wiltshire.gov.uk)
Head of Policy and Support Mrs Mary Liddle BA MCLIP (e-mail:
maryliddle@wiltshire.gov.uk)
Head of Customer Services Ms Joan Davis BALib MCLIP (e-mail:
joandavis@wiltshire.gov.uk)
Head of Learning Services Chris Moore BA(Hons) MSc MCLIP (e-mail:
chrismoore@wiltshire.gov.uk)
Heritage Manager Tom Craig MA BA (e-mail: tomcraig@wiltshire.gov.uk)
Stock Manager David Green BA MCLIP (e-mail: davidgreen@wiltshire.gov.uk)

District libraries
▶ Kennet District: Devizes Library, Sheep Street, Devizes, Wilts SN10 1DL
  ☎(01380 726878/9
  Fax (01380) 722161
  District Manager Maurice Chandler MCLIP (01380 724099; e-mail:
  mauricechandler@wiltshire.gov.uk)
▶ North Wilts District: Chippenham Library, Timber Street, Chippenham, Wilts SN15 3EJ

☎(01249) 650536
Fax (01249) 443793
District Manager Mrs Gail Spence BA(Hons) MCLIP (01249 445005; e-mail:
gailspence@wiltshire.gov.uk)
▶ South and West Area. Salisbury Library, Market Place, Salisbury, Wiltshire SP1 1BL
☎(01722) 324145
Fax (01722) 413214
Area Manager C S Harling BA(Hons) MCLIP (01722 330606; e-mail:
chrisharling@wiltshire.gov.uk)

WINDSOR AND MAIDENHEAD

Authority: Royal Borough of Windsor and Maidenhead
HQ Library and Information Services, Maidenhead Library, St Ives Road, Maidenhead, Berks
SL6 1QU
☎(01628) 796969
Fax (01628) 796971
e-mail: maidenhead.library@rbwm.gov.uk
url: www.rbwm.gov.uk/libraries
Library and Information Services Manager Mark Taylor BA MCLIP (01628 796989;
fax: 01628 796986; e-mail: mark.taylor@rbwm.gov.uk)
Service Development Manager Ms Sara Hudson BA DipLib MCLIP (01628 796742)

Central/largest library

Maidenhead Library, St Ives Road, Maidenhead, Berks SL6 1QU
☎(01628) 796968 (reference), 796969 (issue desk), 796985 (administration)
Fax (01628) 796971
e-mail: maidenhead.library@rbwm.gov.uk
Operations Manager Brian Marpole MCLIP (01628 796976; e-mail:
brian.marpole@rbwm.gov.uk)
Senior Librarian: Local Information and Studies (01628 796979) Vacant
Senior Librarian: Adult Mrs Victoria Law BA (01628 796999)
Senior Librarian: Young People Mrs Angela Gallacher BA (01628 796999; e-mail:
angela.gallacher@rbwm.gov.uk)
Stock Services Officer, Stock Services Section (01628 796987) Vacant
Supervisor: Community Libraries Mrs Margaret Simpson (07747 757919)
Administration Officer Mrs Deepali Soni (01628 796985)

Other libraries

▶ Ascot Library, Winkfield Road, Ascot, Berks SL5 7EX
☎(01344) 620653
▶ Cookham Library, High Road, Cookham Rise, Maidenhead, Berks SL6 9JF
☎(01626) 526147
▶ Datchet Library, Village Hall, Horton Road, Datchet, Berks SL3 9HR
☎(01753) 545310
▶ Dedworth Library, Dedworth County School, Smith's Lane, Windsor, Berks SL4 5PE
☎(01753) 868733
▶ Eton Library, 136 High Street, Eton, Berks SL4 6LT

☎(01753) 860506
▶ Eton Wick Library, Village Hall, Eton Wick, Berks SL4 6LT
☎(01753) 857933
▶ Old Windsor Library, Memorial Hall, Straight Road, Windsor, Berks SL4 2JL
☎(01753) 852098
▶ Sunninghill Library, Reading Room, School Road, Sunninghill, Berks SL5 7AD
☎(01344) 621493
▶ Windsor Library, Bachelors Acre, Windsor, Berks SL4 1ER
☎(01753) 743940

Container Library operating at four sites:
Cox Green (01628 673942)
Holyport (01628 673931)
Sunningdale (01344 626720)
Wraysbury (01784 482431)

Mobile and Home Library Service operating through two vehicles (01628 796314)

WIRRAL

Authority: Metropolitan Borough of Wirral
HQ Education and Cultural Services Department, Hamilton Building, Conway Street,
Birkenhead, Wirral, Cheshire CH41 4FD
☎0151 666 5575
Fax 0151 666 4207
url: www.wirral-libraries.net
Head of Libraries and Halls Ms Sue Powell BA MCLIP (e-mail:
suepowell@wirral.gov.uk)

Central/largest library

Birkenhead Central Library, Borough Road, Birkenhead, Wirral, Cheshire CH41 2XB
☎0151 652 6106 (enquiries), 0151 653 4700 (administration)
Fax 0151 653 7320
e-mail: co-ord@wirral.libraries.net
Principal Librarian, Operational Services John Baxter BA DipLib MCLIP (e-mail:
johnbaxter@wirral.gov.uk)

Regional/district libraries

▶ Bebington Central Library, Civic Way, Bebington, Wirral, Cheshire CH63 7PN
☎0151 643 7219
Fax 0151 643 7231
e-mail: bebington@wirral-library.net
Deputy Area Librarian Ms Clare Oxley (e-mail: clareoxley@wirral-libraries.net)
▶ Wallasey Central Library, Earlston Road, Wallasey, Wirral, Cheshire CH45 5DY
☎0151 639 2334
Fax 0151 691 2040
e-mail: wallasey@wirral-library.net

Principal Librarian, Community Services Paul Irons BA MCLIP (e-mail: paulirons@wirral-libraries.net)
▶ West Kirby Library, The Concourse, West Kirby, Wirral, Cheshire CH48 4HX
☎0151 929 7808
Fax 0151 625 2558
e-mail: west.kirby@wirral-library.net
Team Librarians Mrs Julie Mann BA MCLIP, Mrs Julie Barkway BA DipLib MCLIP

WOKINGHAM

Authority: Wokingham District Council
HQ Libraries and Information Service, Cultural Services and Development, Shute End, Wokingham, Berks RG40 1WN
☎0118 974 6261
e-mail: libraries@wokingham.gov.uk
url: www.wokingham.gov.uk/libraries
Corporate Head of Cultural Services and Development Chris Hamilton MCLIP (0118 974 6261; e-mail: chris.hamilton@wokingham.gov.uk)

Central/largest library

Wokingham Library, Denmark Street, Wokingham, Berks RG40 2BB
☎0118 978 1368
Fax 0118 989 1214

WOLVERHAMPTON

Authority: Wolverhampton City Council
HQ Lifelong Learning – Leisure Services Department, Cultural Services Division, Libraries and Information Services, Central Library, Snow Hill, Wolverhampton WV1 3AX
☎(01902) 552025 (enquiries and administration)
Fax (01902) 552024
e-mail: wolverhampton.libraries@dial.pipex.com
url: www.wolverhampton.gov.uk
City Librarian Mrs Karen Lees BA MCLIP (01902 552010; e-mail: karen.lees@dial.pipex.com)
Assistant City Librarians Graeme Kent BA DipLib (01902 552011; e-mail: gkent@dial.pipex.com), Andrew Scragg MA LLB DipHE MCLIP (01902 552012; e-mail: ascragg@dial.pipex.com), Robert Johnson BA(Hons) (01902 552186; e-mail: robjohnson@dial.pipex.com)

Branch Libraries (Group One)

▶ Ashmore Park Library, Griffiths Drive, Wednesfield, Wolverhampton WV11 2JW
☎(01902) 556296
e-mail: ashmorepark.library@dial.pipex.com
Branch Group Librarian Mrs Kath Fletcher MCLIP (01902 556293)
▶ Collingwood Community Library, 24 The Broadway, Bushbury, Wolverhampton WV10 8EB
☎(01902) 556302

e-mail: collingwood.library@dial.pipex.com
▶ Low Hill Library, Showell Circus, Low Hill, Wolverhampton WV10 9JJ
☎(01902) 556293
e-mail: lowhill.library@dial.pipex.com
▶ Mary Pointon Community Library, Ettingshall Road, Wood Cross, Wolverhampton WV14 9UG
☎(01902) 556263
e-mail: marypointon.library@dial.pipex.com
▶ Pendeford Library, Whitburn Close, Pendeford, Wolverhampton WV9 5NJ
☎(01902) 556250
e-mail: pendeford.library@dial.pipex.com
▶ Penn Library, Coalway Avenue, Penn, Wolverhampton WV3 7LT
☎(01902) 556281
e-mail: penn.library@dial.pipex.com
▶ Whitmore Reans Library, Bargate Drive, Evans Street, Whitmore Reans, Wolverhampton WV4 4PT
☎(01902) 556269
e-mail: whitmorereans.library@dial.pipex.com

Branch Libraries (Group Two)

▶ Bilston Library, Mount Pleasant, Bilston, Wolverhampton WV14 7LU
☎(01902) 556253
e-mail: bilston.library@dial.pipex.com
Branch Group Librarian Kevin Hudson BA (01902 556257)
▶ Daisy Bank Community Library, Ash Street, Bradley, Bilston, Wolverhampton WV14 8UP
☎(01902) 556305
e-mail: daisybank.library@dial.pipex.com
▶ Eastfield Library, Hurstbourne Crescent, Eastfield, Wolverhampton WV1 2EE
☎(01902) 556257
e-mail: eastfield.library@dial.pipex.com
▶ Finchfield Library, White Oak Drive, Finchfield, Wolverhampton WV3 9AF
☎(01902) 556260
e-mail: finchfield.library@dial.pipex.com
▶ Heath Town Community Library, Tudor Road, Heath Town, Wolverhampton WV10 0LT
☎(01902) 556266
e-mail: heathtown.library@dial.pipex.com
▶ Oxley Library, Probert Road, Oxley, Wolverhampton WV10 6UF
☎(01902) 556287
e-mail: oxley.library@dial.pipex.com
▶ Tettenhall Library, Upper Street, Tettenhall, Wolverhampton WV6 8QF
☎(01902) 556308
e-mail: tettenhall.library@dial.pipex.com

Branch libraries (Group Three)

▶ Bradmore Community Library, Bantock House, Bradmore Road, Wolverhampton WV3 9BH
☎(01902) 556299
e-mail: bradmore.library@dial.pipex.com

Branch Group Librarian Mrs Denise Jones BA (01902 556284)

▶ Long Knowle Library, Wood End Road, Wednesfield, Wolverhampton WV11 1YG
☎(01902) 556290
e-mail: longknowle.library@dial.pipex.com

▶ Scotlands Community Library, Masefield Road, Wolverhampton WV10 8SA
☎(01902) 552199
e-mail: scotlands.library@dial.pipex.com

▶ Spring Vale Library, Bevan Avenue, Wolverhampton WV4 6SG
☎(01902) 556284
e-mail: springvale.library@dial.pipex.com

▶ Warstones Library, Pinfold Grove, Penn, Wolverhampton WV4 9PT
☎(01902) 556275
e-mail: warstones.library@dial.pipex.com

▶ Wednesfield Library, Church Street, Wednesfield, Wolverhampton WV11 1SR
☎(01902) 556278
e-mail: wednesfield.library@dial.pipex.com

WORCESTERSHIRE

Authority: Worcestershire County Council
HQ Libraries and Information Service, Cultural Services, County Hall, Spetchley Road, Worcester WR5 2NP
☎(01905) 766231
Fax (01905) 766244
e-mail: librarieshq@worcestershire.gov.uk
url: www.worcestershire.gov.uk/libraries
Library Services Manager Mrs Cathy Evans MCLIP FISCT (01905 766232; e-mail: cevans@worcestershire.gov.uk)
Strategic Library Manager (North + Young People, Lifelong Learning, Performance, Quality) Mrs Carmel Reed BA DMS MCLIP (01905 766233; e-mail: creed@worcestershire.gov.uk)
Strategic Library Manager (South + Stock, Social Inclusion, Special Services) Nigel Preedy BSc MCLIP (01905 766239; e-mail: npreedy@worcestershire.gov.uk)

Libraries Development Team, Libraries Service, Sherwood Lane, Lower Wick, Worcester WR2 4NU
☎(01905) 428945
Fax (01905) 748619
Area Co-ordinator: North Mrs Jane McCallum MCLIP (e-mail: jmccallum@worcestershire.gov.uk)
Area Co-ordinator: South Mrs Ruth Foster BA MCLIP MCMI (e-mail: refoster@worcestershire.gov.uk)
Service Development Manager: Stock, Social Inclusion, Special Services David Pearson BA MCLIP (e-mail: dpearson@worcestershire.gov.uk)
Service Development Manager: Young People, Lifelong Learning, Performance/Quality Vacant

Service Development Manager: Information, ICT, E-gov, Marketing, Training Mrs Carol Woolley BA MCLIP MCMI (e-mail: cwoolley@worcestershire.gov.uk), Dr Christine Tootill MCLIP MCMI (e-mail: ctootill@worcestershire.gov.uk)

Main libraries

▶ Bromsgrove Library, Stratford Road, Bromsgrove, Worcs B60 1AP
☎(01527) 575855 575856 (outside office hours)
Fax (01905) 575855
e-mail: bromsgrovelib@worcestershire.gov.uk
Bromsgrove Librarian Vacant

▶ Countywide Information Service (Intranet and Website), Information and Business Systems Division, County Hall, Spetchley Road, Worcester WR5 2NP
☎(01905) 766927
url: www.worcestershire.gov.uk
Web Manager Paul Taylor (e-mail: ptaylor@worcestershire.gov.uk)

▶ Droitwich Library, Victoria Square, Droitwich, Worcs WR9 8DQ
☎(01905) 773292
Fax (01905) 797401
e-mail: droitwichlib@worcestershire.gov.uk
Droitwich Librarian Miss Val Booler MCLIP

▶ Evesham Library, Oat Street, Evesham, Worcs WR11 4JP
☎(01386) 442291/41348
Fax (01386) 765855
e-mail: eveshamlib@worcestershire.gov.uk
Evesham Librarian Mrs Lynda Downes MCLIP

▶ Kidderminster Library, Market Street, Kidderminster, Worcs DY10 1PE
☎(01562) 824500
Fax (01562) 512907
e-mail: kidderminsterlib@worcestershire.gov.uk
Kidderminster Librarian Kurt Sidaway BA(Hons) MCLIP

▶ Malvern Library, Graham Road, Malvern, Worcs WR14 2HU
☎(01902) 552199
Fax (01684) 892999
e-mail: malvernlib@worcestershire.gov.uk
Malvern Librarian Keith Barber BA MCLIP

▶ Redditch Library, 15 Market Place, Redditch, Worcs B98 8AR
☎(01527) 63291
Fax (01527) 68571
e-mail: redditchlib@worcestershire.gov.uk
Redditch Librarian Mrs Elaine Cooper BA MCLIP

▶ Worcester Library, Foregate Street, Worcester WR1 1DT
☎(01905) 765314
Fax (01905) 726664
e-mail: worcesterlib@worcestershire.gov.uk
Worcester Librarian Ms Nicki Hitchcock BA DipILS MCLIP

YORK

Authority: City of York Council
HQ York Library, Museum Street, York YO1 7DS
☎ (01904) 655631
Fax (01904) 611025
e-mail: lending@york.gov.uk
url: www.york.gov.uk/libraries
Head of Libraries and Heritage Ms Fiona Williams BA(Hons) DipLib MCLIP

BELFAST EDUCATION AND LIBRARY BOARD

Authority: Belfast Education and Library Board
HQ Belfast Public Libraries, Central Library, Royal Avenue, Belfast BT1 1EA
☎028 9050 9150
Fax 028 9033 2819
e-mail: info.belfast@ni-libraries.net
url: www.belb.org.uk
Chief Librarian Ms Linda Houston BLS MCLIP MBA (e-mail: linda.houston@ni-libraries.net)

NORTH EASTERN EDUCATION AND LIBRARY BOARD

Authority: North Eastern Education and Library Board
HQ Area Library HQ, Demesne Avenue, Ballymena, Co Antrim BT43 7BG
☎028 2566 4100
Fax 028 2563 2038
e-mail: info.neelb@ni-libraries.net
url: www.ni-libraries.net
Director of Libraries and Corporate Services Mrs Anne Connolly BA(Hons) MA MBA
Assistant Chief Librarian (Development and Support) Mrs Mandy Bryson BA MCLIP (028 2566 4104)
Assistant Chief Librarian (Community and Learning) Michael McFaul MBA(Hons) DipM MCLIP (028 2566 4103)

Group libraries

▶ Antrim Group Library, 7 High Street, Antrim, Co Antrim BT41 4AX
  ☎028 9446 8125
  Group Librarian Ms Linda Clarke BSc MCLIP
▶ Ballymena Group Library, Central Library, 5 Pat's Brae, Ballymena, Co Antrim BT43 5AX
  ☎028 2563 3959
  Group Librarian Mrs Jennifer Stafford PGDipLib MCLIP MBA
▶ Carrickfergus Group Library, Joymount Court, Carrickfergus BT38 7DQ
  ☎028 9336 2261
  Group Librarian Mrs Jennifer Austin BA MCLIP
▶ Coleraine Group Library, County Hall, Castlerock Road, Coleraine BT1 3HP
  ☎028 7032 0201
  Group Librarian Ms Nicola McNee BA MCLIP
▶ Magherafelt Group Library, The Bridewell Centre, 6 Church Street, Magherafelt BT45 6AN
  ☎028 7963 4887
  Group Librarian Brian Porter BSc MCLIP

SOUTH EASTERN EDUCATION AND LIBRARY BOARD

Authority: South Eastern Education and Library Board
HQ Library Headquarters, Windmill Hill, Ballynahinch, Co Down BT24 8DH
☎028 9756 6400
Fax 028 9756 5072
e-mail: info.seelb@ni-libraries.net
url: www.seelb.org.uk; www.ni-libraries.net
Chief Librarian Mrs Beth Porter BA(Hons) DipLibStud MCLIP (028 9756 6402)
Assistant Chief Librarians Mrs Laura Plummer BA(Hons) DipLibStud MCLIP (028 9756 6406), Ms Adrienne Adair BA(Hons) MPhil DipLibStud MCLIP (028 9756 6408)
Front Line Services Manager Mrs Norma Millar BA(Hons) DipLibStud MCLIP (028 9042 5708)

Area libraries

▶ Colin Glen Library, Colin Centre, Unit 17, Stewartstown Road, Dunmurry, Belfast BT17 0AW
☎028 9043 1266
Fax 028 9043 1278
e-mail: colinglenlibrary@ni-libraries.net
Group Library Manager Mrs Margaret Bell BLS MCLIP
▶ Downpatrick Library, Market Street, Downpatrick, Co Down BT30 6LZ
☎028 4461 2895
Fax 028 4461 1444
e-mail: downpatricklibrary@ni-libraries.net
Group Library Manager Mrs Pamela Cooper BLS PGDipA&LS MCLIP
▶ Holywood Library, Sullivan Building, 86-88 High Street, Holywood, Co Down BT18 9AE
☎028 9042 4232
Fax 028 9042 4194
e-mail: holywoodlibrary@ni-libraries.net
Group Library Manager Mrs Sheila Scarlett DipLibStud MCLIP
▶ Tullycarnet Library, Kinross Avenue, Kings Road, Belfast BT5 7GF
☎028 9048 5079
Fax 028 9048 2342
e-mail: tullycarnetlibrary@ni-libraries.net
Group Library Manager Ms Rosemary Wright BLS MCLIP

SOUTHERN EDUCATION AND LIBRARY BOARD

Authority: Southern Education and Library Board
HQ Library Headquarters, 1 Markethill Road, Armagh, Co Armagh BT60 1NR
☎028 3752 5353
Fax 028 3752 6879
url: www.selb.org
Head of Libraries Mrs Kathleen Ryan BA MBA FCLIP
Assistant Chief Librarian Philip Reid MCLIP (028 3752 0707)

Principal Librarian Public Services Miss Janet Blair MCLIP (028 3752 0715)
Education Services Manager Gerry Burns BA (028 3752 0754)
Communities, Learning & Access Manager Ms Anne McCart BA MCLIP
(028 3752 0760)
Operations Manager Ms Christina Sloan MBE BA DipLib St MCLIP (028 3752 0740)

Group library headquarters

▶ Lurgan Group Library Headquarters, Carnegie Street, Lurgan, Co Armagh BT66 6AS
  ☎028 3834 2907
  Fax 028 3834 6116
  Group Librarian Brendan McGeown BA(Hons) MBA
▶ Newry Group Library Headquarters, 79 Hill Street, Newry, Co Down BT34 1DG
  ☎028 3026 1652
  Fax 028 3025 1739
  Group Librarian Micky Doran MSc MCLIP

Specialist Library

▶ Irish and Local Studies Service, 39c Abbey Street, Armagh, Co Armagh BT61 7EB
  ☎028 3752 7851
  Fax 028 3752 7127
  Irish and Local Studies Librarian Ms Mary McVeigh BA MSSc(Irish Studies) DipLib

WESTERN EDUCATION AND LIBRARY BOARD

Authority: Western Education and Library Board
HQ Library Headquarters, 1 Spillars Place, Omagh, Co Tyrone BT78 1HL
☎028 8224 4821
Fax 028 8224 6716
e-mail: info.welb@ni-libraries.net
url: www.welbni.org
Omagh District Librarian Mrs M Cummings MBE DLibStud
Assistant Chief Librarians Ms A Peoples BA MCLIP DMS, Ms T Ward BLS MCLIP MBA
Head of Libraries and Information Ms H Osborn MLib MCLIP

Central/largest library

Central Library, Foyle Street, Londonderry BT48 1AL
☎028 7127 2310
Fax 028 7126 9084
Librarian Mrs M Craig

District libraries

▶ Enniskillen Library, Halls Lane, Enniskillen, Co Fermanagh BT74 7DR
  ☎028 6632 2886
  Fax 028 6632 4685
  Librarian S Bleakley BA(Hons) DLS
▶ Limavady Library, 5 Connell Street, Limavady, Londonderry BT47 0EA
  ☎028 7776 2540
  Fax 028 7772 2006

Librarian Mrs L Brown BA MCLIP

▶ Omagh Library, 1 Spillars Place, Omagh, Co Tyrone BT78 1HL
☎028 8224 4821
Fax 028 8224 6772
Librarian Mrs M Cummings MBE DLibStud

▶ Strabane Library, 1 Railway Road, Strabane, Co Tyrone BT82 8AW
☎028 7138 3686
Fax 028 7138 2745
Librarian Mrs M Coyle

ABERDEEN

Authority: Aberdeen City Council
HQ Aberdeen City Library and Information Services, Central Library, Rosemount Viaduct, Aberdeen AB25 1GW
☎(01224) 652500 (enquiries and administration)
Fax (01224) 641985
e-mail: centlib@aberdeencity.gov.uk
url: www.aberdeencity.gov.uk
Service Manager, Library and Sports Facilities Neil M Bruce MA DipLib LLM FCLIP (01224 652536; e-mail: NeilBr@aberdeencity.gov.uk)
Public Services Librarian (Lending) John Grant BA MCLIP (01224 652549; e-mail: Jogrant@aberdeencity.gov.uk)
Public Services Librarian (Information) Ms Susan Bell BA MCLIP (01224 652552; e-mail: Sbell@aberdeencity.gov.uk)

ABERDEENSHIRE

Authority: Aberdeenshire Council
HQ Library and Information Service, Meldrum Meg Way, Oldmeldrum, Aberdeenshire AB51 0GN
☎(01651) 872707 (enquiries and administration)
Fax (01651) 872142
e-mail: alis@aberdeenshire.gov.uk
url: www.aberdeenshire.gov.uk/alis
Libraries and Heritage Manager Gerald Moore BA MCLIP (01651 871202; e-mail: gerald.moore@aberdeeenshire.gov.uk)
Media Resources Manager Vacant
Central Support Services Manager Mrs Anne A M Harrison MCLIP (01651 871210; fax: 01651 872142; e-mail: anne.harrison@aberdeenshire.gov.uk)
Client Services Librarians Mrs Helen W Dewar MA MCLIP (01358 729208; fax: 01358 722864; e-mail: helen.dewar@aberdeenshire.gov.uk), Rufus A de Silva BA MEd MBA MCLIP (01330 823784; fax: 01330 824516; e-mail: rufus.de.silva@aberdeenshire.gov.uk)

ANGUS

Authority: Angus Council
HQ Cultural Services Department, County Buildings, Market Street, Forfar, Angus DD8 3WF
☎(01307) 461460
Fax (01307) 462590
e-mail: cultural.services@angus.gov.uk
url: www.angus.gov.uk
Head of Cultural Services Norman K Atkinson DipEd AMA FMA

Libraries Manager John Doherty BSc MCLIP
Arts and Resources Manager Colin Dakers BA MCLIP

Central/largest library

Library Support Services, 50 West High Street, Forfar, Angus DD8 1BA
☎(01307) 466966
Fax (01307) 468451
e-mail: librarysupport.services@angus.gov.uk
Support Services Librarian Jim Fraser BA DipLib MCLIP

Area libraries

▶ Arbroath Library, Hill Terrace, Arbroath, Angus DD11 1AH
☎(01241) 872248
Fax (01241) 434396
e-mail: arbroath.library@angus.gov.uk
Librarian Ms Teresa A Roby BA MCLIP
▶ Brechin Library, 10 St Ninian's Square, Brechin, Angus DD9 7AA
☎(01356) 622687
Fax (01356) 624271
e-mail: brechin.library@angus.gov.uk
Librarian Gavin Hunter MA MCLIP
▶ Carnoustie Library, 21 High Street, Carnoustie, Angus DD7 6AN
☎(01241) 859620
e-mail: carnoustie.library@angus.gov.uk
Librarian Alasdair Sutherland BA MCLIP
▶ Forfar Library, 50-56 West High Street, Forfar, Angus DD8 1BA
☎(01307) 466071
Fax (01307) 468451
e-mail: forfar.library@angus.gov.uk
Librarian Ian K Neil MA MCLIP
▶ Kirriemuir Library, Town Hall, 28/30 Reform Street, Kirriemuir, Angus DD8 4BS
☎(01575) 572357
Librarian Ms Christine Sharp BA MCLIP
▶ Monifieth Library, High Street, Monifieth, Angus DD5 4AE
☎(01382) 533819
e-mail: monifieth.library@angus.gov.uk
Librarian Ms Hazel Cook BA MCLIP
▶ Montrose Library, 214 High Street, Montrose, Angus DD10 8PH
☎(01674) 673256
Fax (01674) 671810
e-mail: montrose.library@angus.gov.uk
Librarian Ms Victoria Fraser BA MCLIP

ARGYLL AND BUTE

Authority: Argyll and Bute Council
HQ Library and Information Service HQ, Highland Avenue, Sandbank, Dunoon, Argyll
PA23 8PB

☎(01369) 703214
Fax (01369) 705797
url: www.argyll-bute.gov.uk
Culture and Libraries Manager Andy I Ewan MCLIP (e-mail:
andy.ewan@argyll-bute.gov.uk)

Area libraries
▶ Campbeltown Library, Hall Street, Campbeltown, Argyll PA28 6BS
☎(01586) 552366 ext 2237
Fax (01586) 552938
Area Librarian Ms Sue Fortune MCLIP
▶ Dunoon Library, 248 Argyll Street, Dunoon, Argyll PA23 7LT
☎(01369) 703735 ext 7522
Fax (01369) 701323
Area Librarian Ms Pauline Flynn BA MCLIP
▶ Helensburgh Library, West King Street, Helensburgh, Dunbartonshire G84 8EB
☎(01436) 674626
Fax (01436) 679567
Area Librarian/IT Systems Development Manager Pat McCann BA MCLIP
▶ Oban Library, Corran Halls, Oban, Argyll PA34 5AB
☎(01631) 571444
Fax (01631) 571372
Area Librarian Kevin Baker BA DipLib MCLIP
▶ Rothesay Library, Moat Centre, Stuart Street, Rothesay, Bute PA20 0BX
☎(01700) 503266
Fax (01700) 500511
Branch Librarian Eddie Monaghan MCLIP

CLACKMANNANSHIRE

Authority: Clackmannanshire Council
HQ Clackmannanshire Libraries, Alloa Library, 26-28 Drysdale Street, Alloa,
Clackmannanshire FK10 1JL
☎(01259) 722262
Fax (01259) 219469
e-mail: libraries@clacks.gov.uk
url: www.clacksweb.org.uk/dyna/library
Team Leader, Community Library Service John A Blake BSc DipLib MCLIP DipEdTech
(ext 220)
Training and Stock Circulation Librarian Ms Helen Finlayson MA DipLib MCLIP
Information Librarian and Archivist Ian D Murray MA DipLib MCLIP DAA
Mobile Librarian Alex Pollock

Branches within community access points
▶ Alva Community Access Point, 153 West Stirling Street, Alva, Clackmannanshire
☎(01259) 760652
Fax (01259) 760354
Senior Community Access Officer Ms N Foster

▶ Clackmannan Community Access Point, Main Street, Clackmannan
☎(01259) 721579
Fax (01259) 212493
Senior Community Access Officer Ms J Laird

▶ Dollar Community Access Point, Dollar Civic Centre, Park Place, Dollar,
Clackmannanshire
☎(01259) 743253
Fax (01259) 743328
Senior Community Access Officer Mrs K Waddell

▶ Menstrie Community Access Point, The Dumyat Leisure Centre, Main Street East,
Menstrie, Clackmannanshire
☎(01259) 769439
Fax (01259) 762941
Senior Community Access Officer Mrs K Waddell

▶ Sauchie Community Access Point, 42-48 Main Street, Sauchie, Clackmannanshire
☎(01259) 721679
Fax (01259) 218750
Senior Community Access Officer Ms M Hunter

▶ Tillicoultry Branch Library, 99 High Street, Tillicoultry, Clackmannanshire
☎(01259) 751685 (tel/fax)
Branch Library Co-ordinator Ms L Paterson

▶ Tullibody Library, Leisure Centre, Abercromby Place, Tullibody, Clackmannanshire
☎(01259) 218725
Branch Library Co-ordinator Ms I Dykes

COMHAIRLE NAN EILEAN SIAR

Authority: Comhairle nan Eilean Siar
HQ Public Library, 19 Cromwell Street, Stornoway, Isle of Lewis, Hebrides HS1 2DA
☎(01851) 708631
Fax (01851) 708677
url: www.cne-siar.gov.uk
Chief Librarian R M Eaves BA DipEd MCLIP (e-mail: bobeaves@cne-siar.gov.uk)
Senior Librarian, Adult Services D J Fowler MCLIP (e-mail: dfowler@cne-siar.gov.uk)

Area libraries

▶ Community Library, Castlebay Community School, Castlebay, Isle of Barra, Hebrides
HS9 5XD
☎(01871) 810471
Fax (01871) 810650
e-mail: castlebaylibrary@eileanansiar.fnes.net
Senior Library Assistant Mrs L Mackinnon

▶ Community Library, Daliburgh School, Daliburgh, Isle of South Uist, Hebrides HS8 5SS
☎(01878) 700673
Library Assistant Mrs M Walker (e-mail: mwalker1c@eileanansiar.fnes.net)

▶ Community Library, Sgoil Lionacleit, Liniclate, Isle of Benbecula, Hebrides HS7 5PJ
☎(01870) 603532
Fax (01870) 602817

e-mail: lionacleitlibrary@eileanansiar.fnes.net

Community Librarian Mrs J F Bramwell BA DipLib MCLIP (e-mail: fbramwell1a@fnes.net)

▶ Community Library, Sgoil Shiaboist, Shawbost, Isle of Lewis, Hebrides HS2 9PQ
☎(01851) 710213
e-mail: shawlib@eileanansiar.fnes.net

Library Assistant Mrs C A Campbell

▶ Community Library, Sir E Scott School, Tarbert, Isle of Harris, Hebrides HS3 3BG
☎(01859) 502926

Library Assistant Mrs F Morrison MA (e-mail: fmmorrison1b@eileanansiar.fnes.net)

DUMFRIES AND GALLOWAY

Authority: Dumfries and Galloway Council
HQ Libraries, Information and Archives, Central Support Unit, Catherine Street, Dumfries DG1 1JB
☎(01387) 253820 (enquiries), 01387 252070 (administration)
Fax (01387) 260294
e-mail: libs&i@dumgal.gov.uk
url: www.dumgal.gov.uk
Operations Manager, Cultural Services A R Johnston BA MCLIP FSA(Scot)

District libraries

▶ Annan Library, Charles Street, Annan, Dumfries and Galloway DG12 5AG
☎(01461) 202809 (tel/fax)

▶ Archive Centre, 33 Burns Street, Dumfries DG1 2PS
☎(01387) 269254
Fax (01387) 264126

▶ Castle Douglas Library, Market Hill, King Street, Castle Douglas, Dumfries and Galloway DG7 1AE
☎(01556) 502643 (tel/fax)

▶ Dalbeattie Library, 23 High Street, Dalbeattie, Dumfries and Galloway DG5 4AD
☎(01556) 610898 (tel/fax)

▶ Dalry Library, Main Street, Dalry, Castle Douglas, Dumfries and Galloway DG7 3UP
☎(01644) 430234 (tel/fax)

▶ Eastriggs Library, Eastriggs Community School, Eastriggs, Annan, Dumfries and Galloway DG12 6PZ
☎(01461) 40844 (tel/fax)

▶ Ewart Library, Catherine Street, Dumfries DG1 1JB
☎(01387) 253820/252070/260000
Fax (01387) 260294

▶ Gatehouse Library, 63 High Street, Gatehouse of Fleet, Dumfries and Galloway DG7 2HS
☎(01557) 814646 (tel/fax)

▶ Georgetown Library, Gillbrae Road, Georgetown, Dumfries DG1 4EJ
☎(01387) 256059 (tel/fax)

▶ Gretna Library, The Richard Greenhow Centre, Central Avenue, Gretna, Dumfries and Galloway DG16 5AQ
☎(01461) 338000 (tel/fax)

▶ Kirkconnel Library, Greystone Avenue, Kelloholm, Dumfries and Galloway DG4 6RA
☎(01659) 67191 (tel/fax)

▶ Kirkcudbright Library, Sheriff Court House, High Street, Kirkcudbright, Dumfries and Galloway DG6 4JW
☎(01557) 331240 (tel/fax)

▶ Langholm Library, Charles Street, Old Langholm, Dumfries and Galloway DG13 0AA
☎(01387) 380040 (tel/fax)

▶ Lochmaben Library, Masonic Hall, High Street, Lochmaben, Lockerbie, Dumfries and Galloway DG11 1NQ
☎(01387) 811865 (tel/fax)

▶ Lochside Library, Lochside Road, Dumfries DG2 0LW
☎(01387) 268751 (tel/fax)

▶ Lochthorn Library, Lochthorn, Dumfries DG1 1UF
☎(01387) 265780
Fax (01387) 266424

▶ Lockerbie Library, 31–33 High Street, Lockerbie, Dumfries and Galloway DG11 2JL
☎(01576) 203380 (tel/fax)

▶ Moffat Library, Town Hall, High Street, Moffat, Dumfries and Galloway DG10 9HF
☎(01683) 220952 (tel/fax)

▶ Newton Stewart Library, Chuch Street, Newton Stewart, Dumfries and Galloway DG8 6ER
☎(01671) 403450 (tel/fax)

▶ Port William Library, Church Street, Port William, Newton Stewart, Dumfries and Galloway DG8 9QJ
☎(01988) 700406 (tel/fax)

▶ Sanquhar Library, 106 High Street, Sanquhar, Dumfries and Galloway DG4 6DZ
☎(01659) 50626 (tel/fax)

▶ Stranraer Library, North Strand Street, Stranraer, Dumfries and Galloway DG9 7LD
☎(01776) 707400/707440
Fax (01776) 703565

▶ Thornhill Library, Townhead Street, Thornhill, Dumfries and Galloway DG3 5NW
☎(01848) 330654 (tel/fax)

▶ Whithorn Library, St John's Street, Whithorn, Dumfries and Galloway DG8 8PF
☎(01988) 500406 (tel/fax)

▶ Wigtown Library, County Buildings, Wigtown, Dumfries and Galloway DG8 9JH
☎(01988) 403329 (tel/fax)

DUNDEE

Authority: Dundee City Council
HQ Communities Department Head Office, Central Library Level 3, The Wellgate, Dundee DD1 1DB
☎(01382) 307460
Fax (01382) 307487
url: www.dundeecity.gov.uk/communities
Head of Communities Department Stewart Murdoch MSc DPSE DipYCW (e-mail: stewart.murdoch@dundeecity.gov.uk)

Senior Manager Communities Mrs Moira Methven MCLIP (e-mail: moira.methven@dundeecity.gov.uk)

Central/largest library

Central Library, The Wellgate, Dundee DD1 1DB
☎(01382) 431500 (enquiries), (01382) 431501 (administration)
Fax (01382) 434642
url: www.dundeecity.gov.uk/library
Section Leader Mrs Judy Dobbie MA MCLIP (01382 431526; e-mail: judy.dobbie@dundeecity.gov.uk)
Unit Leader (Reader Services) Ms Christine Ferguson MA MCLIP (01382 431549; e-mail: christine.ferguson@dundeecity.gov.uk)
Community Information Team Leader Mrs Frances Robertson MA MCLIP (01382 431533; e-mail: frances.robertson@dundeecity.gov.uk)
Reference Services Team Leader David Kett MCLIP (01382 431516; e-mail: david.kett@dundeecity.gov.uk)
Senior Library and Information Worker (Central Library) Ms Amina Shah MCLIP (01382 431523; e-mail: amina.shah@dundeecity.gov.uk)
Section Leader (Libraries and Learning Centres) Ms Frances Foster MCLIP (01382 436360; e-mail: frances.foster@dundeecity.gov.uk)
Senior Library and Information Worker (Community Outreach Team) Ms Jayne Gair BA MCLIP (01382 438894; e-mail: jayne.gair@dundeecity.gov.uk)
Senior Library and Information Worker (Community Learning Team) Ms Fiona Macpherson MA MCLIP (01382 438833; e-mail: fiona.macpheson@dundeecity.gov.uk)
Senior Library and Information Worker (Marketing and Promotion Team) Ms Lynn Moy BA MCLIP (01382 438889; e-mail: lynn.moy@dundeecity.gov.uk)
Senior Library and Information Worker (Stock Management Team) Ms Janis Milne BA MCLIP (01382 431535; e-mail: janis.milne@dundeecity.gov.uk)
Staff Development Worker Mrs Frances Scott MCLIP (01382 438891; e-mail: frances.scott@dundeecity.gov.uk)

Community libraries

▶ Ardler Community Library, Ardler Complex, Turnberry Avenue, Ardler, Dundee DD2 3TP
☎(01382) 432863
Fax (01382) 436446
e-mail: ardler.library@dundeecity.gov.uk
Library and Information Worker Ms Susan Ferguson
▶ Arthurstone Community Library, Arthurstone Terrace, Dundee DD4 6RT
☎(01382) 438881
Fax (01382) 438886
e-mail: arthurstone.library@dundeecity.gov.uk
Library and Information Worker Mrs Shona Wood
▶ Blackness Community Library, 225 Perth Road, Dundee DD2 1EJ
☎(01382) 435936
Fax (01382) 435942
e-mail: blackness.library@dundeecity.gov.uk
Library and Information Worker Ms Karen Duffy

▶ Broughty Ferry Community Library, Queen Street, Broughty Ferry, Dundee DD5 2HN
☎(01382) 436919
Fax (01382) 436913
e-mail: broughty.library@dundeecity.gov.uk
Library and Information Worker Mrs Sandra Westgate

▶ Charleston Community Library, 60 Craigowan Road, Dundee DD2 4NL
☎(01382) 432798
Fax (01382) 432671
e-mail: charleston.library@dundeecity.gov.uk
Library and Information Worker Ian Cranmer MCLIP

▶ Coldside Neighbourhood Library, 150 Strathmartine Road, Dundee DD3 7SE
☎(01382) 432849
Fax (01382) 432850
e-mail: coldside.library@dundeecity.gov.uk
Library and Information Worker Ms Barbara Cook

▶ Douglas Community Library, Balmoral Place, Douglas, Dundee DD4 8SH
☎(01382) 436915
Fax (01382) 436922
e-mail: douglas.library@dundeecity.gov.uk
Library and Information Worker Mrs Lorraine Kell

▶ Fintry Community Library, Finmill Centre, Findcastle Street, Dundee DD4 9EW
☎(01382) 432560
Fax (01382) 432559
e-mail: fintry.library@dundeecity.gov.uk
Library and Information Worker Vacant

▶ Hub Community Library and Learning Centre, Pitkerro Road, Dundee DD4 8ES
☎(01382) 438648
Fax (01382) 438627
e-mail: hub.library@dundeecity.gov.uk
Library and Information Worker Ms Liz Young

▶ Kirkton Community Library, Derwent Avenue, Dundee DD3 0BW
☎(01382) 432851
Fax (01382) 432852
e-mail: kirkton.library@dundeecity.gov.uk
Library and Information Worker Mrs Ann Smith

▶ Lochee Community Library, High Street, Lochee, Dundee DD2 3AU
☎(01382) 431835
Fax (01382) 431827
e-mail: lochee.library@dundeecity.gov.uk
Library and Information Worker Mrs Joan Rodger

▶ Menzieshill Community Library, Orleans Place, Menzieshill, Dundee DD2 4BH
☎(01382) 432945
Fax (01382) 432948
e-mail: menzieshill.library@dundeecity.gov.uk
Library and Information Worker Ms Lorraine Andrews

▶ Whitfield Community Library and Learning Centre, Whitfield Drive, Dundee DD4 0DX
☎(01382) 432561
Fax (01382) 432562

e-mail: whitfield.library@dundeecity.gov.uk
Library and Information Worker Mrs Ruth McDowall

EAST AYRSHIRE

Authority: East Ayrshire Council
HQ Library, Registration and Information Services, Dick Institute, 14 Elmbank Avenue,
Kilmarnock, Ayrshire KA1 3BU
☎(01563) 554300 (general enquiries)
Fax (01563) 554311
e-mail: libraries@east-ayrshire.gov.uk
url: www.east-ayrshire.gov.uk/comser/libraries/libraries.asp
Library, Registration and Information Services Manager Gerard Cairns BA DipLib
MCLIP DMS (e-mail: gerard.cairns@east-ayrshire.gov.uk)
Senior Librarian Mrs Elaine Gray MA DipLib MCLIP (e-mail:
elaine.gray@east-ayrshire.gov.uk)
Senior Librarian John Laurenson BSc DipLib MCLIP (e-mail:
john.laurenson@east-ayrshire.gov.uk)
Support Services Librarian Mrs Julia A Harvey MA(Hons) DipLib MCLIP (e-mail:
julia.harvey@east-ayrshire.gov.uk)
Information Officer Ms Dawn Vallance BA(Hons) DipLib MCLIP (e-mail:
dawn.vallance@east-ayrshire.gov.uk)
Community Librarian (Staff Development) Mrs Lynn Mee BA(Hons) MCLIP (e-mail:
lynn.mee@east-ayrshire.gov.uk)
Marketing and Development Officer Ms Charlotte Connor BSc(Hons) MSc ACIM
(e-mail: charlotte.connor@east-ayrshire.gov.uk)
Community Librarian (Heritage Services) Mrs Anne Geddes MCLIP (e-mail:
baird.institute@east-ayrshire.gov.uk)
Community Librarian (Operations) Hugh MacLean MA(Hons) DipLib MCLIP (e-mail:
hugh.maclean@east-ayrshire.gov.uk)
Education Liaison Officer Miss Pat Standen BA MCLIP (e-mail:
pat.standen@east-ayrshire.gov.uk)

EAST DUNBARTONSHIRE

Authority: East Dunbartonshire Council
HQ Strategic Directorate: Community: Department of Social Inclusion and Community
Development, William Patrick Library, 2 West High Street, Kirkintilloch, East
Dunbartonshire G66 1AD
☎0141 776 5666
Fax 0141 776 0408
e-mail: libraries@eastdunbarton.gov.uk
url: www.eastdunbarton.gov.uk
Information and Lifelong Learning Manager Ms Elizabeth Brown MA MCLIP (0141
775 4501; e-mail: elizabeth.brown@eastdunbarton.gov.uk)
Assistant Manager, Adult Lending and Support Services David Kenvyn BA MCLIP
(0141 775 4519; e-mail: david.kenvyn@eastdunbarton.gov.uk)

Support Services Librarian Ms Anne Hamilton BA MCLIP (0141 775 4511; e-mail: anne.hamilton@eastdunbarton.gov.uk)
Assistant Manager, Learning and Outreach Gerry Kiernan (0141 775 4546; e-mail: gerry.kiernan@eastdunbarton.gov.uk)
Assistant Manager, Information and Archives Don Martin FCLIP (0141 775 4529; e-mail: don.martin@eastdunbarton.gov.uk)
Bibliographical Services Librarian Ms Sandra Busby BA MCLIP (0141 775 4512; e-mail: sandra.busby@eastdunbarton.gov.uk)
Young People's Resource Coordinator Mrs Frances MacArthur MA MCLIP (0141 775 4526; e-mail: frances.macarthur@eastdunbarton.gov.uk)
Area Librarian Ms Isabel Alexander MCLIP (0141 775 4510; e-mail: isabel.alexander@eastdunbarton.gov.uk)

Central/largest library
William Patrick Library, 2-4 West High Street, Kirkintilloch, East Dunbartonshire G66 1AD
☎0141 775 4524 (Lending Library)
Community Librarians Mrs Doreen Fergusson, Mrs Eryl Morris BA (job-share)
Information and Local Studies Librarian Mrs Christine Miller BA DipLib MCLIP (0141 775 4537; e-mail: christine.miller@eastdunbarton.gov.uk)
Assistant Information and Local Studies Librarian David Smith DipLib MCLIP (0141 776 8090; e-mail: david.smith@eastdunbarton.gov.uk)
Archivist Ms Sarah Chubb UDIP RMSA (0141 775 4573; e-mail: sarah.chubb@eastdunbarton.gov.uk)
Freedom of Information Officer David Powell MARM (e-mail: david.powell@eastdunbarton.gov.uk)

Branch libraries
▶ Bishopbriggs Library, 170 Kirkintilloch Road, Bishopbriggs, East Dunbartonshire G64 2LX
☎0141 772 4513
Fax 0141 762 5363
Community Librarians Mrs Elaine Clifford MCLIP, Mrs Fiona Warner BA MCLIP (job-share)
▶ Brookwood Library, 166 Drymen Road, Bearsden, Glasgow G61 3RJ
☎0141 942 6811
Fax 0141 943 1119
Community Librarian Vacant
▶ Craighead Library, Craighead Road, Milton of Campsie, East Dunbartonshire G65 8DL
☎(01360) 311925
Assistant in Charge Mrs May Newton, Mrs Sandra Vernon (job-share)
▶ Lennoxtown Library, Main Street, Lennoxtown, East Dunbartonshire G65 7DG
☎(01360) 311436 (tel/fax)
Senior Library Supervisor Ms Elsa Gordon
▶ Lenzie Library, 13 Alexandra Avenue, Lenzie, East Dunbartonshire G66 5BG
☎0141 776 3021
Library Supervisor Ms Lesley Finlayson
▶ Milngavie Library, Community Centre, Allander Way, Milngavie, Glasgow G62 8PN
☎0141 956 2776
Fax 0141 570 0052

Community Librarian John Murray MCLIP
▶ Westerton Library, 82 Maxwell Avenue, Bearsden, Glasgow G61 1NZ
☎0141 943 0780
Library Supervisor Ms Elizabeth Bushfield

EAST LOTHIAN

Authority: East Lothian Council
HQ Library and Museum Headquarters, Dunbar Road, Haddington, East Lothian EH41 3PJ
☎(01620) 828205 (enquiries), (01620) 828200 (administration)
Fax (01620) 828201
e-mail: libraries@eastlothian.gov.uk (for general enquiries)
url: www.eastlothian.gov.uk
Principal Libraries Officer Ms Alison Hunter

Largest library

Musselburgh Library, 10 Bridge Street, Musselburgh, East Lothian EH21 6AG
☎0131 665 2183
e-mail: musselburgh.library@eastlothian.gov.uk
Area Librarian Mrs Dorothy Elliott MA DipLib

Branch libraries

▶ Dunbar Library, Castellau, Belhaven Road, Dunbar, East Lothian EH42 1DA
☎(01368) 863521
e-mail: dunbar.library@eastlothian.gov.uk
Assistant i/c Mrs Anne Hampshire
▶ East Linton Library, 60A High Street, East Linton, East Lothian EH40 3BX
☎(01620) 860015
e-mail: eastlinton.library@eastlothian.gov.uk
Assistant i/c Ms Barbel Burns
▶ Gullane Library, East Links Road, Gullane, East Lothian EH31 2AF
☎(01620) 842073
e-mail: gullane.library@eastlothian.gov.uk
Assistant i/c Ms Avril Stevens
▶ Haddington Library, Newton Port, Haddington, East Lothian EH41 3NA
☎(01620) 822531 (tel/fax)
e-mail: haddington.library@eastlothian.gov.uk
Area Librarian Ms Trina Gavan MCLIP
▶ Longniddry Library, Church Way, Longniddry, East Lothian EH32 0LW
☎(01875) 852735
e-mail: longniddry.library@eastlothian.gov.uk
Assistant i/c Ms Anne Sturgeon
▶ North Berwick Library, The Old School, School Road, North Berwick, East Lothian
EH39 4JU
☎(01620) 893470
e-mail: northberwick.library@eastlothian.gov.uk
Branch Librarian Ms Jane Paterson BA DipLib
▶ Ormiston Library, 5A Meadowbank, Ormiston, East Lothian EH35 5LQ

☎(01875) 616675
e-mail: ormiston.library@eastlothian.gov.uk
Assistant i/c Bill Wilson
▶ Port Seton Library, Community Centre, South Seton Park, Port Seton, East Lothian EH32 0BG
☎(01875) 811709
Fax (01875) 815177
e-mail: portseton.library@eastlothian.gov.uk
Assistant i/c Mrs Irene Muir
▶ Prestonpans Library, West Loan, Prestonpans, East Lothian EH32 9NX
☎(01875) 810788
e-mail: prestonpans.library@eastlothian.gov.uk
Branch Librarian Ms Erica Thomson BA MCLIP
▶ Tranent Library, 3 Civic Square, Tranent, East Lothian EH33 1LH
☎(01875) 610254
e-mail: tranent.library@eastlothian.gov.uk
Branch Librarian Ms Marjory Daly MCLIP
▶ Wallyford Library, 3 Fa'side Buildings, Wallyford, East Lothian EH21 8BA
☎0131 653 2035
e-mail: wallyford.library@eastlothian.gov.uk
Assistant i/c Ms Kate Shilton

Specialist library
▶ Local History Centre, Newton Port, Haddington, East Lothian EH41 3NA
☎(01620) 823307
Local History Librarian Ms Sheila Millar (e-mail: smillar@eastlothian.gov.uk)

EAST RENFREWSHIRE

Authority: East Renfrewshire Council
HQ Cultural Services, Glen Street, Barrhead, East Renfrewshire G78 1QA
☎0141 577 3500 (enquiries)
Fax 0141 577 3501
url: www.eastrenfrewshire.gov.uk
Head of Culture and Sport Ken McKinlay MA(Hons) PGDipLib MCLIP (0141 577 3103; e-mail: ken.mckinlay@eastrenfrewshire.gov.uk)
Libraries and Information Services Manager Mrs Liz McGettigan BA MCLIP (0141 577 3503; e-mail: liz.mcgettigan@eastrenfrewshire.gov.uk)
Operations Manager Eric Fox MCLIP (0141 577 3512; e-mail: eric.fox@eastrenfrewshire.gov.uk)
Learning Services Ms Janice Weir BA MCLIP (0141 577 3515; e-mail: janice.weir@eastrenfrewshire.gov.uk)
Information Access Officer Scott Simpson BA PGDipIT MCLIP (0141 577 3509; e-mail: scott.simpson@eastrenfrewshire.gov.uk)
Service Improvement Officer Ms Claire Scott (0141 577 3531; e-mail: claire.scott@eastrenfrewshire.gov.uk)

Community libraries

▶ Barrhead Community Library, Glen Street, Barrhead, East Renfrewshire G78 1QA
☎0141 577 3518
e-mail: barrheadl@eastrenfrewshire.gov.uk

▶ Busby Community Library, Duff Memorial Hall, Main Street, Busby, East Renfrewshire G76 8DX
☎0141 577 4971
e-mail: busbyl@eastrenfrewshire.gov.uk

▶ Clarkston Community Library, Clarkston Road, Clarkston, East Renfrewshire G76 8NE
☎0141 577 4972
Fax 0141 577 4973
e-mail: clarkstonl@eastrenfrewshire.gov.uk

▶ Eaglesham Community Library, Montgomerie Hall, Eaglesham, Eaglesham, East Renfrewshire G76 0LH
☎(01355) 302649 (tel/fax)
e-mail: eagleshaml@eastrenfrewshire.gov.uk

▶ Giffnock Community Library, Station Road, Giffnock, East Renfrewshire G46 6JF
☎0141 577 4976
Fax 0141 577 4978
e-mail: giffnockl@eastrenfrewshire.gov.uk

▶ Mearns Community Library, McKinley Place, Newton Mearns, East Renfrewshire G77 6EZ
☎0141 577 4979
Fax 0141 577 4980
e-mail: mearnsl@eastrenfrewshire.gov.uk

▶ Neilston Community Library, Main Street, Neilston, East Renfrewshire G78 3NN
☎0141 577 4981
Fax 0141 577 4982
e-mail: neilstonl@eastrenfrewshire.gov.uk

▶ Netherlee Library Centre, Netherlee Pavilion, Linn Park Avenue, East Renfrewshire G44 3PH
☎0141 637 1301

▶ Thornliebank Community Library, 1 Spiersbridge Road, Thornliebank, East Renfrewshire G46 7SJ
☎0141 577 4983
Fax 0141 577 4816
e-mail: thornliebankl@eastrenfrewshire.gov.uk

▶ Uplawmoor Library Centre, Mure Hall, Tannoch Road, Uplawmoor, East Renfrewshire G78 4AF
☎(01505) 850564

EDINBURGH

Authority: City of Edinburgh Council
HQ Central Library, George IV Bridge, Edinburgh EH1 1EG
☎0131 242 8000
Fax 0131 242 8009
e-mail: eclis@edinburgh.gov.uk

url: www.edinburgh.gov.uk
Head of Libraries and Information Services W Wallace MA MCLIP
Central Library and Information Services Manager Ms M Corr BA DipLib MCLIP
Service Development Manager M Hinds BA DipLib MCLIP
Community Libraries Manager Ms G McCaig DipLib MCLIP

Divisional libraries

▶ East Division. Newington Library, 17 Fountainhall Road, Edinburgh EH9 2LN
☎0131 529 5536
Fax 0131 667 5491
e-mail: newington.library@edinburgh.gov.uk
Principal Library Officer M Spells
▶ North Division. Leith Library, 28 Ferry Road, Edinburgh EH6 5AE
☎0131 529 5517
Fax 0131 554 2720
e-mail: leith.library@edinburgh.gov.uk
Principal Library Officer Ms M McChrystal BLib MCLIP
▶ South Division. Wester Hailes Library, 1 Westside Plaza, Wester Hailes, Edinburgh
EH14 2FT
☎0131 529 5667
Fax 0131 529 5671
e-mail: westerhailes.library@edinburgh.gov.uk
Principal Library Officer Ms L Spells BSc DipLib MCLIP
▶ West Division. Blackhall Library, 56 Hillhouse Road, Edinburgh EH4 5EG
☎0131 529 5595
Fax 0131 336 5419
e-mail: blackhall.library@edinburgh.gov.uk
Principal Library Officer Ms E Kilmurry BA MCLIP

FALKIRK

Authority: Falkirk Council
HQ Library, Victoria Buildings, Queen Street, Falkirk FK2 7AF
☎(01324) 506800
Fax (01324) 506801
url: www.falkirk.gov.uk
Libraries Manager Mrs Irene McIntyre MCLIP (e-mail: irene.mcintyre@falkirk.gov.uk)

Central/largest library

Falkirk Library, Hope Street, Falkirk FK1 5AU
☎(01324) 503605
Fax (01324) 503606
e-mail: falkirk.library@falkirk.gov.uk
Principal Librarian Ms Anna Herron MA DipLib MCLIP

Other libraries

▶ Bo'ness Library, Scotland's Close, Bo'ness, Falkirk EH51 0AH
☎(01506) 778520

Fax (01506) 778521
e-mail: bo'ness.library@falkirk.gov.uk
Librarians Ruaraidh Murray MCLIP, Miss Christine Simm BA MCLIP
▶ Bonnybridge Library, Bridge Street, Bonnybridge, Falkirk FK4 1AD
☎(01324) 503295
Fax (01324) 503296
e-mail: bonnybridge.library@falkirk.gov.uk
Librarian Ms Vikki Ring BA MCLIP
▶ Denny Library, 49 Church Walk, Denny, Falkirk FK6 6DF
☎(01324) 504242
Fax (01324) 504240
e-mail: denny.library@falkirk.gov.uk
Librarians Mrs Lorraine Alexander BA MCLIP, Mrs Shona Hill BA MCLIP
▶ Grangemouth Library, Bo'ness Road, Grangemouth, Falkirk FK3 8AG
☎(01324) 504690
Fax (01324) 504691
e-mail: grangemouth.library@falkirk.gov.uk
Senior Librarians Mrs Sharon Woodforde MCLIP, Mrs Rachel Williams BSc(Hons) DipLib
▶ Larbert Library, Main Street, Stenhousemuir, Larbert, Falkirk FK5 3JX
☎(01324) 503590
Fax (01324) 503592
e-mail: larbert.library@falkirk.gov.uk
Senior Librarians Mrs Karyn Jaffray BA MCLIP, Miss Tanya Milligan MA MCLIP, Ms Fiona Fraser BA MCLIP
▶ Slamannan Library, The Cross, Slamannan, Falkirk FK1 3EX
☎(01324) 851373
Fax (01324) 851862
e-mail: slamannan.library@falkirk.gov.uk
Librarian Mrs Gil Vick BA MCLIP

FIFE

Authority: Fife Council
HQ Arts, Libraries and Museums, Town House, Kirkcaldy, Fife KY1 1XW
☎(01592) 417823
Fax (01592) 417847
e-mail: fife.libraries@fife.gov.uk
url: www.fifedirect.org.uk
Service Manager, Arts, Libraries, Museums Iain Whitelaw (e-mail: iain.whitelaw@fife.gov.uk)

Area libraries
▶ Central Area Library HQ, East Fergus Place, Kirkcaldy, Fife KY1 1XT
☎(01592) 412930
Fax (01592) 412941
Libraries Cultural Services Co-ordinator David Spalding MCLIP (e-mail: david.spalding@fife.gov.uk)

▶ East Area Library HQ, Area Library, County Buildings, St Catherine Street, Cupar, Fife KY15 4TA
☎(01334) 412737
Fax (01334) 412941
Libraries Systems and Support Co-ordinator David Burns (e-mail: david.burns@fife.gov.uk)

▶ West Area Library HQ, Carnegie Library, Abbot Street, Dunfermline, Fife KY12 7NL
☎(01383) 312605
Fax (01383) 314314
Libraries Policy and Learning Services Co-ordinator Ms Dorothy Browse MBA MA MCLIP (e-mail: dorothy.browse@fife.gov.uk)

Area/group libraries

▶ Cupar Library, 33-35 Crossgate, Cupar, Fife KY15 5AS
☎(01334) 412285
Fax (01334) 412467
Community Librarian David Castle-Smith MCLIP

▶ Dalgety Bay Library, Regents Way, Dalgety Bay, Fife KY11 5UY
☎(01383) 318981
Fax (01383) 318988
Library Supervisor Ms Brenda Gilmour

▶ Glenwood Library, Glenwood Shopping Centre, Glenrothes, Fife KY6 1PA
☎(01592) 416840
Fax (01592) 416843
Library Supervisor Ms Maria Cook

▶ Kirkcaldy Central Library, War Memorial Gardens, Kirkcaldy, Fife KY1 1YG
☎(01592) 412878
Fax (01592) 412750
Customer Services Librarian Ms T Steedman MCLIP

▶ Leven Library, Durie Street, Leven, Fife KY8 4HE
☎(01333) 592650
Fax (01333) 592655
Library Supervisor Ms Loraine McIntosh

▶ Methil Library, Wellesley Road, Methil, Fife KY8 3QR
☎(01333) 592470
Fax (01333) 592415
Library Supervisor Ms Heather Kirkwood

▶ Rosyth Library, Parkgate Community Centre, Rosyth, Fife KY11 2JW
☎(01383) 313560
Fax (01383) 313562
Library Supervisor Ms Daphne Hutton

▶ St Andrews Library, Church Square, St Andrews, Fife KY16 9NN
☎(01334) 412687
Fax (01334) 413029
Community Librarian Ms Lindsey Cordiner MCLIP

GLASGOW

Authority: Glasgow City Council
HQ Cultural and Leisure Services, Libraries, Information and Learning, The Mitchell Library, North Street, Glasgow G3 7DN
☎0141 287 2999 (enquiries), 0141 287 2870 (service development)
Fax 0141 287 2815
e-mail: lil@cls.glasgow.gov.uk
url: www.glasgowlibraries.org
Head of Libraries, Information and Learning Ms Karen Cunningham MA DipLib MCLIP (0141 287 5114; fax: 0141 287 5151; e-mail: karen.cunningham@cls.glasgow.gov.uk) (located at 20 Trongate, Glasgow G1 1LX)
Service Development Manager Gordon Anderson BA MCLIP (0141 287 2949; e-mail: gordon.anderson@cls.glasgow.gov.uk)
Information Services Manager Ms Pamela Tulloch MA MBA DipLib MCLIP (0141 287 2862; e-mail: pamela.tulloch@cls.glasgow.gov.uk)
Community Libraries Network Manager Ms Wilma Moore MCLIP (0141 287 2806; e-mail: wilma.moore@cls.glasgow.gov.uk)
Community Learning Manager Ms Jane Edgar DipYCW (0141 287 2881; e-mail: jane.edgar@cls.glasgow.gov.uk)

Community libraries

▶ Anderston Library, Berkeley Street, Glasgow G3 7DN
  ☎0141 287 2872 (tel/fax)
▶ Anniesland Library, 833 Crow Road, Glasgow G13 1LE
  ☎0141 954 5687
  Fax 0141 954 5548
▶ Baillieston Library, 141 Main Street, Glasgow G69 6AA
  ☎0141 771 2433 (tel/fax)
▶ Barmulloch Library, Wallacewell Quadrant, Glasgow G21 3DY
  ☎0141 558 1772
  Fax 0141 558 8294
▶ Bridgeton Library, 23 Landressy Street, Glasgow G40 1BP
  ☎0141 554 0217 (tel/fax)
▶ Cardonald Library, 1113 Mosspark Drive, Glasgow G52 3BU
  ☎0141 882 1381
  Fax 0141 810 5490
▶ Castlemilk Library, 100 Castlemilk Drive, Glasgow G45 9TN
  ☎0141 634 2066 (tel/fax)
▶ Couper Institute Library, 84 Clarkston Road, Glasgow G44 3DA
  ☎0141 637 1544 (tel/fax)
▶ Dennistoun Library, 2a Craigpark, Glasgow G31 2NA
  ☎0141 554 0055
  Fax 0141 551 9971
▶ Drumchapel Library, 65 Hecla Avenue, Glasgow G15 8LX
  ☎0141 944 5698 (tel/fax)
▶ Easterhouse Library, 5 Shandwick Street, Glasgow G34 9DP
  ☎0141 771 5986

145

Fax 0141 771 5643

▶ Elder Park Library, 228a Langlands Road, Glasgow G51 3TZ
☎0141 445 1047 (tel/fax)

▶ Gorbals Library and Cybercafé, Crown Street, Glasgow G5
☎0141 429 0949
Fax 0141 429 0167

▶ Govanhill Library, 170 Langside Road, Glasgow G42 7JU
☎0141 423 0335 (tel/fax)

▶ Hillhead Library, 348 Byres Road, Glasgow G12 8AP
☎0141 339 7223
Fax 0141 337 2783

▶ Ibrox Library, 1 Midlock Street, Glasgow G51 1SL
☎0141 427 5831
Fax 0141 427 1139

▶ Knightswood Library, 27 Dunterlie Avenue, Glasgow G13 3BB
☎0141 959 2041 (tel/fax)

▶ Langside Library, 2 Sinclair Drive, Glasgow G42 9QE
☎0141 632 0810
Fax 0141 632 8982

▶ Library@Goma, Queen Street, Glasgow G1 3AZ
☎0141 248 0143
Fax 0141 249 9943

▶ Maryhill Library, 1508 Maryhill Road, Glasgow G20 9AD
☎0141 946 2348 (tel/fax)

▶ Milton Library, 163 Ronaldsay Street, Glasgow G22 7AP
☎0141 772 1410 (tel/fax)

▶ Parkhead Library, 64 Tollcross Road, Glasgow G31 4XA
☎0141 554 0198 (tel/fax)

▶ Partick Library, 305 Dumbarton Road, Glasgow G11 6AB
☎0141 339 1303 (tel/fax)

▶ Pollok Library, Cowglen Road, Glasgow G53 6DW
☎0141 881 3540 (tel/fax)

▶ Pollokshaws Library, 50-60 Shawbridge Street, Glasgow G43 1RW
☎0141 632 3544 (tel/fax)

▶ Pollokshields Library, 30 Leslie Street, Glasgow G41 2LF
☎0141 423 1460 (tel/fax)

▶ Possilpark Library, 127 Allander Street, Glasgow G22 5JJ
☎0141 336 8110 (tel/fax)

▶ Riddrie Library, 1020 Cumbernauld Road, Glasgow G33 2QS
☎0141 770 4043 (tel/fax)

▶ Royston Library, 67 Royston Road, Glasgow G21 2QW
☎0141 552 1657 (tel/fax)

▶ Service Development, The Mitchell Library, North Street, Glasgow G3 7DN
☎0141 287 2870
Fax 0141 287 2815

▶ Shettleston Library, 154 Wellshot Road, Glasgow G32 7AX
☎0141 778 1221
Fax 0141 778 9004

▶ Sighthill Drop-in Centre, Sighthill Library, Fountainwell Square, Glasgow G21 1RF
☎0141 557 0710
Fax 0141 558 9087

▶ Springburn Library, Kay Street, Glasgow G21
☎0141 577 5878
Fax 0141 557 5893

▶ Whiteinch Library, 14 Victoria Park Drive South, Glasgow G14 9RL
☎0141 959 1376 (tel/fax)

▶ Woodside Library, 343 St George's Road, Glasgow G3 6JQ
☎0141 832 1808 (tel/fax)

HIGHLAND

Authority: The Highland Council
HQ Education, Culture and Sport Service, Glenurquhart Road, Inverness IV3 5NX
☎(01463) 702046
Fax (01463) 711177
Lifelong Learning Manager Christopher Phillips (BA DipLib MCLIP)
(christopher.phillips@highland.gov.uk)

Library Support Unit, 31A Harbour Road, Inverness IV1 1UA
☎(01463) 235713
Fax (01463) 236986
e-mail: libraries@highland.gov.uk
url: www.highland.gov.uk
Library and Information Services Co-ordinator Ms Joyce Watson BA MCLIP (e-mail:
joyce.watson@highland.gov.uk)

Area libraries

Inverness
▶ Culloden Library, Keppoch Road, Culloden, Inverness IV1 2LL
☎(01463) 792531
Fax (01463) 739162
e-mail: culloden.library@highland.gov.uk
Librarian Mrs Angela Donald MCLIP
▶ Inverness Library, Farraline Park, Inverness IV1 1NH
☎(01463) 236463
Fax (01463) 237001
e-mail: inverness.library@highland.gov.uk
Libraries Officer Ms Carol Goodfellow MA MCLIP (e-mail:
carol.goodfellow@highland.gov.uk)
Assistant Librarian Sam McDowell BA MCLIP (e-mail:
sam.mcdowell@highland.gov.uk)
Reference Librarian Ms Edwina Burridge BA MCLIP (e-mail:
edwina.burridge@highland.gov.uk)

Lochaber

▶ Fort William Library, Education Culture and Sport Service, Airds Crossing, Fort William, Inverness-shire PH33 6EU
☎(01397) 703552
Fax (01397) 703528
e-mail: fortwilliam.library@highland.gov.uk
Area Libraries Officer, Lochaber Ms Maggie Wright BA(Hons) MCLIP (e-mail: maggie.wright@highland.gov.uk)

Ross and Cromarty

▶ Dingwall Library, Old Academy Buildings, Tulloch Street, Dingwall, Ross-shire IV15 9JZ
☎(01349) 863163
Fax (01349) 865239
e-mail: dingwall.library@highland.gov.uk
Libraries Officer Ms Charlotte MacArthur MCLIP (e-mail: charlotte.macarthur@highland.gov.uk)
Librarian Ms Sheena Paterson MCLIP (e-mail: sheena.paterson@highland.gov.uk)
▶ Invergordon Library, High Street, Invergordon, Ross-shire IV18 0DG
☎(01349) 852698 (tel/fax)
e-mail: invergordon.library@highland.gov.uk
Librarian Vacant
▶ Ullapool Library, Ullapool High School, Mill Street, Ullapool, Ross-shire IV26 2UN
☎(01854) 612543 (tel/fax)
e-mail: ullapool.library@highland.gov.uk
Librarian Vacant

Caithness

▶ Thurso Library, Davidson's Lane, Thurso, Caithness KW14 7AF
☎(01847) 893237
Fax (01847) 896114
e-mail: thurso.library@highland.gov.uk
Libraries Officer Vacant
▶ Wick Library, Sinclair Terrace, Wick, Caithness KW1 5AB
☎(01955) 602864
Fax (01955) 603000
e-mail: wick.library@highland.gov.uk
Assistant Librarian Vacant

Skye and Lochalsh

▶ Portree Library, Bayfield Road, Portree, Isle of Skye, Inverness-shire IV51 9EL
☎(01478) 612697
Fax (01478) 613314
e-mail: portree.library@highland.gov.uk
Libraries Officer David Linton MCLIP (01478 614060; fax: 01478 613289; e-mail: david.linton@highland.gov.uk) (Based at The Highland Council, Elgin Hostel, Dunvegan Road, Portree, Isle of Skye IV51 9EE)

Badenoch and Strathspey

▶ Grantown-on-Spey Library, The YMCA Building, 80 High Street, Grantown-on-Spey, Perthshire PH26 3HB
☎(01479) 873175 (tel/fax)
e-mail: grantown.library@highland.gov.uk
Libraries Officer Ms Eleanor Somerville BEd DipLib MCLIP (based at Nairn Library, details below)

Nairn

▶ Nairn Library, 68 High Street, Nairn, Nairnshire IV12 4AU
☎(01667) 458506
Fax (01667) 458548
e-mail: nairn.library@highland.gov.uk
Libraries Officer Ms Eleanor Somerville BEd DipLib MCLIP (e-mail: eleanor.somerville@highland.gov.uk)
Assistant Librarian Mrs Jennifer Murdoch MCLIP BA (e-mail: jennifer.murdoch@highland.gov.uk)

Sutherland

▶ Dornoch Library, Carnegie Building, High Street, Dornoch, Sutherland IV25 3SH
☎(01862) 811585
Fax (01862) 811079
e-mail: dornoch.library@highland.gov.uk
Libraries Officer Mrs Alison Forrest BA MCLIP (e-mail: alison.forrest@highland.gov.uk)

INVERCLYDE

Authority: Inverclyde Council
HQ Central Library, Clyde Square, Greenock, Renfrewshire PA15 1NA
☎(01475) 712323
Fax (01475) 712339
e-mail: library.central@inverclyde.gov.uk
url: www.inverclyde.gov.uk
Libraries Manager Miss Sandra MacDougall MA(Hons) MCLIP (e-mail: sandra.macdougall@inverclyde.gov.uk)

MIDLOTHIAN

Authority: Midlothian Council
HQ Library HQ, 2 Clerk Street, Loanhead, Midlothian EH20 9DR
☎0131 271 3980
Fax 0131 440 4635
e-mail: library.hq@midlothian.gov.uk
url: www.midlothian.gov.uk/library/
Library Services Manager Alan Reid MA MCLIP

Central/largest library

Dalkeith Library, White Hart Street, Dalkeith, Midlothian EH22 1AE
☎0131 663 2083
Fax 0131 654 9029
e-mail: dalkeith.library@midlothian.gov.uk
Senior Librarian Thomas Regan BA MCLIP

Branch libraries

▶ Bonnyrigg Library, Polton Street, Bonnyrigg, Midlothian EH19 3HB
☎0131 663 6762
Fax 0131 654 9019
e-mail: bonnyrigg.library@midlothian.gov.uk
Senior Librarian David Stevenson BA MCLIP
▶ Danderhall Library, 1A Campview, Danderhall, Midlothian EH22 1QD
☎0131 663 9293
e-mail: danderhall.library@midlothian.gov.uk
Assistant i/c Ms Jannette Brown
▶ Gorebridge Library, Hunterfield Road, Gorebridge, Midlothian EH23 4TT
☎(01875) 820630
Fax (01875) 823657
e-mail: gorebridge.library@midlothian.gov.uk
Assistant i/c Ms Janette Hamilton
▶ Loanhead Library, George Avenue, Loanhead, Midlothian EH20 9HD
☎0131 440 0824
e-mail: loanhead.library@midlothian.gov.uk
Assistant i/c Ms Gillian Renwick
▶ Local Studies, 2 Clerk Street, Loanhead, Midlothian EH20 9DR
☎0131 271 3976
Fax 0131 440 4635
e-mail: local.studies@midlothian.gov.uk
Local Studies Officer Dr Kenneth Bogle MA MCLIP PhD
▶ Mayfield Library, Stone Avenue, Mayfield, Dalkeith, Midlothian EH22 5PB
☎0131 663 2126
e-mail: mayfield.library@midlothian.gov.uk
Assistant i/c Ms Isobel Allen
▶ Newtongrange Library, St Davids, Newtongrange, Midlothian EH22 4LG
☎0131 663 1816
Fax 0131 654 1990
e-mail: newtongrange.library@midlothian.gov.uk
Assistant i/c Ms Jacqueline Elliot
▶ Penicuik Library, Bellmans Road, Penicuik, Midlothian EH26 0AB
☎(01968) 672340
Fax (01968) 679968
e-mail: penicuik.library@midlothian.gov.uk
Assistant Librarian Ms Frances Bell BA MCLIP
▶ Roslin Library, 9 Main Street, Roslin, Midlothian EH25 9LD
☎0131 448 2781
e-mail: roslin.library@midlothian.gov.uk

Assistant i/c Vacant

▶ Woodburn Library, Dalkeith Comunity Centre, 6 Woodburn Road, Dalkeith, Midlothian EH22 2AR
☎0131 663 3445
e-mail: woodburn.library@midlothian.gov.uk
Assistant i/c Ms Isobel Allen, Ms Jannette Brown

MORAY

Authority: The Moray Council
HQ Educational Services Department, Council Office, High Street, Elgin, Moray IV30 1BX
☎(01343) 562600 (enquiries), 01343 563398 (administration)
Fax (01343) 563478
url: www.moray.gov.uk
Libraries and Museums Manager G Alistair Campbell MA BCom MCLIP
(e-mail: campbea@moray.gov.uk)

Central/largest library

Elgin Library, Cooper Park, Elgin, Moray IV30 1HS
☎(01343) 562600
Fax (01343) 562630
e-mail: elgin.library@moray.gov.uk
Principal Librarian (Central Services) Ms Sheila Campbell MCLIP (e-mail:
sheila.campbell@moray.gov.uk)

Area libraries

▶ Buckie Library, Cluny Place, Buckie, Banffshire AB56 1HB
☎(01542) 832121
Fax (01542) 835237
e-mail: buckie.library@moray.gov.uk
Senior Librarian (Buckie) Ms Eleanor Kidd MA MCLIP
▶ Forres Library, Forres House, High Street, Forres, Moray IV36 0BU
☎(01309) 672834
Fax (01309) 675084
e-mail: forres.library@moray.gov.uk
Community Librarian (Forres) Ms Elizabeth Parker MCLIP (e-mail:
elizabeth.parker@moray.gov.uk)
▶ Keith Library, Union Street, Keith, Banffshire AB55 5DP
☎(01542) 882223
Fax (01542) 882177
e-mail: keith.library@moray.gov.uk
Senior Librarian (Keith) Ms Susan Butts MA(Hons) MCLIP

NORTH AYRSHIRE

Authority: North Ayrshire Council
HQ Library, 39-41 Princes Street, Ardrossan, Ayrshire KA22 8BT
☎(01294) 469137

Fax (01294) 604236
e-mail: libraryhq@north-ayrshire.gov.uk
url: www.north-ayrshire.gov.uk
Information and Resource Manager Ms Marion McLarty MA MCLIP (e-mail:
mmclarty@north-ayrshire.gov.uk)
Area Officer (Three Towns and Arran) Mrs Marilyn Vint MCLIP (01294 469137; fax:
01294 604236; e-mail: mvint@north-ayrshire.gov.uk)
Area Officer (Irvine/Kilwinning) Miss Sandra Kerr MCLIP (01294 554699; fax: 01294
557628; e-mail: skerr@north-ayrshire.gov.uk)
Area Officer (North Coast and Garnock Valley) Paul Cowan BEd DipLib MCLIP
(01505 503613; fax: 01505 503417; e-mail: pcowan@north-ayrshire.gov.uk)

Central/largest library

Irvine Library, Cunninghame House, Irvine, Irvine, Ayrshire KA12 8EE
☎(01294) 324251
Fax (01294) 324252
e-mail: irvinelibrary@north-ayrshire.gov.uk
Senior Librarian Miss Mary-Anne Scott MCLIP

Area libraries

▶ Largs Library, Allanpark Street, Largs, Ayrshire KA30 9AS
  ☎(01475) 673309 (tel/fax)
  e-mail: largslibrary@north-ayrshire.gov.uk
  Senior Librarian John West BA DipLib MCLIP
▶ Saltcoats Library, Springvale Place, Saltcoats, Ayrshire KA21 5LS
  ☎(01294) 469546 (tel/fax)
  e-mail: saltcoatslibrary@north-ayrshire.gov.uk
  Senior Librarian Jim Macaulay MCLIP DipLib

NORTH LANARKSHIRE

Authority: North Lanarkshire Council
HQ Dept of Community Services, Buchanan Tower, Buchanan Business Park, Cumbernauld
Road, Stepps, Glasgow G33 6HR
☎0141 304 1800
Fax 0141 304 1902
url: www.northlan.gov.uk
Libraries and Information Manager John Fox DMS MCLIP (e-mail:
foxj@northlan.gov.uk)

Central/largest library

Motherwell Library, 35 Hamilton Road, Motherwell, North Lanarkshire ML1 3BZ
☎(01698) 332626
Fax (01698) 332625
Information Services Manager Charles Bennett BA MCLIP (e-mail:
bennettc@northlan.gov.uk)
Lending Services Manager Mrs Catriona Wales BA MCLIP (e-mail:
walesc@northlan.gov.uk)

Area libraries

▶ Coatbridge Library, 25 Academy Street, Coatbridge, North Lanarkshire ML5 3AW
☎(01236) 424150
Fax (01236) 437997
Lending Services Manager Central Danny McGuinness MCLIP (e-mail: mcguinnessd@northlan.gov.uk)

▶ Cumbernauld Library, 8 Allander Walk, Cumbernauld, North Lanarkshire G67 6EE
☎(01236) 725664
Fax (01236) 458350
Lending Services Manager North Mrs Wendy Bennett BA MCLIP (e-mail: bennettw@northlan.gov.uk)

ORKNEY

Authority: Orkney Islands Council
HQ The Orkney Library and Archive, 44 Junction Road, Kirkwall, Orkney KW15 1AG
☎(01856) 873166 (enquiries and administration)
Fax (01856) 875260
e-mail: general.enquiries@orkneylibrary.org.uk
url: www.orkneylibrary.org.uk
Library and Archive Manager Vacant
Principal Librarian Ms Karen I Walker BA (e-mail: karen.walker@orkneylibrary.org.uk)
Principal Archivist Ms Alison Fraser (e-mail: alison.fraser@orkneylibrary.org.uk)

PERTH AND KINROSS

Authority: Perth and Kinross Council
HQ The A K Bell Library, York Place, Perth, Perthshire PH2 8EP
☎(01738) 444949
Fax (01738) 477010
e-mail: library@pkc.gov.uk
url: www.pkc.gov.uk/library
Community Libraries Manager Ms Caroline Beaton (e-mail: cfbeaton@pkc.gov.uk)
Principal Librarian Iain MacRae BA MCLIP (e-mail: imacrae@pkc.gov.uk)

Area libraries

▶ Auchterarder Library, Aytoun Hall, Chapel Wynd, Auchterarder, Perthshire PH3 1BL
☎(01764) 663850
Fax (01764) 663917
Branch Librarian Mrs Kirsty Mayall BA

▶ Blairgowrie Library, 46 Leslie Street, Blairgowrie, Perthshire PH10 6AW
☎(01250) 872905 (tel/fax)
Branch Librarian Simon McGowan MA

▶ Crieff Library, 6 Comrie Street, Crieff, Perthshire PH7 4AX
☎(01764) 653418 (tel/fax)
Branch Librarian Ms Marilyn Gordon BA

▶ Kinross Library, 27 High Street, Kinross, Kinross-shire KY13 8AW
☎(01577) 864202

Branch Library Assistant Ms Marion Garden
▶ Scone Library, Sandy Road, Scone, Perth, Perthshire PH2 6LJ
☎(01738) 553029 (tel/fax)
Branch Librarian Mrs Elaine Wallace BA

RENFREWSHIRE

Authority: Renfrewshire Council
HQ Library Services, Abbey House, 8A Seedhill Road, Paisley, Renfrewshire PA1 1AJ
☎0141 840 3003
Fax 0141 840 3004
url: www.renfrewshire.gov.uk
Libraries Manager Ms Vivian Kerr BA MCLIP MSc MIM (0141 840 3003; e-mail:
vivian.kerr@renfrewshire.gov.uk)

Central/largest library

Paisley Central Library, High Street, Paisley, Renfrewshire PA1 2BB
☎0141 887 3672 (lending services), 0141 889 2360 (ref/info/local studies)
Fax 0141 887 6468
e-mail: ce.els@renfrewshire.gov.uk (lending services); locstuds.els@renfrewshire.gov.uk
(local studies); ref.els@renfrewshire.gov.uk (ref/info services)

Community libraries

▶ Johnstone Community Library, Houston Court, Johnstone, Renfrewshire PA5 8DL
☎(01505) 329726
Fax (01505) 336657
e-mail: jo.els@renfrewshire.gov.uk
▶ Renfrew Community Library, Paisley Road, Renfrew, Renfrewshire PA4 8LJ
☎0141 886 3433
Fax 0141 886 1660
e-mail: rw.els@renfrewshire.gov.uk

SCOTTISH BORDERS

Authority: Scottish Borders Council
HQ Scottish Borders Library Service, St Mary's Mill, Selkirk TD7 5EW
☎(01750) 20842
Fax (01750) 22875
url: www.scotborders.gov.uk
Head of Community Services Alan Hasson MA MBA DipLib MCLIP MIMgt
Library and Information Services Manager Ms Margaret Menzies BA MLib MCLIP
Community and Operations Librarian Ms Gillian McNay MA MCLIP DipLib
Information Systems Librarian Ms Sheena Milne MA MCLIP DipLib

Area libraries

▶ Galashiels Library, Lawyer's Brae, Galashiels, Selkirkshire TD1 3JQ
☎(01896) 752512
Fax (01896) 753575

e-mail: libgalashiels@scotborders.gov.uk

Area Librarian Miss Caroline R Letton MA FSA(Scot) MCLIP DipLib

▶ Hawick Library, North Bridge Street, Hawick, Roxburghshire TD9 9QT
☎(01450) 372637
Fax (01450) 370991
e-mail: libhawick@scotborders.gov.uk

Area Librarian John Beedle BA MCLIP

▶ Peebles Library, Chambers Institute, High Street, Peebles, Peeblesshire EH45 8AG
☎(01721) 720123
Fax (01721) 724424
e-mail: libpeebles@scotborders.gov.uk

Area Librarian Paul Taylor BSc FSA MCLIP

Branch libraries

▶ Archive & Local History Centre, St Mary's Mill, Selkirk TD7 5EW
☎(01750) 20842
Fax (01750) 22875
e-mail: archives@scotborders.gov.uk

Librarian Miss Helen Darling BA(Hons) MCLIP

▶ Coldstream Library, Gateway Centre, Coldstream, Scottish Borders TD12 4AE
☎(01890) 883314 (tel/fax)
e-mail: libcoldstream@scotborders.gov.uk

Branch Librarian Iain Hope

▶ Duns Library, 49 Newtown Street, Duns, Berwickshire TD11 3AU
☎(01361) 882622
Fax (01361) 884104
e-mail: libduns@scotborders.gov.uk

Branch Librarian Ms Joan B Sanderson BA MCLIP

▶ Earlston Library, High School, Earlston, Scottish Borders TD4 6ED
☎(01896) 849282
Fax (01896) 848918
e-mail: libearlston@scotborders.gov.uk

Branch Librarian Mrs Anne Taitt

▶ Eyemouth Library, Manse Road, Eyemouth, Scottish Borders TD14 5JE
☎(01890) 750300
Fax (01890) 751633
e-mail: libeyemouth@scotborders.gov.uk

Branch Librarian Mrs Joan Thomas, Mrs Alison Fowler

▶ Innerleithen Library, Buccleuch Street, Innerleithen, Scottish Borders EH44 6LA
☎(01896) 830789 (tel/fax)
e-mail: libinnerleithen@scotborders.gov.uk

Branch Librarian Mrs Elaine Hogarth

▶ Jedburgh Library, Castlegate, Jedburgh, Scottish Borders TD8 6AS
☎(01835) 863592 (tel/fax)
e-mail: libjedburgh@scotborders.gov.uk

Branch Librarian Mrs Carol Chisholm

▶ Kelso Library, Bowmont Street, Kelso, Roxburghshire TD5 7JH
☎(01573) 223171

Fax (01573) 226618
e-mail: libkelso@scotborders.gov.uk
Branch Librarian Mrs Ruth Holmes
▶ Melrose Library, 18 Market Square, Melrose, Scottish Borders TD6 9PN
☎(01896) 823052 (tel/fax)
e-mail: libmelrose@scotborders.gov.uk
Branch Librarian Mrs Mairi Wight
▶ Selkirk Library, Ettrick Terrace, Selkirk TD7 4LE
☎(01750) 20267 (tel/fax)
e-mail: libselkirk@scotborders.gov.uk
Branch Librarian Mrs Jean Gammie BSc MCLIP

SHETLAND ISLANDS

Authority: Shetland Islands Council
HQ Shetland Library, Lower Hillhead, Lerwick, Shetland ZE1 0EL
☎(01595) 693868 (enquiries and administration)
Fax (01595) 694430
e-mail: shetlandlibrary@sic.shetland.gov.uk
Online catalogue: http://library.shetland.gov.uk/TalisPrism
Library and Information Services Manager Ms Silvija Crook
Support Services Librarian Douglas Garden (e-mail:
douglas.garden@sic.shetland.gov.uk)
Customer Services Librarian Ms Karen Fraser
Secretary/Administration Assistant Mrs Agnes Anderson (e-mail:
agnes.anderson@sic.shetland.gov.uk)
Administration Assistant Miss Katrina Williamson (e-mail:
katrina.a.williamson@sic.shetland.gov.uk)
Learning Services Librarian Miss Aileen Paterson (e-mail:
aileen.paterson@sic.shetland.gov.uk)

SOUTH AYRSHIRE

Authority: South Ayrshire Council
HQ Library HQ, 26 Green Street, Ayr KA8 8AD
☎(01292) 288820
Fax (01292) 619019
url: www.south-ayrshire.gov.uk
Libraries and Galleries Manager Charles Deas BA MCLIP (e-mail:
charles.deas@south-ayrshire.gov.uk)

Central/largest library
Carnegie Library, 12 Main Street, Ayr KA8 8ED
☎(01292) 286385
Fax (01292) 611593
e-mail: carnegie.library@south-ayrshire.gov.uk

SOUTH LANARKSHIRE

Authority: South Lanarkshire Council
HQ Libraries and Community Learning Service, Education Resources, Council Offices, Almada Street, Hamilton, South Lanarkshire ML3 0AA
☎(01698) 454545
Fax (01698) 454465
url: www.southlanarkshire.gov.uk
Libraries and Community Learning Service Manager Ms D Barr BA MCLIP MIMgt
(01698 454412; e-mail: diana.barr@southlanarkshire.gov.uk)
Information Services Co-ordinator John McGarrity BA MCLIP (01698 452220; e-mail: john.mcgarrity@library.s-lanark.org.uk)
Service Development Co-ordinator Ms Frances Roberts BA MCLIP (01698 452144; e-mail: frances.roberts@library.s-lanark.org.uk)
Literacy Development Co-ordinator Ms Margaret Cowan MCLIP (01355 248581; e-mail: margaret.cowan@southlanarkshire.gov.uk)

Central/largest library

East Kilbride Central Library, 40 The Olympia, East Kilbride, South Lanarkshire G74 1PG
☎(01355) 220046
Fax (01355) 229365
e-mail: libek@slc-learningcentres.org.uk
Libraries Co-ordinator D Leitch MCLIP

Divisional libraries

▶ Hamilton Central Library, 98 Cadzow Street, Hamilton, South Lanarkshire ML3 6HQ
☎(01698) 452299
Fax (01698) 286334
e-mail: libhc@slc-learningcentres.org.uk
Libraries Co-ordinator Ms I Walker MCLIP
▶ Lanark Library, Hope Street, Lanark, Lanarkshire ML11 7NH
☎(01555) 661144
Fax (01555) 665884
e-mail: libln@slc-learningcentres.org.uk
Libraries Co-ordinator Ms F Renfrew BA MCLIP
▶ Rutherglen Library, 163 Main Street, Rutherglen, Glasgow G73 2HB
☎0141 647 6453
Fax 0141 647 5164
e-mail: librg@slc-learningcentres.org.uk
Libraries Co-ordinator D Moncrieff MCLIP

STIRLING

Authority: Stirling Council
HQ Library HQ, Borrowmeadow Road, Springkerse, Stirling FK7 7TN
☎(01786) 432383 (enquiries/administration)
Fax (01786) 432395
e-mail: libraryheadquarters@stirling.gov.uk

url: www.stirling.gov.uk
Head of Libraries, Learning, Communities and Culture Ms Susan Carragher
BA(Hons) MCLIP (01786 443388) (Based at Stirling Council, Viewforth, Stirling FK8 2ET)
Service Development Librarian Steven J Dolman BA(Hons) MCLIP (01786 432388)
Operations Librarian Andrew Muirhead MA MLitt MCLIP (01786 432386)

Central/largest library

Central Library, Corn Exchange Road, Stirling FK8 2HX
☎(01786) 432106/7 (enquiries), (01786) 432108 (administration)
Fax (01786) 473094
e-mail: centrallibrary@stirling.gov.uk
Area Librarians Ms Elizabeth Farr BA MCLIP,. 2 posts vacant

WEST DUNBARTONSHIRE

Authority: West Dunbartonshire Council
HQ West Dunbartonshire Libraries, Levenford House, Helenslee Road, Dumbarton G82 4AH
☎(01389) 608041 (enquiries and administration)
Fax (01389) 608044
url: www.wdcweb.info
Head of Service, Education & Cultural Services Vacant

Area libraries

▶ Clydebank Library, Dumbarton Road, Clydebank, Dumbarton G81 1XH
☎0141 952 1416 (enquiries)
Fax 0141 951 8275
Team Leader (Libraries) Miss Fiona MacDonald MA MCLIP
▶ Dumbarton Library, Strathleven Place, Dumbarton G82 1BD
☎(01389) 763129 (enquiries), (01389) 608038 (administration)
Fax (01389) 607302
Area Librarian Ms Fiona Matheson MCLIP

WEST LOTHIAN

Authority: West Lothian Council
HQ Library HQ, Connolly House, Hopefield Road, Blackburn, West Lothian EH47 7HZ
☎(01506) 776336 (enquiries), (01506) 776342 (administration)
Fax (01506) 776345
e-mail: library.info@westlothian.gov.uk
url: www.wlonline.org.uk/libraries
Library Services Manager Misss Jeanette Castle MA(Hons) DipILS MCLIP (e-mail:
jeanette.castle@westlothian.gov.uk)
Support Services Manager Ms Anne Hunt MA DipLib MCLIP (01506 776325; e-mail:
anne.hunt@westlothian.gov.uk)
Area Manager Mrs Irene Brough (01506 776327; e-mail:
irene.brough@westlothian.gov.uk)
Acting Area Manager Mrs Hilda Gibson (01506 776326; e-mail:
hilda.gibson@westlothian.gov.uk)

Acting Area Manager Mrs Mary Shelton MCLIP (01501 776350; e-mail: mary.shelton@westlothian.gov.uk)

Central/largest library

Carmondean Library, Carmondean Centre, Livingston, West Lothian EH54 8PT
☎(01506) 777602 (enquiries)
e-mail: carmondean.lib@wled.org.uk
Library Manager Stephen Harris MA MSc MCLIP

Branch libraries

▶ Almondbank Library, The Mall, Craigshill, Livingston, West Lothian EH54 5EJ
☎(01506) 777500
e-mail: almondbank.lib@wled.org.uk
Library Manager Ms Helen Dobie MA DipLib MCLIP
▶ Armadale Library, West Main Street, Armadale, West Lothian EH48 3JB
☎(01501) 778400
e-mail: armadale.lib@wled.org.uk
Library Manager Mrs Betty Hunter MCLIP
▶ Bathgate Library, 66 Hopetoun Street, Bathgate, West Lothian EH48 1TD
☎(01506) 776400
e-mail: bathgate.lib@wled.org.uk
Library Managers Mrs Anne Mackintosh BA MCLIP, Mrs Margaret Armstrong MCLIP
(job-share)
▶ Blackburn Library, Ash Grove, Blackburn, West Lothian EH47 7LJ
☎(01506) 776500
e-mail: blackburn.lib@wled.org.uk
Library Manager Mrs Fiona Aitken
▶ Blackridge Library, Craig Inn Centre, Blackridge, West Lothian EH48 3RJ
☎(01501) 752396
e-mail: blackridge.lib@wled.org.uk
Library Manager Ms Moira McCabe
▶ Broxburn Library, West Main Street, Broxburn, West Lothian EH52 5RH
☎(01506) 775600
e-mail: broxburn.lib@wled.org.uk
Library Manager Ms Gillian Gillespie BA MCLIP
▶ East Calder Library, Main Street, East Calder, West Lothian EH53 0EJ
☎(01506) 883633
e-mail: eastcalder.lib@wled.org.uk
Library Manager Ms Gillian Downie BA MCLIP
▶ Fauldhouse Library, Lanrigg Road, Fauldhouse, West Lothian EH47 9JA
☎(01501) 770358
e-mail: fauldhouse.lib@wled.org.uk
Library Manager Ms Marilyn James
▶ Lanthorn Library, Lanthorn Centre, Kenilworth Rise, Dedridge, Livingston, West Lothian
EH54 6NY
☎(01506) 777700
e-mail: lanthorn.lib@wled.org.uk
Library Manager Ms Gillian Downie BA MCLIP

▶ Linlithgow Library, The Vennel, Linlithgow, West Lothian EH49 7EX
☎(01506) 775490
e-mail: linlithgow.lib@wled.org.uk
Library Manager Mrs Kay Ali BA MCLIP

▶ Public Reference Library, West Lothian College, Almondvale Cresent, Livingston, West Lothian EH54 7DN
☎(01506) 427601
Library Manager Ms Linda Hartley

▶ Pumpherston Library, Pumpherston Primary School, 18 Uphall Station Road, Pumpherston, West Lothian EH53 0LP
☎(01506) 435837
e-mail: pumpherston.lib@wled.org.uk
Library Manager Mrs Ruth Forsythe MCS

▶ West Calder Library, Main Street, West Calder, West Lothian EH55 8BJ
☎(01506) 871371
e-mail: westcalder.lib@wled.org.uk
Library Manager Ms Gillian Gillespie BA MCLIP

▶ Whitburn Library, Union Road, Whitburn, West Lothian EH47 0AR
☎(01506) 778050
e-mail: whitburn.lib@wled.org.uk
Acting Library Manager Ms Sandra Valentis

WESTERN ISLES *see* COMHAIRLE NAN EILEAN SIAR

ANGLESEY, ISLE OF

Authority: Isle of Anglesey County Council
HQ Department of Education and Leisure, Parc Mownt, Fford Glanhwfa, Llangefni, Ynys Môn LL77 7EY
☎(01248) 752092 (enquiries); (01248) 752908 (administration)
Fax (01248) 752999
url: www.ynysmon.gov.uk
Corporate Director: Education and Leisure Richard Jones MA (01248 752900; e-mail: rpjed@ynysmon.gov.uk)
Head of Service: Lifelong Learning and Information John Rees Thomas BSc(Econ) DipLib MCLIP (01248 752908; e-mail: jrtlh@ynysmon.gov.uk)
Principal Librarian David Evans BA DipLib MCLIP
Archivist Ms Anne Venables BA DipAA (01248 752080)

Central/largest library

Llangefni Central Library, Lôn-y-Felin, Llangefni, Ynys Môn LL77 7RT
☎(01248) 752092
Fax (01248) 750197
e-mail: dhelh@ynysmon.gov.uk

Branch libraries

▶ Amlwch Library, Lôn Parys, Amlwch, Ynys Môn LL68 9EA
☎(01407) 830145 (tel/fax)
e-mail: kbxlh@ynysmon.gov.uk
▶ Holyhead Library, Newry Fields, Holyhead, Ynys Môn LL65 1LA
☎(01407) 762917
Fax (01407) 769616
e-mail: kpxlh@ynysmon.gov.uk
▶ Menai Bridge Library, Ffordd y Ffair, Menai Bridge, Ynys Môn LL59 5AS
☎(01248) 712706 (tel/fax)
e-mail: dbxlh@ynysmon.gov.uk
▶ Record Office, Shirehall, Glanhwfa Street, Llangefni, Ynys Môn LL77 7TW
☎(01248) 752083
Fax (01248) 751289
e-mail: archives@ynysmon.gov.uk

BLAENAU GWENT

Authority: Blaenau Gwent County Borough Council
HQ Library Headquarters, Central Depot, Barleyfields Industrial Estate, Brynmawr, Blaenau Gwent NP23 4YF
☎(01495) 355318 (enquiries), (01495) 355319 (administration)
Fax (01495) 312357

url: www.blaenau-gwent.gov.uk/library.htm
Information Officer Steve Hardman BSc(Econ) (01495 355318; e-mail:
steve.hardman@blaenau-gwent.gov.uk)

Central/largest library

Ebbw Vale Library, 21 Bethcar Street, Ebbw Vale, Blaenau Gwent NP23 6HS
☎(01495) 303069
Fax (01495) 350547
Library Manager Mrs Sue White MCLIP (01495 301122; e-mail:
sue.white@blaenau-gwent.gov.uk)
Librarian Ms Julie Davies BA MCLIP

Area libraries

▶ Abertillery Library, Station Hill, Abertillery, Blaenau Gwent NP13 1UJ
☎(01495) 212332/217640
Fax (01495) 320995
Library Manager Ms Karen Ross (01495 217698; e-mail:
karen.ross@blaenau-gwent.gov.uk)
Librarian Miss Jane Corey BSc MCLIP
▶ Acquisitions Dept, c/o Abertillery Library, Station Hill, Abertillery, Blaenau Gwent
NP13 1UJ
☎(01495) 217640
Fax (01495) 320995
Acquisitions Librarian Peter Marley BA MCLIP
▶ Blaina Library, Reading Institute, High Street, Blaina, Blaenau Gwent NP13 3BN
☎(01495) 290312
Fax (01495) 290312
Librarian John Leacy BA MCLIP
▶ Brynmawr Library, Market Square, Brynmawr, Brynmawr, Blaenau Gwent
NP23 4AJ
☎(01495) 310045
Fax (01495) 310045
Librarian John Leacy BA MCLIP
▶ Cwm Library, Canning Street, Cwm, Blaenau Gwent NP23 7RW
☎(01495) 370454
Fax (01495) 370454
Librarian Miss Janet Karn BA MCLIP
▶ Llanhilleth Library, Workmen's Institute, Llanhilleth, Blaenau Gwent NP13 2JH
☎(01495) 214485
Fax (01495) 214485
Librarian Peter Marley BA MCLIP
▶ Reaching Out/Mobile, c/o Brynmawr Library, Market Square, Brynmawr, Blaenau Gwent
NP23 4AJ
☎(01495) 722687
Fax (01495) 717018
Special Services Librarian Miss Jane Corey BSc MCLIP
▶ Tredegar Library, The Circle, Tredegar, Blaenau Gwent NP22 3PS
☎(01495) 722687

Fax (01495) 717018
Librarian Miss Janet Karn BA MCLIP

BRIDGEND

Authority: Bridgend County Borough Council
HQ Library and Information Service, Coed Parc, Park Street, Bridgend CF31 4BA
☎(01656) 767451
Fax (01656) 645719
e-mail: blis@bridgendlib.gov.uk
url: www.bridgend.gov.uk/english/library
County Borough Librarian John C Woods BSc MCLIP (e-mail: woodsjc@bridgend.gov.uk)

Central/largest libraries

▶ Bridgend Lending Library, Wyndham Street, Bridgend CF31 1EF
☎(01656) 653444
Fax (01656) 667886
e-mail: bridgendlib@bridgend.gov.uk
Site Librarian Mrs Diana Apperley MA
▶ Maesteg Library, North's Lane, Maesteg, Glamorgan CF34 9AA
☎(01656) 733201
Fax (01656) 731098
e-mail: maestlib@bridgend.gov.uk
Branch Librarian Ms Helen Pridham BA DipIS MCLIP
▶ Pencoed Library, Penybont Road, Pencoed, Glamorgan CF35 5RA
☎(01656) 860358
Fax (01656) 863042
e-mail: penclib@bridgend.gov.uk
Branch Librarian Mrs Alison Nicholas BA MCLIP
▶ Porthcawl Library, Church Place, Porthcawl, Glamorgan CF36 3AG
☎(01656) 782059
Fax (01656) 722745
e-mail: porthcawllib@bridgend.gov.uk
Branch Librarian Mrs Lesley A Milne BA MCLIP
▶ Pyle Library, Pyle Life Centre, Helig Fan, Pyle, Glamorgan CF33 6BS
☎(01656) 740631
Fax (01656) 744865
e-mail: pylelib@bridgend.gov.uk
Life Centre Manager Mrs Janet Arbery
▶ Reference and Information Centre, Coed Parc, Park Street, Bridgend CF31 4BA
☎(01656) 661813
Fax (01656) 645719
e-mail: blis@bridgend.gov.uk
url: www.bridgend.gov.uk/english/library
Reference Librarian Mrs Christine Phillips BA MCLIP

CAERPHILLY

Authority: Caerphilly County Borough Council
HQ Lifelong Learning and Leisure, Unit 7, Woodfieldside Business Park, Penmaen Road, Pontllanfraith, Blackwood, Caerphilly NP12 2DG
☎(01495) 235587
Fax (01495) 235567
e-mail: libraries@caerphilly.gov.uk
url: www.caerphilly.gov.uk/learning/libraries
Principal Officer: Libraries Ms Mary Palmer MLib MCLIP
Assistant Director Peter Gomer

Area libraries

▶ Blackwood Library, 192 High Street, Blackwood, Caerphilly NP12 1AJ
☎(01495) 233000
Fax (01495) 233002
Area Manager: North Mrs Dianne Madhavan MCLIP
▶ Caerphilly Library, Morgan Jones Park, Caerphilly CF8 1AP
☎029 208 52543
Fax 029 2086 5585
Area Manager: South Mrs Yvonne Harris MCLIP
▶ Risca Library, Park Place, Risca, Caerphilly NP11 6AS
☎(01633) 600920
Fax (01633) 600922
Area Manager: Central Mrs Marion Davies MCLIP

CARDIFF

Authority: Cardiff Council
HQ Cardiff Libraries and Information Service, Central Library, St David's Link, Frederick Street, Cardiff CF10 2DU
☎029 2038 2116
Fax 029 208 71599
e-mail: centrallibrary@cardiff.gov.uk
url: www.cardiff.gov.uk/libraries
Operational Manager Lifelong Learning Vacant
Central Library Manager Rob Boddy BA MCLIP (e-mail: rboddy@cardiff.gov.uk)
Libraries and Information Development Manager Ms Elspeth Morris BA MCLIP (e-mail: emorris@cardiff.gov.uk)
Branch Libraries Manager Ms Fiona Bailey (e-mail: fbailey@cardiff.gov.uk)
Stock Manager Ms Siân Best (e-mail: sbest@cardiff.gov.uk)

CARMARTHENSHIRE

Authority: Carmarthenshire County Council
HQ Library HQ, Block 1, Parc Myrddin, Richmond Terrace, Carmarthen, Carmarthenshire SA31 1DS
☎(01267) 228203

Fax (01267) 238584
url: www.libraries.carmarthenshire.gov.uk
Head of Libraries and Community Learning Dewi P Thomas BA DipLib MCLIP
(e-mail: dpthomas@sirgar.gov.uk)

Area libraries
▶ Ammanford Area Library, 3 Wind Street, Ammanford, Carmarthenshire SA18 3DN
☎(01269) 598150
Fax (01269) 598151
Area Librarian Myrddin Morgan
▶ Carmarthen Area Library, St Peter's Street, Carmarthen SA31 1LN
☎(01267) 224824
Fax (01267) 221839
Area Librarian William T Phillips BA DipLib MCLIP
▶ Llanelli Area Library, Vaughan Street, Llanelli, Carmarthenshire SA15 3AS
☎(01554) 773538
Fax (01554) 750125
Area Librarian Mark Jewell

CEREDIGION

Authority: Ceredigion County Council
HQ Public Library, Corporation Street, Aberystwyth, Ceredigion SY23 2BU
☎(01970) 633703; 633716
Fax (01970) 625059
url: www.ceredigion.gov.uk
Assistant Director (Cultural Services) D Geraint Lewis MA MCLIP
County Libraries Officer W H Howells BA MLib MCLIP (e-mail:
williamh@ceredigion.gov.uk)

Branch library
▶ Branch Library, Canolfan Teifi, Pendre, Ceredigion SA43 1JL
☎(01239) 612578
Fax (01239) 612285
e-mail: teifillb@ceredigion.gov.uk
Branch Librarian D G Evans MCLIP

CONWY

Authority: Conwy County Borough Council
HQ Library, Information and Culture Service, Bodlondeb, Conwy LL32 8DU
☎(01492) 576140
Fax (01492) 592061
e-mail: llyfr.lib.pencadlys.hq@conwy.gov.uk
url: www.conwy.gov.uk/library
Head of Service Ms Rona Aldrich MLib MCLIP (e-mail: rona.aldrich@conwy.gov.uk)
Principal Librarian Ms Rhian G Williams BA DipLib MCLIP (01492 576139; e-mail:
rhian.williams@conwy.gov.uk)

Corporate Information Manager David J Smith BA(Hons) DMS MCLIP MCMI (01492 576137; e-mail: david.smith@conwy.gov.uk)

Regional/community libraries
▶ Abergele Library, Market Street, Abergele, Abergele, Conwy LL22 7BP
☎(01745) 832638
Fax (01745) 823376
e-mail: llyfr.lib.abergele@conwy.gov.uk
▶ Colwyn Bay Library, Woodland Road West, Colwyn Bay, Conwy LL29 7DH
☎(01492) 532358
Fax (01492) 534474
e-mail: llyfr.lib.baecolwynbay@conwy.gov.uk
▶ Conwy Library, Civic Hall, Castle Street, Conwy LL32 6AY
☎(01492) 596242
Fax (01492) 582359
e-mail: llyfr.lib.conwy@conwy.gov.uk
▶ Llandudno Library, Mostyn Street, Llandudno, Conwy LL30 2RP
☎(01492) 574010/574020
Fax (01492) 876826
e-mail: llyfr.lib.llandudno@conwy.gov.uk
▶ Llanrwst Library, Plas yn Dre, Station Road, Llanrwst, Conwy LL26 0DF
☎(01492) 640043
Fax (01492) 642316
e-mail: llyfr.lib.llanrwst@conwy.gov.uk

DENBIGHSHIRE

Authority: Denbighshire County Council
HQ Library and Information Service, Directorate of Lifelong Learning, Yr Hen Garchar, Clwyd Street, Ruthin, Denbighshire LL15 1HP
☎(01824) 708205 (enquiries)
Fax (01824) 708202
url: www.denbighshire.gov.uk/libraries
Assistant Director, Culture and Leisure Dr Ann Gosse (01824 708200; e-mail: ann.gosse@denbighshire.gov.uk)
Principal Librarian Robat Arwyn Jones BMus MCLIP DipLib (01824 708203; e-mail: arwyn.jones@denbighshire.gov.uk)

Central/largest library
Rhyl Library, Museum and Arts Centre, Church Street, Rhyl, Denbighshire LL18 3AA
☎(01745) 353814
Fax (01745) 331438
e-mail: rhyl.library@denbighshire.gov.uk
Principal Community Librarian Alastair Barber BSc DipLib MCLIP

FLINTSHIRE

Authority: Flintshire County Council
HQ Library and Information Service, Library Headquarters, County Hall, Mold, Flintshire CH7 6NW
☎(01352) 704400
Fax (01352) 753662
e-mail: libraries@flintshire.gov.uk
url: www.flintshire.gov.uk
Head of Libraries, Culture and Heritage L Rawsthorne MLib FCLIP MIMgt
Principal Librarian, Community Libraries and Arts Mrs S Kirby MCLIP (01352 704402)
Senior Information Librarian Mrs G Fraser BA MCLIP (01352 704416)

Group libraries

▶ Broughton Library, Broughton Hall Road, Broughton, Nr Chester, Flintshire CH4 0QQ
   ☎(01244) 533727
   Community Librarian Miss Kathleen Morris BA DipLib MCLIP
▶ Buckley Library, Museum and Gallery, The Precinct, Buckley, Flintshire CH7 2EF
   ☎(01244) 549210
   Fax (01244) 548850
   Community Librarian Mrs Penelope Corbett MLib MCLIP
▶ Connah's Quay Library, Wepre Drive, Connah's Quay, Deeside, Flintshire CH5 4HA
   ☎(01244) 830485
   Fax (01244) 856672
   Community Librarian Mrs Carol A Guy BA MCLIP
▶ Flint Library, Church Street, Flint, Flintshire CH6 5AP
   ☎(01352) 703737
   Fax (01352) 731010
   Community Librarian Mrs Elizabeth A Martin BLib MCLIP
▶ Holywell Library, North Road, Holywell, Flintshire CH8 7TQ
   ☎(01352) 713157
   Fax (01352) 710744
   Community Librarian Mrs Catherine E Barber MCLIP, Mrs Morwenna Wallbank MCLIP
▶ Mold Library, Museum and Gallery, Earl Road, Mold, Flintshire CH7 1AP
   ☎(01352) 754791
   Fax (01352) 754655
   Community Librarian Miss Nia W Jones BLib MCLIP

GWYNEDD

Authority: Gwynedd Council
HQ Council Offices, Caernarfon, Gwynedd LL55 1SH
☎(01286) 679504
Fax (01286) 677347
e-mail: llyfrgell@gwynedd.gov.uk
url: www.gwynedd.gov.uk/library
Principal Librarian Hywel James BA DipLib MCLIP

Central/largest library

Caernarfon Library, Pavilion Hill, Caernarfon, Gwynedd LL55 1AS
☎(01286) 679463
Fax (01286) 671137
e-mail: llyfrgellcaernarfon@gwynedd.gov.uk
Community Librarian Mrs Eirlys Thomas MCLIP

Community libraries

▶ Bangor Library, Ffordd Gwynedd, Bangor, Gwynedd LL57 1DT
☎(01248) 353479
Fax (01248) 370149
e-mail: llyfrgellbangor@gwynedd.gov.uk
Community Librarian Ms Rhiannon Clifford Jones MCLIP
▶ Dolgellau Library, Ffordd y Bala, Dolgellau, Gwynedd LL40 2YF
☎(01341) 422771
Fax (01341) 423560
e-mail: llyfrgelldolgellau@gwynedd.gov.uk
Community Librarian Elwyn Evans MCLIP
▶ Porthmadog Library, Stryd Wesla, Porthmadog, Gwynedd LL49 9BT
☎(01766) 514091
Fax (01766) 513821
e-mail: llyfrgellporthmadog@gwynedd.gov.uk
Community Librarian Ms Anna Yardley Jones BA DipLib MCLIP

MERTHYR TYDFIL

Authority: Merthyr Tydfil County Borough Council
HQ Central Library, High Street, Merthyr Tydfil CF47 8AF
☎(01685) 723057
Fax (01685) 370690
e-mail: library.services@merthyr.gov.uk
url: www.merthyr.gov.uk
Head of Libraries Geraint James BA MCLIP

Area libraries

▶ Dowlais Library, Church Street, Merthyr Tydfil CF48 3HS
☎(01685) 723051
Fax (01685) 723051
(Enquiries to Central Library)
▶ Treharris Library, Perrott Street, Treharris, Merthyr Tydfil CF46 5ET
☎(01443) 410517
Fax (01443) 410675
(Enquiries to Central Library)

MONMOUTHSHIRE

Authority: Monmouthshire County Council
HQ Libraries and Information Service, Chepstow Library, Manor Way, Chepstow,

Monmouthshire NP16 5HZ
☎(01291) 635731 (enquiries), 01291 635649 (administration)
Fax (01291) 635736
url: http://libraries.monmouthshire.gov.uk
Principal Librarian Mrs Ann Jones MLib MCLIP (e-mail:
annjones@monmouthshire.gov.uk)

Area libraries

Bryn-a-Cwm Area
▶ Abergavenny Library, Baker Street, Abergavenny, Monmouthshire NP7 5BD
☎(01873) 735980
Fax (01873) 735985
e-mail: abergavennylibrary@monmouthshire.gov.uk
Community Library Managers Mrs Julia Greenway MCLIP, Mrs Alison Newsam BA
DipLIS MCLIP

Central Monmouthshire Area
▶ Monmouth Library, Rolls Hall, Whitecross Street, Monmouth NP25 3BY
☎(01600) 775215
Fax (01600) 775218
e-mail: monmouthlibrary@monmouthshire.gov.uk
Community Library Manager Mrs Vivienne Thomas BA BD MCLIP

Lower Wye Area
▶ Chepstow Library, Manor Way, Chepstow, Monmouthshire NP16 5HZ
☎(01291) 635730
Fax (01291) 635736
e-mail: chepstowlibrary@monmouthshire.gov.uk
Community Library Manager Mrs Margaret Stimson

Severnside Area
▶ Caldicot Library, Woodstock Way, Caldicot, Monmouthshire NP26 4DB
☎(01291) 426425
Fax (01291) 426426
e-mail: caldicotlibrary@monmouthshire.gov.uk
Community Library Managers Dr Kay Flatten BSc MSc PED MCLIP, Richard Skinner
MCLIP

NEATH PORT TALBOT

Authority: Neath Port Talbot County Borough Council
HQ Library and Information Services, Reginald Street, Velindre, Port Talbot SA13 1YY
☎(01639) 899829
Fax (01639) 899152
e-mail: npt.libhq@npt.gov.uk
url: www.npt.gov.uk
Cultural Services Co-ordinator J L Ellis BA MCLIP (e-mail: j.l.ellis@npt.gov.uk)

Central/largest libraries

Neath Library, Victoria Gardens, Neath, Neath Port Talbot SA11 3BA
☎(01639) 644604/635017
Fax (01639) 641912
e-mail: neath.library@npt.gov.uk
Branch Library Manager Wayne John MCLIP (e-mail: w.john@npt.gov.uk)

Port Talbot Library, Aberavon Shopping Centre (1st Floor), Port Talbot SA13 1PB
☎(01639) 763490/1
Fax (01639) 763489
e-mail: porttalbot.library@npt.gov.uk

NEWPORT

Authority: Newport City Council
HQ Community Learning and Libraries Service, Central Library, John Frost Square, Newport, Gwent NP20 1PA
☎(01633) 656656 (enquiries and administration)
Fax (01633) 222615
e-mail: central.library@newport.gov.uk
url: www.newport.gov.uk/libraries
Community Learning and Libraries Manager Mrs Gill John MBA MCLIP

PEMBROKESHIRE

Authority: Pembrokeshire County Council
HQ County Library, Dew Street, Haverfordwest, Pembrokeshire SA61 1SU
☎(01437) 775244 (enquiries), (01437) 775241 (administration)
Fax (01437) 767092
url: www.pembrokeshire.gov.uk
Cultural Services Manager Neil Bennett BSc DMS MCLIP (01437 775240; e-mail: neil.bennett@pembrokeshire.gov.uk)
Group Librarian, Central Mrs Sandra Matthews MCLIP (01437 775242; e-mail: sandra.matthews@pembrokeshire.gov.uk)
Group Librarian, Haven Clive Richards MCLIP (01646 692892; e-mail: clive.richards@pembrokeshire.gov.uk)
Group Librarian, North Mrs Anita Thomas MCLIP (01348 875464; e-mail: anita.thomas@pembrokeshire.gov.uk)
Group Librarian, East Mrs Eleri Evans MCLIP (01834 861781; e-mail: eleri.evans@pembrokeshire.gov.uk)
Support Librarian, Central George Edwards MCLIP (01437 775243; e-mail: george.edwards@pembrokeshire.gov.uk)
Support Librarian, Reference & Local Studies Ms Sue Armour MCLIP (01437 775245; e-mail: sue.armour@pembrokeshire.gov.uk)

Community libraries

▶ Fishguard Library, High Street, Fishguard, Pembrokeshire SA65 9AR
☎(01348) 872694 (tel/fax)

Support Librarian Ms Wendy Davies
▶ Haverfordwest Library, Dew Street, Haverfordwest, Pembrokeshire SA61 1SU
☎(01437) 775244
Senior Library Assistant Mrs Annabel Haywood
▶ Milford Haven Library, Hamilton Terrace, Milford Haven, Pembrokeshire SA73 3HP
☎(01646) 692892 (tel/fax)
Group Librarian, Haven Clive Richards MCLIP (e-mail:
clive.richards@pembrokeshire.gov.uk)
▶ Pembroke Dock Library, Water Street, Pembroke Dock, Pembrokeshire SA72 6DW
☎(01646) 686356
Fax (01646) 687071
Support Librarian Ms Gill Gilliland (e-mail: gill.gilliland@pembrokeshire.gov.uk)
▶ Tenby Library, Green Hill Avenue, Tenby, Pembrokeshire SA70 7LB
☎(01834) 843934 (tel/fax)
Senior Library Assistant Mrs Julie Sutcliffe

POWYS

Authority: Powys County Council
HQ County Library HQ, Cefnllys Road, Llandrindod Wells, Powys LD1 5LD
☎(01597) 826860 (general enquiries)
Fax (01597) 826872
url: www.powys.gov.uk
County Librarian Miss Tudfil L Adams BA MCLIP

Management/Administrative Centre, Children, Families and Lifelong Learning Directorate,
County Hall, Llandrindod Wells, Powys LD1 5LG
☎(01597) 826105
Fax (01597) 826243
Principal Librarian (Field Services) Mrs Helen Edwards BLib MCLIP
Principal Librarian (Education, Schools and Children) Mrs Dianne Jones MCLIP

Main libraries
▶ Brecon Library, Ship Street, Brecon, Powys LD3 9AE
☎(01874) 623346
Fax (01874) 622818
Group Librarian Ms Deborah Cogger MCLIP
▶ Llandrindod Wells Library, Cefnllys Lane, Llandrindod Wells, Powys LD1 5LD
☎(01597) 826870
Fax (01597) 826872
Group Librarian Miss Rebecca Lewis
▶ Newtown Library, Park Lane, Newtown, Powys SY16 1EJ
☎(01686) 626934
Fax (01686) 624935
Group Librarian Gareth Griffiths BA MCLIP

RHONDDA CYNON TAFF

Authority: Rhondda Cynon Taff County Borough Council
HQ Education Department, Ty Trevithick, Abercynon, Mountain Ash, Rhondda Cynon Taff
CF45 4UQ
☎(01443) 744029
Fax (01443) 744023
url: www.rhondda-cynon-taff.gov.uk
Head of Libraries and Museums Ms Gill Evans BA DipLib MCLIP (01443 744023;
e-mail: Gillian.M.Evans@rhondda-cynon-taff.gov.uk)
Information Services Development Librarian Leon Hughes (01443 778951;
e-mail: Leon.J.Hughes@rhondda-cynon-taff.gov.uk) (based at Treorchy Library)
Principal Librarian (Reader Services) Mrs Norma Jones MSc MCLIP (01685 880060;
e-mail: Norma.D.Jones@rhondda-cynon-taff.gov.uk) (based at Aberdare Library)
Area Librarian (North) Mrs Ros Williams MSc MCLIP (01443 778952; e-mail:
Ros.Williams@rhondda-cynon-taff.gov.uk) (based at Treorchy Library)
Area Librarian (South) Mrs Lindsay Morris BA MCLIP (01443 492138; e-mail:
Lindsay.M.Morris@rhondda-cynon-taff.gov.uk) (based at Pontypridd Library)

Largest library

Aberdare Library, Green Street, Aberdare, Rhondda Cynon Taff CF44 7AG
☎(01685) 885318
Fax (01685) 881188
Branch Librarian Ms Catherine Langdon BA MCLIP

Regional libraries

▶ Pontypridd Library, Library Road, Pontypridd, Rhondda Cynon Taff CF37 2DY
☎(01443) 486850
Fax (01443) 493258
Branch Librarian Ms Linda Jones MCLIP, Mrs Edwina Smart BA MCLIP(job-share)
▶ Treorchy Library, Station Road, Treorchy, Rhondda Cynon Taff CF42 6NN
☎(01443) 773204
Fax (01443) 777047
Branch Librarian Dean Price BSc(Econ)

SWANSEA

Authority: City and County of Swansea
HQ Library HQ, County Hall, Oystermouth Road, Swansea SA1 3SN
☎(01792) 636430
Fax (01792) 636235
e-mail: swansea.libraries@swansea.gov.uk
url: www.swansea.gov.uk/libraries
Head of Libraries and Lifelong Learning Peter Gaw BA MCLIP (01792 636656; e-mail:
peter.gaw@swansea.gov.uk)
Assistant Head of Libraries Ms Karen Bewen-Chappell MCLIP (01792 636809; e-mail:
karen.bewen-chappell@swansea.gov.uk), Ms Caroline Tomlin MCLIP (e-mail:
caroline.tomlin@swansea.gov.uk)

Senior Manager: Resources Mrs Julie Clement BLib MCLIP (01792 636628; e-mail: julie.clement@swansea.gov.uk)
Senior Manager: Customer Services Mrs Jayne James BA DipLib MCLIP (01792 636938; e-mail: jayne.james@swansea.gov.uk)
Senior Manager: Information and Learning Ms Glynis James (01792 637220; e-mail: glynis.james@swansea.gov.uk)
Senior Manager: Development and Support Ms Rebecca Williams MA/MSc ILM (DL) (01792 637132; e-mail: rebecca.williams@swansea.gov.uk)

Central/largest library

Swansea Library, Alexandra Road, Swansea SA1 5DX
☎(01792) 516750/516751
Fax (01792) 516759
e-mail: central.library@swansea.gov.uk
Library Manager Chris Burton
Knowledge Team Leader Ms Marilyn Jones

Branch libraries

▶ Gorseinon Library, 15 West Street, Gorseinon, Swansea SA4 4AA
  ☎(01792) 516780
  Fax (01792) 516772
  e-mail: gorseinon.library@swansea.gov.uk
  Library Manager Mrs Carole Bonham
▶ Morriston Library, Treharne Road, Morriston, Swansea SA6 7AA
  ☎(01792) 516770
  Fax (01792) 516771
  e-mail: morriston.library@swansea.gov.uk
  Library Manager Peter Matthews
▶ Oystermouth Library, Dunns Lane, Mumbles, Swansea SA3 4AA
  ☎(01792) 368380
  Fax (01792) 369143
  e-mail: oystermouth.library@swansea.gov.uk
  Library Manager Miss Vicky Blewett

TORFAEN

Authority: Torfaen County Borough Council
HQ Torfaen Libraries HQ, Civic Centre, Pontypool, Torfaen, Gwent NP4 6YB
☎(01633) 628941
Fax (01633) 628935
url: www.torfaen.gov.uk
Cultural Services Manager Ms Sue Johnson MCLIP (e-mail: sue.johnson@torfaen.gov.uk)
Principal Librarian Mrs Christine George BA DipLib MCLIP

Central/largest library

Cwmbran Library, Gwent House, Cwmbran, Torfaen, Gwent NP44 1XQ
☎(01633) 483240
Fax (01633) 838609

e-mail: cwmbranlibrary@torfaen.gov.uk
Senior Librarian Ms Sandra Miller MCLIP

Group library

▶ Pontypool Library, Hanbury Road, Pontypool, Torfaen, Gwent NP4 6JL
☎(01495) 762820
Fax (01495) 752530
e-mail: pontypoollibrary@torfaen.gov.uk
Senior Librarian Mark Tanner BA DipLib MCLIP

VALE OF GLAMORGAN

Authority: Vale of Glamorgan Council
HQ Directorate of Learning and Development, Civic Offices, Holton Road, Barry, Vale of Glamorgan CF63 4RU
☎(01446) 709381
url: www.valeofglamorgan.gov.uk/libraries
Chief Librarian Ms Sian E Jones BSc(Econ) MSc(Econ) MCLIP (e-mail: sjones@valeofglamorgan.gov.uk)
Principal Librarian Christopher Edwards BA DipLib MCLIP (e-mail: cdedwards@valeofglamorgan.gov.uk)

Central/largest library

Barry Library, Leisure Centre, Greenwood Street, Barry, Vale of Glamorgan CF63 4RW
☎(01446) 735722
Senior Librarian Ms Sandra Wildsmith MCLIP (e-mail: smwildsmith@valeofglamorgan.gov.uk)
Information Librarian Ms Katherine Owen MCLIP (e-mail: kowen@valeofglamorgan.gov.uk)

Main libraries

▶ Cowbridge Library, Old Hall, Cowbridge, Vale of Glamorgan CF7 7AH
☎(01446) 773941
Community Librarian Ms Melanie Weeks (e-mail: mpweeks@valeofglamorgan.gov.uk)
▶ Dinas Powys Library, The Murch, Dinas Powys, Vale of Glamorgan CF64 4QU
☎029 2051 2556
Community Librarian Vacant
▶ Llantwit Major Library, Boverton Road, Llantwit Major, Vale of Glamorgan CF61 9XZ
☎(01446) 792700
Community Librarian Ms Ronni Allen MCLIP (e-mail: rallen@valeofglamorgan.gov.uk)
▶ Penarth Library, Stanwell Road, Penarth, Vale of Glamorgan CF64 2YT
☎029 2070 8438
Senior Librarian Marcus Payne BA DipLib MCLIP (e-mail: mmpayne@valeofglamorgan.gov.uk)

WREXHAM

Authority: Wrexham County Borough Council
HQ Education and Leisure Service, Ty Henblas, Queen's Square, Wrexham LL13 8AZ
☎(01978) 297430
Fax (01978) 297422
url: www.wrexham.gov.uk
Chief Leisure, Libraries and Culture Officer Alan Watkin BA DipLib FCLIP MIM FRSA
Libraries Officer Dylan Hughes BA DipLib MCLIP (01978 297442)

Central/largest library

Wrexham Library, Rhosddu Road, Wrexham LL11 1AU
☎(01978) 292090
Fax (01978) 292611
e-mail: reference.library@wrexham.gov.uk
Community Librarian Hedd ap Emlyn BA DipLib MCLIP

Group/branch libraries

▶ Brynteg Library, Quarry Road, Brynteg, Wrexham LL11 6AB
  ☎(01978) 759523
  Community Librarian Mrs Marina Thomas MCLIP
▶ Rhosllanerchrugog Library, Princes Road, Rhos, Wrexham LL14 1AB
  ☎(01978) 840328
  Community Librarian Miss Ann Hughes MA MCLIP

CROWN DEPENDENCIES

ALDERNEY

HQ Alderney Library, Church Street, Alderney, Channel Islands GY9 3TE
☎(01481) 824178
e-mail: info@alderneylibrary.org
url: www.alderneylibrary.org
Chairman, Alderney Library Committee Mrs Joan Birmingham
(Alderney Library is a voluntary organization)

GUERNSEY

HQ Guille-Allès Library, Market Street, St Peter Port, Guernsey, Channel Islands GYI IHB
☎(01481) 720392
Fax (01481) 712425
e-mail: ga@library.gg
url: www.library.gg
Chief Librarian Miss Maggie Falla BA MA MLib MCLIP (e-mail: maggiefalla@library.gg)

Priaulx Library, Candie Road, St Peter Port, Guernsey, Channel Islands GYI IUG
☎(01481) 721998
Fax (01481) 713 804
e-mail: priaulx.library@gov.gg
url: www.guernseyonthemap.co.uk
Acting Chief Librarian Ms Amanda Bennett MA MCLIP
(The Priaulx Library is a reference and lending library specializing in local history and family history research in the Channel Islands)

ISLE OF MAN

HQ Douglas Borough Library, Henry Bloom Noble Library, 10/12 Victoria Street, Douglas, Isle of Man IMI 2LH
☎(01624) 696461
Fax (01624) 696400
url: www.douglas.org.im
Acting Librarian Ms Susan Caley (e-mail: scaley@douglas.org.im)

Castletown Library, Farrants Way, Castletown, Isle of Man IM9 INR
☎(01624) 829355
e-mail: library@castletown.org.im
Librarian Ms Pauline Cringle

George Herdman Library, Bridson Street, Port Erin, Isle of Man IM9 6AL
☎(01624) 832365
e-mail: gh_library@hotmail.com
Librarian Miss Angela Dryland BSc

Nobles Hall Library (Junior and Mobile), Westmoreland Road, Douglas, Isle of Man IM1 1RL
☎(01624) 673123
Fax (01624) 671043
Librarian (Junior Library) Ms Mary Cousins (e-mail: marycousins.sch@gov.im)
Librarian (Mobile Library) Mrs Sandra Henderson MCLIP
Assistant Librarian Mrs Linda Strickett

Onchan Library, Willow House, 61-69 Main Road, Onchan, Isle of Man IM3 1AJ
☎(01624) 621228
Fax (01624) 663482
e-mail: onchan.library@onchan.org.im
url: www.library.onchan.org.im
Librarian Mrs Pam Hand

Ramsey Town Library, Town Hall, Parliament Square, Ramsey, Isle of Man IM8 1RT
☎(01624) 810146
e-mail: rtc@mcb.net
Librarian Paul Boulton BA

Ward Library, 38 Castle Street, Peel, Isle of Man IM5 1AL
☎(01624) 843533
e-mail: ward_library@hotmail.com
Librarian Mrs Carol Horton

JERSEY

HQ Jersey Library, Halkett Place, St Helier, Jersey, Channel Islands JE2 4WH
☎(01534) 759991 (enquiries), (01534) 759992 (reference), (01534) 759993
(administration)
Fax (01534) 769444
e-mail: library@jsylib.gov.je
url: www.jsylib.gov.je
Chief Librarian Mrs Pat Davis MCLIP

Public Libraries in the Republic of Ireland

CARLOW

Authority: Carlow County Council
HQ Carlow Central Library, Tullow Street, Carlow, Republic of Ireland
☎(00 353 59) 917 0094
Fax (00 353 59) 914 0548
e-mail: library@carlowcoco.ie
url: www.carlow.ie
County Librarian Tom King MA DipLib
Executive Librarian Ms Deirdre Condron BComm DipLib
Assistant Librarian Ms Carmel Flahavan BA(Open) DipLib
Assistant Librarian John Shortall BA MSc(Econ)

CAVAN

Authority: Cavan County Council
HQ Cavan County Library, Farnham Street, Cavan, Republic of Ireland
☎(00 353 49) 433 1799
Fax (00 353 49) 437 1832
e-mail: cavancountylibrary@eircom.net
url: www.cavancoco.ie
County Librarian Ms Josephine Brady BA DLIS
Executive Librarian Tom Sullivan DLIS
Assistant Librarians Mrs Teresa Treacy BA DLIS, Ms Emma Clancy BA DLIS
ICT Officer Brian Connolly

CLARE

Authority: Clare County Council
HQ Clare County Library HQ, Mill Road, Ennis, Co Clare, Republic of Ireland
☎(00 353 65) 684 2461/684 6350
Fax (00 353 65) 684 2462
e-mail: mailbox@clarelibrary.ie
url: www.clarelibrary.ie
County Librarian Noel Crowley FLAI

Central/largest library
De Valera Branch Library, Ennis, Co Clare, Republic of Ireland
☎(00 353 65) 684 6353

Area libraries
▶ Kilfinaghty Library, Church Street, Sixmile Bridge, Co Clare, Republic of Ireland
☎(00 353 61) 369678
▶ Kilrush Library, Kilrush, Co Clare, Republic of Ireland
☎(00 353 65) 905 1504
▶ The Library, The Square, Ennistymon, Co Clare, Republic of Ireland
☎(00 353 65) 707 1245

▶ The Library, Kilnasoolagh Park, Newmarket-on-Fergus, Co Clare, Republic of Ireland
☎(00 353 61) 368411

▶ The Library, The Lock House, Killaloe, Co Clare, Republic of Ireland
☎(00 353 61) 376062

▶ The Library, Ballard Road, Miltown Malbay, Co Clare, Republic of Ireland
☎(00 353 65) 708 4822

▶ Local Studies Centre, The Manse, Harmony Row, Ennis, Co Clare, Republic of Ireland
☎(00 353 65) 684 6271

▶ Sean Lemass Library, Town Centre, Shannon, Co Clare, Republic of Ireland
☎(00 353 61) 364266

▶ Sweeney Memorial Library, O'Connell Street, Kilkee, Co Clare, Republic of Ireland
☎(00 353 65) 905 6034

CORK CITY

Authority: Cork City Council
HQ Cork City Library, Grand Parade, Cork, Republic of Ireland
☎(00 353 21) 492 4900
Fax (00 353 21) 427 5684
e-mail: citylibrary@corkcity.ie
url: www.corkcitylibrary.ie
City Librarian Liam Ronayne BCL DipLib ALAI

Branch libraries

▶ Douglas Library, Village Shopping Centre, Douglas, Cork, Republic of Ireland
☎(00 353 21) 492 4932
Fax (00 353 21) 427 5684
e-mail: douglas_library@corkcity.ie

▶ Hollyhill Library, Shopping Centre, Hollyhill, Cork, Republic of Ireland
☎(00 353 21) 492 4928
Fax (00 353 21) 439 3032
e-mail: hollyhill_library@corkcity.ie

▶ Mayfield Library, Old Youghal Road, Cork, Republic of Ireland
☎(00 353 21) 492 4935
Fax (00 353 21) 427 5684
e-mail: mayfield_library@corkcity.ie

▶ St Mary's Road Library, Cork, Republic of Ireland
☎(00 353 21) 492 4933
Fax (00 353 21) 427 5684
e-mail: stmarys_library@corkcity.ie

▶ Tory Top Road Library, Ballyphehane, Cork, Republic of Ireland
☎(00 353 21) 492 4934
Fax (00 353 21) 427 5684
e-mail: torytop_library@corkcity.ie

CORK COUNTY

Authority: Cork County Council
HQ Cork County Library, Model Business Park, Model Farm Road, Cork, Republic of Ireland
☎(00 353 21) 454 6499
Fax (00 353 21) 434 3254
e-mail: corkcountylibrary@corkcoco.ie
url: www.corkcoco.ie
County Librarian Ms Ruth Flanagan BA DipLib ALAI

DONEGAL

Authority: Donegal County Council
HQ Donegal County Library Admin. Centre, Rosemount, Letterkenny, Co Donegal, Republic of Ireland
☎(00 353 74) 912 1968 (enquiries and administration)
Fax (00 353 74) 912 1740
e-mail: library@donegalcoco.ie
url: www.donegallibrary.ie
County Librarian and Divisional Manager, Cultural Services Ms Eileen Burgess

Central/largest library

Central Library & Arts Centre, Oliver Plunkett Road, Letterkenny, Co Donegal, Republic of Ireland
☎(00 353 74) 912 4950
Fax (00 353 74) 912 4950
e-mail: central@donegallibrary.ie
Assistant Librarian Ms Maureen Kerr

DUBLIN

Authority: Dublin City Council
HQ Dublin City Public Libraries, Dublin City Council Library and Archive, 138–144 Pearse Street, Dublin 2, Republic of Ireland
☎(00 353 1) 674 4800
Fax (00 353 1) 674 4880
e-mail: dublinpubliclibraries@dublincity.ie
url: www.dublincity.ie
City Librarian and Director Ms Deirdre Ellis-King BA DipLib ALAI MPhil
Deputy City Librarian Ms Margaret Hayes BA DipLib HDipEd ALAI

Central/largest library

Central Public Library, ILAC Centre, Henry Street, Dublin 1, Republic of Ireland
☎(00 353 1) 873 4333
Fax (00 353 1) 872 1451
e-mail: central.library@dublincity.ie

DÚN LAOGHAIRE–RATHDOWN

Authority: Dún Laoghaire–Rathdown County Council
HQ Public Library Service, Duncairn House, 14 Carysfort Avenue (First Floor), Blackrock, Co Dublin, Republic of Ireland
☎(00 353 1) 278 1788
Fax (00 353 1) 278 1792
e-mail: libraries@dlrcoco.ie
url: www.dlrcoco.ie/library
County Librarian Muiris Ó Raghaill BSc(Econ) MCLIP
Senior Librarian, Bibliographic Services Ms Orla Gallagher BSocSc DLT
Senior Librarian, Administration, Staff and Policy Co-ordination Ms Mairead Owens BA DLIS
Senior Librarian (ICT) Ms Monica Boyle BSocSc(InfStud) MA (LocGvtMgt)
Senior Librarian, Culture Ms Marian Keyes BA MA DLIS
Librarian, Staff and Interlibrary loans Ms Audrey Geraghty BA DLIS
Librarian, Finance Ms Anne Millane BA DLIS
Librarian, Cataloguing Pat Walsh BA HDipEd DLIS

Branch libraries

▶ Blackrock Library, Main Street, Blackrock, Co Dublin, Republic of Ireland
☎(00 353 1) 288 8117
Librarian Ms Detta O'Connor BA HDipEd DLIS
▶ Cabinteely Library, Old Bray Road, Cabinteely, Dublin 18, Republic of Ireland
☎(00 353 1) 285 5363
Librarian Ms Susan Lynch BA DLIS
Librarian Ms Eithne Prout BA DLIS
▶ Dalkey Library, Castle Street, Dalkey, Co Dublin, Republic of Ireland
☎(00 353 1) 285 5277
Librarian Ms Oonagh Brennan BA DLIS
▶ Deansgrange Library, Clonkeen Drive, Deansgrange, Dublin 18, Republic of Ireland
☎(00 353 1) 285 0860
Senior Librarian Ms Kathleen Guinan BA DLIS
Librarian Ms Patricia Corish BA DLIS
▶ Dun Laoghaire Library, Lower George's Street, Dun Laoghaire, Co Dublin, Republic of Ireland
☎(00 353 1) 280 1147
Librarian Ms Susan Lynch BA DLIS
▶ Dundrum Library, Upper Churchtown Road, Dublin 14, Republic of Ireland
☎(00 353 1) 298 5000
Senior Librarian Tony Curran BA DLIS
Librarian Ms Geraldine McHugh MA DLIS ALAI
▶ Sallynoggin Library, Senior College, Sallynoggin, Co Dublin, Republic of Ireland
☎(00 353 1) 285 0127
Librarian Nigel Curtin BA DLIS
▶ Shankill Library, Library Road, Shankill, Co Dublin, Republic of Ireland
☎(00 353 1) 282 3081
Librarian Ms Ciara Jones BA DLIS

▶ Stillorgan Library, St Laurence's Park, Stillorgan, Co Dublin, Republic of Ireland
☎(00 353 1) 288 9655
Senior Librarian D Griffin BA DLT
Librarian Ms Frances Fox BSocSc(InfStud)

FINGAL

Authority: Fingal County Council
HQ Fingal County Libraries, Lower Ground Floor, County Hall, Swords, Co Dublin,
Republic of Ireland
☎(00 353 1) 890 5524
Fax (00 353 1) 890 5599
e-mail: libraries@fingalcoco.ie
url: www.fingalcoco.ie
County Librarian Paul Harris DLIS ALAI
Senior Librarian (Personnel & Finance) Ms Phyllis Carter
Senior Librarian (Circulations & Acquisitions) Ms Rina Mullet

Central/largest library
Blanchardstown Library, Civic Centre, Blanchardstown Centre, Dublin 15, Republic of
Ireland
☎(00 353 1) 890 5560
Fax (00 353 1) 890 5571
e-mail: blanchlib@fingalcoco.ie
Senior Librarians Ms Evelyn Conway (Children's), Ms Marion Coakley (Adult Lending),
Ms Anne Finn (Reference & Research)

Branch libraries
▶ Balbriggan Library, St George's Square, Balbriggan, Co Dublin, Republic of Ireland
☎(00 353 1) 841 1128
Fax (00 353 1) 841 2101
e-mail: balbrigganlibrary@fingalcoco.ie
Senior Librarian Jim Walsh
▶ County Archives, 11 Parnell Square, Dublin 1, Republic of Ireland
☎(00 353 1) 872 7968
Fax (00 353 1) 878 6919
Archivist Colm McQuinn (e-mail: colmmcquinn@fingalcoco.ie)
▶ Housebound Services, Unit 34, Coolmine Industrial Estate, Coolmine, Dublin 15,
Republic of Ireland
☎(00 353 1) 860 4290
Fax (00 353 1) 822 1568
Librarian Ms Josephine Knight (e-mail: josephine.knight@fingalcoco.ie)
▶ Howth Library, Main Street, Howth, Co Dublin, Republic of Ireland
☎(00 353 1) 832 2130
Fax (00 353 1) 832 2277
e-mail: howthlibrary@fingalcoco.ie
Librarian Ms Helen Hughes
▶ Local Studies, 11 Parnell Square, Dublin 1, Republic of Ireland

☎(00 353 1) 878 6910
Fax (00 353 1) 878 6919
e-mail: localstudies@fingalcoco.ie
Librarian Jeremy Black
▶ Malahide Library, Main Street, Malahide, Co Dublin, Republic of Ireland
☎(00 353 1) 845 2026
Fax (00 353 1) 845 2199
e-mail: malahidelibrary@fingalcoco.ie
Senior Librarian Ms Marjory Sliney
▶ Mobile Library Services, Unit 34, Coolmine Industrial Estate, Coolmine, Dublin 15, Republic of Ireland
☎(00 353 1) 822 1564
Fax (00 353 1) 822 1568
e-mail: coolminelibrary@fingalcoco.ie
Senior Librarian Dermot Bregazzi (e-mail: dermot.bregazzi@fingalcoco.ie)
▶ Skerries Library, Strand Street, Skerries, Co Dublin, Republic of Ireland
☎(00 353 1) 849 1900
Fax (00 353 1) 849 5142
e-mail: skerrieslibrary@fingalcoco.ie
Librarian Ms Geraldine Bollard
▶ Swords Library, Swords Shopping Centre, Rathbeale Road, Swords, Co Dublin, Republic of Ireland
☎(00 353 1) 840 4179
Fax (00 353 1) 840 4417
e-mail: swordslibrary@fingalcoco.ie
Senior Librarian Ms Yvonne Reilly (e-mail: yvonne.reilly@fingalcoco.ie)

GALWAY

Authority: Galway County Council
HQ Galway County Library HQ, Island House, Cathedral Square, Galway, Republic of Ireland
☎(00 353 91) 562471
Fax (00 353 91) 565039
e-mail: info@galwaylibrary.ie
url: www.galwaylibrary.ie
County Librarian Pat McMahon DipLib
Deputy Librarian Ms Maureen Moran
Librarian, Branch System Peter Rabbitt
Librarian, ICT John Fitzgibbon

Central/largest library
Galway City Library, Hynes Building, St Augustine Street, Galway, Republic of Ireland
☎(00 353 91) 561666
Executive Librarian, Galway City Services Mrs Bernie Kelly BA DipLib
Assistant Librarian Mrs Josephine Vahey

Branch libraries

▶ Public Library, Athenry, Co Galway, Republic of Ireland
Branch Librarian Ms Imelda Hussey

▶ Public Library, Fairgreen, Ballinasloe, Co Galway, Republic of Ireland
☎(00 353 905) 43464
Assistant Librarian Mrs Mary Dillon

▶ Public Library, Clifden, Co Galway, Republic of Ireland
☎(00 353 95) 21092
Senior Library Assistant Paul Keogh

▶ Public Library, Gort, Co Galway, Republic of Ireland
Branch Librarian Mrs Jo Hickey

▶ Public Library, Loughrea, Co Galway, Republic of Ireland
Senior Library Assistant Ms Anne Callanan

▶ Public Library, Oranmore, Co Galway, Republic of Ireland
Senior Library Assistant Ms Eileen O'Connor

▶ Public Library, Portumna, Co Galway, Republic of Ireland
☎(00 353 509) 41261
Library Assistant Ms Theresa Tierney

▶ Public Library, Tuam, Co Galway, Republic of Ireland
☎(00 353 93) 24287
Senior Library Assistant Ms Sheila Roche

KERRY

Authority: Kerry County Council
HQ Kerry County Library, Moyderwell, Tralee, Co Kerry, Republic of Ireland
☎(00 353 66) 712 1200
Fax (00 353 66) 712 9202
e-mail: info@kerrycolib.ie
url: www.kerrycolib.ie
Chief Librarian Mrs Kathleen Browne FLAI

Area libraries

▶ Ballybunion Branch Library, Ballybunion, Co Kerry, Republic of Ireland
☎(00 353 68) 27615
e-mail: ballybunion@kerrycolib.ie

▶ Caherciveen Branch Library, Caherciveen, Co Kerry, Republic of Ireland
☎(00 353 66) 947 2287
e-mail: caherciveen@kerrycolib.ie

▶ Castleisland Branch Library, Castleisland, Co Kerry, Republic of Ireland
☎(00 353 66) 714 1485
e-mail: castleisland@kerrycolib.ie

▶ Dingle Branch Library, Dingle, Co Kerry, Republic of Ireland
☎(00 353 66) 915 1499
e-mail: dingle@kerrycolib.ie

▶ Kenmare Branch Library, Kenmare, Co Kerry, Republic of Ireland
☎(00 353 64) 41416
e-mail: kenmare@kerrycolib.ie

▶ Killarney Branch Library, Killarney, Co Kerry, Republic of Ireland
☎(00 353 64) 32655
Fax (00 353 64) 36065
e-mail: killarney@kerrycolib.ie

▶ Killorglin Branch Library, Killorglin, Co Kerry, Republic of Ireland
☎(00 353 66) 976 1272
e-mail: killorglin@kerrycolib.ie

▶ Listowel Branch Library, Listowel, Co Kerry, Republic of Ireland
☎(00 353 68) 23044
e-mail: listowel@kerrycolib.ie

▶ Mobile Library Services
Contact details as HQ above

KILDARE

Authority: Kildare County Council
HQ Kildare County Library Service, Riverbank Arts Centre, Main Street, Newbridge, Co Kildare, Republic of Ireland
☎(00 353 45) 431109/431486 (enquiries)
Fax (00 353 45) 432490
e-mail: colibrary@kildarecoco.ie
url: www.kildare.ie
County Librarian Ms Breda Gleeson

Main branch libraries

▶ Community Library, Town Hall, Athy, Co Kildare, Republic of Ireland
☎(00 353 45) 863 1144
Fax (00 353 45) 863 1809
Librarian in charge Ms Nuala Hartnett

▶ Branch Library, St Patrick's Park, Celbridge, Co Kildare, Republic of Ireland
☎(00 353 1) 627 2207
Librarian in charge Ms Aisling Donnelly

▶ Branch Library, Newtown House, Leixlip, Co Kildare, Republic of Ireland
☎(00 353 1) 624 4240
Librarian in charge Ms Anne Myler
(This library is currently closed. New building under construction)

▶ Branch Library, Main Street, Maynooth, Co Kildare, Republic of Ireland
☎(00 353 1) 628 5530
Librarians in charge Ms Lorraine Daly, Ms June Branigan

▶ Branch Library, Canal Harbour, Naas, Co Kildare, Republic of Ireland
☎(00 353 45) 879111
Fax (00 353 45) 881766
Librarian in charge Ms Eimear McGinn

▶ Branch Library, Athgarvan Road, Newbridge, Co Kildare, Republic of Ireland
☎(00 353 45) 436453
Librarian in charge Ms Mary Coughlan

KILKENNY

Authority: Kilkenny County Council
HQ Kilkenny County Library, 6 Rose Inn Street, Kilkenny, Republic of Ireland
☎(00 353 56) 779 4160 (enquiries, local studies and administration)
Fax (00 353 56) 779 4168
e-mail: info@kilkennylibrary.ie
url: www.kilkennylibrary.ie
County Librarian James Fogarty DLIS ALAI (e-mail: jim.fogarty@kilkennylibrary.ie)

Central/largest library

Kilkenny City Library, John's Quay, Kilkenny, Republic of Ireland
☎(00 353 56) 779 4174
e-mail: citylibrary@kilkennylibrary.ie
Senior Library Assistants Ms Catriona Kenneally
Assistant Librarians Declan Macaulay BSc DLIS, Ms Dorothy O'Reilly DLIS ALAI, Ms Brenda Ward BA DLIS

Area libraries

▶ Castlecomer Library, Kilkenny Street, Castlecomer, Co Kilkenny, Republic of Ireland
☎(00 353 56) 444 0561
e-mail: castlecomer@kilkennylibrary.ie
Senior Library Assistant Ms Mary Morrissey
▶ Graiguenamanagh Library, Convent Road, Graiguenamanagh, Co Kilkenny, Republic of Ireland
☎(00 353 56) 779 4178
e-mail: graiguenamanagh@kilkennylibrary.ie
Acting Senior Library Assistant Ms Majella Byrne
▶ Urlingford Library, The Courthouse, Urlingford, Co Kilkenny, Republic of Ireland
☎(00 353 56) 779 4182
e-mail: urlingford@eircom.net
Branch Librarians Ms Helen Muldowney, Ms Annette Purcell

LAOIS

Authority: Laois County Council
HQ Laois County Library, Aras An Chontae, JFL Avenue, Portlaoise, Co Laois, Republic of Ireland
☎(00 353 502) 74315
Fax (00 353 502) 74381
url: www.laois.ie/library
County Librarian G Maher LLB(Hons) DLIS (e-mail: gmaher@laoiscoco.ie)

Central/largest library

Portlaoise Branch Library, Dunamase House, Portlaoise, Co Laois, Republic of Ireland
☎(00 353 502) 22333
Assistant Librarian Walter Lawlor

Branch libraries

▶ Abbeyleix Branch Library, Abbeyleix, Co Laois, Republic of Ireland
☎(00 353 502) 30020
Branch Librarian Ms E Sutton

▶ Clonaslee Branch Library, Clonaslee, Co Laois, Republic of Ireland
☎(00 353 505) 48397
Branch Librarian Ms M Cusack

▶ Mountmellick Branch Library, Mountmellick, Co Laois, Republic of Ireland
☎(00 353 502) 24733
Branch Librarian Ms F Lynch

▶ Mountrath Branch Library, Mountrath, Co Laois, Republic of Ireland
☎(00 353 502) 56046
Branch Librarian Ms J Phelan

▶ Portarlington Branch Library, Portarlington, Co Laois, Republic of Ireland
☎(00 353 502) 43751
Branch Librarian Ms B Doris

▶ Rathdowney Branch Library, Rathdowney, Co Laois, Republic of Ireland
☎(00 353 505) 46852
Branch Librarian Mrs C Fitzpatrick

▶ Stradbally Branch Library, Stradbally, Co Laois, Republic of Ireland
☎(00 353 502) 25005
Branch Librarian Ms P Norton

▶ Timahoe Branch Library, Timahoe, Co Laois, Republic of Ireland
☎(00 353 502) 27231
Branch Librarian Ms M Scully

LEITRIM (LEABHARLANN CHONTAE LIATROMA)

Authority: Leitrim County Council
HQ Leitrim County Library, Main Street, Ballinamore, Co Leitrim, Republic of Ireland
☎(00 353 71) 964 5582
Fax (00 353 71) 964 5572
e-mail: leitrimlibrary@eircom.net
url: www.leitrim.ie
County Librarian Seán Ó Suilleabháin DLT FLAI ALAI

LIMERICK CITY

Authority: Limerick City Council
HQ Limerick City Library, The Granary, Michael Street, Limerick, Republic of Ireland
☎(00 353 61) 407510
Fax (00 353 61) 411506
e-mail: citylib@limerickcity.ie
url: www.limerickcity.ie
City Librarian Ms Dolores Doyle BA FLAI ALAI (e-mail: ddoyle@limerickcity.ie)

LIMERICK COUNTY

Authority: Limerick County Council
HQ Limerick County Library HQ, 58 O'Connell Street, Limerick, Republic of Ireland
☎(00 353 61) 496526 (enquiries and administration)
Fax (00 353 61) 318570
e-mail: colibrar@limerickcoco.ie
Executive Librarian Damien Brady BA DLIS
Executive Librarians Ms Anne Bennett BA DLIS, Ms Helen Walsh DLIS LAI

Central/largest library

Dooradoyle Branch Library, Crescent Shopping Centre, Dooradoyle Road, Limerick,
Republic of Ireland
☎(00 353 61) 301101
Executive Librarian Ms Noreen O'Neill BA DLIS

Branch libraries

▶ Abbeyfeale Branch Library, Bridge Street, Abbeyfeale, Co Limerick, Republic of Ireland
☎(00 353 68) 32488
Senior Library Assistant Mike McInerney
▶ Adare Branch Library, Adare, Co Limerick, Republic of Ireland
☎(00 353 61) 396822
Assistant Librarian Ms Margaret O'Reilly BA DLIS
▶ Foynes Branch Library, Foynes, Co Limerick, Republic of Ireland
☎(00 353 69) 65365
Assistant Librarian Ms Sarah Prendiville DLIS
▶ Newcastlewest Branch Library, Newcastlewest, Co Limerick, Republic of Ireland
☎(00 353 69) 62273
Executive Librarian Ms Aileen Dillane BA DLIS

LONGFORD

Authority: Longford County Council
HQ Longford County Library Arts and Archives Services, Town Centre, Longford, Co
Longford, Republic of Ireland
☎(00 353 43) 41124
Fax (00 353 43) 48576
e-mail: library@longfordcoco.ie
url: www.longfordlibrary.ie
County Librarian Ms Mary Carleton-Reynolds DLIS ALAI

Central/largest library

Longford Library, Town Centre, Longford, Co Longford, Republic of Ireland
☎(00 353 43) 41125
e-mail: longfordlibrary@longfordcoco.ie
Librarian Willie O'Dowd BComm LLB MLIS

Branch libraries

▶ Ballymahon Library, Main Street, Ballymahon, Co Longford, Republic of Ireland
☎(00 353 90) 643 2546
e-mail: ballymahonlibrary@longfordcoco.ie
Branch Librarian Ms Carmel Kelly

▶ Drumlish Library, Drumlish, Co Longford, Republic of Ireland
☎(00 353 43) 24760
e-mail: drumlishlibrary@longfordcoco.ie
Branch Librarian Ms Isabella Mallon

▶ Edgeworthstown Library, Edgeworthstown, Co Longford, Republic of Ireland
☎(00 353 43) 71927
e-mail: edgeworthstownlibrary@longfordcoco.ie
Branch Librarian Ms Sheila Walsh

▶ Granard Library, Granard, Co Longford, Republic of Ireland
☎(00 353 43) 86164
e-mail: granardlibrary@longfordcoco.ie
Branch Librarian Ms Rosemary Gaynor

▶ Lanesboro Library, Lanesboro, Co Longford, Republic of Ireland
☎(00 353 43) 24760
e-mail: lanesborolibrary@longfordcoco.ie
Branch Librarian Ms Stella O'Sullivan

LOUTH

Authority: Louth
HQ Louth County Library, Roden Place, Dundalk, Co Louth, Republic of Ireland
☎(00 353 42) 935 3190
Fax (00 353 42) 933 7635
url: www.louthcoco.ie
County Librarian Miss Ann Ward BA DLT (e-mail: ann.ward@louthcoco.ie)

MAYO

Authority: Mayo County Council
HQ Mayo County Library, Library HQ, Mountain View, Castlebar, Co Mayo, Republic of Ireland
☎(00 353 94) 904 7573 (enquiries and administration)
Fax (00 353 94) 902 4774
url: www.mayolibrary.ie
County Librarian Austin Vaughan BA DLIS (e-mail: avaughan@mayococo.ie)

Central/largest library

Mayo Central Library, The Mall, Castlebar, Co Mayo, Republic of Ireland
☎(00 353 94) 904 7557
Fax (00 353 94) 904 6491
e-mail: avaughan@mayococo.ie

MEATH

Authority: Meath County Council
HQ Meath County Library, Railway Street, Navan, Co Meath, Republic of Ireland
☎(00 353 46) 902 1134; 902 1451
e-mail: colibrar@meathcoco.ie
url: www.meath.ie/library
County Librarian Ciaran Mangan BA MLIS
Executive Librarian Ms Geraldine Donnelly DLIS, Ms Dympna Herward BA DLIS

Branch libraries

▶ Ashbourne Library, 1-2 Killegland Court, Ashbourne, Co Meath, Republic of Ireland
☎(00 353 1) 835 8185
Executive Librarian Ms Mary Murphy
▶ Athboy Library, Main Street, Athboy, Co Meath, Republic of Ireland
☎(00 353 46) 943 2539
Branch Librarian Ms Teresa Doherty
▶ Duleek Library, Main Street, Duleek, Co Meath, Republic of Ireland
☎(00 353 41) 988 0709
Library Assistant Ms Noirin Clarke
▶ Dunboyne Library, Castleview, Dunboyne, Co Meath, Republic of Ireland
☎(00 353 1) 825 1248
Assistant Librarian Tom French BA DLIS
▶ Dunshaughlin Library, Main Street, Dunshaughlin, Co Meath, Republic of Ireland
☎(00 353 1) 825 0504
Senior Library Assistant Vacant
▶ Kells Library, Maudlin Street, Kells, Co Meath, Republic of Ireland
☎(00 353 46) 924 1592
Branch Librarian Ms Rose Grimes
▶ Laytown Library, Laytown, Co Meath, Republic of Ireland
Branch Librarian Ms Iris Cunningham
▶ Nobber Library, Nobber, Co Meath, Republic of Ireland
☎(00 353 46) 905 2732
Branch Librarian Ms Imelda Griffin
▶ Oldcastle Library, Millbrook Road, Oldcastle, Co Meath, Republic of Ireland
☎(00 353 49) 854 2084
Library Assistant Ms Claudine O'Brien
▶ Slane Library, Castle Hill, Slane, Co Meath, Republic of Ireland
☎(00 353 41) 982 4955
Branch Librarian Ms Kathleen Nally
▶ Trim Library, High Street, Trim, Co Meath, Republic of Ireland
☎(00 353 46) 943 6014
Assistant Librarian Ms Maedhbh Rogan

MONAGHAN

Authority: Monaghan County Council
HQ Monaghan County Library, The Diamond, Clones, Co Monaghan, Republic of Ireland

☎(00 353 47) 51143
Fax (00 353 47) 51863
e-mail: moncolib@monaghancoco.ie
url: www.monaghan.ie
County Librarian Joe McElvaney DLIS (e-mail: jmcelvaney@monaghancoco.ie)
Executive Librarian Ms Catherine Elliott BSocSc

Central/largest library
Monaghan Branch Library, North Road, Monaghan Town, Monaghan Town, Republic of Ireland
☎(00 353 47) 81830
e-mail: monaghan@eircom.net
Senior Library Assistant Ms Suzanne Buckley (e-mail: sbuckley@monaghancoco.ie)

Branch libraries
▶ Ballybay Library, Main Street, Ballybay, Co Monaghan, Republic of Ireland
☎(00 353 42) 974 1256
e-mail: ballybaylibrary@eircom.net
Branch Librarian Mrs Rosemary McDonnell
▶ Carrickmacross Branch Library, Market Square, Carrickmacross, Co Monaghan, Republic of Ireland
☎(00 353 42) 966 1148
e-mail: cmxlibrary@eircom.net
Senior Library Assistant Ms Breda Moore (e-mail: bmoore@monaghancoco.ie)
▶ Castleblayney Branch Library, Unit 3, Castleblayney Enterprise Centre, Dublin Road, Castleblayney, Co Monaghan, Republic of Ireland
☎(00 353 42) 974 0281
e-mail: castleblayneylibrary@eircom.net
Branch Librarian Ms Pauline Duffy
▶ Clones Branch Library, The Diamond, Clones, Co Monaghan, Republic of Ireland
☎(00 353 47) 51143
Fax (00 353 47) 51863
Senior Library Assistant Ms Lorna Greenan

OFFALY

Authority: Offaly County Council
HQ Offaly County Library, O'Connor Square, Tullamore, Co Offaly, Republic of Ireland
☎(00 353 506) 46834
Fax (00 353 506) 52769
e-mail: colibrar@offalycoco.ie
url: www.offaly.ie
County Librarian Ms Anne M Coughlan DLT MCLIP
Executive Librarian Diarmaid Bracken BA DLIS

ROSCOMMON

Authority: Roscommon County Council
HQ Roscommon County Library, Abbey Street, Roscommon, Republic of Ireland
☎(00 353 90) 663 7272/7273 (enquiries and administration)
Fax (00 353 90) 663 7101
url: www.roscommoncoco.ie/home.htm
County Librarian Richie Farrell BA DLIS (e-mail: rfarrell@roscommoncoco.ie)

Central/largest library
Roscommon Branch Library, Abbey Street, Roscommon, Republic of Ireland
☎(00 353 90) 663 7277
Fax (00 353 90) 663 7101

Branch libraries
▶ Ballaghaderreen Branch Library, Barrack Street, Ballaghaderreen, Co Roscommon,
Republic of Ireland
☎(00 353 94) 987 7044
e-mail: dbllib@eircom.net
Senior Library Assistant Ms Maureen Moran
▶ Ballyforan Branch Library, Ballyforan, Co Roscommon, Republic of Ireland
Branch Librarian Ms Rebecca Thompson
▶ Boyle Branch Library, The King House, Boyle, Co Roscommon, Republic of Ireland
☎(00 353 71) 966 2800
e-mail: bbllib@eircom.net
Senior Library Assistant Matthew Gammon
▶ Castlerea Branch Library, Main Street, Castelrea, Co Roscommon, Republic of Ireland
☎(00 353 94) 962 0745
e-mail: cbllib@eircom.net
Branch Librarian Ms Maura Carroll
▶ Elphin Branch Library, Main Street, Elphin, Co Roscommon, Republic of Ireland
☎(00 353 71) 963 5775
e-mail: ebllib@eircom.net
Branch Librarian Ms Mary Walsh
▶ Strokestown Branch Library, Elphin Street, Strokestown, Co Roscommon, Republic of
Ireland
☎(00 353 71) 963 4027
e-mail: sbllib@eircom.net
Branch Librarian Ms Moya Lane

SLIGO

Authority: Sligo County Council
HQ Sligo County Library, The Westward Town Centre, Bridge Street, Sligo, Republic of
Ireland
☎(00 353 71) 914 7190
Fax (00 353 71) 914 6798
e-mail: sligolib@sligococo.ie

url: www.sligococo.ie
County Librarian Donal Tinney BA DLIS ALAI
Executive Librarian Ms Pauline Brennan DLIS
Assistant Librarians Patrick Gannon BA DLIS, Fran Hegarty DipLib
Senior Library Assistant Ms Frances Walsh

Central/largest library

Sligo City Library, Stephen Street, Sligo, Republic of Ireland
☎(00 353 71) 914 2212
Fax (00 353 71) 914 6798
Senior Library Assistant Ms Caroline Morgan FLAI

SOUTH DUBLIN

Authority: South Dublin County Council
HQ Unit 1, The Square Industrial Complex, Tallaght, Dublin 24, Republic of Ireland
☎(00 353 1) 459 7834
Fax (00 353 1) 459 7872
e-mail: library@sdublincoco.ie
url: www.sdublincoco.ie
County Librarian Ms Teresa Walsh

Central/largest library

County Library, County Hall, Tallaght, Dublin 24, Republic of Ireland
☎(00 353 1) 462 0073
Fax (00 353 1) 414 9207
e-mail: talib@sdublincoco.ie
Senior Librarian Ms Coleesa Humphries

Branch libraries

▶ Ballyroan Library, Orchardstown Avenue, Rathfarnham, Dublin 14, Republic of Ireland
  ☎(00 353 1) 494 1900
  Fax (00 353 1) 494 7083
  e-mail: ballyroan@sdublincoco.ie
  Senior Librarians Ms Una Phelan, Ms Rosena Hand
▶ Castletymon Library, Castletymon Shopping Centre, Tymon Road North, Tallaght,
  Dublin 24, Republic of Ireland
  ☎(00 353 1) 452 4888
  Fax (00 353 1) 459 7873
  e-mail: castletymon@sdublincoco.ie
  Librarian Ms Ann Dunne
▶ Clondalkin Library, Monastry Road, Clondalkin, Dublin 22, Republic of Ireland
  ☎(00 353 1) 459 3315
  Fax (00 353 1) 459 5509
  e-mail: clondalkin@sdublincoco.ie
  Acting Senior Librarian Vincent Allen
▶ John J Jennings Library, Stewarts Hospital, Palmerstown, Dublin 20, Republic of Ireland
  ☎(00 353 1) 626 4444 (ext 1129)

Fax (00 353 1) 626 1707
e-mail: johnjjlib@eircom.net
Senior Librarian Ms Siobhan O'Neill
▶ Lucan Library, Superquinn Shopping Centre, Newcastle Road, Lucan, Co Dublin, Republic of Ireland
☎(00 353 1) 621 6422
Fax (00 353 1) 621 6433
e-mail: lucan@sdublincoco.ie
Acting Senior Librarian Ms Mary Byron
▶ Mobile Library Service, Unit 1, The Square Industrial Complex, Tallaght, Dublin 24, Republic of Ireland
☎(00 353 1) 459 7834
Fax (00 353 1) 459 7872
e-mail: mobiles@sdublincoco.ie
Senior Librarian Ms Breid Ryan
▶ Whitechurch Library, Taylor's Lane, Rathfarnham, Dublin 16, Republic of Ireland
☎(00 353 1) 493 0199
e-mail: whitechurch@sdublincoco.ie
Branch Librarian Ms Breda Bollard

TIPPERARY

Authority: Tipperary County Council
HQ Tipperary County Library, Castle Avenue, Thurles, Co Tipperary, Republic of Ireland
☎(00 353 504) 21555
Fax (00 353 504) 23442
e-mail: info@tipperarylibraries.ie
url: www.tipperarylibraries.ie
County Librarian Martin Maher

Branch libraries
▶ Borrisokane Library, Main Street, Borrisokane, Co Tipperary, Republic of Ireland
☎(00 353 67) 27199
Branch Librarian Mrs Frankie O'Carroll
▶ Cahir Library, The Square, Cahir, Co Tipperary, Republic of Ireland
☎(00 353 52) 42075
Branch Librarian Mrs Ann Tuohy
▶ Carrick-on-Suir Library, Fair Green, Carrick-on-Suir, Co Tipperary, Republic of Ireland
☎(00 353 51) 640591 (tel/fax)
Senior Library Assistant Oliver Corbett
▶ Cashel Library, Friar Street, Cashel, Co Tipperary, Republic of Ireland
☎(00 353 62) 63825
Fax (00 353 62) 63948
e-mail: cashel@tipperarylibraries.ie
Assistant Librarian Ms Margaret Ryan
▶ Clonmel Library, Emmet Street, Clonmel, Co Tipperary, Republic of Ireland
☎(00 353 52) 24545
Fax (00 353 52) 27336

e-mail: clonmel@tipperarylibraries.ie

Assistant Librarian Mrs Marie Boland

▶ Cloughjordan Library, Main Street, Cloughjordan, Co Tipperary, Republic of Ireland
☎(00 353 505) 42425

Branch Librarian Mrs Marie Brady

▶ Killenaule Library, Bailey Street, Killenaule, Co Tipperary, Republic of Ireland
☎(00 353 52) 56028

Branch Librarian Mrs Rena Lahart

▶ Nenagh Library, O'Rahilly Street, Nenagh, Co Tipperary, Republic of Ireland
☎(00 353 67) 34404
Fax (00 353 67) 34405
e-mail: nenagh@tipperarylibraries.ie

Assistant Librarian Ms Breffni Hannon

▶ Roscrea Library, Birr Road, Roscrea, Co Tipperary, Republic of Ireland
☎(00 353 505) 22032 (tel/fax)

Assistant Librarian Ms Aine Beausang

▶ Templemore Library, Old Mill Court, Templemore, Co Tipperary, Republic of Ireland
☎(00 353 504) 32555/6
Fax (00 353 504) 32545
e-mail: templemore@tipperarylibraries.ie

Senior Library Assistant Pat Bracken

▶ Thurles Library, Castle Avenue, Thurles, Co Tipperary, Republic of Ireland
☎(00 353 504) 20638
Fax (00 353 504) 23442
e-mail: thurles@tipperarylibraries.ie

Senior Library Assistant Ms Gemma Larkin

▶ Tipperary Library, Dan Breen House, Tipperary, Republic of Ireland
☎(00 353 62) 51761 (tel/fax)

Branch Librarian Ms Nollaig Butler, Ms Gerardine Hughes

WATERFORD CITY

Authority: Waterford City Council
HQ Central Library, Lady Lane, Waterford, Republic of Ireland
☎(00 353 51) 849839
Fax (00 353 51) 850031
e-mail: citylibrary@waterfordcity.ie
url: www.waterfordcity.ie/library.htm
City Librarian Ms Jane Cantwell
Acting Executive Librarian Ms Mary Conway
Assistant Librarians Ms Katherine Collins, Ms Melanie Cunningham, Ms Ann Marie Brophy

Central/largest library

Central Library, Lady Lane, Waterford City, Waterford, Republic of Ireland
☎(00 353 51) 849975
Fax (00 353 51) 850031
e-mail: library@waterfordcity.ie
Acting Executive Librarian Ms Mary Conway

Other libraries

▶ Ardkeen Library, Ardkeen Shopping Centre, Dunmore Road, Waterford, Republic of Ireland
☎(00 353 51) 849755
Fax (00 353 51) 874100
e-mail: library@waterfordcity.ie
Assistant Librarian Ms Katherine Collins

▶ Brown's Road Library, Paddy Brown's Road, Waterford, Republic of Ireland
☎(00 353 51) 860845
e-mail: library@waterfordcity.ie

WATERFORD COUNTY

Authority: Waterford County Council
HQ Waterford County Library, West Main Street, Lismore, Co Waterford, Republic of Ireland
☎(00 353 58) 54128/54830
Fax (00 353 58) 54797
e-mail: libraryhq@waterfordcoco.ie
url: www.waterfordcountylibrary.ie
County Librarian Donal Brady (e-mail: dbrady@waterfordcoco.ie)
Assistant Librarian Ger Croughan (e-mail: gcroughan@waterfordcoco.ie)
Systems Administrator Eddie Byrne (e-mail: ebyrne@waterfordcoco.ie)

Central/largest library

Dungarvan Branch Library, Davitt's Quay, Dungarvan, Dungarvan, Co Waterford, Republic of Ireland
☎(00 353 58) 41231
e-mail: dungarvanlibrary@waterfordcoco.ie
Librarian Ms Margaret O'Brien (e-mail: mgtobrien@waterfordcoco.ie)

Area libraries

▶ Cappoquin Branch Library, Cappoquin, Waterford, Republic of Ireland
☎(00 353 58) 52263
e-mail: cappoquinlibrary@waterfordcoco.ie
Branch Librarian Mrs Mary Tobin

▶ Dunmore Branch Library, Dunmore East, Waterford, Republic of Ireland
☎(00 353 51) 383211
e-mail: dunmorelibrary@waterfordcoco.ie
Branch Librarian Ms Claire O Mullain

▶ Kilmacthomas Branch Library, Kilmacthomas, Waterford, Republic of Ireland
☎(00 353 51) 294270
e-mail: kilmacthomaslibrary@waterfordcoco.ie
Branch Librarian Ms Laura Kirwan

▶ Lismore Branch Library, Main Street, Lismore, Waterford, Republic of Ireland
☎(00 353 58) 54128
e-mail: lismorelibrary@waterfordcoco.ie
Branch Librarian Ms Jennifer Nolan

▶ Portlaw Branch Library, The Square, Portlaw, Waterford, Republic of Ireland
☎(00 353 51) 387402
e-mail: portlawlibrary@waterfordcoco.ie
Branch Librarian Ms Loretta Kinsella

▶ Tallow Branch Library, Convent Street, Tallow, Waterford, Republic of Ireland
☎(00 353 58) 56347
e-mail: tallowlibrary@waterfordcoco.ie
Branch Librarian Ms Sheila Curtin

▶ Tramore Branch Library, Market Square, Tramore, Waterford, Republic of Ireland
☎(00 353 51) 381479
e-mail: tramorelibrary@waterfordcoco.ie
Librarian Ms Kate Murphy (e-mail: kmurphy@waterfordcoco.ie)

WESTMEATH

Authority: Westmeath County Council
HQ Westmeath County Library HQ, Dublin Road, Mullingar, Co Westmeath, Republic of Ireland
☎(00 353 44) 40781/2/3 (enquiries and administration)
Fax (00 353 44) 41322
url: www.westmeathcoco.ie/services/library/
County Librarian Miss Mary Farrell BA HDE DLIS ALAI (e-mail:
mfarrell@westmeathcoco.ie)
Executive Librarian Ms Mary Stuart DLIS (e-mail: mstuart@westmeathcoco.ie)

Branch libraries

▶ Castlepollard Library, Civic Offices, Castlepollard, Co Westmeath, Republic of Ireland
☎(00 353 44) 32199
Senior Library Assistant Ms Nicola Brennan-Gavin (e-mail:
ngavin@westmeathcoco.ie)

▶ Eidan Heavey Public Library, Athlone Civic Centre, Church Street, Athlone, Co Westmeath, Republic of Ireland
☎(00 353 90) 644 2157/8/9
e-mail: athlib@eircom.net
Executive Librarian Gearoid O'Brien DLIS FLAI (e-mail: gobrien@westmeathcoco.ie)

▶ Kilbeggan Library, Tullamore Road, Kilbeggan, Co Westmeath, Republic of Ireland
☎(00 353 506) 32001
Branch Librarian Ms Elizabeth Gorman (e-mail: lgorman@westmeathcoco.ie)

▶ Killucan Library, Rathwire Hall, Killucan, Co Westmeath, Republic of Ireland
☎(00 353 44) 74260
Branch Librarian Ms Geraldine Corroon (e-mail: gcorroon@westmeathcoco.ie)

▶ Moate Library, The Courthouse, Main Street, Moate, Co Westmeath, Republic of Ireland
☎(00 353 90) 648 1888 (tel/fax)

▶ Mullingar Library, Church Avenue, Mullingar, Co Westmeath, Republic of Ireland
☎(00 353 44) 48278
Assistant Librarian Tony Cox DLIS (e-mail: tcox@westmeathcoco.ie)

WEXFORD

Authority: Wexford County Council
HQ Library Management Services, The Kent Building, Ardcavan, Co Wexford, Republic of Ireland
☎(00 353 53) 24922/24928
Fax (00 353 53) 21097
e-mail: libraryhq@wexfordcoco.ie
url: www.wexford.ie
County Librarian Ms Fionnuala Hanrahan BA DLIS MLIS MCLIP MCLIPI

Central/largest library

Wexford Town Library, Selskar House, McCauley's Carpark, off Redmond Square, Co Wexford, Republic of Ireland
☎(00 353 53) 21637
Fax (00 353 53) 21639
e-mail: wexfordlib@wexfordcoco.ie
Librarian Ms Susan Kelly BA DLIS

Area libraries

▶ Enniscorthy Branch Library, Lymington Road, Enniscorthy, Co Wexford, Republic of Ireland
☎(00 353 54) 36055
e-mail: enniscorthylib@wexfordcoco.ie
Librarian Ms Clare Kelly BA DLIS
▶ New Ross Branch Library, Barrack Lane, New Ross, Co Wexford, Republic of Ireland
☎(00 353 51) 421877
e-mail: newrosslib@eircom.net
Senior Library Assistant Ms Joan Lambert

WICKLOW

Authority: Wicklow County Council
HQ Wicklow County Library, Library HQ, Boghall Road, Bray, Co Wicklow, Republic of Ireland
☎(00 353 1) 286 6566 (enquiries and administration)
Fax (00 353 1) 286 5811
e-mail: wcclhq@eircom.net
url: www.wicklow.ie
County Librarian Brendan Martin BA DLIS
Executive Librarian (Schools and Outreach) Ms Noelle Murray BA DLIS
Assistant Librarian (IT) Ms Mary O'Driscoll BSocSc DLIS
Executive Librarian (Administration) Ms Carmel Moore DLIS

Largest library

Bray Public Library, Eglinton Road, Bray, Co Wicklow, Republic of Ireland
☎(00 353 1) 286 2600
Branch Librarian Ms Gillean Misstear BA MA

Area libraries

▶ Arklow Public Library, St Mary's Road, Arklow, Co Wicklow, Republic of Ireland
☎(00 353 40) 239977
Senior Library Assistant Ms Pamela Taner

▶ Ballywaltrim Public Library, Boghall Road, Bray, Co Wicklow, Republic of Ireland
☎(00 353 1) 272 3205
Assistant Librarian Ms Mary Murphy

▶ Greystones Public Library, Church Road, Greystones, Co Wicklow, Republic of Ireland
☎(00 353 1) 287 3548
Assistant Librarian Ms Fiona Scannell

▶ Wicklow Public Library, Market Square, Co Wicklow, Republic of Ireland
☎(00 353 40) 467025
Senior Library Assistant Ms Anne Murdiff

Children's, Youth and Schools Library Services in the United Kingdom, the Channel Islands and the Isle of Man

England
Scotland
Wales
Crown Dependencies

For Northern Ireland please see entries under Northern Ireland Education and Library Boards in the Public Libraries section

BARKING AND DAGENHAM

Authority: London Borough of Barking and Dagenham
Barking Central Library, Unit 53, Vicarage Field Shopping Centre, Barking, Essex IG11 8DQ
☎020 8724 1321 (School Library Service 020 8724 1320)
Fax 020 8724 1316
Principal Librarian, Learning and Development Ms Susan Leighton MA MCLIP (e-mail: susan.leighton@lbbd.gov.uk)
Senior Librarian, Young People and Schools Ms Vashti Thorne MCLIP (e-mail: vashti.thorne@lbbd.gov.uk)
(Temporary change of address)

BARNET

Authority: London Borough of Barnet
Cultural Services, North London Business Park, Oakleigh Road South, London N11 1NP
☎020 8359 7779
Principal Librarian: Children and Youth Ms Hannah Richens DipILM MCLIP

School Libraries Resources Service, Grahame Park Library, The Concourse, Grahame Park, London NW9 5XL
☎020 8200 8948
Fax 020 8201 3018
e-mail: slrs@barnet.gov.uk
url: www.libraries.barnet.gov.uk
Manager Neil Angrave BA MCLIP (e-mail: neil.angrave@barnet.gov.uk)

BARNSLEY

Authority: Barnsley Metropolitan Borough Council
Central Library, Shambles Street, Barnsley, South Yorks S70 2JF
☎(01226) 773952/773920
Fax (01226) 773955
e-mail: barnsleylibraryenquiries@barnsley.gov.uk
url: www.barnsleylibraries.gov.uk/service/libraries/index.asp
Children's Services Officer Mrs Jane E Matthews BLib(Hons) MCLIP (e-mail: JaneMatthews@barnsley.gov.uk)

BATH AND NORTH EAST SOMERSET

Authority: Bath and North East Somerset Council
Central Library, The Podium, Northgate Street, Bath BA1 5AN
☎(01225) 787402
Fax (01225) 787426
Children's Librarians Mrs Lynne S Hamer MCLIP (e-mail: lynne_hamer@bathnes.gov.uk), Vacant

BEDFORDSHIRE

Authority: Bedfordshire County Council
Kempston Library, Halsey Road, Kempston, Bedford MK42 8AU
☎(01234) 853092
Fax (01234) 841476
Principal Librarian, Youth Services Ms Kerry O'Neil BA(Hons) MCLIP (e-mail:
oneilk@bedfordshire.gov.uk)

Leighton Buzzard Library, Lake Street, Leighton Buzzard, Beds LU7 1RX
☎(01525) 371788
Fax (01525) 851368
Senior Librarian, Youth Services Ms Vicky Fox MCLIP (e-mail:
foxv@bedfordshire.gov.uk)

Schools Library Service, Riverside Building, County Hall, Cauldwell Street, Bedford
MK42 9AP
☎(01234) 228755
Fax (01234) 228666
e-mail: bedfsls@bedfordshire.gov.uk
Senior Librarian, Schools Library Service Mrs Caroline Coombs BA(Hons) MCLIP

BEXLEY

Authority: London Borough of Bexley
Bexley Library Service, Footscray Offices, Maidstone Road, Sidcup, Kent DA14 5HS
☎020 8309 4138
Fax 020 8309 4142
e-mail: libraries@bexley.gov.uk
Youth Services Librarians Mrs Frances Mason BA MCLIP (e-mail:
frances.mason@bexley.gov.uk), Mrs Ruth White BA MA MCLIP (e-mail:
ruth.white@bexley.gov.uk) (job-share)

BIRMINGHAM

Authority: Birmingham City Council
Central Library, Chamberlain Square, Birmingham B3 3HQ
☎0121 303 2418
Fax 0121 233 9702
Head of Children's, Youth and Education Library Services Mrs Patsy Heap BA MCLIP
(e-mail: patsy.heap@birmingham.gov.uk)

Schools Library Service, Ellen Street, Hockley, Birmingham B18 6QZ
☎0121 464 1900/0757
Fax 0121 464 1852
e-mail: sls@birmingham.gov.uk
url: www.schoolslibraryservice.co.uk
Managers, Schools Library Service Mrs Sue Rogers BA MCLIP, Mrs Sue Needham MCLIP

BLACKBURN WITH DARWEN

Authority: Blackburn with Darwen Borough Council

Children's and Schools' Services, Blackburn Central Library, Town Hall Street, Blackburn, Lancashire BB2 1AG

☎(01254) 587937

Fax (01254) 679565

Literacy Development and Resources Manager Miss Jean Gabbatt BLib MCLIP (e-mail: jean.gabbatt@blackburn.gov.uk)

BLACKPOOL

Authority: Blackpool Borough Council

Leisure, Culture and Community Learning, Progress House, Clifton Road, Blackpool, Lancashire FY4 4US

☎(01253) 478111 (enquiries), (01253) 478105 (administration)

Fax (01253) 478071

e-mail: library.info@blackpool.gov.uk

Children's Library Services Manager Mrs Lynne Cowap-French MCLIP (01253 478096; fax: 01253 478082)

Senior Librarian, Schools' Library Services Mrs Liz Lawson (01253 476627; fax: 01253 476628)

BOLTON

Authority: Bolton Metropolitan Borough Council

Community and Access, Castle Hill Centre, Castleton Street, Bolton, Lancashire BL2 2JW

☎(01204) 338120

Fax (01204) 338128

url: www.bolton.gov.uk/library

Community and Access Team Leader Ms Mary Keane BA(Hons) DipLib MCLIP (e-mail: mary.keane@bolton.gov.uk)

Schools' Library Service, Castle Hill Centre, Castleton Street, Bolton, Lancs BL2 2JW

☎(01204) 338121

Fax (01204) 338128

url: www.bolton.gov.uk/library

Schools' Library Service Team Leader Mrs Kath Morgan MCLIP (e-mail: kath.morgan@bolton.gov.uk)

BOURNEMOUTH

Authority: Bournemouth Borough Council

Children and Learning, The Bournemouth Library, 22 The Triangle, Bournemouth BH2 5RQ

☎(01202) 454827

Fax (01202) 454830

e-mail: bournemouth@bournemouthlibraries.org.uk

url: www.bournemouth.gov.uk/libraries

Libraries Officer, Children and Learning Ms Heather Young BA DipIM MCLIP (e-mail: heather.young@bournemouthlibraries.org.uk)
(Bournemouth has joint provision with Dorset for school library services: see Dorset)

BRACKNELL FOREST

Authority: Bracknell Forest Borough Council
Bracknell Library, Town Square, Bracknell, Berks RG12 1BH
Fax (01344) 411392
e-mail: bracknell.library@bracknell-forest.gov.uk
url: www.bracknell-forest.gov.uk/libraries
Senior Librarian Ms Fiona Atkinson BA(Hons) MA MCLIP (01344 352404; e-mail: fiona.atkinson@bracknell-forest.gov.uk)
Head of Service Ms Ruth Burgess BLib MCLIP (01344 353134; e-mail: ruth.burgess@bracknell-forest.gov.uk)

Berkshire Education Library Service (Berkshire Authorities), 2-4 Darwin Close, Reading RG2 0TB
☎0118 901 5989
Fax 0118 901 5988
e-mail: els@bracknell-forest.gov.uk
url: www.berkshire-ers.gov.us
Head of Service Jeremy Saunders BA MCLIP (0118 901 5990; e-mail: jeremy.sanders@bracknell-forest.gov.uk)

BRADFORD

Authority: City of Bradford Metropolitan District Council
Central Library, Princes Way, Bradford BD1 1NN
☎(01274) 433600
Development Officer: Young People's Services Mrs Christinea Donnelly BA(Hons) MLib (01274 433915; e-mail: christinea.donnelly@bradford.gov.uk)
Principal Libraries Officer: Operations Mrs Marilyn Rogerson BA MCLIP (e-mail: marilyn.rogerson@bradford.gov.uk)

Education Library Service, Education Bradford, Serco Learning, Future House, Bolling Road, Bradford BD4 7EB
☎(01274) 385580
Fax (01274) 385588
Principal Librarian Robert Wilkes BEd FCLIP (e-mail: bob.wilkes@educationbradford.com)

BRENT

Authority: London Borough of Brent
Children and Young People Services, Willesden Green Library, 95 High Road, Willesden, London NW10 2ST
☎020 8937 3419

e-mail: willesdengreenlibrary@brent.gov.uk
url: www.brent.gov.uk/libraryservice
Children and Young People Services' Coordinator Ms Sarah Smith BSc MA MCLIP
(e-mail: sarah.smith@brent.gov.uk)

Library Service, 4th Floor, Chesterfield House, 9 Park Lane, Wembley, Middlesex HA9 7RW
☎020 8937 3143
Fax 020 8937 3008

BRIGHTON AND HOVE

Authority: Brighton and Hove City Council
Jubilee Library, Jubilee Street, Brighton BN1 1GE
☎(01273) 290800
Fax (01273) 296976
url: www.citylibraries.info
Community and Development Manager Alan Issler BA MCLIP (e-mail:
alan.issler@brighton-hove.gov.uk)
(Brighton and Hove has joint provision with East Sussex for schools library services: see
East Sussex)

BRISTOL

Authority: Bristol City Council
Cheltenham Road Library, Cheltenham Road, Bristol BS6 5QX
☎0117 903 8565 (tel/fax)
Children's and Young People's Adviser Mrs Janet Randall MCLIP (e-mail:
janet_randall@bristol-city.gov.uk)

Bristol School Library Service, Unit 1, Bristol Vale Trading Estate, Hartcliffe Way,
Bedminster, Bristol BS3 5RJ
☎0117 903 8534
Fax 0117 903 8535
e-mail: bristolschool_libraryservice@bristol-city.gov.uk
Service Manager Ms Dianne Southcombe BA(Hons)

BROMLEY

Authority: London Borough of Bromley
Central Library, High Street, Bromley, Kent BR1 1EX
☎020 8461 7193
Fax 020 8313 9975
url: www.bromley.gov.uk
Service Manager (Children & Learning) Ian Dodds BSc(Hons) MA MCLIP (e-mail:
ian.dodds@bromley.gov.uk)

BUCKINGHAMSHIRE

Authority: Buckinghamshire County Council
County Library HQ, Walton Street, Aylesbury, Buckinghamshire HP20 1UU
☎(01296) 383230
Fax (01296) 382259
e-mail: library@buckscc.gov.uk
url: www.buckscc.gov.uk/libraries
Children and Family Learning Manager Ms S A Hyland BA MCLIP (01296 383161;
e-mail: shyland@buckscc.gov.uk)

Great Missenden Library, High Street, Great Missenden, Bucks HP16 0AL
District Children's Co-ordinator (Wycombe/South Bucks District) Ms Judy Ottaway
MCLIP (01494 866641; e-mail: jottaway@buckscc.gov.uk)

Long Crendon Library, High Street, Long Crendon, Bucks HP18 9AF
District Children's Co-ordinator (Aylesbury Vale/Chiltern District) Mrs G Clipsham
MCLIP (01296 208997; e-mail: gclipsham@buckscc.gov.uk)

Library and Information Service for Schools (LISS), County Library HQ, Walton Street,
Aylesbury, Bucks HP20 1UU
☎(01296) 382268
Fax (01296) 382122
e-mail: liss@buckscc.gov.uk
Children and Family Learning Manager Ms S A Hyland BA MCLIP (01296 383161;
e-mail: shyland@buckscc.gov.uk)

BURY

Authority: Bury Metropolitan Borough Council
Learning Support Services, Unsworth Library, Sunnybank Road, Bury, Greater Manchester
BL9 8EB
☎0161 253 7561
Fax 0161 253 7564
Assistant Principal Librarian for Learning Support and Children's Services Mrs
Christine Almond (0161 253 7561; e-mail: c.almond@bury.gov.uk)

CALDERDALE

Authority: Calderdale Metropolitan Borough Council
Children's and Schools' Library Service, Central Library, Northgate, Halifax, Yorkshire
HX1 1UN
☎(01422) 392618
Fax (01422) 392615
Principal Librarian, Children's Services Ms Lynne Hackett MSc MCLIP (e-mail:
lynne.hackett@calderdale.gov.uk)

CAMBRIDGESHIRE

Authority: Cambridgeshire County Council
Schools Library Service, Units 1-3, Springwater Business Park, Station Road, Whittlesey,
Cambs PE7 2EU
☎(01733) 758016
Fax (01733) 758015
url: www.cambridgeshire.gov.uk/sls
Manager Ms Ann Leeming MCLIP (e-mail: ann.leeming@cambridgeshire.gov.uk)

CAMDEN

Authority: London Borough of Camden
Reader Development and Community Learning Team, Holborn Library, 3rd Floor, 32-38
Theobalds Road, London WC1X 8PA
☎020 7974 3675
Fax 020 7974 6356
e-mail: holbornlibrary@camden.gov.uk
url: www.camden.gov.uk
Principal Librarian, Reader Development Ms Felicity Page BA MCLIP (e-mail:
felicity.page@camden.gov.uk)

Schools Library Service, Swiss Cottage Library, 88 Avenue Road, London NW3 3HA
☎020 7974 6510
Fax 020 7974 6521
e-mail: sls@camden.gov.uk
Principal Librarian, Schools Library Service Ms Stella Richards (e-mail:
stella.richards@camden.gov.uk)

CHESHIRE

Authority: Cheshire County Council
Libraries, Information and Culture, 3rd Floor, County Hall, Chester CH1 1SQ
☎(01244) 606023
Fax (01244) 602478
url: www.cheshire.gov.uk/library
Resources and Development Manager Hedley Skinner DipEdTech MCLIP (e-mail:
hedley.skinner@cheshire.gov.uk)

Education Library Service, Browning Way, Woodford Park Industrial Estate, Winsford,
Cheshire CW7 2JN
☎(01606) 557126
Fax (01606) 861412
e-mail: educationlibraryservice@cheshire.gov.uk
url: www.cheshire.gov.uk/els
Young People's Services Officer Mrs Lesley Simons MCLIP (e-mail:
lesley.simons@cheshire.gov.uk)

Secondary School Specialist Mrs Ann Cowsill BA DipLib MCLIP (e-mail: ann.cowsill@cheshire.gov.uk)

Primary School Specialist Ms Carol Shaw BA (e-mail: carol.shaw@cheshire.gov.uk)

Young People's Specialists Ms Shan Wilkinson (0151 357 4686; e-mail: shan.wilkinson@cheshire.gov.uk) (Ellesmere Port Library), Ms Clare Ashbee (01606 552065; e-mail: clare.ashbee@cheshire.gov.uk) (Winsford Library), Ms Joan Roberts (01625 528977; e-mail: joan.roberts@cheshire.gov.uk) (Wilmslow Library), Ms Helena Jones (e-mail: helena.jones@cheshire.gov.uk) (Macclesfield Library), Ms Carol Maplesden (0151 357 4686; e-mail: carol.maplesden@cheshire.gov.uk) (Ellesmere Port Library)

CORNWALL

Authority: Cornwall County Council

Education Library Services, Unit 17, Threemilestone, Truro, Cornwall TR4 9LD

☎(01872) 323456

Fax (01872) 223509/323819

e-mail: els@library.cornwall.gov.uk

Head of Young People's Services Ms Susan McCulloch BA MCLIP (e-mail: smcculloch@cornwall.gov.uk)

COVENTRY

Authority: Coventry City Council

School Library Service, Central Library, Smithford Way, Coventry CV1 1FY

☎024 7683 2338

Fax 024 7683 2338

e-mail: sls@coventry.gov.uk

url: www.coventry.gov.uk/ccm/navigation/education-and learning/school-library-service

Learning Resources Manager, Teaching and Learning Service Mrs Joy Court BA(Hons) DipLib (e-mail: joy.court@coventry.gov.uk)

CROYDON

Authority: London Borough of Croydon

Central Library, Katharine Street, Croydon CR9 1ET

☎020 8686 4433 ext 61051

Fax 020 8253 1004

url: www.croydon.gov.uk/libraries

Children's Services Manager Ms Margaret Fraser MA MCLIP (e-mail: margaret.fraser@croydon.gov.uk), Ms Grace McElwee BA(Hons) DipLib MCLIP (e-mail: grace.mcelwee@croydon.gov.uk) (job-share)

CUMBRIA

Authority: Cumbria County Council

Library HQ, Arroyo Block, The Castle, Carlisle, Cumbria CA3 8UR

☎(01228) 607338

Fax (01228) 607299

County Library Operations Manager Mrs Liz Bowe MCLIP (e-mail:
liz.bowe@cumbriacc.gov.uk)

Library Services for Schools HQ, Botchergate, Carlisle CA1 1RZ
☎(01228) 607273
Fax (01228) 607275
School Library Services Manager Mrs Ann Singleton MCLIP (e-mail:
ann.singleton@cumbriacc.gov.uk)

DARLINGTON

Authority: Darlington Borough Council
Education Department, Darlington Library, Crown Street, Darlington DL1 1ND
☎(01325) 462034
Fax (01325) 381556
e-mail: crown.street.library@darlington.gov.uk
url: www.darlington.gov.uk/education/library
Libraries Manager Mrs Lynne Litchfield

DERBY

Authority: Derby City Council
Department of Development and Cultural Services, Room C526, Roman House, Friar
Gate, Derby DE1 1XB
☎(01332) 716604
Fax (01332) 715549
url: www.derby.gov.uk/libraries
Senior Librarian, Children and Education Mrs Hilary Marshall BA MCLIP (e-mail:
hilary.marshall@derby.gov.uk)
(Derby has joint provision with Derbyshire for schools library services: see Derbyshire)

DERBYSHIRE

Authority: Derbyshire County Council
Libraries and Heritage Division, Cultural and Community Services Department,
Chatsworth Hall, Chesterfield Road, Matlock, Derbyshire DE4 3FW
☎(01629) 585182
Fax (01629) 585917
url: www.derbyshire.gov.uk
Service Manager (Young People and Policy Development) Ms Annie Everall OBE
BA(Hons)Lib MCLIP (e-mail: annie.everall@derbyshire.gov.uk)

School Library Service, Kedleston Road Centre, 184 Kedleston Road, Derby DE22 1GT
☎(01332) 371921
Fax (01332) 371381
School Library Service Manager Ms Denise Pritchard (e-mail:
denise.pritchard@derbyshire.gov.uk)

DEVON

Authority: Devon County Council
North Devon Library and Record Office, Tuly Street, Barnstaple, Devon EX31 1EL
☎(01271) 388622
Fax (01271) 388619
url: www.devon.gov.uk/libraries
Group Librarian, North & West Devon (i/c Children's Services) Ian Tansley MCLIP
(e-mail: ian.tansley@devon.gov.uk)

School Library Service, Great Moor House, Bittern Road, Sowton, Exeter, Devon EX2 7NL
☎(01392) 384304
Fax (01392) 381392
url: www.devon.gov.uk/school_library_service
Head of School Library Service Ms Lynne Medlock BEd MCLIP (e-mail:
lynne.medlock@devon.gov.uk)

DONCASTER

Authority: Doncaster Metropolitan Borough Council
Education and Young People's Service, Top Road, Barnby Dun, Doncaster DN3 1DB
☎(01302) 881787 (tel/fax)
Manager Ms Donna Peverley MCLIP (e-mail: donna.peverley@doncaster.gov.uk)

DORSET

Authority: Dorset County Council
County Library HQ, Colliton Park, Dorchester, Dorset DT1 1XJ
☎(01305) 224455 (enquiries), (01305) 224450 (administration)
Fax (01305) 224344
e-mail: dorsetlibraries@dorsetcc.gov.uk
Senior Manager (Stock and Children's Services) Ms Sharon Kirkpatrick BLS MCLIP
(e-mail: s.d.kirkpatrick@dorsetcc.gov.uk)
Service Development Manager (Young People) Ms Sharon Holmes BA(Hons) MA
MCLIP (e-mail: s.e.holmes@dorsetcc.gov.uk)

School Library Service, Education Resources Centre, College Road, Blandford Camp,
Blandford, Dorset DT11 8BG
☎(01258) 451151
Fax (01258) 480076
e-mail: school_library_service@dorsetcc.gov.uk
url: www.dorsetcc.gov.uk/schoollibraryservice
School Library Service Manager Ms Alison Burgess BA DipLib MCLIP MLib
(Dorset has joint provision with Bournemouth and Poole for schools library services)

DUDLEY

Authority: Dudley Metropolitan Borough Council
Schools Library and Information Service, Milton Crescent, Lower Gornal, Dudley, West Midlands DY3 3EE
☎(01384) 812850
Fax (01384) 812851
e-mail: schools.library@dudley.gov.uk
Principal Librarian Mrs Dilys M Ward MCLIP (e-mail: dilys.ward@dudley.gov.uk)

DURHAM

Authority: Durham County Council
Leisure and Culture, County Hall, Durham DH1 5TY
☎0191 383 4459
Fax 0191 383 3858
url: www.durham.gov.uk/dlr
Youth Services Manager Peter Burns MCLIP (e-mail: peter.burns@durham.gov.uk)
(Includes responsibility for schools library services)

EALING

Authority: London Borough of Ealing
Library Support Centre, Ealing Central Sports Ground, Horsenden Lane South, Greenford, Middlesex UB6 8AP
☎020 8810 7650
Fax 020 8810 7651
url: www.ealing.gov.uk
Young People's Collection Development Librarian Ms Caroline Downie BA (e-mail: downiec@ealing.gov.uk)

EAST RIDING OF YORKSHIRE

Authority: East Riding of Yorkshire Council
Library and Information Services, Council Offices, Main Road, Skirlaugh, East Riding of Yorks HU11 5HN
☎(01482) 392726 (office)
Fax (01482) 392710
Schools Library Service Manager Mrs Ann Walker (01482 392725; e-mail: annm.walker@eastriding.gov.uk)

EAST SUSSEX

Authority: East Sussex County Council
Libraries, Information and Arts, G Floor Centre Block, County Hall, St Anne's Crescent, Lewes, East Sussex BN7 1UE
Manager, Schools Library Service and Young People's Services Ms Michele Eaton BA(Hons) MCLIP (e-mail: michele.eaton@eastsussex.gov.uk)

Schools Library Service, Hammonds Drive, Lottbridge Drove, Hampden Park, Eastbourne, East Sussex BN23 6PW
☎(01323) 416324
Fax (01323) 412806
e-mail: sls@eastsussex.gov.uk
Manager, Schools Library Service and Young People's Services Ms Michele Eaton BA(Hons) MCLIP (01323 416324; e-mail: michele.eaton@eastsussex.gov.uk)

ENFIELD

Authority: London Borough of Enfield
PO Box 58, Civic Centre, Silver Street, Enfield, Middlesex EN1 3XJ
☎020 8379 3748
Fax 020 8379 3777
Principal Librarian, Children and Education Ms Lucy Love BA(Hons) DipLib MCLIP
(e-mail: lucy.love@enfield.gov.uk)

Schools Library Service, Library Resources Unit, Southgate Town Hall, Green Lanes, Palmers Green, London N13 4XD
☎020 8379 2708
Fax 020 8379 2761
e-mail: sls@enfield.gov.uk
url: www.enfield.gov.uk
Schools Library Service Librarian Ms Liz Day (e-mail: liz.day@enfield.gov.uk)

ESSEX

Authority: Essex County Council
Essex Libraries, Goldlay Gardens, Chelmsford, Essex CM2 0EW
☎(01245) 244955
Fax (01245) 492780
Strategic Manager Reading and Learning Mrs Moira Tarrant (e-mail: moira.tarrant@essexcc.gov.uk)

School Library Service, 3 Atholl Road, Dukes Park Industrial Estate, Chelmsford, Essex CM2 6TB
☎(01245) 542600
Fax (01245) 542601
e-mail: sls@essexcc.gov.uk
School Library Service Manager Ms Carolyn Hughes

GATESHEAD

Authority: Gateshead Metropolitan Borough Council
Youth Services Team, Dryden PDC, Evistones Road, Gateshead, Tyne and Wear NE9 5UR
☎0191 433 8527/8
Fax 0191 487 1895

Youth Services Manager Mrs Barbara Wood BA MCLIP (0191 433 8529; e-mail: barbarawood@gateshead.gov.uk)

GLOUCESTERSHIRE

Authority: Gloucestershire County Council
Libraries and Information, Quayside House, Shire Hall, Gloucester GL1 2HY
☎(01452) 426557
Fax (01452) 425042
e-mail: libhelp@gloucestershire.gov.uk
url: www.gloucestershire.gov.uk
Policy Development Officer: Children and Young People Mrs Helen Briggs BA DMS MIMgt MCLIP (01452 425030; e-mail: helen.briggs@gloucestershire.gov.uk)

Library Services for Education, Hucclecote Centre, Churchdown Lane, Hucclecote, Gloucester GL3 3QL
☎(01452) 427247
Fax (01452) 427243
e-mail: lse@gloucestershire.gov.uk
Manager Mrs Susan C Westwood BA MCLIP (e-mail: susan.westwood@gloucestershire.gov.uk)

GREENWICH

Authority: London Borough of Greenwich
Children's and Young People's Service, Support Services, Plumstead Library, Plumstead High Street, London SE18 1JL
☎020 8317 4466
Fax 020 8317 4868
Group Library Manager Martin Stone (e-mail: martin.stone@greenwich.gov.uk)

Schools Library Service, West Greenwich Library, Greenwich High Road, Greenwich, London SE10 8NN
☎020 8853 1691
Fax 020 8858 3512
e-mail: projectloans.library@greenwich.gov.uk
Group Library Manager Martin Stone (e-mail: martin.stone@greenwich.gov.uk)

HACKNEY

Authority: London Borough of Hackney
Development, Homerton Library, Homerton High Street, London E9 6AS
Fax 020 8356 1693
Development Manager, Libraries Ms Anita Kane (020 8356 1696; e-mail: anita.kane@hackney.gov.uk)

Stoke Newington Library, Stoke Newington Church Street, London N16 0JS
☎020 8356 5237 (tel/fax)

Acting Children and Young People's Co-ordinator Ms Dawn Hendrickson (e-mail: dawn.hendrickson@hackney.gov.uk)

HALTON

Authority: Halton Borough Council
Halton Lea Library, Halton Lea, Runcorn, Cheshire WA7 2PF
☎(01928) 715351
Fax (01928) 790221
Young Persons Officers Mrs Allyson Watt BA(Hons) MCLIP (e-mail:
allyson.watt@halton.gov.uk), Mrs Jennie Archer MCLIP (e-mail:
jennie.archer@halton.gov.uk)
(Schools library services provided by Education Library Service, Cheshire: see Cheshire)

HAMMERSMITH AND FULHAM

Authority: London Borough of Hammersmith and Fulham
Hammersmith Library, Shepherds Bush Road, Hammersmith, London W6 7AT
☎020 8753 3811
Fax 020 8753 3815
Library Development Manager Ms Amanda Stirrup BA MCLIP (e-mail:
amanda.stirrup@lbhf.gov.uk)

HAMPSHIRE

Authority: Hampshire County Council
Library and Information Service HQ, 81 North Walls, Winchester, Hants SO23 8BY
☎(01962) 826660
Fax (01962) 856615
url: www.hants.gov.uk/library/index.html
Head of Children's, Youth and Schools Service Anne Marley BA MCLIP (01962
826658; e-mail: anne.marley@hants.gov.uk)

HARINGEY

Authority: London Borough of Haringey
Hornsey Library, Haringey Park, Hornsey, London N8 9JA
☎020 8489 1428
Fax 020 8374 6942
Senior Librarian, Children (Hornsey Area) Sean Edwards BA (e-mail:
sean.edwards@haringey.gov.uk)

Marcus Garvey Library, Tottenham Green Centre, 1 Philip Lane, London N15 4JA
☎020 8489 5360
Fax 020 8489 5338
Senior Librarian, Children (Tottenham Area) Mrs Claire Stalker-Booth (e-mail:
claire.stalker-booth@haringey.gov.uk)

Wood Green Central Library, High Road, Wood Green, London N22 6XD
☎020 8489 2776
Fax 020 8489 2722
url: www.haringey.gov.uk/libraries
Principal Librarian, Children's Services Mrs Valerie Ross BA MCLIP (e-mail: val.ross@haringey.gov.uk)
Senior Librarian, Children (Wood Green Area) Meaza Abrahaley-Mebrahtu (e-mail: meaza.abrahaley-mebrahtu@haringey.gov.uk)

Schools Library Service, Professional Development Centre, Downhills Park Road, London N17 6AR
☎020 8489 5043
Fax 020 8489 5004
e-mail: sls@haringey.gov.uk
School Services Librarian Ms Catherine Collingborn (e-mail: catherine.collingborn@haringey.gov.uk)

HARROW

Authority: London Borough of Harrow
Young People's and School Library Services, Civic Centre Library, PO Box 4, Civic Centre, Harrow, Middlesex HA1 2UU
☎020 8424 1052
Fax 020 8424 1971
Principal Librarian, Young People's Services and Lifelong Learning Mrs Gill Polding MCLIP (e-mail: gill.poulding@harrow.gov.uk)

HARTLEPOOL

Authority: Hartlepool Borough Council
Central Library, 124 York Road, Hartlepool, Cleveland TS26 9DE
☎(01429) 272905
Fax (01429) 275685
e-mail: infodesk@hartlepool.gov.uk
Children and Young Person's Librarian Mrs Gill Slimings (e-mail: gillian.slimings@hartlepool.gov.uk)
Schools Resources Service: see Redcar & Cleveland (cooperative service with Middlesbrough, Redcar & Cleveland and Stockton-on-Tees)

HAVERING

Authority: London Borough of Havering
Central Library, St Edwards Way, Romford, Essex RM1 3AR
Fax (01708) 432391
Children's Services Manager Mrs Ruth Gedalovitch BA(Hons) MCLIP (01708 432380; e-mail: ruth.gedalovitch@havering.gov.uk)
Schools Library Service Manager Mrs Anne Lehva BA(Hons) MCLIP (01708 432397; e-mail: anne.lehva@havering.gov.uk)

HEREFORDSHIRE

Authority: Herefordshire Council
Schools Library Service, Shirehall, Hereford HR1 2HY
☎(01432) 260661
e-mail: sls@herefordshire.gov.uk
Access and Learning Manager Mrs Julia Radburn BA PGCE DipLib MCLIP, Ms Sarah Chedgzoy BA MCLIP DipLib(job-share)
Schools Library Service Librarian Mrs Rosemarie Fleming BA MCLIP

HERTFORDSHIRE

Authority: Hertfordshire County Council
Community Information: Libraries, New Barnfield, Travellers Lane, Hatfield, Herts AL10 8XG
☎(01438) 737333
Fax (01707) 281514
Service Development Manager Ms Sue Jones MA MCLIP (01707 281630; fax: 01707 281611; e-mail: sue.jones@herts-sls.org.uk)

HILLINGDON

Authority: London Borough of Hillingdon
Central Library, 14-15 High Street, Uxbridge, Middlesex UB8 1HD
☎(01895) 250715/250600
Fax (01895) 811164/239794 (Hillingdon Libraries)
e-mail: clibrary@hillingdongrid.org
url: www.hillingdon.gov.uk
Outreach Manager Ms Liz McMillan MCLIP (01895 250703; e-mail: lmcmillan@hillingdongrid.org)
Resource and Development Manager Ms Eileen Smyth MCLIP (01895 250701; e-mail: esmyth@hillingdongrid.org)

HOUNSLOW

Authority: London Borough of Hounslow
Young People's Library Service, Centrespace, 24 Treaty Centre, High Street, Hounslow, Middlesex TW3 1ES
☎0845 456 2921
Fax 0845 456 2928
url: www.cip.com
Principal Librarian, Library Management Group Ms Frances Stanbury MCLIP (e-mail: frances-stanbury@cip.org.uk)

ISLE OF WIGHT

Authority: Isle of Wight Council
Young People's Library Service, Thompson House, Sandy Lane, Newport, Isle of Wight PO30 3NA

☎(01983) 525731
Fax (01983) 529463
e-mail: ypls@iow.gov.uk
Young People's Services Librarian Mrs Elspeth Jackson (e-mail:
elspeth.jackson@iow.gov.uk)

ISLINGTON

Authority: London Borough of Islington
Central Library, 2 Fieldway Crescent, London N5 1PF
☎020 7527 6997
url: www.islington.gov.uk/libraries
Manager, Library Services to Children and Young People Geoff James BA(Hons)
DipLib MCLIP (e-mail: geoff.james@islington.gov.uk)

Education Library Service, Block D, Barnsbury Complex, Barnsbury Park, London N1 1QG
☎020 7527 5827
Fax 020 7527 5564
Head of Education Library Service Ms Pam Dix (e-mail: pam.dix.cea@islington.gov.uk)
Senior Librarian Ms Sue Adler (e-mail: sue.adler.cea@islington.gov.uk)

KENSINGTON AND CHELSEA

Authority: Royal Borough of Kensington and Chelsea
Children and Schools Library Service, Kensington Central Library, Phillimore Walk, London
W8 7RX
☎020 7361 2029
Fax 020 7361 2225
Service Development Manager for Schools, Children and Young People Ms Sue
Riley MLS MCLIP (e-mail: sue.riley@rbkc.gov.uk)

KENT

Authority: Kent County Council
Kent Libraries and Archives, Gibson Drive, Kings Hill, West Malling, Kent ME19 4AL
☎(01622) 605213
Fax (01622) 605221
url: www.kent.gov.uk/e&l/artslib
Family and Lifelong Learning Services Manager Mrs Janet Davies BA MCLIP (01622
605211; e-mail: janet.davies@kent.gov.uk), Ms L Prestage BA MA MCLIP DipMgt (01622
605211; e-mail: lindsay.prestage@kent.gov.uk) (job-share)

KINGSTON UPON HULL

Authority: Kingston upon Hull City Council
Hull Central Library, Albion Street, Kingston upon Hull HU1 3TF
☎(01482) 616846
Fax (01482) 616827

url: www.hullcc.gov.uk
Specialist Librarian – Children and Young People Mrs Janis Wilson BA MCLIP (e-mail: janis.wilson@hullcc.gov.uk)

KINGSTON UPON THAMES

Authority: Royal Borough of Kingston upon Thames
Kingston Library, Fairfield Road, Kingston upon Thames, Surrey KT1 2PS
☎020 8408 9100
Fax 020 8547 6426
url: www.kingston.gov.uk/libs
Senior Team Librarian, Children's and Schools Services Michael Treacy (020 8408 9100; e-mail: michael.treacy@rbk.kingston.gov.uk), Mrs Jane Richardson (020 8547 6422; e-mail: jane.richardson@rbk.kingston.gov.uk) (job-share)

KIRKLEES

Authority: Kirklees Metropolitan Council
Cultural Services HQ, Red Doles Lane, Huddersfield, Yorkshire HD2 1YF
☎(01484) 226365 (direct), (01484) 226300
Fax (01484) 226342
e-mail: kinfo@kirklees.gov.uk
url: www.kirklees.gov.uk/libraries
Assistant Head, Culture and Leisure Services Rob Warburton BA MCLIP (e-mail: rob.warburton@kirklees.gov.uk)

KNOWSLEY

Authority: Knowsley Metropolitan Borough Council
Page Moss Library, Stockbridge Lane, Huyton, Knowsley, Merseyside L36 3SA
☎0151 482 1304
Learning Services Manager Ms Pam Jones BA MCLIP (e-mail: pam.jones.dlcs@knowsley.gov.uk)
Children's and School Services Manager Ms Geraldine Williams BA (0151 482 1849; e-mail: gerry.williams.dlcs@knowsley.gov.uk)

Kirkby Library, Newtown Gardens, Kirkby, Knowsley, Merseyside L32 8RR
☎0151 443 4285
e-mail: school.library.service.dlcs@knowsley.gov.uk
School Library Service Manager Ms Julie Mansfield, Ms Pat Harrison (job-share)

LAMBETH

Authority: London Borough of Lambeth
Tate Library Brixton, Brixton Oval, London SW2 1JQ
☎020 7926 1104
Senior Children and Young People's Services Librarian Ms Sandra Davidson (e-mail: sdavidson@lambeth.gov.uk)

Lambeth Libraries, Arts and Archives, 3rd Floor, International House, Canterbury Crescent, London SW9 7QE
☎020 7926 0750
Fax 020 7926 0751
url: www.lambeth.gov.uk
Development Manager, Learning and Access Ms Susan Doyle MCLIP (020 7926 0518; fax: 020 7926 0751; e-mail: sdoyle@lambeth.gov.uk)

LANCASHIRE

Authority: Lancashire County Council
School Library Service, 218-222 North Road, Preston, Lancashire PR1 1SY
☎(01772) 534041
Fax (01772) 533391
e-mail: preston.sls@lcl.lancscc.gov.uk
County Library Manager David G Lightfoot MA DMS MCLIP (e-mail: david.lightfoot@lcl.lancscc.gov.uk)
Manager, Young People's Services Mrs J Wolstenholme DMS MCLIP (01772 534040)

LEEDS

Authority: Leeds City Council
Library and Information Services HQ, 32 York Road, Leeds LS9 8TD
☎0113 214 3346
Fax 0113 214 3339
url: www.leeds.gov.uk
Young People's Services Manager Mrs Sarah Kift BA MCLIP (e-mail: sarah.kift@leeds.gov.uk)

School Library Service, Foxcroft Close, Leeds LS6 3NT
☎0113 214 4531
Fax 0113 214 4532
e-mail: schoollibrariesleeds@talk21.com
School Library Service Manager Mrs Margaret Drinkwater MA MCLIP

LEICESTER

Authority: Leicester City Council
Libraries and Information Services, Fosse Library, Mantle Road, Leicester LE3 5HG
☎0116 225 4997
Fax 0116 225 4999
Community Library Manager (Children and Young People Services) Paul Gobey
(Leicester has joint provision for schools library services with Leicestershire: see Leicestershire)

LEICESTERSHIRE

Authority: Leicestershire County Council
Library Services for Education, Rothley Crossroads, 929-931 Loughborough Road, Rothley, Leics LE7 7NH
☎0116 267 8000
Fax 0116 267 8039
e-mail: lse@leics.gov.uk
Learning and Information Development Manager Mrs Glenys Willars MA MCLIP
(0116 267 8008; e-mail: ghwillars@leics.gov.uk)

LEWISHAM

Authority: London Borough of Lewisham
Education and Culture Library Service, 1st Floor, Town Hall Chambers, Catford, London SE6 4RU
☎020 8314 8026
Fax 020 8314 3229
Head of Libraries and Information Service Ms Julia Newton MCLIP (e-mail: julia.newton@lewisham.gov.uk)

Lewisham Libraries and Information Service, 1st Floor, Town Hall Chambers, Rushey Green, Catford, London SE6 4RU
☎020 8314 7189
Fax 020 8314 3229
url: www.lewisham.gov.uk/learning/index.asp
Children and Young Persons Librarian Ms Joanne Moulton BA DipIM MCLIP (020 8314 7189; fax: 020 8314 3229; e-mail: joanne.moulton@lewisham.gov.uk)

LINCOLNSHIRE

Authority: Lincolnshire County Council
Libraries Special Services, Eastgate Centre, 105 Eastgate, Sleaford, Lincs NG34 7EN
Fax (01522) 550372
Acting Libraries Special Services Managers Ms Wendy Bond BA MCLIP (01522 550379; e-mail: wendy.bond@lincoln.gov.uk), Ms Toni Franck (01522 550378; e-mail: toni.franck@lincoln.gov.uk)

LIVERPOOL

Authority: Liverpool City Council
Children's Support Services, Central Library, William Brown Street, Liverpool L3 8EW
☎0151 233 5841
Fax 0151 233 5801
e-mail: css@liverpool.gov.uk
url: www.liverpool.gov.uk
Librarian, Children's Support Services Mrs Irene Mandelkow BA MCLIP, Mrs Patricia Lee MCLIP

LONDON, CITY OF

Authority: Corporation of London
Barbican Library, Barbican Centre, London EC2Y 8DS
☎020 7628 9447
Fax 020 7638 2249
e-mail: barbicanlib@corpoflondon.gov.uk
url: www.cityoflondon.gov.uk/barbicanlibrary
Children's Librarian Mrs M-A Stevens BA MCLIP (e-mail:
mary-ann.stevens@corpoflondon.gov.uk)

LUTON

Authority: Luton Borough Council
Children & Young People's Service, Luton Central Library, St George's Square, Luton,
Bedfordshire LU1 2NG
☎(01582) 547466
Fax (01582) 547461
url: www.lutonlibrary.com
Principal Librarian (Children, Young People and Schools Library Service) Mrs Jane
Humm MCLIP (e-mail: hummj@luton.gov.uk)

Schools Library Service, Leagrave Library, Marsh Road, Luton, Bedfordshire LU3 2NL
☎(01582) 598065
Fax (01582) 847077
e-mail: sls@luton.gov.uk
Senior Librarian, Schools Library Service Ms Linda Bukumunhe BSc MA (e-mail:
bukumunhel@luton.gov.uk)
Library Service Manager Mrs Judy Neal (e-mail: nealj@luton.gov.uk)

MANCHESTER

Authority: Manchester City Council
North District Libraries, Crumpsall Library, Abraham Moss Centre, Crescent Road,
Manchester M8 5UF
☎0161 908 1911
Fax 0161 908 1912
Library and Information Officer, Children and Young People's Services Ms Fozia
Pasha (e-mail: foziap@libraries.manchester.gov.uk)

MEDWAY

Authority: Medway Council
Young People's Services, Gillingham Library, High Street, Gillingham, Kent ME7 1BG
☎(01634) 281066
Fax (01634) 855814
url: www.medway.gov.uk
Area Librarian Chatham D Mead BA MCLIP (e-mail: duncan.mead@medway.gov.uk)

(with responsibility for Young People's Services)

Young People's Services, Strood Library, Bryant Road, Strood, Rochester, Kent ME2 3EP
☎(01634) 718161 (tel/fax)
e-mail: strood.library@medway.gov.uk
Senior Librarian (Services to Schools) Mrs Greta Paterson MA DipLib MCLIP DMS
(e-mail: greta.paterson@medway.gov.uk)
(Medway shares a learning resources service provided by Kent: see Kent)

MERTON

Authority: London Borough of Merton
Libraries and Heritage Services, Apollo House, 66a London Road, Morden, Surrey SM4 5BE
☎020 8545 4083
Fax 020 8545 3237
Young People's Services Development Manager Mrs Janet Graves BA MCLIP (e-mail:
janet.graves@merton.gov.uk)

MIDDLESBROUGH

Authority: Middlesbrough Borough Council
Young People's Services, c/o Central Library, Victoria Square, Middlesbrough TS1 2AY
☎(01642) 729421
Fax (01642) 729953
Young People's Library Manager Ms Caryn Annal BA(Hons) (e-mail:
caryn_annal@middlesbrough.gov.uk), Ms Rita Wilson BA DipLib MCLIP (e-mail:
rita_wilson@middlesbrough.gov.uk) (job-share)
(Schools Resources Service: see Redcar and Cleveland. Cooperative service with
Hartlepool, Redcar & Cleveland, and Stockton-on-Tees)

MILTON KEYNES

Authority: Milton Keynes Council
Central Library, 555 Silbury Boulevard, Milton Keynes MK9 3HL
☎(01908) 254050
Fax (01908) 254089
e-mail: central.library@milton-keynes.gov.uk
Children's Librarian Mrs Emma Carrick BA MCLIP (e-mail:
emma.carrick@milton-keynes.gov.uk), Mrs Michelle Herriman BA DipLib MCLIP (01908
254081; e-mail: michelle.herriman@milton-keynes.gov.uk) (job share)

School Library Service, Bletchley Library, Westfield Road, Bletchley, Milton Keynes MK2 2RA
☎(01908) 647611 (tel/fax)
e-mail: sls@milton-keynes.gov.uk
url: www.mkweb.co.uk/sls
Principal Librarian (School Library Service) Mrs Elizabeth Brand BA MCLIP

NEWCASTLE UPON TYNE

Authority: Newcastle upon Tyne City Council
Access to Learning, Brinkburn Centre, Brinkburn Street, Newcastle upon Tyne NE6 2AR
☎0191 278 4200
Fax 0191 278 4202
Access to Learning Manager Mrs Janice Hall MCLIP (e-mail:
janice.hall@newcastle.gov.uk)

NEWHAM

Authority: London Borough of Newham
Culture and Community, Libraries HQ, 292 Barking Road, East Ham, London E6 3BA
☎020 8430 3993
Children and Young People's Service Manager, Libraries Ms Jacky Appleton (e-mail:
jacky.appleton@newham.gov.uk)

School Library Service, Canning Town Library, Barking Road, London E16 4HQ
☎020 7476 2925
Fax 020 7511 8693 (mark for attention of SLS)
Resources Manager Ms Zainab Umar (e-mail: zainab.umar@newham.gov.uk)

NORFOLK

Authority: Norfolk County Council
Library and Information Service, County Hall, Martineau Lane, Norwich NR1 2UA
☎(01603) 222049
Fax (01603) 222422
url: www.library.norfolk.gov.uk
Head of Libraries Mrs Jennifer Holland BA(Hons) MCLIP MCMI (01603 222272; e-mail:
jennifer.holland@norfolk.gov.uk)
Development Officer Ms Lorna Payne MA MCLIP (01603 222273; fax: 01603 222422;
e-mail: lorna.payne@norfolk.gov.uk)
Senior Librarian, Young People's Services Dr Dorne Fraser BA MCLIP (01603 222270;
e-mail: dorne.fraser@norfolk.gov.uk)

School Library Service, County Hall, Martineau Lane, Norwich NR1 2UA
☎(01603) 222266
Fax (01603) 222264
url: www.norfolk.gov.uk/sls
School Library Service Manager Philip Cocker (01603 222266; e-mail:
philip.cocker.lib@norfolk.gov.uk)

NORTH EAST LINCOLNSHIRE

Authority: North East Lincolnshire Council
Schools Library Service, Western Primary School Campus, Broadway, Grimsby, Lincs
DN34 5RS

☎(01472) 323654
Fax (01472) 323653
e-mail: schoolslib@hotmail.com
Young People and Children's Development Officer Ms Sue Wink (01472 323621;
e-mail: sue.wink@nelincs.gov.uk)
Schools Service Librarian Mike Grubb BEd (01472 323654)

NORTH LINCOLNSHIRE

Authority: North Lincolnshire Council
Young People's Services, Riddings Library, Willoughby Road, Scunthorpe, Lincs DN17 2NW
☎(01724) 856034
Librarian, Young People's Services Mrs Rosie Scotting BLib MCLIP (e-mail:
rosie.scotting@northlincs.gov.uk)

Scunthorpe Central Library, Carlton Street, Scunthorpe, North Lincs DN15 6TX
☎(01724) 860161 (tel/fax)
url: www.northlincs.gov.uk/library
Senior Librarian, Young People's Services Colin Brabazon BA DipLib MCLIP (e-mail:
colin.brabazon@northlincs.gov.uk)

NORTH SOMERSET

Authority: North Somerset Council
Department of Development and Environment (Libraries), Weston Library, The Boulevard,
Weston-super-Mare, Somerset BS23 1PL
☎(01934) 620373/636638
Fax (01934) 413046
e-mail: weston.library@n-somerset.gov.uk
Librarian for Services to Children and Young People (South Area) Mrs Maura
Coleman MCLIP (e-mail: maura.coleman@n-somerset.gov.uk)

NORTH TYNESIDE

Authority: North Tyneside Council
North Tyneside Children and Young People's Library Service, Wallsend Library, Ferndale
Avenue, Wallsend, Tyne and Wear NE28 7NB
☎0191 200 7339
Fax 0191 200 6967
e-mail: cypls@northtyneside.gov.uk
url: www.northtyneside.gov.uk
Senior Librarian for Children's Services Mrs Gaye Jamieson BA(Hons) MCLIP (0191
200 6974; e-mail: gaye.jamieson@northtyneside.gov.uk)
(Includes a support service to schools)

NORTH YORKSHIRE

Authority: North Yorkshire County Council
Business and Community Services HQ, 21 Grammar School Lane, Northallerton, North
Yorks DL6 1DF
☎(01609) 533848
Fax (01609) 780793
e-mail: libraries@northyorks.gov.uk
url: www.northyorks.gov.uk
Manager: Children and Schools Mrs B Hooper BSc MCLIP (01609 533849; e-mail:
brenda.hooper@northyorks.gov.uk)

NORTHAMPTONSHIRE

Authority: Northamptonshire County Council
Libraries and Information Service, PO Box 216, John Dryden House, 8-10 The Lakes,
Northampton NN4 7DD
☎(01604) 236236
Fax (01604) 237937
Principal Libraries and Information Officer (Service Development) Ms E Jarvis BA
MA DipLib MCLIP DMS (e-mail: ejarvis@northamptonshire.gov.uk)
Learning Resources Manager Ms Tricia Adams BA MCLIP (e-mail:
paadams@northamptonshire.gov.uk)

Learning Resources for Education, Booth Meadow House, Museum Way, Riverside Park,
Northampton NN3 9ZD
☎(01604) 773930
Fax (01604) 773939
Principal Libraries and Information Officer (Service Delivery) Nick L Matthews BA
MCLIP DMS (e-mail: nmatthews@northamptonshire.gov.uk)
Learning Resources Manager Ms Tricia Adams BA MCLIP (e-mail:
paadams@northamptonshire.gov.uk)

NORTHUMBERLAND

Authority: Northumberland County Council
County Library HQ, The Willows, Morpeth, Northumberland NE61 1TA
☎(01670) 534507
Fax (01670) 534521
e-mail: reference@northumberland.gov.uk
Principal Library and Archive Officer Chris Baker MCLIP (e-mail:
cbaker@northumberland.gov.uk)

Schools Library Service, Hepscott Park, Stannington, Morpeth, Northumberland
NE61 6NF
☎(01670) 534354
Fax (01670) 533591
e-mail: generalsls@northumberland.gov.uk

url: www.northumberland.gov.uk
Senior Education Librarian Ms Ann Kirton BA DipLib MCLIP

NOTTINGHAM

Authority: City of Nottingham Council
Libraries, Information and Communication Services, Isabella Street, Nottingham NG1 6AT
☎0115 915 8720
Service Manager Vacant
Children's Services Librarians Ms Deborah Sheppard MCLIP, Ms Elaine Dykes BA
MCLIP(job-share)
(Schools Library Service offered in partnership with Nottinghamshire County Council: see
Nottinghamshire)

NOTTINGHAMSHIRE

Authority: Nottinghamshire County Council
Education Library Service, Glaisdale Parkway, Nottingham NG8 4GP
☎0115 985 4200
Fax 0115 928 6400
e-mail: elsg@nottscc.gov.uk
Principal Libraries Officer (Resources and Commissioning) Philip Marshall BA DipLib
MCLIP (0115 985 4201; e-mail: philip.marshall@nottscc.gov.uk)
Principal Librarian (Advisory) Mrs Carole Brittan MA MCLIP (0115 985 4200; e-mail:
carole.brittan@nottscc.gov.uk)
Principal Librarian (Resources) Mrs Janet Huffer BA DipLib MCLIP (0151 985 4202;
e-mail: janet.huffer@nottscc.gov.uk)

OLDHAM

Authority: Oldham Metropolitan District Council
Children's Library Service, Oldham Library, Union Street, Oldham, Lancashire OL1 1DN
☎0161 911 4641
Fax 0161 911 4630
Children's Services Librarian Mrs Beverley Fitzsimons (0161 911 4080; e-mail:
ecs.beverley.fitzsimons@oldham.gov.uk)

OXFORDSHIRE

Authority: Oxfordshire County Council
Cultural Services, Holton, Oxford OX33 1QQ
☎(01865) 810220
Fax (01865) 810207
url: www.oxfordshire.gov.uk/libraries_and_information
County Children's and Youth Librarian Ms Carol Stitson BA DipLib MCLIP (e-mail:
carol.stitson@oxfordshire.gov.uk)

PETERBOROUGH

Authority: Peterborough City Council
Reader Services, Central Library, Broadway, Peterborough PE1 1RX
☎(01733) 742700
Fax (01733) 319140
e-mail: reader.services@peterborough.gov.uk
url: www.peterborough.gov.uk
Reading Services and Marketing Manager Ms Heather Walton BLS MCLIP (e-mail:
heather.walton@peterborough.gov.uk)
(Schools Library Service shared with Cambridgeshire County Council: see Cambridgeshire)

PLYMOUTH

Authority: Plymouth City Council
Schools Library Centre, Chaucer Way, Manadon, Plymouth PL5 3EJ
☎(01752) 780713
Fax (01752) 767623
e-mail: sls@plymouth.gov.uk
url: www.pgfl.gov.uk/sls
Coordinator of Library Services to Young People Mrs Amanda Gerrard BA MCLIP (e-
mail: amanda.gerrard@plymouth.gov.uk), Mrs Sally Walsh BA MCLIP (e-mail:
sally.walsh@plymouth.gov.uk) (job share)
Centre Manager Mrs Anne Smith (e-mail: anne.smith@plymouth.gov.uk)

POOLE

Authority: Borough of Poole
Children and Youth Services, Parkstone Library, Britannia Road, Parkstone, Poole, Dorset
BH14 8AZ
☎(01202) 261650
url: www.boroughofpoole.com/libraries
Children and Youth Services Librarian Mrs Marguerite C Dike MCLIP (e-mail:
m.dike@poole.gov.uk)
(Schools library service provided by Dorset: see Dorset)

PORTSMOUTH

Authority: Portsmouth City Council
Children's Library Service, Central Library, Guildhall Square, Portsmouth PO1 2DX
☎023 9281 9311
Fax 023 9283 9855
Lifelong Learning and Children's Services Manager Mrs Lindy Elliott BA MCLIP (023
9286 8030; e-mail: lindy.elliott@portsmouthcc.gov.uk)

School Library Service, Saxon Shore Infant School, Jubilee Avenue, Paulsgrove, Portsmouth
PO6 4QJ
☎023 9232 6612

Fax 023 9237 5245
School Library Service Manager Peter Bone BA MCLIP (e-mail: peter.bone@portsmouthcc.gov.uk)

READING

Authority: Reading Borough Council
Central Library, Abbey Square, Reading RG1 3BQ
☎0118 939 9849
url: www.readinglibraries.org.uk
Senior Young Persons Development Librarian Ms Suzan Davis BA MCLIP (e-mail: suzan.davis@reading.gov.uk), Ms Nicci Shepherd BA MCLIP (e-mail: nicci.shepherd@reading.gov.uk)
Children's Librarian Simon Smith BA MCLIP (e-mail: simon.smith@reading.gov.uk)
(Shared Education Library Resource Centre: see Bracknell Forest)

REDBRIDGE

Authority: London Borough of Redbridge
Central Library, Clements Road, Ilford, Essex IG1 1EA
☎020 8708 2422
Fax 020 8708 2571
Senior Children's and Schools' Librarian Ms Anne Fowler BA MCLIP (020 8708 2422; e-mail: anne.fowler@redbridge.gov.uk)

REDCAR AND CLEVELAND

Authority: Redcar and Cleveland Borough Council
Library Service, Redcar and Cleveland House, PO Box 86, Kirkleatham Street, Redcar, Cleveland TS10 1XX
☎(01642) 444357
Fax (01642) 444341
url: www.redcar-cleveland.gov.uk
Head of Information and Communications Mrs Carol Barnes BA DipLib (e-mail: carol_barnes@redcar-cleveland.gov.uk)
Children's and Special Services Officer Mrs Janet Richardson (01642 444319; e-mail: janet_richardson@redcar-cleveland.gov.uk)

Schools Resources Service, The Cooper Centre, Beech Grove, South Bank, Middlesbrough TS6 6SU
☎(01642) 289199
Fax (01642) 287811
e-mail: resources_schools@redcar-cleveland.gov.uk
Schools Resources Officer Mrs Carolyn Rimmington MCLIP
(Cooperative service with Hartlepool, Middlesbrough and Stockton-on-Tees)

RICHMOND UPON THAMES

Authority: London Borough of Richmond upon Thames
Young People's Services, The Cottage, Little Green, Richmond upon Thames, Surrey
TW9 1QL
☎020 8940 0590
Fax 020 8940 8030
e-mail: yps@richmond.gov.uk
url: www.richmond.gov.uk/libraries
Young People's Library Services Manager Ms Joss Green MCLIP (e-mail:
j.green@richmond.gov.uk)

ROCHDALE

Authority: Rochdale Metropolitan Borough Council
Wheatsheaf Library, Wheatsheaf Shopping Centre, Baillie Street, Rochdale, Greater
Manchester OL16 1JZ
☎(01706) 864972
Fax (01706) 864992
e-mail: libraryservice@rochdale.gov.uk
Community Services Manager Mrs Freda Fletcher MCLIP (01706 864964; e-mail:
freda.fletcher@rochdale.gov.uk)
Children's Services Manager Ray Stearn BA MCLIP (01706 864972; e-mail:
ray.stearn@rochdale.gov.uk)

ROTHERHAM

Authority: Rotherham Metropolitan Borough Council
Education and Young People's Services, Maltby Library HQ, High Street, Maltby,
Rotherham, South Yorks S66 8LD
☎(01709) 815123; (01709) 813034 (Schools Library Service)
Fax (01709) 818051
Manager, Services to Children and Young People Ms Marcia Newton BA MCLIP
(e-mail: marcia.newton@rotherham.gov.uk)

RUTLAND

Authority: Rutland County Council
Children and Young People's Service, Oakham Library, Catmose Street, Oakham, Rutland
LE15 6HW
☎(01572) 722918
Fax (01572) 724906
e-mail: oakhamlibrary@rutnet.co.uk
Children and Young People's Librarian Ms Diane Wright BA(Hons) MCLIP

ST HELENS

Authority: Metropolitan Borough of St Helens
The Rivington Centre, Rivington Road, St Helens, Merseyside WA10 4ND
☎(01744) 455412
Fax (01744) 455413
e-mail: libraryservicesschools@sthelens.gov.uk
Senior Libraries Manager, Social Inclusion Ms Kathryn Boothroyd BA(Hons) MCLIP
(01744 675236; e-mail: kathrynboothroyd@sthelens.gov.uk)
Schools Library Service Manager Mrs Judith Lilley BA(Hons) DipLib (01744 455412)

SALFORD

Authority: Salford City Council
Swinton Library, Chorley Road, Swinton, Manchester M27 4AE
☎0161 793 3568
Fax 0161 727 7071
url: www.salford.gov.uk/library/Services/childservices.htm
Senior Librarian, Children and Young People Mrs Pamela Manley BA MLS PGDipLib
MA(Ed) (e-mail: pamela.manley@salford.gov.uk)

Schools' Library Service, Broadwalk Centre, Belvedere Road, Salford, Manchester M6 5EJ
☎0161 778 0936
Senior Librarian, Children and Young People Mrs Pamela Manley BA MLS PGDipLib
MA(Ed) (e-mail: pamela.manley@salford.gov.uk)

SANDWELL

Authority: Sandwell Metropolitan Borough Council
Central Library, High Street, West Bromwich, West Midlands B70 8DZ
☎0121 569 4933
Fax 0121 525 9465
url: www.sandwell.gov.uk/libraries
Management Support Librarian – Client Groups Mrs Diane Edlin (e-mail:
diane.edlin@sandwell.gov.uk)

Training & Development Centre, Popes Lane, Oldbury, West Midlands B69 4PJ
☎0121 569 4415
Fax 0121 569 4481
e-mail: resource.matters@sandwell.gov.uk
url: www.sandwell.gov.uk/libraries
Schools Library Service Manager Ms Judith Bird MA DipLib MCLIP

SEFTON

Authority: Sefton Council
Leisure Services Department, Pavilion Buildings, 99–105 Lord Street, Southport PR8 1RJ
☎0151 934 2376

e-mail: library.service@leisure.sefton.gov.uk

Principal Development Manager (Community Cohesion) Ms Zoë Clarke BA MA MCLIP (e-mail: zoe.clarke@leisure.sefton.gov.uk)

SHEFFIELD

Authority: Sheffield City Council

Learning and Young People's Unit, Bannerdale Education Centre, 125 Carter Knowle Road, Sheffield S7 1EX

☎0114 250 6840

Fax 0114 250 6841

e-mail: schoolslibservice@sheffield.gov.uk

Young People's Library Service Manager Ms Diane Kostka BA MA (0114 250 6839; e-mail: diane.kostka@sheffield.gov.uk)

SHROPSHIRE

Authority: Shropshire County Council

Shropshire County Library Service, The Annexe, Shirehall, Abbey Foregate, Shrewsbury SY2 6ND

☎(01743) 255030

Fax (01743) 255050

e-mail: libraries@shropshire-cc.gov.uk

url: www.shropshire-cc.gov.uk/library.nsf

Principal Librarian: Young People and Access Gordon Dickins BA MCLIP (01743 255005)

SLOUGH

Authority: Slough Borough Council

Slough Library, High Street, Slough SL1 1EA

☎(01753) 535166

Fax (01753) 825050

url: www.sloughlibrary.org.uk

Library Services Manager: Operations Ms Jackie Menniss BA(Hons) DipIM MCLIP (01753 787506; e-mail: jackie.menniss@slough.gov.uk)

Principal Librarian: Children and Young People Ms Liz Broekmann BA HDipLib (01753 787530; e-mail: liz.broekmann@slough.gov.uk)

(Shared Education Library Resource Centre: see Bracknell Forest)

SOLIHULL

Authority: Solihull Metropolitan Borough Council

Central Library, Homer Road, Solihull, West Midlands B91 3RG

☎0121 704 8401

Fax 0121 704 6991

Children's Family Learning and Schools Services Manager Ms Trish Botten BA(Hons) (e-mail: tbotten@solihull.gov.uk)

Learning Resources and Advice Service – Bookstart, Family Learning and Schools, Central Library, Homer Road, Solihull, West Midlands B91 3RG
☎0121 704 6984
Fax 0121 704 6991
url: www.solihull.gov.uk
LRAS Coordinator – Bookstart, Family Learning and Schools Vacant

SOMERSET

Authority: Somerset County Council
Libraries, Arts and Information Admin Centre, Mount Street, Bridgwater, Somerset TA6 3ES
☎(01278) 451201
Fax (01278) 452787
url: www.somerset.gov.uk/libraries
Assistant County Librarian, Policy and Development Miss Rachel Boyd BA MCLIP (e-mail: rboyd@somerset.gov.uk)

Resources for Learning, Parkway, Bridgwater, Somerset TA6 4RL
☎(01278) 421015
e-mail: rfl@somerset.gov.uk
Manager, Resources for Learning (Schools Library Service) Christopher Jones BSc PGCE DMS MCLIP (e-mail: cbjones@somerset.gov.uk)
Senior Schools Librarian: Operations Nick Rowe MCLIP (e-mail: nrowe@somerset.gov.uk)
Senior Assistant: Administration Ms Anne-Marie Moares
Senior Assistant: Operations Ms Sasha Appleby BA

SOUTH GLOUCESTERSHIRE

Authority: South Gloucestershire Council
Downend Library, Buckingham Gardens, Downend, South Glos BS16 5TW
☎(01454) 868451
Children and Young People's Librarian Ms Wendy Nicholls MCLIP (e-mail: wendy.nicholls@southglos.gov.uk)

SOUTH TYNESIDE

Authority: South Tyneside Metropolitan Borough Council
Central Library, Prince George Square, South Shields, Tyne and Wear NE33 2PE
☎0191 424 7884
Fax 0191 455 8085
Young People's Services Co-ordinator Ms K Armstrong MA MCLIP (e-mail: kathryn.armstrong@s-tyneside-mbc.gov.uk)

School Library Service, Chuter Ede Education Centre, Galsworthy Road, South Shields, Tyne and Wear NE34 9UG
☎0191 426 8110

Fax 0191 519 0600
Schools Librarian Miss Karen Hall BA MCLIP (e-mail: karen.hall@s-tyneside-mbc.gov.uk)

SOUTHAMPTON

Authority: Southampton City Council
Central Children's Library, Civic Centre, Southampton SO14 7LW
☎023 8083 2598
Fax 023 8033 6305
e-mail: childrens.library@southampton.gov.uk
url: www.southampton.gov.uk/libraries/
Principal Children's Librarian Clive Barnes BA MA MCLIP (023 8083 2163; e-mail:
clive.barnes@southampton.gov.uk)

School Library Service Centre, Warren Crescent, Shirley Warren, Southampton SO16 6AY
☎023 8078 0507
Fax 023 8070 2783
Senior Schools Librarian Miss Chris Thomas MCLIP (e-mail:
christobel.thomas@southampton.gov.uk)

SOUTHEND ON SEA

Authority: Southend on Sea Borough Council
Southend Library, Victoria Avenue, Southend on Sea, Essex SS2 6EX
☎(01702) 612621
Fax (01702) 469241
Head of Children's and Access Services Mark Thres BA MCLIP

SOUTHWARK

Authority: London Borough of Southwark
Southwark Environment and Leisure, 15 Spa Road, London SE16 3QW
☎020 7525 3920
Fax 020 7525 1568
Head of Libraries and Lifelong Learning Adrian Olsen BA MCLIP (e-mail:
adrian.olsen@southwark.gov.uk)
Library Operations Manager Ms Christine Brown BA MCLIP MLib (e-mail:
christine.brown@southwark.gov.uk)
Libraries Development and Support Manager Ms Claire Styles BA(Hons) MSc(Econ)
MCLIP (e-mail: claire.styles@southwark.gov.uk)

Education Library Service, Learning and Business Centre, Cator Street (off Commercial
Way), Peckham, London SE15 6AA
☎020 7525 2830
Fax 020 7525 2837
Manager Ms Elvena Brumant (e-mail: elvena.brumant@southwark.gov.uk)

STAFFORDSHIRE

Authority: Staffordshire County Council
Education and Lifelong Learning Directorate, Library and Information Services, Tipping Street, Stafford ST16 2DH
Service Advisor: Children and Young People Mrs B W Kettle MCLIP (01785 854170; e-mail: beryl.kettle@staffordshire.gov.uk)
Service Development Officer, Learning, Knowledge and Resources Ms Sue Ball BA MCLIP (01785 854170; e-mail: sue.ball@staffordshire.gov.uk)

Schools Library Service, Staffordshire Library and Information Service, Friars Terrace, Stafford ST17 4AY
☎(01785) 278340/1
Fax (01785) 278421
e-mail: sls@staffordshire.gov.uk
Senior Librarians, School Library Service Mrs Ann Barlow BA MA, Mrs Pat Morris MCLIP

STOCKPORT

Authority: Stockport Metropolitan Borough Council
School Library Service, Dialstone Centre, Lisburne Lane, Stockport SK2 7LL
☎0161 474 2253
Fax 0161 474 2257
e-mail: sls@stockport.gov.uk
url: www.stockport.gov.uk
Head of Library Services to Children Ms Andrea Ellison BA MA (e-mail: andrea.ellison@stockport.gov.uk), Judith Lynch (e-mail: judith.lynch@stockport.gov.uk) (job share)

STOCKTON-ON-TEES

Authority: Stockton-on-Tees Borough Council
Children and Youth Services, East Precinct, Town Centre, Billingham, Stockton-on-Tees TS23 2JZ
☎(01642) 526520
Children's and Young Persons Librarian Ms Karen Morris
Children and Youth Services Officer Tony Quantrill (01642 526995)
(Schools Resources Service: see Redcar & Cleveland. Cooperative service with Middlesbrough, Hartlepool and Redcar & Cleveland)

STOKE-ON-TRENT

Authority: Stoke-on-Trent City Council
Children's and Youth Service, Floor F, Hanley Library, Bethesda Street, Hanley, Stoke-on-Trent ST1 3RS
☎(01782) 238496
url: www.stoke.gov.uk/council/libraries

Principal Children's and Young People's Librarian Mrs Caroline Lovatt BA MCLIP
(e-mail: caroline.lovatt@stoke.gov.uk)
(Shared school library service with Staffordshire: see Staffordshire)

SUFFOLK

Authority: Suffolk County Council
Libraries and Heritage, Endeavour House, 8 Russell Road, Ipswich IP1 2BX
☎(01473) 264623
url: www.suffolkcc.gov.uk/libraries_and_heritage/
Head of Childeren and Young People's Services Ms Helen Boothroyd BA MCLIP
(e-mail: helen.boothroyd@libher.suffolkcc.gov.uk)

SUNDERLAND

Authority: City of Sunderland Metropolitan District Council
City Library and Arts Centre, 30-32 Fawcett Street, Sunderland SR1 1RE
☎0191 514 1235
Fax 0191 514 8444
url: www.sunderland.gov.uk/libraries
Assistant Head of Culture and Tourism (Libraries, Heritage and Information)
Mrs Jane F Hall BA(Hons) MCLIP (e-mail: Jane.Hall@sunderland.gov.uk)

Sandhill Centre Library of EVH, Grindon Lane, Sunderland SR3 4EN
☎0191 553 8870
Fax 0191 553 8873
Library Manager Ms Caroline Gray

SURREY

Authority: Surrey County Council
Ewell Library, Bourne Hall, Spring Street, Ewell, Surrey KT17 1UF
☎020 8786 7361
Fax 020 8873 3835
e-mail: libraries@surreycc.gov.uk
Library Service Development Manager, Lifelong Learning and Children's Services
Mrs Sue Gent BA MCLIP (e-mail: sue.gent@surreycc.gov.uk)

SUTTON

Authority: London Borough of Sutton
Children's Library Service, Central Library, St Nicholas Way, Sutton, Surrey SM1 1EA
☎020 8770 4766
Fax 020 8770 4777
Children's Services Manager Mrs Pauline Deakin BA MCLIP (020 8770 4622; e-mail:
pauline.deakin@sutton.gov.uk), Mrs Jane Allen BA MCLIP (020 8770 4622; e-mail:
jane.allen@sutton.gov.uk) (job-share)

Schools Library Service, Central Library, St Nicholas Way, Sutton, Surrey SM1 1EA
☎020 8770 4754
Fax 020 8770 4777
e-mail: schools.libraryservice@sutton.gov.uk
Schools Library Service Manager Mrs Angela McNally MCLIP

SWINDON

Authority: Swindon Borough Council
Central Library, Regent Circus, Swindon, Wilts SN1 1QG
☎(01793) 464202
Fax (01793) 541319
Librarian Ms Rebecca Bolton BA(Hons) MLib MCLIP (e-mail: rbolton@swindon.gov.uk)

North Swindon Library, Orbital Retail Park, Thamesdown Drive, Swindon SN25 4AN
Librarian Ms Rachel Douglass MSc MCLIP (01793 707131; e-mail:
rdouglass@swindon.gov.uk)
(School Library Service provided by Wiltshire: see Wiltshire – Wiltshire & Swindon
Learning Resources)

TAMESIDE

Authority: Tameside Metropolitan Borough Council
Young People's Services, Central Library, Old Street, Ashton-under-Lyne, Tameside OL6 7SG
☎0161 342 2664
Fax 0161 330 4762
Young People's Services Co-ordinator Mrs Ruth Lomas (e-mail:
ruth.lomas@tameside.gov.uk)

School Library Services, Dukinfield Town Hall, King Street, Dukinfield, Tameside SK16 4LA
☎0161 342 5091
Fax 0161 342 5089
e-mail: schoollibraryservice@tameside.gov.uk
School Libraries Consultant Ms Lynne Craigs MCLIP (e-mail:
lynne.craigs@tameside.gov.uk)

TELFORD AND WREKIN

Authority: Borough of Telford and Wrekin
Customer, Community and Culture, Civic Offices, PO Box 59, Telford, Shropshire TF3 4WZ
☎(01952) 292151
Fax (01952) 290317
Senior Librarian, Children and Young People Mrs Jo Heaton (01952 202747; e-mail:
jo.heaton@telford.gov.uk)
(Schools library service offered in partnership with Shropshire County Council: see
Shropshire)

THURROCK

Authority: Thurrock Council
Libraries and Cultural Services Department, Grays Library, Orsett Road, Grays, Essex
RM17 5DX
☎(01375) 383611 (enquiries), (01375) 382555 ext 221 (administration)
Fax (01375) 370806
url: www.thurrock.gov.uk/libraries
Children's Services Manager Miss Rosalyn Jones BA(Hons) DipLib (e-mail:
rjones@thurrock.gov.uk)

TORBAY

Authority: Torbay Council
Young People's Services, Torquay Central Library, Lymington Road, Torquay, Devon TQI
3DT
Fax (01803) 208311
Young People's Services Librarian Ms Helen Cunningham BA(Hons) DipLib (01803
208289; e-mail: helen.cunningham@torbay.gov.uk), Mrs Tracey Dickinson BA(Hons) MCLIP
(e-mail: tracey.dickinson@torbay.gov.uk) (job-share)

Devon School Library Service, Torquay Central Library, Lymington Road, Torquay, Devon
TQI 3DT
☎(01803) 208293
Fax (01803) 208311
e-mail: sls.south@devon.gov.uk
Centre Manager Miss M Granata
Senior Schools Librarian Mrs J Hyde MCLIP
School Librarian Mrs C Kennett MA DipLib MCLIP

TOWER HAMLETS

Authority: London Borough of Tower Hamlets
Children's Library Service, Whitechapel Library, 77 Whitechapel High Street, London E1 7QX
☎020 7247 9510
Fax 020 7247 5731
e-mail: childrenslibrary@towerhamlets.gov.uk
Co-ordinator, Children's Library Service Giles Harrison BSc(Econ) MSc MCLIP
GradCertEd

Schools Library Services, Tower Hamlets Professional Development Centre, English Street,
London E3 4TA
☎020 7364 6428
Fax 020 7364 6422
e-mail: schoolslibraryservices@towerhamlets.gov.uk
Head of Schools Library Services Ms G Harris MA MCLIP

TRAFFORD

Authority: Trafford Metropolitan Borough Council
Schools Library Service, Davyhulme Library Site, Hayeswater Road, Davyhulme, Greater Manchester M41 7BL
☎0161 912 2894
Fax 0161 912 2895
Education Services Librarian Mrs Jenny Brooks BA(Hons) MCLIP (e-mail: jenny.brooks@trafford.gov.uk)

WAKEFIELD

Authority: Wakefield Metropolitan District Council
Featherstone Library and Community Centre, Station Lane, Featherstone, West Yorks WF7 5BB
☎(01977) 722745
Fax (01977) 722749
e-mail: featherstonelibrary@wakefield.gov.uk
Senior Librarian, Children's Services Andrew Wright BMus(Hons) DipLib

Library HQ, Balne Lane, Wakefield, Yorkshire WF2 0DQ
☎(01924) 302238
Fax (01924) 302245
url: www.wakefield.gov.uk/sls
Senior Librarian, Schools Library Service Ms Lesley Marshall BA MCLIP (e-mail: lesleymarshall@wakefield.gov.uk)

WALSALL

Authority: Walsall Metropolitan Borough Council
Children's and Schools Library Support Services, Manor Farm Centre, King George Crescent, Rushall, Walsall, West Midlands WS4 1EG
☎(01922) 724995
Fax (01922) 659559
e-mail: slss@walsallgfl.org.uk
Children's and School Library Services Manager Ms Louise Davies BA (e-mail: ldavies@walsallgfl.org.uk)

WALTHAM FOREST

Authority: London Borough of Waltham Forest
Administrative Office, Walthamstow Library, High Street, London E17 7JN
url: www.lbwf.gov.uk
Social Inclusion Manager Les Armstrong (020 8496 1124; e-mail: les.armstrong@walthamforest.gov.uk)

WANDSWORTH

Authority: London Borough of Wandsworth
Children's Library Service, Battersea Library, Lavender Hill, London SW11 1JB
☎020 8871 7466
Fax 020 7978 4376
url: www.wandsworth.gov.uk
Library Service Development Manager, Children and Young People Miss Hilary
Manning BA(Hons) MA MCLIP (e-mail: hmanning@wandsworth.gov.uk)

WARRINGTON

Authority: Warrington Borough Council
Young People's Services, Warrington Library, Museum Street, Warrington, Cheshire WA1 1JB
☎(01925) 442889 (switchboard), (01925) 443232 (specialist services)
Fax (01925) 443257
url: www.libraryatwarrington.gov.uk
Young People's Services Manager Mrs Christine Everett BA MCLIP (e-mail:
ceverett@warrington.gov.uk)
(Schools library services provided by Education Library Service, Cheshire: see Cheshire)

WARWICKSHIRE

Authority: Warwickshire County Council
Schools Library Service, Unit 11b, Montague Road, Warwick CV34 5LT
☎(01926) 413461/2
Fax (01926) 413438
e-mail: schoolslibraryservice@warwickshire.gov.uk
Managers Mrs Angela Ballard BA MCLIP, Mrs Celia Merriman BA MCLIP
Resource Manager Mrs Karen Jones BA MCLIP

WEST BERKSHIRE

Authority: West Berkshire District Council
Newbury Library, The Wharf, Newbury, Berkshire RG14 5AU
☎(01635) 519900
Fax (01635) 519906
e-mail: newburylibrary@westberks.gov.uk
url: www.westberks.gov.uk
Children's Services Librarian Ms Susan Deering-Punshon BLib(Hons) MCLIP (e-mail:
Sdeeringpunshon@westberks.gov.uk), Mrs Ros Preuss BA(Hons) MCLIP (e-mail:
Rpreuss@westberks.gov.uk)
Team Leader: Reader Development and Children's Services Mrs Felicity Harrison
BA(Hons) MPhil MCLIP (e-mail: Fharrison@westberks.gov.uk), Mrs Barbara Magee
BA(Hons) MA MCLIP (e-mail: Bmagee@westberks.gov.uk)
(Shared Education Library Resource Centre: see Bracknell Forest)

WEST SUSSEX

Authority: West Sussex County Council
West Sussex County Library Services, Tower Street, Chichester, West Sussex PO19 1QJ
☎(01243) 382557
Fax (01243) 382554
Assistant County Librarian, Reading and Learning Ms Lesley Sim BA MCLIP (e-mail: lesley.sim@westsussex.gov.uk)

School Library Service, Administration Centre, Willow Park, 4B Terminus Road, Chichester, West Sussex PO19 8EQ
☎(01243) 816755
Fax (01243) 816752
Head of Schools Library Service Ms S A Heyes BA(Hons) CertEd MCLIP (e-mail: susan.heyes@westsussex.gov.uk)

WESTMINSTER

Authority: Westminster City Council
Children's Library Services, 4th Floor, City Hall, 65 Victoria Street, London SW1E 6QP
☎020 7641 1782
url: www.westminster.gov.uk/libraries
Local Area Manager: Children and Lifelong Learning John Hughes BA(Hons) DipLib
(e-mail: jhughes1@westminster.gov.uk)

Schools Library Service, 62 Shirland Road, London W9 2EH
☎020 7641 4321
Fax 020 7641 4322
Schools Library Service Manager Nick Fuller BA(Hons) AgDipLib MCLIP (e-mail: nfuller@westminster.gov.uk)

WIGAN

Authority: Wigan Council
Wigan Leisure and Culture Trust, Children and Young People's Library Service, Leigh Library, Turnpike Centre, Civic Square, Market Street, Leigh, Lancashire WN7 1EB
Children and Youth Services Co-ordinator Ms Chris Appleton BA(Hons) DipLib
MCLIP (01942 404555; e-mail: chris.appleton@wlct.org)
Children's Officers Ms Yvonne Wilson BA(Hons) MCLIP (01942 404477), Mrs Rita Hackett (01942 404477)

Wigan Leisure and Culture Trust, Schools Library Service, Shevington Library, Gathurst Lane, Shevington, Wigan WN6 8HA
☎(01257) 253269
Schools Library Service Manager Mrs Tracey Stirrup BA(Hons) (e-mail: t.stirrup@wlct.org)

WILTSHIRE

Authority: Wiltshire County Council
Children's Library Services, c/o Westbury Library, Edward Street, Westbury, Wilts BA13 3BD
☎(01373) 865602
Fax (01373) 859208
County Children's Librarian Miss Sarah Hillier BA PGCE MCLIP (e-mail:
sarahhillier@wiltshire.gov.uk)

Wiltshire & Swindon Learning Resources, Counties and Heritage HQ, Bythesea Road,
Trowbridge, Wilts BA14 8BS
☎(01225) 713744
Fax (01225) 350029
Acting Head of Wiltshire & Swindon Learning Resources (School Library Service)
Ms Lesley Hughes BA DipLib MCLIP (01225 713742; e-mail:
lesleyhughes@wiltshire.gov.uk)
(Shared service with Swindon)

WINDSOR AND MAIDENHEAD

Authority: Royal Borough of Windsor and Maidenhead
Maidenhead Central Library, St Ives Road, Maidenhead, Berks SL6 1QU
☎(01628) 685641
Fax (01628) 796971
e-mail: maidenhead.library@rbwm.gov.uk
url: www.rbwm.gov.uk
Senior Librarian, Young People Mrs Angela Gallacher BA(Hons) AUDIS (e-mail:
angela.gallacher@rbwm.gov.uk)
(Shared Education Library Resource Centre: see Bracknell Forest)

WIRRAL

Authority: Metropolitan Borough of Wirral
Education and Cultural Services Department, Hamilton Building, Conway Street,
Birkenhead, Wirral, Cheshire CH41 4FD
☎0151 666 5575
Fax 0151 666 4207
url: www.wirral-libraries.net
Head of Libraries and Halls Ms Sue Powell BA MCLIP (e-mail:
suepowell@wirral.gov.uk)

Wirral Schools Library Service, Wirral Education Centre, Acre Lane, Bromborough, Wirral,
Cheshire CH62 7BZ
☎0151 346 6502
Fax 0151 346 6739
e-mail: sls@wirral.gov.uk
url: www.wirral-mbc.gov.uk
Schools' Librarian Ms Mary Bryning BA DipLib (e-mail: marybryning@wirral.gov.uk)

WOKINGHAM

Authority: Wokingham District Council
Wokingham Library, Denmark Street, Wokingham, Berks RG40 2BB
☎0118 978 1368
url: www.wokingham.gov.uk/libraries
Community Librarian: Children and Young People Mrs Rachel Maskelyne BA(Hons)
MA (0118 979 3474; e-mail: rachel.maskelyne@wokingham.gov.uk)

Woodley Library, Headley Road, Woodley, Reading RG5 4JA
☎0118 969 0304
Community Librarian Vacant
Team Librarian Ms Elizabeth McDonald (e-mail: elizabeth.mcdonald@wokingham.gov.uk)

WOLVERHAMPTON

Authority: Wolverhampton City Council
Central Library, Snow Hill, Wolverhampton WV1 3AX
☎(01902) 552013
Fax (01902) 556235
Children and Young People's Service Manager Mrs Marion Cockin MCLIP (e-mail:
marion.cockin@dial.pipex.com)

Education Library Service, Jennie Lee Professional Centre, Lichfield Road, Wednesfield,
Wolverhampton WV11 3HT
☎(01902) 555906
Fax (01902) 555265
Senior Librarian, Children's and Young People's Services Mrs Sylvia Jenkins
BA(Hons) (e-mail: sylvia.jenkins@dial.pipex.com)

WORCESTERSHIRE

Authority: Worcestershire County Council
Cultural Services, County Hall, Spetchley Road, Worcester WR5 2NP
☎(01905) 766233
Fax (01905) 766244
Strategic Library Manager Mrs Carmel Reed BA DMS MCLIP (e-mail:
creed@worcestershire.gov.uk)

Schools Libraries Service, Sherwood Lane, Lower Wick, Worcester WR2 4NU
☎(01905) 420273
Fax (01905) 748619
e-mail: slslib@worcestershire.gov.uk
url: www.worcestershire.gov.uk/home/lib-index/lib-schools.htm
Schools Library Service Manager Mrs Dawn Woods BA MCLIP (e-mail:
dwoods@worcestershire.gov.uk)

YORK

Authority: City of York Council
Acomb Library, Front Street, Acomb, York YO24 3BZ
☎(01904) 787511 (tel/fax)
Community Development Librarians Ms Ann Masters BSc(Hons) DipLib MCLIP
(e-mail: ann.masters@york.gov.uk), Ms Sue Matthews BA(Hons) DipLib (e-mail:
sue.matthews@york.gov.uk)

Clifton Library, Rawcliffe Lane, York YO30 5SJ
☎(01904) 693979 (tel/fax)
Community Development Librarians Ms Frances Postlethwaite BA(Hons) CertEd
MCLIP (e-mail: frances.postlethwaite@york.gov.uk), Mrs Charlotte Maitland MA (e-mail:
charlotte.maitland@york.gov.uk)

ABERDEEN

Authority: Aberdeen City Council
Arts & Recreation Department (Libraries), Central Library, Rosemount Viaduct, Aberdeen
AB25 1GW
☎(01224) 652500
Fax (01224) 641985
Children's Services Librarian Ms Ann Stephen BEd MCLIP (e-mail:
annstephen@aberdeencity.gov.uk)
Assistant Librarian, Central Ms Marion Wands MA (e-mail:
mwands@aberdeencity.gov.uk)

Curriculum Resources and Information Service, Summerhill Centre, Stronsay Drive,
Aberdeen AB15 6JA
☎(01224) 346114
Fax (01224) 346116
e-mail: cris@aberdeencity.gov.uk
Principal Officer Mrs Alison Turriff BA MEd FCLIP (01224 346110; e-mail:
aturriff@aberdeencity.gov.uk)

ABERDEENSHIRE

Authority: Aberdeenshire Council
Aberdeenshire Library & Information Service, Meldrum Meg Way, The Meadows Industrial
Estate, Oldmeldrum, Aberdeenshire AB51 0GN
☎(01651) 872707
Fax (01651) 872142
Young People and Schools Resources Librarian Mrs Fiona Gillies BA MCLIP (e-mail:
fiona.gillies@aberdeenshire.gov.uk), Mrs Susan McKay BA MCLIP (e-mail:
susan.mckay@aberdeenshire.gov.uk)
Primary School Librarian Mrs Angela Hogg BA (e-mail:
angela.hogg@aberdeenshire.gov.uk)

ANGUS

Authority: Angus Council
Cultural Services Department, County Buildings, Market Street, Forfar, Angus DD8 3WF
☎(01307) 461460
Fax (01307) 462590
e-mail: cultural@angus.gov.uk
Head of Cultural Services Norman K Atkinson DipEd AMA FMA

Educational Resources Service, Bruce House, Wellgate, Arbroath, Angus DD11 3TL
☎(01241) 435045

e-mail: cularbers@angus.gov.uk
Educational Resources Librarian Ms Moyra Hood BSc(Hons) PGDipLib MCLIP (e-mail: hoodm@angus.gov.uk)

ARGYLL AND BUTE

Authority: Argyll and Bute Council
Library HQ, Highland Avenue, Sandbank, Dunoon, Argyll PA23 8PB
☎(01369) 703214
Fax (01369) 705797
Youth Services Librarian Ms Dorothy A McLennan MA(Hons) MCLIP (e-mail: Dorothy.McLennan@argyll-bute.gov.uk)

CLACKMANNANSHIRE

Authority: Clackmannanshire Council
Library Services, 26-28 Drysdale Street, Alloa, Clackmannanshire FK10 1JL
☎(01259) 722262
Fax (01259) 219469
e-mail: libraries@clacks.gov.uk
Team Leader (Community Services) John Blake BSc DipLib DipEdTech MCLIP (ext 220; e-mail: jblake@clacks.gov.uk)
Team Leader (Childrens Services) Ms Anne Fulton BSc DipLib MCLIP (ext 219; e-mail: afulton@clacks.gov.uk)
Children's Librarian Ms Chris Pairman BA MCLIP (ext 221; e-mail: cpairman@clacks.gov.uk), Vacant (job-share)

COMHAIRLE NAN EILEAN SIAR

Authority: Comhairle nan Eilean Siar
Public Library, 19 Cromwell Street, Stornoway, Isle of Lewis, Hebrides HS1 2DA
☎(01851) 708649
Fax (01851) 708677
Senior Librarian, Youth Services Mrs M Ferguson MA MCLIP (e-mail: mary-ferguson@cne-siar.gov.uk)

Education Development Centre Library, Kenneth Street, Stornoway, Isle of Lewis, Hebrides HS1 2DP
☎(01851) 708646
Fax (01851) 708677
Senior Library Assistant Ms Kay MacKinnon (e-mail: kay-mackinnon@cne-siar.gov.uk)

DUMFRIES AND GALLOWAY

Authority: Dumfries and Galloway Council
Lochthorn Library, Lochthorn, Dumfries DG1 1UF
☎(01387) 265780
Fax (01387) 266424

Section Librarian, Young People Ms Christine Johnston (e-mail: christinejo@dumgal.gov.uk)

Central Support Unit, Catherine Street, Dumfries DG1 1JB
☎(01387) 253820
Fax (01387) 260294
e-mail: libs&i@dumgal.gov.uk
Children's Librarian Mrs Allyson Jardine BA MCLIP

DUNDEE

Authority: Dundee City Council
Children's Department, Central Library, The Wellgate, Dundee DD1 1DB
☎(01382) 431529
Fax (01382) 431558
e-mail: central.childrens@dundeecity.gov.uk
url: www.dundeecity.gov.uk
Library and Information Worker Ms Shona Donaldson BSc (e-mail: shona.donaldson@dundeecity.gov.uk)

Communities Department, Library and Information Services, Arthurstone Neighbourhood Library, Arthurstone Terrace, Dundee DD4 6RT
☎(01382) 438892
Fax (01382) 438885
url: www.dundeecity.gov.uk/library
Senior Library and Information Worker Ms Lynn Moy BA MCLIP (e-mail: lynn.moy@dundeecity.gov.uk)

School Library Service, Central Library, The Wellgate, Dundee DD1 1DB
☎(01382) 431546
Fax (01382) 431558
e-mail: schools.service@dundeecity.gov.uk
Senior Library and Information Worker Stuart Syme BA MCLIP (01382 431546; e-mail: stuart.syme@dundeecity.gov.uk)

EAST AYRSHIRE

Authority: East Ayrshire Council
Council Offices, Lugar, Cumnock, Ayrshire KA18 3JQ
☎(01563) 555457
Fax (01563) 555455
Education Liaison Officer Miss Pat Standen BA MCLIP (01563 555451; e-mail: pat.standen@east-ayrshire.gov.uk)
Community Librarians (Young People) Mrs Ailsa McInnes BA DipLib MCLIP (e-mail: ailsa.mcinnes@east-ayrshire.gov.uk)
Community Librarians (Young People) Mrs Margaret Patterson BA MCLIP (e-mail: margaret.patterson@east-ayrshire.gov.uk)

EAST DUNBARTONSHIRE

Authority: East Dunbartonshire Council
Information and Lifelong Learning, Library Headquarters, 2 West High Street, Kirkintilloch, Dunbartonshire G66 IAD
☎0141 776 5666
Fax 0141 776 0408
e-mail: libraries@eastdunbarton.gov.uk
url: www.eastdunbarton.gov.uk
Young People's Resource Co-ordinator Mrs Frances MacArthur MA MCLIP (e-mail: frances.macarthur@eastdunbarton.gov.uk)
Assistant Librarian, Young People's Services Ian Gibson BA MCLIP (e-mail: ian.gibson@eastdunbarton.gov.uk)

Educational Resource Service, Brookwood Villa, 166 Drymen Road, Bearsden, Glasgow G61 3RJ
☎0141 570 2300
Fax 0141 943 1688
Education Resource Officers Mrs Linda Owens, Mrs Linda Farrar

EAST LOTHIAN

Authority: East Lothian Council
Library and Museum HQ, Dunbar Road, Haddington, East Lothian EH41 3PJ
☎(01620) 828212 (Senior Librarian), (01620) 828213 (Librarian)
Fax (01620) 828201
Senior Librarian, Young People's Services Ms Ruth Collin BA MCLIP (e-mail: rcollin@eastlothian.gov.uk)
Librarian, Young People's Services Mrs Louise Nowell (e-mail: lnowell@eastlothian.gov.uk), Mrs Elaine Young (e-mail: eyoung@eastlothian.gov.uk)

EAST RENFREWSHIRE

Authority: East Renfrewshire Council
Cultural Services, Glen Street, Barrhead, East Renfrewshire G78 1QA
☎0141 577 3513
Fax 0141 577 3501
url: www.eastrenfrewshire.gov.uk
Lifelong Learning Officer Ms Janice Weir BA MCLIP (0141 577 3516; e-mail: janice.weir@eastrenfrewshire.gov.uk)
Library Development Worker Ms Mary Curran, Ms Elissa Wilson

EDINBURGH

Authority: City of Edinburgh Council
Central Library, George IV Bridge, Edinburgh EH1 1EG
☎0131 242 8120
Fax 0131 242 8127

e-mail: eclis@edinburgh.gov.uk
url: www.edinburgh.gov.uk/libraries
Principal Library Officer, Youth Services Ms Brenda Rowan BA MCLIP (e-mail:
brenda.rowan@edinburgh.gov.uk)

Learning and Information Resources, Education Service Centre, 154 McDonald Road,
Edinburgh EH7 4NN
☎0131 469 2960
Fax 0131 469 2961
Principal Officer, Learning and Information Ms Valerie Walker (e-mail:
valerie.walker@educ.edin.gov.uk)

FALKIRK

Authority: Falkirk Council
Library Services, Victoria Buildings, Queen Street, Falkirk FK2 7AF
☎(01324) 506800
Fax (01324) 506801
Convenor, Young People's Services Team Ms Yvonne Manning MA DipLib MCLIP
(e-mail: yvonne.manning@falkirk.gov.uk)

FIFE

Authority: Fife Council
Central Area Library Services, Library HQ, East Fergus Place, Kirkcaldy, Fife KY1 1XT
☎(01592) 412930
Fax (01592) 412941
Community Librarian, Young People's Services Ms Ella Dickson (e-mail:
ella.dickson@fife.gov.uk)

East Area Library Services, Library HQ, County Building, Cupar, Fife KY15 4TA
☎(01334) 412943
Fax (01334) 412941
Learning Services Librarian Ms Margaret Nikolic (e-mail: margaret.nikolic@fife.gov.uk)

West Area Library Services, Carnegie Library, 1 Abbot Street, Dunfermline, Fife KY12 7NL
☎(01383) 312986
Fax (01383) 314314
e-mail: dunfermline.library@fife.gov.uk
url: www.fifedirect.org.uk/libraries
Community Librarian, Young People's Services Miss Christine Chambers BA(Hons)
MA MCLIP (e-mail: christine.chambers@fife.gov.uk)

Schools Library Service, Auchterderran Centre, Woodend Road, Cardenden, Fife KY5 0NE
☎(01592) 414610
Fax (01592) 414641
Young People's Services Librarian Mrs Maggie Gray (e-mail: maggie.gray@fife.gov.uk)

GLASGOW

Authority: Glasgow City Council
Libraries, Information and Learning, The Mitchell Library, North Street, Glasgow G3 7DN
☎0141 287 2867
Fax 0141 287 2815
Young People's Services Coordinator Ms Pamela McClean BA MCLIP MSc (e-mail:
pamela.mcclean@clsglasgow.gov.uk)

Education Resource Service, School Library Service, 97 Scone Street, Glasgow G21 1JF
☎0141 336 7407
Fax 0141 336 7412
e-mail: ers@ea.glasgow.sch.uk
url: www.easyweb.easynet.co.uk/~ersglasgow/home
Principal Resources Development Officer Ms Frances Walker MEd MCLIP
Resource Centre Manager Ms Marie Ward BA(Hons) MCLIP
Educational Resource Librarians Ms Elaine Galt BA MCLIP, Ms Laura Hogg BA(Hons)
MCLIP

HIGHLAND

Authority: The Highland Council
Council Offices, High Street, Dingwall, Ross-shire IV15 9QN
☎(01349) 868460
Fax (01349) 863107
Ross & Cromarty Area Libraries Officer Mrs Charlotte E Macarthur BA(Hons) DipLib
MCLIP (e-mail: charlotte.macarthur@highland.gov.uk)

Elgin Hostel, Dunvegan Road, Portree, Isle of Skye, Hebrides IV51 9EE
☎(01478) 614050
Fax (01478) 613289
Skye & Lochalsh Area Libraries Officer David Linton MCLIP (01478 614060; fax:
01478 613751; e-mail: david.linton@highland.gov.uk)

Dornoch Library, Carnegie Building, High Street, Dornoch, Sutherland IV25 3SH
☎(01862) 811585 (tel/fax)
Sutherland Area Libraries Officer Mrs Alison Forrest BA MCLIP (e-mail:
alison.forrest@highland.gov.uk)

Education, Culture and Sport Services, Fort William Library, Airds Crossing, High Street,
Fort William, Inverness-shire PH33 6EU
☎(01397) 703552
Fax (01397) 703538
e-mail: fortwilliam.library@highland.gov.uk
Lochaber Area Libraries Officer Ms Maggie Wright BA(Hons) MCLIP (e-mail:
maggie.wright@highland.gov.uk)

Inverness Library, Farraline Park, Inverness IVI 1NH
☎(01463) 236463
Fax (01463) 237001
e-mail: inverness.library@highland.gov.uk
Inverness Area Libraries Officer Ms Carol Goodfellow MA MCLIP (e-mail:
carol.goodfellow@highland.gov.uk)
Assistant Librarian Sam McDowell BA MCLIP (e-mail: sam.mcdowell@highland.gov.uk)
Reference Librarian Ms Edwina Burridge BA MCLIP (e-mail:
edwina.burridge@highland.gov.uk)

Library Support Unit, 31A Harbour Road, Inverness IVI 1UA
☎(01463) 235713
Fax (01463) 236986
url: www.highland.gov.uk/educ/publicservices/librariesdetails/libraries_index_allareas.htm
Senior Librarian, Stock Co-ordinator Mrs Carol Hart BA(Hons) DipLib MCLIP (e-mail:
carol.hart@highland.gov.uk)
Principal Schools Librarian Miss Stephanie E. Hoyle MA MCLIP (01463 251269; e-mail:
stephanie.hoyle@highland.gov.uk)

Nairn Library, 68 High Street, Nairn IV12 4AU
☎(01667) 458506
Fax (01667) 458548
Nairn + Badenoch & Strathspey Area Libraries Officer Ms Eleanor Somerville BEd
DipLib MCLIP (e-mail: eleanor.somerville@highland.gov.uk)
Nairn + Badenoch & Strathspey Area Assistant Librarian Mrs Jennifer Murdoch
MCLIP BA (e-mail: jennifer.murdoch@highland.gov.uk)

Thurso Library, Davidson's Lane, Thurso, Caithness KW14 7AF
☎(01847) 893237
Fax (01847) 896114
e-mail: thurso.library@highland.gov.uk
Caithness Area Libraries Officer Vacant

Ullapool Community Library, Mill Street, Ullapool, Ross-shire IV26 2UN
☎(01854) 612543 (tel/fax)
West Ross Librarian Mrs Charlotte E Macarthur BA(Hons) DipLib MCLIP (e-mail:
charlotte.macarthur@highland.gov.uk)

INVERCLYDE

Authority: Inverclyde Council
Central Library, 1 Clyde Square, Greenock, Renfrewshire PA15 1NA
☎(01475) 712323
Fax (01475) 712334
e-mail: library.central@inverclyde.gov.uk
url: www.inverclyde.gov.uk/libraries
Readers' Services Librarian Ms Bernadette Fisher BA(Hons) MSc (e-mail:
bernadette.fisher@inverclyde.gov.uk)

Education Resource Service, Port Glasgow High School, Marloch Avenue, Port Glasgow, Renfrewshire PA14 6PP
☎(01475) 714660
Fax (01475) 715201
Education Resource Service Librarian Mrs Irene Gilchrist MA(Hons) DipLib MCLIP
(e-mail: irene.gilchrist@inverclyde.gov.uk)

MIDLOTHIAN

Authority: Midlothian Council
Library HQ, 2 Clerk Street, Loanhead, Midlothian EH20 9DR
☎0131 271 3980
Fax 0131 440 4635
e-mail: library.hq@midlothian.gov.uk
url: www.midlothian.gov.uk
Assistant Librarian, School Library Service Ms Rachel Dryburgh MA DipLib MCLIP
Children's Mobile Librarian A A Scobbie JP BA(Hons) MCLIP, Ms A Guyon MSc

MORAY

Authority: The Moray Council
Education Library Services, Elgin Library, Cooper Park, Elgin, Moray IV30 1HS
☎(01343) 562611
Fax (01343) 562630
Principal Librarian, Young People's Services Ms Helen Adair BA(Hons) MCLIP (e-mail: helen.adair@moray.gov.uk)

NORTH AYRSHIRE

Authority: North Ayrshire Council
Library HQ, 39-41 Princes Street, Ardrossan, Ayrshire KA22 8BT
☎(01294) 469137
Fax (01294) 604236
e-mail: librarychildrens@north-ayrshire.gov.uk
url: www.north-ayrshire.gov.uk
Children's Librarian Mrs Mhairi Cook BA MCLIP

Education Resource Service, Greenwood Teachers' Centre, Dreghorn, Irvine, Ayrshire KA11 4HL
☎(01294) 212716
Fax (01294) 222509
e-mail: nacers@netcentral.co.uk
url: www.ers.north-ayrshire.gov.uk
Information and Resource Manager Ms Marion McLarty MA MCLIP (e-mail: mmclarty@north-ayrshire.gov.uk)

NORTH LANARKSHIRE

Authority: North Lanarkshire Council
Community Services Dept, Buchanan Tower, Buchanan Business Park, Cumbernauld Road, Stepps, Glasgow G33 6HR
☎0141 304 1843
Fax 0141 304 1902
Libraries and Information Manager John Fox DMS MCLIP (e-mail: foxj@northlan.gov.uk)
Young Persons Services Librarian Ms Margaret Bell MCLIP (e-mail: bellm@northlan.gov.uk)

Education Department, Education Resource Service, 8 Kildonan Street, Coatbridge, Lanarkshire ML5 3LP
☎(01236) 434377
Fax (01236) 436224
e-mail: ERSmail@northlan.gov.uk
Principal Librarian Russell Brown BA(Hons) MCLIP
Senior Resource Development Officer Ms Alison MacPhail MA(Hons) PGDip MCLIP

ORKNEY

Authority: Orkney Islands Council
The Orkney Library and Archive, 44 Junction Road, Kirkwall, Orkney KW15 1AG
☎(01856) 873166
Fax (01856) 875260
e-mail: general.enquiries@orkneylibrary.org.uk
Assistant Librarian Ms Karen Miller BSc(Econ) PGAG MCLIP (e-mail: karen.miller@orkneylibrary.org.uk)

PERTH AND KINROSS

Authority: Perth and Kinross Council
Education and Children's Service, Libraries and Lifelong Learning, A K Bell Library, York Place, Perth PH2 8EP
☎(01738) 477039
Fax (01738) 477046
Senior Librarian, Children's Services Ms Morag Kelly MA DipLib MCLIP (e-mail: makelly@pkc.gov.uk)
Librarian, Children's Services Ms Amanda Pirie BSc(Hons) DipLib (01738 477023; e-mail: apirie@pkc.gov.uk)
Assistant Children's and Schools' Librarian Ms Elaine Hallyburton MA(Hons) DipLib (01738 477040; e-mail: ehallyburton@pkc.gov.uk)

RENFREWSHIRE

Authority: Renfrewshire Council
Education Resource Service, Abbey House, 8A Seedhill Road, Paisley, Renfrewshire PA1 1AJ

☎0141 840 3009
Fax 0141 840 3004
Education and Children's Services Co-ordinator Miss Linda Dawson MCLIP (e-mail: linda.dawson@renfrewshire.gov.uk)

SCOTTISH BORDERS

Authority: Scottish Borders Council
Library HQ, St Mary's Mill, Selkirk TD7 5EW
☎(01750) 20842
Fax (01750) 22875
e-mail: libraries@scotborders.gov.uk
url: www.scotborders.gov.uk/libraries
Young People's Services Co-ordinator Ms Gill Swales BA MCLIP DipLib (e-mail: gswales@scotborders.gov.uk)

SHETLAND ISLANDS

Authority: Shetland Islands Council
Shetland Library, Lower Hillhead, Lerwick, Shetland ZE1 0EL
☎(01595) 693868
Fax (01595) 694430
Young People's Services Librarian Mrs Morag Nicolson BA DipLib MCLIP (e-mail: morag.nicolson@sic.shetland.gov.uk)

SOUTH AYRSHIRE

Authority: South Ayrshire Council
Carnegie Library, 12 Main Street, Ayr KA8 8EB
☎(01292) 286385
Fax (01292) 611593
url: www.south-ayrshire.gov.uk/libraries/index.htm
Children's Services Librarian Mrs Geraldine Downie BA MCLIP (e-mail: geraldine.downie@south-ayrshire.gov.uk)

Library HQ, 26 Green Street, Ayr KA8 8AD
☎(01292) 288820
Fax (01292) 619019
Libraries and Galleries Manager Charles Deas BA MCLIP (e-mail: charles.deas@south-ayrshire.gov.uk)

SOUTH LANARKSHIRE

Authority: South Lanarkshire Council
East Kilbride Central Library, The Olympia, East Kilbride, Lanarkshire G74 1PG
☎(01355) 243652/220046
Fax (01355) 229365
e-mail: libek@slc-learningcentres.org.uk

Literacy Development Coordinator Ms Margaret Cowan MCLIP (e-mail: margaret.cowan@southlanarkshire.gov.uk)

STIRLING

Authority: Stirling Council
Educational Resources and Information Service, Resource Centre, Modan Road, Stirling FK7 9BS
☎(01786) 474974
Fax (01786) 474980
e-mail: eris@stirling.gov.uk
Principal Librarian Ms Mary Murray BA MCLIP (e-mail: murrayma@stirling.gov.uk)

WEST DUNBARTONSHIRE

Authority: West Dunbartonshire Council
Children's Libraries, Edinbarnet Campus, Craigpark Street, Clydebank, West Dunbartonshire G81 5BS
☎(01389) 890011
Fax (01389) 891414
Children's Librarian Ms Sarah Inglis
Children's Library Assistant Ms Sophie Hawkey-Edwards

Young People's Library Service, Schools and Libraries, Edinbarnet Campus, Craigpark Street, Clydebank, Dunbartonshire G81 5BS
☎(01389) 890011; Mobile 07795 602320
Fax (01389) 891414
Senior Officer, Young People's Librarian Ms Anne Louise McGough (e-mail: annelouise.mcgough@west-dunbarton.gov.uk)

Education Resource Service, Edinbarnet Campus, Craigpark Street, Faifley, Dunbartonshire G81 5BS
☎(01389) 890011
Fax (01389) 891414
Librarian Ms Mary O'Donnell BA DipLib (e-mail: mary.odonnell@west-dunbarton.gov.uk)

WEST LOTHIAN

Authority: West Lothian Council
Library HQ, Connolly House, Hopefield Road, Blackburn, West Lothian EH47 7HZ
☎(01506) 776336
Fax (01506) 776345
url: www.westlothian.gov.uk/libraries
Library Services Manager Miss Jeanette Castle MA(Hons) DipILS MCLIP
Support Services Manager Ms Anne Hunt MA DipLib MCLIP (e-mail: anne.hunt@westlothian.gov.uk)
Area Managers (Children's Services) Mrs Irene Brough, Mrs Mary Shelton MCLIP

ANGLESEY, ISLE OF

Authority: Isle of Anglesey County Council
Llangefni Library, Lôn-y-Felin, Llangefni, Anglesey LL77 7RT
☎(01248) 752088
Fax (01248) 750197
url: www.ynysmon.gov.uk
Children and Young People's Librarian Mrs Glenda Williams BA DipLib MCLIP (e-mail: gwxlh@ynysmon.gov.uk)
Education Librarian Mrs Katherine Laundy Parri BA MLS (01248 752096; e-mail: clplh@ynysmon.gov.uk)

BLAENAU GWENT

Authority: Blaenau Gwent County Borough Council
Ebbw Vale Library, 21 Bethcar Street, Ebbw Vale, Blaenau Gwent NP23 6HH
☎(01495) 303069
Fax (01495) 350547
Library Manager Ms Sue White MCLIP (01495 301122; e-mail: sue.white@blaenau-gwent.gov.uk)
(Blaenau Gwent has joint provision with Caerphilly for schools library services: see Caerphilly)

BRIDGEND

Authority: Bridgend County Borough Council
Bridgend Library and Information Service, Coed Parc, Park Street, Bridgend CF31 4BA
☎(01656) 767451
Fax (01656) 645719
e-mail: blis@bridgendlib.gov.uk
url: www.bridgend.gov.uk/english/library
Children's/Promotions Librarian Mrs Margaret Griffiths BLib MCLIP (e-mail: griffma@bridgend.gov.uk)

CAERPHILLY

Authority: Caerphilly County Borough Council
Youth and Schools, Library HQ, Unit 4, Woodfieldside Business Park, Penmaen Road, Pontllanfraith, Blackwood, Caerphilly NP12 2DG
☎(01495) 235565
Fax (01495) 235566
Children's and Youth Services Manager Mrs Lesley Case MCLIP (01495 235562; e-mail: casel@caerphilly.gov.uk)
Schools Library Service Manager Ms Christine Selby MSc(Econ) MCLIP (01495 235563; e-mail: selbyc@caerphilly.gov.uk)

CARDIFF

Authority: Cardiff Council
Central Library, St David's Link, Frederick Street, Cardiff CF10 2DU
☎029 2038 2116
Fax 029 2087 1599
e-mail: centrallibrary@cardiff.gov.uk
url: www.cardiff.gov.uk/libraries
Operational Manager Lifelong Learning Vacant
Childrens Services Manager Mrs Heather Noble (e-mail: hnoble@cardiff.gov.uk)

CARMARTHENSHIRE

Authority: Carmarthenshire County Council
Children's and Schools Library Service, Carmarthen Area Library, St Peter's Street,
Carmarthen SA31 1LN
☎(01267) 224832
Fax (01267) 221839
url: www.carmarthenshire.gov.uk
Children's/Schools Librarian Mrs Sheila Jones MCLIP (e-mail:
shejones@carmarthenshire.gov.uk)

CEREDIGION

Authority: Ceredigion County Council
Public Library, Corporation Street, Aberystwyth, Ceredigion SY23 2BU
☎(01970) 633720/633703
Fax (01970) 625059
Assistant Librarian, Primary Schools J Leeding MCLIP

CONWY

Authority: Conwy County Borough Council
Services to Children and Young People, Llandudno Library, Victoria Centre, Mostyn Street,
Llandudno, Conwy LL30 2RP
☎(01492) 574010
Fax (01492) 876826
url: www.conwy.gov.uk
Lifelong Learning Librarian Ms Bethan Tobin (e-mail: bethan.tobin@conwy.gov.uk)
(Schools Library Service: see Flintshire. Cooperative service with Denbighshire, Flintshire
and Wrexham)

DENBIGHSHIRE

Authority: Denbighshire County Council
Library Service, Yr Hen Garchar, 46 Clwyd Street, Ruthin, Denbighshire LL15 1HP
☎(01824) 708207
Fax (01824) 708202

e-mail: library.services@denbighshire.gov.uk
url: www.denbighshire.gov.uk/libraries
Children and Young People and Welsh Services Library Adviser Ms Bethan M
Hughes BA DipLib MCLIP (e-mail: bethan.hughes@denbighshire.gov.uk)
(Schools Library Service: see Flintshire. Cooperative service with Conwy, Flintshire and
Wrexham)

FLINTSHIRE

Authority: Flintshire County Council
Library HQ, County Hall, Mold, Flintshire CH7 6NW
☎(01352) 704411
Fax (01352) 753662
Lifelong Learning Librarian Mrs Gina Maddison (01352 704405; e-mail:
gina.maddison@flintshire.gov.uk)

North East Wales Schools Library Service, c/o Library and Information HQ, County Hall,
Mold, Flintshire CH7 6NW
☎(01352) 704441
Fax (01352) 753662
e-mail: newalessls@flintshire.gov.uk
Schools Library Service Manager David C Barker BA MCLIP (e-mail:
david_barker@flintshire.gov.uk)
(Cooperative service with Conwy, Denbighshire and Wrexham)

GWYNEDD

Authority: Gwynedd Council
Children's and Schools' Library Service, Caernarfon Library Centre, Pavilion Hill,
Caernarfon, Gwynedd LL55 1AS
☎(01286) 679465
Fax (01286) 671137
e-mail: llyfrgell@gwynedd.gov.uk
url: www.gwynedd.gov.uk/library
Children and Young People's Librarian Ms Nia Gruffydd MLib MCLIP (e-mail:
NiaGruffydd@gwynedd.gov.uk)

MERTHYR TYDFIL

Authority: Merthyr Tydfil County Borough Council
Central Library, High Street, Merthyr Tydfil CF47 8AF
☎(01685) 723057
Fax (01685) 370690
e-mail: library.services@merthyr.gov.uk
Head of Libraries Geraint James BA MCLIP
All enquiries to Head of Libraries

MONMOUTHSHIRE

Authority: Monmouthshire County Council
Chepstow Library, Manor Way, Chepstow, Monmouthshire NP16 5HZ
☎(01291) 635730
Fax (01291) 635736
e-mail: infocentre@monmouthshire.gov.uk
url: http://libraries.monmouthshire.gov.uk
Reading and Youth Manager Ms Fiona Ashley BLib MCLIP (e-mail:
fionaashley@monmouthshire.gov.uk)

Schools Library Service, Croesyceiliog, County Hall, Cwmbran, Torfaen, Gwent NP44 2XH
☎(01633) 644565
Fax (01633) 644564
Schools Library Service Manager Ms Angela Noble BA PGCE DipLib MCLIP (e-mail:
angelanoble@monmouthshire.gov.uk)
Librarian, Schools Library Service Ms Emma Stevens (e-mail:
emmastevens@monmouthshire.gov.uk)
(Schools library service in partnership with Newport and Torfaen)

NEATH PORT TALBOT

Authority: Neath Port Talbot County Borough Council
Library and Cultural Services HQ, Reginald Street, Velindre, Port Talbot, Neath Port Talbot
SA13 1YY
☎(01639) 899829
Fax (01639) 899152
e-mail: npt.libhq@neath-porttalbot.gov.uk
Senior Assistant Librarian (Children's Services) Ms Jayne O'Brien (e-mail:
j.obrien@neath-porttalbot.gov.uk)

Education, Library and Resource Service, Reginald Street, Velindre, Port Talbot, Neath Port
Talbot SA13 1YY
☎(01639) 889900
Fax (01639) 889909
e-mail: npt.elrs@neath-porttalbot.gov.uk
Manager, Education, Library and Resource Service Clive Biscoe MCLIP (e-mail:
c.biscoe@neath-porttalbot.gov.uk)
(Schools library service in partnership with Swansea)

NEWPORT

Authority: Newport City Council
Central Library, John Frost Square, Newport, Gwent NP20 1PA
☎(01633) 656656
Fax (01633) 222615
e-mail: central.library@newport.gov.uk
url: www.newport.gov.uk/libraries

Children and Young People's Services Manager Ms Tracey Paddon BSc(Hons) MSc(Econ) DipAppSc MCLIP (e-mail: tracey.paddon@newport.gov.uk) (Schools library service in partnership with Monmouthshire and Torfaen: see Monmouthshire)

PEMBROKESHIRE

Authority: Pembrokeshire County Council
Narberth Library, St James' Street, Narberth, Pembrokeshire SA67 7BU
☎(01834) 861781 (tel/fax)
Group Librarian, East Mrs Eleri Evans MCLIP (e-mail: eleri.evans@pembrokeshire.gov.uk)

POWYS

Authority: Powys County Council
Education, Schools' and Children's Services, County Library HQ, Cefnllys Road, Llandrindod Wells, Powys LD1 5LD
☎(01597) 826866
Fax (01597) 826872
Principal Librarian Mrs Dianne Jones MCLIP (01597 826867; e-mail: diannej@powys.gov.uk)

RHONDDA CYNON TAFF

Authority: Rhondda Cynon Taff County Borough Council
Mountain Ash Library, Knight Street, Mountain Ash, Rhondda Cynon Taff CF45 3EY
☎(01443) 478463
Fax (01443) 477270
Senior Librarian, Children's/Youth Services Ms Ceri Roberts MCLIP DipEd (e-mail: ceri.w.roberts@rhondda-cynon-taff.gov.uk)
Librarian, Schools and Related Services Ms Wendy Cole MCLIP (e-mail: schools.library@rhondda-cynon-taff.gov.uk)

SWANSEA

Authority: City and County of Swansea
Library and Information Service, Library HQ, County Hall, Oystermouth Road, Swansea SA1 3SN
☎(01792) 636430
Fax (01792) 636235
url: www.swansea.gov.uk/libraries
Senior Manager: Children's Youth and Inclusion Ms Emma Rees MA DipLIS (01792 636610; e-mail: emma.rees@swansea.gov.uk)
Children's Librarian Ms Carole Billingham (e-mail: carole.billingham@swansea.gov.uk)
Youth Librarian Ms Jean Meredith (e-mail: jean.meredith@swansea.gov.uk)
(Schools library service in partnership with Neath Port Talbot: see Neath Port Talbot)

TORFAEN

Authority: Torfaen County Borough Council
Pontypool Library, Hanbury Road, Pontypool, Gwent NP4 6JL
☎(01495) 762820
Fax (01495) 752530
e-mail: pontypool.library@torfaen.gov.uk
url: www.torfaen.gov.uk
Senior Librarian Mark Tanner BA(Hons) DipLib MCLIP (e-mail:
mark.tanner@torfaen.gov.uk)
(Schools library service in partnership with Newport and Monmouthshire: see
Monmouthshire)

VALE OF GLAMORGAN

Authority: Vale of Glamorgan Council
Barry Library@the Leisure Centre, Greenwood Street, Barry, Glamorgan CF63 4RU
☎(01446) 709737
Fax (01446) 709377
e-mail: barrylibrary@valeofglamorgan.gov.uk
Children's Librarian Ms Gillian Southby BA(Hons) PGDipILM (01446 709764)

WREXHAM

Authority: Wrexham County Borough Council
Children's and Young People's Service, Wrexham Library, Rhosddu Road, Wrexham
LL11 1AU
☎(01978) 292643
Fax (01978) 292611
e-mail: library@wrexham.gov.uk
url: www.wrexham.gov.uk/libraries
Children's Librarian Ms S Kensall DipLib MCLIP
(Schools Library Service: see Flintshire. Co-operative service with Conwy, Denbighshire
and Flintshire)

CROWN DEPENDENCIES

GUERNSEY

Guille-Allès Library, Market Street, St Peter Port, Guernsey, Channel Islands GY1 1HB
☎(01481) 720392
Fax (01481) 712425

Schools' Library Service
☎(01481) 714098
Fax (01481) 714436
Other details as above
Head of Services to Education and Young People Mrs Jane Falla BA DipLib MCLIP
(e-mail: jfalla@library.gg)

ISLE OF MAN

Nobles Library, Junior and Mobile Services, Nobles Hall, Westmoreland Road, Douglas, Isle of Man IM1 1RL
☎(01624) 673123
Fax (01624) 671043
Librarian (Mobile Library) Mrs Sandra Henderson MCLIP
Librarian - Junior Library Ms Mary Cousins
Assistant Librarian Mrs Linda Strickett, Ms Kath Garret

JERSEY

Library Service, Jersey Library, Halkett Place, St Helier, Jersey, Channel Islands JE2 4WH
☎(01534) 759991
Fax (01534) 769444
e-mail: jsylib@gov.je
url: www.jsylib.gov.je
Principal Librarian, Young People's Services and Schools Resources Ms Jaci Graham MCLIP (e-mail: j.graham03@jsylib.gov.je)
Senior Librarian, Young Readers Miss Cathy Bithell BSc MSc(Econ) MCLIP (e-mail: c.bithell03@jsylib.gov.je)

Children's, Youth and Schools Library Services in the Republic of Ireland

(listed under public library authority)

In the Republic of Ireland, local authority public library services generally provide a service to primary schools on an agency basis for the Department of Education (there is no similar service for second level schools). Within public libraries it is not usual for staff to be appointed with specific responsibility for children's or youth libraries. Please contact the appropriate library authority as listed in the Public Libraries in the Republic of Ireland section for information. The exceptions that follow are Dublin, Dún Laoghaire, Fingal, Galway, Kerry, Longford, South Dublin, Wexford and Wicklow.

DUBLIN

Children's and Schools' Section, Cabra Bibliographic Section, Cabra Public Library, Navan Road, Dublin 7, Republic of Ireland
☎(00 353 1) 674 4840
Fax (00 353 1) 869 1412
e-mail: childrens.library@dublincity.ie
url: www.dublincity.ie/living_in_the_city/libraries/
Senior Librarian, Children's and Schools' Section Ms Anne-Marie Kelly BSc MLIS MCLIP (e-mail: annemarie.kelly@dublincity.ie)

DÚN LAOGHAIRE–RATHDOWN

Duncairn House, 14 Carysfort Avenue, Blackrock, Co Dublin, Republic of Ireland
☎(00 353 1) 278 1788
Fax (00 353 1) 278 1792
e-mail: libraries@dlrcoco.ie
Librarian, Young People and Schools Ms Patricia Byrne BSocSci(LIS)(Hons)

FINGAL

Schools' Library Service, Unit 34, Coolmine Industrial Estate, Coolmine, Dublin 15, Republic of Ireland
☎(00 353 1) 822 5056
Fax (00 353 1) 822 1568
e-mail: schoolslibrary@fingalcoco.ie
Librarian Ms Caroline McLoughlin BA HDipEd DipLIS

GALWAY

Galway County Library HQ, Island House, Cathedral Square, Galway, Republic of Ireland
☎(00 353 91) 562471
Fax (00 353 91) 565039
e-mail: info@galwaylibrary.ie
url: www.galwaylibrary.ie
Librarian, Schools Library Service Martin Keating

KERRY

Schools Library Services, Kerry County Library, Moyderwell, Tralee, Co Kerry, Republic of Ireland
☎(00 353 66) 712 1200
Fax (00 353 66) 712 9202
e-mail: info@kerrycolib.ie
url: www.kerrycolib.ie
Chief Librarian Mrs Kathleen Browne FLAI

LONGFORD

Schools Library Service, Longford County Library, Main Street, Longford, Co Longford, Republic of Ireland
☎(00 353 43) 41124/5
Fax (00 353 43) 48576
Librarian Ms Grainne Milner (e-mail: gmilner@longfordcoco.ie)

SOUTH DUBLIN

Schools Library Service, Unit 1, The Square Industrial Complex, Tallaght, Dublin 24, Republic of Ireland
☎(00 353 1) 459 7834
Fax (00 353 1) 459 7872
e-mail: schools@sdublincoco.ie
Librarian Ms Maria O'Sullivan, Ms Laura Joyce (job-share)

WEXFORD

Library Management Services, Kent Building, Ardcavan, Co Wexford, Republic of Ireland
☎(00 353 53) 24922
Fax (00 353 53) 21097
e-mail: libraryhq@wexfordcoco.ie
url: www.wexford.ie/library
County Librarian Ms Fionnuala Hanrahan BA DLIS MLIS MCLIP MCLIPI
Schools and Children's Librarian Ms Patricia Keenan BSocSci (e-mail: patricia.keenan@wexfordcoco.ie)

WICKLOW

Wicklow County Library, Library HQ, Boghall Road, Bray, Co Wicklow, Republic of Ireland
☎(00 353 1) 286 6566
Fax (00 353 1) 286 5811
e-mail: library@wicklowcoco.ie
Executive Librarian (Schools and Outreach) Ms Noelle Murray BA DLIS

Libraries in Academic Institutions in the United Kingdom

ABERDEEN UNIVERSITY

Directorate of Information Systems and Services: Library Services, Aberdeen University, Queen Mother Library, Meston Walk, Aberdeen AB24 3UE
☎(01224) 273330 (enquiries/help desk), (01224) 272573 (administration)
Fax (01224) 487048
e-mail: library@abdn.ac.uk
url: www.abdn.ac.uk/diss/library
Director, Information Systems and Services Graham Pryor BA(Hons) DipLib FRSA
(e-mail: g.pryor@abdn.ac.uk)

Site libraries

▶ Medical Library, Aberdeen University, Polwarth Building, Foresterhill, Aberdeen AB25 2ZD
☎(01224) 681818 ext 52488 (enquiries), ext 52740 (administration)
Fax (01224) 685157
e-mail: medlib@abdn.ac.uk
Site Services Manager Ms Melanie Bickerton BA
▶ Special Libraries and Archives, Aberdeen University, King's College, Aberdeen AB24 3SW
☎(01224) 272598 (enquiries)
Fax (01224) 273891
e-mail: speclib@abdn.ac.uk
Manager, Historic Collections Alan Knox BSc PhD
▶ Taylor Library and European Documentation Centre, Aberdeen University, Taylor Building, Aberdeen AB24 3UB
☎(01224) 272601 (law enquiries), 273334 (European Union enquiries), 273892 (administration)
Fax (01224) 273893
e-mail: lawlib@abdn.ac.uk
Site Services Manager Ms Liz Mackie BA

UNIVERSITY OF ABERTAY DUNDEE

Information Services, University of Abertay Dundee, Bell Street, Dundee DD1 1HG
☎(01382) 308899
Fax (01382) 308877
e-mail: infodesk@abertay.ac.uk
url: http://vlib.abertay.ac.uk/
Head of Information Services Ivor G Lloyd BA DipLib MLib MCLIP (e-mail: i.lloyd@abertay.ac.uk)

ANGLIA POLYTECHNIC UNIVERSITY

University Library, Anglia Polytechnic University, Rivermead Campus, Bishop Hall Lane, Chelmsford, Essex CM1 1SQ
☎(01245) 493131
url: http://libweb.apu.ac.uk
University Librarian Ms Nicky Kershaw BA CertEd MCLIP (ext 3762; e-mail: n.j.kershaw@apu.ac.uk)

Campus Library Manager Ms Margaret March BA MA MCLIP (ext 4644; e-mail: m.march@apu.ac.uk)
Electronic Services and Systems Manager Graham Howorth BA MSc MCLIP (ext 3145; e-mail: g.howorth@apu.ac.uk)

University Library, Anglia Polytechnic University, Cambridge Campus, East Road, Cambridge CB1 1PT
☎(01223) 363271
url: http://libweb.apu.ac.uk
Campus Library Manager Roddie Shepherd BA DipLib MCLIP (ext 2310; e-mail: r.c.shepherd@apu.ac.uk)

ARTS INSTITUTE AT BOURNEMOUTH

AIB Library Ltd, The Arts Institute at Bournemouth, Wallisdown Road, Poole, Dorset BH12 5HH
☎(01202) 363256
Fax (01202) 537729
e-mail: library@aib.ac.uk
url: www.aib.ac.uk
Librarian Ms Julia Waite BSc(Econ) MSc MCLIP

ASTON UNIVERSITY

Library & Information Services, Aston University, Aston Triangle, Birmingham B4 7ET
☎0121 204 4525 (enquiries), 0121 204 4509 (administration)
Fax 0121 204 4530
e-mail: library@aston.ac.uk
url: www.aston.ac.uk/lis/
Director Nick Smith BSc MSc PhD MCLIP
Head of Information Resources Mrs Jackie Brocklebank BA MIL DipLib MCLIP, Mrs Heather Whitehouse BSc DipInfSc (job share)
Head of Public Services Mrs Jill Lambert BSc DipLib MA MCLIP (e-mail: j.lambert@aston.ac.uk)

BATH SPA UNIVERSITY COLLEGE

Library, Bath Spa University College, Newton Park, Newton St Loe, Bath BA2 9BN
☎(01225) 875490
Fax (01225) 875493
url: www.bathspa.ac.uk
Head of Library and Information Services Mrs Julie Parry MLib MCLIP (01225 875634; e-mail: j.parry@bathspa.ac.uk)
Head of Academic Library Services Nick Drew BA MLib MCLIP (01225 875477; e-mail: n.drew@bathspa.ac.uk)
Head of Library Systems Ms Ann Siswell BA DipLib MCLIP (01225 875678; e-mail: a.siswell@bathspa.ac.uk)

Information Managers Mrs Barbara Molloy BA MCLIP (01225 875430; e-mail: b.molloy@bathspa.ac.uk), Mrs Marilyn Floyd MCLIP (01225 875476; e-mail: m.floyd@bathspa.ac.uk)

Campus library

▶ Library, Bath Spa University College, 8 Somerset Place, Bath BA1 5SF
☎(01225) 875648
Fax (01225) 427080
Campus Librarians Ms Helen Rayner BA(Hons) DipInf (01225 875648; e-mail: h.rayner@bathspa.ac.uk), Ms Nicola Morrison BA(Hons) MCLIP (01225 875648; e-mail: n.morrison@bathspa.ac.uk)

(Subject to approval, Bath Spa University College will become Bath Spa University in Autumn 2005)

UNIVERSITY OF BATH

Library and Learning Centre, University of Bath, Bath BA2 7AY
☎(01225) 386835 (enquiries), (01225) 386084 (administration)
Fax (01225) 386229
e-mail: library@bath.ac.uk
url: www.bath.ac.uk/library
University Librarian Howard Nicholson MA MCLIP FRSA

BELL COLLEGE

Library, Bell College, Hamilton Campus, Almada Street, Hamilton, Lanarkshire ML3 0JB
☎(01698) 894424
Fax (01698) 286856
e-mail: library@bell.ac.uk
url: www.bell.ac.uk/library.htm
College Librarian Ms Barbara Catt BA MCLIP

Campus library

Dumfries Campus Library, Bell College, Maxwell House, Crichton University Campus, Dumfries DG1 4UQ
☎(01387) 702084
Fax (01387) 702082
e-mail: library@bell.ac.uk
Campus Librarian Ms Judith Anderson MA MCLIP

BIRMINGHAM COLLEGE OF FOOD, TOURISM AND CREATIVE STUDIES

Birmingham College of Food, Tourism and Creative Studies, Summer Row, Birmingham B3 1JB
☎0121 604 1000

Fax 0121 608 7100
Head of Library Services Ms Stephanie Holliday MSc AdDipEd (e-mail:
s.holliday@bcftcs.ac.uk)

Birmingham College of Food, Tourism and Creative Studies, Richmond House, Newhall
Street, Birmingham B3 1PB
☎0121 604 1000
Fax 0121 608 7100
Library Manager Miss Debbie Findlay BA (e-mail: d.findlay@bcftcs.ac.uk)

UNIVERSITY OF BIRMINGHAM

Main Library, Information Services, University of Birmingham, Edgbaston, Birmingham
B15 2TT
☎0121 414 5828 (enquiries)
Fax 0121 471 4691
url: www.is.bham.ac.uk
Director of Information Services Ms Michele Shoebridge (e-mail:
m.i.shoebridge@bham.ac.uk)
Head of Library Services Ms Elizabeth Warner-Davies BSc DipLib DipHECouns

Site libraries

▶ Barber Fine Art Library, University of Birmingham, Edgbaston, Birmingham B15 2TT
☎0121 414 7334
e-mail: fine-arts-library@bham.ac.uk
Librarian James Shaw BA MA
▶ Barber Music Library, University of Birmingham, Edgbaston, Birmingham B15 2TT
☎0121 414 5852
e-mail: music-library@bham.ac.uk
Librarian James Shaw BA MA
▶ Barnes Library (Medicine, Health Sciences, Life Sciences), University of Birmingham,
Edgbaston, Birmingham B15 2TT
☎0121 414 3567
e-mail: ba-lib@bham.ac.uk
Librarian Ms Jean Scott BA DipLib
▶ Chemical Engineering Library, University of Birmingham, Edgbaston, Birmingham B15 2TT
☎0121 414 5321
e-mail: garner@bham.ac.uk
Librarian Ms Jean Scott BA DipLib
▶ Education Library, University of Birmingham, Edgbaston, Birmingham B15 2TT
☎0121 414 4869
e-mail: edlib@bham.ac.uk
Librarian Ms Dorothy Vuong BSocSc PGDip
▶ Electronic and Electrical Engineering Library, University of Birmingham, Edgbaston,
Birmingham B15 2TT
☎0121 414 4321
e-mail: elecenglib@bham.ac.uk
Librarian Ms Jean Scott BA DipLib

▶ European Resource Centre, University of Birmingham, Edgbaston, Birmingham B15 2TT
☎0121 414 3614
Librarian Geoff Price MCLIP
▶ Harding Law Library, University of Birmingham, Edgbaston, Birmingham B15 2TT
☎0121 414 5865
Librarian Geoff Price MCLIP
▶ Orchard Learning Resources Centre, University of Birmingham, Hamilton Drive,
Weoley Park Road, Selly Oak, Birmingham B29 6QW
☎0121 415 8454
e-mail: olrc@bham.ac.uk
Manager Ms Dorothy Vuong BSocSc PGDip
▶ Ronald Cohen Dental Library, Birmingham Dental Hospital, University of Birmingham,
St Chad's Queensway, Birmingham B4 6NN
☎0121 237 2859
e-mail: dllib@bham.ac.uk
Librarian Ms Jean Scott BA DipLib
▶ Shakespeare Institute Library, University of Birmingham, Shakespeare Institute, Church
Street, Stratford upon Avon, Warwicks CV37 6HP
☎(01789) 293384
e-mail: silib@bham.ac.uk
Librarian James Shaw BA MA
▶ Special Collections, University of Birmingham, Edgbaston, Birmingham B15 2TT
☎0121 414 5838
e-mail: special-collections@bham.ac.uk
Head of Special Collections Ms Christine Penney BA DipLib MCLIP MSocArch

BISHOP GROSSETESTE COLLEGE

Sibthorp Library, Bishop Grosseteste College, Newport, Lincoln LN1 3DY
☎(01522) 530771/527347
url: www.bgc.ac.uk
Director of Library and Knowledge Services Ms Emma Sansby BA(Hons) MA MCLIP
(ext 312; e-mail: emma.sansby@bgc.ac.uk)
Assistant Librarian Chris Browning MA BA (ext 227; e-mail:
christopher.browning@bgc.ac.uk)

UNIVERSITY OF BOLTON (formerly Bolton Institute)

Eagle Learning Support Centre, University of Bolton, Deane Road, Bolton, Lancashire
BL3 5AB
☎(01204) 903092 (enquiries), (01204) 903160 (administration)
Fax (01204) 903166
url: www.bolton.ac.uk/learning/
Head of Learning Support Services Mrs Karen Senior BA MCLIP MLib (01204 903160;
e-mail: k.senior@bolton.ac.uk)

Chadwick Learning Support Centre, University of Bolton, Chadwick Street, Bolton,
Greater Manchester BL2 1JW

☎(01204) 903262
Senior library staff as above

BOURNEMOUTH UNIVERSITY

Library and Learning Centre, Bournemouth University, Talbot Campus, Fern Barrow,
Poole, Dorset BH12 5BB
☎(01202) 965083 (enquiries), (01202) 965044 (administration)
Fax (01202) 965475
e-mail: jascott@bournemouth.ac.uk
url: www.bournemouth.ac.uk/library
Acting Head of Academic Services and University Librarian David Ball

Site library
▶ Bournemouth House Library, Bournemouth University, Bournemouth House, 19
   Christchurch Road, Bournemouth BH1 3LG
   ☎(01202) 967301 (enquiries)
   Fax (01202) 967298
   User Services Manager Ms Rachel Geeson (01202 967297)

UNIVERSITY OF BRADFORD

J B Priestley Library, University of Bradford, Bradford BD7 1DP
☎(01274) 233301
Fax (01274) 233398
e-mail: library@bradford.ac.uk
url: www.brad.ac.uk/lss/library/
Director of Learning Support Services Dr Stanley J Houghton (01274 233303; e-mail:
s.j.houghton@bradford.ac.uk)
University Librarian (Academic Services) John J Horton MA MPhil MCLIP (01274
233375; e-mail: j.j.horton@bradford.ac.uk)
University Librarian (Resources Management) Peter M Ketley BA MA (01274 233366;
e-mail: p.m.ketley@bradford.ac.uk)

UNIVERSITY OF BRIGHTON

Information Services, University of Brighton, Moulsecoomb, Brighton BN2 4GJ
☎(01273) 600900
Fax (01273) 642988
url: www.brighton.ac.uk
Director of Information Services Mark Toole MA(Cantab)

Central/largest library
The Aldrich Library, Information Services, University of Brighton, Cockcroft Building,
Lewes Road, Brighton BN2 4GJ
☎(01273) 642760
Fax (01273) 642988
Librarian i/c Ms Lyn Turpin MA MCLIP

Site libraries

▶ Information Services, University of Brighton, St Peter's House, 16-18 Richmond Place, Brighton BN2 2NA
☎(01273) 643221
Librarian i/c Mrs Louise Tucker BA

▶ Information Services, University of Brighton, Falmer, Brighton BN1 9PH
☎(01273) 643569
Librarian i/c Keith Baxter

▶ Information Services, University of Brighton, Queenwood Library, Darley Road, Eastbourne, East Sussex BN20 7UN
☎(01273) 643822
Librarian i/c Michael Ainscough BA MCLIP

UNIVERSITY OF BRISTOL

Arts and Social Sciences Library, University of Bristol, Tyndall Avenue, Bristol BS8 1TJ
☎0117 928 9000 ext 8000, 0117 928 8004 (administration)
Fax 0117 925 5334
e-mail: library@bris.ac.uk
url: www.bris.ac.uk/is
Director of Library Services Peter King BA MA PhD

Site libraries

▶ Biological Sciences Library, University of Bristol, Woodland Road, Bristol BS8 1UG
☎0117 928 7943

▶ Chemistry Library, University of Bristol, School of Chemistry, Cantocks Close, Bristol BS8 1TS
☎0117 928 8984

▶ Continuing Education Library, University of Bristol, 10 Berkeley Square, Bristol BS8 1HH
☎0117 928 7177

▶ Dental Library, University of Bristol, Lower Maudlin Street, Bristol BS1 2LY
☎0117 928 4419

▶ Education Library, University of Bristol, 35 Berkeley Square, Bristol BS8 1JA
☎0117 928 7070

▶ Geography Library, University of Bristol, University Road, Bristol BS8 1SS
☎0117 928 8116

▶ Medical Library, University of Bristol, Medical School, University Walk, Bristol BS8 1TD
☎0117 928 7945

▶ Physics Library, University of Bristol, H. H. Wills Physics Laboratory, Tyndall Avenue, Bristol BS8 1TL
☎0117 928 7960

▶ Queen's Library (Engineering, Mathematics, Computer Science), University of Bristol, Queen's Building, University Walk, Bristol BS8 1TR
☎0117 928 7628

▶ Veterinary Science Library, University of Bristol, School of Veterinary Science, Churchill Building, Langford, Bristol BS40 5DU
☎0117 928 9205

▶ Wills Memorial Library (Law, Earth Sciences, EDC), University of Bristol, Wills Memorial Building, Queen's Road, Bristol BS8 1RJ
☎0117 954 5398

BRUNEL UNIVERSITY

Library, Brunel University, Middlesex UB8 3PH
☎(01895) 266154 (enquiries), (01895) 266145 (administration)
Fax (01895) 269741
e-mail: library@brunel.ac.uk
url: www.brunel.ac.uk/about/pubfac/library
Director of Library Services Nick Bevan BSc MSc(Econ) DipLib MSc(InfSc) MCLIP
Assistant Director: User Services and Staff Development Ms Liz Annetts BA MCLIP
Assistant Director: Systems and Resource Management Malcolm Emmett BSc MCLIP
Team Leader: Subject Librarians and Information Services John Aanonson BSc MSc MCLIP

Campus libraries
▶ Osterley Campus Library, Brunel University, Borough Road, Isleworth, Middlesex TW7 5DU
☎020 8891 0121
Fax 020 8891 8251
Principal Library Assistant Ms Pam Singh (e-mail: parminder.singh@brunel.ac.uk)

UNIVERSITY OF BUCKINGHAM

University Library, University of Buckingham, Hunter Street, Buckingham MK18 1EG
☎(01280) 814080
Fax (01280) 820312
e-mail: library@buckingham.ac.uk
url: www.buckingham.ac.uk

Site libraries
▶ Franciscan Library, University of Buckingham, London Road, Buckingham MK18 1EG
☎(01280) 814080
Fax (01280) 828288
Librarian (Law and Science) L M Hammond BSc
▶ Hunter Street Library, University of Buckingham, Hunter Street, Buckingham MK18 1EG
☎(01280) 814080
Fax (01280) 820312
Librarian (Business and Humanities) S H Newell BA DipLib LLB

BUCKINGHAMSHIRE CHILTERNS UNIVERSITY COLLEGE

Learning Resource Centre, Buckinghamshire Chilterns University College, Queen Alexandra Road, High Wycombe, Bucks HP11 2JZ

☎(01494) 522141 ext 5107 (enquiries), ext 3270 (administration)
Fax (01494) 450774
e-mail: hwlib@bcuc.ac.uk
url: www.bcuc.ac.uk
Head of Learning and Information Services Dr Helen Fletcher (ext 5064; e-mail:
helen.fletcher@bcuc.ac.uk)
Learning Resources Manager Mrs Ann Badhams MCLIP (ext 3027; e-mail:
ann.badhams@bcuc.ac.uk)

Campus libraries

▶ Campus Library, Buckinghamshire Chilterns University College, Wellesbourne Campus,
  Kingshill Road, High Wycombe, Bucks HP13 5BB
  ☎(01494) 522141 ext 4055
  Fax (01494) 450774
  Faculty Librarian Ms Lisa Hodgkins BA MLS MCLIP (e-mail: lhodgk@bcuc.ac.uk)
▶ Campus LRC, Buckinghamshire Chilterns University College, Chalfont Campus,
  Newland Park, Gorlands Road, Chalfont St Giles, Bucks HP8 4AD
  ☎(01494) 522141 ext 5137
  Fax (01494) 603082
  Learning Resources Manager Mrs Ann Badhams MCLIP (ext 3081; e-mail:
  ann.badhams@bcuc.ac.uk)

UNIVERSITY OF CAMBRIDGE

Cambridge University Library, University of Cambridge, West Road, Cambridge CB3 9DR
☎(01223) 333000
Fax (01223) 333160
e-mail: library@lib.cam.ac.uk
url: www.lib.cam.ac.uk
Librarian Peter K Fox MA AKC MCLIP
Deputy Librarian Ms Anne Murray MA

Dependent libraries

▶ Betty and Gordon Moore Library, University of Cambridge, Wilberforce Road,
  Cambridge CB3 0WD
  ☎(01223) 765670
  Fax (01223) 765678
  e-mail: moore-library@lib.cam.ac.uk
  Librarian Michael L Wilson MA
▶ Scientific Periodicals Library, University of Cambridge, Benet Street, Cambridge CB2 3PY
  ☎(01223) 334744
  Fax (01223) 334748
  e-mail: lib-spl-inquiries@lists.cam.ac.uk
  Librarian Michael L Wilson MA
▶ Squire Law Library, University of Cambridge, 10 West Road, Cambridge CB3 9DZ
  ☎(01223) 330077
  Fax (01223) 330048
  e-mail: sql1@lib.cam.ac.uk

Librarian David F Wills BA MCLIP
▶ University Medical Library, University of Cambridge, Addenbrooke's Hospital, Hills Road, Cambridge CB2 2SP
☎(01223) 336757
Fax (01223) 331918
e-mail: library@medschl.cam.ac.uk
Librarian Peter B Morgan MA MCLIP

College, Institute and Departmental

Cambridge Union Society
Keynes Library, Cambridge Union Society, 9(A) Bridge Street, Cambridge CB2 1UB
☎(01223) 566423
Fax (01223) 566444
e-mail: paa22@cam.ac.uk
url: www.cambridge-union.org
Senior Librarian Ms Patricia Aske MA
Assistant Librarian James Noyes MSc MA
(Members only)

Christ's College
Library, Christ's College, Cambridge CB2 3BU
☎(01223) 334950/334905
Fax (01223) 334967
e-mail: library@christs.cam.ac.uk
url: www.christs.cam.ac.uk
College Librarian Miss Candace J E Guite MA(Ord) MCLIP LTCL MA (e-mail: cjeg2@cam.ac.uk)

Churchill College
Library, Churchill College, Storey's Way, Cambridge CB3 0DS
☎(01223) 336138
Fax (01223) 336160
url: www.chu.cam.ac.uk/members/library
Librarian Ms Mary Kendall MA MCLIP (e-mail: librarian@chu.cam.ac.uk)
(NB The Library is available to College Members only)

Clare College
▶ Fellows' Library, Clare College, Cambridge CB2 1TL
☎(01223) 333202
Fax (01223) 765560
url: www.clare.cam.ac.uk/academic/libraries/fellows-library.html
Fellows' Librarian Dr Hubertus F Jahn PhD (e-mail: hfj21@cam.ac.uk)
▶ Forbes Mellon Library, Clare College, Cambridge CB3 9AJ
☎(01223) 333202
Fax (01223) 765560
url: www.clare.cam.ac.uk/academic/libraries/forbes-mellon-library.html
Librarian Mrs Anne C Hughes MA

Corpus Christi College
Parker Library, Corpus Christi College, Trumpington, Cambridge CB2 1RH
☎(01223) 338025
Fax (01223) 338041
e-mail: parker-library@corpus.cam.ac.uk
url: www.corpus.cam.ac.uk
Librarian Dr C de Hamel
Sub-Librarian Mrs G C Cannell (e-mail: gc110@cam.ac.uk)

Darwin College
Library, Darwin College, Silver Street, Cambridge CB3 9EU
☎(01223) 763547
Fax (01223) 335667
e-mail: librarian@dar.cam.ac.uk
url: www.dar.cam.ac.uk
Fellow Librarian Dr Anne Ferguson-Smith MA PhD
Student Librarian Ms Ariane Kossack

Department of Land Economy Library
Mill Lane Library, Department of Land Economy Library, 8 Mill Lane, Cambridge CB2 1RX
☎(01223) 337110
Fax (01223) 337130
url: www.landecon.cam.ac.uk/library/library.htm
Librarian Ms Wendy Thurley BA ALAA (e-mail: wt10000@cam.ac.uk)
(Mill Lane Library also houses the Centre of Latin American Studies and the Centre of
International Studies and Development Studies)

Downing College
The Maitland Robinson Library, Downing College, Regent Street, Cambridge CB2 1DQ
☎(01223) 334829 (enquiries), (01223) 335352 (College Librarian)
Fax (01223) 363852
url: www.dow.cam.ac.uk
Librarian Dr Ian James MA PhD
College Librarian Ms Karen Lubarr BA (e-mail: karen.lubarr@dow.cam.ac.uk)

Emmanuel College
Library, Emmanuel College, Cambridge CB2 3AP
☎(01223) 334233
e-mail: library@emma.cam.ac.uk
url: www.emma.cam.ac.uk
College Librarian H C Carron BA MA MPhil PhD MCLIP
Assistant Librarian C E P Bonfield BA

Faculty of Education
Library and Information Service, Faculty of Education, 184 Hills Road, Cambridge CB2 2PQ
☎(01223) 767700 (enquiries)
Fax (01223) 767602
e-mail: library@educ.cam.ac.uk

url: www.educ.cam.ac.uk/library
Librarian Ms Angela Cutts BA DipLib MCLIP
Deputy Librarian Ms Emma Jane Batchelor BA DipILS MCLIP

Faculty of Music
Pendlebury Library of Music, Faculty of Music, 11 West Road, Cambridge CB3 9DP
☎(01223) 335182
Fax (01223) 335183
url: www.mus.cam.ac.uk
Librarian Ms Anna Pensaert LIC

Faculty of Oriental Studies
Library, Faculty of Oriental Studies, Sidgwick Avenue, Cambridge CB3 9DA
☎(01223) 335112 (enquiries)
Fax (01223) 335110
e-mail: library@oriental.cam.ac.uk
url: www.oriental.cam.ac.uk/guide1.html
Librarian Ms Françoise Simmons MA(Cantab) MA(UCL) (01223 335111)

Fitzwilliam College
Library, Fitzwilliam College, Cambridge CB3 0DG
☎(01223) 332042
Fax (01223) 477976
e-mail: library@fitz.cam.ac.uk
url: www.fitz.cam.ac.uk
Librarian Miss Marion A MacLeod MA DipLib

Girton College
Library, Girton College, Cambridge CB3 0JG
☎(01223) 338970
Fax (01223) 339890
e-mail: library@girton.cam.ac.uk
url: www.lib.girton.cam.ac.uk/
Fellow and Librarian F Gandy BA MA MCLIP
Assistant Librarian Ms Jenny Blackhurst MA MA MCLIP
Archivist Mrs K M Perry

Gonville and Caius College
Library, Gonville and Caius College, Cambridge CB2 1TA
☎(01223) 332419
Fax (01223) 332430
e-mail: library@cai.cam.ac.uk
url: www.cai.cam.ac.uk/library/index.php
Librarian J H Prynne MA
Sub-Librarian M S Statham MA MCLIP
(Working library open to members of the College only. Old library open to scholars by appointment. All enquiries should be addressed to the Sub-Librarian)

Homerton College

Library, Homerton College, Mary Allan Building, Hills Road, Cambridge CB2 2PH
☎(01223) 507259
url: www.homerton.cam.ac.uk
College Librarian Geoff Mizen (e-mail: gm10009@cam.ac.uk)

Institute of Criminology

Radzinowicz Library of Criminology, Institute of Criminology, Sidgwick Avenue, Cambridge
CB3 9DT
☎(01223) 335375
Fax (01223) 335356
e-mail: crimlib@hermes.cam.ac.uk
url: www.crim.cam.ac.uk
Librarian Mrs H Krarup BA(Open) MSc
Senior Assistant Librarian Mrs M Gower MCLIP

Jesus College

▶ Quincentenary Library, Jesus College, Jesus Lane, Cambridge CB5 8BL
  ☎(01223) 339451
  Fax (01223) 324910
  url: www.jesus.cam.ac.uk/library.index.html
  Quincentenary Librarian Ms Rhona Watson BA(Hons) DipLib MCLIP (e-mail:
  r.watson@jesus.cam.ac.uk)
▶ The Old Library, Jesus College, Jesus Lane, Cambridge CB5 8BL
  ☎(01223) 339405
  Keeper of the Old Library Dr Stephen Heath
  Assistant to the Keeper and Archivist Dr Frances Willmoth
  (Apply in writing)

King's College Cambridge

Library, King's College Cambridge, Cambridge CB2 1ST
☎(01223) 331232
Fax (01223) 331891
e-mail: library@kings.cam.ac.uk
url: www.kings.cam.ac.uk/library/
Librarian Peter Jones

Lucy Cavendish College

Library, Lucy Cavendish College, Lady Margaret Road, Cambridge CB3 0BU
☎(01223) 332183
Fax (01223) 332178
e-mail: library@lucy-cav.cam.ac.uk
url: www.lucy-cav.cam.ac.uk
Librarian Ms C A Reid BSc MSc MCLIP
Assistant Librarian Ms J M Harris BA
(The Library is open only to the members of the College; it is essentially an undergraduate
library)

Magdalene College

Libraries, Magdalene College, Cambridge CB3 0AG
☎(01223) 332100
e-mail: magd-lib@lists.cam.ac.uk
url: www.magd.cam.ac.uk
College Librarian N G Jones MA LLM PhD
Pepys Librarian R Luckett MA PhD
(College Library: available only to members of the College. The Old Library: readers by
appointment in writing. The Pepys Library: readers by appointment in writing, and open to
visitors during full term only in Oct–Mar 2.30–3.30; Apr-Aug 11.30–12.30 and 2.30–3.30;
parties by appointment. Application for the Old and Pepys Libraries to R Luckett MA PhD
(fax 01223 332187)

New Hall

Rosemary Murray Library, New Hall, Huntingdon Road, Cambridge CB3 0DF
☎(01223) 762202
Fax (01223) 763110
e-mail: library@newhall.cam.ac.uk
url: www.newhall.cam.ac.uk/facilities/library/
Librarian Ms Alison Wilson BA MLitt MSc MCLIP
(Admittance to New Hall members only; for special collections, please write to the
Librarian)

Newnham College

Library, Newnham College, Sidgwick Avenue, Cambridge CB3 9DF
☎(01223) 335740/335739
url: www.newn.cam.ac.uk/nclcl
Librarian Ms Deborah Hodder MA MCLIP (e-mail: librarian@newn.cam.ac.uk)

Pembroke College

Library, Pembroke College, Cambridge CB2 1RF
☎(01223) 338100
Fax (01223) 338163
e-mail: lib@pem.cam.ac.uk
url: www.pem.cam.ac.uk
Librarian Prof T R S Allan MA BCL(Oxon)
Assistant Librarian Ms Patricia Aske MA

Peterhouse

Ward and Perne Libraries, Peterhouse, Cambridge CB2 1RD
☎(01223) 338218 (Ward Library); (01223) 338233 (Perne Library)
e-mail: lib@pet.cam.ac.uk
url: www.pet.cam.ac.uk
Ward Librarian M S Golding MA
Assistant Librarian E A McDonald BA MA MCLIP
Project Cataloguer Dr S Preston MA PhD DipLIS
Perne Librarian S H Mandelbrote MA
(Perne library by appointment only)

Queens' College
Library, Queens' College, Silver Street, Cambridge CB3 9ET
☎(01223) 335549, Porter's Lodge (01223) 335511
Fax (01223) 335522
e-mail: library@quns.cam.ac.uk
url: www.quns.cam.ac.uk
College Librarian Mrs Karen E Begg MSc(Econ) (e-mail: keb36@cam.ac.uk)
Fellow Librarian Dr Ian Patterson

Robinson College
Library, Robinson College, Cambridge CB3 9AN
☎(01223) 339124
url: www.robinson.cam.ac.uk
College Librarian Miss L Read MA BA MCLIP

St Catharine's College
Library, St Catharine's College, Cambridge CB2 1RL
☎(01223) 338343
Fax (01223) 338340
url: www.caths.cam.ac.uk/library
Fellow Librarian Dr R S K Barnes
Librarian Mrs S N T Griffiths MA MCLIP (e-mail: sntg100@cam.ac.uk)

St Edmund's College
Library, St Edmund's College, Mount Pleasant, Cambridge CB3 0BN
☎(01223) 336250 (switchboard)
Fax (01223) 762822
url: www.st-edmunds.cam.ac.uk
Fellow Librarian Dr Peta Dunstan MA PhD (e-mail: librarian@st-edmunds.cam.ac.uk)
(Please write in with enquiries)

St John's College
Library, St John's College, Cambridge CB2 1TP
☎(01223) 338661 (administration), (01223) 338662 (enquiries)
Fax (01223) 337035
e-mail: library@joh.cam.ac.uk
url: www.joh.cam.ac.uk/library
Librarian Dr Mark Nicholls MA PhD

Scott Polar Research Institute
Library, Scott Polar Research Institute, Lensfield Road, Cambridge CB2 1ER
☎(01223) 336552
Fax (01223) 336549
e-mail: library@spri.cam.ac.uk
url: www.spri.cam.ac.uk
Librarian Mrs Heather E Lane MA(Oxon) DipLiS MCLIP (e-mail: hel20@cam.ac.uk)

Selwyn College

Library, Selwyn College, Grange Road, Cambridge CB3 9DQ
☎(01223) 335880
Fax (01223) 335837
e-mail: lib@sel.cam.ac.uk
url: www.sel.cam.ac.uk/library
College Librarian Mrs Sarah Stamford BA(Hons) MA
Assistant Librarian M P Wilson BA(Hons) MA

Sidney Sussex College

Library, Sidney Sussex College, Cambridge CB2 3HU
☎(01223) 338800 (enquiries), (01223) 338852 (administration)
Fax (01223) 338884
e-mail: librarian@sid.cam.ac.uk
url: www.sid.cam.ac.uk/indepth/lib/library.html
Librarian Mrs C E Ratcliff (e-mail: cer34@cam.ac.uk)

Section library

▶ Archive and Muniment Room, Sidney Sussex College, Cambridge CB2 3HU
    ☎(01223) 338824
    Fax (01223) 338884
    e-mail: archivist@sid.cam.ac.uk
    Research Assistant Nicholas J Rogers MA MLitt (01223 338824; e-mail:
    njr1002@cam.ac.uk)

Trinity College

Library, Trinity College, Cambridge CB2 1TQ
☎(01223) 338488
Fax (01223) 338532
e-mail: jeb30@hermes.cam.ac.uk
url: www.trin.cam.ac.uk
Librarian Dr D J McKitterick FBA
(Undergraduate Library open to members of the College only. Wren Library: readers by
appointment. Visitors: Mon–Fri 12–2pm; Sat 10.30–12.30, full term only)

Trinity Hall

Library, Trinity Hall, Trinity Lane, Cambridge CB2 1TJ
☎(01223) 332546
Fax (01223) 332537
College Librarians Dr A C Lacey PhD (e-mail: ad28@cam.ac.uk), Mrs A M Hunt
BA(Hons) MCLIP (e-mail: amh55@cam.ac.uk)

Wolfson College

The Lee Library, Wolfson College, Barton Road, Cambridge CB3 9BB
☎(01223) 335965 (direct), (01223) 335900 (Porters' Lodge)
Fax (01223) 335937
e-mail: library@wolfson.cam.ac.uk

url: www.wolfson.cam.ac.uk
Librarian Mrs Anna Jones MA(Oxon) MA(Lond) MPhil(Cantab)

CANTERBURY CHRIST CHURCH UNIVERSITY

Library, Canterbury Christ Church University, North Holmes Road, Canterbury, Kent
CT1 1QU
☎(01227) 782514 (enquiries), (01227) 782403 (administration)
Fax (01227) 767530
e-mail: lib1@canterbury.ac.uk
url: www.cant.ac.uk
Acting Director of Library Services Pete Ryan BA(Hons) MCLIP (e-mail:
p.j.ryan@canterbury.ac.uk)

Site libraries
▶ Salomons Hayloft Library, Canterbury Christ Church University, David Salomons Estate,
  Broomhill Road, Southborough, Tunbridge Wells, Kent TN3 0TG
  ☎(01892 507514
  Fax (01892 507501
  e-mail: hayloftlibrary@canterbury.ac.uk
  Librarian Ms Andrea Ford BA DipLib MCLIP (e-mail: a.ford@canterbury.ac.uk)
▶ Salomons Mansion Library, Canterbury Christ Church University, David Salomons
  Estate, Broomhill Road, Southborough, Tunbridge Wells, Kent TN3 0TG
  ☎(01892) 507717
  Fax (01892) 507719
  e-mail: salomons_library@canterbury.ac.uk
  Site Librarian Mrs Kathy Chaney MCLIP (e-mail: k.v.chaney@canterbury.ac.uk)
▶ St Augustines Library, Canterbury Christ Church University, Burgate House, The
  Precincts, Canterbury, Kent CT1 2EH
  ☎(01227) 865338
  Librarian Ms Karen Erskine BA MCLIP (e-mail: k.j.erskine@canterbury.ac.uk)
▶ Thanet Learning Centre, Canterbury Christ Church University, Northwood Road,
  Broadstairs, Kent CT10 2WA
  ☎(01843 609121
  Fax (01843 609130
  e-mail: thanetlc@canterbury.ac.uk
  Learning Centre Manager Dennis Corn (e-mail: d.corn@canterbury.ac.uk)

CARDIFF UNIVERSITY

Information Services, Cardiff University, 40-41 Park Place, Cardiff CF10 3BB
e-mail: library@cardiff.ac.uk
url: www.cardiff.ac.uk/schoolsanddivisions/divisions/insrv/index.html
Director of Information Services Martyn Harrow
Deputy Director and University Librarian Steve Pritchard BA MCLIP (029 2087 9362)

Following the merger of activities between Cardiff University and the University of Wales College of Medicine on 1 August 2004, the University Library Service has 18 principal service points:
Aberconway; Archie Cochrane; Architecture; Arts and Social Sciences; Biomedical Sciences; Brian Cooke Dental; Bute; Cancer Research Wales; Law; Legal Practice; Music; Nursing and Healthcare; Nursing and Midwifery; Science; Senghennydd; Sir Herbert Duthie; Trevithick; Whitchurch Postgraduate Medical Centre. During the period of transition, please see the website for contact details.

UNIVERSITY OF CENTRAL ENGLAND IN BIRMINGHAM

Library Services, University of Central England in Birmingham, Perry Barr, Birmingham B42 2SU
☎0121 331 5289 (enquiries), 0121 331 5300 (administration)
Fax 0121 356 2875
e-mail: kenrick.library.enquiry.desk@uce.ac.uk
url: http://library.uce.ac.uk
Director of Library Services Ms Judith Andrews MA DipLib MCLIP (e-mail: judith.andrews@uce.ac.uk)

UNIVERSITY OF CENTRAL LANCASHIRE

Library and Learning Resource Services, University of Central Lancashire, Preston, Lancs PR1 2HE
☎(01772) 892284 (enquiries), (01772) 892260 (administration)
Fax (01772) 892937
e-mail: helpdesk@uclan.ac.uk
url: www.uclan.ac.uk
Head of Library and Learning Resource Services Kevin Ellard BA MA DMS MCLIP (01772 892261; e-mail: krellard@uclan.ac.uk)
Head of Information Services Jeremy Andrew BSc (01772 892264; e-mail: jsandrew@uclan.ac.uk)
Head of User Support Vacant
Head of Specialized Learning Resource Unit Ms K McCrea (01772 892272; e-mail: kmccrea@uclan.ac.uk)
Head of Specialized Learning Resource Unit Ms Kay Mason (01772 892294; e-mail: kmason1@uclan.ac.uk)
Acting Head of Bibliographic and Support Services Ms Sharon Whiteside (01772 892141; e-mail: smwhiteside@uclan.ac.uk)
Acting Head of Systems Stephen Mossop (01772 892692; e-mail: samossop@uclan.ac.uk)

Site libraries
▶ Blackburn Clinical Library, Education Centre, University of Central Lancashire, Blackburn Royal Infirmary, Bolton Road, Blackburn, Lancs BB2 3LR
   ☎(01254) 294312

Fax (01254) 261504
e-mail: lblackburn1@uclan.ac.uk

▶ Blackpool Clinical Library, University of Central Lancashire, Health Professionals Education Centre, Blackpool Victoria Hospital, Whinney Heys Road, Blackpool, Lancs FY3 8NR
☎(01253) 303831
Fax (01253) 303818
e-mail: lblackpool1@uclan.ac.uk

▶ Burnley Clinical Library, Education Centre, University of Central Lancashire, Burnley General Hospital, Casterton Avenue, Burnley, Lancs BB10 2PQ
☎(01282) 474699
Fax (01282) 838916
e-mail: lburnley.uclan.ac.uk

▶ Carlisle Campus Library, University of Central Lancashire, Milbourne Street, Carlisle CA2 5XB
☎(01228) 404660; (01772) 895230
Fax (01228) 404669; (01772) 895239
e-mail: lcarlisle1@uclan.ac.uk

▶ Cumbria Campus Library, University of Central Lancashire, Cumbria Campus, Newton Rigg, Penrith, Cumbria CA11 0AH
☎(01772) 894200
Fax (01772) 894991
Librarian/Resource Centre Manager David Singleton BSc MA DipLib MCLIP (01772 894201; e-mail: dsingleton@uclan.ac.uk)

▶ Ormskirk Clinical Library, Learning Resource Centre, University of Central Lancashire, Southport and Ormskirk District General Hospital, Wigan Road, Ormskirk, Lancs L39 2AZ
☎(01695) 656790
Fax (01695) 581459
e-mail: lormskirk@uclan.ac.uk

▶ Wigan Clinical Library, Wigan Education Centre, University of Central Lancashire, Bernard Surgeon Suite, RAE Infirmary, Wigan Lane, Wigan WN1 2NN
☎(01942) 822162
Fax (01942) 829583
e-mail: lwigan@uclan.ac.uk

CENTRAL SCHOOL OF SPEECH AND DRAMA

Learning and Information Services, Central School of Speech and Drama, Embassy Theatre, 64 Eton Avenue, London NW3 3HY
☎020 7559 3942 (enquiries)
Fax 020 7722 4132
e-mail: library@cssd.ac.uk
url: www.cssd.ac.uk
Head of Learning and Information Services Vacant
Library Services Manager Peter Collett BA PGDipLib MCLIP (020 7559 3996; e-mail: p.collett@cssd.ac.uk)

Systems Manager Brian Harry BSc (020 7559 3969; e-mail: b.harry@cssd.ac.uk)
Media Services Manager Roger West (020 7559 3934; e-mail: r.west@cssd.ac.uk)

UNIVERSITY COLLEGE CHESTER

Library/Learning Resources, University College Chester, Parkgate Road, Chester CH1 4BJ
☎(01244) 375444 ext 3301 (enquiries)
Fax (01244) 392811
url: www.chester.ac.uk/lr
Director of Learning Resources Mrs Christine Stockton BA MBA MCLIP (ext 3300;
e-mail: c.stockton@chester.ac.uk)
Deputy Director (Academic and User Services) Mrs Angela Walsh BLib MA MCLIP
(ext 3308; e-mail: a.walsh@chester.ac.uk)
Deputy Director (Health, Social Care and Development) Mrs Wendy Fiander BSc
MA MCLIP (ext 3793; e-mail: w.fiander@chester.ac.uk)

Nursing and midwifery site libraries

▶ JET (Joint Education and Training) Library, University College Chester, Leighton
Hospital, Middlewich Road, Crewe, Cheshire CW1 4QJ
☎(01270) 255141 ext 2538/2705
Librarian Vacant
▶ Library, University College Chester, School of Health and Social Care, Arrowe Park
Hospital, Upton, Wirral, Cheshire CH49 5PE
☎0151 604 7291
Fax 0151 678 5322
Librarian Mrs Christine Holly BSc (e-mail: c.holly@chester.ac.uk)
▶ Library, University College Chester, School of Health and Social Care, Bache Education
Centre, Countess Way, Chester CH2 1BR
☎(01244) 364664
Librarian Mrs Elisa Dowey BA MCLIP (e-mail: e.dowey@chester.ac.uk)

(Subject to approval, University College Chester will become University of Chester in
Autumn 2005)

UNIVERSITY COLLEGE CHICHESTER

Learning Resources Centre, University College Chichester, Bishop Otter Campus, College
Lane, Chichester, West Sussex PO19 6PE
☎(01243) 816089 (enquiries), (01243) 816091 (administration)
Fax (01243 816080
url: www.ucc.ac.uk
Director of Information Services Terry A Hanson BA DipLib (01243 816150; e-mail:
t.hanson@ucc.ac.uk)
Head of Library Services Scott O Robertson MA MEd MCLIP (01243 816090; e-mail:
s.robertson@ucc.ac.uk)

Campus library
▶ Library, University College Chichester, Bognor Regis Campus, Upper Bognor Road, Bognor Regis, West Sussex PO21 1HR
☎(01243) 816099
Fax (01243) 816081
Campus Librarian Ms Norma Leigh BLib MA MCLIP (01243 816082; e-mail: n.leigh@ucc.ac.uk)

(Subject to approval, University College Chichester will become University of Chichester in Autumn 2005)

CITY UNIVERSITY

University Library, City University, Northampton Square, London EC1V 0HB
☎020 7040 4061 (enquiries)
Fax 020 7040 8194
e-mail: library@city.ac.uk
url: www.city.ac.uk/library
Director of Library and Information Services Brendan Casey BA DipLib
Senior Associate Director Ms Liz Harris

Site libraries
▶ Department of Radiography Library, City University, Rutland Place, Charterhouse Square, London EC1M 6PA
☎020 7040 5653 (enquiries)
Fax 020 7040 5691
▶ Learning Resource Centre, City University, Cass Business School, 106 Bunhill Row, London EC1Y 8TZ
☎020 7040 8787 (enquiries)
Fax 020 7638 1080
e-mail: cklib@city.ac.uk
url: www.city.ac.uk/library/ckl
Senior Associate Director Leslie Baldwin
▶ Library and Information Services, City University, Inns of Court School of Law, 4 Gray's Inn Place, Gray's Inn, London WC1R 5DX
☎020 7400 3605 (enquiries)
Fax 020 7831 3193
e-mail: ltrc@icsl.ac.uk
url: www.city.ac.uk/icsl/ltrc/
Associate Director Paul Banks
▶ West Smithfield Site Library, City University, St Bartholomew's School of Nursing and Midwifery, 20 Bartholomew Close, London EC1A 7QN
☎020 7040 5759 (enquiries)
url: www.city.ac.uk/library/sonm
Associate Director Mrs Helen Alper
▶ Whitechapel Site Library, City University, Alexandra Building, Philpot Street, London E1 2EA

☎020 7040 5859 (enquiries)
url: www.city.ac.uk/library/sonm

COVENTRY UNIVERSITY

Lanchester Library, Coventry University, Frederick Lanchester Building, Gosford Street, Coventry CVI 5DD
☎024 7688 7575
Fax 024 7688 7525
url: www.coventry.ac.uk
University Librarian Pat Noon BA MBA DipLib MCLIP (e-mail: p.noon@coventry.ac.uk)

CRANFIELD UNIVERSITY

Kings Norton Library, Cranfield University, Cranfield, Beds MK43 0AL
☎(01234) 754444 (general enquiries)
Fax (01234) 752391
url: www.cranfield.ac.uk/library/
University Librarian Dr Hazel Woodward PhD BA MCLIP (e-mail: h.woodward@cranfield.ac.uk)
Deputy University Librarian Stephen Town MA DipLib FCLIP MIMgt (e-mail: stown@rmcs.cranfield.ac.uk)

Other libraries
▶ Library, Cranfield University, Cranfield University at Silsoe, Silsoe, Beds MK45 4DT
   ☎(01525) 863022
   Fax (01525) 863001
   Librarian Chris Napper BA DipLib MCLIP (e-mail: c.napper@cranfield.ac.uk)
▶ Management Information Resource Centre, Cranfield University, Cranfield, Beds MK43 0AL
   ☎(01234) 754440
   Fax (01234) 751806
   Head Ms Louise Edwards BA(Hons) DipLib MCLIP (e-mail: l.edwards@cranfield.ac.uk)
▶ Royal Military College of Science, Cranfield University, Library, Shrivenham, Swindon SN6 8LA
   ☎(01793) 785484 (general enquiries)
   Fax (01793) 785555
   e-mail: library2@rmcs.cranfield.ac.uk
   Director of Information Services at Shrivenham Stephen Town MA DipLib FCLIP MIMgt (01793 785480; e-mail: stown@rmcs.cranfield.ac.uk)

CUMBRIA INSTITUTE OF THE ARTS

Library, Cumbria Institute of the Arts, Brampton Road, Carlisle CA3 9AY
☎(01228) 400312
Fax (01228) 514491
url: www.cumbria.ac.uk
College Librarian Ms Clare Daniel BA MA MCLIP (e-mail: clare.daniel@cumbria.ac.uk)

DARTINGTON COLLEGE OF ARTS

Library, Dartington College of Arts, Totnes, Devon TQ9 6EJ
☎(01803) 861651
Fax (01803) 861666
e-mail: library@dartington.ac.uk
url: www.dartington.ac.uk/library/index.asp
Director of Academic Services Chris Pressler BA(Hons) MA MSc MCLIP (e-mail:
c.pressler@dartington.ac.uk)
Deputy Librarian John Sanford (e-mail: j.sanford@dartington.ac.uk)

DE MONTFORT UNIVERSITY

Kimberlin Library, De Montfort University, The Gateway, Leicester LE1 9BH
☎0116 257 7165
Fax 0116 257 7046
url: www.library.dmu.ac.uk
Director of Library Services Ms Kathryn Arnold BA DipLib MCLIP (e-mail:
karnold@dmu.ac.uk)
Library Services Manager (Leics) Vacant
Quality and Staff Resources Manager Ms Margaret Oldroyd BA(Hons) MLib MCLIP
(e-mail: meo@dmu.ac.uk)

Campus libraries

▶ Bedford Library, De Montfort University, Polhill Avenue, Bedford MK41 9EA
☎(01234) 351671
Fax (01234) 217738
Library Services Manager (Bedford) Ms Diana Saulsbury BA MA PGDipLib
CertEdFE (e-mail: ds@dmu.ac.uk)
▶ Charles Frears Campus Library, De Montfort University, 266 London Road, Leicester
LE2 1RQ
☎0116 270 0661
Fax 0116 270 9722
Campus Librarian Ms Barbara Freeman BA MCLIP

UNIVERSITY OF DERBY

Learning and Information Services, University of Derby, Kedleston Road, Derby DE22 1GB
☎(01332) 591205
Fax (01332) 597767
e-mail: enquirydesk@derby.ac.uk
url: http://lib.derby.ac.uk/library/homelib.html
Director of Learning and Information Services Richard Maccabee MA
(e-mail: r.maccabee@derby.ac.uk)
University Librarian Richard Finch MA DipLib DMS MCLIP (e-mail: r.finch@derby.ac.uk)

DUNDEE UNIVERSITY

University Library, Dundee University, Small's Wynd, Dundee DD1 4HN
☎(01382) 344087 (enquiries), (01382) 344084 (administration)
Fax (01382) 229190
e-mail: library@dundee.ac.uk
url: www.dundee.ac.uk/Library
Librarian John Bagnall MA DipLib MCLIP

Site libraries

▶ Book and Paper Conservation Studio, Dundee University, Dundee DD1 4HN
☎(01382) 344094
Fax (01382) 345614
e-mail: conservation@dundee.ac.uk
Conservator Mrs Ylva Player-Dahnsjo MA AKC HND

▶ Duncan of Jordanstone Faculty of Art Library, Dundee University, Matthew Building,
13 Perth Road, Dundee DD1 4HT
☎(01382) 345255 (enquiries)
Fax (01382) 229283
e-mail: doj-library@dundee.ac.uk
College Librarian Ms Marie Simmons BA MCLIP

▶ Faculty of Education and Social Work Library, Dundee University, Gardyne Road
Campus, Gardyne Road, Dundee DD5 1NY
☎(01382) 464267
Fax (01382) 464255
e-mail: gardyne-library@dundee.ac.uk
Librarian John McCaffery BA DipLib MCLIP

▶ Law Library, Dundee University, Scrymgeour Building, Dundee DD1 4HN
☎(01382) 344100
Fax (01382) 228669
e-mail: law-library@dundee.ac.uk
Librarian David Hart MA MCLIP

▶ Ninewells Medical Library, Dundee University, Ninewells Hospital and Medical School,
Dundee DD1 9SY
☎(01382) 632519
Fax (01382) 566179
e-mail: ninewells-medical-library@dundee.ac.uk
Librarian Donald Orrock MA

▶ Nursing and Midwifery Library, Dundee University, Tayside Campus,
Tayside School of Nursing and Midwifery, Ninewells Hospital and Medical School,
Dundee DD1 9SY
☎(01382) 632012
e-mail: snm-tayside-library@dundee.ac.uk
Learning Resources Manager Andrew Jackson BA(Hons) MCLIP

▶ Nursing and Midwifery Library, Fife Campus, Dundee University, Fife School of Nursing
and Midwifery, Forth Avenue, Kirkcaldy, Fife KY2 5YS
☎(01382) 345930
Fax (01382) 345931

e-mail: snm-fife-library@dundee.ac.uk
Librarian Ms Margaret Forrest MA(Hons) MSc DipLib FCLIP FSA(Scot)

UNIVERSITY OF DURHAM

University Library, University of Durham, Stockton Road, Durham DH1 3LY
☎0191 334 2968
Fax 0191 334 2971
e-mail: main.library@durham.ac.uk
url: www.dur.ac.uk/library
Chief Librarian John T D Hall MA PhD

Departmental libraries

▶ Library, University of Durham, Education Section, Leazes Road, Durham DH1 1TA
☎0191 334 8137
Fax 0191 334 8311
Site Supervisor Mrs Susan McBreen

▶ Library, University of Durham, Palace Green Section (Law, Music, Archives & Special Collections), Palace Green, Durham DH1 3RN
☎0191 334 2932
Fax 0191 334 2942
Sub-Librarian, Heritage Collections Mrs Sheila M Hingley MA MCLIP
Site Supervisor Mrs Anne E Farrow MA MCLIP

▶ Library, University of Durham, Stockton Campus Section, University Boulevard, Stockton-on-Tees, Co Durham TS17 6BH
☎0191 334 0270
Fax 0191 334 0271
e-mail: stockton.library@durham.ac.uk
Site Supervisor Ms Jane A Hodgson

UNIVERSITY OF EAST ANGLIA

Library, University of East Anglia, Norwich NR4 7TJ
☎(01603) 592421 (enquiries), (01603) 592407 (administration)
Fax (01603) 591010
e-mail: library@uea.ac.uk
url: www.lib.uea.ac.uk
Director of Information Services and Librarian Mrs Jean Steward BA MA MCLIP
(01603 592424; e-mail: j.steward@uea.ac.uk)
Director of Library Resources Ms Kitty Inglis BA DipLib (01603 592430; e-mail: k.inglis@uea.ac.uk)
User Services Director Vacant
ISD Administrator Mrs Christine Christopher BA(Hons) PGCE (01603 592407; e-mail: c.christopher@uea.ac.uk)
Subject Librarian (Arts and Humanities) Alex Noel-Tod MA DipLib (01603 592428; e-mail: a.noel-tod@uea.ac.uk)
Subject Librarian (Social Sciences) Bill Marsh BSc(Econ) MA DipLib (01603 592431; e-mail: j.marsh@uea.ac.uk)

Subject Librarian (Sciences) Dr Elizabeth Clarke BSc PhD (01603 591249; e-mail:
e.clarke@uea.ac.uk)
Subject Librarian (Arts and Humanities and Social Sciences) Ms Sarah Elsegood BSc
MCLIP ILTM
Subject Librarian (Health) William Jones BSc DipLib MCLIP
Interlending and Document Supply Services David Palmer BA LLB MLS
Acquisitions Librarian Mrs Anne Baker BA MCLIP (01603 592429; e-mail:
a.b.baker@uea.ac.uk)
Circulation Librarian Mrs Caroline Reeman (01603 592414; e-mail:
c.reeman@uea.ac.uk)
IT Systems Director Iain Reeman (01603 592423; e-mail: i.reeman@uea.ac.uk)
Electronic Resources Librarian Nicholas Lewis BA PGCE MA (01603 592382; e-mail:
nicholas.lewis@uea.ac.uk)

Nursing library
▶ NAM Library, Peddars Centre, University of East Anglia, Hellesdon, Drayton High Road,
Norwich NR6 5BE
☎(01603) 421527
e-mail: a.cook@uea.ac.uk

UNIVERSITY OF EAST LONDON

Learning Support Services, University of East London, Longbridge Road, Dagenham, Essex
RM8 2AS
☎020 8223 2614 (enquiries), 020 8223 2619 (administration)
Fax 020 8223 2804
url: www.uel.ac.uk
Director of Learning Support Services Prof Andrew McDonald FCLIP (020 8223 2620;
e-mail: a.mcdonald@uel.ac.uk)

Campus learning resource centres
▶ Barking LRC, University of East London, Longbridge Road, Dagenham, Essex RM8 2AS
☎020 8223 2614 (enquiries)
▶ Docklands LRC, University of East London, Docklands Campus, Royal Albert Way,
London E16 2QJ
☎020 8223 3434
Campus LRC Manager Ms Judith Preece BA MCLIP
▶ Duncan House LRC, University of East London, Duncan House, High Street, Stratford,
London E15 2JA
☎020 8223 3346 (enquiries)
Site Manager Ms Maureen Azubike BA MCLIP
▶ Stratford LRC, University of East London, University House, Romford Road, Stratford,
London E15 4LZ
☎020 8223 4224 (enquiries)
Campus LRC Manager Paul Chopra MA PGDipLib MCLIP

EDGE HILL COLLEGE OF HIGHER EDUCATION

Learning Services, Edge Hill College of Higher Education, St Helens Road, Ormskirk, Lancs L39 4QP
☎(01695) 584286 (enquiries), (01695) 584284 (administration)
Fax (01695) 584592
url: www.edgehill.ac.uk/ls/
Head of Learning Services Ms Sue Roberts BA(Hons) DipLib MA (01695 584284; e-mail: robertss@edgehill.ac.uk)
Academic Support Manager Ms Dawn McLoughlin (01695 584518; e-mail: mcloughd@edgehill.ac.uk)
User Services Manager Ms Coral Black BA(Hons) (01695 584334; e-mail: blackc@edgehill.ac.uk)

Site libraries

▶ Learning Services, Edge Hill College of Higher Education, Woodlands Campus, Southport Road, Chorley, Lancs PR7 1QR
  ☎(01257) 517136
  Learning Services Manager Ms Ruth Wilson BA DipLib MCLIP (01257 517137; e-mail: wilsonr@edgehill.ac.uk)
▶ The Library and Information Resource Centre, Edge Hill College of Higher Education, Clinical Sciences Centre, University Hospital Aintree, Longmoor Lane, Liverpool L9 7AL
  LIRC Manager Ms Rachel Bury BA(Hons) MCLIP (0151 529 5857; e-mail: buryr@edgehill.ac.uk)

EDINBURGH COLLEGE OF ART

Lauriston Place Library, Edinburgh College of Art, Lauriston Place, Edinburgh EH3 9DF
☎0131 221 6034
Fax 0131 221 6033
url: www.lib.eca.ac.uk
Principal Librarian Wilson Smith MA DipLib (e-mail: w.smith@eca.ac.uk)

UNIVERSITY OF EDINBURGH

Edinburgh University Library, University of Edinburgh, George Square, Edinburgh EH8 9LJ
☎0131 650 3409 (Access and Lending Services); 0131 650 8379 (Special Collections)
Fax 0131 667 9780/650 3380
e-mail: library@ed.ac.uk; lib-ref@ed.ac.uk; eishelp@ed.ac.uk
url: Library Online: www.lib.ed.ac.uk/
Director of Library Services Mrs Sheila E Cannell MA MCLIP (e-mail: s.cannell@ed.ac.uk)

Site libraries

▶ Law & Europa Library, University of Edinburgh, Old College, South Bridge, Edinburgh EH8 9YL
  ☎0131 650 2044
  Fax 0131 650 6343

Site and Services Supervisor Ms Teresa Jones (e-mail: teresa.jones@ed.ac.uk)
▶ Medical Libraries, University of Edinburgh, George Square, Edinburgh EH8 9LJ
☎0131 650 3690
Fax 0131 667 9780
College Librarian Ms Irene McGowan BA MCLIP (e-mail: irene.mcgowan@ed.ac.uk)
▶ Moray House Library (Education), University of Edinburgh, Dalhousie Land, St John
Street, Edinburgh EH8 8AQ
☎0131 651 6193
Fax 0131 557 3458
Site and Services Supervisor David Fairgrieve MA DipLib MCLIP (e-mail:
david.fairgrieve@ed.ac.uk)
▶ New College Library (Divinity), University of Edinburgh, Mound Place, Edinburgh
EH1 2LU
☎0131 650 8957
Fax 0131 650 7952
Site and Services Supervisor Ms Sheila Dunn BA (e-mail: sheila.dunn@ed.ac.uk)
▶ Science Libraries, University of Edinburgh, Edinburgh University Library, West Mains
Road, Edinburgh EH9 3JF
☎0131 650 5205
Fax 0131 650 6702
College Librarian Richard Battersby BA DipLib MCLIP (e-mail: r.battersby@ed.ac.uk)
▶ Veterinary Libraries, University of Edinburgh, Summerhall, Edinburgh EH9 1QH
☎0131 650 6175
Fax 0131 650 6593
Liaison Librarian Mrs Fiona Brown MA (e-mail: f.brown@ed.ac.uk)
(site also at Easter Bush, Roslin, Midlothian EH25 9RG)

ESSEX UNIVERSITY

The Albert Sloman Library, Essex University, Wivenhoe Park, Colchester, Essex CO4 3SQ
☎(01206) 873188
Fax (01206) 872289
url: www.essex.ac.uk
Librarian Robert Butler MSc

UNIVERSITY OF EXETER

University Library, University of Exeter, Stocker Road, Exeter, Devon EX4 4PT
☎(01392) 263873 (enquiries), (01392) 263869 (administration)
Fax (01392) 263871
e-mail: library@exeter.ac.uk
url: www.exeter.ac.uk/library/
Librarian Alasdair T Paterson MA ALAI

Departmental libraries
▶ Law Library, University of Exeter, Amory Building, Rennes Drive, Exeter, Devon EX4 4RJ
☎(01392) 263356
Librarian Lee Snook LLB MSc MCLIP

▶ St Luke's Campus Library, University of Exeter, Exeter, Devon EX1 2LU
  ☎(01392) 264785
  Librarian Roy Davies BSc DipLib DipCompSci MCLIP

UNIVERSITY COLLEGE FALMOUTH
(formerly Falmouth College of Arts)

Learning Resources Centre, University College Falmouth, Tremough Campus, Treliever Road, Penryn, Cornwall TR10 9EZ
☎(01326) 370441
Fax (01326) 370437
e-mail: library@falmouth.ac.uk
url: www.falmouth.ac.uk
Head of Library and Information Services Ms Doreen Pinfold BA(Hons) PGDipLib
Visual Resources Librarian Ms Rebecca Ball BA(Hons) PGDipLib (e-mail: rebeccab@falmouth.ac.uk)
User Services Librarian Ms Christina Lake MA (e-mail: christinal@falmouth.ac.uk)
Systems Librarian Steve Pellow BA(Hons) PGCE (e-mail: stevep@falmouth.ac.uk)
Technical Services Librarian Stephen Atkinson BSc DipLib MCLIP (e-mail: stephena@falmouth.ac.uk)
(Tremough Campus LRC also serves University of Exeter in Cornwall)

Library and Information Services, University College Falmouth, Woodlane Campus Library, Falmouth, Cornwall TR11 4RA
☎(01326) 213815
Fax (01326) 211205
e-mail: library@falmouth.ac.uk
url: www.falmouth.ac.uk
Senior Art and Design Librarian Roger Towe BA PGDipLib (e-mail: rogert@falmouth.ac.uk)
Cataloguing Librarian Stephen Gibson BA (e-mail: stepheng@falmouth.ac.uk)
Campus Librarian Ms Rosalind Tyley MA

UNIVERSITY OF GLAMORGAN

Learning Resources Centre, University of Glamorgan, Pontypridd, Rhondda Cynon Taff CF37 1DL
☎(01443) 482625 (enquiries)
Fax (01443) 482629
e-mail: lrcenq@glam.ac.uk
url: www.glam.ac.uk/lrc
Head of Learning Resources Centre Jeremy Atkinson BSc MPhil DipLib MCLIP
Deputy Head of Learning Resources Centre Steve Morgan BA MEd MBA FCLIP

GLASGOW CALEDONIAN UNIVERSITY

Caledonian Library and Information Centre, Glasgow Caledonian University, Cowcaddens Road, Glasgow G4 0BA

☎0141 273 1000
Fax 0141 331 8549
e-mail: library@gcal.ac.uk
url: www.lib.gcal.ac.uk
Director, Learner Support Tom Finnigan BSc DipEdComp MA MEd MIIT ILTM FRSA

GLASGOW SCHOOL OF ART

Library, Glasgow School of Art, 167 Renfrew Street, Glasgow G3 6RQ
☎0141 353 4551
Fax 0141 353 4670
url: www.gsa.ac.uk/library/
Head of Learning Resources Ms Catherine Nicholson MA DipLib MCLIP (e-mail:
c.nicholson@gsa.ac.uk)

GLASGOW UNIVERSITY

University Library, Glasgow University, Hillhead Street, Glasgow G12 8QE
☎0141 330 6704/5 (enquiries), 0141 330 5634 (administration)
Fax 0141 330 4952
e-mail: library@lib.gla.ac.uk
url: www.lib.gla.ac.uk
Director of Library Services Chris Bailey MA DipLib MCLIP

Site/departmental libraries
▶ Adam Smith Library, Glasgow University, Adam Smith Building, Bute Gardens, Hillhead,
  Glasgow G12 8RT
  ☎0141 330 5648
  Librarian Kerr Ross
▶ Chemistry Branch, Glasgow University, Joseph Black Building, Glasgow G12 8QQ
  ☎0141 330 5502
  e-mail: library@lib.gla.ac.uk
  Librarian Mrs Denise Currie
▶ James Herriot Library, Glasgow University, Veterinary School, Garscube Estate,
  Bearsden, Glasgow G61 1QH
  ☎0141 330 5708
  e-mail: vetlib@lib.gla.ac.uk
  Librarian Mrs Maureen McGovern
▶ James Ireland Memorial Library, Glasgow University, Dental School and Hospital,
  Sauchiehall Street, Glasgow G2 3JZ
  ☎0141 211 9705
  e-mail: library@dental.gla.ac.uk
  Librarian Ms Beverley Rankin

UNIVERSITY OF GLOUCESTERSHIRE

Learning Centre, University of Gloucestershire, The Park, Cheltenham, Glos GL50 2RH
☎(01242) 543458

Fax (01242) 543492
e-mail: lcinfopark@glos.ac.uk
url: www.glos.ac.uk/lis/
Head of Learning and Information Services Ms Ann Mathie BA MPhil MCLIP
Learning Centre Manager Terry Smith

Site libraries

▶ Learning Centre, University of Gloucestershire, Francis Close Hall, Swindon Road,
Cheltenham, Glos GL50 4AZ
☎(01242) 532913
e-mail: lcinfofch@glos.ac.uk
Learning Centre Manager Mrs Ann Cummings BA

▶ Learning Centre, University of Gloucestershire, Pittville Campus, Albert Road,
Cheltenham, Glos GL52 3JG
☎(01242) 532259
e-mail: lcinfopitt@glos.ac.uk
Learning Centre Manager Terry Smith

▶ Learning Centre, University of Gloucestershire, Oxstalls Campus, Oxstalls Lane,
Gloucester GL2 9HW
☎(01452) 876602
e-mail: lcinfoox@glos.ac.uk
Learning Centre Manager Mrs Ann Cummings BA

▶ Learning Centre, University of Gloucestershire, Urban Learning Foundation, Bede
House, 56 East India Dock Road, London E14 6JE
☎020 7536 7002
Fax 020 7536 0107
e-mail: lcinfoulf@glos.ac.uk

UNIVERSITY OF GREENWICH

Maritime Greenwich Campus Library, University of Greenwich, Old Royal Naval College,
Park Row, Greenwich, London SE10 9LS
☎020 8331 8000
url: www.gre.ac.uk/lib
Director of Information and Library Services Denis Heathcote MA MCLIP (e-mail:
d.heathcote@gre.ac.uk)
Head of Learning Services Ms Ann Murphy BA DipLib (020 8331 8196; e-mail:
a.e.murphy@gre.ac.uk)

Campus libraries

▶ Avery Hill Campus Library, University of Greenwich, Bexley Road, London SE9 2PQ
☎020 8331 8484
Fax 020 8331 9645
Campus Librarian Ms Rosemary Moon BA DipLib (e-mail: r.m.moon@gre.ac.uk)

▶ Dreadnought Library, University of Greenwich, Maritime Greenwich Campus, Old
Royal Naval College, Park Row, Greenwich, London SE10 9LS
☎020 8331 7788
Fax 020 8331 7775

Campus Librarian Ms Teri Harland BSc MCLIP (e-mail: c.m.harland@gre.ac.uk)

▌ Medway Campus Library, University of Greenwich, Nelson Building, Chatham Maritime, Central Avenue, Chatham, Kent ME4 4TB
☎020 8331 9617
Fax 020 8331 9837
Campus Librarian Ms Virginia Malone

GUILDHALL SCHOOL OF MUSIC AND DRAMA

Library, Guildhall School of Music and Drama, Silk Street, Barbican, London EC2Y 8DT
☎020 7382 7178 (direct)
Fax 020 7786 9378 (direct)
e-mail: library@gsmd.ac.uk
url: www.gsmd.ac.uk
Senior Librarian Mrs Kate Eaton BA(Hons) MA

HARPER ADAMS UNIVERSITY COLLEGE

Library, Harper Adams University College, Edgmond, Newport, Shropshire TF10 8NB
☎(01952) 820280
e-mail: libhelp@harper-adams.ac.uk
url: www.harper-adams.ac.uk
Librarian Ms Kathryn Greaves BLib(Hons) MCLIP

HERIOT-WATT UNIVERSITY

University Library, Heriot-Watt University, Edinburgh EH14 4AS
☎0131 451 3571
Fax 0131 451 3164
e-mail: library@hw.ac.uk
url: www.hw.ac.uk/library
Librarian Michael Breaks BA DipLib (e-mail: m.l.breaks@hw.ac.uk)

UNIVERSITY OF HERTFORDSHIRE

Learning and Information Services, University of Hertfordshire, College Lane, Hatfield, Herts AL10 9AB
☎(01707) 284678
Fax (01707) 284666
e-mail: lisadmin@herts.ac.uk
url: www.herts.ac.uk/lis
Dean of Learning and Information Services Ms Di Martin MA DipLib MCLIP CertEd MCIPD

Learning resources centres

▌ Hatfield College Lane Campus Learning Resources Centre, University of Hertfordshire, College Lane, Hatfield, Herts AL10 9AB
☎(01707) 284678

Campus LIS Manager Mrs Cathy Parr MA MCLIP
▶ Hatfield de Havilland Campus Learning Resources Centre, University of Hertfordshire, Hatfield, Herts AL10 9AB
☎(01707) 284678
Campus LIS Manager Neil Allen BA MCLIP
(post c/o College Lane address above)
▶ St Albans Campus Learning Resources Centre, University of Hertfordshire, 7 Hatfield Road, St Albans, Hertfordshire AL1 3RS
☎(01707) 284678
Campus LIS Manager Nick Goodfellow MA MCLIP CertEd

UNIVERSITY OF HUDDERSFIELD

Learning Centre, University of Huddersfield, Queensgate, Huddersfield, Yorkshire HD1 3DH
☎(01484) 473830 (enquiries), (01484) 473838 (administration)
Fax (01484) 472385
e-mail: ills@hud.ac.uk
url: www.hud.ac.uk
Director of Computing and Library Services Prof John Lancaster MPhil MCLIP
Deputy Director of Computing and Library Services Ms Sue White BA DipLib MCLIP
Head of Communications and Information Technology Brian Hackett BA MCLIP

UNIVERSITY OF HULL

The Brynmor Jones Library, University of Hull, Cottingham Road Campus, Cottingham Road, Kingston upon Hull HU6 7RX
☎(01482) 466581
Fax (01482) 466205
e-mail: libhelp@hull.ac.uk
url: www.hull.ac.uk/lib
Director of Academic Services and Librarian R G Heseltine BA DPhil DipLib

Campus library

▶ Keith Donaldson Library, University of Hull, Scarborough Campus, Filey Road, Scarborough, North Yorks YO11 3AZ
☎(01723) 357277
Fax (01723) 357328
e-mail: libhelp-scar@hull.ac.uk
Library Manager Ms J Crowther (01723 357254)

ISLE OF MAN COLLEGE

Library, Isle of Man College, Homefield Road, Douglas, Isle of Man IM2 6RB
☎(01624) 648207
Fax (01624) 663675
e-mail: libiomc@manx.net

Senior Librarian Miss Carole Graham BA MCLIP MSc (e-mail: Carole.Graham@iomcollege.ac.im)
College Librarian Tim Kenyon BA MCLIP MA (e-mail: Tim.Kenyon@iomcollege.ac.im)

KEELE UNIVERSITY

Department of Information Services, Keele University, Keele, Staffs ST5 5BG
☎(01782) 583535 (enquiries), (01782) 583232 office
Fax (01782) 711553
e-mail: kis@keele.ac.uk
url: www.keele.ac.uk/depts/li/lihome.html
Director of Information Services A Foster BA FCLIP (e-mail: a.j.foster@keele.ac.uk)
Assistant Director (Library Services) P Reynolds MA MCLIP (e-mail: p.r.reynolds@keele.ac.uk)

Departmental library
▶ Health Library, Keele University, Clinical Education Centre, University Hospital of North Staffordshire, Newcastle Road, Stoke-on-Trent ST4 6QG
☎(01782) 556565
Fax (01782) 556582
Health Faculty Librarian D Bird BA MA MA (e-mail: d.t.bird@keele.ac.uk)

UNIVERSITY OF KENT

Templeman Library, University of Kent at Canterbury, Canterbury, Kent CT2 7NU
☎(01227) 823570 (enquiries), 823565 (administration)
Fax (01227) 823984
e-mail: library@kent.ac.uk
url: www.kent.ac.uk/library
Director of Information Services John Sotillo BSc
Librarian Vacant

Site libraries
▶ Drill Hall Library, Universities at Medway, University of Kent at Medway, Lower Pembroke, Chatham Maritime, Chatham, Kent ME4 4AG
☎(01634) 888999
Library Manager Ms Virginia Malone
(Shared library with Canterbury Christ Church University and University of Greenwich)
▶ Library, University Centre Tonbridge, University of Kent at Tonbridge, Avebury Avenue, Tonbridge, Kent TN9 1TG
☎(01732) 368449
Library Supervisor Mrs Denyse Straker

KENT INSTITUTE OF ART AND DESIGN

Library, Kent Institute of Art and Design, Oakwood Park, Maidstone, Kent ME16 8AG
☎(01622) 757286
Fax (01622) 621100

e-mail: librarymaid@kiad.ac.uk
url: www.kiad.ac.uk
Head of Library and Learning Resources Ms Vanessa Crane MBA BA MCLIP (e-mail:
vcrane@kiad.ac.uk)
Librarian, Maidstone Mrs Annamarie McKie MA MCLIP (e-mail: amckie@kiad.ac.uk)

Campus libraries
▶ Library, Kent Institute of Art and Design, Canterbury Campus, New Dover Road,
Canterbury, Kent CT1 3AN
☎(01227) 769371
Fax (01227) 817500
e-mail: librarycant@kiad.ac.uk
Librarian, Canterbury Mrs Kathleen Godfrey MA(Ed) MCLIP (e-mail:
kgodfrey@kiad.ac.uk)
▶ Library, Kent Institute of Art and Design, Rochester Campus, Design Fort Pitt,
Rochester, Kent ME1 1DZ
☎(01634) 830022
Fax (01634) 820300
e-mail: libraryroch@kiad.ac.uk
Librarian, Rochester Mrs Pauline Sowry BA MCLIP (e-mail: psowry@kiad.ac.uk)

Please note: The Kent Institute of Art & Design and The Surrey Institute of Art & Design,
University College merged on 1 August 2005 and became the University College for the
Creative Arts at Canterbury, Epsom, Farnham, Maidstone and Rochester

KING ALFRED'S COLLEGE WINCHESTER *see* UNIVERSITY COLLEGE WINCHESTER

KINGSTON UNIVERSITY

Library Services, Kingston University, Penrhyn Road, Kingston upon Thames, Surrey KT1 2EE
☎020 8547 7101 (enquiries), 020 8547 7105 (administration)
Fax 020 8547 7111
e-mail: library@kingston.ac.uk
url: www.kingston.ac.uk/library
Director of Library Services Graham Bulpitt MA MCLIP CertEd (020 8547 7100; e-mail:
g.bulpitt@kingston.ac.uk)
Head of Learning and Research Support Mrs Jane Savidge MA MCLIP (020 8547 7503;
e-mail: j.savidge@kingston.ac.uk)
Head of E-strategy and Collection Management Mrs Elizabeth Malone BA(Hons)
DipLib MCLIP (020 8547 7814; e-mail: e.malone@kingston.ac.uk)
Head of Finance, Planning and Resources Simon Mackie (020 8547 7110; e-mail:
s.mackie@kingston.ac.uk)

Campus libraries
▶ Library Services, Kingston University, Kingston Hill, Kingston upon Thames, Surrey KT2 7LB

☎020 8547 7384
Fax 020 8547 7312

▸ Library Services, Kingston University, Knights Park, Kingston upon Thames, Surrey KT1 2QJ
☎020 8547 7057
Fax 020 8547 8039

▸ Library Services, Kingston University, Penrhyn Road, Kingston upon Thames, Surrey KT1 2EE
☎020 8547 7101
Fax 020 8547 8115

▸ Library Services, Kingston University, Roehampton Vale, Friars Avenue, London SW15 3DW
☎020 8547 7903 (tel/fax)

UNIVERSITY OF LANCASTER

University Library, University of Lancaster, Bailrigg, Lancaster LA1 4YH
☎(01524) 592517 (enquiries), 01524 592535 (administration)
Fax (01524) 65719
e-mail: lbrusrvs@exchange.lancs.ac.uk (Library user services)
url: www.libweb.lancs.ac.uk
University Librarian Ms Jacqueline Whiteside MA MCLIP FRSA (e-mail:
j.whiteside@lancaster.ac.uk)

LEEDS METROPOLITAN UNIVERSITY

Learning and Information Services, Leeds Metropolitan University, Leslie Silver Building,
Civic Quarter, Leeds LS1 3HE
☎0113 283 5956
Fax 0113 283 6779
url: www//leedsmet.ac.uk/lis/lss
Head of Learning Support Services Ms Jo Norry BA(Hons) MA DipLib PGDip MCLIP
ILTM (0113 283 5966; e-mail: j.norry@leedsmet.ac.uk)
E-Services Development Manager Vacant

Campus libraries

▸ Civic Quarter Library, Leeds Metropolitan University, Leslie Silver Building, Woodhouse
Lane, Leeds LS1 3HE
☎0113 283 3106 (counter), 0113 283 5968 (enquiries)
Fax 0113 283 3123
Campus Library Manager Ms Dilys Young BA DMS MSc(Econ) MLIS ILTM (0113 283
2600, ext 3975; e-mail: d.a.young@leedsmet.ac.uk)

▸ Harrogate College Library, Leeds Metropolitan University, Hornbeam Park, Harrogate,
Yorkshire HG2 8QT
☎(01423) 878216/878213
Campus Library Manager Arthur Sargeant MA BA(Hons) CertFE (0113 283 2600,
ext 8282; e-mail: a.sargeant@leedsmet.ac.uk)

▸ Headingley Library, Leeds Metropolitan University, Beckett Park, Leeds LS6 3QS
☎0113 283 3164 (counter), 0113 283 7467 (enquiries)
Fax 0113 283 3211

Campus Library Manager Ms Wendy Luker BA(Hons) PGDip MCLIP (0113 283 2600, ext 7468; e-mail: w.luker@leedsmet.ac.uk)

UNIVERSITY OF LEEDS

University Library, University of Leeds, Leeds LS2 9JT
☎0113 343 5663 (general enquiries), 0113 343 5507 (administration)
Fax 0113 343 5561
e-mail: library@library.leeds.ac.uk
url: www.leeds.ac.uk/library/library.html
The Librarian/Head of the Brotherton Collection Ms Margaret Coutts MA(Glas) MA(Sheff) MCLIP

UNIVERSITY OF LEICESTER

University Library, University of Leicester, PO Box 248, University Road, Leicester LE1 9QD
☎0116 252 2043 (general enquiries), 0116 252 2031 (Librarian's secretary)
Fax 0116 252 2066
e-mail: libdesk@leicester.ac.uk
url: www.le.ac.uk/library/
University Librarian Mrs Christine Fyfe BA MA MBA

Site libraries

▶ Clinical Sciences Library, University of Leicester, Clinical Sciences Building, Leicester Royal Infirmary, PO Box 65, Leicester LE2 7LX
☎0116 252 3104
Fax 0116 252 3107
Librarian i/c Miss Joanne E Dunham BA DipLib

▶ Education Library, University of Leicester, 21 University Road, Leicester LE1 7RF
☎0116 252 3738
Fax 0116 252 5798
Librarian i/c Roy W Kirk BA MCLIP HonFLA

UNIVERSITY OF LINCOLN

University Library, Learning and Information Services, University of Lincoln, Brayford Pool, Lincoln LN6 7TS
☎(01522) 886222 (general enquiries)
Fax (01522) 886047
e-mail: pyoung@lincoln.ac.uk; nrogers@lincoln.ac.uk
url: www.lincoln.ac.uk
Head of Learning Resources Ms Michelle Anderson BA(Hons) MA
Administrative Officer Ms Pat Hughes (e-mail: phughes@lincoln.ac.uk)

LIVERPOOL HOPE UNIVERSITY COLLEGE

Sheppard–Worlock Library, Liverpool Hope University College, PO Box 95, Hope Park, Liverpool L16 9JD

☎0151 291 2000 (issue desk), 0151 291 2001 (administration), 0151 291 2041 (enquiries), 0151 291 2038 IT help desk
Fax 0151 291 2037
url: www.hope.ac.uk/library
Director of Library, Learning and Information Services Ms Linda J Taylor MEd BA MCLIP ILTM (0151 291 3528; e-mail: taylorl@hope.ac.uk)
Library Manager Ms Susan Murray MA BSc MCLIP ILTM (0151 291 2002; e-mail: murrays@hope.ac.uk)
Academic Services Managers Mrs Angela Duckworth BA MCLIP ILTM (0151 291 2008; e-mail: duckwoa@hope.ac.uk), Mrs Ruth Keane MA BA BPhil DipLib MCLIP ILTM (0151 291 2008; e-mail: keaner@hope.ac.uk job-share) (job-share)
Technical Services Manager Mrs Colette Hughes BA(Hons) MCLIP ILTM (0151 291 2016; e-mail: hughesc@hope.ac.uk)

(Subject to approval, Liverpool Hope University College will become Liverpool Hope University in Autumn 2005)

LIVERPOOL INSTITUTE FOR PERFORMING ARTS

Learning Services, Liverpool Institute for Performing Arts, Mount Street, Liverpool L1 9HF
☎0151 330 3111
Fax 0151 330 3110
url: www.lipa.ac.uk
Director of Information Services and Technical Support Ken O'Donoghue BA MA DLIS CertEd (0151 330 3250; e-mail: k.odonoghue@lipa.ac.uk)
Learning Services Manager Ms C Holmes BA(Hons) PGDipLib (0151 332 3111; e-mail: c.holmes@lipa.ac.uk)

LIVERPOOL JOHN MOORES UNIVERSITY

Learning and Information Services, Liverpool John Moores University, Aldham Robarts Learning Resource Centre, Mount Pleasant, Liverpool L3 5UZ
☎0151 231 3544/3682
Fax 0151 231 3113
url: www.livjm.ac.uk
Director of Learning and Information Services Ms Maxine Melling BA PGDipLib MLib MCLIP (0151 231 3682; e-mail: m.melling@livjm.ac.uk)
Computing Services Manager Graham Chan MSc BSc MCLIP (0151 231 3178; e-mail: g.k.chan@livjm.ac.uk)
Customer Services Manager Mrs Brigid Badger BA DipLib (0151 231 4008; e-mail: b.j.badger@livjm.ac.uk)
Facilities Services Manager Jim Ainsworth BA MCLIP (0151 231 4020/5300; e-mail: j.w.ainsworth@livjm.ac.uk)
Academic Services Manager Ms Valerie Stevenson BA(Hons) (0151 231 4456; e-mail: v.stevenson@livjm.ac.uk)

Site libraries

▶ Aldham Robarts Learning Resource Centre, Liverpool John Moores University, Mount Pleasant, Liverpool L3 5UZ
☎0151 231 3634/3701
Fax 0151 707 1307

▶ Avril Robarts Learning Resource Centre, Liverpool John Moores University, Tithebarn Street, Liverpool L2 2ER
☎0151 231 4022
Fax 0151 231 4479

▶ I M Marsh Learning Resource Centre, Liverpool John Moores University, Barkhill Road, Liverpool L17 6BD
☎0151 231 5216
Fax 0151 231 5378

UNIVERSITY OF LIVERPOOL

University Library, University of Liverpool, Liverpool L69 3DA
☎0151 794 2679 (enquiries), 0151 794 2674 (administration)
Fax 0151 794 2681/5417
url: www.liv.ac.uk/library
University Librarian Phil Sykes BA MCLIP

Site libraries

▶ Continuing Education Library, University of Liverpool, 126 Mount Pleasant, Liverpool L69 3DA
☎0151 794 3285
Continuing Education Librarian Ms Linda Crane BA(Hons) MCLIP (e-mail: lcrane@liv.ac.uk)

▶ Harold Cohen Library (Science, Medicine, Engineering, Veterinary and Dental Science), University of Liverpool, Ashton Street, Liverpool L69 3DA
☎0151 794 5411
Fax 0151 794 5417
User Services Manager Mrs Laura Oldham BA DipLib (e-mail: loldham@liv.ac.uk)

▶ Law Library, University of Liverpool, Chatham Street, Liverpool L69 3DA
☎0151 794 2832
e-mail: qlis07@liv.ac.uk
Law Librarian Mrs Wendy Spalton BA DipLib

▶ Sydney Jones Library (Humanities, Social Sciences, Special Collections and Archives), University of Liverpool, Chatham Street, Liverpool L69 3DA
☎0151 794 2679
Fax 0151 794 2681
User Services Manager Ms Carol Kay BA MA DipLib (e-mail: c.kay@liv.ac.uk)

LONDON CONTEMPORARY DANCE SCHOOL

Library, London Contemporary Dance School, The Place, 16 Flaxman Terrace, London WC1H 9AT
☎020 7387 0152 (direct)

Fax 020 7387 3976 (direct)
Librarian Ms Sasi del Bono (e-mail: sasi.delbono@theplace.org.uk)

LONDON METROPOLITAN UNIVERSITY

Systems and Services, London Metropolitan University, London North Campus, 236–250 Holloway Road, London N7 6PP
☎020 7133 2100 (enquiries), 020 7133 5148 (central administration)
Fax 020 7133 2066
url: www.londonmet.ac.uk/library
Director of Systems and Services Kevin Harrigan
Associate Director, Systems and Services: ICT & General Management
Miss Maureen E Castens BSc MA MCLIP DMS (e-mail: m.castens@londonmet.ac.uk)
(Based at London City Campus)
Associate Director, Systems and Services: Libraries, Media and Print Roy Williams
BA MCLIP DipLib GradIPM (e-mail: r.williams@londonmet.ac.uk)

London City Campus

Systems and Services, London City Campus, Calcutta House, Old Castle Street, London E1 7NT
☎020 7320 1173 (administration)
url: www.londonmet.ac.uk
Head of Library Services and Media Services (City) Ms Ann Constable BA DipLib
MCLIP (e-mail: a.constable@londonmet.ac.uk)

Site/departmental libraries

▶ Calcutta House Library, London City Campus, Old Castle Street, London E1 7NT
☎020 7320 1185
Fax 020 7320 1182
Learning Resources Manager Ms Helen Dalton BSc MCLIP (e-mail:
h.dalton@londonmet.ac.uk)
▶ Commercial Road Library, London City Campus, 41-71 Commercial Road, London E1 1LA
☎020 7320 1869
Fax 020 7320 2831
Learning Resources Manager Ms Catherine Walsh (e-mail:
c.walsh@londonmet.ac.uk)
▶ Moorgate Library, London City Campus, 84 Moorgate, London EC2M 6SQ
☎020 7320 1567
Fax 020 7320 1565
Learning Resources Manager Vacant
(See also The Women's Library in Selected Government, National and Special Libraries section)

London North Campus

Systems and Services, London North Campus, Learning Centre, 236-250 Holloway Road, London N7 6PP
☎020 7133 2100 (enquiries), 020 7133 5148 (central administration)

Fax 020 7133 2066
url: www.londonmet.ac.uk/library
Head of Library Services, North Campus Ms Julie Howell BSc(SocSci)Hons DipLib
(020 7133 2450; e-mail: j.howell@londonmet.ac.uk)

Holloway Road Learning Centre Teams

▶ Academic Information Services Team, London North Campus, 236-250 Holloway Road,
London N7 6PP
☎020 7133 2101
Fax 020 7133 2066
Team Manager Ms Susan Davy BSc MCLIP (020 7133 2101; e-mail:
s.davy@londonmet.ac.uk)
▶ Operations Team, London North Campus, 236-250 Holloway Road, London N7 6PP
☎020 7133 2089
Fax 020 7133 2066
Team Manager Peter Bowbeer BA(Hons) DipInfSci (020 7133 2089; e-mail:
p.bowbeer@londonmet.ac.uk)

Special Collections

▶ European Documentation Centre, London North Campus, Holloway Road Learning
Centre, 236-250 Holloway Road, London N7 6PP
☎020 7133 2718
Fax 020 7133 2066
Subject Librarian Ms Ruth Newton (e-mail: r.newton@londonmet.ac.uk)
▶ TUC Library Collections, London North Campus, Holloway Road Learning Centre,
236-250 Holloway Road, London N7 6PP
☎020 7133 2260
Fax 020 7133 2569
e-mail: tuclib@londonmet.ac.uk
url: www.londonmet.ac.uk/library/tuc
Librarian Ms Christine Coates MA MCLIP (e-mail: c.coates@londonmet.ac.uk)

Ladbroke House Library Team

Ladbroke House Team, London North Campus, Ladbroke House Library, 62-66 Highbury
Grove, London N5 2AD
☎020 7133 5149
Fax 020 7133 5100
Team Manager Ms Bridget Shersby BA (e-mail: b.shersby@londonmet.ac.uk)

LONDON SOUTH BANK UNIVERSITY

Perry Library, London South Bank University, 250 Southwark Bridge Road, London SE1 6NJ
☎020 7815 6607 (enquiries), 020 7815 6602 (administration)
Fax 020 7815 6699
url: www.lisa.lsbu.ac.uk
Head of Learning and Information Services John Akeroyd MPhil BSc MCLIP DipLIS
(e-mail: akeroyj@lsbu.ac.uk)

Site libraries

▶ Library, London South Bank University, Harold Wood Hospital, Gubbins Lane, Romford, Essex RM3 0BE
☎020 7815 5982
Fax 020 7815 4786
Site Manager Ms Patricia Noble MCLIP (e-mail: noblep@lsbu.ac.uk)

▶ Library, London South Bank University, Whipps Cross Education Centre, Whipps Cross Hospital, Leytonstone, London E11 1NR
☎020 7815 4747
Fax 020 7815 4777
Deputy Site Manager Ms Diana Watmough MCLIP CLTHE (e-mail: watmoudj@lsbu.ac.uk)

UNIVERSITY OF LONDON

Senate House Library, University of London, Senate House, Malet Street, London WC1E 7HU
☎020 7862 8461 (enquiries), 020 7862 8432 (administration)
Fax 020 7862 8480
e-mail: enquiries@shl.lon.ac.uk
url: www.shl.lon.ac.uk
Director, University of London Research Library Services David Pearson MA FCLIP (e-mail: dpearson@lon.ac.uk)
Senior Sub-Librarian, Academic Services Paul McLaughlin MA MCLIP (020 7862 8413; e-mail: pmclaughlin@lon.ac.uk)
Sub-Librarian, Administration, Planning and Resources Mrs Gail Duggett BA MA MSc MBA MCHI FRSA (020 7862 8412; e-mail: gduggett@lon.ac.uk)
Sub-Librarian, Information Strategy Steve Clews MA DipLib (020 7862 8452; e-mail: sclews@lon.ac.uk)
Head of Historic Collections Services Mrs Christine Wise (020 7862 8471; e-mail: cwise@lon.ac.uk)

(Includes libraries of the Institute of United States Studies, the Institute for English Studies, the Institute of Romance Studies, and of the Australian and Canadian High Commissions)

Depository Library, University of London, Spring Rise, Egham, Surrey TW20 9PP
☎(01784) 434560 (tel/fax)
Depository Librarian T West BA MCLIP (e-mail: twest@lon.ac.uk/dpmail@lon.ac.uk)

College, Institute and Departmental

Each College listed below is an independent self-governing institution funded, where applicable, by HEFCE, and awarding degrees of the University of London, of which each is a member.

Australian High Commission Library

See University of London, Senate House

Birkbeck College
Library, Birkbeck College, Malet Street, London WC1E 7HX
☎020 7631 6064 (administration), 020 7631 6063/6239 (enquiries)
Fax 020 7631 6066
e-mail: libhelp@bbk.ac.uk
url: www.bbk.ac.uk/lib/
Librarian Philip Payne BA MCLIP (020 7631 6250; e-mail: p.payne@bbk.ac.uk)
Deputy Librarian Robert Atkinson MA DipLib MCLIP (020 7631 6366; e-mail:
r.atkinson@bbk.ac.uk)

Canadian High Commission Library
See University of London, Senate House

Courtauld Institute of Art
Library, Courtauld Institute of Art, Somerset House, Strand, London WC2R 0RN
☎020 7848 2701 (enquiries)
Fax 020 7848 2887
e-mail: booklib@courtauld.ac.uk
url: www.courtauld.ac.uk
Book Librarian Tim Davies (020 7848 2706)

Goldsmiths College
Information Services Department, Goldsmiths College, New Cross, London SE14 6NW
☎020 7919 7150 (enquiries), 020 7919 7161 (administration)
Fax 020 7919 7165
e-mail: library@gold.ac.uk
url: http://libweb.gold.ac.uk
Director of Information Services Ms Joan Pateman BSc

Heythrop College
Library, Heythrop College, Kensington Square, London W8 5HQ
☎020 7795 4250 (enquiries), 020 7795 4251 (administration)
Fax 020 7795 4253
e-mail: library@heythrop.ac.uk
url: www.heythrop.ac.uk
Librarian Christopher J Pedley SJ BA(Econ) BA MTh ThM MA (e-mail:
c.pedley@heythrop.ac.uk)

Imperial College London
Central Library, Imperial College London, South Kensington, London SW7 2AZ
☎020 7594 8820 (enquiries), 020 7594 8816 (administration)
Fax 020 7594 8876
e-mail: library@imperial.ac.uk
url: www.imperial.ac.uk/library
Director of Library Services Ms Clare Jenkins BA DipLib MCLIP (020 7594 8881; e-mail:
c.jenkins@imperial.ac.uk)
Assistant Director, Faculty Support Services for Learning and Research Ms Liz
Davis BSc MCLIP (020 7594 8877; e-mail: e.davis@imperial.ac.uk)

Assistant Director, e-Strategy, Information Resources and Systems Management (ESIRSM) Ms Janet Evans BA DipLib MCLIP (020 7594 8829; e-mail: janet.evans@imperial.ac.uk)
Assistant Director, Administration and Planning Ms Susan Howard BA MSc DipLib MCLIP (020 7594 8622; e-mail: s.howard@imperial.ac.uk)

Departmental libraries

▶ Aeronautics Department Library, Imperial College London, South Kensington Campus, London SW7 2AZ
☎020 7594 5069
Fax 020 7584 8120
e-mail: aerolib@imperial.ac.uk
▶ Chemical Engineering and Chemical Technology Department Library, Imperial College London, South Kensington Campus, London SW7 2AZ
☎020 7594 5598
Fax 020 7594 5604
e-mail: chemenglib@imperial.ac.uk
▶ Civil and Environmental Engineering Department Library, Imperial College London, South Kensington Campus, London SW7 2AZ
☎020 7594 6007
Fax 020 7225 2716
e-mail: civenglib@imperial.ac.uk
▶ Electrical and Electronic Engineering Department Library, Imperial College London, South Kensington Campus, London SW7 2AZ
☎020 7594 6182
Fax 020 7823 8125
e-mail: eeelib@imperial.ac.uk
▶ Mathematics Library, Imperial College London, South Kensington Campus, London SW7 2AZ
☎020 7594 8542
Fax 020 7594 8517
e-mail: mathslib@imperial.ac.uk
▶ Mechanical Engineering Library, Imperial College London, South Kensington Campus, London SW7 2AZ
☎020 7594 7166
Fax 020 7594 8845
e-mail: mechenglibrary@imperial.ac.uk

Medical libraries

▶ Charing Cross Campus Library, Imperial College London, Charing Cross Campus, St Dunstan's Road, London W6 8RP
☎020 7594 0755
Fax 020 7594 0851
e-mail: librarycx@imperial.ac.uk
▶ Chelsea and Westminster Campus Library, Imperial College London, Chelsea and Westminster Campus, Fulham Road, London SW10 9NH
☎020 8746 8107
Fax 020 8746 8215

e-mail: librarycw@imperial.ac.uk
▶ Hammersmith Campus Library, Imperial College London, Hammersmith Campus, Du Cane Road, London W12 0NN
☎020 8383 3246
Fax 020 8383 2195
e-mail: lib.hamm@imperial.ac.uk
▶ Royal Brompton Campus Library, Imperial College London, Royal Brompton Campus, Dovehouse Street, London SW3 6LY
☎020 7351 8150
Fax 020 7351 8117
e-mail: br.library@imperial.ac.uk
▶ St Mary's Campus Library, Imperial College London, St Mary's Campus, Norfolk Place, London W2 1PG
☎020 7594 3692
Fax 020 7402 3971
e-mail: sm-lib@imperial.ac.uk
▶ Silwood Park Campus Library, Imperial College London, Silwood Park Campus, Buckhurst Road, Ascot, Berks SL5 7TE
☎(01491) 829112
Fax (01491) 829123
e-mail: mway.library@imperial.ac.uk
▶ Wye Campus Library, Imperial College London, Wye Campus, High Street, Wye, Ashford, Kent TN25 5AH
☎020 7594 2915
Fax 020 7594 2929
e-mail: wyelibrary@imperial.ac.uk

Institute for English Studies
See University of London, Senate House

Institute for the Study of the Americas
Library, Institute for the Study of the Americas, School of Advanced Study, 31 Tavistock Square, London WC1H 9HA
☎020 7862 8501
Fax 020 7862 8971
e-mail: latam@sas.ac.uk
url: www.americas.sas.ac.uk
Information Resources Manager Ms Sarah Pink BA MA MCLIP (e-mail: sarah.pink@sas.ac.uk)

Institute of Advanced Legal Studies
Library, Institute of Advanced Legal Studies, School of Advanced Study, 17 Russell Square, London WC1B 5DR
☎020 7862 5800
Fax 020 7862 5770
e-mail: ials@sas.ac.uk
url: www.ials.sas.ac.uk
Librarian Jules R Winterton BA LLB MCLIP

Deputy Librarian and Academic Services Manager David R Gee BA MA MCLIP
Information Systems Manager Steve J Whittle BA MA
Information Resources Manager Ms Lesley Young BA DipLib MCLIP

Institute of Cancer Research
Library, Institute of Cancer Research, Chester Beatty Labs, 237 Fulham Road, London SW3 6JB
☎020 7153 5123
Fax 020 7153 5143
e-mail: fullib@icr.ac.uk
url: www.icr.ac.uk
Librarian Barry Jenkins BA DipLib
Assistant Librarian Ms June Greenwood

Site library
▶ Library, Institute of Cancer Research, Brookes Lawley Building, 15 Cotswold Road, Belmont, Sutton, Surrey SM2 5NG
☎020 8722 4230
Fax 020 8722 4323
e-mail: sutlib@icr.ac.uk
Librarian Barry Jenkins BA DipLib
Library Information Officer Mrs Sue Rogers

Institute of Classical Studies
Institute of Classical Studies Library and Joint Library of the Hellenic and Roman Societies, Institute of Classical Studies, Senate House, Malet Street, London WC1E 7HU
☎020 7862 8709
Fax 020 7862 8724
url: www.sas.ac.uk/icls/default.htm
Librarian Colin H Annis MA MCLIP (e-mail: colin.annis@sas.ac.uk)

Institute of Commonwealth Studies
Library, Institute of Commonwealth Studies, School of Advanced Study, 28 Russell Square, London WC1B 5DS
☎020 7862 8842 (library enquiries)
Fax 020 7862 8820
e-mail: icommlib@sas.ac.uk
url: www.sas.ac.uk/commonwealthstudies
Information Resources Manager/Librarian David Clover DipLib MA (020 7862 8840; e-mail: david.clover@sas.ac.uk)

Institute of Education
Information Services, Institute of Education, 20 Bedford Way, London WC1H 0AL
☎020 7612 6080 (enquiries)
Fax 020 7612 6093
e-mail: lib.enquiries@ioe.ac.uk
url: www.ioe.ac.uk

Head of Information Services Stan Smith BSc (020 7612 6052; e-mail: stan.smith@ioe.ac.uk)
Library Manager Stephen Pickles (020 7612 6064; e-mail: s.pickles@ioe.ac.uk)

Institute of Germanic Studies
Library, Institute of Germanic Studies, 29 Russell Square, London WC1B 5DP
☎020 7862 8965 (administration), 020 7862 8967 library
Fax 020 7862 8970
e-mail: igslib@sas.ac.uk
url: www.sas.ac.uk/gs
Librarian William Abbey BA

Institute of Historical Research
Library, Institute of Historical Research, School of Advanced Study, Senate House, Malet Street, London WC1E 7HU
☎020 7862 8760
Fax 020 7862 8762
e-mail: IHR.Library@sas.ac.uk
url: www.history.ac.uk/ihrlibrary/
Librarian Robert Lyons BA DipLib

Institute of Ophthalmology and Moorfields Eye Hospital NHS Foundation Trust
Joint Library, Institute of Ophthalmology and Moorfields Eye Hospital NHS Foundation Trust, 11-43 Bath Street, London EC1V 9EL
☎020 7608 6814 (tel/fax)
e-mail: ophthlib@ucl.ac.uk
url: www.ucl.ac.uk/ioo/library
Librarian Ms Debbie Heatlie BA (020 7608 6815)
Assistant Librarian Vacant

Institute of Romance Studies
Institute of United States Studies
See University of London, Senate House

King's College Institute of Psychiatry
Library, King's College Institute of Psychiatry, De Crespigny Park, London SE5 8AF
☎020 7848 0204
Fax 020 7703 4515
e-mail: spyllib@kcl.ac.uk
url: www.iop.ac.uk
Librarian Martin Guha BA MCLIP
Deputy Librarian Ms Clare Martin BA MCLIP

King's College London
King's College London, Strand, London WC2R 2LS
☎020 7848 2139/2140 (administration)
Fax 020 7848 1777

e-mail: issenquiry@kcl.ac.uk
url: www.kcl.ac.uk/iss
Director of Information Services and Systems Ms Margaret Haines BA MLS FCLIP
(e-mail: margaret.haines@kcl.ac.uk)
Site Services Manager Mrs Vivien Robertson BA MCLIP (e-mail:
vivien.robertson@kcl.ac.uk)
(There is no longer a library at this site. Library now located at Chancery Lane: see Strand
Campus below)

For site information contact
Site Services Manager Mrs Vivien Robertson BA MCLIP (e-mail:
vivien.robertson@kcl.ac.uk)
☎020 7848 2424
Fax 020 7848 2277

Guy's Campus
▶ Information Services Centre, King's College London, New Hunt's House, Guy's
Campus, London SE1 1UL
☎020 7848 6600
Fax 020 7848 6743
▶ Warner Library and Information Centre, King's College London, Guy's Tower, Guy's
Campus, London SE1 9RT
☎020 7188 3169
Fax 020 7188 3265

King's Denmark Hill Campus
▶ Information Services Centre, King's College London, Weston Education Centre,
Cutcombe Road, London SE5 9RJ
☎020 7848 5541/5542
Fax 020 7848 5550

Strand Campus
▶ Maughan Library and Information Services Centre, King's College London, Chancery
Lane, London WC2A 1LR
☎020 7848 2424
Fax 020 7848 2277

St Thomas' Campus
▶ Medical Library, King's College London, Block 9, Sherrington Building, St Thomas'
Hospital, Lambeth Palace Road, London SE1 7EH
☎020 7188 3740
Fax 020 7401 3932

Waterloo Campus
▶ Information Services Centre, King's College London, Franklin-Wilkins Building, 150
Stamford Street, London SE1 9NH
☎020 7848 4378
Fax 020 7848 4290

London Business School
Library, London Business School, 25 Taunton Place, London NW1 6HB
☎020 7262 5050 (switchboard)
Fax 020 7706 1897
e-mail: library@london.edu
url: www.london.edu/library/
Director, Information Systems Russell Altendorff
Head of Information Services Ms Helen Edwards BA MCLIP

Business Information Service, London Business School, 25 Taunton Place, London NW1 6HB
☎020 7723 3404
Fax 020 7706 1897
e-mail: infoserve@london.edu
url: www.bestofbiz.com
Manager Ms Sue Watt DipLib MCLIP

(Note: Main postal address of the London Business School is Regent's Park, London
NW1 4SA)

London School of Economics and Political Science
Library of the London School of Economics and Political Science (British Library of Political
and Economic Science), London School of Economics and Political Science, 10 Portugal
Street, London WC2A 2HD
☎020 7955 7229 (enquiries), 020 7955 7219 (administration)
Fax 020 7955 7454
e-mail: library.information.desk@lse.ac.uk
url: www.library.lse.ac.uk
Librarian and Director of Information Services Ms Jean Sykes MA MLitt DipLib MCLIP
(020 7955 7218; e-mail: j.sykes@lse.ac.uk)
Deputy Librarian Ms Maureen Wade BA DipLib MCLIP (020 7955 7224; e-mail:
m.wade@lse.ac.uk)
Information Services Manager Ms Kate Sloss BA PGDip MCLIP (020 7955 7217; e-mail:
k.sloss@lse.ac.uk)
Technical Services Manager Glyn Price BA DipLib MCLIP (020 7995 6755; e-mail:
g.price@lse.ac.uk)
User Services Manager Ms Helen Cocker BA MPhil (020 7955 6336; e-mail:
h.cocker@lse.ac.uk)
Archivist Ms Sue Donnelly BA DipArchiveAdmin (020 7955 7223; e-mail:
document@lse.ac.uk)
Library IT Manager Tim Green DipCompStud (020 7955 6140; e-mail:
t.green@lse.ac.uk)
Communications and Marketing Manager Ms Marysia Henty DipDM (020 7852 3525;
e-mail: m.henty@lse.ac.uk)
Library Administrator Ms Val Straw BA (020 7955 7238; e-mail: v.straw@lse.ac.uk)

London School of Hygiene & Tropical Medicine
Library, London School of Hygiene & Tropical Medicine, Keppel Street, London WC1E 7HT
☎020 7927 2276 (enquiries), 020 7927 2283 (administration)

Fax 020 7927 2273
e-mail: library@lshtm.ac.uk
url: www.lshtm.ac.uk/as/library/libintro.htm
Head of Library Services Ms Caroline Lloyd BA MA MCLIP

London School of Jewish Studies

Library, London School of Jewish Studies, Schaller House, 44A Albert Road, London
NW4 2SJ
☎020 8203 6427
Fax 020 8203 6420
e-mail: enquiries@lsjs.ac.uk
Librarians Aron Prys BA MPhil DipLib MCLIP, Mrs Erla Zimmels DipLib

Moorfields Eye Hospital see University of London Institute of Ophthalmology and Moorfields Eye Hospital

Queen Mary

Library, Queen Mary, Mile End Road, London E1 4NS
☎020 7882 3300 (enquiries), 020 7882 3302 (administration)
Fax 020 8981 0028
e-mail: library@qmul.ac.uk
url: www.library.qmul.ac.uk/
Director of Information Services Brian Murphy BA MCLIP (020 7882 5004; e-mail:
b.murphy@qmul.ac.uk)
Main Library Manager Neil Entwistle BA MA MCLIP (020 7882 3304; e-mail:
n.w.entwistle@qmul.ac.uk)
Assistant Library Manager Ms June Hayles BA MCLIP (020 7882 3323; e-mail:
j.m.hayles@qmul.ac.uk)
Medical Librarian Paul Hockney BSc MCLIP (020 7882 7114; e-mail:
p.s.hockney@qmul.ac.uk)

Site libraries
▶ Medical and Dental Library (Whitechapel), Queen Mary, Turner Street, London E1 2AD
 ☎020 7882 7115
 Fax 020 7882 7113
 e-mail: library@qmul.ac.uk
 Site Librarian Ms Jacqueline Thomas BSc DipLib (020 7882 7116; e-mail:
 j.h.thomas@qmul.ac.uk)
▶ Medical Library (West Smithfield), Queen Mary, West Smithfield, London EC1A 7BA
 ☎020 7601 7849
 Fax 020 7601 7853
 Site Librarian Ms Marie Montague BEd MCLIP (e-mail: m.b.montague@qmul.ac.uk)

Royal Holloway

Library, Royal Holloway, University of London, Egham, Surrey TW20 0EX
☎(01784) 443823 (enquiries), 443334 (administration)
Fax (01784) 477670
e-mail: library@rhbnc.ac.uk

url: www.rhul.ac.uk (College); www.rhul.ac.uk/information-services/library/
Librarian and Deputy Director of Information Services Ms Sarah E Gerrard BA
DipLib MCLIP (01784 443330; e-mail: s.gerrard@rhul.ac.uk)
Academic Services Manager Vacant
Services Manager (Operations) Ms Emma Bull BA(Hons) DipInf MCLIP (01784 414066;
e-mail: emma.bull@rhul.ac.uk)

Music Library, Royal Holloway, University of London, Egham, Surrey TW20 0EX
☎(01784) 443560
Fax (01784) 477670
e-mail: library@rhbnc.ac.uk
Music Librarian Matthew Brooke BA(Hons) MA (01784 443759; e-mail:
m.brooke@rhul.ac.uk)

Royal Veterinary College
Library, Royal Veterinary College, Royal College Street, London NW1 0TU
☎020 7468 5162
Fax 020 7468 5162
e-mail: library@rvc.ac.uk
url: www.rvc.ac.uk
Assistant Librarian Ms Kate Warner MA (e-mail: kwarner@rvc.ac.uk)

Campus library
▶ Hawkshead Campus Library, Royal Veterinary College, Eclipse Building, RVC,
Hawkshead Lane, North Mimms, Hatfield, Herts AL9 7TA
☎(01707) 666214 (tel/fax)
College Librarian Simon Jackson MA MCLIP (e-mail: sjackson@rvc.ac.uk)
Senior Assistant Librarian Ms Elspeth Keith MCLIP

St George's Hospital Medical School
St George's Library, St George's Hospital Medical School, Hunter Wing, Cranmer Terrace,
London SW17 0RE
☎020 8725 5466 (direct line)
Fax 020 8725 3863
url: www.sgul.ac.uk/depts/is/
Library Services Manager Ms Marina Logan Bruce BA(Hons) (e-mail: logan@sgul.ac.uk)

School of Oriental and African Studies
Library, School of Oriental and African Studies, Thornhaugh Street, Russell Square, London
WC1H 0XG
☎020 7898 4163 (enquiries), 020 7898 4160 (library office)
Fax 020 7898 4159
url: www.soas.ac.uk/library/
Head of Library Services Mrs Anne Poulson BA(Oxon) MA MPhil (020 7898 4161;
e-mail: ap45@soas.ac.uk)

School of Pharmacy
Library, School of Pharmacy, 29-39 Brunswick Square, London WC1N 1AX

☎020 7753 5833
Fax 020 7753 5947
e-mail: library@ulsop.ac.uk
url: www.ulsop.ac.uk
Head of Library and Information Services Mrs Linda Lisgarten BA

UCL (University College London)
Library Services, UCL (University College London), Gower Street, London WC1E 6BT
☎020 7679 7700 (enquiries), 020 7679 7051 (administration)
Fax 020 7679 7373
e-mail: library@ucl.ac.uk
url: www.ucl.ac.uk/library
Director of Library Services P Ayris MA PhD
Deputy Director of Library Services: Group Manager, Subjects and Sites
Ms E A Chapman MA FCLIP BA DipLib FECert (020 7679 7907; e-mail:
elizabeth.chapman@ucl.ac.uk)
Group Manager, Planning and Resources Mrs J Percival MA DipArchAdmin (020 7679
7791; e-mail: j.percival@ucl.ac.uk)
Group Manager, IT Services Mrs J Cropper MSc DipLib (020 7679 7833; e-mail:
j.cropper@ucl.ac.uk)
Group Manager, Reader Services V Matthews BSc(Econ) MA MA PhD (020 7679 2607;
e-mail: v.matthews@ucl.ac.uk)
Group Manager, Bibliographic Services Ms D Mercer MSc DipLib (020 7679 2625;
e-mail: d.mercer@ucl.ac.uk)

Sectional libraries
▶ Cruciform Library, UCL (University College London), Cruciform Building, Gower
   Street, London WC1E 6BT
   ☎020 7679 6079
   e-mail: clinscilib@ucl.ac.uk
   Librarian i/c Ms K Cheney BA MSc MCLIP
▶ Environmental Studies Library, UCL (University College London), Faculty of the Built
   Environment, Wates House, 22 Gordon Street, London WC1H 0QB
   ☎020 7679 4900
   e-mail: library@ucl.ac.uk
   Librarian i/c Ms S Page BA(Hons) MSc
▶ Information Centre, Eastman Dental Institute for Oral Health Care Sciences, UCL
   (University College London), 256 Grays Inn Road, London WC1X 8LD
   ☎020 7915 1045/1262
   Fax 020 7915 1147
   e-mail: ic@eastman.ucl.ac.uk
   Librarian G Bissels
▶ Institute of Archaeology Library, UCL (University College London), 31-34 Gordon
   Square, London WC1H 0PY
   ☎020 7679 4788
   e-mail: library@ucl.ac.uk
   Librarian i/c R T Kirby MA

▶ Institute of Child Health Library, UCL (University College London), 30 Guilford Street, London WC1N 1EH
☎020 7242 9789 ext 2424
Fax 020 7831 0488
e-mail: library@ich.ucl.ac.uk
Librarian i/c J Clarke MA DipLib

▶ Institute of Laryngology and Otology Library, UCL (University College London), Royal National Throat, Nose and Ear Hospital, Gray's Inn Road, London WC1X 8EE
☎020 7915 1445
e-mail: ilolib@ucl.ac.uk
Librarian i/c Alex Stagg MA

▶ Institute of Neurology, UCL (University College London), Rockefeller Medical Library, The National Hospital, Queen Square, London WC1N 3BG
☎020 7829 8709
Fax 020 7278 1371
e-mail: library@ion.ucl.ac.uk
Manager, Libraries and Computing Services (ION) and Librarian (Nat Hosp)
Mrs L J Shepherd BA (e-mail: l.shepherd@ion.ucl.ac.uk)

▶ Institute of Ophthalmology Library, UCL (University College London), 11-43 Bath Street, London EC1V 9EL
☎020 7608 6814 (tel/fax)
e-mail: ophthlib@ucl.ac.uk
Librarian Ms Debbie Heatlie BA

▶ Institute of Orthopaedics Library, UCL (University College London), Royal National Orthopaedic Hospital, Brockley Hill, Stanmore, Middlesex HA7 4LP
☎020 8909 5351
Fax 020 8954 1213
Librarian i/c Ms Julie Noren

▶ Library, School of Slavonic and East European Studies, UCL (University College London), 2nd Floor, Senate House North Wing, Malet Street, Malet Street, London WC1E 7HU
☎020 7862 8525
e-mail: ssees-library@ssees.ac.uk
Librarian and Director of Information Services Ms Lesley Pitman BA DipLib
(e-mail: l.pitman@ssees.ac.uk)

▶ Medical Library, Royal Free and University College Medical School, UCL (University College London), Royal Free Hospital, Rowland Hill Street, Rowland Hill Street, London NW3 2PF
☎020 7794 0500 ext 3202
Fax 020 7794 3534
e-mail: library@rfc.ucl.ac.uk
Librarian Ms B Anagnostelis BSc(Hons) MSc DipLib (e-mail: b.anagnostelis@ucl.ac.uk)

▶ National Information Centre for Speech–Language Therapy (NIC&ST) Library, Department of Human Communication Science, UCL (University College London), Chandler House, 2 Wakefield Street, London WC1N 1PF
☎020 7679 4207
Fax 020 7713 0861
e-mail: hcs.library@ucl.ac.uk

url: www.hcs.ucl.ac.uk
Librarian i/c Ms S Russell DipLib

▶ Royal National Institute for Deaf People Library, UCL (University College London), Royal National Throat, Nose and Ear Hospital, Gray's Inn Road, London WC1X 8EE
☎020 7915 1553
Fax 020 7915 1443
Librarian i/c Alex Stagg MA

Warburg Institute

Library, Warburg Institute, Warburg Institute, School of Advanced Study, Woburn Square, London WC1H 0AB
☎020 7862 8935/6 (Reading Room)
Fax 020 7862 8939
e-mail: warburg.library@sas.ac.uk
url: www.sas.ac.uk/warburg/
telnet (for library): library.sas.ac.uk
Librarian Prof Jill Kraye

LOUGHBOROUGH UNIVERSITY

Pilkington Library, Loughborough University, Loughborough, Leics LE11 3TU
☎(01509) 222360 (enquiries), (01509) 222341 (administration)
Fax (01509) 223993
e-mail: library@lboro.ac.uk
url: www.lboro.ac.uk/library
University Librarian Mrs Mary Morley BA DipLib MCLIP

UNIVERSITY OF LUTON

Learning Resources Centre, University of Luton, Park Square, Luton, Bedfordshire LU1 3JU
☎(01582) 743262 (library), (01582) 489398 (administration)
Fax (01582) 489325
e-mail: geraldine.kiernan@luton.ac.uk (administration)
url: www.luton.ac.uk/studentresources/lrc.shtml
Director of Learning Resources Tim Stone MA MCLIP (01582 489310)
Bedfordshire Health Librarian Ms Hilary Johnson

Site libraries

▶ Healthcare Library, University of Luton, School of Community and Mental Health, Britannia Road, Bedford MK40 2NU
☎(01234) 792215

▶ Healthcare Library, University of Luton, Lovelock-Jones Nurse Education Centre, Barracks Road, High Wycombe, Bucks HP11 1QN
☎(01494) 425137

▶ Healthcare Library, University of Luton, Nuffield Research Centre, Stoke Mandeville Hospital, Mandeville Road, Aylesbury, Buckinghamshire HP21 8AL
☎(01296) 315900

▶ Healthcare Library, School of Acute Care/Midwifery, University of Luton, Luton and Dunstable Hospital, Lewsey Road, Luton, Bedfordshire LU4 0DT
☎(01582) 497296
▶ Putteridge Bury Resource Centre, University of Luton, Hitchin Road, Luton, Bedfordshire LU2 8LE
☎(01582) 489079
Academic Liaison Librarian (Luton Business School) Mrs Audrey Stewart MCLIP
(e-mail: audrey.stewart@luton.ac.uk)

MANCHESTER METROPOLITAN UNIVERSITY

Library, Manchester Metropolitan University, All Saints, Manchester M15 6BH
☎0161 247 3096
Fax 0161 247 6349
url: www.mmu.ac.uk/library
Chief Librarian Prof Colin G S Harris BA MA MLS BPhil PhD FCLIP (0161 247 6100;
e-mail: c.harris@mmu.ac.uk)
Deputy Librarian Mrs Gill R Barry BA MSc MCLIP (0161 247 6101; e-mail:
g.r.barry@mmu.ac.uk)
Faculty Librarian (Crewe & Alsager) Dr Margaret Robinson BA DipLib MCLIP (0161
247 5138; e-mail: m.g.robinson@mmu.ac.uk)

Site libraries
▶ Alsager Library, Manchester Metropolitan University, Hassall Road, Alsager, Stoke-on-Trent ST7 2HL
☎0161 247 5356
Site Manager Ms Mary Pickstone BSc DipLib MCLIP (0161 247 5355; e-mail:
m.pickstone@mmu.ac.uk)
▶ Aytoun Library, Manchester Metropolitan University, Aytoun Street, Manchester M1 3GH
☎0161 247 3093
Library Services Manager Mrs Kate Morrison BA (0161 247 3091; e-mail:
k.morrison@mmu.ac.uk), Mrs Diana Massam BA PGDip MCLIP (0161 247 3091;
e-mail: d.massam@mmu.ac.uk)
▶ Crewe Library, Manchester Metropolitan University, Crewe Green Road, Crewe, Cheshire CW1 1DU
☎0161 247 5002
Site Manager Mrs Fiona Hughes BA MLib MCLIP (0161 247 5012; e-mail:
f.hughes@mmu.ac.uk)
▶ Didsbury Library, Manchester Metropolitan University, 799 Wilmslow Road, Manchester M20 8RR
☎0161 247 6126
Library Services Manager Ms Jayne Evans BA MLib (0161 247 6120; e-mail:
j.e.h.evans@mmu.ac.uk)
▶ Elizabeth Gaskell Library, Manchester Metropolitan University, Hathersage Road, Manchester M13 0JA
☎0161 247 6134
Library Services Manager Ms Alison Mackenzie BA (0161 247 6561; e-mail:
a.mackenzie@mmu.ac.uk)

▶ Hollings Library, Manchester Metropolitan University, Old Hall Lane, Manchester
M14 6HR
☎0161 247 6119
Library Services Manager Ian Harter BSc DipLib (e-mail: i.harter@mmu.ac.uk)

THE UNIVERSITY OF MANCHESTER

The John Rylands University Library, The University of Manchester, Main Library, Oxford
Road, Manchester M13 9PP
☎0161 275 3751
url: www.manchester.ac.uk/library
University Librarian and Director of The John Rylands Library William G Simpson
BA MA MCLIP FRSA (e-mail: bill.simpson@manchester.ac.uk)
**Deputy University Librarian (Information Resources and Academic Supoport) and
Associate Director of The John Rylands Library** Dr Diana M Leitch BSc PhD FRSC
(e-mail: diana.leitch@manchester.ac.uk)
**Deputy University Librarian (Infrastructure and Planning Support) and Associate
Director of The John Rylands Library** Michael P Day BSc MSc (e-mail:
m.p.day@manchester.ac.uk)

Site libraries
▶ The John Rylands University Library, Special Collections Division, The University of
Manchester, Main Library, Oxford Road, Manchester M13 9PP
☎0161 275 3764
Head of Special Collections and Principal Keeper Ms Stella Butler BSc PhD AMA
(e-mail: stella.butler@manchester.ac.uk)
▶ The Joule Library, The University of Manchester, PO Box 88, Sackville Street,
Manchester M60 1QD
☎0161 306 4924
Head of Public Services and Joule Site Librarian Ms Jessie Kurtz BA BEd MLS
(e-mail: jessie.kurtz@manchester.ac.uk)
▶ The Eddie Davies Library, Manchester Business School, The University of Manchester,
Booth Street West, Manchester M15 6PB
☎0161 275 6507 (enquiries), 0161 275 6500 (administration)
Fax 0161 275 6505
e-mail: libdesk@mbs.ac.uk
url: www.mbs.ac.uk/services/library-services
Librarian Ms Kathy Kirby MA MCLIP PGCE (e-mail: kathy.kirby@mbs.ac.uk)

MIDDLESEX UNIVERSITY

Library Services, Middlesex University, North London Business Park, Oakleigh Road South,
New Southgate, London N11 1NP
☎020 8411 5234
Fax 020 8411 5163
url: www.lr.mdx.ac.uk
Head of Learning Resources and University Librarian William Marsterson MA MCLIP
(020 8411 5234; e-mail: w.marsterson@mdx.ac.uk)

Assistant Head of Learning Resources Ms Judith Cattermole BA MCLIP (020 8411 6947; e-mail: j.cattermole@mdx.ac.uk)

Bibliographical Services, Middlesex University, North London Business Park, Oakleigh Road South, New Southgate, London N11 1NP
☎020 8411 5254 (direct)
e-mail: libbg1@mdx.ac.uk
Bibliographical Services Librarian Mrs Liz Barton BSc MCLIP

Campus libraries

▶ Health Campus Library, Middlesex University, Chase Farm Education Centre, Chase Farm Hospital, The Ridgeway, Enfield, Middlesex EN2 8JL
☎020 8366 9112
e-mail: libcf1@mdx.ac.uk
Site Librarian Ms Sue Hill BA DMS MCLIP
▶ Health Campus Library, Middlesex University, Royal Free Education Centre, Royal Free Hospital, Pond Street, London NW3 2XA
☎020 7830 2788
e-mail: librf1@mdx.ac.uk
Site Librarian Ms Yvette Dickerson BA MCLIP
▶ Library, Middlesex University at Cat Hill, Middlesex University, Barnet, Herts EN4 8HT
☎020 8411 5042 (direct)
e-mail: libch1@mdx.ac.uk
Campus Librarian Ms Nazlin Bhimani BMus MA MCLIP
▶ Library, Middlesex University at Enfield, Middlesex University, Queensway, Enfield, Middlesex EN3 4SF
☎020 8411 5334 (direct)
e-mail: liben1@mdx.ac.uk
Campus Librarian Ms Kathy McGowan MA MCLIP
▶ Library, Middlesex University at Hendon, Middlesex University, The Burroughs, London NW4 4BT
☎020 8411 5852 (direct)
e-mail: libhe1@mdx.ac.uk
Campus Librarian Ms Hilary Cummings BSc DipLib, Mrs Caroline Fletcher BA (job share)
▶ Library, Middlesex University at Trent Park, Middlesex University, Bramley Road, London N14 4XS
☎020 8411 5646 (direct)
e-mail: libtp1@mdx.ac.uk
Campus Librarian Ms Sue Fellows PGDipAS MCLIP

(The Health Campus libraries are also served by multidisciplinary libraries at:

David Ferriman Library, North Middlesex Hospital, Sterling Way, London N18 1QX (020 8887 2223; e-mail: libnm1@mdx.ac.uk, libnm2@mdx.ac.uk) and The Archway Healthcare Library, Holborn Union Building, The Archway Campus, Highgate Hill, London N19 3UA (020 7288 3567; e-mail: libwh1@mdx.ac.uk, libwh2@mdx.ac.uk)

NAPIER UNIVERSITY

Main library
Craiglockhart Campus Library, Napier University, Craiglockhart Campus, Edinburgh EH14 1DJ
☎0131 455 4260
Fax 0131 455 4276
url: www.napier.ac.uk/
Director of Learning Information Services C Pinder BA MLib DipLib FCLIP (0131 455 4270)
Head of Customer Services and Deputy Director M Lobban MA DipLib DipEdTech MCLIP (0131 455 4272)
Head of Information Services M Jones BA DipLib MCLIP (0131 455 2693)
Research Support Advisor Dr D Cumming BSc DipLib MLib PhD MCLIP FGS (0131 455 2368; fax: 0131 455 2358)

Campus libraries

▶ Canaan Lane Library, Napier University, Canaan Lane Campus, Edinburgh EH9 2TB
☎0131 455 5616
Fax 0131 455 5608
Librarian

▶ Comely Bank Library, Napier University, Comely Bank Campus, Edinburgh EH4 2LD
☎0131 455 5319
Fax 0131 455 5358
Librarian

▶ Craighouse Library, Napier University, Craighouse Campus, Edinburgh EH10 5LG
☎0131 455 6020
Fax 0131 455 6022
Librarian

▶ Livingston Library, Napier University, Livingston Campus, West Lothian EH54 6PP
☎(01506) 422831
Fax (01506) 422833
Librarian

▶ Melrose Library, Napier University, Melrose Campus, Melrose, Scottish Borders TD6 9BS
☎(01896) 661632
Fax (01896) 823869

▶ Merchiston Library, Napier University, Merchiston Campus, Edinburgh EH10 5DT
☎0131 455 2582
Fax 0131 455 2377
Librarian

UNIVERSITY OF NEWCASTLE UPON TYNE

Robinson Library, University of Newcastle upon Tyne, Newcastle upon Tyne NE2 4HQ
☎0191 222 7662 (enquiries), 0191 222 7674 (administration)
Fax 0191 222 6235
e-mail: library@newcastle.ac.uk
url: www.ncl.ac.uk/library/
Librarian Thomas W Graham MA PhD DipLib MCLIP

Divisional libraries

▶ Law Library, University of Newcastle upon Tyne, Newcastle Law School, 22-24 Windsor Terrace, Newcastle upon Tyne NE1 7RU
☎0191 222 7944
Librarian Mrs Linda Kelly BA MCLIP

▶ The Walton Library (Medical and Dental), University of Newcastle upon Tyne, The Medical School, Framlington Place, Newcastle upon Tyne NE2 4HH
☎0191 222 7550
Librarian Ms Erika Gwynnett BA(Hons) MA DipLib

NEWMAN COLLEGE OF HIGHER EDUCATION

Library, Newman College of Higher Education, Genners Lane, Bartley Green, Birmingham B32 3NT
☎0121 476 1181 ext 2208
e-mail: library@newman.ac.uk
url: www.newman.ac.uk/library
Head of Library and Learning Services Ms Christine Porter BA MLib MCLIP (ext 2327; e-mail: c.porter@newman.ac.uk)

NORTH EAST WALES INSTITUTE OF HIGHER EDUCATION

Information and Student Services, North East Wales Institute of Higher Education, Plas Coch, Mold Road, Wrexham LL11 2AW
☎(01978) 293250
Fax (01978) 293435
url: www.newi.ac.uk
User Services Manager P Jeorrett BA MCLIP (e-mail: p.jeorrett@newi.ac.uk)
Academic Liaison Co-ordinator N Watkinson BSc MCLIP ILTM (e-mail: nicolaw@newi.co.uk)

UNIVERSITY COLLEGE NORTHAMPTON

Park Campus Library, University College Northampton, Boughton Green Road, Northampton NN2 7AL
☎(01604) 735500 ext 2477 (enquiries), ext 2046 (administration)
Fax (01604) 718819
url: www.northampton.ac.uk
Chief Librarian Ms Hilary Johnson BA MA MCLIP (ext 2045; e-mail: hilary.johnson@northampton.ac.uk)
Deputy Librarian Vacant

Avenue Campus Library, University College Northampton, Maidwell Building, St George's Avenue, Northampton NN2 6JD
☎(01604) 735500 ext 3900
Fax (01604) 719618
Other details as above

NORTHERN SCHOOL OF CONTEMPORARY DANCE

Library, Northern School of Contemporary Dance, 98 Chapeltown Road, Leeds LS7 4BH
☎0113 219 3020
Fax 0113 219 3030
url: www.nscd.ac.uk
Librarian Miss Samantha King BA(Hons) (e-mail: sam.king@nscd.ac.uk)
Library Assistant Miss Laura Ager (e-mail: laura.ager@nscd.ac.uk)

NORTHUMBRIA UNIVERSITY

University Library and Learning Services, Northumbria University, City Campus Library, Ellison Place, Newcastle upon Tyne NE1 8ST
☎0191 227 4125 (enquiries), 0191 227 4143 (administration)
Fax 0191 227 4563
url: www.unn.ac.uk/sd/central/library
Director of ULLS Prof Jane Core

Site library
▶ Coach Lane Library, Northumbria University, Coach Lane, Newcastle upon Tyne NE7 7XA
 ☎0191 215 6540
 Fax 0191 215 6560

NORWICH SCHOOL OF ART AND DESIGN

Library, Norwich School of Art and Design, 3–7 Redwell Street, Norwich NR2 4SN
☎(01603) 610561
Fax (01603) 615728
url: www.nsad.ac.uk
Librarian Tim Giles BA (e-mail: t.giles@nsad.ac.uk)
Assistant Librarians Ms Kitty Guiver MA MCLIP (e-mail: k.guiver@nsad.ac.uk), Ms Jan McLachlan BA(Hons) DipLIS (e-mail: j.mclachlan@nsad.ac.uk)

NOTTINGHAM TRENT UNIVERSITY

Department of Libraries and Learning Resources, Nottingham Trent University, Goldsmith Street, Nottingham NG1 5LS
☎0115 848 6494
Fax 0115 848 2286
url: www.ntu.ac.uk
Director of Libraries and Knowledge Resources Ms Sue McKnight BBus MPA AALIA AFAIM (e-mail: sue.mcknight@ntu.ac.uk)

Site libraries
▶ The Boots Library, Nottingham Trent University, Goldsmith Street, Nottingham NG1 5LS

☎0115 848 2175 (enquiries)
Fax 0115 848 2286

▶ Brackenhurst Campus Library, Nottingham Trent University, Southwell Road, Southwell, Notts NG25 0QF
☎(01636) 817049 (enquiries)
Fax (01636) 817077

▶ Clifton Campus Library, Nottingham Trent University, Clifton Lane, Nottingham NG11 8NS
☎0115 848 3570/3246
Fax 0115 848 6304

UNIVERSITY OF NOTTINGHAM

Information Services, University of Nottingham, University Park, Nottingham NG7 2RD
url: www.nottingham.ac.uk/is
Chief Information Officer Ms Karen Stanton BA MEd DipLib (0115 951 3502; e-mail: karen.stanton@nottingham.ac.uk)
Deputy Chief Information Officer and Director, Research and Learning Resources Stephen Pinfield MA MA MCLIP (0115 951 5109; e-mail: stephen.pinfield@nottingham.ac.uk)
Director, Customer Services Graham Moore BA (0115 951 4535; e-mail: graham.moore@nottingham.ac.uk)
Director, IT Systems Ms Lynne Tucker (0115 951 3352; e-mail: lynne.tucker@nottinghamac.uk)
Assistant Director, Planning and Quality Ms Paula Manning BA PGDip (0115 951 4547; e-mail: paula.manning@nottingham.ac.uk)

Library sites

▶ Business Library, University of Nottingham, Business School, Jubilee Campus, Wollaton Road, Nottingham NG8 1BB
☎0115 846 8069
Fax 0115 846 8064

▶ Djanogly LRC (Education, Business, Computer Science), University of Nottingham, Jubilee Campus, Wollaton Road, Nottingham NG8 1FF
☎0115 846 6700
Fax 0115 846 6705

▶ George Green Library of Science and Engineering, University of Nottingham, University Park, Nottingham NG7 2RD
☎0115 951 4570
Fax 0115 951 4578

▶ Greenfield Medical Library, University of Nottingham, Queen's Medical Centre, Nottingham NG7 2UH
☎0115 970 9435
Fax 0115 970 9449

▶ Hallward Library (Arts, Law, Social Sciences), University of Nottingham, University Park, Nottingham NG7 2RD
☎0115 951 4557
Fax 0115 951 4558

▶ Hallward Library (Department of Manuscripts and Special Collections), University of Nottingham, University Park, Nottingham NG7 2RD
☎0115 951 4565
Fax 0115 951 4558
Keeper D B Johnston BA PhD DipLib (0115 951 4563)

▶ James Cameron-Gifford Library of Agricultural and Food Sciences, University of Nottingham, Sutton Bonington Campus, Sutton Bonington, nr Loughborough, Leics LE12 5RD
☎0115 951 6390
Fax 0115 951 6389

▶ School of Nursing Library (Derby), University of Nottingham, Derby Centre, Derbyshire Royal Infirmary, London Road, Derby DE1 2QY
☎(01332) 347141 ext 2561
Fax (01332) 290321

▶ School of Nursing Library (Mansfield), University of Nottingham, Mansfield Education Centre, Dukeries Centre, Kings Mill Hospital, Mansfield Road, Sutton-in-Ashfield, Notts NG17 4JL
☎(01623) 465634
Fax (01623) 465601

▶ Shakespeare Street Learning Resource Centre, University of Nottingham, Adult Education Centre, 14-22 Shakespeare Street, Nottingham NG1 4FQ
☎0115 951 6510
Fax 0115 947 2977

OPEN UNIVERSITY

Library and Learning Resources Centre, Open University, Walton Hall, Milton Keynes MK7 6AA
☎(01908) 653138
Fax (01908) 653571
e-mail: oulibrary@open.ac.uk
url: www.open.ac.uk/library
Director of Library Services Mrs Nicky Whitsed MSc FCLIP (01908 653254; e-mail: n.whitsed@open.ac.uk)
Assistant Director of Library Services Ms Ann Davies BSc MSc (01908 652057; e-mail: ann.davies@open.ac.uk)
Head of Business Services Ms Mary Hunt MCLIP (01908 652672; e-mail: m.e.hunt@open.ac.uk)
Head of Library, Learning and Teaching Services Ms Patricia Heffernan BA(Hons) DipLib MCLIP (01908 654850; e-mail: p.a.heffernan@open.ac.uk)
Head of Strategic and Service Development Ms Gill Needham BA(Hons) DipLib CertMan MSc(Econ) (01908 658369; e-mail: g.needham@open.ac.uk)

OXFORD BROOKES UNIVERSITY

Headington Library, Oxford Brookes University, Headington Campus, Gipsy Lane, Headington, Oxford OX3 0BP
☎(01865) 483156 (enquiries), (01865) 483130 (administration)

Fax (01865) 483998
e-mail: library@brookes.ac.uk
url: www.brookes.ac.uk/services/library
Director of Learning Resources and University Librarian Dr Helen M Workman PhD MCLIP
Head of Academic Library Services Ms Jan Haines BLib MA DipM MCLIP
Head of Administration Tony Robbins BA MSc MCLIP

Site libraries
▶ Harcourt Hill Library, Oxford Brookes University, Harcourt Hill Campus, Oxford OX2 9AT
☎(01865) 488222
Fax (01865) 488224
Head of Learning Resources: Harcourt Hill and Wheatley Ms Claire M Jeffery BSc DipLib DMS MCLIP
▶ Wheatley Library, Oxford Brookes University, Wheatley Campus, Wheatley, Oxford OX33 1HX
☎(01865) 485869
Fax (01865) 485750
Head of Learning Resources: Harcourt Hill and Wheatley Ms Claire M Jeffery BSc DipLib DMS MCLIP

UNIVERSITY OF OXFORD

Oxford University Library Services
Bodleian Library, University of Oxford, Broad Street, Oxford OX1 3BG
☎(01865) 277000 (enquiries), (01865) 277170 (administration)
Fax (01865) 277182
e-mail: enquiries@bodley.ox.ac.uk
Director of University Library Services and Bodley's Librarian Dr Reg P Carr MA FRSA BA MA(Man) MA (Camb) HonDLitt
Acting Director of University Library Services and Bodley's Librarian Ronald R Milne MA MA(Edin) MA(Lond) FCLIP FRSA
Acting Deputy Director of University Library Services and Bodley's Librarian David E Perrow MA MCLIP

▶ Accessible Resources Acquisition and Creation Unit, University of Oxford, Ewert House, Ewert Place, Oxford OX2 7BZ
☎(01865) 280880
Fax (01865) 280912
e-mail: ourb@bodley.ox.ac.uk
Director/Manager Ms E Burgess
▶ Bodleian Japanese Library at the Nissan Institute, University of Oxford, 27 Winchester Road, Oxford OX2 6NA
☎(01865) 284506
Fax (01865) 284500
e-mail: japanese@bodley.ox.ac.uk

url: www.bodley.ox.ac.uk/dept/oriental/bjl.htm
Librarian Mrs Izumi Tytler MA

▶ Bodleian Law Library, University of Oxford, St Cross Building, Manor Road, Oxford OX1 3UR
☎(01865) 271462
Fax (01865) 271475
e-mail: law.library@bodley.ox.ac.uk
url: www.bodley.ox.ac.uk/dept/law
Law Librarian Ms Ruth Bird BA TSTC GradDipLib (e-mail: ruth.bird@ouls.ox.ac.uk)

▶ Bodleian Library of Commonwealth and African Studies at Rhodes House, University of Oxford, Rhodes House, South Parks Road, Oxford OX1 3RG
☎(01865) 270908
Fax (01865) 270912
e-mail: rhodes.house.library@bodley.ox.ac.uk
Librarian John Pinfold MA

▶ Department for Continuing Education Library, University of Oxford, Rewley House, 1 Wellington Square, Oxford OX1 2JA
☎(01865) 270454
Fax (01865) 270309
e-mail: library@conted.ox.ac.uk
url: www.lib.ox.ac.uk
Librarian Mrs A E Rees

▶ Department of Educational Studies Library, University of Oxford, 15 Norham Gardens, Oxford OX2 6PY
☎(01865) 274028 (library)
Fax (01865) 274027 (department)
e-mail: library@edstud.ox.ac.uk
url: www.edstud.ox.ac.uk/Library/webpage_main.htm
Librarian Ms Judy Reading MA MCLIP

▶ Department of Experimental Psychology, Library, University of Oxford, South Parks Road, Oxford OX1 3UD
☎(01865) 271312
Fax (01865) 310447
e-mail: library@psy.ox.ac.uk
url: www.psych.ox.ac.uk/library/
Librarian Ms Karine Barker

▶ English Faculty Library, University of Oxford, St Cross Building, Manor Road, Oxford OX1 3UQ
☎(01865) 271050
Fax (01865) 271054
e-mail: library@music.oc.ac.uk
url: www.efl.ox.ac.uk/
English Librarian Ms Sue Usher BA(Hons) DipLib MCLIP

▶ Faculty of Music Library, University of Oxford, St Aldate's, Oxford OX1 1DB
☎(01865) 276146 (librarian), (01865) 276148 (enquiries)
Fax (01865) 286260
url: www.music.ox.ac.uk/library/
Subject Librarian Peter Ward Jones (e-mail: pwj@bodley.ox.ac.uk)

▶ History Faculty Library, University of Oxford, Broad Street, Oxford OX1 3DB
☎(01865) 277262
e-mail: library@history.ox.ac.uk
url: history.ox.ac.uk/libraryit/faclib/
Librarian Ms Isabel Holowaty BA(Hons) MSc (e-mail: isabel.holowaty@ouls.ox.ac.uk)

▶ Hooke Library, University of Oxford, South Parks Road, Oxford OX1 3UB
☎(01865) 272812
Fax (01865) 272821
e-mail: hooke.library@bodley.ox.ac.uk
Hooke Librarian Ms Juliet Ralph BA MSc MCLIP

▶ Indian Institute Library, University of Oxford, New Bodleian Library, Broad Street,
Oxford OX1 3BG
☎(01865) 277082
Fax (01865) 277182
e-mail: indian.institute@bodley.ox.ac.uk
Librarian Dr Gillian Evison MA MPhil DPhil

▶ Institute for Chinese Studies Library, University of Oxford, Walton Street, Oxford
OX1 2HG
☎(01865) 280430
Fax (01865) 280431
e-mail: chinese.studies.library@bodley.ox.ac.uk
url: www.bodley.ox.ac.uk/dept.oriental.cs.htm
Librarian Minh Chung MA

▶ Latin American Centre, St Antony's College, University of Oxford, 1 Church Walk,
Oxford OX2 6JF
☎(01865) 274483
Fax (01865) 274489
Librarian Mrs Ruth Hodges MA DipLib (e-mail: ruth.hodges@lac.ox.ac.uk or
laura.salinas@lac.ox.ac.uk)

▶ Oriental Institute Library, University of Oxford, Pusey Lane, Oxford OX1 2LE
☎(01865) 278202
Fax (01865) 278204
e-mail: library@orinst.ox.ac.uk
Librarian Martyn Minty MA MCLIP

▶ Philosophy Library, University of Oxford, 10 Merton Street, Oxford OX1 4JJ
☎(01865) 276927
Fax (01865) 276932
e-mail: phillib@bodley.ox.ac.uk
Librarian Dr Hilla A Wait

▶ Radcliffe Science Library, University of Oxford, Parks Road, Oxford OX1 3QP
☎(01865) 272800
Fax (01865) 272821
e-mail: rsl.enquiries@bodley.ox.ac.uk
url: www.bodley.ox.ac.uk/dept/rsl
Keeper of Scientific Books Dr Judith M Palmer MA PhD FCLIP MIIS

▶ Refugee Studies Centre, Library, University of Oxford, Queen Elizabeth House, 21 St
Giles, Oxford OX1 3LA
☎(01865) 270298

Fax (01865) 270721
e-mail: rsclib@qeh.ox.ac.uk
url: www.rsc.ox.ac.uk
Librarian Ms Sarah Rhodes BA DipLib MA (e-mail: sarah.rhodes@qeh.ox.ac.uk)

▶ Sackler Library, University of Oxford, 1 St John Street, Oxford OX1 2LG
☎(01865) 278092
Fax (01865) 278098
e-mail: enquiries@saclib.ox.ac.uk; librarian@saclib.ox.ac.uk
url: www.saclib.ox.ac.uk
Librarian James Legg MA MA(Lond) (e-mail: james.legg@ouls.ox.ac.uk)
(Access to the Library is limited to members of Oxford University and holders of
Bodleian Library reader's tickets)

▶ Sainsbury Library, University of Oxford, Park End Street, Oxford OX1 1HP
☎(01865) 288880
Fax (01865) 288805
e-mail: library@sbs.ox.ac.uk
url: www.sbs.ox.ac.uk/html/about_facilities_library.asp
Librarian Ms Fiona Richardson

▶ School of Geography and the Environment Library, University of Oxford, Mansfield
Road, Oxford OX1 3TB
☎(01865) 271912
Fax (01865) 271929
e-mail: library@geog.ox.ac.uk
url: www.geog.ox.ac.uk/facilities/library/index.html
Librarian Mrs Linda S Atkinson BSc MSc MCLIP

▶ Social Sciences Library, University of Oxford, Manor Road Building, Manor Road,
Oxford OX1 3UQ
☎(01865) 271071 (Librarian), (01865) 271093 (Library)
Fax (01865) 271072
e-mail: library@ssl.ox.ac.uk
url: www.ssl.ox.ac.uk
Librarian Ms Margaret Robb BS MA MLS MCLIP (e-mail: margaret.robb@ssl.ox.ac.uk)

▶ Taylor Institution, Library, University of Oxford, St Giles, Oxford OX1 3NA
☎(01865) 278154 (office), 278158/278161 (main desk)
Fax (01865) 278165
e-mail: enquiries@taylib.ox.ac.uk
url: www.taylib.ox.ac.uk
Librarian i/c Ms Amanda Peters MA DipLib
(The Taylor Institution Modern Languages Faculty Library can also be found at this location; the Taylor Institution Slavonic, East European and Modern Greek Library can be
found at 47 Wellington Square, Oxford OX1 2JF; tel: 01865 270464)

▶ Theology Faculty Library, University of Oxford, 41 St Giles', Oxford OX1 3LW
☎(01865) 270731
Fax (01865) 270795
url: www.theology.ox.ac.uk/resource/library.shtml
Librarian Ms Kate Alderson-Smith BA MA (e-mail:
kate.alderson-smith@theology.ox.ac.uk)

▶ Vere Harmsworth Library (Rothermere American Institute), University of Oxford, 1A South Parks Road, Oxford OX1 3TG
☎(01865) 282700
Fax (01865) 282709
e-mail: vhl@bodley.ox.ac.uk
Librarian John Pinfold MA

▶ Zoology Library, University of Oxford, Tinbergen Building, South Parks Road, Oxford OX1 3PS
☎(01865) 271141-3
Fax (01865) 310447
e-mail: zoolib@zoo.ox.ac.uk
url: http://users.ox.ac.uk/~zoolib/
Librarian Dr Linda Birch

Health Care Libraries

▶ Cairns Library, University of Oxford, Oxford Radcliffe Hospitals NHS Trust, The John Radcliffe Hospital, Headley Way, Headington, Oxford OX3 9DU
☎(01865) 221936
Fax (01865) 221941
e-mail: library@hcl.ox.ac.uk
url: www.medicine.ox.ac.uk/cairns
Head of Health Care Libraries Dr Donald Mackay MA(Hons) MA MCLIP

▶ Health Care Library, University of Oxford, Research Institute, The Churchill Hospital, Oxford OX3 7LJ
☎(01865) 225815
Fax (01865) 225834
e-mail: library@cairns-library.ox.ac.uk
url: www.medicine.ox.ac.uk/cairns
Manager Dr Donald Mackay MA(Hons) MA MCLIP

▶ Health Care Library, University of Oxford, Radcliffe Infirmary, Woodstock Road, Oxford OX2 6HE
☎(01865) 224478
Fax (01865) 224789
e-mail: library@cairns-library.ox.ac.uk
url: www.medicine.ox.ac.uk/cairns/
Manager Dr Donald Mackay MA(Hons) MA MCLIP

▶ Health Care Library, University of Oxford, Old Road, Headington, Oxford OX3 7LG
☎(01865) 226688
Fax (01865) 226619
e-mail: old-road-library@hcl.ox.ac.uk
Librarian Nia Wyn Robert

College, Institute and Departmental

All Souls College
Codrington Library, All Souls College, Oxford OX1 4AL
☎(01865) 279318
Fax (01865) 279299

e-mail: codrington.library@all-souls.ox.ac.uk
url: www.all-souls.ox.ac.uk
Librarian in Charge Dr Norma Aubertin-Potter BA PhD MCLIP

Balliol College
Library, Balliol College, Oxford OX1 3BJ
☎(01865) 277709
Fax (01865) 277803
e-mail: library@balliol.ox.ac.uk
url: www.balliol.ox.ac.uk
Librarian Dr P A Bulloch MCLIP FSA
Assistant Librarian Alan Tadiello BA

Brasenose College
Library, Brasenose College, Oxford OX1 4AJ
☎(01865) 277827
Fax (01865) 277831
e-mail: library@bnc.ox.ac.uk
url: www.bnc.ox.ac.uk
Fellow Librarian Dr Ed Bispham
College Librarian Ms Liz Kay

Campion Hall
Library, Campion Hall, Brewer Street, Oxford OX1 1QS
☎(01865) 286100
url: www.campion.ox.ac.uk
Librarian Revd Peter Edmonds (01865 286106)
Assistant Librarian Laurence Weeks MA

Christ Church
Library, Christ Church, Oxford OX1 1DP
☎(01865) 276169
e-mail: library@christ-church.ox.ac.uk
url: www.chch.ox.ac.uk
Assistant Librarians Mrs J E McMullin MA MCLIP, C M Neagu DPhil MCLIP

Corpus Christi College
Library, Corpus Christi College, Merton Street, Oxford OX1 4JF
☎(01865) 276744
Fax (01865) 276767
e-mail: library.staff@ccc.ox.ac.uk
url: www.ccc.ox.ac.uk/library/library.htm
Librarian Miss Joanna Snelling MA MCLIP (e-mail: joanna.snelling@ccc.ox.ac.uk)

Exeter College
Library, Exeter College, Turl Street, Oxford OX1 3DP
☎(01865) 279600 (switchboard), (01865) 279657 (direct)
Fax (01865) 279630

e-mail: library@exeter.ox.ac.uk
url: www.exeter.ox.ac.uk
Fellow Librarian Dr J R Maddicott DPhil FBA
Sub-Librarian Ms J Chadwick

Green College (at the Radcliffe Observatory)
Library, Green College (at the Radcliffe Observatory), Woodstock Road, Oxford OX2 6HG
☎(01865) 274788 (library), (01865) 274770 (lodge)
Fax (01865) 274796
url: www.green.ox.ac.uk
Assistant Librarian Ms Gill Edwards BSc (e-mail: gill.edwards@green.ox.ac.uk)

Harris Manchester College
Library, Harris Manchester College, Mansfield Road, Oxford OX1 3TD
☎(01865) 271016 (enquiries), (01865) 281472 (administration)
Fax (01865) 271012
e-mail: librarian@hmc.ox.ac.uk
url: www.hmc.ox.ac.uk
Fellow Librarian Ms Sue Killoran BA MA(Oxon) PGDipLib MCLIP

Hertford College
Library, Hertford College, Catte Street, Oxford OX1 3BW
☎(01865) 279409
Fax (01865) 279466
e-mail: library@hertford.ox.ac.uk
url: www.hertford.ox.ac.uk
Fellow Librarian Dr S R West FBA (e-mail: stephanie.west@hertford.ox.ac.uk)
Librarian Mrs S Griffin BA DipLib (e-mail: susan.griffin@hertford.ox.ac.uk)

Jesus College
Library, Jesus College, Oxford OX1 3DW
☎(01865) 279704
Fax (01865) 279687 attn. Librarian)
e-mail: library@jesus.ox.ac.uk
url: www.jesus.ox.ac.uk
Fellow Librarian T J Horder MA PhD
College Librarian Miss S A Cobbold MA DipLib
Archivist Miss R Dunhill OBE FSA MA
(Visits by bona fide scholars are available only by prior appointment with the College
Librarian or Archivist as appropriate)

Keble College
Library, Keble College, Oxford OX1 3PG
☎(01865) 272797
e-mail: library@keb.ox.ac.uk
url: www.keble.ox.ac.uk
Librarian Mrs Margaret Ann Sarosi BA HDipLib

Lady Margaret Hall

Library, Lady Margaret Hall, Norham Gardens, Oxford OX2 6QA
☎(01865) 274361
Fax (01865) 511069
url: www.lmh.ox.ac.uk
Librarian Miss Roberta Staples BA (e-mail: roberta.staples@lmh.ox.ac.uk)
Archivist Mrs J Courtenay BA
(The library is for the use of members of college only, though bona fide researchers may be allowed access to books by arrangement with the Librarian)

Linacre College

Library, Linacre College, St Cross Road, Oxford OX1 3JA
☎(01865) 271661
Fax (01865) 271668
e-mail: library@linacre.ox.ac.uk
url: www/linacre.ox.ac.uk
Fellow Librarian Ms Margaret Robb BS MA MLS MCLIP (e-mail: margaret.robb@ssl.ox.ac.uk)
Assistant Librarian Ms L Trevelyan (e-mail: louise.trevelyan@linacre.ox.ac.uk)

Lincoln College

Library, Lincoln College, Turl Street, Oxford OX1 3DR
☎(01865) 279831
e-mail: library@lincoln.ox.ac.uk
url: www.lincoln.ox.ac.uk
Librarian Mrs Fiona Piddock BA DipLib

Magdalen College

Library, Magdalen College, Oxford OX1 4AU
☎(01865) 276045 (direct)
Fax (01865) 276057
e-mail: library@magd.ox.ac.uk
url: www.magd.ox.ac.uk
Fellow Librarian Dr C Y Ferdinand BA MA MA MA DPhil
Assistant Librarian Mrs Hilary Pattison MA MA

Mansfield College

Library, Mansfield College, Mansfield Road, Oxford OX1 3TF
☎(01865) 270975
Fax (01865) 270970
url: www.mansfield.ox.ac.uk
Fellow Librarian Dr K Gleadle PhD (e-mail: kathryn.gleadle@mansfield.ox.ac.uk)
Librarian Ms A Jenner (e-mail: alma.jenner@mansfield.ox.ac.uk)

Merton College

Library, Merton College, Oxford OX1 4JD
☎(01865) 276380
Fax (01865) 276361

e-mail: library@admin.merton.ox.ac.uk
url: www.merton.ox.ac.uk
Librarian Ms Julia Walworth BA MA PhD
Assistant Librarian Mrs Catherine Lewis BA DipLib MCLIP

New College
Library, New College, Oxford OX1 3BN
☎(01865) 279580 (enquiries and administration)
Fax (01865) 279590
url: www.new.ox.ac.uk
Librarian Mrs Naomi van Loo MA BA MCLIP (e-mail: naomi.vanloo@new.ox.ac.uk)

Nuffield College
Library, Nuffield College, New Road, Oxford OX1 1NF
☎(01865) 278550
Fax (01865) 278621
e-mail: library-enquiries@nuf.ox.ac.uk
url: www.nuff.ox.ac.uk/library
Librarian Ms Elizabeth Martin DipLib MA MCLIP (e-mail: librarian@nuf.ox.ac.uk)

Oriel College
Library, Oriel College, Oxford OX1 4EW
☎(01865) 276558 (direct)
e-mail: library@oriel.ox.ac.uk
url: www.oriel.ox.ac.uk
Librarian Mrs Marjory Szurko BA MRes DipLib MCLIP

Pembroke College
McGowin Library, Pembroke College, Oxford OX1 1DW
☎(01865) 276409 (direct)
Fax (01865) 276418
e-mail: library@pembroke.oxford.ac.uk
url: www.pmb.ox.ac.uk/library/index.html
Fellow Librarian Dr Christopher Melchert BA MA PhD
Librarian Mrs Lucie Walker MA BA BSc

Plant Sciences Library and Oxford Forest Information Service
Plant Sciences Library and Oxford Forest Information Service, Plant Sciences Library and
Oxford Forest Information Service, Oxford University Library Services, South Parks Road,
Oxford OX1 3RB
☎(01865) 275087
Fax (01865) 275095
e-mail: enquiries@plantlib.ox.ac.uk
url: www.plantlib.ox.ac.uk
Librarian Roger Mills MA MCLIP (01865 275080; e-mail: roger.mills@ouls.ox.ac.uk)

The Queen's College
Library, The Queen's College, Oxford OX1 4AW

☎(01865) 279130
Fax (01865) 289064
e-mail: library@queens.ox.ac.uk
url: www.queens.ox.ac.uk/library/
Librarian Ms Amanda Saville MA MCLIP (01865 279213)
Reader Services Librarian Ms Tessa Shaw BA DipLib
Technical Services Librarian Michael Williams BSc MSc
Historic Collections Assistant Mrs Veronika Vernier BA
Fellow Librarian Dr John Blair BA DPhil FSA

Regent's Park College

Library, Regent's Park College, Pusey Street, Oxford OX1 2LB
☎(01865) 288120; (01865) 288142 (Angus Library direct line)
Fax (01865) 288121
url: www.rpc.ox.ac.uk/; www.lib.ox.ac.uk/libraries/guides/REG.html
Librarian Mrs Susan J Mills MA MA MCLIP (e-mail: sue.mills@regents-park.oxford.ac.uk)
(General College Library open to members of College only. The Angus Library, a research
library for Baptist history, incorporating the former libraries of the Baptist Union of Great
Britain and the Baptist Historical Society, and the archives of the Baptist Missionary Society
on deposit, available by appointment to bona fide researchers)

St Anne's College

Library, St Anne's College, Woodstock Road, Oxford OX2 6HS
☎(01865) 274810
Fax (01865) 274899
e-mail: library@st-annes.ox.ac.uk
url: www.st-annes.ox.ac.uk/content/inf/lib.htm
Librarian Dr David Smith MA DPhil MCLIP (e-mail: david.smith@st-annes.ox.ac.uk)

St Antony's College

Library, St Antony's College, Oxford OX2 6JF
☎(01865) 274480
Fax (01865) 310518
url: www.sant.ox.ac.uk
Librarian R Campbell

St Benet's Hall

Library, St Benet's Hall, 38 St Giles, Oxford OX1 3LN
☎(01865) 280556
e-mail: michael.black@stb.ox.ac.uk
url: www.st-benets.ox.ac.uk
Master Father Leo Chamberlain

St Catherine's College

Library, St Catherine's College, Manor Road, Oxford OX1 3UJ
☎(01865) 271707
url: www.stcatz.ox.ac.uk
Librarian Dr Gervaise Rosser MA PhD

Assistant Librarian Mrs Sally Collins (e-mail: sally.collins@stcatz.ox.ac.uk)

St Cross College
Library, St Cross College, St Giles, Oxford OX1 3LZ
☎(01865) 278481
e-mail: librarian@stx.ox.ac.uk
url: www.users.ox.ac.uk/~scrostud/library.html
Librarian Mrs Sheila Allcock BSc

St Edmund Hall
Library, St Edmund Hall, Oxford OX1 4AR
☎(01865) 279000
url: www.seh.ox.ac.uk/index.cfm?do=library
Librarian Ms Deborah Eaton BA MA
(The Library is for the use of members of St Edmund Hall only. Housed in 12th century church of historical interest. Visitors welcome but only by prior application to the Librarian; groups shown round only during vacations.)

St Hilda's College
Library, St Hilda's College, Cowley Place, Oxford OX4 1DY
☎(01865) 276848/276849 (general enquiries)
e-mail: library@st-hildas.ox.ac.uk
url: www.st-hildas.ox.ac.uk
Librarian Miss Maria Croghan MA MCLIP (e-mail: maria.croghan@st-hildas.ox.ac.uk)

St Hugh's College
Library, St Hugh's College, St Margaret's Road, Oxford OX2 6LE
☎(01865) 274900 (enquiries), (01865) 274938 (administration)
Fax (01865) 274912
e-mail: library@st-hughs.ox.ac.uk
url: www.st-hughs.ox.ac.uk
Librarian Miss Deborah Quare BA MLitt MCLIP

St John's College
Library, St John's College, Oxford OX1 3JP
☎(01865) 277300 (main lodge), (01865) 277330/1 (direct to library)
Fax (01865) 277435 (College office)
e-mail: library@sjc.ox.ac.uk
url: www.sjc.ox.ac.uk
Fellow Librarian Dr P M S Hacker MA DPhil
Librarian Mrs Catherine Hilliard MA MLIS
Library Administrator Mrs Ruth Ogden BA DipLib

St Peter's College
Library, St Peter's College, New Inn Hall Street, Oxford OX1 2DL
☎(01865) 278882
Fax (01865) 278855
e-mail: library@spc.ox.ac.uk

url: www.spc.ox.ac.uk
Librarian David Johnson MA(Lond) DPhil(Oxon) (e-mail: david.johnson@st-peters.ox.ac.uk)

Somerville College
Library, Somerville College, Oxford OX2 6HD
☎(01865) 270694
Fax (01865) 270620
e-mail: library@somerville.ox.ac.uk
url: www.some@ox.ac.uk
Librarian Miss Pauline Adams BLitt MA DipLib (01865 270694)
Assistant Librarian Miss Susan Purver MA DipLIS (01865 270694)

Templeton College
Information Centre, Templeton College, Kennington, Oxford OX1 5NY
☎(01865) 422564
Fax (01865) 422501
e-mail: infocent@templeton.oxford.ac.uk
url: www.templeton.ox.ac.uk
Information Centre Manager Miss E Havard
(Restricted access: enquiries to Information Centre helpdesk as above)

Trinity College
Library, Trinity College, Oxford OX1 3BH
☎(01865) 279863 (enquiries and administration)
Fax (01865) 279911
url: www.trinity.ox.ac.uk
Librarian Ms Alison Selstead

University College
Library, University College, Oxford OX1 4BH
☎(01865) 276621
Fax (01865) 276987
e-mail: library@university-college.ox.ac.uk
url: www.lib.ox.ac.uk/guides/colleges/uni.htm
Fellow Librarian Dr Bill Child MA BPhil DPhil(Oxon)
Librarian Miss Christine M Ritchie MA(Aber) MA(Lond) MCLIP

Wadham College
Library, Wadham College, Oxford OX1 3PN
☎(01865) 277900
Fax (01865) 277937
e-mail: library@wadh.ox.ac.uk
url: www.wadham.ox.ac.uk
Librarian Ms Sandra Bailey BA MA DipLib

Wolfson College
The Library, Wolfson College, Oxford OX2 6UD
☎(01865) 274076

e-mail: library@wolfson.ox.ac.uk
url: www.wolfson.ox.ac.uk/library/
Librarian Ms Fiona E Wilkes BA MA DipLib MCLIP
(Open to members of College and Common Room only)

Worcester College
Library, Worcester College, Walton Street, Oxford OX1 2HB
☎(01865) 278354 (library); (01865) 278300 (porter's lodge)
Fax (01865) 278387
url: www.worcester.ox.ac.uk
Librarian Dr Joanna Parker MA DPhil

UNIVERSITY OF PAISLEY

Library, University of Paisley, Paisley, Renfrewshire PA1 2BE
☎0141 848 3758 (enquiries), 0141 848 3751 (administration)
Fax 0141 848 3761
e-mail: library@paisley.ac.uk
url: www.library.paisley.ac.uk/index.htm
Librarian Stuart James BA FCLIP FRSA (e-mail: stuart.james@paisley.ac.uk)

Site libraries
▶ Ayr Campus Library, University of Paisley, Beech Grove, Ayr KA8 0SR
☎(01292) 886000
Fax (01292) 886006
Librarian Ms Teresa Gilbert BA DipLib (e-mail: teresa.gilbert@paisley.ac.uk)
▶ Library, University of Paisley, Royal Alexandra Hospital, Corsebar Road, Paisley,
Renfrewshire PA2 9BN
☎0141 580 4757
Fax 0141 887 4962
Librarian Ms Ruth Robinson BA DipLib MCLIP (e-mail: ruth.robinson@paisley.ac.uk)

UNIVERSITY OF PLYMOUTH

Library, University of Plymouth, Drake Circus, Plymouth PL4 8AA
☎(01752) 232323/232307 (enquiries); (01752) 232352 (administration)
Fax (01752) 232340
url: www.plymouth.ac.uk
Acting Director of Information and Learning Services Ms Penny Holland BA DipLib
MCLIP (e-mail: penny.holland@plymouth.ac.uk)
Head of Learning and Research Support Ms Jane Gosling BSc DipLib MCLIP (e-mail:
jane.gosling@plymouth.ac.uk)
Head of Customer Services Vacant

Campus libraries
▶ Library, University of Plymouth, Earl Richards Road North, Exeter, Devon EX2 6AS
☎(01392) 475049
Fax (01392) 475058

Senior Subject Librarian Ms Amanda Russell MSc MCLIP (e-mail: amanda.russell@plymouth.ac.uk)

▶ Library, University of Plymouth, Douglas Avenue, Exmouth, Devon EX8 2AT
☎(01395) 255331
Fax (01395) 255337
ILS Co-ordinator Ms Rosemary Smith BA(Hons) DLIS MCLIP (e-mail: rosemary.smith@plymouth.ac.uk)

UNIVERSITY OF PORTSMOUTH

Frewen Library, University of Portsmouth, Cambridge Road, Portsmouth PO1 2ST
☎023 9284 3228/9 (enquiries), 023 9284 3222 (administration)
Fax 023 9284 3233
e-mail: library@port.ac.uk
url: www.port.ac.uk
University Librarian Ian Bonar BSc

QUEEN MARGARET UNIVERSITY COLLEGE

Library, Queen Margaret University College, Clerwood Terrace, Edinburgh EH12 8TS
☎0131 317 3300
Fax 0131 339 7057
e-mail: Library_Enquiries@qmuc.ac.uk
url: www.qmuc.ac.uk/lb
Acting Librarian Ms Barbara Smith BSc MCLIP ILTM (e-mail: bsmith@qmuc.ac.uk)

Leith Campus Library
▶ Library, Queen Margaret University College, Leith Campus, Duke Street, Edinburgh EH6 8HF
☎0131 317 3308
Fax 0131 317 3308
Librarian Miss Vicki Cormie MSc MCLIP

QUEEN'S UNIVERSITY OF BELFAST

University Library, Queen's University of Belfast, Belfast BT7 1LS
☎028 9097 5020
Fax 028 9097 3072
url: www.qub.ac.uk/lib/
Director of Information Services Norman Russell BA MPhil (e-mail: n.russell@qub.ac.uk)
Assistant Director (Library Services) Ms Elizabeth Traynor BA MA MCLIP (e-mail: e.traynor@qub.ac.uk)

RAVENSBOURNE COLLEGE OF DESIGN AND COMMUNICATION

Library, Ravensbourne College of Design and Communication, Walden Road, Chislehurst, Kent BR7 5SN
☎020 8289 4900 ext 8117
Fax 020 8325 8320
url: www.rave.ac.uk
Head of Learning Resource Centre Stephen A Bowman BA(Hons) MA MCLIP (e-mail: s.bowman@rave.ac.uk)
Media Librarian P Rogers (e-mail: p.rogers@rave.ac.uk)
Information Services Officer Ms D Fitzgerald (e-mail: d.fitzgerald@rave.ac.uk)
Library Services Officer Ms R Todd BA MA (e-mail: r.todd@rave.ac.uk)

THE UNIVERSITY OF READING

Reading University Library, The University of Reading, Whiteknights, PO Box 223, Reading RG6 6AE
☎0118 378 8770 (enquiries), 0118 378 8773 (administration)
Fax 0118 378 6636
e-mail: library@reading.ac.uk
url: www.library.rdg.ac.uk
University Librarian Mrs Julia Munro BSc MSc MBA MCLIP (0118 378 8774; e-mail: j.h.munro@reading.ac.uk)
Head of Collections Rupert Wood BPhil MA DipLib ILTM (0118 378 6784; e-mail: r.j.m.wood@rdg.ac.uk)
Head of Systems and Services Miss Celia A Ayres BSc DipInfSc MCLIP (0118 378 8781; e-mail: c.a.ayres@reading.ac.uk)
Support Services Manager Ian Burn BA (0118 378 8775; e-mail: i.j.burn@reading.ac.uk)

Site libraries

▶ Bulmershe Library, The University of Reading, Bulmershe Court, Woodlands Avenue, Earley, Reading RG6 1HY
☎0118 378 8652
Fax 0118 378 8651
Bulmershe Librarian Gordon Connell MA MSc MCLIP (0118 378 8652 ext 5820; e-mail: g.connell@reading.ac.uk)

ROBERT GORDON UNIVERSITY

The Georgina Scott Sutherland Library, The Robert Gordon University, Garthdee Road, Aberdeen AB10 7QE
☎(01224) 263451
Fax (01224) 263455
e-mail: library@rgu.ac.uk
url: www.rgu.ac.uk/library
Director of Knowledge and Information Services Ms Carole Munro MA DipLib

(e-mail: c.munro@rgu.ac.uk)
Depute Librarian Ms Diane M Devine MA MCLIP (e-mail: d.devine@rgu.ac.uk)
Senior Librarian Dr Susan Copeland MA MPhil PhD MCLIP (e-mail:
s.copeland@rgu.ac.uk)
Senior Librarian Ms Judith Brown MA MCLIP (e-mail: j.brown@rgu.ac.uk)

Site library
▶ St Andrew Street Library, The Robert Gordon University, St Andrew Street, Aberdeen
AB25 1HG
☎(01224) 262888
Fax (01224) 262889
e-mail: saslibrary@rgu.ac.uk
url: www.rgu.ac.uk/library
Site Librarian Keith G Fraser BA DMS MCLIP (e-mail: k.fraser@rgu.ac.uk)

ROEHAMPTON UNIVERSITY

Roehampton Lane Learning Resources Centre, Roehampton University, Digby Stuart
College, Roehampton Lane, London SW15 5SZ
☎020 8392 3770 (enquiries), 020 8392 3053 (administration)
Fax 020 8392 3026
e-mail: edesk@roehampton.ac.uk
url: www.roehampton.ac.uk/support/infoserv/index.asp
Director of Information Services Ms Sue Clegg BA MBA MCLIP (020 8392 3051;
e-mail: s.clegg@roehampton.ac.uk)
Assistant Director Paul Scarsbrook BA MA (020 8392 3052; e-mail:
p.scarsbrook@roehampton.ac.uk)
Head of Academic Liaison and Customer Development Adam Edwards BA MSc
MCLIP (020 8392 3551; e-mail: adam.edwards@roehampton.ac.uk)

ROSE BRUFORD COLLEGE

Learning Resources Centre, Rose Bruford College, Lamorbey Park, Sidcup, Kent DA15 9DF
☎020 8308 2626 (enquiries), 020 8300 3024 (administration)
Fax 020 8308 0542
url: www.bruford.ac.uk
College Librarian John Collis BA MCLIP ARCM (e-mail: john.collis@bruford.ac.uk)

ROYAL ACADEMY OF DRAMATIC ART

Library, Royal Academy of Dramatic Art, 18 Chenies Street, London WC1E 7PA
☎020 7636 7076
e-mail: library@rada.ac.uk
url: www.rada.org
Consultant Librarian Ms Claire Hope BA MCLIP
Library Manager James Thornton

ROYAL ACADEMY OF MUSIC

Library, Royal Academy of Music, Marylebone Road, London NW1 5HT
☎020 7873 7323 (enquiries and administration)
Fax 020 7873 7322
e-mail: library@ram.ac.uk
url: www.ram.ac.uk
Librarian Ms Kathryn Adamson BA MA DipLib HonARAM

ROYAL AGRICULTURAL COLLEGE

Library, Royal Agricultural College, Stroud Road, Cirencester, Glos GL7 6JS
☎(01285) 652531 ext 2274
Fax (01285) 889844
e-mail: library@rac.ac.uk
url: www.rac.ac.uk/library
Head of Library Services Ms Sarah Howie BA MPhil DipLib MCLIP (01285 655214 ext 2276)

ROYAL COLLEGE OF ART

College Library, Royal College of Art, Kensington Gore, London SW7 2EU
☎020 7590 4224 (enquiries)
Fax 020 7590 4500
e-mail: info@rca.ac.uk
url: www.rca.ac.uk
Head of Information and Learning Services Peter Hassell MCLIP (e-mail: peter.hassell@rca.ac.uk)
Library Manager Ms Pauline Rae (e-mail: pauline.rae@rca.ac.uk)
Special Collections and Services Manager Ms Darlene Maxwell (e-mail: darlene.maxwell@rca.ac.uk)

ROYAL COLLEGE OF MUSIC

Library, Royal College of Music, Prince Consort Road, London SW7 2BS
☎020 7591 4325
Fax 020 7589 7740
e-mail: library@rcm.ac.uk
url: www.rcm.ac.uk
Chief Librarian Ms Pamela Thompson BA (020 7591 4323; e-mail: pthompson@rcm.ac.uk)
Reference Librarian Dr Peter Horton (020 7591 4324; e-mail: phorton@rcm.ac.uk)

ROYAL COLLEGE OF NURSING OF THE UNITED KINGDOM

Library and Information Services, Royal College of Nursing of the United Kingdom, 20 Cavendish Square, London W1G 0RN
☎020 7647 3610
Fax 020 7647 3420
e-mail: rcn.library@rcn.org.uk
url: www.rcn.org.uk
Head of Library and Information Services Ms Jackie Lord BA(Hons) DipLib MCLIP
(Access for non-members is by appointment)

ROYAL NORTHERN COLLEGE OF MUSIC

Library, Royal Northern College of Music, 124 Oxford Road, Manchester M13 9RD
☎0161 907 5243
Fax 0161 273 7611
e-mail: library@rncm.ac.uk
url: www.rncm.ac.uk
Librarian Miss A E Smart BA MA MCLIP
Deputy Librarian G Thomason MusB MusM ARCM LTCL DipLib

ROYAL SCOTTISH ACADEMY OF MUSIC AND DRAMA

Whittaker Library, Royal Scottish Academy of Music and Drama, 100 Renfrew Street, Glasgow G2 3DB
☎0141 270 8268
Fax 0141 270 8353
e-mail: library@rsamd.ac.uk
url: www.rsamd.ac.uk
Head of Information Services Ms Caroline Cochrane (0141 270 8269; e-mail: c.cochrane@rsamd.ac.uk)

ROYAL WELSH COLLEGE OF MUSIC AND DRAMA

Library, Royal Welsh College of Music and Drama, Castle Grounds, Cathays Park, Cardiff CF10 3ER
☎029 2034 2854
Fax 029 2039 1304
url: www.library.rwcmd.ac.uk
Librarian Mrs Judith Agus BA BMus MCLIP (029 2039 1330; e-mail: agusjm@rwcmd.ac.uk)

RUSKIN COLLEGE

College Library, Ruskin College, Walton Street, Oxford OX1 2HE
☎(01865) 554331
Fax (01865) 554372
e-mail: library@ruskin.ac.uk
url: www.ruskin.ac.uk
Librarian Ms Valerie Moyses BA(Hons) MCLIP DipLib
(Admission by appointment only)

UNIVERSITY OF ST ANDREWS

Library and Information Services, University of St Andrews, University Library, North
Street, St Andrews, Fife KY16 9TR
☎(01334 462281 (enquiries and administration), 01334 462301 management
Fax (01334) 462282
e-mail: lis.library@st-and.ac.uk
url: www.st-andrews.ac.uk
Acting Librarian Mrs Christine Gascoigne BA MA

COLLEGE OF ST MARK AND ST JOHN

Library, College of St Mark and St John, Derriford Road, Plymouth PL6 8BH
☎(01752) 636845 (enquiries), (01752) 636700 ext 4206 (administration)
Fax (01752) 636712
url: www.marjon.ac.uk
Director of Information Services Frank Clements FCLIP (01752 636700 ext 4215;
e-mail: fclements@marjon.ac.uk)
Librarian Ms Wendy Evans ILTA MCLIP (ext 4200; e-mail: wevans@marjon.ac.uk)

ST MARTIN'S COLLEGE

Harold Bridges Library, St Martin's Services Ltd, St Martin's College, St Martin's College
(Lancaster), Bowerham Road, Lancaster LA1 3JD
☎(01524) 384238
Fax (01524) 384588
url: www.ucsm.ac.uk/library/
Head of Library Services Ms Margaret Weaver BA MSc MCLIP ILTM (01524 384238;
e-mail: m.weaver@ucsm.ac.uk)

Site libraries
▶ Charlotte Mason Library, St Martin's Services Ltd, St Martin's College, St Martin's
College (Ambleside), Rydal Road, Ambleside, Cumbria LA22 9BB
☎(01539) 430274
Fax (01539) 430371
e-mail: amb.library@ucsm.ac.uk
Site Librarian Ms Sarah Ruston BA(Hons) PGCE MCLIP (01539 430244; e-mail:
s.e.l.ruston@ucsm.ac.uk)

▶ Harold Bridges Library, St Martin's Services Ltd, St Martin's College, St Martin's College (Lancaster), Bowerham Road, Lancaster LA1 3JD
☎(01524) 384319
Fax (01524) 384588
e-mail: library@ucsm.ac.uk/library
Site Library Manager Ms Lisa Toner BA DipLib MCLIP (01524 384254; e-mail: l.toner@ucsm.ac.uk)

▶ Library, St Martin's Services Ltd, St Martin's College, St Martin's College (Carlisle), Fusehill Street, Carlisle CA1 2HG
☎(01228) 616218
Fax (01228) 616263
e-mail: car.library@ucsm.ac.uk
Senior Information Officer Ms Shirley Green BA MCLIP (01228 616219; e-mail: s.h.green@ucsm.ac.uk)

ST MARY'S COLLEGE, STRAWBERRY HILL

Learning Resources Centre, St Mary's College, Strawberry Hill, Waldegrave Road, Strawberry Hill, Twickenham, Middlesex TW1 4SX
☎020 8240 4097
Fax 020 8240 4270
e-mail: enquiry@smuc.ac.uk
url: www.smuc.ac.uk
Director of Information Services and Systems Ms Maire Lanigan BSc(Hons) DipLib
Assistant Director Martin Scarrott BA DipLib MCLIP ILTM

UNIVERSITY OF SALFORD

Information Services Division, University of Salford, Clifford Whitworth Building, Salford, Manchester M5 4WT
☎0161 295 2444
Fax 0161 295 5888
e-mail: helpdesk-isd@salford.ac.uk
url: www.isd.salford.ac.uk
Director of Information Services Division Tony Lewis BA(Hons) MSc CEng MICE MIWEM
Deputy Director Mrs Margaret Duncan BA(Hons) MCLIP (0161 295 5180)
Head of Customer Services Ms Liz Jolly BA(Hons) DipILS MCLIP
Head of Liaison and Planning Mrs Julie Berry BA DMS MCLIP
Head of Learning Resources Mrs Wendy Carley BA MA MCLIP

Campus libraries

▶ Adelphi Library, University of Salford, Adelphi Building, Peru Street, Salford, Manchester M3 6EQ
☎0161 295 6084
Fax 0161 295 6083

▶ Allerton Library, University of Salford, Allerton Building, Frederick Road, Salford, Manchester M6 6PU

☎0161 295 2435
Fax 0161 295 2437
▶ Clifford Whitworth Library, University of Salford, Salford, Manchester M5 4WT
☎0161 295 5535
Fax 0161 295 5888
Resource Delivery Manager Ms Geraldine Barlow
▶ Irwell Valley Library, University of Salford, Irwell Valley Campus, Blandford Road,
Salford, Manchester M6 6BD
☎0161 295 6083
Fax 0161 295 2361

SCOTTISH AGRICULTURAL COLLEGE

The Agriculture Library, Scottish Agricultural College, Peter Wilson Building, Kings Buildings,
West Mains Road, Edinburgh EH9 3JG
☎0131 535 4117 (enquiries), 0131 535 4116 (administration)
Fax 0131 535 4246
e-mail: library@ed.sac.ac.uk
url: www.sac.ac.uk/library/External/Edin/
Site Librarian Miss Ishbel K Leggat MA PGDipLib (e-mail: ishbel.leggat@sac.ac.uk)

Campus libraries

▶ SAC Library, Scottish Agricultural College, Ferguson Building, Craibstone Estate,
Aberdeen AB21 9YA
☎(01224) 711039
Fax (01224) 711291
e-mail: library@ab.sac.ac.uk
url: www.sac.ac.uk/library/External/Ab/intro.htm
Head Librarian Mrs Elizabeth Buchan BA(Hons) (e-mail: elizabeth.buchan@sac.ac.uk)
▶ SAC Library, Scottish Agricultural College, Donald Hendrie Building, Auchincruive,
Ayrshire KA6 5HW
☎(01292) 525209
Fax (01292) 525211
e-mail: library@au.sac.ac.uk
url: www.sac.ac.uk/library/External/Au/default.htm
Site Librarian Ms Elaine P Muir MA PGDipLib MCLIP (e-mail: elaine.muir@sac.ac.uk)

SHEFFIELD HALLAM UNIVERSITY

Learning Centre, Sheffield Hallam University, City Campus, Sheffield S1 1WB
☎0114 225 2103
Fax 0114 225 3859
e-mail: learning.centre@shu.ac.uk
url: http://students.shu.ac.uk/lc/
Chief Information Officer John Hemingway MBA MSc BSc MIEE CEng
Head of Academic Services and Development Ms B M Fisher MLib MCLIP (e-mail:
b.m.fisher@shu.ac.uk)
Head of Technical Services and Development E Oyston BA MSc MCLIP

Campus Learning Centres

▶ Learning Centre, Sheffield Hallam University, Collegiate Crescent Campus, Sheffield
S10 2BP
☎0114 225 2474
Fax 0114 225 2476

▶ Learning Centre, Sheffield Hallam University, Psalter Lane Campus, Sheffield
S11 8UZ
☎0114 225 2721
Fax 0114 225 2717

THE UNIVERSITY OF SHEFFIELD

Main Library, The University of Sheffield, Western Bank, Sheffield S10 2TN
☎0114 222 7200 (general enquiries); 0114 222 7224 library (administration)
Fax 0114 222 7290
e-mail: library@sheffield.ac.uk
url: www.shef.ac.uk/library
Director of Library Services and University Librarian Martin J Lewis MA DipLib
MCLIP

Major libraries

▶ Health Sciences Library, The University of Sheffield, Royal Hallamshire Hospital,
Sheffield S10 2JF
☎0114 271 2030
Fax 0114 278 0923
e-mail: hsl.rhh@sheffield.ac.uk

▶ St George's Library (Engineering & Management), The University of Sheffield, Mappin
Street, Sheffield S1 4DT
☎0114 222 7301
Fax 0114 279 6406
e-mail: sgl@sheffield.ac.uk

SOUTHAMPTON INSTITUTE

Mountbatten Library, Southampton Institute, Southampton SO14 0RJ
☎023 8031 9681 (enquiries), 023 8031 9248 (administration)
Fax (023 8031 9672
url: www.solent.ac.uk/library/
Information Services Manager Robert Burrell MSc(Econ) MCLIP (023 8031 9342;
e-mail: robert.burrell@solent.ac.uk)

Site library

▶ Warsash Library, Southampton Institute, Newtown Road, Warsash, Southampton
SO31 9ZL
☎(01489) 556269

(Subject to approval, Southampton Institute will become Southampton Solent University in
Autumn 2005)

UNIVERSITY OF SOUTHAMPTON

Hartley Library, University of Southampton, Highfield, Southampton SO17 1BJ
☎023 8059 2180 (enquiries), 023 8059 3450 (administration)
Fax 023 8059 5451
e-mail: library@soton.ac.uk
url: www.library.soton.ac.uk/
University Librarian Mark Brown MA PhD DipLib DipMgmt MCLIP (023 8059 2677;
e-mail: mlb@soton.ac.uk)
Deputy Librarian Richard Wake MA MA CertMgmt MCLIP (023 8059 2371; e-mail:
rlw1@soton.ac.uk)
Head of Archives and Special Collections Christopher Woolgar BA PhD
DipArchAdmin FSA FRHistS (023 8059 2721; e-mail: cmw@soton.ac.uk)

Site libraries
▶ Biomedical Sciences Library, University of Southampton, Biomedical Sciences Building,
  Bassett Crescent East, Highfield, Southampton SO16 7PX
  ☎023 8059 4215
  Fax 023 8059 3251
  e-mail: bslenqs@soton.ac.uk
  url: www.library.soton.ac.uk/bsl
  Head of Biomedical Sciences Library Miss Adrienne Norman BA DipLib MCLIP
▶ Health Services Library MP 883, University of Southampton, Level A, South Academic
  Block, Southampton General Hospital, Tremona Road, Southampton SO16 6YD
  ☎023 8079 6547
  Fax 023 8079 8939
  e-mail: hslib@soton.ac.uk
  url: www.library.soton.ac.uk/hsl
  Head of MHLS Library Services Ms Christine Fowler BSc(Hons) MA MCLIP
▶ Library, University of Southampton, Winchester School of Art, Park Avenue,
  Winchester, Hants SO23 8DL
  ☎023 8059 6986
  e-mail: wsaenqs@soton.ac.uk
  url: www.library.soton.ac.uk/wsal
  Head of Library and Information Services Ms Linda Newington BA(Hons) PGDip
  MCLIP (e-mail: lan1@soton.ac.uk)
▶ National Oceanographic Library, University of Southampton, Southampton
  Oceanography Centre, Waterfront Campus, European Way, Southampton SO14 3ZH
  ☎023 8059 6111 (marine information and advisory service), 023 8059 6116 (general)
  Fax 023 8059 6115
  e-mail: mias@soc.soton.ac.uk (marine inf/adv serv); nol@soc.soton.ac.uk (general)
  url: www.library.soton.ac.uk/nol
  Head of Information Services Mrs Pauline Simpson BA MCLIP (e-mail:
  ps@soc.soton.ac.uk)
▶ New College Library, University of Southampton, New College, The Avenue,
  Southampton SO17 1BG
  ☎023 8059 7220
  Fax 023 8059 7339

e-mail: nclib@soton.ac.uk
url: www.library.soton.ac.uk/ncl
Head of Library and Information Services Ms Gail McFarlane (e-mail:
egm@soton.ac.uk)

SPURGEON'S COLLEGE

Library, Spurgeon's College, 189 South Norwood Hill, London SE25 6DJ
☎020 8653 0850
Fax 020 8771 0959
e-mail: library@spurgeons.ac.uk
url: www.spurgeons.ac.uk
Librarian Mrs J C Powles BA MCLIP (e-mail: j.powles@spurgeons.ac.uk)

STAFFORDSHIRE UNIVERSITY

Information Services, Staffordshire University, PO Box 335, Beaconside, Stafford ST16 9DQ
☎(01782) 294000
Fax (01785) 353410
e-mail: library@staffs.ac.uk
url: www.staffs.ac.uk
Director of Information Services Ms Liz Hart BA(Hons) DipLib FCLIP (e-mail:
l.hart@staffs.ac.uk)

Site libraries
▶ Health Library, Staffordshire University, School of Health, Royal Shrewsbury Hospital
(North), Mytton Oak Road, Shrewsbury SY3 8XQ
☎(01743) 261440
Fax (01743) 261061
Subject and Learning Support Librarian Mrs Shirley Kennedy
▶ Law Library, Staffordshire University, Leek Road, Stoke-on-Trent, Staffs ST4 2DF
☎(01782) 294307
Fax (01782) 294306
Site Operations Manager Mrs Nicola Adams
▶ Nelson Library, Staffordshire University, PO Box 368, Beaconside, Stafford ST18 0YU
☎(01785) 353236
Fax (01785) 251058
Site Operations Manager Mrs Gill Edwards
▶ Thompson Library, Staffordshire University, PO Box 664, College Road, Stoke-on-Trent
ST4 2XS
☎(01782) 295770
Fax (01782) 295799
Site Operations Manager Mrs Janice Broad

UNIVERSITY OF STIRLING

University Library, University of Stirling, Stirling FK9 4LA
☎(01786 467235 (Information Centre), 01786 467227 (administration)

Fax (01786) 466866
e-mail: liby1@stir.ac.uk
url: www.library.stir.ac.uk
Director of Information Services Peter Kemp MA PhD (e-mail: pk2@stir.ac.uk)

Campus library
▶ Highland Health Sciences Library, University of Stirling, Highland Campus, Inverness
IV2 3UJ
☎(01463) 705269
Librarian Mrs A Gillespie BA DipLibStud MCLIP (e-mail: ag5@stir.ac.uk)

UNIVERSITY OF STRATHCLYDE

Andersonian Library, University of Strathclyde, Curran Building, 101 St James' Road,
Glasgow G4 0NS
☎0141 548 3701 (enquiries), ext 4621 (administration)
Fax 0141 552 3304
e-mail: library@strath.ac.uk
url: www.lib.strath.ac.uk/home
Librarian and Director of Information Strategy Prof Derek Law DUniv MA DipLib
FCLIP FKC FRSE (0141 548 4997; e-mail: d.law@strath.ac.uk)
Director of Library Services Keith R Davis BA DipLib (0141 548 4619; e-mail:
k.r.davis@strath.ac.uk)

Constituent libraries
▶ Jordanhill Library, University of Strathclyde, 76 Southbrae Drive, Glasgow G13 1PP
☎0141 950 3000
Fax 0141 950 3150
e-mail: jordanhill.library@strath.ac.uk
Librarian Mrs Margaret Harrison MA MCLIP (e-mail: m.harrison@strath.ac.uk)
▶ Law Library, University of Strathclyde, Stenhouse Building, 173 Cathedral Street,
Glasgow G4 0RQ
☎0141 552 3701 ext 3293
Librarian Mrs Christina C MacSween MA DipLib (e-mail: c.macsween@strath.ac.uk)

UNIVERSITY OF SUNDERLAND

Student and Learning Support, University of Sunderland, Chester Road, Sunderland SR1 3SD
☎0191 515 2900 (enquiries)
Fax 0191 515 2904
url: www.sunderland.ac.uk
Director of Student and Learning Support Vacant

Site libraries
▶ Ashburne Library, University of Sunderland, Sunderland SR2 7EG
☎0191 515 2119
Fax 0191 515 3166

Site Librarian Ms J Dodshon BA(Hons) DipLib (0191 515 2120; e-mail: jan.dodshon@sunderland.ac.uk)
▶ The Murray Library, University of Sunderland, Chester Road, Sunderland SR1 3SD
☎0191 515 2900
Fax 0191 515 2904
Site Librarian Ms J Archer BA (0191 515 3272; e-mail: julie.archer@sunderland.ac.uk)
▶ St Peter's Library, University of Sunderland, Prospect Building, St Peter's Riverside Campus, St Peter's Way, Sunderland SR6 0DD
☎0191 515 3059
Fax 0191 515 3061
Site Librarian Mrs E Astan BA MCLIP (e-mail: elizabeth.astan@sunderland.ac.uk)

SURREY INSTITUTE OF ART AND DESIGN, UNIVERSITY COLLEGE

Library, Surrey Institute of Art and Design, University College, Falkner Road, The Hart, Farnham, Surrey GU9 7DS
☎(01252) 892709
Fax (01252) 892725
url: www.surrart.ac.uk
Institute Librarian Ms Rosemary Lynch BA(Hons) MALib MCLIP
Deputy Librarian Ms Gwynneth Wilkey BA(Hons) DipLib MCLIP

Site library
▶ Library, Surrey Institute of Art and Design, University College, Epsom Campus, Ashley Road, Epsom, Surrey KT18 5BE
☎(01372) 202458
Fax (01372) 747050
Site Librarian Ms Christina Gregory BSc(Hons) PGDipILM MCLIP

Please note: The Surrey Institute of Art & Design, University College and The Kent Institute of Art & Design merged on 1 August 2005 and became the University College for the Creative Arts at Canterbury, Epsom, Farnham, Maidstone and Rochester

UNIVERSITY OF SURREY

University Library, University of Surrey, George Edwards Building, Guildford, Surrey GU2 7XH
☎(01483 683325 (enquiries), 01483 689232 (administration)
Fax (01483) 689500
e-mail: library-enquiries@surrey.ac.uk
url: www.surrey.ac.uk/library
Head of Library Services Robert B Hall BA MA MCLIP

UNIVERSITY OF SUSSEX

University Library, University of Sussex, Falmer, Brighton BN1 9QL
☎(01273) 678163 (enquiries), (01273) 678797 (administration)

Fax (01273) 678441
e-mail: library@sussex.ac.uk
url: www.sussex.ac.uk/library/
University Librarian Mrs Deborah Shorley BA FCLIP

Institute of Development Studies, British Library for Development Studies, University of Sussex, Falmer, Brighton BN1 9RE
☎(01273) 678263 (enquiries), 606261 (administration)
Fax (01273) 621202
e-mail: blds@ids.ac.uk
url: www.ids.ac.uk/blds/
Librarian Michael Bloom BA DipLib

SPRU – The Keith Pavitt Library, University of Sussex, Freeman Centre, Falmer, Brighton BN1 9QE
☎(01273) 678178 (enquiries), (01273) 678066 (administration)
Fax (01273) 685865
e-mail: spru_library@sussex.ac.uk
url: www.sussex.ac.uk/spru/1-6.html; www.sprulib.central.sussex.ac.uk/ (for catalogue)
Librarian Ms Barbara Merchant BSc MCLIP (e-mail: b.a.merchant@sussex.ac.uk)
Information Officer Ms Maureen Winder BA MSc MCLIP (e-mail: m.e.winder@sussex.ac.uk)

SWANSEA INSTITUTE OF HIGHER EDUCATION

Townhill Campus Library, Swansea Institute of Higher Education, Townhill Road, Swansea SA2 0UT
☎(01792) 481000 ext 2293
Fax (01792) 298017
e-mail: library2@sihe.ac.uk
url: www.sihe.ac.uk
Head of Library and Learning Resources Tony Lamb BA MCLIP GradCertEd (e-mail: tony.lamb@sihe.ac.uk)

Site libraries
▶ Owen Library, Swansea Institute of Higher Education, Mount Pleasant, Swansea SA1 6ED
  ☎(01792) 481000 ext 4221
▶ Thompson Library, Swansea Institute of Higher Education, Mount Pleasant, Swansea SA1 6ED
  ☎(01792) 481000 ext 4141
  Site Librarian Ms Anne Harvey LLB (e-mail: anne.harvey@sihe.ac.uk)

UNIVERSITY OF TEESSIDE

Library and Information Services, Learning Resource Centre, University of Teesside, Middlesbrough TS1 3BA
☎(01642) 342100 (enquiries), (01642) 342103 (administration)
Fax (01642) 342190

url: www.tees.ac.uk/lis/
Director of Library & Information Services Ian C Butchart MSc BA PGCE MCLIP
(e-mail: ian.butchart@tees.ac.uk)

THAMES VALLEY UNIVERSITY

Learning and Research Support, Thames Valley University, St Mary's Road, Ealing, London
W5 5RF
☎020 8231 2248 (enquiries), 020 8231 2246 (administration)
Fax 020 8231 2631
url: www.tvu.ac.uk/lrs
Head of Learning and Research Support John Wolstenholme BA (020 8231 2678;
e-mail: john.wolstenholme@tvu.ac.uk)

Learning resource centres
▶ Paul Hamlyn LRC, Thames Valley University, Wellington Street, Slough SL1 1YG
☎(01753) 697536
Fax (01753) 697538
LRC Manager Michael Sharrocks (e-mail: michael.sharrocks@tvu.ac.uk)
▶ Royal Berkshire Hospital LRC, Thames Valley University, Royal Berkshire Hospital,
London Road, Reading RG1 5AN
☎0118 332 7661
Fax 0118 332 8675
LRC Manager Felix Oliver-Tasker (e-mail: felix.oliver-tasker@tvu.ac.uk)
▶ St Mary's Road LRC, Thames Valley University, Ealing, London W5 5RF
☎020 8231 2401
Fax 020 8231 2631
LRC Manager David McGrath BA (e-mail: david.mcgrath@tvu.ac.uk)
▶ Westel House Health Sciences LRC, Thames Valley University, Westel House, 32
Uxbridge Road, Ealing, London W5 2BS
☎020 8280 5043
Fax 020 8280 5045
LRC Manager Ms Gillian Briggs (e-mail: gillian.briggs@tvu.ac.uk)

TRINITY AND ALL SAINTS COLLEGE

Library, Trinity and All Saints College, Brownberrie Lane, Horsforth, Leeds LS18 5HD
☎0113 283 7244
Fax 0113 283 7200
url: www.tasc.ac.uk/library
Director of Information Support Services Edward Brush BA(Hons) FIDPM (e-mail:
e_brush@tasc.ac.uk)
Librarian Ms Elizabeth Murphy MA MCLIP (e-mail: e_murphy@tasc.ac.uk)

TRINITY COLLEGE CARMARTHEN

Learning Resources Centre, Trinity College Carmarthen, College Road, Carmarthen
SA31 3EP

☎(01267) 676780 (Library), (01267) 676786 (Teaching Resources Centre)
Fax (01267) 676766
e-mail: library@trinity-cm.ac.uk (Library), trc@trinity-cm.ac.uk (Teaching Resources Centre)
url: www.trinity-cm.ac.uk/english/lrc
Director of Learning Resources Ms Sally Wilkinson BA DipLib MCLIP (e-mail: s.a.wilkinson@trinity-cm.ac.uk)

UHI MILLENNIUM INSTITUTE

Directorate Office, UHI Millennium Institute, Ness Street, Inverness IV3 5SQ
☎(01463) 279000
Fax (01463) 279001
url: www.uhi.ac.uk
Learning Resources Contact Ms Gillian Anderson

Site libraries
▶ Library, UHI Millennium Institute, Highland Theological College, Dingwall, Inverness IV15 9HA
  ☎(01349) 780207
  Fax (01349) 867555
  Learning Resources Contact Martin Cameron, Fraser Jackson
▶ Library, UHI Millennium Institute, Inverness College, 3 Longman Road, Longman Road South, Inverness IV1 1SA
  ☎(01463) 273248
  Fax (01463) 711977
  Learning Resources Contact Ms Sue Cromar
▶ Library, UHI Millennium Institute, Lews Castle College, Stornoway, Isle of Lewis, Hebrides HS2 0XR
  ☎(01851) 770409
  Fax (01851) 770001
  Learning Resources Contact Ms Erica McLeod
▶ Library, UHI Millennium Institute, Lochaber College, An Aird, Fort William, Lochaber, Inverness-shire PH33 6AN
  ☎(01397) 774264
  Fax (01397) 701886
  Learning Resources Contact Dagan Lev
▶ Library, UHI Millennium Institute, Moray College, Elgin, Elgin, Moray IV30 1JJ
  ☎(01343) 576206
  Fax (01343) 576001
  Learning Resources Contact Ms Angie Mackenzie
▶ Library, UHI Millennium Institute, North Atlantic Fisheries College, Port Arthur, Scalloway, Shetland ZE1 0UN
  ☎(01595) 772350
  Fax (01595) 880549
  Learning Resources Contact Ms Maureen Grant
▶ Library, UHI Millennium Institute, North Highland College, Ormlie Road, Thurso, Caithness KW14 7EE

☎(01847) 889292
Fax (01847) 889001
Learning Resources Contact Ms Rhona Mason
▶ Library, UHI Millennium Institute, Orkney College, Kirkwall, Orkney KW15 1LX
☎(01856) 569272
Fax (01856) 569001
Learning Resources Contact Ms Annette Andersen
▶ Library, UHI Millennium Institute, Perth College, Crieff Road, Perth PH1 2NX
☎(01738) 877710/877708
Fax (01738) 631364
Learning Resources Contact Ms Jennifer Louden
 Ms Jackie Proven
▶ Library, UHI Millennium Institute, Sabhal Mor Ostaig, An Teanga, Sleite, Isle of Skye,
Hebrides IV44 8BQ
☎(01471) 888431
Fax (01473) 888001
Learning Resources Contact Ms Christine Cain
▶ Library, UHI Millennium Institute, Seafish Aquaculture, Marine Farming Unit, Ardtoe,
Acharacle, Argyll PH36 4LD
☎(01967) 875000
Fax (01967) 875001
Learning Resources Contact Vacant
▶ Library, UHI Millennium Institute, Shetland College, Gremista, Lerwick, Shetland ZE1 0PX
☎(01595) 771258
Fax (01595) 694830
Learning Resources Contact Ms Elizabeth McHugh
▶ Library, UHI Millennium Institute, SAMS – Dunstaffnage Marine Laboratory, PO Box 3,
Oban, Argyll PA34 4AD
☎(01631) 559000
Fax (01631) 559001
Learning Resources Contact Ms Trisha Thompson
▶ Library, UHI Millennium Institute, Argyll College, Dunoon Learning Centre, West Bay,
Dunoon, Argyll PA23 7HP
☎(01369) 707183

UNIVERSITY OF ULSTER

LRC, University of Ulster, Shore Road, Jordanstown, Newtownabbey, Co Antrim BT37 0QB
☎028 9036 6370
Fax 028 9036 6849
url: www.ulster.ac.uk
Assistant Director, Library Mrs Elaine Urquhart MA DipLibInfoStud MCLIP (028 9036
6370; e-mail: ee.urquhart@ulster.ac.uk)

Campus libraries
▶ Library, Faculty of Art and Design, University of Ulster at Belfast, University of Ulster,
York Street, Belfast BT15 1ED
☎028 9026 7269

Fax 028 9026 7278

Belfast Campus Contact Mrs Marion Khorshidian BA DipLIS MCLIP (e-mail: m.khorshidian@ulster.ac.uk)

▶ Library, University of Ulster at Coleraine, University of Ulster, Cromore Road, Coleraine BT52 ISA
☎028 7032 4364
Fax 028 7032 4928

Coleraine Campus Contact David McClure BA(Hons) DipEd DLS (e-mail: dj.mcclure@ulster.ac.uk)

▶ LRC, University of Ulster at Jordanstown, University of Ulster, Shore Road, Jordanstown, Newtownabbey, Co Antrim BT37 0QB
☎028 9036 6929
Fax 028 9036 6849

Jordanstown Campus Contact Mrs Mary McCullough BA DipLibStud (e-mail: m.mccullough@ulster.ac.uk)

▶ LRC, University of Ulster at Magee, University of Ulster, Northland Road, Londonderry BT48 7JL
☎028 7137 5386
Fax 028 7137 5626

Magee Campus Contact Mrs Stephanie McLaughlin BA LibStud (e-mail: sa.mclaughlin@ulster.ac.uk)

UNIVERSITY OF THE ARTS LONDON

Library and Learning Resources, University of the Arts London, 65 Davies Street, London WIK 5DA
☎020 7514 6000
url: www.arts.ac.uk/library

Director of Library and Learning Resources Ms Mary J Auckland OBE MSc HonFCLIP (020 7514 8072; e-mail: m.auckland@arts.ac.uk)

College/site libraries

Camberwell College of Arts

Library and Learning Resources, Camberwell College of Arts, 43-45 Peckham Road, London SE5 8UF
☎020 7514 6349
Fax 020 7514 6324

Head of Learning Resources Ms Liz Kerr BA PGDip (Photography) PGDip (Library & Archive Studies) MCLIP (e-mail: l.kerr@camberwell.arts.ac.uk)

Central Saint Martins College of Art and Design

Library and Learning Resources, Central Saint Martins College of Art and Design, Southampton Row, London WCIB 4AP
☎020 7514 7037
Fax 020 7514 7033
url: www.csm.arts.ac.uk

Head of Learning Resources Ms Pat Christie BA MCLIP

Library and Learning Resources, Central Saint Martins College of Art and Design,
107 Charing Cross Road, London WC2H 0DU
☎020 7514 7190
Fax 020 7514 7189
Site Librarian Ms Arja Huxstep BA(Hons) MA DipLib

Chelsea College of Art and Design
Library and Learning Resources, Chelsea College of Art and Design, Millbank, London
SW1P 4RJ
☎020 7514 7780
Fax 020 7514 7785
url: www.arts.ac.uk/library
Acting Head of Library and Learning Resources Ms E Ward BA MA

London College of Communication
Library and Learning Resources, London College of Communication, Elephant and Castle,
London SE1 6SB
☎020 7514 6527 (enquiries), 020 7514 6581 (administration)
Fax 020 7514 6597
e-mail: ec-lib@linst.ac.uk
url: www.arts.ac.uk/library
Deputy Head of Learning Resources Ms Jacky Camroux MSc DipEdTech MCLIP

London College of Fashion
Library and Learning Resources, London College of Fashion, 20 John Princes Street,
Oxford Circus, London W1G 0BJ
☎020 7514 7455/7543
Fax 020 7514 7580
Library Manager Ms Diane Mansbridge BA MA MCLIP (e-mail:
d.mansbridge@fashion.arts.ac.uk)

UNIVERSITY OF WALES ABERYSTWYTH

Hugh Owen Library, University of Wales Aberystwyth, Penglais, Aberystwyth, Ceredigion
SY23 3DZ
☎(01970) 622399 (enquiries), (01970) 622391 (administration)
Fax (01970) 622404
e-mail: libinfo@aber.ac.uk
url: www.aber.ac.uk
Director of Information Services Mike Hopkins BA PhD MCLIP

Site/departmental libraries
▶ Education Library, University of Wales Aberystwyth, Old College, King Street,
  Aberystwyth, Ceredigion SY23 2AX
  ☎(01970) 622130
  Librarian i/c Elgan Davies BA DipLib
▶ Law Library, University of Wales Aberystwyth, The Hugh Owen Building, Penglais,
  Aberystwyth, Ceredigion SY23 3DZ

☎(01970) 622401
e-mail: libinfo@aber.ac.uk
Librarian i/c Mrs Lillian Stevenson LLB DipLib MCLIP
▶ Physical Sciences Library (Mathematics, Computer Sciences and Physics), University of Wales Aberystwyth, 4th Floor, Physical Sciences Building, Penglais, Aberystwyth, Ceredigion SY23 3BZ
☎(01970) 622407
e-mail: libinfo@aber.ac.uk
Librarian i/c Mrs Tegwen Meredith
▶ Thomas Parry Library, University of Wales Aberystwyth, Llanbadarn Fawr, Aberystwyth, Ceredigion SY23 3AS
☎(01970) 622412 (enquiries), (01970) 622417 (administration)
Fax (01970) 622190
e-mail: parrylib@aber.ac.uk
Librarian i/c Alan Clark BSocSci DipLib MCLIP

UNIVERSITY OF WALES BANGOR

Library, Archives and Records Management Service, University of Wales Bangor, College Road, Bangor, Gwynedd LL57 2DG
☎(01248) 382980 (enquiries), (01248) 383772 (secretary)
Fax (01248) 382979
e-mail: library@bangor.ac.uk; ill@bangor.ac.uk (interlibrary loans)
url: www.bangor.ac.uk/is/library
Head of Library, Archives and Records Management Service Vacant
Information Support Group Manager Angela Jones-Evans BLib(Hons) PhD PGCED MCLIP (e-mail: a.jones-evans@bangor.ac.uk)
Lending and Access Services Manager Vacant
Systems and Technical Services Manager Mieko Yamaguchi BA MA DipLib (e-mail: m.yamaguchi@bangor.ac.uk)
Welsh and Special Collections Manager Ellen Parry Williams BA (e-mail: e.p.williams@bangor.ac.uk)
University Archivist Einion Wyn Thomas BA DAA (e-mail: e.w.thomas@bangor.ac.uk)
University Records Manager Gwenan Owen BA(Hons) (e-mail: gwenan.owen@bangor.ac.uk)

Site libraries
▶ Education Site Library, University of Wales Bangor, Safle'r Normal, Holyhead Road, Bangor, Gwynedd LL57 2PX
☎(01248) 383048
Subject Librarian Bethan Wyn Jones BA DipLib MCLIP (e-mail: b.w.jones@bangor.ac.uk)
▶ Health Studies Library, University of Wales Bangor, Archimedes Centre, Technology Park, Wrexham LL13 7YP
☎(01978) 316370
Subject Librarian Gwyneth Haylock BA DipLib (e-mail: g.d.haylock@bangor.ac.uk)
▶ Health Studies Library, University of Wales Bangor, Fron Heulog, Holyhead Road, Bangor, Gwynedd LL57 2EF

☎(01248) 383131
Subject Librarian Marion Poulton BA MEd DipLib MCLIP (e-mail:
m.poulton@bangor.ac.uk)
▶ Law Library, University of Wales Bangor, College Road, Bangor, Gwynedd LL57 2DG
☎(01248) 382983
Subject Librarian Mairwen Owen BA (e-mail: mairwen.owen@bangor.ac.uk)
▶ Main Library, University of Wales Bangor, College Road, Bangor, Gwynedd LL57 2DG
☎(01248) 382983
Subject Librarians Paul Rolfe BA MA CertEd DipLib MCLIP (e-mail:
p.rolfe@bangor.ac.uk), Eileen Tilley MA CertEd MCLIP (e-mail: e.f.tilley@bangor.ac.uk)
▶ Ocean Sciences Library, University of Wales Bangor, Wolfson Building, Askew Street,
Menai Bridge LL59 5EY
☎(01248) 382985
Librarian Paul Rolfe BA MA CertEd DipLib MCLIP (e-mail: p.rolfe@bangor.ac.uk)
▶ Science Library, University of Wales Bangor, Adeilad Deiniol, Deiniol Road, Bangor,
Gwynedd LL57 2UX
☎(01248) 382984
Subject Librarian Stephen Harling MA DipLib MA (e-mail: s.t.harling@bangor.ac.uk)

UNIVERSITY OF WALES COLLEGE OF MEDICINE
see CARDIFF UNIVERSITY

UNIVERSITY OF WALES INSTITUTE, CARDIFF

Library Division, University of Wales Institute, Cardiff, Llandaff Campus, Western Avenue,
Cardiff CF5 2YB
☎029 2041 6240
Fax 029 2041 6908
url: www.uwic.ac.uk/library
Head of Library Division Paul Riley BA(Hons) (029 2041 6240; e-mail: priley@uwic.ac.uk)

UNIVERSITY OF WALES LAMPETER

The Library, University of Wales Lampeter, Lampeter, Ceredigion SA48 7ED
☎(01570 424772 (enquiries/Librarian)
Fax (01570) 424997
e-mail: library@lamp.ac.uk
url: www.lamp.ac.uk/library
Systems Librarian Ms Miriam Perrett MA DipLib (e-mail: m.perrett@lamp.ac.uk)
Library Administrator Ms Jennie Bracher (e-mail: j.bracher@lamp.ac.uk)

UNIVERSITY OF WALES NEWPORT

(formerly University of Wales College, Newport)

Library and Information Services, University of Wales Newport, Caerleon Campus, PO
Box 179, Newport, Gwent NP18 3YG

☎(01633) 432652
Fax (01633) 432920
e-mail: lis@newport.ac.uk
url: http://lis.newport.ac.uk
Director of Library and Information Services Mrs Janet Peters BA MLS MCLIP ILTM
(e-mail: janet.peters@newport.ac.uk)

Campus libraries
▶ Caerleon Campus, University of Wales Newport, PO Box 179, Newport, Gwent
NP18 3YG
☎(01633) 432294
Head of Library Services Mrs Lesley May BA DipLib MCLIP PGCE(FE) ILTM (e-mail:
lesley.may@newport.ac.uk)
▶ Allt-yr-yn Campus, University of Wales Newport, PO Box 180, Newport, Gwent
NP20 5XR
☎(01633) 432310
Quality Manager Ms Dawne Leatherdale MBA MCLIP (e-mail:
dawne.leatherdale@newport.ac.uk)

UNIVERSITY OF WALES SWANSEA

Library and Information Centre, University of Wales Swansea, Singleton Park, Swansea
SA2 8PP
☎(01792) 295697 (enquiries), (01792) 295175 (administration)
Fax (01792) 295851
e-mail: library@swansea.ac.uk
url: www.swan.ac.uk/lis/index.htm
Director of Library and Information Services Christopher West MA BA MCLIP

Branch libraries
▶ Education Library, University of Wales Swansea, Hendrefoelan House, Gower Road,
Swansea SA2 7NB
☎(01792) 518659
e-mail: edmail@swansea.ac.uk
Branch Librarian Ms Madeleine M Rogerson BA DipLib PGCE(FE)
▶ Natural Sciences Library, University of Wales Swansea, Singleton Park, Swansea SA2 8PP
☎(01792) 295024
e-mail: nslmail@swansea.ac.uk
Science and Engineering Librarian Alasdair B Montgomery BSc DipLib MCLIP
▶ Nursing Library, University of Wales Swansea, Morriston Hospital, Morriston, Swansea
SA6 6NL
☎(01792) 703767
e-mail: s.m.storey@swansea.ac.uk
Health and Clinical Sciences Librarian Ms Lori D Havard MLS BA
▶ South Wales Miners' Library, University of Wales Swansea, Hendrefoelan House, Gower
Road, Swansea SA2 7NB
☎(01792) 518603

e-mail: miners@swansea.ac.uk
Branch Librarian Ms Siân F Williams BSc MCLIP

UNIVERSITY OF WARWICK

Library, University of Warwick, Gibbet Hill Road, Coventry CV4 7AL
☎024 7652 4103
Fax 024 7652 4211
e-mail: library@warwick.ac.uk
url: library.warwick.ac.uk
Librarian Ms Anne Bell BA MA MCLIP

UNIVERSITY OF THE WEST OF ENGLAND, BRISTOL

Library Services, University of the West of England, Bristol, Frenchay Campus,
Coldharbour Lane, Bristol BS16 1QY
☎0117 328 2576 (enquiries), 0117 328 2404 (administration)
Fax 0117 328 2407
url: www.uwe.ac.uk/library
Head of Library Services Mrs Cathy Rex BSc DMS MAML MCLIP

UNIVERSITY OF WESTMINSTER

Information Systems and Library Services, University of Westminster, 115 New Cavendish
Street, London W1W 6UW
☎020 7911 5095
Fax 020 7911 5093
url: www.wmin.ac.uk
Director of Information Systems and Library Services (ISLS) Ms Suzanne Enright BA
DipLib MCLIP (e-mail: s.enright@wmin.ac.uk)

Campus libraries

▶ Cavendish Campus Library, University of Westminster, 115 New Cavendish Street,
London W1W 6UW
☎020 7911 5000 ext 3613
Fax 020 7911 5871
Library Manager Ms Ann Sainsbury BA MCLIP (e-mail: a.sainsbury@wmin.ac.uk)
▶ Harrow LRC, Harrow Campus, University of Westminster, Watford Road, Northwick
Park, Harrow, Middlesex HA1 3TP
☎020 7911 5000 ext 4664
Fax 020 7911 5952
Library Manager Ms Carole Symes BA MCLIP (e-mail: c.symes@wmin.ac.uk)
▶ Marylebone Campus Library, University of Westminster, 35 Marylebone Road, London
NW1 5LS
☎020 7911 5000 ext 3212
Fax 020 7911 5058

Library Manager Ms Jane Harrington BA MLib MCLIP (e-mail: j.harrington@wmin.ac.uk)

▶ Regent Campus Library, University of Westminster, 4-12 Little Titchfield Street, London WIW 7UW
☎020 7911 5000 ext 2537
Fax 020 7911 5846
Library Manager Ms Elaine Salter BA DipLib MLib (e-mail: e.salter@wmin.ac.uk)

▶ University Archives, University of Westminster, Regent Campus, 4-12 Little Titchfield Street, London WIW 7UW
☎020 7911 5000 ext 2524
Fax 020 7911 5846
Archivist Ms Brenda Weeden MA MSc DipArchAdmin (e-mail: b.c.weeden@wmin.ac.uk)

WIMBLEDON SCHOOL OF ART

Library, Wimbledon School of Art, Merton Hall Road, London SW19 3QA
☎020 8408 5027 (enquiries)
Fax 020 8408 5050
url: www.wimbledon.ac.uk/low/resource/resource.html
Head of Learning Resources Peter Jennett MA MCLIP (e-mail: pjennett@wimbledon.ac.uk)
Librarian Ms Helen Davies BA(Hons) MCLIP (e-mail: hdavies@wimbledon.ac.uk)
Assistant Librarian Peter Crollie BA(Hons) (e-mail: pcrollie@wimbledon.ac.uk)

UNIVERSITY COLLEGE WINCHESTER

(formerly King Alfred's College, Winchester)

Library, University College Winchester, Sparkford Road, Winchester, Hants SO22 4NR
☎(01962) 827306
Fax (01962) 827443
url: www.winchester.ac.uk/library
Librarian David Farley BA(Hons) CertMan(OU) MCLIP (01962 827229; e-mail: david.farley@winchester.ac.uk)
Deputy Librarian Ms Liz Fletcher BA(Hons) MA (01962 827374; e-mail: liz.fletcher@winchester.ac.uk)
School Resources Librarian Ms Sybil Bunn BA MCLIP (e-mail: sybil.bunn@winchester.ac.uk)

(Subject to approval, University College Winchester will become the University of Winchester in Autumn 2005)

UNIVERSITY OF WOLVERHAMPTON

Harrison Learning Centre, University of Wolverhampton, St Peter's Square, Wolverhampton WVI IRH
☎(01902) 322300 (enquiries), 01902 322302 (administration)
Fax (01902) 322668

e-mail: lib@wlv.ac.uk
Director of Learning Centres Ms Mary Heaney BA DipLib MCLIP FRSA MILTHE
Assistant Director of Learning Centres (Resources) Ms Fiona Mill MA DipLib
Assistant Director of Learning Centres (Operations) Clive Evans MCLIP MLS

Site libraries

▶ Compton Learning Centre, University of Wolverhampton, Compton Road West,
Wolverhampton WV3 9DX
☎(01902) 323642
Fax (01902) 323702
Learning Centre Manager Mrs Linda Thomas MCLIP

▶ Harrison Learning Centre, University of Wolverhampton, St Peter's Square,
Wolverhampton WV1 1RH
☎(01902) 322300
Fax (01902) 322194
Learning Centre Manager Mrs Irene Ordidge BSc PGDipLib

▶ Telford Learning Centre, University of Wolverhampton, Old Shifnal Road, Priorslee,
Telford, Shropshire TF2 9NT
☎(01902) 323983
Fax (01902) 323985
Learning Centre Manager David W Clare BA MCLIP

▶ Walsall Learning Centre, University of Wolverhampton, Gorway, Walsall, West Midlands
WS1 3BD
☎(01902) 323275
Fax (01902) 323079
Learning Centre Manager Mrs Gill Hughes BLib MCLIP

School of Health site library

▶ Burton Learning Centre, University of Wolverhampton, Burton Nurse Education
Centre, Belvedere Road, Burton upon Trent, Staffs DE13 0RB
☎(01283) 566333 ext 2217/2237
Fax (01283) 515978
Site Librarian Ms Liz Watson BA(Hons) PGDipLib MCLIP

UNIVERSITY COLLEGE WORCESTER

Peirson Library, University College Worcester, Peirson Building, Henwick Grove,
Worcester WR2 6AJ
☎(01905) 855341 (enquiries), (01905) 855338 (administration)
Fax (01905) 855132
url: www2.worc.ac.uk/ils/
Director of Information and Learning Services Ms Anne Hannaford BA(Hons) DipLib
(e-mail: a.hannaford@worc.ac.uk)
Issue Desk Manager Ms Lissa O'Grady (e-mail: l.o'grady@worc.ac.uk)

WRITTLE COLLEGE

Library, Writtle College, Chelmsford, Essex CM1 3RR

☎(01245) 424245
Fax (01245) 420456
e-mail: library@writtle.ac.uk
url: www.writtle.ac.uk
Head of Learning Information Services Mrs R M Hewings BSc(Econ) DMS DipLib
MCLIP (ext 26009; e-mail: rmh@writtle.ac.uk)
Subject Librarian (Science) Ms J Lamb BA(Hons) DipLib MCLIP (ext 26008; e-mail:
jl@writtle.ac.uk)
Subject Librarian (Business and Leisure Management) Mrs J V Scully BA MCLIP
(ext 26008; e-mail: jvs@writtle.ac.uk)

YORK ST JOHN COLLEGE

Library and Information Services, York St John College, Fountains Learning Centre, Lord
Mayor's Walk, York YO31 7EX
☎(01904) 716700
Fax (01904) 716324
e-mail: library@yorksj.ac.uk
url: www.yorksj.ac.uk/library/learningcent/
College Librarian Tony Chalcraft BA MA MCLIP (01904 716701; e-mail:
a.chalcraft@yorksj.ac.uk)
Deputy College Librarian Ms Helen Westmancoat BA MCLIP (e-mail:
h.westmancoat@yorksj.ac.uk)
Academic Liaison Librarians Ms Jane Munks BA MCLIP (e-mail: j.munks@yorksj.ac.uk),
John Hagart BA MCLIP (e-mail: j.hagart@yorksj.ac.uk), Ms Fiona Ware BA MCLIP (e-mail:
f.ware@yorksj.ac.uk), Ms Lottie Alexander BA (e-mail: l.alexander@yorksj.ac.uk)
Acquisitions Librarian Bryan Jones BA (e-mail: b.jones@yorksj.ac.uk)
Special Collections Librarian Roger Wolfe BA (e-mail: r.wolfe@yorksj.ac.uk)
Database Librarian Ms Ruth Mardall BA MA (e-mail: r.mardall2@yorksj.ac.uk)

UNIVERSITY OF YORK

J B Morrell and Raymond Burton Libraries, University of York, Heslington, York
YO10 5DD
☎(01904) 433865 (enquiries), (01904) 433863 (administration)
Fax (01904) 433866
e-mail: lib-enquiry@york.ac.uk
url: www.york.ac.uk/services/library/
University Librarian Ms Elizabeth Heaps BA MA DipLib (e-mail: aemh1@york.ac.uk)

Branch/department libraries

▶ King's Manor Library, University of York, The King's Manor, York YO1 7EP
☎(01904) 433969
Fax (01904) 433949
Librarian Ms Pat Haywood BA MA (e-mail: ph16@york.ac.uk)
▶ Library and Information Service, University of York, The Strayside Education Centre,
Harrogate District Hospital, Lancaster Park Road, Harrogate, Yorkshire HG2 7SX
☎(01423) 553104

e-mail: hslibhg@york.ac.uk
Manager of Library and Information Service Mrs Gillian Jarrett BA (e-mail: gj7@york.ac.uk)

Selected Government, National and Special Libraries in the United Kingdom

ACAS

Information Centre, ACAS, Brandon House, 180 Borough High Street, London SE1 1LW
☎020 7210 3911 (enquiries)
Fax 020 7210 3615
url: www.acas.org.uk
Information Centre Manager Ms Alison Matthews MA (020 7210 3917; e-mail:
amatthews@acas.org.uk)
Specialism(s): Advisory, conciliation and arbitration service; UK employment relations

ADVISORY, CONCILIATION AND ARBITRATION SERVICE *see* ACAS

ADVOCATES LIBRARY

Advocates Library, Parliament House, Edinburgh EH1 1RF
☎0131 260 5683 (enquiries), 0131 260 5637 (Librarian)
Fax 0131 260 5663 (9am–5pm weekdays)
url: www.advocates.org.uk
Librarian Ms Andrea Longson BSc DipLib (e-mail: andrea.longson@advocates.org.uk)
Open to members only. Non-members may access stock at the National Library of
Scotland.
Specialism(s): Law

ALDERSHOT MILITARY MUSEUM

Military Museum and Archive, Aldershot Military Museum, Evelyn Woods Road, Queens
Avenue, Aldershot, Hants GU11 2LG
☎(01252) 314598
Fax (01252) 342942
url: www.hants.gov.uk/museum/aldershot
Curator Ms Sally Day BA MCLIP (e-mail: sally.1.day@hants.gov.uk)
(Accessible to enquirers by appointment)
Specialism(s): Military history; Local history

AMBLESIDE'S ARMITT MUSEUM AND LIBRARY

Ambleside's Armitt Museum and Library, Rydal Road, Ambleside, Cumbria LA22 9BL
☎(01539) 431212
Fax (01539) 431313
e-mail: info@armitt.com
url: www.armitt.com
Curator Ms Michelle Kelly BA
Specialism(s): Specialist Lake District collection (literature, topography, natural history);
Cumbria; Mountaineering; Kurt Schwitters; Beatrix Potter

AMBLESS SOCIETY LIBRARY

Ambless Society Library, Shalom House, Lower Celtic Park, Enniskillen, Co Fermanagh
BT74 6HP
☎028 6632 0320; Ambless Accident Supportline: 028 6632 0321 (phone/fax)
Fax 028 6632 0320
url: www.ukselfhelp.info.ambless
Librarian John Wood
Specialism(s): Private research library working closely with the charity Ambless, which
offers care and support to accident sufferers and their families

AMERICAN MUSEUM IN BRITAIN

Library, American Museum in Britain, Claverton Manor, Bath BA2 7BD
☎(01225) 823016
Fax (01225) 469160
url: www.americanmuseum.org
Librarian Mrs Anne Armitage BA (e-mail: anne.armitage@americanmuseum.org)
Specialism(s): American history and decorative arts; Religions, e.g. Shakers; North American
Indians

ASSOCIATION OF COMMONWEALTH UNIVERSITIES

Reference Library, Association of Commonwealth Universities, John Foster House, 36
Gordon Square, London WC1H 0PF
☎020 7380 6700
Fax 020 7387 2655
e-mail: info@acu.ac.uk
url: www.acu.ac.uk
Librarian N Mulhern
Specialism(s): Higher Education in the Commonwealth

BABRAHAM INSTITUTE

Library, The Babraham Institute, Babraham Research Campus, Cambridge CB2 4AT
☎(01223) 496214 (enquiries)
Fax (01223) 496027
e-mail: babraham.library@bbsrc.ac.uk
url: www.babraham.ac.uk
Librarian Miss Jennifer R Maddock BA DipLib MCLIP (01223 496235; e-mail:
jennifer.maddock@bbsrc.ac.uk)
Library Assistants Ms Suzanne Morley BA MA, Mrs Arwen E Spicer BA
Specialism(s): Journals in cell biology, Genetics, Immunology, Molecular biology and
Neuroscience

BANK OF ENGLAND

Information Centre, Bank of England, Threadneedle Street, London EC2R 8AH
☎020 7601 4715 (enquiries), 020 7601 4668 (administration)
Fax 020 7601 4356
e-mail: informationcentre@bankofengland.co.uk
url: www.bankofengland.co.uk
Information Centre Manager Ms Penny Hope BA MA MSc DipLib MCLIP
Specialism(s): Economics; Central banking

BG GROUP PLC

Information Centre, BG Group plc, Faraday Building 2, 100 Thames Valley Park Drive,
Reading RG6 1PT
☎(0118) 929 2496 (enquiries and administration)
Fax (0118) 929 2414
url: www.bg-group.com
Information Analysts P Cronin (0118 929 2496; e-mail: padraig.cronin@bg-group.com),
D Freemantle (0118 929 2497; e-mail: david.freemantle@bg-group.com)
Specialism(s): Reference collection, mainly energy industry

BIRMINGHAM AND MIDLAND INSTITUTE

The Birmingham Library, Birmingham and Midland Institute, 9 Margaret Street, Birmingham
B3 3BS
☎0121 236 3591
Fax 0121 212 4577
e-mail: admin@bmi.org.uk
url: www.bmi.org.uk
Librarian Mrs Sheila Utley BA
(Private members' library)
Specialism(s): History; Literature; Natural history; Science; Travel; Fiction; Biography; Music

BISHOPSGATE INSTITUTE

Bishopsgate Library, Bishopsgate Institute, 230 Bishopsgate, London EC2M 4QH
☎020 7392 9270
Fax 020 7392 9275
e-mail: library@bishopsgate.org.uk
url: www.bishopsgate.org.uk
Library Manager Jeff Abbott BA(Hons)
Specialism(s): London history and topography; Labour history; 19thC trades union history;
Co-operative movement; Freethought movement

BOOKTRUST

Children's Reference Library, Booktrust, Book House, 45 East Hill, London SW18 2QZ
☎020 8516 2977

Fax 020 8516 2978
e-mail: ed@booktrust.org.uk
url: www.booktrust.org.uk; www.booktrusted.com
Children's Librarian Vacant
(Note: the collection is to be relocated during 2005/6. For further information see website)

BRITANNIA ROYAL NAVAL COLLEGE

College Library, Britannia Royal Naval College, Dartmouth, Devon TQ6 0HJ
☎(01803) 677279/677278
Fax (01803) 677015
url: www.brnc.org.uk
Librarian Richard Kennell MCLIP (e-mail: r.kennell@brnc.ac.uk)
Assistant Librarian Vacant
(Prior appointment necessary)
Specialism(s): Strategic studies; Naval history; Marine environment

BRITISH ANTARCTIC SURVEY

Library, British Antarctic Survey, High Cross, Madingley Road, Cambridge CB3 0ET
☎(01223) 221617
Fax (01223) 362616
url: www.antarctica.ac.uk
Librarian Ms Christine Phillips MA MCLIP (e-mail: cmp@bas.ac.uk)
Specialism(s): Geology; Geophysics; Glaciology; Climatology; Upper atmosphere physics;
Marine and terrestrial biology (all with accent on Antarctic region)

BRITISH BROADCASTING CORPORATION

BBC Information and Archives, British Broadcasting Corporation, 3rd Floor, Broadcast
Centre, 201 Wood Lane, London W12 7TP
☎020 8008 2288
Fax 020 8008 2272
e-mail: Research-Central@bbc.co.uk
url: www.bbcresearchcentral.com
Head of Media Asset Management Ms Sarah Hayes
Business Development Manager, Information and Archives Guy Strickland

BRITISH COUNCIL

Knowledge and Information Services, British Council, Bridgewater House, 58 Whitworth
Street, Manchester M1 6BB
☎0161 957 7755 (enquiries), 0161 957 7170 (administration)
Fax 0161 957 7762 (enquiries), 0161 957 7168 (administration)
e-mail: general.enquiries@britishcouncil.org
url: www.britishcouncil.org
Director Ms Neeta Patel (e-mail: neeta.patel@britishcouncil.org)

Senior Management Team
Director Knowledge and Information Services Operations Ms Judy Ugonna (e-mail: judy.ugonna@britishcouncil.org)
Director Knowledge Management Ms Bonnie Cheuk (e-mail: bonnie.cheuk@britishcouncil.org)
Director Knowledge Resources David Skinner (e-mail: david.skinner@britishcouncil.org)

British Council enquiries (e-mail: general.enquiries@britishcouncil.org)
(For details of British Council information services in 110 countries see website: www.britishcouncil.org)

BRITISH DENTAL ASSOCIATION

BDA Information Centre, British Dental Association, 64 Wimpole Street, London W1G 8YS
☎020 7563 4545
Fax 020 7935 6492
e-mail: infocentre@bda.org
url: www.bda.org.uk
Head of Library Services R Farbey BA DipLib MCLIP (e-mail: r.farbey@bda.org)

BRITISH EMPIRE AND COMMONWEALTH MUSEUM

British Empire and Commonwealth Museum, Clock Tower Yard, Temple Meads, Bristol
BS1 6QH
☎0117 925 4980
Fax 0117 925 4983
e-mail: admin@empiremuseum.co.uk
url: www.empiremuseum.co.uk
Director Dr Gareth Griffiths
Collections Development Officer Dr John McAleer
Specialism(s): Commonwealth literature, archives and resources; Colonial and Empire history

BRITISH FILM INSTITUTE

BFI National Library, British Film Institute, 21 Stephen Street, London W1T 1LN
☎020 7255 1444 (enquiries), ext 2264 (administration)
Fax 020 7436 2338
e-mail: library@bfi.org.uk
url: www.bfi.org.uk/nationallibrary/
Head of Collections and Information Darren Long
Deputy Head (User Services) David Sharp BA MCLIP
Deputy Head (Technical Services) Stephen Pearson BA MLS CertEd MCLIP
(Incorporates Independent Television Commission Library collections)
Specialism(s): the moving image (national film and television collection and archives)

BRITISH GEOLOGICAL SURVEY

Library and Information Services, British Geological Survey, Kingsley Dunham Centre, Keyworth, Notts NG12 5GG
☎0115 936 3205 (enquiries), 0115 936 3472 (Chief Librarian)
Fax (0115 936 3015
e-mail: libuser@bgs.ac.uk
url: www.bgs.org.uk
Chief Librarian Ken Hollywood BA(Hons) DipLib MSc MCLIP

Branch libraries
▶ Library, British Geological Survey, Scottish Regional Office, Murchison House, West Mains Road, Edinburgh EH9 3LA
☎0131 667 1000, 0131 650 0322 (direct dial)
Fax 0131 668 2683
e-mail: librarymh@bgs.ac.uk
Site Librarian Bob McIntosh BSc DipLib
▶ London Information Office, British Geological Survey, Natural History Museum, Exhibition Road, South Kensington, London SW7 2DE
☎020 7589 4090
Fax 020 7584 8270
e-mail: bgslondon@bgs.ac.uk
Officer-in-Charge Ms Clare Tombleson (e-mail: cto@bgs.ac.uk)

BRITISH HOROLOGICAL INSTITUTE

Library, British Horological Institute, Upton Hall, Upton, Newark, Notts NG23 5TE
☎(01636) 813795
Fax (01636) 812258
e-mail: services@bhi.co.uk; clocks@bhi.co.uk
url: www.bhi.co.uk
Librarian and Curator Viscount Alan Midleton FBHI

BRITISH LIBRARY

British Library, 96 Euston Road, London NW1 2DB
☎020 7412 7332 (general and visitor enquiries), 0870 444 1500 (switchboard)
url: www.bl.uk
Chairman Lord Eatwell
Chief Executive Mrs Lynne Brindley
Acting Director of Finance and Corporate Resources Robert Kirton
Director of Operations and Services Ms Natalie Ceeney
Director of Scholarship and Collections Dr Clive Field
Director of Strategic Marketing and Communications Ms Jill Finney
Director of e-Strategy and Information Systems Richard Boulderstone

Enquiry points
The following are based at 96 Euston Road, London NW1 2DB. Admission to the Library's

London reading rooms is by pass only. Most of the Library's catalogues are available on its website, www.bl.uk. For general enquiries about the collection, reader services and advance reservations, tel: 020 7412 7676, e-mail: reader-services-enquiries@bl.uk

Other useful numbers/e-mail addresses
Reader Admissions (advice on who may use the Library and how to apply for a reader's pass)
☎020 7412 7677, e-mail: Reader-Admissions@bl.uk
Visitor Services (for general enquiries and details of exhibitions, events)
☎020 7412 7332, e-mail: Visitor-Services@bl.uk

Northern Site, British Library, Boston Spa, Wetherby, West Yorks LS23 7BQ
☎0870 444 1500
e-mail: dsc-customer-services@bl.uk

St Pancras Reading Rooms
Librarianship and Information Science Service (LIS)
☎020 7412 7676; e-mail: lis@bl.uk
Maps
☎020 7412 7702; e-mail: maps@bl.uk
Music Collections
☎020 7412 7772; e-mail: music-collections@bl.uk
Sound Archive
☎020 7412 7440; e-mail: nsa@bl.uk
Asia, Pacific and Africa Collections (formerly Oriental and India Office Collections)
☎020 7412 7873; e-mail: oioc-enquiries@bl.uk
Philatelic
☎020 7412 7635; e-mail: philatelic@bl.uk
Rare Book Collections
☎020 7412 7676; e-mail: rare-books@bl.uk
Science, Technology and Medicine Information
☎020 7412 7676; e-mail: scitech@bl.uk
Manuscripts
☎020 7412 7513; e-mail: mss@bl.uk

Other Reading Rooms
British Library Newspapers, Colindale Avenue, London NW9 5HE
☎020 7412 7353/7356; e-mail: newspaper@bl.uk

For material in Document Supply
Boston Spa, Wetherby, West Yorks LS23 7BQ
☎(01937) 546060; e-mail: dsc-customer-services@bl.uk

BRITISH MEDICAL ASSOCIATION

BMA Library, British Medical Association, BMA House, Tavistock Square, London WC1H 9JP
☎020 7383 6625

Fax 020 7388 2544
e-mail: bma-library@bma.org.uk/library
url: www.bma.org.uk/library
Librarian Ms Jane Smith BA(Hons)

BRITISH MUSEUM

Anthropology Library, Centre for Anthropology, British Museum, Great Russell Street,
London WC1B 3DG
☎020 7323 8031
Fax 020 7323 8049
e-mail: anthropologylibrary@thebritishmuseum.ac.uk
Senior Librarian Ms Sheila Mackie BA DipEd DipLib MCLIP (020 7323 8069; e-mail:
smackie@thebritishmuseum.ac.uk)
(The Anthropology Library incorporates the former library of the Royal Anthropological
Institute and covers every aspect of anthropology – cultural anthropology (with an emphasis on material culture), archaeology, some biological anthropology and linguistics and such
related fields as history and travel. It also houses a Pictorial Collection containing about
150,000 items. The Library is open to both researchers and the public without appointment)

Paul Hamlyn Library, British Museum, Great Russell Street, London WC1B 3DG
☎020 7323 8838
e-mail: readingroom@thebritishmuseum.ac.uk
url: www.thebritishmuseum.ac.uk
The Fleming Librarian Ms Pam Smith (020 7323 8907; e-mail:
psmith@thebritishmuseum.ac.uk)
(The Paul Hamlyn Library is an open access public reference library on subjects relating to
the Museum's collections, e.g. ancient history, archaeology, art history, museology. The
Library is freely open to the public without any membership or prior appointment.)

BRITISH NATIONAL SPACE CENTRE

Information Unit, British National Space Centre, 151 Buckingham Palace Road, London
SW1W 9SS
☎020 7215 0901 (enquiries)
Fax 020 7215 0936
e-mail: bnscinfo@bnsc.gsi.gov.uk
url: www.bnsc.gov.uk
Librarian Stuart Grayson BSc DipLib
Specialism(s): Space exploration, science and earth observation to support UK civil space
activity

BRITISH PSYCHOLOGICAL SOCIETY

Psychology Library, British Psychological Society, Senate House Library, University of
London, Malet Street, London WC1E 7HU
☎020 7862 8451/8461

Fax 020 7862 8480
e-mail: enquiries@shl.lon.ac.uk
url: www.shl.lon.ac.uk
Psychology Librarian, University of London Library Mrs Susan E Tarrant BA MCLIP
(The BPS collection of periodicals is held at the Psychology Library and amalgamated with
the University of London Library collection of psychology periodicals.)

BRITISH STANDARDS INSTITUTION

Library, British Standards Institution, 389 Chiswick High Road, London W4 4AL
☎020 8996 7004
Fax 020 8996 7005
e-mail: library@bsi-global.com
url: www.bsi-global.com
Library Manager Ms Mary Yates BSc DipLib (020 8996 7041)
(The Library may be used for reference free of charge by members and students. For non-
members there is a charge)
Specialism(s): Standards; Technical regulations; Quality and environmental management

BRITISH UNIVERSITIES FILM & VIDEO COUNCIL

Information Service, British Universities Film & Video Council, 77 Wells Street, London
WIT 3QJ
☎020 7393 1500
Fax 020 7393 1555
e-mail: ask@bufvc.ac.uk
url: www.bufvc.ac.uk
Head of Information Luke McKernan PhD
Specialism(s): Film; Television; Radio

THE BRITTEN-PEARS LIBRARY

The Britten-Pears Library, The Red House, Golf Lane, Aldeburgh, Suffolk IP15 5PZ
☎(01728) 451700
Fax (01728) 453076
e-mail: library@brittenpears.org
url: www.brittenpears.org
Librarian Dr Christopher Grogan BMus PhD DipLIS (01728 451707)

BROMLEY HOUSE LIBRARY

Bromley House Library, Bromley House, Angel Row, Nottingham NG1 6HL
☎0115 947 3134
e-mail: nsl@bromho.freeserve.co.uk
Librarian Mrs Carol Allison BSc DipLib MA MCLIP
(Subscription library available to the public for reference purposes only, by prior appointment)

CANCER RESEARCH UK

Library and Information Services, Cancer Research UK, 44 Lincoln's Inn Fields, London
WC2A 3PX
☎020 7269 3206 (enquiries), 020 7269 2868 (administration)
Fax 020 7269 3084
e-mail: lib.info@cancer.org.uk
url: www.science.cancerresearchuk.org/; www.cancerresearchuk.org/
LIS Resources Manager Chris Wilson BA DipLib (e-mail: chris.wilson@cancer.org.uk)

CANCERBACUP

Library and Information Service, CancerBacup, 3 Bath Place, Rivington Street, London
EC2A 3JR
☎020 7696 9003
Fax 020 7696 9002
url: www.cancerbacup.org.uk
Library and Information Service Manager Ms Fiona McLean (e-mail:
fmclean@cancerbacup.org))

CANTERBURY CATHEDRAL

Cathedral Library, Canterbury Cathedral, The Precincts, Canterbury, Kent CT1 2EH
☎(01227) 865287
e-mail: library@canterbury-cathedral.org
url: www.canterbury-cathedral.org/library.html
Cathedral Librarian K M C O'Sullivan MA MSc(Econ) MCLIP (e-mail:
keith@canterbury-cathedral.org)
Specialism(s): Theology; Liturgy; Church history; Local (Kentish) history; Anti-slavery movement; Catholic and anti-Catholic history; Natural history

CCLRC (COUNCIL FOR THE CENTRAL LABORATORY OF THE RESEARCH COUNCILS)

Chadwick Library, CCLRC (Council for the Central Laboratory of the Research Councils),
Daresbury Laboratory, Daresbury, Warrington, Cheshire WA4 4AD
☎(01925) 603397 (enquiries)
Fax (01925) 603779
e-mail: library@dl.ac.uk
url: www.cclrc.ac.uk/Activity/ACTIVITY=LIS
Library Services Development Manager, CCLRC Mrs Debbie Franks BSc MCLIP
(01925 603189)

Library, CCLRC (Council for the Central Laboratory of the Research Councils), Rutherford
Appleton Laboratory, Chilton, Didcot, Oxon OX11 0QX
☎(01235) 445384 (general enquiries)
Fax (01235) 446403

e-mail: library@rl.ac.uk
url: www.cclrc.ac.uk/Activity/ACTIVITY=LIS
Library Systems Development Manager, CCLRC Mrs Catherine Jones BSc MCLIP
(01235 445402)

CENTRAL POLICE TRAINING AND DEVELOPMENT AUTHORITY

National Police Library, Central Police Training and Development Authority, Centrex
Bramshill, Bramshill, Hook, Hants RG27 0JW
☎(01256) 602650 (enquiries), (01256) 602100 (main switchboard)
Fax (01256) 602285
e-mail: library@centrex.pnn.police.uk
url: www.centrex.police.uk
Chief Librarian Mrs Sue King MCLIP

CENTRE FOR ECOLOGY AND HYDROLOGY

Library, Centre for Ecology and Hydrology, Centre for Ecology and Hydrology Edinburgh,
Bush Estate, Penicuik, Midlothian EH26 0QB
☎0131 445 4343
Fax 0131 445 3943
url: http://library.ceh.ac.uk
Librarian and Head of CEH Library Service Steve Prince BSc DipLib MCLIP (e-mail:
sjpr@ceh.ac.uk)

Research station libraries
▶ Library, Centre for Ecology and Hydrology Banchory, Centre for Ecology and
Hydrology, Hill of Brathens, Glassel, Banchory, Kincardineshire AB31 4BY
☎(01330) 826300
Fax (01330) 823303
Librarian Ms Alison Odds (e-mail: ao@ceh.ac.uk)
▶ Library, Centre for Ecology and Hydrology Bangor, Centre for Ecology and Hydrology,
Orton Building, University of Wales, Deiniol Road, Bangor, Gwynedd LL57 2UP
☎(01248) 370045
Fax (01248) 355365
Librarian Ms Jackie Cooper (e-mail: jrco@ceh.ac.uk)
▶ Library, Centre for Ecology and Hydrology Dorset, Centre for Ecology and Hydrology,
Winfrith Technology Centre, Winfrith Newburgh, Dorchester, Dorset DT2 8ZD
☎(01305) 213550
Fax (01305) 213600
Librarian Ms Stephanie Smith (e-mail: ssmi@ceh.ac.uk)
▶ Library, Centre for Ecology and Hydrology Lancaster, Centre for Ecology and
Hydrology, Lancaster Environment Centre, Library Avenue, Bailrigg, Lancaster LA1 4AP
☎(01524) 595800
Fax (01524) 61536
Librarian Ian McCulloch (e-mail: idm@ceh.ac.uk)

▶ Library, Centre for Ecology and Hydrology Monks Wood, Centre for Ecology and Hydrology, Abbots Ripton, Huntingdon, Cambs PE28 2LS
☎(01487) 773381
Fax (01487) 773467
Librarian Ms Pam Moorhouse (e-mail: pmo@ceh.ac.uk)

▶ Library, Centre for Ecology and Hydrology Oxford, Centre for Ecology and Hydrology, Mansfield Road, Oxford OX1 3SR
☎(01865) 281630
Fax (01865) 281696
Librarian Christopher Wilson (e-mail: cjw@ceh.ac.uk)

▶ Library, Centre for Ecology and Hydrology Wallingford, Centre for Ecology and Hydrology, Maclean Building, Crowmarsh Gifford, Wallingford, Oxon OX10 8BB
☎(01491) 838800
Fax (01491) 692424
Librarian Adrian Smith BSc AIMgt MCLIP (e-mail: apsm@ceh.ac.uk)
Specialism(s): Enviroment (esp. terrestrial and freshwater sciences)

CENTRE FOR POLICY ON AGEING

Library, Centre for Policy on Ageing, 25–31 Ironmonger Row, London EC1V 3QP
☎020 7553 6500
Fax 020 7553 6501
e-mail: cpa@cpa.org.uk
url: www.cpa.org.uk
Director Ms Gillian Crosby BA MCLIP (e-mail: gcrosby@cpa.org.uk)
Librarian Ms Ruth Hayes BA MCLIP
Information Officer Ms Kate Jones BA MCLIP

THE CHARTERED INSTITUTE OF LOGISTICS AND TRANSPORT IN THE UK

(formerly The Chartered Institute of Transport and Logistics)

Logistics and Transport Centre, The Chartered Institute of Logistics and Transport in the UK, Earlstrees Court, Earlstrees Road, Corby, Northants NN17 4AX
☎(01536) 740112 or 740139 (library), (01536) 740100 (reception)
Fax (01536) 740102 (FAO Knowledge Centre Manager)
url: www.ciltuk.org.uk
Knowledge Centre Manager Peter Huggins MA (e-mail: peter.huggins@ciltuk.org.uk)
Knowledge Centre Assistant Ms Lynn Mentiply (e-mail: lynn.mentiply@ciltuk.org.uk)
(Access: free to Institute members and full-time students; a charge is made for non-member usage. London Reading Room open to members only – for details contact The Knowledge Centre Manager)
Specialism(s): Logistics; Supply-chain; Passenger transport

CHARTERED INSTITUTE OF MANAGEMENT ACCOUNTANTS (CIMA)

Technical Information Service, Chartered Institute of Management Accountants (CIMA), 26 Chapter Street, London SW1P 4NP
☎020 7663 5441
Fax 020 8849 2464
e-mail: tis@cimaglobal.com
url: www.cimaglobal.com
Information Manager Mrs Denise Metcalf BSc(Hons)
(Please note that this is an information service for CIMA members only)

CHARTERED INSTITUTE OF PERSONNEL AND DEVELOPMENT

Library and Information Services, Chartered Institute of Personnel and Development, 151 The Broadway, London SW19 1JQ
☎020 8612 6210 (enquiries), 020 8612 6641 (administration)
Fax 020 8612 6232
e-mail: lis@cipd.co.uk
url: www.cipd.co.uk
Head of Library and Information Services Ms Barbara Salmon

CHARTERED INSURANCE INSTITUTE

CII Information Services, Chartered Insurance Institute, 20 Aldermanbury, London EC2V 7HY
☎020 7417 4415/4416
Fax 020 7972 0110
e-mail: is@cii.co.uk
url: www.cii.co.uk/is
Head of Information Services Robert Cunnew BA FCLIP
Specialism(s): Insurance, risk and related financial services

CHARTERED MANAGEMENT INSTITUTE

Management Information Centre, Chartered Management Institute, Management House, Cottingham Road, Corby, Northants NN17 1TT
☎(01536) 204222 (switchboard), (01536) 207400 (enquiries)
Fax (01536) 401013
e-mail: mic.enquiries@managers.org.uk
url: www.managers.org.uk
Professional Services Manager Bob Norton BA FCLIP
(Information services, principally to Institute members)
Specialism(s): Management theory, practice and techniques

CHETHAM'S LIBRARY

Chetham's Library, Long Millgate, Manchester M3 1SB
☎0161 834 7961
Fax 0161 839 5797
e-mail: librarian@chethams.org.uk
url: www.chethams.org.uk
Chetham's Librarian Michael Powell BD PhD
Specialism(s): Rare books; Local history

CHILD ACCIDENT PREVENTION TRUST

Resource Centre, Child Accident Prevention Trust, 4th Floor, Clerk's Court, 22-26
Farringdon Lane, London EC1R 3AJ
☎020 7608 3828 (switchboard)
Fax 020 7608 3674
e-mail: safe@capt.org.uk
url: www.capt.org.uk
Information Officer Vacant

CILIP: THE CHARTERED INSTITUTE OF LIBRARY AND INFORMATION PROFESSIONALS

Information Team, CILIP: the Chartered Institute of Library and Information Professionals,
7 Ridgmount Street, London WC1E 7AE
☎020 7255 0620
Fax 020 7255 0501
e-mail: info@cilip.org.uk
url: www.cilip.org.uk
Textphone 020 7255 0505
Information Manager Ms Caroline Nolan MA MCLIP
Specialism(s): Library and information management

CILT, THE NATIONAL CENTRE FOR LANGUAGES

CILT Resources Library, CILT, the National Centre for Languages, 20 Bedfordbury, London
WC2N 4LB
☎020 7379 5110
Fax 020 7379 5082
e-mail: library@cilt.org.uk
url: www.cilt.org.uk; http://www.cilt.org.uk/libcat (library catalogue)
Librarian Michael Hammond BA MCLIP (e-mail: michael.hammond@cilt.org.uk)
Specialism(s): Language teaching methodology and materials

CIVIL AVIATION AUTHORITY

Library and Information Centre, Civil Aviation Authority, Aviation House, Gatwick Airport
South, West Sussex RH6 0YR

☎(01293) 573725
Fax (01293) 573181
e-mail: infoservices@caa.co.uk
url: www.caa.co.uk
Library Manager Ms Carol Cairns BA(Hons) DipLib MLib MCLIP (e-mail:
carol.cairnssrg@caa.co.uk)
Specialism(s): UK aviation and aviation safety

COLLEGE OF OCCUPATIONAL THERAPISTS

Library, College of Occupational Therapists, 106–114 Borough High Street, Southwark,
London SE1 1LB
☎020 7450 2303/2320/2316
Fax 020 7450 2364
e-mail: library@cot.co.uk
url: www.cot.org.uk
Librarian Ms Ann Mason BA(Hons) MCLIP
Deputy Librarian Ms Lorna Rutherford BA(Hons) PGDip

COMMONWEALTH SECRETARIAT

Library, Commonwealth Secretariat, Marlborough House, Pall Mall, London SW1Y 5HX
☎020 7747 6164
Fax 020 7747 6168
e-mail: library@commonwealth.int
url: www.thecommonwealth.org
Librarian David Blake BA DipLib MSc MCLIP (e-mail: d.blake@commonwealth.int)
Specialism(s): The Commonwealth (politics, economics, health, education, science and
gender)

COMPETITION COMMISSION

Information Centre, Competition Commission, Victoria House, Southampton Row, London
WC1B 4AD
☎020 7271 0243
Fax 020 7271 0367
e-mail: info@competition-commission.gsi.gov.uk
url: www.competition-commission.org.uk
Information Centre Manager Miss L J Fisher MA MCLIP
Press and Publicity Officer F Royle
(Open to government libraries by appointment. Not open to the public, but deals with
public telephone and written enquiries.)

CONSERVATIVE RESEARCH DEPARTMENT

Library, Conservative Research Department, Conservative Party, 25 Victoria Street,
London SW1H 0DL
☎020 7222 9000 (main)

Fax 020 7984 8273
url: www.conservatives.com
Researcher Sheridan Westlake MA(Oxon) MSc MPhil
(Not open to the public)

CORUS UK LTD, RESEARCH, DEVELOPMENT AND TECHNOLOGY

Library and Information Services, Corus UK Ltd, Research, Development and Technology, Swinden Technology Centre, Moorgate, Rotherham, South Yorks S60 3AR
☎(01709) 820166, (01642) 467144
Fax (01709) 825337
e-mail: stc.library@corusgroup.com
url: www.corusgroup.com
Manager, Customised Information Services Ms Carol Patton
Specialism(s): Steel

COUNTRYSIDE AGENCY

Library, Countryside Agency, John Dower House, Crescent Place, Cheltenham, Glos GL50 3RA
☎(01242) 533311
Fax (01242) 584270
e-mail: info@countryside.gov.uk
url: www.countryside.gov.uk
Librarian Ms Jean Bacon MSc MCLIP

COUNTRYSIDE COUNCIL FOR WALES (CYNGOR CEFN GWLAD CYMRU)

Library, Countryside Council for Wales (Cyngor Cefn Gwlad Cymru), Hafod Elfyn, Ffordd Penrhos, Bangor, Gwynedd LL57 2BQ
☎(01248) 385522
Fax (01248) 385510
e-mail: library@ccw.gov.uk
url: www.ccw.gov.uk
Librarian Ms Dwynwen Lloyd BA MCLIP

CPRE (CAMPAIGN TO PROTECT RURAL ENGLAND)

Library and Information Unit, CPRE (Campaign to Protect Rural England), 128 Southwark Street, London SE1 0SW
☎020 7981 2800
Fax 020 7981 2899
e-mail: library@cpre.org.uk

url: www.cpre.org.uk
Library and Information Services Officer Oliver Hilliam BA
Specialism(s): Planning; Environment; Transport

CROWN PROSECUTION SERVICE

Library Information Services, Crown Prosecution Service, 50 Ludgate Hill, London
EC4M 7EX
☎020 7796 8320/8364
url: www.cps.gov.uk
CPS Librarian Robert Brall BA DipLib MCLIP (e-mail: robert.brall@cps.gsi.gov.uk)

DEPARTMENT FOR CONSTITUTIONAL AFFAIRS

HQ Library, Department for Constitutional Affairs, Selborne House, 54–60 Victoria Street,
London SW1E 6QW
☎020 7210 1671/1656
Fax 020 7210 1617
e-mail: dca.library@dca.gsi.gov.uk
url: www.dca.gov.uk
Librarian Miss Christine Younger BLib MCLIP TEM
Assistant Librarians Mrs Katherine Marsterson BSc MSc, Miss Kathy Turner BSc MSc

DEPARTMENT FOR CULTURE, MEDIA AND SPORT

Information Centre, Department for Culture, Media and Sport, 2-4 Cockspur Street,
London SW1Y 5DH
☎020 7211 6200 (enquiries), 020 7211 6041 (administration)
Fax 020 7211 6032
e-mail: enquiries@culture.gov.uk
url: www.culture.gov.uk
Manager Ms Abigail Humber BA(Hons) MA MCLIP

DEPARTMENT FOR EDUCATION AND SKILLS (DFES)

Library, Department for Education and Skills (DfES), LG.01, Sanctuary Buildings, Great
Smith Street, London SW1P 3BT
☎020 7925 5040 (enquiries); 0870 000 2288 (Public Enquiry Unit)
Fax 020 7925 5085
e-mail: enquiries.library@dfes.gsi.gov.uk
url: www.dfes.gov.uk
Chief Librarian/Information Architect John Quinn (020 7925 5058; e-mail:
john.quinn@dfes.gsi.gov.uk)
Electronic Resources Senior Librarian/Information Architect Ms Gill Baker (020
7925 5451; e-mail: gill.baker@dfes.gsi.gov.uk)

Information Services Librarian (London) Ms Jane Wardlaw (020 7925 5798; e-mail: jane.wardlaw@dfes.gsi.gov.uk)

Site library

Library, Department for Education and Skills (DfES), Room E3, Moorfoot, Sheffield S1 4PQ
☎0114 259 3338 (enquiries); 0870 000 2288 (Public Enquiry Unit)
Fax 0114 259 3564
e-mail: enquiries.library@dfes.gsi.gov.uk
Deputy Chief Librarian/Information Architect Ms Julia Reed BA MA MA(InfSc) MCLIP (0114 259 3339; e-mail: julia.reed@dfes.gsi.gov.uk)
Information Services Librarian (Sheffield) Miss Helen Challinor BA(Hons) (0114 259 4450; e-mail: helen.challinor@dfes.gsi.gov.uk)
Specialism(s): Education theory and policy

DEPARTMENT FOR ENVIRONMENT, FOOD AND RURAL AFFAIRS (DEFRA)

Information Resource Centre, Department for Environment, Food and Rural Affairs (Defra), Lower Ground Floor, Ergon House, c/o Nobel House, 17 Smith Square, London SW1P 3JR
☎020 7238 6575
Fax 020 7238 6609
e-mail: defra.library@defra.gsi.gov.uk
url: www.defra.gov.uk
Senior Librarian Mark Maidment
(Visitors must give 24 hours' notice)
Specialism(s): Environment; Farming; Food; Rural issues; Agriculture

DEPARTMENT FOR INTERNATIONAL DEVELOPMENT

DFID Library, Department for International Development, Room 503, Abercrombie House, Eaglesham Road, East Kilbride, Lanarkshire G75 8EA
☎0845 300 4100 (public enquiries), (01355) 843880 (library enquiries)
Fax (01355) 843632
e-mail: library@dfid.gov.uk
url: www.dfid.gov.uk
Assistant Librarian Robert Martin

DFID Library, Department for International Development, 1 Palace Street, London SW1E 5HE
DFID Library Manager Ms Sharon Skelton

DEPARTMENT FOR REGIONAL DEVELOPMENT

Library, Department for Regional Development, Room G-40, Clarence Court, 10-18 Adelaide Street, Belfast BT2 8GB

☎028 9054 1045/6
Fax 028 9054 1081
e-mail: library@drdni.gov.uk
url: www.drdni.gov.uk
Librarian Ms Fiona Sawey BA
Assistant Librarian Ms Gillian Conroy MA(Hons) MA

DEPARTMENT FOR WORK AND PENSIONS (DWP)

Adelphi Information Centre, Department for Work and Pensions (DWP), Room 114, The
Adelphi, 1-11 John Adam Street, London WC2N 6HT
☎020 7712 2500
Fax 020 7962 8491
e-mail: library@dwp.gsi.gov.uk
url: www.dwp.gov.uk
Information Centre Team Manager Ms Melanie Harris BA(Hons) DipLib MCLIP
Information Centre Manager Ms Angela Tailby BA(Hons)
Acquisitions (Books) Librarian Philip Warnock MA
Acquisitions (Serials) Librarian Ms Vanessa Whittle BHort MLIS
Cataloguer Alan Pratt BA(Hons) DipLib
Assistant Librarians Ms Andria Lannon BA(Hons) MA DipLib MCLIP, Mrs Anoja Fernando
Intranet Senior Librarian Cliff Sheppard MSc
Information Management and Research Team Manager Ms Julia Lewis MA

Legal Information Centre, Department for Work and Pensions (DWP), 4th Floor, New
Court, 48 Carey Street, London WC2A 2LS
☎020 7412 1333
Fax 020 7412 1324
Legal Information Manager Ms Liz Murray BA DipInf MCLIP
Assistant Librarians Ms Carol Gurajena, Ms Amanda Cole

Sheffield Information Centre, Department for Work and Pensions (DWP), Porterbrook
House, 8 Pear Street, Sheffield
☎0114 259 6082
Information Centre Manager Ms Karen Gommersall

DEPARTMENT OF HEALTH

Library, Department of Health, Skipton House, 80 London Road, London SE1 6LH
☎020 7972 6541
Fax 020 7972 5976
e-mail: library.skh@dh.gsi.gov.uk (library); dhmail@dh.gsi.gov.uk (DoH)
url: www.dh.gov.uk
Head of Library and Information Services Mrs Pek Lan Bower BA(Hons) DipLib
MCLIP
Senior Librarian (London) James Denmead BA(Hons) MA
Senior Librarian (Leeds) Miss Kerry Hanson BA(Hons) PGCert MCLIP
Customer Services Librarian (London) Miss Lesley Vickers BA(Hons) (020 7972 5992)

Associated library

▶ Library, Department of Health, Room 5W58A, Quarry House, Quarry Hill, Leeds LS2 7UE
☎0113 254 5080/1
Fax 0113 254 5084
e-mail: libqh@dh.gsi.gov.uk
Customer Services Librarian (Leeds) Mrs Jennifer Goodfellow MA(Hons) MA MCLIP

Agency libraries

▶ Medicines and Healthcare Products Regulatory Agency – Information Centre, Department of Health, Market Towers, 1 Nine Elms Lane, London SW8 5NQ
☎020 7084 2000
Fax 020 7084 2353
e-mail: info@mhra.gsi.gov.uk
url: www.mhra.gov.uk/
Head of Information and Communications Diane Leakey BPharm MSc MRPharmS MCLIP MCPP MIPR (020 7084 2678)
Librarian (Medicines) Ed Scully BA(Hons) DipLib MCLIP (020 7084 2678)
Librarian (Devices) Mrs Karen Morgan BSc(Hons) MSc MCLIP (020 7084 3075)
▶ NHS Estates Information Centre, Department of Health, 1 Trevelyan Square, Boar Lane, Leeds LS1 6AE
☎0113 254 7070
Fax 0113 254 7167
e-mail: nhs.estates@dh.gov.uk
url: www.nhsestates.gov.uk
Head of Information Centre Mrs Catherine Russell (0113 254 7088)
Specialism(s): Public health, health services, health services policy and management, medicine, hospitals, social care

DEPARTMENT OF TRADE AND INDUSTRY

Department of Trade and Industry, 1 Victoria Street, London SW1H 0ET
url: www.dti.gov.uk
Minicom 020 7215 6740
Assistant Director, Information Services Mrs Anne Bridge OBE MA MCLIP
Head of Information and Library Services Miss Alison Cotterill BLib(Hons) MA MCLIP

Information and Library Services, Department of Trade and Industry, 1 Victoria Street, London SW1H 0ET
☎020 7215 5006 (enquiries)
Fax 020 7215 5665
Information Services Manager Ms Diane Rowland BLib(Hons) MSc MCLIP
(Limited public access by appointment only)

ENERGY INSTITUTE

Library and Information Service, Energy Institute, 61 New Cavendish Street, London
WIG 7AR
☎020 7467 7113/4/5 (enquiries), 020 7467 7111 (administration)
Fax 020 7255 1472
e-mail: lis@energyinst.org.uk
url: www.energyinst.org.uk
Library and Information Service Manager Mrs C M Cosgrove BSc(Hons) BA MCLIP
FEI
Senior Information Officer Chris L Baker BA(Hons) MEI
Information Officer Miss Deborah Wilson BA(Hons)

ENGLISH FOLK DANCE AND SONG SOCIETY

Vaughan Williams Memorial Library, English Folk Dance and Song Society, Cecil Sharp
House, 2 Regent's Park Road, London NWI 7AY
☎020 7485 2206 exts 18/19
Fax 020 7284 0523
e-mail: library@efdss.org
url: www.efdss.org
Librarian Malcolm Taylor BA(Lib) MCLIP OBE
Assistant Librarian Ms Elaine Bradtke PhD, Ms Peta Webb
Audio Technician Tony Black
Specialism(s): Traditional music and folk culture

ENGLISH HERITAGE

Library, English Heritage, Room B01, Fortress House, 23 Savile Row, London WIS 2ET
☎020 7973 3031 (general enquiries)
Fax 020 7973 3001
e-mail: library@english-heritage.org.uk
url: www.english-heritage.org.uk
Librarian Ms Jane Trodd MA
Assistant Librarian Ms Karen Horn MA
Library Assistant Ms Liz Poirier BA(Hons)
(Prior appointment necessary for members of the public)

Library, English Heritage, National Monuments Record Centre, Kemble Drive, Swindon
SN2 2GZ
☎(01793) 414632
Fax (01793) 414801
e-mail: nmrinfo@english-heritage.org.uk
url: www.english-heritage.org.uk/nmr
Librarians Ms Felicity Gilmour MA(Hons), Ms Diana Thomas BSc(Hons) (job-share)
Specialism(s): English archaeology and architecture

ENGLISH NATURE

Information and Library Service, Information Management Team, English Nature, Northminster House, Peterborough PE1 1UA
☎(01733) 455094 (library enquiry desk), (01733) 455000 (switchboard)
Fax (01733) 568834 (library)
e-mail: enquiries@english-nature.org.uk
url: www.english-nature.org.uk
Team Manager Jonathan Budd
Library Enquiries and Records Manager Ms Isabel Chivers BA(Hons) DipLib MCLIP
Enquiry Service Manager Dick Seamons BSc DipLib
Specialism(s): Nature conservation; Biodiversity

ENGLISH-SPEAKING UNION

Page Memorial Library, English-Speaking Union, Dartmouth House, 37 Charles Street, London W1J 5ED
☎020 7529 1550
Fax 020 7495 6108
e-mail: library@esu.org
url: www.esu.org
Librarian/Information Officer Ms Gill Hale, Ms Jeanne Huse
Specialism(s): Specialist collection on the USA (politics, sociology, history and literature (including fiction))

EQUAL OPPORTUNITIES COMMISSION

Information Centre, Equal Opportunities Commission, Arndale House, Arndale Centre, Manchester M4 3EQ
☎0161 838 8324
Fax 0161 838 8303
url: www.eoc.org.uk
Librarian Ms Julie Foster BA MCLIP (e-mail: julie.foster@eoc.org.uk)
Specialism(s): Sex discrimination and gender equality

EUROPEAN COMMISSION REPRESENTATION IN THE UNITED KINGDOM

Network Support Section, The European Commission Representation in the United Kingdom, 8 Storey's Gate, London SW1P 3AT
☎020 7973 1992
Fax 020 7973 1975
url: www.cec.org.uk
Librarian Mrs Marguerite-Marie Brenchley (e-mail: marguerite-marie.brenchley@cec.eu.int)

(Enquiries may only be referred to this library via a recognized EPIC (European Public Information Centre, formerly known as PiR). For details of your nearest centre please contact your local library or check on www.europe.org.uk)
Specialism(s): All EU legislation and information

FOOD STANDARDS AGENCY

The FSA Library and Information Service, Food Standards Agency, Aviation House, 125 Kingsway, London WC2B 6NH
☎020 7276 8181/2
Fax 020 7276 8069
e-mail: Library&info@foodstandards.gsi.gov.uk
url: www.food.gov.uk
Head of Library and Information Service Aadil Bashir
Specialism(s): Food and nutrition

FOREIGN AND COMMONWEALTH OFFICE

Main Library, Foreign and Commonwealth Office, King Charles Street, London SW1A 2AH
☎020 7008 3925 (enquiries)
Fax 020 7008 3270
e-mail: library.enquiries@fco.gov.uk
Librarian Ms Carryl Allardice BA HDipLib BA(Hons) MA MBA FCLIP

Departmental library

Legal Library, Foreign and Commonwealth Office, Room K168, King Charles Street, London SW1A 2AH
☎020 7008 3050 (enquiries)
Fax 020 7008 4259
Legal Librarian Vacant
Specialism(s): International relations; International law; Diplomacy and politics

FORESTRY COMMISSION

Library, Forestry Commission, Forest Research Station, Alice Holt Lodge, Wrecclesham, Farnham, Surrey GU10 4LH
☎(01420) 22255, (01420) 526216 (direct line)
Fax (01420) 23653
e-mail: library@forestry.gsi.gov.uk
url: www.forestry.gov.uk
Librarian Miss Catherine Oldham BA MA DipLib MCLIP (e-mail: catherine.oldham@forestry.gsi.gov.uk)
Specialism(s): Forestry; Arboriculture; Plant sciences

FRANCIS SKARYNA BELARUSIAN LIBRARY AND MUSEUM

Francis Skaryna Belarusian Library and Museum, 37 Holden Road, London N12 8HS

☎020 8445 5358
Fax 020 8445 5358
e-mail: library@skaryna.org
url: www.skaryna.org
Librarian Mgr Alexander Nadson
Specialism(s): Books, periodicals and archives relating to Belarus

FRESHWATER BIOLOGICAL ASSOCIATION

Library, Freshwater Biological Association, Ferry House, Far Sawrey, Ambleside, Cumbria
LA22 0LP
☎(01539) 442468
Fax (01539) 446914
e-mail: wilib@ceh.ac.uk
url: www.fba.org.uk
Librarian I McCulloch BA(Hons) DipLIS
Specialism(s): Freshwater biology; Water chemistry; Algology; Ichthyology

GEOLOGICAL SOCIETY OF LONDON

Library, Geological Society of London, Burlington House, Piccadilly, London W1J 0BG
☎020 7432 0999
Fax 020 7439 3470
e-mail: library@geolsoc.org.uk
url: www.geolsoc.org.uk
Librarian Miss S Meredith

GERMAN HISTORICAL INSTITUTE LONDON

Library, German Historical Institute London, 17 Bloomsbury Square, London WC1A 2NJ
☎020 7309 2019/2022 (enquiries), 020 7309 2020 (administration)
Fax 020 7404 5573
e-mail: library@ghil.ac.uk
url: www.ghil.ac.uk
Head Librarian Dr Michael Schaich
Librarians Ms A-M Klauk, C Schönberger, Mrs Barbara Bültmann

GOETHE-INSTITUT LONDON

Library, Goethe-Institut London, 50 Princes Gate, Exhibition Road, London SW7 2PH
☎020 7596 4040 (brief enquiries), 020 7596 4044 (information service)
Fax 020 7594 0230
e-mail: library@london.goethe.org
url: www.goethe.de/london
Head Librarian Ms G Buck DiplBibl (e-mail: buck@london.goethe.org)
Specialism(s): German culture, literature and language

GREATER LONDON AUTHORITY

Research Library, Greater London Authority, City Hall, The Queen's Walk, London SE1 2AA
☎020 7983 4000 (GLA switchboard), 020 7983 4455 (library enquiries)
Fax 020 7983 4674
e-mail: rlinfo@london.gov.uk
url: www.london.gov.uk
Head of Research Library Ms Annabel Davies BA(Hons) MCLIP
Information Services Manager Andy Land BA(Hons) PGDipIM MCLIP

GUILDFORD INSTITUTE

Library, Guildford Institute of the University of Surrey, Ward Street, Guildford, Surrey
GU1 4LH
☎(01483) 562142
Fax (01483) 451034
Librarian Mrs E C Miles BA AMA (e-mail: c.miles@surrey.ac.uk)
Specialism(s): General collection of literature, humanities and science work dating from late
Victorian period to present; Local history collections of Surrey and Guildford. Lending
service to members. Research enquiries welcomed by appointment.

HEALTH AND SAFETY EXECUTIVE

Information Services, Health and Safety Executive, Magdalen House, Trinity Road, Bootle,
Merseyside L20 3QZ
☎0151 951 3332
Fax 0151 951 3674
url: www.hse.gov.uk
Head of Information Services Ms Sandie Brown (e-mail: sandie.brown@hse.gsi.gov.uk)

Information centres

▶ Information Centre, Nuclear Safety Division, Health and Safety Executive, St Peter's
House, Balliol Road, Bootle, Merseyside L20 3LZ
☎0151 951 4042
Fax 0151 951 4004
Site Manager Ms E Dearden
▶ Information Services, Health and Safety Executive, Magdalen House, Trinity Road,
Bootle, Merseyside L20 3QZ
☎0151 951 4382
Fax 0151 951 3674
Site Manager Miss Janice Martin MA DipLib MCLIP

(General requests for information on health and safety at work should be referred to the
HSE Infoline on 0845 345 0055. Written enquiries to HSE Information Services, Caerphilly
Business Park, Caerphilly CF83 3GG; e-mail: hseinformationservices@natbrit.com; fax: 029
2085 9260)

HEALTH DEVELOPMENT AGENCY see NATIONAL INSTITUTE FOR HEALTH AND CLINICAL EXCELLENCE (NICE)

HEALTH MANAGEMENT LIBRARY

Health Management Library, Scottish Health Service Centre, Crewe Road South, Edinburgh EH4 2LF
☎0131 623 2535
Fax 0131 315 2369
e-mail: library@shsc.csa.scot.nhs.uk
url: www.healthmanagementonline.co.uk
Library Services Manager Ms Gill Earl BA MCLIP
Librarian Mrs Alison Bogle MA DipLib MCLIP
Assistant Librarian Ms Frances Schofield BA MSc
Specialism(s): Health care management

HEALTH PROTECTION AGENCY

Library, Health Protection Agency, 61 Colindale Avenue, London NW9 5HT
☎020 8200 4400 ext 7616 (enquiries), ext 7617 (Librarian)
Fax 020 8200 7875
url: www.hpa.org.uk
Librarian David Keech (e-mail: david.keech@hpa.org.uk)
Specialism(s): Microbiology, infectious diseases

HEREFORD CATHEDRAL

Library, Hereford Cathedral, The Cathedral, Hereford HR1 2NG
☎(01432) 374225/6
Fax: (01432) 374220
e-mail: library@herefordcathedral.org
url: www.herefordcathedral.org/library.asp
Librarian James Anthony MA MA (e-mail: james.anthony@herefordcathedral.org)
(Open to the public)

HIGH COMMISSION OF INDIA

Library, High Commission of India, India House, Aldwych, London WC2B 4NA
☎020 7632 3166 (Direct Line)
Fax 020 7632 3204
e-mail: info@hcilondon.net
Librarian Murari Lal
Hon Librarian Miss M S Travis
(Staff library only)

HIGHGATE LITERARY AND SCIENTIFIC INSTITUTION

Library, Highgate Literary and Scientific Institution, 11 South Grove, Highgate, London N6 6BS
☎020 8340 3343
Fax 020 8340 5632
e-mail: librarian@hlsi.net
url: www.hlsi.net
Librarian Ms Margaret Mackay DipLib BEd(Hons) MCLIP
(Public access allowed for reference)
Specialism(s): Biography; Fiction; London/local history; Samuel Taylor Coleridge; John Betjeman

HIGHWAYS AGENCY

Highways Agency Information Point, Highways Agency, Broadway, Broad Street, Birmingham B15 1BL
☎0121 678 8059
Fax 0121 687 4092
e-mail: information point-birmingham@highways.gsi.gov.uk
url: www.highways.gov.uk
Information Point Team Leader Richard McIntosh (e-mail: richard.mcintosh@highways.gsi.gov.uk)

HISPANIC AND LUSO-BRAZILIAN COUNCIL

Canning House Library, Hispanic and Luso-Brazilian Council, 2 Belgrave Square, London SW1X 8PJ
☎020 7235 2303
Fax 020 7235 3587
e-mail: library@canninghouse.com
url: www.canninghouse.com
Information Services Managers Ms Irene Barranco Garcia (e-mail: ibarranco@canninghouse.com), Alan Biggins BSc DipLib MCLIP (e-mail: abiggins@canninghouse.com) (job-share)
Specialism(s): Latin America, Spain, Portugal (history, literature, art, linguistics, culture, travel, sociology, politics and economics)

HISTORIC SCOTLAND

Technical Conservation, Research and Education (TCRE) Resource Centre, Historic Scotland, Room G55, Longmore House, Salisbury Place, Edinburgh EH9 1SH
☎0131 668 8642
Fax 0131 668 8669
url: www.historic-scotland.gov.uk
Resource Centre Manager Ms Lisa Perry (e-mail: lisa.perry@scotland.gsi.org.uk)

Specialism(s): Built heritage; History; Traditional building materials; Conservation science; Paintings conservation; Museums collections and conservation; Objects conservation

HM REVENUE AND CUSTOMS

Library, HM Revenue and Customs, LG73, 100 Parliament Street, London SW1A 2BQ
☎020 7147 2193
Fax 020 7147 0232
e-mail: libraryenquiries@hmrc.gsi.gov.uk
url: www.hmce.gov.uk
Head of Library Services Ms Lorna Bankes BA(Hons) MCLIP (0161 827 0465)

HM TREASURY AND CABINET OFFICE

Library and Information Service, HM Treasury and Cabinet Office, Information Gateway Team, 1 Horse Guards Road, London SW1A 2HQ
☎020 7270 5289 (enquiries)
Fax 020 7270 5681
e-mail: library@hm-treasury.x.gsi.gov.uk
url: www.hm-treasury.gov.uk
Director of Information Gateway Ms Jenny Coombes
Library Services Manager Ms Sandra Horsell
Specialism(s): Economics and finance; Public administration; Parliamentary material

HMS SULTAN

Library, HMS Sultan, Military Road, Gosport, Hants PO12 3BY
☎023 9254 2678
Fax (023 9254 2555
e-mail: sultan-librarian@nrta.mod.uk
url: www.royal-navy.mod.uk
Librarian Jim Quibell BA MCLIP
(Visits by arrangement)
Specialism(s): Mechanical, electrical, marine and aeronautical engineering; Naval science, technology and history

HOME OFFICE

Information Services Unit, Home Office, Communication Directorate, Lower Ground Floor, Seacole Building, 2 Marsham Street, London SW1P 4DF
☎020 7035 4041/2 (enquiries)
Fax 020 7035 4022
e-mail: library@homeoffice.gsi.gov.uk
url: www.homeoffice.gov.uk
Head of Library and Information Team Ms Karen George BA PGDipLib
Reader Services Librarian Vacant

HORTICULTURE RESEARCH INTERNATIONAL *see* WARWICK HRI

HOUSE OF COMMONS

Department of the Library, House of Commons, London SW1A 0AA
☎020 7219 4272
Fax 020 7219 5839
e-mail: hcinfo@parliament.uk
url: www.parliament.uk
Librarian of the House of Commons John Pullinger MA
(There are specialist sections which deal with enquiries from Members of Parliament only. Outside enquirers should approach the Department's public interface, the House of Commons Information Office (contact details as above))
Head of the Information Office Stephen McGinness

HOUSE OF LORDS

Library, House of Lords, London SW1A 0PW
☎020 7219 5242 (enquiries), 020 7219 3240 (administration)
Fax 020 7219 6396
e-mail: hllibrary@parliament.uk
url: www.parliament.uk/about_lords/about_lords.cfm
Librarian David L Jones MA FSA FRHistS MCLIP

HULTON/ARCHIVE

Hulton/Archive, Unique House, 21-31 Woodfield Road, London W9 2BA
☎020 7579 5777 (Research), 020 7579 5700 (Reception)
Fax 020 7266 3154
e-mail: archiveresearch@getty-images.com
url: www.gettyimages.com
Research Manager Ms Caroline Theakstone
Curator Ms Sarah McDonald
(Hulton/Archive is part of Getty Images)
Specialism(s): Social history; Personalities; Entertainment; Sport; War; Royalty; Events up to 1980s

THE IEE (INSTITUTION OF ELECTRICAL ENGINEERS)

Library, The IEE (Institution of Electrical Engineers), Savoy Place, London WC2R 0BL
☎020 7344 5461 (enquiries and administration), 020 7344 5451 (management)
Fax 020 7497 3557
e-mail: libdesk@iee.org
url: www.iee.org/library

Head of Library Services John Coupland BA MCLIP (020 7344 5451; e-mail: jcoupland@iee.org.uk)
Specialism(s): Electrical, electronic, control and manufacturing engineering; Telecommunications, computing and information technology

IGER (INSTITUTE OF GRASSLAND AND ENVIRONMENTAL RESEARCH)

Stapledon Library and Information Service, IGER (Institute of Grassland and Environmental Research), Plas Gogerddan, Ceredigion SY23 3EB
☎(01970) 823053 (library desk)
Fax (01970) 828357
e-mail: igerlib.igerlib-wpbs@bbsrc.ac.uk
url: www.iger.bbsrc.ac.uk
Institute Librarian Steve Smith BSc DipLib MCLIP
Collections Librarian Paul Drew BLib MPhil
Specialism(s): Grasses; Plant genetics, physiology and breeding; Livestock; Animal nutrition; Cell biology; Ecology

IMPERIAL WAR MUSEUM

Department of Printed Books, Imperial War Museum, Lambeth Road, London SE1 6HZ
☎020 7416 5342
Fax 020 7416 5246
e-mail: books@iwm.org.uk
url: www.iwm.org.uk
Keeper of Printed Books R Golland BA DipLib MCLIP
Head of Public Services C J V Hunt BA (020 7416 5341)
Head of Acquisitions, Cataloguing and Computing Ms M Wilkinson BA DipLib (020 7416 5348)
(Services: Reading Room (appointment required) Mon–Sat 10–5; telephone enquiry service Mon–Fri.))
Specialism(s): Conflicts since 1914 involving Great Britain and Commonwealth countries – military, civilian and social historical aspects

INSTITUT FRANÇAIS D'ÉCOSSE (FRENCH INSTITUTE)

Library, Institut français d'Écosse (French Institute), 13 Randolph Crescent, Edinburgh EH3 7TT
☎0131 225 5366
Fax 0131 220 0648
e-mail: library@ifecosse.org.uk
url: www.ifecosse.org.uk
Librarian Ms A-M Usher
Specialism(s): French language and culture

INSTITUT FRANÇAIS DU ROYAUME-UNI

The Multi-Media Library, Institut français du Royaume-Uni, 17 Queensberry Place, London SW7 2DT
☎020 7073 1350
Fax 020 7073 1363
e-mail: library@ambafrance.org.uk
url: www.institut-francais.org.uk
Head Librarian Mme Isabel Fernandez

Children's Library, Institut français du Royaume-Uni, 32 Harrington Road, London SW7 3HD
☎020 7073 1350
Deputy Head Mme Chantal Morel
Specialism(s): French literature, art, cinema, music

INSTITUTE OF ACTUARIES

Library, Institute of Actuaries, Napier House, 4 Worcester Street, Oxford OX1 2AW
☎(01865) 268206/7
Fax (01865) 268211
e-mail: libraries@actuaries.org.uk
url: www.actuaries.org.uk
Information Manager Ms Sally Grover MA MCLIP
Deputy Librarian Ms Fiona J McNeil BA MCLIP
Specialism(s): Actuarial science; Pensions; Insurance; Finance and investment; Demography

INSTITUTE OF CHARTERED ACCOUNTANTS IN ENGLAND AND WALES

Library and Information Service, Institute of Chartered Accountants in England and Wales, Chartered Accountants' Hall, PO Box 433, Moorgate Place, London EC2P 2BJ
☎020 7920 8620
Fax 020 7920 8621
e-mail: library@icaew.co.uk
url: www.icaew.co.uk/library
Head of Library and Information Services Ms S P Moore BA(Hons)Lib MCLIP
Deputy Head of LIS Ms A Dennis BA(Hons) DipLib MCLIP
Customer Services Manager N Williams BA(Hons)Lib MCLIP
Collection Manager Ms S Robertson MA MA MCLIP
(The Library is for members of the ICAEW and ICAEW registered students; ACT members and non-members by arrangement and paying a daily or weekly fee for access.)
Specialism(s): Accountancy; Auditing; Taxation; Law; Company information; Finance; Management; IT

INSTITUTE OF CHARTERED SECRETARIES AND ADMINISTRATORS

Information Centre, Institute of Chartered Secretaries and Administrators, 16 Park Crescent, London W1B 1AH
☎020 7580 4741*
Fax 020 7612 7034
e-mail: informationcentre@icsa.co.uk
url: www.icsa.org.uk
Information Centre Manager Andrew Tillbrook
(*Technical enquiries should be sent by letter, fax or e-mail)
Specialism(s): Company law; Corporate governance; Company secretarial practice; Charity law

INSTITUTE OF CLINICAL RESEARCH

Resource Centre, Institute of Clinical Research, PO Box 2962, Marlow, Bucks SL7 1XH
☎(01628) 899755
Fax (01628) 899766
e-mail: resources@instituteofclincalresearch.org
url: www.instituteofclincalresearch.org
Information Services Officer Ms Helena Korjonen-Close (01628 899764; e-mail: helena.korjonen-close@instituteofclinicalresearch.org)
Specialism(s): Specialist subjects relate to nature of clinical research; regulations; ethical issues, the clinical trial process and the personal development of professionals involved in clinical research; course materials, job descriptions and resource lists

INSTITUTE OF CONSERVATION

Institute of Conservation, 3rd Floor, Downstream Building, 1 London Bridge, London SE1 9BG
☎020 7785 3805
Fax 020 7785 3806
e-mail: info@instituteofconservation.org.uk
url: www.instituteofconservation.org.uk
Chief Executive Alastair McCapra
Specialism(s): Conservation of cultural heritage

The Chantry Library, Grove Cottage, St Cross Road, Oxford OX1 3TX
☎(01865) 251303/271520
e-mail: library@ipc.org.uk
url: www.lib.ox.ac.uk/ipc-chantry/
Librarian Vacant
Specialism(s): Book and paper conservation
Note: The Chantry Library is administered by the Institute of Conservation. Information on the collection is available at the University of Oxford's online system OLIS (Oxford Libraries Information System).

INSTITUTE OF CONTEMPORARY HISTORY AND WIENER LIBRARY

Institute of Contemporary History and Wiener Library, 4 Devonshire Street, London
WIW 5BH
☎020 7636 7247
Fax 020 7436 6428
e-mail: library@wienerlibrary.co.uk
url: www.wienerlibrary.co.uk
Librarian Ms Katharina Hübschmann
Director Ben Barkow
Education Officer Ms Katherine Klinger
Specialism(s): Holocaust; Third Reich; Fascism; Modern German–Jewish history; Anti-semitism

INSTITUTE OF DIRECTORS

IOD Information Centre, Institute of Directors, I Pall Mall East, London SWIY 5AU
☎020 7451 3100
Fax 020 7321 0145
e-mail: businessinfo@iod.com
url: www.iod.com
Head of Information and Advisory Services Mrs A Burmajster MA MCLIP
Specialism(s): Corporate governance; Directorship; Boardroom practice

INSTITUTE OF MATERIALS, MINERALS AND MINING

Minerals and Mining Library, Institute of Materials, Minerals and Mining, I Carlton House
Terrace, London SWIY 5DB
☎020 7451 7300
Fax 020 7451 7406
url: www.iom3.org.uk
Mining and Minerals Information Co-ordinator Mike McGarr BSc (020 7451 7344;
e-mail: mike.mcgarr@iom3.org)
Specialism(s): Economic geology; Mining; Mineral processing; Extractive metallurgy

Materials Library, Institute of Materials, Minerals and Mining, I Carlton House Terrace,
London SWIY 5DB
☎020 7451 7300
Fax 020 7839 1702
url: www.iom3.org.uk
Materials Information Co-ordinator Ms Hilda Kaune BA(Hons) DipLib (020 7451 7360;
e-mail: hilda.kaune@iom3.org)
Specialism(s): Metals; Materials; Polymers and plastics

INSTITUTE OF OCCUPATIONAL MEDICINE

Library, Institute of Occupational Medicine, Research Park North, Riccarton, Edinburgh
EH14 4AP
☎0870 850 5131
Fax 0870 850 5132
e-mail: iom@iomhq.org.uk
url: www.iom-world.org
Scientific Information Officer Ken Dixon MA(Hons) MA MCLIP
Specialism(s): Occupational medicine and environmental issues

INSTITUTE OF PSYCHOANALYSIS

Library, Institute of Psychoanalysis, 112a Shirland Road, Maida Vale, London W9 2EQ
☎020 7563 5008
Fax 020 7563 5001
e-mail: library@iopa.org.uk
url: www.psychoanalysis.org.uk
Library Executive Officer Ms A Chandler DipLIS

INSTITUTION OF CIVIL ENGINEERS

Library, Institution of Civil Engineers, 1 Great George Street, Westminster, London
SW1P 3AA
☎020 7665 2252
Fax 020 7976 7610
e-mail: library@ice.org.uk
url: www.ice.org.uk
Librarian Michael Chrimes BA MLS MCLIP

INSTITUTION OF MECHANICAL ENGINEERS

Information and Library Service, Institution of Mechanical Engineers, 1 Birdcage Walk,
London SW1H 9JJ
☎020 7973 1274
Fax 020 7222 8762
e-mail: library@imeche.org.uk
url: www.imeche.org.uk/library
Head Librarian and Archivist Keith Moore MA
Information Officers Ms Sarah Rogers MA MCLIP, Ms Fenella Philpot MA MCLIP, Ms Lisa
Davies MA
Librarian Mike Claxton BSc

INSTITUTION OF OCCUPATIONAL SAFETY AND HEALTH

Technical Enquiry and Information Service, The Institution of Occupational Safety and
Health, The Grange, Highfield Drive, Wigston, Leics LE18 1NN

☎0116 257 3199; 0116 257 3100 (switchboard)
Fax 0116 257 3107
e-mail: techinfo@iosh.co.uk
url: www.iosh.co.uk
Information Officers Mrs Margaret Griggs (e-mail: margaret.griggs@iosh.co.uk),
Miss Anne Wells (e-mail: anne.wells@iosh.co.uk)

INSTITUTO CERVANTES

Library, Instituto Cervantes, 102 Eaton Square, London SW1W 9AN
☎020 7201 0757
Fax 020 7235 0329
e-mail: biblon@cervantes.es
url: www.cervantes.es; http://londres.cervantes.es
Chief Librarian David Carrión

Site library

Library, Instituto Cervantes, 326-330 Deansgate, Manchester M3 4FN
☎0161 661 4210 (direct)
Fax 0161 661 4203
e-mail: bibman@cervantes.es
Librarian José M Fernández

A further site library (located in Dublin) can be found in Academic, National and Special
Section of the Republic of Ireland.
Specialism(s): Spanish culture, history, literature, language and teaching

THE INTERNATIONAL INSTITUTE FOR STRATEGIC STUDIES (IISS)

Library and Information Department, The International Institute for Strategic Studies (IISS),
Arundel House, 13-15 Arundel Street, London WC2R 3DX
☎020 7395 9122 (library enquiries) or 020 7379 7676 (main switchboard)
Fax 020 7836 3108
e-mail: library@iiss.org
url: www.iiss.org
Chief Librarian Miss Ellena Pike MA(Oxon) MSc
Deputy Librarian Ms Catherine Micklethwaite BSc(Econ) MA
Assistant Librarian James Howarth BA MA MA
Specialism(s): International relations; War studies

INTERNATIONAL MARITIME ORGANIZATION

IMO Library Services, International Maritime Organization, 4 Albert Embankment, London
SE1 7SR
☎020 7735 7611
Fax 020 7587 3210

url: www.imo.org
Librarian Mrs Marianne Harvey (e-mail: mharvey@imo.org)
Specialism(s): Maritime safety; Prevention of pollution from ships; Ship design; Navigation; Technical co-operation; Liability and compensation

ISLE OF MAN FAMILY HISTORY SOCIETY

Library, Isle of Man Family History Society, Above Shoprite, 13 Michael Street, Peel, Isle of Man IM5 1HB
☎(01624) 843105
url: www.isle-of-man.com/interests/geneaology/fhs/
Librarian Mrs D Quayle
(Open Tuesdays, Wednesdays and Saturday afternoons)

ISLE OF MAN GOVERNMENT/LESIGLATURE OF THE ISLE OF MAN

Tynwald Library, Isle of Man Government/Lesiglature of the Isle of Man, Legislative Buildings, Douglas, Isle of Man IM1 3PW
☎(01624) 685520
Fax (01624) 685522
e-mail: library@tynwald.org.im
Librarian Geoffrey Clucas Haywood MCLIP
Deputy Librarian Ms Trudi Thompson BA
Specialism(s): Manx Parliamentary and Isle of Man Government publications and Isle of Man laws

ITALIAN CULTURAL INSTITUTE (ISTITUTO ITALIANO DI CULTURA)

Library, Italian Cultural Institute (Istituto Italiano di Cultura), 39 Belgrave Square, London SW1X 8NX
☎020 7235 1461 (switchboard), 020 7235 1461 ext 203 (library)/204 (information), 020 7396 4425 (library direct line)
Fax 020 7235 4618
e-mail: library@italcultur.org.uk
url: www.italcultur.org.uk
Librarian in charge Dr Luigi Mammolini
Specialism(s): Italian culture and language; Literature and visual arts

JERWOOD LIBRARY OF THE PERFORMING ARTS

Jerwood Library of the Performing Arts, Jerwood Library of the Performing Arts, Trinity College of Music, King Charles Court, Old Royal Naval College, Greenwich, London SE10 9JF
☎020 8305 3950
Fax 020 8305 3999

e-mail: library@tcm.ac.uk
url: www.tcm.ac.uk
Acting Library Manager Miss Claire Kidwell BA(Hons) MA
Administrator (Mander and Mitcheson Theatre Collection) Richard Mangan (020 8305 4426; e-mail: rmangan@tcm.ac.uk)
(Houses the Mander and Mitchenson Theatre Collection)
Specialism(s): Music; Theatre; Performing arts; Sound recording

JOINT SERVICES COMMAND AND STAFF COLLEGE

Library, Joint Services Command and Staff College, Faringdon Road, Watchfield, Swindon SN6 8TS
☎(01793) 788236
Fax (01793) 788281
e-mail: library@jscsc.org
Librarian C M Hobson MCLIP MBE
Specialism(s): Defence studies; International affairs; Military history

THE KENNEL CLUB

The Kennel Club Library & Art Gallery, 1-5 Clarges Street, London W1J 8AB
☎020 7518 1009
Fax 020 7518 1045
e-mail: library@the-kennel-club.org.uk
url: www.the-kennel-club.org.uk/library/library.htm
Library and Collections Manager Mrs Sarah Rogers BA
(Open Mondays to Fridays, 9.30 am–4.30 pm by appointment)
Specialism(s): Canine literature, registrations and show catalogues, canine art

KING'S FUND

Information and Library Service, King's Fund, 11-13 Cavendish Square, London W1G 0AN
☎020 7307 2568/9 (enquiries)
Fax 020 7307 2805
e-mail: library@kingsfund.org.uk
url: www.kingsfund.org.uk/library
Information and Library Service Manager Ms Lynette Cawthra MA DipLib MCLIP
Specialism(s): Health and social care policy/management

LABOUR PARTY

Communications Unit, Labour Party, Eldon House, Regents Centre, Newcastle upon Tyne NE3 3PW
☎08705 900200
Fax 0191 246 5136
e-mail: info@new.labour.org.uk

url: www.labour.org.uk
Communications Unit Manager Ms Zoe Edmonds
Specialism(s): Labour Party and Government policy

LAMBETH PALACE LIBRARY

Lambeth Palace Library, London SE1 7JU
☎020 7898 1400
Fax 020 7928 7932
url: www.lambethpalacelibrary.org
Librarian and Archivist Dr Richard Palmer PhD MCLIP
Specialism(s): History (particularly of the Church of England); Early printed mss; Archives of the Province of Canterbury; Liturgy; Bibliography; Architecture

LAW COMMISSION

Library, Law Commission, Conquest House, 37/38 John Street, Theobalds Road, London WC1N 2BQ
☎020 7453 1241 (enquiries), 020 7453 1242 (administration)
Fax 020 7453 1297
e-mail: library@lawcommission.gsi.gov.uk
url: www.lawcom.gov.uk
Librarian Keith Tree BA

THE LAW SOCIETY

Library, The Law Society, 113 Chancery Lane, London WC2A 1PL
☎0870 606 2511 (enquiries), 020 7320 5699 (administration)
Fax 020 7831 1687
e-mail: lib-enq@lawsociety.org.uk
url: www.library.lawsociety.org.uk
Online catalogue: catalyst.lawsociety.org.uk
Librarian and Head of Information Services Chris Holland BA MCLIP
Specialism(s): Law; Parliamentary material; Historical legal material

THE LIBRARY AND MUSEUM OF FREEMASONRY

The Library and Museum of Freemasonry, Freemasons' Hall, Great Queen Street, London WC2B 5AZ
☎020 7395 9257
Fax 020 7404 7418
e-mail: libmus@ugle.org.uk
url: www.freemasonry.london.museum
Director Ms D Clements
Librarian M Cherry
Curator M Dennis

LIBRARY FOR IRANIAN STUDIES

Library for Iranian Studies, The Woodlands Hall, Crown Street, London W3 8SA
☎020 8993 6384
Fax 020 8752 1300
Librarian Dr Mashala Ajoudani

LINCOLN CATHEDRAL

Lincoln Cathedral Library, The Cathedral, Lincoln LN2 1PZ
☎(01522) 544544
Fax: (01522) 511307
url: www.lincolncathedral.com
Librarian Dr Nicholas Bennett (e-mail: librarian@lincolncathedral.com)

LINEN HALL LIBRARY

The Linen Hall Library, 17 Donegall Square North, Belfast BT1 5GB
☎028 9032 1707
Fax 028 9043 8586
e-mail: info@linenhall.com
url: www.linenhall.com
Librarian John Gray BA DLIS
Specialism(s): Irish history and culture

LINNEAN SOCIETY OF LONDON

Library, Linnean Society of London, Burlington House, Piccadilly, London W1J 0BF
☎020 7434 4479
Fax 020 7287 9364
e-mail: library@linnean.org
url: www.linnean.org
Librarian Ms G Douglas BSc FLS (e-mail: gina@linnean.org)
Deputy Librarian Mrs Lynda Brooks Ba DipLib MCLIP
Specialism(s): Natural history; Taxonomy; Evolutionary ecology; History of natural history; Conservation and environment

LITERARY AND PHILOSOPHICAL SOCIETY OF NEWCASTLE UPON TYNE

Library, Literary and Philosophical Society of Newcastle upon Tyne, 23 Westgate Road, Newcastle upon Tyne NE1 1SE
☎0191 232 0192
Fax 0191 261 4494
e-mail: library@litandphil.org.uk
url: www.litandphil.org.uk
Librarian Ms Kay Easson
Specialism(s): Humanities

LONDON CHAMBER OF COMMERCE AND INDUSTRY

Information Centre, London Chamber of Commerce and Industry, 33 Queen Street, London EC4R IAP
☎020 7248 4444 (members only)
Fax 020 7203 1863
e-mail: info@londonchamber.co.uk
url: www.londonchamber.co.uk
Information Officer Jim Padget
Specialism(s): International trade

LONDON LIBRARY

London Library, 14 St James's Square, London SW1Y 4LG
☎020 7930 7705
Fax 020 7766 4766
e-mail: membership@londonlibrary.co.uk
url: www.londonlibrary.co.uk
Librarian Miss Inez T P A Lynn BA MLitt MCLIP
Specialism(s): History; Literature; The arts; Related subjects in major European languages

LONDON METROPOLITAN ARCHIVES

Library, London Metropolitan Archives, 40 Northampton Road, London EC1R 0HB
☎020 7332 3817
Fax 020 7833 9136
url: www.cityoflondon.gov.uk
Senior Librarian Ms Maxine Miller BA(Hons) DipLib MCLIP (e-mail: maxine.miller@corpoflondon.gov.uk)
Specialism(s): London (local government history; social history); Maps and prints

LONDON'S TRANSPORT MUSEUM

Library, London's Transport Museum, 39 Wellington Street, Covent Garden, London WC2E 7BB
☎020 7565 7280
Fax 020 7565 7252
e-mail: library@ltmuseum.co.uk
url: www.ltmuseum.co.uk
Library and Information Services Manager Ms Caroline Warhurst BA MCLIP
Librarian Ms Helen Kent MA
(Visitors by appointment)
Specialism(s): History and development of London's Transport from 1800 to present day; information about Transport for London, London Transport and predecessor companies; special emphasis on the development of art, architecture and design in London Transport

MANX NATIONAL HERITAGE

Library, Manx National Heritage, Manx Museum, Douglas, Isle of Man IM1 3LY
☎(01624) 648000
Fax (01624) 648001
e-mail: library@mnh.gov.im
url: www.gov.im/mnh
Librarian/Archivist Roger M C Sims BA DAA DPESS RMSA FSA (e-mail:
Roger.Sims@mnh.gov.im)
Librarian Alan G Franklin MA MCLIP (e-mail: alan.franklin@mnh.gov.im)
Archivist Ms Wendy Thirkettle BA DipAS (e-mail: Wendy.Thirkettle@mnh.gov.im)
Specialism(s): History and development of the Isle of Man; Combined local studies, Archive
and diocesan record office

MARINE BIOLOGICAL ASSOCIATION

National Marine Biological Library, Marine Biological Association, Citadel Hill, Plymouth
PL1 2PB
☎(01752) 633266
Fax (01752) 633102
e-mail: nmbl@pml.ac.uk
url: www.mba.ac.uk/nmbl/
Head of Library and Information Services Miss Linda Noble BSc MCLIP (01752
633270; e-mail: lno@pml.ac.uk)
Specialism(s): Marine sciences including marine biology, pollution, oceanography and chemistry; Fisheries dating back to 19th century

MARX MEMORIAL LIBRARY

Marx Memorial Library, 37A Clerkenwell Green, London EC1R 0DU
☎020 7253 1485
Fax 020 7251 6039
e-mail: marx.library@britishlibrary.net
url: www.marxlibrary.net
Librarian Ms Tish Collins BA MSc

MARYLEBONE CRICKET CLUB

Library, Marylebone Cricket Club, Lord's Ground, St John's Wood, London NW8 8QN
☎020 7616 8656
Fax 020 7616 8659
e-mail: museum@mcc.org.uk
url: www.mcc.org.uk
Curator Adam Chadwick (020 7616 8655)
Archivist and Historian Ms Glenys Williams BA MPhil

MET OFFICE

National Meterological Library, Met Office, FitzRoy Road, Exeter, Devon EX1 3PB
☎(01392) 884841 (enquiries)
e-mail: metlib@metoffice.gov.uk
url: www.metoffice.gov.uk
Library and Information Manager Graham Bartlett
Librarian Ms Sara Osman

National Meteorological Archive, Met Office, Devon Record Office, Great Moor House,
Bittern Road, Sowton, Exeter, Devon EX2 7NL
☎(01392) 360987
e-mail: metarc@metoffice.gov.uk
url: www.metoffice.com
Archive Manager Ian MacGregor
(Open to the public)

MINISTRY OF DEFENCE

MOD Information Services, Ministry of Defence, Ground Floor, Zone D, Main Building,
Whitehall, London SW1A 2HB
☎020 7218 4445 (general enquiries), 020 7218 4184 (administration)
Fax 020 7218 5413
e-mail: info-libsvcsgroupmailbox@defence.mod.uk
url: www.mod.uk
Chief Librarian Patrick Ryan BA MBA MCLIP (020 7218 0266; fax: 020 7218 5430;
e-mail: patrick.ryan893@mod.uk)

Site library

Library, Ministry of Defence, Room 1410, Kentigern House, 65 Brown Street, Glasgow
G2 8EX
☎0141 224 2500/1
Fax 0141 224 2257
e-mail: library@khinf.demon.co.uk
Librarian Ms Margaret Gair BA(Hons) DipLib MCLIP

MORRAB LIBRARY

Morrab Library, Morrab Gardens, Penzance, Cornwall TR18 4DA
☎(01736) 364474
url: www.morrablibrary.co.uk
Librarian Mrs Annabelle Read
(Available on payment of an annual subscription or a daily fee)
Specialism(s): Cornish literature and history; Napoleonic collection

MUSEUM OF LONDON

Library, Museum of London, London Wall, London EC2Y 5HN

☎0870 444 3852
Fax 0870 444 3853
e-mail: info@museumoflondon.org.uk
url: www.museumoflondon.org.uk
Library Officer Ms Sally Brooks MA MCLIP
(Readers by appointment only)

MUSEUM OF WELSH LIFE (AMGUEDDFA WERIN CYMRU)

Library, Museum of Welsh Life (Amgueddfa Werin Cymru), St Fagans, Cardiff CF5 6XB
☎029 2057 3446
Fax 029 2057 3490
url: www.nmgw.ac.uk/mwl/collections/library/
Librarian Niclas L Walker MA DipLib MCLIP (e-mail: Nic.Walker@nmgw.ac.uk)
Specialism(s): Material, social and cultural history of Wales

THE NATIONAL ARCHIVES

National Archives: Public Record Office
Resource Centre and Library, National Archives: Public Record Office, Kew, Richmond, Surrey TW9 4DU
☎020 8876 3444 ext 2458 (general library enquiries)
Fax 020 8392 5286
e-mail: enquiry@nationalarchives.gov.uk
url: www.nationalarchives.gov.uk
Head of Resource Centre and Library Ms Helen Pye-Smith MA (020 8392 5278; e-mail: helen.pye-smith@nationalarchives.gov.uk)
Keeper of the Public Record Office and Historical Manuscripts Commissioner Ms Sarah Tyacke CB

National Archives: Historical Manuscripts Commission
National Register of Archives and Manorial Document Register, National Archives: Historical Manuscripts Commission, Kew, Richmond, Surrey TW9 4DU
☎020 8392 5200
Fax 020 8392 5286
e-mail: nra@nationalarchives.gov.uk
url: www.nationalarchives.gov.uk
Head of National Advisory Service Nicholas Kingsley
Senior Curatorial Officer Alex Ritchie MA

NATIONAL ARMY MUSEUM

Reading Room, National Army Museum, Royal Hospital Road, London SW3 4HT
☎020 7730 0717 ext 2222 (enquiries), ext 2215 (administration)
Fax 020 7823 6573

e-mail: info@national-army-museum.ac.uk
url: www.national-army-museum.ac.uk
Head of Department of Printed Books Michael Ball MA AMA
Head of Archives, Photographs, Film and Sound Alastair Massie MA DPhil
Head of Fine and Decorative Art Miss Jenny Spencer-Smith MA AMA
Open Tuesday–Saturday 10am–4.30pm
Specialism(s): Military history; British army; Indian and Commonwealth armies

NATIONAL ART LIBRARY

Word and Image Department, National Art Library, Victoria and Albert Museum, Cromwell
Road, South Kensington, London SW7 2RL
☎020 7942 2400 (enquiries)
Fax 020 7942 2401
e-mail: nal.enquiries@vam.ac.uk
url: www.nal.vam.ac.uk/nal
Keeper Julius Bryant
Deputy Keeper John Meriton

Site library
Archive of Art and Design, National Art Library, 23 Blythe Road, West Kensington, London
W14 0QF
☎020 7603 1514
Fax 020 7602 0980
e-mail: archive@vam.ac.uk
Head of Archives Christopher Marsden
Archivist Ms Alexia Bleathman

NATIONAL ASSEMBLY FOR WALES

Welsh Assembly Government
Assembly Library Services, Welsh Assembly Government, Information Management
Division, Cathays Park, Cardiff CF10 3NQ
☎029 2082 5449/3683
Fax 029 2082 5239
e-mail: assemblylibraryservice@wales.gsi.gov.uk
url: www.wales.gov.uk; www.wales.gov.uk/keypub/index.htm (for Assembly publications)
Head of the Assembly Library Service Ms Rebecca Davies
Specialism(s): Welsh government publications

Presiding Office
Members' Library (Assembly Parliamentary Service), Presiding Office, Cardiff Bay, Cardiff
CF99 1NA
☎029 2089 8097
Fax 029 2089 8229
e-mail: membersresearchserviceresources@wales.gsi.gov.uk
Resources Manager Mrs Stephanie Wilson

Specialism(s): Information resources to support the work of Assembly Members, also the Members' Research Services, which provides a confidential research and information service to individual Assembly Members and the Assembly's Committees

NATIONAL CHILDREN'S BUREAU

Library and Information Service, National Children's Bureau, 8 Wakley Street, London EC1V 7QE
☎020 7843 6008 (enquiry line)
Fax 020 7843 6007
e-mail: library@ncb.org.uk
url: www.ncb.org.uk
Head of Library & Information Ms Nicola Hilliard BA MCLIP

NATIONAL COAL MINING MUSEUM FOR ENGLAND

Library, National Coal Mining Museum for England, Caphouse Colliery, New Road, Overton, West Yorks WF4 4RH
☎(01924) 848806
Fax (01924) 840694
e-mail: info@ncm.org.uk
url: www.ncm.org.uk
Curatorial Librarian Mrs Alison Henesey BA MCLIP (e-mail: curatorial.librarian@ncm.org.uk)

NATIONAL GALLERY

Libraries and Archive, The National Gallery, Trafalgar Square, London WC2N 5DN
☎020 7747 2830
Fax 020 7747 2892
e-mail: lad@ng-london.org.uk
url: www.nationalgallery.org.uk
Head of Libraries and Archive Ms Elspeth Hector MA MCLIP (e-mail: elspeth.hector@ng-london.org.uk)
Archivist Alan Crookham (e-mail: alan.crookham@ng-london.org.uk)
(Readers by appointment only)
Specialism(s): Western European painting 1200–1900

NATIONAL HERITAGE LIBRARY

National Heritage Library, 313–315 Caledonian Road, London N1 1DR
☎020 7609 9639
Founder Director M McNiel
(A comprehensive reference collection covering every aspect of the landscape and culture of the British Isles: open by appointment only)
Specialism(s): The Arts; Environmental, historical, industrial and transport sites

NATIONAL INSTITUTE FOR HEALTH AND CLINICAL EXCELLENCE (NICE)

(formerly Health Development Agency)

Information Services, Clinical and Public Health Directorate, National Institute for Health and Clinical Excellence (NICE), MidCity Place, 71 High Holborn, London WC1V 6NA
☎020 7067 5800
Fax 020 7067 5801
e-mail: nice@nice.org.uk
url: www.nice.org.uk
Associate Director of Information Services Dr Sarah Cumber
Specialism(s): Evidence-based healthcare; Health technology evaluation; Clinical guidelines

NATIONAL INSTITUTE FOR MEDICAL RESEARCH (MEDICAL RESEARCH COUNCIL)

Library, National Institute for Medical Research (Medical Research Council), The Ridgeway, Mill Hill, London NW7 1AA
☎020 8816 2228
Fax 020 8816 2230
e-mail: library@nimr.mrc.ac.uk
url: www.nimr.mrc.ac.uk/library
Librarian Frank Norman BSc DipLib MCLIP
Specialism(s): Physiology; Neuroscience; Immunology; Microbiology; Molecular biology; Cell biology; Biochemistry; Structural biology; Developmental biology

NATIONAL INSTITUTE OF ADULT CONTINUING EDUCATION (NIACE)

Library, National Institute of Adult Continuing Education (NIACE), 21 De Montfort Street, Leicester LE1 7GE
☎0116 204 4200
Fax 0116 204 4253
e-mail: information@niace.org.uk
url: www.niace.org.uk
Librarian Ms Helen Kruse BA(Hons) MCLIP

NATIONAL INSTITUTE OF ECONOMIC AND SOCIAL RESEARCH

Library, National Institute of Economic and Social Research, 2 Dean Trench Street, Smith Square, London SW1P 3HE
☎020 7654 7665
Fax 020 7654 1900
e-mail: library@niesr.ac.uk

url: www.niesr.ac.uk
Librarian Ms Patricia Oliver BA MCLIP (020 7654 1907; e-mail: poliver@niesr.ac.uk)

NATIONAL LIBRARY FOR THE BLIND

National Library for the Blind, Far Cromwell Road, Bredbury, Stockport SK6 2SG
☎0161 355 2000
Fax 0161 355 2098
e-mail: enquiries@nlbuk.org.uk
url: www.nlb-online.org
Minicom: 0161 355 2043
Chief Executive Ms Helen Brazier MA MCLIP (0161 355 2004)
Library and Information Services Director Ms Pat Beech MCLIP
Specialism(s): Braille and Moon books and music; Electronic services for visually impaired people

NATIONAL LIBRARY OF SCOTLAND

National Library of Scotland, George IV Bridge, Edinburgh EH1 1EW
☎0131 226 4531
Fax 0131 622 4803
e-mail: enquiries@nls.uk
url: www.nls.uk
Librarian Martyn Wade MA MLib MCLIP

Branch/regional libraries

▶ Inter-Library Services, National Library of Scotland, 33 Salisbury Place, Edinburgh
  EH9 1SL
  ☎0131 466 3815
  Fax 0131 466 3814
  e-mail: ils@nls.uk
▶ Map Library, National Library of Scotland, 33 Salisbury Place, Edinburgh EH9 1SL
  ☎0131 466 3813
  Fax 0131 466 3812
  e-mail: maps@nls.uk
  Specialism(s): Scottish history and culture

NATIONAL LIBRARY OF WALES: LLYFRGELL GENEDLAETHOL CYMRU

National Library of Wales: Llyfrgell Genedlaethol Cymru, Aberystwyth, Ceredigion
SY23 3BU
☎(01970) 632800
Fax (01970) 615709
e-mail: holi@llgc.org.uk
url: www.llgc.org.uk
Librarian Andrew Green MA DipLib MCLIP

Specialism(s): Legal deposit library housing books, mss, maps, photographs, paintings, audiovisual and electronic materials; an important digitization and exhibitions programme

NATIONAL MARITIME MUSEUM

Caird Library, National Maritime Museum, Greenwich, London SE10 9NF
☎020 8312 6673/6528
Fax 020 8312 6599
e-mail: library@nmm.ac.uk; manuscripts@nmm.ac.uk
url: www.nmm.ac.uk
Head of Library and Manuscripts Mrs Jill Terrell BSc DipLib MCLIP
Librarian Vacant
Manuscripts Archivist Mrs Daphne Knott BA DipArch
Specialism(s): Maritime history; Horology; Astronomy; Shipbuilding; Navigation

NATIONAL MUSEUM OF PHOTOGRAPHY, FILM & TELEVISION

Royal Photographic Society Collection, National Museum of Photography, Film & Television, Bradford BD1 1NQ
☎(01274) 202030 (switchboard)
Fax (01274) 772325
e-mail: rps@nmsi.ac.uk
url: www.nmpft.org.uk
Curator Dr Jane Fletcher (01274 203398; e-mail: jane.fletcher@nmsi.ac.uk)
(Prior appointment essential for members and non-members)

NATIONAL MUSEUMS & GALLERIES OF WALES

Library, National Museums & Galleries of Wales, Cathays Park, Cardiff CF10 3NP
☎029 2057 3202
Fax 029 2057 3216
url: www.nmgw.ac.uk
Librarian John R Kenyon BA MCLIP FSA FRHistS FSA(Scot)
Specialism(s): Archaeology; Fine and decorative arts; Botany; Geology; Zoology; Architecture; Welsh history and topography

NATIONAL MUSEUMS OF SCOTLAND

Library, National Museums of Scotland, Chambers Street, Edinburgh EH1 1JF
☎0131 247 4137 (enquiries), 0131 247 4153 (administration)
Fax 0131 247 4311
e-mail: library@nms.ac.uk
url: www.nms.ac.uk
Head of Information Services Ms Evelyn Simpson
Head of Library Ms Elize Rowan MSc FSAScot
Depute Librarian Ms Andrew Martin MA DipLib FSAScot

Branch library
Library, National Museums of Scotland, National War Museum of Scotland, The Castle,
Edinburgh EH1 2NG
☎0131 225 7534 ext 204
Assistant Curator Mrs Edith Philip
Specialism(s): Decorative arts; Archaeology; Ethnography; History of science and
technology; Natural sciences; Museology; Military history

NATIONAL PHYSICAL LABORATORY

Library, National Physical Laboratory, Hampton Road, Teddington, Middlesex TW11 0LW
☎020 8943 6417
Fax 020 8614 0424
e-mail: library@npl.co.uk
url: www.npl.co.uk
Librarian Ian O'Leary MA DLIS (020 8943 6089)
Specialism(s): Physics; Material science; Mathematics; Metrology

NATIONAL PORTRAIT GALLERY

Heinz Archive and Library, National Portrait Gallery, 2 St Martin's Place, London WC2H 0HE
☎020 7306 0055 ext 257
Fax 020 7306 0056
e-mail: archiveenquiry@npg.org.uk
url: www.npg.org.uk
Head of Archive and Library Robin K Francis BSc(Hons) MA MCLIP
Librarian Ms Antonia Leak BA(Hons) MA MCLIP
(Readers by appointment only)
Specialism(s): British portraiture

NATIONAL RAILWAY MUSEUM

Library and Archive, National Railway Museum, Leeman Road, York YO26 4XJ
☎(01904) 621261 (switchboard); (01904) 686235 (for appointments)
Fax (01904) 611112
e-mail: nrm.researchcentre@nmsi.ac.uk
url: www.nmsi.ac.uk/nrm
Resource Centre Manager Philip Atkins BSc (01904 686208; e-mail:
p.atkins@nmsi.ac.uk)
(Open Mon–Fri 10.00–17.00 by prior appointment)

NATIONAL UNION OF TEACHERS

Library and Information Unit, National Union of Teachers, Hamilton House, Mabledon
Place, London WC1H 9BD
☎020 7380 4713
Fax 020 7387 8458
url: www.teachers.org.uk

Information Officer Ms Janet Friedlander BA MCLIP (e-mail: j.friedlander@nut.org.uk)
Information Assistant Mrs Elizabeth Norfolk (e-mail: e.norfolk@nut.org.uk)

NATIONAL YOUTH AGENCY

Information Centre, National Youth Agency, Eastgate House, 19–23 Humberstone Road,
Leicester LE3 3GI
☎0116 242 7350 (enquiries and administration)
Fax 0116 242 7444
e-mail: dutydesk@nya.org.uk
url: www.nya.org.uk
Library Officer Ms Jo Poultney BA (e-mail: jop@nya.org.uk)
(Information collection on young people, the youth service and youth affairs. Provides a
postal loan and enquiry answering service. Personal visitors welcome, by appointment)

NATURAL HISTORY MUSEUM

Library, Natural History Museum, Cromwell Road, London SW7 5BD
☎020 7942 5460 (general enquiries)
Fax 020 7942 5559
e-mail: library@nhm.ac.uk
url: www.nhm.ac.uk
Head of Library and Information Services Graham Higley BSc
(The Library is divided into four specialist sections at South Kensington: General & Zoology
(020 7942 5460); Botany (020 7942 5685); Entomology (020 7942 5751) and Earth
Sciences (020 7942 5476). There is an out-station library: The Library, The Walter
Rothschild Museum, Akeman Street, Tring, Herts HP23 6AP (020 7942 6159), which
contains the collection of works on ornithology.

NETWORK RAIL INFRASTRUCTURE LTD

Network Rail HQ Library, Network Rail Infrastructure Ltd, 2nd Floor Library, 40 Melton
Street, London NWI 2EE
☎020 7557 8062
Fax 020 7557 9150
url: www.networkrail.co.uk
Librarian Ms Sue Peters (e-mail: sue.peters@networkrail.co.uk)
(Not open to the public but queries welcomed from professional organizations and
researchers.)
Specialism(s): UK railway history, legislation, engineering, health and safety

NHS HEALTH SCOTLAND

Library, NHS Health Scotland, The Priory, Canaan Lane, Edinburgh EH10 4SG
☎0845 912 5442 (enquiries) - Scotland only), 0131 536 5582 (administration), textphone
0131 536 5593
Fax 0131 536 5502
e-mail: library.enquiries@health.scot.nhs.uk

url: www.healthscotland.com/library
Library Services Manager Ms Sharon Jamieson BA(Hons) MSc DipLIS MCLIP
Librarian Ms Julia Green BA DipLib
Specialism(s): Public health; Health promotion and education

NHS NATIONAL SERVICES SCOTLAND

Information Services Division, NHS National Services Scotland, Gyle Square, 1 South Gyle Crescent, Edinburgh EH12 9EB
☎0131 275 6423
Fax 0131 275 7535
e-mail: isdlib@isd.csa.scot.nhs.uk
url: www.isdscotland.org/
Manager, ISD Library Services Alan Jamieson MA DipLib MCLIP (e-mail:
alan.jamieson@isd.csa.scot.nhs.uk)
Specialism(s): Health statistics; Official circulars; Media monitoring

NORTHERN IRELAND ASSEMBLY

Library, Northern Ireland Assembly, Parliament Buildings, Stormont, Belfast BT4 3XX
☎028 9052 1250
Fax 028 9052 1715/1922
e-mail: issuedesk.library@niassembly.gov.uk
url: www.ni-assembly.gov.uk
Resource Team Librarian George D Woodman BA DipLib MCLIP (028 9052 1250;
e-mail: george.woodman@niassembly.gov.uk)
Specialism(s): Legislation and official publications relating especially to N Ireland,
government, politics and Irish history

NORTHERN IRELAND OFFICE

Library, Northern Ireland Office, 11 Millbank, London SW1P 4PN
☎020 7210 0253
Fax 020 7210 0212
url: www.nio.gov.uk
Contact Ms Rose Dines (e-mail: rose.dines@nio.x.gsi.gov.uk)

OFFICE FOR NATIONAL STATISTICS

National Statistics Information and Library Service, Office for National Statistics,
1 Drummond Gate, London SW1V 2QQ
☎0845 601 3034 (enquiries)
Fax (01633) 652747
e-mail: info@statistics.gov.uk
url: www.statistics.gov.uk/services/nslibraryservices.asp; catalogue: http://library.ons.gov.uk
Chief Librarian John Birch BLib MCLIP (020 7533 6250; e-mail: john.birch@ons.gov.uk)
Librarian Alan Cliftlands BA (020 7533 6257; e-mail: alan.cliftlands@ons.gov.uk)

(This library is open to the public by appointment only. Includes most major national statistics series.)

Site libraries

▶ National Statistics Information and Library Service, Office for National Statistics, Room 1.001, Government Buildings, Cardiff Road, Newport, Gwent NP9 1XG
☎0845 601 3034 (enquiries), (01633) 812399 (administration)
Fax (01633) 652747
Librarian Ian W Bushnell BA MCLIP (01633 813033; e-mail: ian.bushnell@ons.gov.uk)
(Library open to the public by appointment only. Specializes in micro-economic data.)

▶ National Statistics Information and Library Service, Office for National Statistics, Segensworth Road, Titchfield, Fareham, Hants PO15 5PR
☎(01329) 813606
Fax (01329) 813406
Librarian Bill Anderson BA MCLIP
(This library is not open to the public.)

OFFICE OF FAIR TRADING

Library and Information Centre, Office of Fair Trading, LC/7 Fleetbank House, 2-6 Salisbury Square, London EC4Y 8JX
☎020 7211 8938/9. For general OFT enquiries 020 7211 8000; OFT Publications orderline 0800 389 3158
Fax 020 7211 8940
e-mail: enquiries@oft.gsi.gov.uk
url: www.oft.gov.uk
Head of Library and Information Services Martin Shrive BA(Hons) MCLIP

OFFICE OF RAIL REGULATION

Library, Office of Rail Regulation, 1 Waterhouse Square, 138-142 Holborn, London EC1N 2TQ
☎020 7282 2001 (direct)
Fax 020 7282 2045
e-mail: rail.library@orr.gsi.gov.uk
url: www.rail-reg.gov.uk
Librarian Ms Sue MacSwan BA MSc

OFFICE OF THE DEPUTY PRIME MINISTER AND DEPARTMENT OF TRANSPORT (ODPM-DFT)

Library and Information Services, Office of the Deputy Prime Minister and Department of Transport (ODPM-DFT), 2/H24 Ashdown House, 123 Victoria Street, London SW1E 6DE
☎020 7944 3333 (public information); 020 7944 3000 (switchboard)
Fax 020 7944 6098
url: www.odpm.gov.uk (ODPM); www.dft.gov.uk (DFT)

Library and Information Services Branch Head Ms Sue Westcott MA DipLib FCLIP (020 7944 5830)

Library and information centre
▶ Ashdown House Information Centre, Office of the Deputy Prime Minister and Department of Transport (ODPM-DFT), 2/H24 Ashdown House, 123 Victoria Street, London SWIE 6DE
☎020 7944 3039 (for external enquiries)
Fax 020 7944 6098
Specialism(s): Housing; Local Government; Planning (ODPM); Transport (DfT)

OFFICE OF THE PARLIAMENTARY AND HEALTH SERVICE OMBUDSMAN (Office of the Parliamentary Commissioner for Administration and Health Service Commissioner for England)

Library and Information Service, Office of the Parliamentary and Health Service Ombudsman (Office of the Parliamentary Commissioner for Administration and Health Service Commissioner for England), 29th Floor, Millbank Tower, Millbank, London SWIP 4QP
☎020 7217 4102/4104
Fax 020 7217 4295
e-mail: library@ombudsman.gsi.gov.uk
url: www.ombudsman.org.uk
Information Manager Ms Suzanne Burge HonFCLIP BA FCLIP
Specialism(s): Ombudsman issues; Maladministration

OFGEM (OFFICE OF GAS AND ELECTRICITY MARKETS)

Research and Information Centre, OFGEM (Office of Gas and Electricity Markets), 9 Millbank, London SWIP 3GE
☎020 7901 7003/7004
Fax 020 7901 7378
e-mail: library@ofgem.gov.uk
url: www.ofgem.gov.uk
Librarian Keith Smith
Assistant Librarian Ms Katy Hamilton
(Open 2pm–4.30pm Monday to Friday. By appointment only: 24 hours notice required.)

OFWAT (OFFICE OF WATER SERVICES)

Library and Information Services, OFWAT (Office of Water Services), Centre City Tower, 7 Hill Street, Birmingham B5 4UA
☎0121 625 1361 (general enquiries)
Fax 0121 625 1362

e-mail: enquiries@ofwat.gsi.gov.uk
url: www.ofwat.gov.uk
Librarian and Information Services Manager Ms Jackie Cranmer BSc MCLIP (0121 625 1361)

OMNIBUS SOCIETY

The John F Parke Memorial Library, The Omnibus Society, Museum of Iron, Coalbrookdale, Ironbridge, Shropshire
url: www.omnibussoc.org
Librarian Alan Mills (01922 631867 (tel/fax); e-mail: alanavrilmills@hotmail.com)
(Manned by volunteers, the Library is currently open to casual callers on the 1st, 3rd and 5th Wednesdays of the month (09.30–16.30), although other weekday appointments can be made by prior arrangement.)
Specialism(s): Road passenger transport; Unique collection of timetables

OPRA see THE PENSIONS REGULATOR

ORDNANCE SURVEY

Library and Information Centre, Ordnance Survey, Room C128, Romsey Road, Southampton SO16 4GU
☎023 8079 2334
Fax 023 8079 2879
url: www.ordnancesurvey.co.uk
Librarian Ms Cathy Layton BSc(Econ) (e-mail: cathy.layton@ordnancesurvey.co.uk)

PARTNERSHIP HOUSE MISSION STUDIES LIBRARY

Partnership House Mission Studies Library, 157 Waterloo Road, London SE1 8XA
☎020 7803 3215
Fax 020 7928 3627
e-mail: library.phmslib@cms-uk.org
url: http://phmsl.soutron.com
Librarian Miss Elizabeth Williams BA MCLIP (e-mail: elizabeth.phmslib@cms-uk.org)
Specialism(s): History and theology of mission of the Anglican Church

THE PENSIONS REGULATOR

(formerly OPRA (Occupational Pensions Regulatory Authority))
Library, The Pensions Regulator, Invicta House, Trafalgar Place, Brighton BN1 4DW
☎(01273) 627686
Fax (01273) 627760
url: www.thepensionsregulator.gov.uk

Information Officer Mrs Jan Godfrey BA(Hons) PGDip Law MCLIP BIALL (e-mail: jan.godfrey@thepensionsregulator.gov.uk)
(The Library is not open to the public.)

PIRA INTERNATIONAL

Information Services, PIRA International, Cleeve Road, Leatherhead, Surrey KT22 7RU
☎(01372) 802050 (enquiries); 802061 (photocopy requests)
Fax (01372) 802239
e-mail: docdel@pira.co.uk
url: www.piranet.com
Business Manager Ms Diana Deavin
Specialism(s): Papermaking; Printing; Packaging; Publishing

PLUNKETT FOUNDATION

Library, Plunkett Foundation, The Quadrangle, Woodstock, Oxon OX20 1LH
☎(01993) 810730
Fax (01993) 810849
e-mail: info@plunkett.co.uk
url: www.plunkett.co.uk
Information Services Manager Ms Elodie Malhomme
Specialism(s): Focus on history and practice of cooperatives and rural enterprise; Agriculture

PLYMOUTH PROPRIETARY LIBRARY

Plymouth Proprietary Library, Alton Terrace, 111 North Hill, Plymouth PL4 8JY
☎(01752) 660515
Librarian John R Smith
Specialism(s): 19th- and early 20th-century classical fiction (available to members only)

POETRY LIBRARY

Poetry Library, Level 5, Royal Festival Hall, London SE1 8XX
☎020 7921 0943/0664
Fax 020 7921 0939
e-mail: info@poetrylibrary.org.uk
url: www.poetrylibrary.org.uk; www.poetrymagazines.org.uk
Librarian Simon Smith BA DipLibInfSci
(The Poetry Library will be closed April 2005–January 2007 for visits from the public. However, enquiries by e-mail, post and telephone will be welcome during this period, Mon–Fri 10am–6pm)
Specialism(s): Modern and contemporary poetry written in or translated into English

POLISH LIBRARY

Polish Library, 238-246 King Street, London W6 0RF

☎020 8741 0474
Fax 020 8741 7724
e-mail: bibliotekapolska@posklibrary.fsnet.co.uk; polish.library@posk.org
Librarian Mrs Jadwiga Szmidt MA

PORTICO LIBRARY AND GALLERY

The Portico Library and Gallery, 57 Mosley Street, Manchester M2 3HY
☎0161 236 6785
Fax 0161 236 6785
url: www.theportico.org.uk
Librarian Miss Emma Marigliano BA(Hons) (e-mail: librarian@theportico.org.uk)
(Tours by arrangement. Nineteenth-century stock available for scholarly research. Gallery open to the public.)

PROUDMAN OCEANOGRAPHIC LABORATORY

Library, Proudman Oceanographic Laboratory, Joseph Proudman Building, 6 Brownlow Street, Liverpool L3 5DA
☎0151 795 4800
Fax 0151 795 4801
url: www.pol.ac.uk
Head of Information and Communications Ms J Martin BA MSc MCLIP (e-mail: jul@pol.ac.uk)
Assistant Librarian Miss Sarah Lewis-Newton BA
Specialism(s): Oceanography and marine science

QINETIQ

Information Centre, Qinetiq, Winfrith Technology Centre, Building A22, Dorchester, Dorset DT2 8XJ
☎(01305) 212218
Fax (01305) 212444
url: www.qinetiq.com
Information Specialist Ms Wendy Gubbels BA (e-mail: wrgubbels@qinetiq.com)
Specialism(s): Sonar and oceanography

RELIGIOUS SOCIETY OF FRIENDS IN BRITAIN (QUAKERS)

Library, Religious Society of Friends in Britain (Quakers), Friends House, 173-177 Euston Road, London NW1 2BJ
☎020 7663 1135
Fax 020 7663 1001
e-mail: library@quaker.org.uk
url: www.quaker.org.uk/library.html
Librarian Ms Heather Rowland BA MCLIP
Specialism(s): Quakerism; Peace and pacifism; Anti-slavery

THE RESEARCH COUNCILS

The Research Councils, Polaris House, North Star Avenue, Swindon, Wilts SN2 1SZ
☎(01793) 442000 (enquiries)
Fax (01793) 442042
url: www.rcuk.ac.uk

The following research councils are based at this site:
▶ Biotechnology and Biological Sciences Research Council (BBSRC), Polaris House, North Star Avenue, Swindon, Wilts SN2 1UH
  url: www.bbsrc.ac.uk
  Information Officer Mrs Carol Milner (01793 414679; e-mail: carol.milner@bbsrc.ac.uk)
▶ Economic and Social Research Council (ESRC), Polaris House, North Star Avenue, Swindon, Wilts SN2 1SZ
  url: www.esrc.ac.uk
  Information Officer Aaron Russell (01793 413051; e-mail: aaron.russell@esrc.ac.uk)
▶ Engineering and Physical Sciences Research Council (EPSRC), Polaris House, North Star Avenue, Swindon, Wilts SN2 1ET
  url: www.epsrc.ac.uk
  Information Officer Alan Holyday (01793 444232; e-mail: alan.holyday:epsrc.ac.uk)
▶ Natural Environment Research Council (NERC), Polaris House, North Star Avenue, Swindon, Wilts SN2 1EU
  url: www.nerc.ac.uk
  Information Officer John Mason (01793 411782; e-mail: john.mason@nerc.ac.uk)

ROTHAMSTED LIBRARY – ROTHAMSTED RESEARCH

Rothamsted Library – Rothamsted Research, Harpenden, Herts AL5 2JQ
☎(01582) 763133
Fax (01582) 760981
url: www.res.bbsrc.ac.uk/library/tlibindex.html; www.rothamsted.ac.uk
Librarian Mrs S E Allsopp BA DipLib (e-mail: liz.allsopp@bbsrc.ac.uk)
Specialism(s): Arable crops research; Sustainable land development

ROYAL ACADEMY OF ARTS

Library, Royal Academy of Arts, Burlington House, Piccadilly, London W1J 0BD
☎020 7300 5737 (enquiries), 020 7300 5740 (administration)
Fax 020 7300 5765
e-mail: library@royalacademy.org.uk
url: www.royalacademy.org.uk
Head of Library Services A M Waterton
Assistant Librarian Mrs L Macpherson
Specialism(s): British art and artists from 18th century to present; History of the Academy since 1768

ROYAL AERONAUTICAL SOCIETY

Library, Royal Aeronautical Society, 4 Hamilton Place, London W1J 7BQ
☎020 7670 4362
Fax 020 7670 4359
url: www.aerosociety.com
Librarian Brian Riddle (e-mail: brian.riddle@raes.org.uk)
Specialism(s): Extensive collection of material relating to the development and recent
technical advances in aeronautics, aviation and aerospace technology

ROYAL AIR FORCE COLLEGE

College Library, Royal Air Force College, Cranwell, Sleaford, Lincs NG34 8HB
☎(01400) 266329
Fax (01400) 266266
e-mail: college.library@dial.pipex.com
College Librarian & Archivist Ms Mary Guy BA(Hons) DipLib MCLIP (e-mail:
collegelibrarian@cranwell.raf.mod.uk)

ROYAL AIR FORCE MUSEUM

Royal Air Force Museum, Grahame Park Way, Hendon, London NW9 5LL
☎020 8205 2266 ext 4873
Fax 020 8200 1751
e-mail: research@rafmuseum.org
url: www.rafmuseum.org
Senior Keeper P J V Elliott MA BSc MCLIP
(Prior appointment necessary)
Specialism(s): Military aviation

ROYAL ASTRONOMICAL SOCIETY

Library, Royal Astronomical Society, Burlington House, Piccadilly, London W1J 0BQ
☎020 7734 3307/4582
Fax 020 7494 0166
e-mail: info@ras.org.uk
url: www.ras.org.uk
Librarian Peter D Hingley BA MCLIP RD (e-mail: pdh@ras.org.uk)
Assistant Librarian Miss Mary Chibnall BA MCLIP (e-mail: mic@ras.org.uk)
(Extensive archive and rare book collection covering astronomy and geophysics. Enquiries
in writing or by e-mail preferred, access by appointment)

ROYAL BOTANIC GARDEN, EDINBURGH

Library, Royal Botanic Garden, Edinburgh, 20A Inverleith Row, Edinburgh EH3 5LR
☎0131 248 2853 (enquiries), 0131 248 2850 (administration)
Fax 0131 248 2901
e-mail: library@rbge.org.uk

url: www.rbge.org.uk
Head of Library Mrs Jane Hutcheon BSc MCLIP (e-mail: j.hutcheon@rbge.org.uk)
Specialism(s): Botany; Horticulture; Garden history and botanical art

ROYAL BOTANIC GARDENS, KEW

Library & Archives, Royal Botanic Gardens, Kew, Richmond, Surrey TW9 3AE
☎020 8332 5000
Fax 020 8332 5197
e-mail: library@kew.org
url: www.rbgkew.org.uk
Head of Library and Archives John Flanagan MCLIP (020 8332 5412; fax: 020 8332 5430; e-mail: j.flanagan@rbgkew.org.uk)
Archivist Mrs Kate Pickard MA MArAd
Illustrations Curator Miss Marilyn Ward

ROYAL COLLEGE OF PHYSICIANS AND SURGEONS OF GLASGOW

Library, Royal College of Physicians and Surgeons of Glasgow, 232-242 St Vincent Street, Glasgow G2 5RJ
☎0141 227 3204 (enquiries), 0141 221 6072 (administration)
Fax 0141 221 1804
e-mail: library@rcpsg.ac.uk
url: www.rcpsg.ac.uk
Librarian James Beaton MA(Hons) DipLib MCLIP (e-mail: james.beaton@rcpsg.ac.uk)
Archivist Mrs Carol Parry BA(Hons) DAA FETC (e-mail: carol.parry@rcpsg.ac.uk)
Assistant Librarian Mrs Valerie McClure MA(Hons) MSc (e-mail: valerie.mcclure@rcpsg.ac.uk)
Cataloguer Ms Julie Wands BSc(Hons) DipLib MCLIP (e-mail: julie.wands@rcpsg.ac.uk)
Specialism(s): History of medicine

ROYAL COLLEGE OF PHYSICIANS OF EDINBURGH

Library, Royal College of Physicians of Edinburgh, 9 Queen Street, Edinburgh EH2 1JQ
☎0131 225 7324
Fax 0131 220 3939
e-mail: library@rcpe.ac.uk
url: www.rcpe.ac.uk
Head of Library and Information Services Iain A Milne MLib MCLIP

ROYAL COLLEGE OF PHYSICIANS OF LONDON

Library, Royal College of Physicians of London, 11 St Andrews Place, Regent's Park, London NW1 4LE
☎020 7935 1174 ext 312

Fax 020 7486 3729
e-mail: info@rcplondon.ac.uk
url: www.rcplondon.ac.uk
Minicom 020 7486 5687
Manager, Heritage Centre Ms Caroline Moss-Gibbons BLib(Hons) PGCE
Manager, Information Centre Mrs Julie Beckwith BA MSc MCLIP
Specialism(s): UK health policy; History of medicine

ROYAL COLLEGE OF PSYCHIATRISTS

Library and Information Service, Royal College of Psychiatrists, 17 Belgrave Square, London SW1X 8PG
☎020 7235 2351 ext 138/152
Fax 020 7259 6303
e-mail: infoservices@rcpsych.ac.uk
url: www.rcpsych.ac.uk
Librarian Mrs Morwenna Rogers BSc MSc
Honorary Librarian Dr David Tate
Specialism(s): Antiquarian psychiatry textbooks dating from 15th century

ROYAL COLLEGE OF SURGEONS OF ENGLAND

Library and Lumley Study Centre, Royal College of Surgeons of England, 35-43 Lincoln's Inn Fields, London WC2A 3PE
☎020 7869 6555/6556 (enquiries), 020 7405 3474 (College switchboard)
Fax 020 7405 4438
e-mail: library@rcseng.ac.uk
url: www.rcseng.ac.uk
Head of Library and Information Services Mrs Thalia Knight MA MA DipLib MCLIP
Deputy Head of Library and Information Services Ms Tina Craig BA(Hons) MA DipLib
Information Services Manager Tom Bishop BA(Hons) MA

ROYAL COLLEGE OF VETERINARY SURGEONS

RCVS Trust Library, Royal College of Veterinary Surgeons, Belgravia House, 62-64 Horseferry Road, London SW1P 2AF
☎020 7222 2021
Fax 020 7202 0751
e-mail: library@rcvstrust.org.uk
url: www.rcvstrust.org.uk
Librarian Brendan McDonagh BLS MSLS MPhil (e-mail: b.mcdonagh@rcvstrust.org.uk)

ROYAL COMMISSION ON THE ANCIENT AND HISTORICAL MONUMENTS OF WALES

Publications and Outreach Branch, Royal Commission on the Ancient and Historical Monuments of Wales, Crown Building, Plas Crug, Aberystwyth, Ceredigion SY23 1NJ

☎(01970) 621200
Fax (01970) 627701
e-mail: nmr.wales@rcahmw.gov.uk
url: www.rcahmw.gov.uk
Secretary Peter White BA FSA
Librarian and Head of Reader Services Ms Patricia Moore BA MCLIP
Specialism(s): Archaeology; Architectural history and heritage of Wales

ROYAL ENGINEERS LIBRARY

Royal Engineers Library, Brompton Barracks, Chatham, Kent ME4 4UG
☎(01634) 822416
Fax (01634) 822419
url: www.army.mod.uk/royalengineers/library
Library Curator Ms M Lindsay Roxburgh

ROYAL ENTOMOLOGICAL SOCIETY

Library, Royal Entomological Society, 41 Queen's Gate, London SW7 5HR
☎020 7584 8361
Fax 020 7581 8505
e-mail: lib@royensoc.co.uk
url: www.royensoc.co.uk
Librarian Ms Berit Pedersen BA(Hons) MCLIP

ROYAL GEOGRAPHICAL SOCIETY (with the Institute of British Geographers)

Foyle Reading Room, Royal Geographical Society (with the Institute of British Geographers), 1 Kensington Gore, London SW7 2AR
☎020 7591 3044
Fax 020 7591 3001
e-mail: enquiries@rgs.org
url: www.rgs.org
Principal Librarian E Rae MA DipLIS
Reader Services Librarian Miss J C Turner BA(Hons)
Curator of Maps Francis Herbert
Specialism(s): Geography; Travel; Exploration

ROYAL HORTICULTURAL SOCIETY

The Lindley Library, Royal Horticultural Society, 80 Vincent Square, London SW1P 2PE
☎020 7821 3050
Fax 020 7828 3022
e-mail: library.london@rhs.org.uk
url: www.rhs.org.uk/libraries/libraries_london.asp
Librarian and Archivist Dr Brent Elliott BA MA PhD

ROYAL INSTITUTE OF BRITISH ARCHITECTS

British Architectural Library, Royal Institute of British Architects, 66 Portland Place, London
WIB IAD
☎020 7307 3707 (24-hr recorded information service); 020 7580 5533 (switchboard)
Fax 020 7631 1802
e-mail: info@inst.riba.org
url: www.architecture.com
Public information line (calls 50p per min): (0906) 302 0400
Director Dr Irena Murray

Branch library

British Architectural Library Drawings Collection, Royal Institute of British Architects,
Henry Cole Wing, Victoria and Albert Museum, Exhibition Road, London SW7 2RL
☎020 7307 3708 (Study Room)
e-mail: drawings&archives@inst.riba.org
Assistant Director, Special Collections and Curator, Drawings Collection C Hind
MA DipLib MCLIP
(The Drawings Collection is located at the address above from Autumn 2004 and will be
fully operational from January 2005)

ROYAL INSTITUTE OF INTERNATIONAL AFFAIRS

Library, Royal Institute of International Affairs, Chatham House, 10 St James's Square,
London SWIY 4LE
☎020 7957 5723 (enquiries)
Fax 020 7314 2796
e-mail: libenquire@chathamhouse.org.uk
url: www.riia.org
Head of Library and Information Services Mrs C Hume BA DipLib MSc MCLIP (020
7957 5720; e-mail: chume@riia.org)
Deputy Librarian Mrs M Bone BSc (020 7314 2775; e-mail: mbone@riia.org)
Specialism(s): International affairs; Politics; Economics; Security; Environment

ROYAL INSTITUTE OF NAVIGATION

Library, Royal Institute of Navigation, 1 Kensington Gore, London SW7 2AT
☎020 7591 3130
Fax 020 7591 3131
e-mail: info@rin.org.uk
url: www.rin.org.uk
Librarian
(The library stocks 2000 titles on land, sea and air navigation. It is free to members and
open to the public on an appointment-only basis)

ROYAL INSTITUTION OF GREAT BRITAIN

Library, Royal Institution of Great Britain, 21 Albemarle Street, London WIS 4BS

☎020 7670 2939
Fax 020 7629 3569
e-mail: ril@ri.ac.uk
url: www.rigb.org
Head of Collections and Heritage Prof Frank James (020 7670 2924; e-mail: fjames@ri.ac.uk)
(Please note that the Library will be closed from January 2005 for approximately one year)

ROYAL INSTITUTION OF NAVAL ARCHITECTS

Library, Royal Institution of Naval Architects, 10 Upper Belgrave Street, London SW1X 8BQ
☎020 7235 4622
Fax 020 7259 5912
e-mail: hq@rina.org.uk
url: www.rina.org.uk
IT Manager Ms Debra Greene

ROYAL MILITARY ACADEMY SANDHURST

Central Library, Royal Military Academy Sandhurst, Camberley, Surrey GU15 4PQ
☎(01276) 412367
Fax (01276) 412538
url: www.atra.mod.uk
Senior Librarian Andrew Orgill MA DipLib MCLIP (e-mail: senlibrarian@rmas.mod.uk)
Specialism(s): Military history and international affairs

ROYAL NATIONAL INSTITUTE FOR DEAF PEOPLE

RNID Library, UCL Ear Institute, 330-332 Gray's Inn Road, London WC1X 8EE
☎020 7915 1553
Fax 020 7915 1443
e-mail: rnidlib@ucl.ac.uk
url: www.ucl.ac.uk/library/rnid
Librarian Alex Stagg MA
Specialism(s): Hearing, speech and language and their disorders; Deafness

ROYAL NATIONAL INSTITUTE OF THE BLIND

Research Library, Royal National Institute of the Blind, 105 Judd Street, London WC1H 9NE
☎020 7391 2052
Fax 020 7388 2034
e-mail: library@rnib.org.uk
url: www.rnib.org.uk/researchlibrary
Research Library Manager Ms Penny J Sturgess BSc (020 7391 2060; e-mail: penny.sturgess@rnib.org.uk)
Librarian Robert Saggers (e-mail: robert.saggers@rnib.org.uk)

Library Services
RNIB Braille Library; RNIB Cassette Library; RNIB Talking Books Library: contact 0845 702 3153 (customer services)

Library Services, Royal National Institute of the Blind, PO Box 173, Peterborough PE2 6WS
☎(01733) 375333
Fax (01733) 375001
e-mail: libraryinfo@rnib.org.uk
Library Services Manager John Crampton MCLIP

ROYAL PHARMACEUTICAL SOCIETY OF GREAT BRITAIN

Library, Royal Pharmaceutical Society of Great Britain, 1 Lambeth High Street, London SE1 7JN
☎020 7735 9141 (switchboard); 020 7572 2300 (direct)
Fax 020 7572 2499
e-mail: library@rpsgb.org
url: www.rpsgb.org
Head of Information Centre Roy T Allcorn BSc MCLIP
Librarian Vacancy
Assistant Librarian Miss Karen Poole BA MSc
Specialism(s): Pharmacy; Medicines; Therapeutics; Historical information; Pharmaceutical science

ROYAL SOCIETY

Library, Royal Society, 6–9 Carlton House Terrace, London SW1Y 5AG
☎020 7451 2606
Fax 020 7930 2170
e-mail: library@royalsoc.ac.uk
url: www.royalsoc.ac.uk
Head of Library and Information Services Keith Moore

ROYAL SOCIETY FOR THE PREVENTION OF ACCIDENTS

Information Centre, Royal Society for the Prevention of Accidents, Edgbaston Park, 353 Bristol Road, Birmingham B5 7ST
☎0121 248 2063/6
Fax 0121 248 2081
e-mail: infocentre@rospa.com
url: www.rospa.com
Information Services Manager Mrs Lisa Lawson BSocSc MA (0121 248 2063; e-mail: llawson@rospa.com)
Information Officer (Statistics) Ms Dianne Hooper BA(Hons) (0121 248 2064; e-mail: d.hooper@rospa.com)

Assistant Information Manager Ms Louise Neel BA PGDip (0121 248 2066; e-mail: lneel@rospa.com)

ROYAL SOCIETY OF CHEMISTRY

Library and Information Centre, Royal Society of Chemistry, Burlington House, Piccadilly, London W1J 0BA
☎020 7437 8656; 020 7440 3373 (direct)
Fax 020 7287 9798
e-mail: e-mail: library@rsc.org
url: www.rsc.org/library
Librarian Nigel Lees MSc MCLIP

ROYAL SOCIETY OF MEDICINE

Library, Royal Society of Medicine, 1 Wimpole Street, London W1G 0AE
☎020 7290 2940 (enquiries), 020 7290 2931 (administration)
Fax 020 7290 2939 (requests), 020 7290 2976 (administration)
e-mail: library@rsm.ac.uk
url: www.rsm.ac.uk
Director of Information Services Ian Snowley BA MBA MCLIP FRSA

ROYAL STATISTICAL SOCIETY

Royal Statistical Society, 12 Errol Street, London EC1Y 8LX
☎020 7638 8998
url: www.rss.org.uk
Consultant Archivist Ms Janet Foster (e-mail: j.foster@rss.org.uk)
(Pre-1800 books and Society archives. Viewing by appointment only)

Albert Sloman Library, Royal Statistical Society, University of Essex, Wivenhoe Park, Colchester, Essex CO4 3SQ
☎(01206) 873181/873172 (enquiries)
Deputy Librarian Nigel Cochrane (e-mail: nigelc@essex.ac.uk)
Assistant Librarian Ms Sandy Macmillen (e-mail: amacmi@essex.ac.uk)
(Houses the historical collection of the RSS)
Specialism(s): Statistics; Social history

ROYAL TOWN PLANNING INSTITUTE

Library, Royal Town Planning Institute, 41 Botolph Lane, London EC3R 8DL
☎020 7929 9452
Fax 020 7929 9490
e-mail: library@rtpi.org.uk
url: www.rtpi.org.uk
Information Manager Ms Melissa Wyatt BA

RSA

Library, RSA, 8 John Adam Street, London WC2N 6EZ
☎020 7451 6874 (Library), 020 7451 6847 (Archive)
Fax 020 7839 5805
e-mail: library@rsa.org.uk; archive@rsa.org.uk
url: www.theRSA.org/library
Librarian and Knowledge Manager Matthew McCarthy
Archivist Nicola Allen
(Access by appointment)

ST DEINIOL'S RESIDENTIAL LIBRARY

St Deiniol's Residential Library, Church Lane, Hawarden, Flintshire CH5 3DF
☎(01244) 532350
Fax (01244) 520643
e-mail: deiniol.warden@btconnect.com
url: www.st-deiniols.org
Warden The Very Revd P B Francis MTheol
Librarian Miss P J Williams BA DipLib
(This is a residential library specializing in theology, history and Victorian studies. The collection of over 250,000 volumes includes W E Gladstone's personal library. Modern residential accommodation is available at modest charges. Day readers welcome. Testimonial required)

SCIENCE FICTION FOUNDATION COLLECTION

Science Fiction Foundation Collection, University of Liverpool Library, PO Box 123, Liverpool L69 3DA
☎0151 794 2696 (library)
Fax 0151 794 2681
url: http://sca.lib.liv.ac.uk/collections/index.html
Librarian/Administrator Andy Sawyer MPhil MCLIP (0151 794 3142; e-mail: asawyer@liverpool.ac.uk)

SCIENCE MUSEUM LIBRARY

Science Museum Library, Imperial College Road, London SW7 5NH
☎020 7942 4242
Fax 020 7942 4243
e-mail: smlinfo@nmsi.ac.uk
url: www.sciencemuseum.org.uk/library/
Acting Manager of Library Services Ian E D Carter BSc DipLib MCLIP (e-mail: ian.carter@nmsi.ac.uk)
(A national library for the history and public understanding of science and technology. Open free to the public. Enquiries accepted in person, and by e-mail, letter and telephone. Some services are run jointly with Imperial College London Central Library.)

SCOTTISH ASSOCIATION FOR MARINE SCIENCE

Library, Scottish Association for Marine Science, Dunstaffnage Marine Laboratory, Oban,
Argyll PA37 1QA
☎(01631) 559000
Fax (01631) 559001
url: www.sams.ac.uk
Library Assistant Ms Patricia Thomson (e-mail: tricia.thomson@sams.ac.uk)

SCOTTISH BOOK TRUST

Children's Reference Library, Scottish Book Trust, Sandeman House, Trunks Close, 55 High
Street, Edinburgh EH1 1SR
☎0131 524 0160
Fax 0131 524 0161
e-mail: info@scottishbooktrust.com
url: www.scottishbooktrust.com
Library Development Officer Vacant

SCOTTISH ENTERPRISE

The Knowledge Exchange, Scottish Enterprise, 150 Broomielaw, Glasgow G2 8LU
☎0141 248 2700 (main), 0141 228 2268 (direct line)
Fax 0141 228 2818
url: www.scottish-enterprise.com
Manager Mrs Gail Rogers MA DipLib (e-mail: gail.rogers@scotent.co.uk)
Specialism(s): Business information

SCOTTISH EXECUTIVE

Information and Library Services Centre, Scottish Executive, K Spur, Saughton House,
Broomhouse Drive, Edinburgh EH11 3XD
☎0131 244 4565
Fax 0131 244 4545
e-mail: library@scotland.gsi.gov.uk
Chief Librarian/Head of Information Resources Ms Anne Martin BA MA MCLIP
Specialism(s): Scottish Executive and official publications

SCOTTISH NATURAL HERITAGE

Library Services, Scottish Natural Heritage, 2 Anderson Place, Edinburgh EH6 5NP
☎0131 446 2479 (enquiries), 0131 446 2478 (library management)
Fax 0131 446 2405
e-mail: library@snh.gov.uk
url: www.snh.org.uk
Library Manager Ms A Coupe MCLIP (e-mail: alwyn.coupe@snh.gov.uk)

SCOTTISH PARLIAMENT

Scottish Parliament Information Centre (SPICe), Scottish Parliament, Edinburgh EH99 1SP
☎0131 348 5000
Fax 0131 348 5378
e-mail: spice@scottish.parliament.uk
url: www.scottish.parliament.uk
Head of Research and Information Services Ms Janet Seaton FCLIP

SIGNET LIBRARY

Signet Library, Parliament Square, Edinburgh EH1 1RF
☎0131 225 4923
Fax 0131 220 4016
e-mail: library@wssociety.co.uk
url: www.signetlibrary.co.uk
Librarian Ms Audrey Walker BA MCLIP
Specialism(s): Scottish law

SOCIÉTÉ JERSIAISE

Lord Coutanche Library, Société Jersiaise, 7 Pier Road, St Helier, Jersey, Channel Islands
JE2 4XW
☎(01534) 730538 (enquiries), (01534) 633392 (administration)
Fax (01534) 888262
e-mail: library@societe-jersiaise.org
url: www.societe-jersiaise.org
Librarian Mrs Brenda Ross MA(Hons)
Specialism(s): Local studies; Local and family history; Maps, prints, newspapers and
ephemera

SOCIETY FOR COOPERATION IN RUSSIAN AND SOVIET STUDIES

Library, Society for Cooperation in Russian and Soviet Studies, 320 Brixton Road, London
SW9 6AB
☎020 7274 2282
Fax 020 7274 3230
e-mail: ruslibrary@scrss.org.uk
url: www.scrss.org.uk
Hon. Librarian Ms J Rosen BA(Hons) DipLib
Specialism(s): Literature, arts and history of Russia/Soviet Union in the 20th century

SOCIETY OF ANTIQUARIES OF LONDON

Library, Society of Antiquaries of London, Burlington House, Piccadilly, London W1J 0BE
☎020 7479 7084

Fax 020 7287 6967
e-mail: library@sal.org.uk
url: www.sal.org.uk
Librarian Bernard Nurse MA FSA MCLIP
Specialism(s): Archaeology; Antiquities and historic monuments in Britain and Europe

SOCIETY OF GENEALOGISTS

Library, Society of Genealogists, 14 Charterhouse Buildings, Goswell Road, London
EC1M 7BA
☎020 7251 8799
Fax 020 7250 1800
e-mail: library@sog.org.uk
url: www.sog.org.uk
Librarian Ms Sue Gibbons BA MCLIP
Specialism(s): Family, local and national history; Topography; Biography; Heraldry;
Demography

SUPREME COURT LIBRARY

Supreme Court Library, Royal Courts of Justice, Department for Constitutional Affairs,
Queens Building, Strand, London WC2A 2LL
☎020 7947 6587 (enquiries), 020 7947 7198 (administration)
Fax 020 7947 6661
url: www.courtservice.gov.uk; www.dca.gov.uk
Supreme Court Librarian Ms J M Robertson BA MCLIP

TATE BRITAIN

The Hyman Kreitman Research Centre for the Tate Library and Archive, Tate Britain,
Millbank, London SW1P 4RG
☎020 7887 8838
Fax 020 7887 3952
e-mail: research.centre@tate.org.uk
url: www.tate.org.uk/research services
Head of Library and Archive Ms Beth Houghton DipAD
Librarian Ms Meg Duff BA DipEd DipNZLS
Archivist Ms Sue Breakell MA MArAd
Head of Readers' Services Tim Pate BA(Hons) MSc(Hons) ILM
(Readers by appointment only)
Specialism(s): British art and international modern art

TAVISTOCK AND PORTMAN NHS TRUST

Tavistock and Portman NHS Trust Library, 120 Belsize Lane, London NW3 5BA
☎020 7447 3776 (direct line)
Fax 020 7447 3734
e-mail: library@tavi-port.org

url: www.tavi-port.org
Head of Library Services Ms Angela Douglas MCLIP BSc MA
Specialism(s): Psychoanalysis; Psychotherapy; Educational psychology

THEATRE MUSEUM

The Theatre Museum Research Department, Theatre Museum, 1E Tavistock Street,
London WC2E 7PR
☎020 7943 4700
Fax 020 7943 4777
url: www.theatremuseum.org
Head of Information Services and Collections Management Ms C Hudson BA MCLIP
Specialism(s): Performing arts; Stage design

TPS CONSULT LTD

The Information Centre, TPS Consult Ltd, Centre Tower, Whitgift Centre, Croydon CR9 0AU
☎020 8256 4110
Fax 0870 128 4894
url: www.tpsconsult.co.uk
Marketing and Information Services Manager Gursel Ziynettin (e-mail:
ziynettin.gursel@tpsconsult.co.uk)

TRADES UNION CONGRESS

(see also London Metropolitan University)
TUC Library Collections, Trades Union Congress, London Metropolitan University, London
North Campus, Learning Centre, 236–250 Holloway Road, London N7 6PP
☎020 7133 2260
Fax 020 7133 2529
e-mail: tuclib@londonmet.ac.uk
url: www.londonmet.ac.uk/libraries/tuc; www.unionhistory.info
Librarian Ms Christine Coates MA MCLIP (e-mail: c.coates@londonmet.ac.uk)
Specialism(s): Trade unions; Industrial relations; Politics; Economic history; International
affairs

UK TRADE AND INVESTMENT

Information Centre, UK Trade and Investment, Kingsgate House, 66-74 Victoria Street,
London SW1E 6SW
☎020 7215 8000
Fax 020 7215 4231
e-mail: 'Contact us' on www.uktradeinvest.gov.uk
url: www.uktradeinvest.gov.uk
Senior Manager, Information Centre and Enquiries Miss Ann Hughes BA(Hons) MLIS
Manager, Information Centre Miss Diane Brodie MA DipLib
Manager, Information Resources Mrs Cass Martin BA(Hons) MA MA
Manager, Enquiries Ms Eleanora Small

Specialism(s): Over 15 online commercial databases containing information relating to export and investment overseas, including trade, production and official statistics together with market-research reports

UNITED STATES EMBASSY

Information Resource Center, American Embassy, 24 Grosvenor Square, London WIA IAE
☎020 7894 0925 (10am–12 noon, (public enquiries), 020 7499 9000 ext 2643 (administration)
Fax 020 7629 8288
e-mail: reflond@state.gov
url: www.usembassy.org.uk
Director Ms Anna Girvan
Specialism(s): US government and foreign policy; Current affairs

VETERINARY LABORATORIES AGENCY

Library, Veterinary Laboratories Agency, New Haw, Addlestone, Surrey KT15 3NB
☎(01932) 357314 (enquiries), (01932) 357603 (administration)
Fax (01932) 357608
e-mail: enquiries@vla.defra.gsi.gov.uk
url: www.defra.gov.uk/corporate/vla
Senior Librarian Mrs Heather Hulse BA(Hons)
Deputy Librarian Ms Ellen Howard BA(Hons) MA
Specialism(s): Veterinary science and medicine; Animal husbandry; Diseases of commercial farm animals

WARWICK HRI

(formerly Horticulture Research International)

Library, Warwick HRI, Wellesbourne, Warwick CV35 9EF
☎024 7657 4455
Fax 024 7657 4500
e-mail: wellesbourne.library@warwick.ac.uk
url: www.warwickhri.ac.uk
Head of Academic Support Hywel Williams (e-mail: hywel.williams@warwick.ac.uk)
Specialism(s): Horticulture research

WELLCOME LIBRARY FOR THE HISTORY AND UNDERSTANDING OF MEDICINE

Wellcome Library for the History and Understanding of Medicine, 210 Euston Road, London NW1 2BE
☎020 7611 8722
url: http://library.wellcome.ac.uk
Librarian Ms Frances Norton DipLib MA
Head of Public Services Ms Wendy Fish BA DipLib

History of Medicine/Science and Society collections
☎020 7611 8722 (enquiries)
Fax 020 7611 8369
e-mail: library@wellcome.ac.uk

Medical Photographic Library
☎020 7611 8348
Fax 020 7611 8577
e-mail: photolib@wellcome.ac.uk

Medical Film and Audio Collections
☎020 7611 8766
Fax 020 7611 8577
e-mail: mfac@wellcome.ac.uk
Specialism(s): History of medicine and allied science subjects

WESTMINSTER ABBEY

Muniment Room and Library, Westminster Abbey, London SW1P 3PA
☎020 7654 4830
Fax 020 7654 4827
e-mail: library@westminster-abbey.org
url: www.westminster-abbey.org
Librarian Dr Tony Trowles MA DPhil
Specialism(s): History of Westminster Abbey; Coronations; Theology (pre-1800)

WILLIAM SALT LIBRARY

William Salt Library, 19 Eastgate Street, Stafford ST16 2LZ
☎(01785) 278372
Fax (01785) 278414
e-mail: william.salt.library@staffordshire.gov.uk
url: www.staffordshire.gov.uk/salt
Librarian Mrs Thea Randall BA DAS
Specialism(s): Staffordshire local history

DR WILLIAMS'S LIBRARY

Dr Williams's Library, 14 Gordon Square, London WC1H 0AR
☎020 7387 3727
e-mail: enquiries@dwlib.co.uk
url: www.dwlib.co.uk
Director of Dr Williams's Trust and Library D L Wykes BSc PhD FRHistSoc
(The Congregational Library at 15 Gordon Square is administered by Dr Williams's Library, to whom any application should be made. Other details are the same)
Specialism(s): History and theology of religious dissent

WOMEN'S LIBRARY

The Women's Library, The Women's Library, London Metropolitan University, City
Campus, Old Castle Street, London E1 7NT
☎020 7320 2222
Fax 020 7320 2333
e-mail: enquirydesk@thewomenslibrary.ac.uk
url: www.thewomenslibrary.ac.uk
Head of Library Services Ms Beverley Kemp

WORKING CLASS MOVEMENT LIBRARY

Working Class Movement Library, Jubilee House, 51 The Crescent, Salford, Greater
Manchester M5 4WX
☎0161 736 3601
Fax 0161 737 4115
e-mail: enquiries@wcml.org.uk
url: www.wcml.org.uk
Librarian/Keeper Alain Kahan BA MCLIP
Library Assistant Patrick Ward
Specialism(s): Labour history; Communism; Socialism; Labour Party; ILP; Anarchism; Trades
Unions; Working class autobiography

YORK MINSTER

Library, York Minster, Dean's Park, York YO1 7JQ
☎(01904) 625308 (library); (01904) 611118 (archives)
Fax (01904) 611119
Acting Librarian John S Powell MA MCLIP (e-mail: jsp5@york.ac.uk)
Archivist Peter Young BA(Hons)
Open to the public Mon–Thurs 9am–5pm, Fri 9am–12 noon.
Specialism(s): Early printed books; Theology; Church history; Yorkshire history; Stained
glass; York Minster archives

ZOOLOGICAL SOCIETY OF LONDON

Library, Zoological Society of London, Regent's Park, London NW1 4RY
☎020 7449 6293
Fax 020 7586 5743
e-mail: library@zsl.org
url: www.zsl.org; https://library.zsl.org (library catalogue)
Librarian Ms A Sylph MSc MCLIP
Specialism(s): Zoology; Animal conservation

Academic, National and Special Libraries in the Republic of Ireland

ARCHBISHOP MARSH'S LIBRARY

Archbishop Marsh's Library, St Patrick's Close, Dublin 8, Republic of Ireland
☎(00 353 1) 454 3511 (enquiries and administration)
Fax (00 353 1) 454 3511
url: www.marshlibrary.ie
Keeper Dr Muriel McCarthy MA LLD (e-mail: keeper@marshlibrary.ie)
(Archbishop Marsh's Library is a 300-year-old research library with a magnificent collection of 16th and 17th century books. The library also has a book conservation bindery, which includes a flat paper conservation service.)

CDVEC CURRICULUM DEVELOPMENT UNIT

Library/Resource Centre, CDVEC Curriculum Development Unit, Sundrive Road, Crumlin, Dublin 12, Republic of Ireland
☎(00 353 1) 453 5487
Fax (00 353 1) 453 7659
url: www.curriculum.ie
Librarian Ms Eva Hornung DiplBibl MLIS ALAI (e-mail: eva.hornung@cdu.cdvec.ie)

CENTRAL CATHOLIC LIBRARY

Central Catholic Library, 74 Merrion Square, Dublin 2, Republic of Ireland
☎(00 353 1) 676 1264 (enquiries and administration)
Fax (00 353 1) 678 7618
e-mail: catholicresearch@eircom.net
url: www.catholiclibrary.ie
Librarian Ms Teresa Whitington MA DLIS DipTrans

CHESTER BEATTY LIBRARY

Chester Beatty Library, The Clocktower Building, Dublin Castle, Dublin 2, Republic of Ireland
☎(00 353 1) 407 0750
Fax (00 353 1) 407 0760
e-mail: info@cbl.ie
url: www.cbl.ie
Director and Librarian Dr Michael Ryan (e-mail: mryan@cbl.ie)
Reference Librarian Ms Celine Ward BA MLIS (e-mail: cward@cbl.ie)

AN CHOMHAIRLE LEABHARLANNA (THE LIBRARY COUNCIL)

Research Library, An Chomhairle Leabharlanna (The Library Council), 53-54 Upper Mount Street, Dublin 2, Republic of Ireland
☎(00 353 1) 678 4900/676 1167
Fax (00 353 1) 676 6721

e-mail: info@librarycouncil.ie
url: www.librarycouncil.ie
Research & Information Officer Alun Bevan MLib (00 353 1 678 4905; fax: 00 353 1
676 6721; e-mail: abevan@librarycouncil.ie)

DUBLIN CITY UNIVERSITY

Library, Dublin City University, Dublin 9, Republic of Ireland
☎(00 353 1) 700 5418 (enquiries); (00 353 1) 700 5212 (administration)
Fax (00 353 1) 700 5010
url: www.dcu.ie/~library/
Director of Library Services P Sheehan (e-mail: paul.sheehan@dcu.ie)

DUBLIN INSTITUTE OF TECHNOLOGY

Central Services Unit, Dublin Institute of Technology, Rathmines Road, Dublin 6, Republic
of Ireland
☎(00 353 1) 402 7800 (enquiries), 7801 (administration)
Fax (00 353 1) 402 7802
e-mail: csu.library@dit.ie
url: www.dit.ie/library
Head of Library Services Dr Philip Cohen BA PhD DipLib MCLIP (e-mail:
philip.cohen@dit.ie)
Senior Librarian, Collection Development Ms Ann McSweeney BA DLIS MLIS (00 353
1 402 7804; e-mail: ann.mcsweeney@dit.ie)
Senior Librarian, Systems Development Ms Ursula Gavin BA DLIS MLIS (00 353 1 402
7805; e-mail: ursula.gavin@dit.ie)
Faculty Librarian Ms Yvonne Desmond BA DLIS (00 353 1 402 7807; e-mail:
yvonne.desmond@dit.ie)

Library, Dublin Institute of Technology, Bolton Street, Dublin 1, Republic of Ireland
☎(00 353 1) 402 3681
Fax (00 353 1) 402 3995
e-mail: bst.library@dit.ie
Faculty Librarian Peter Cahalane BA DipLib (00 353 1 402 3682; e-mail:
peter.cahalane@dit.ie)

Library, Dublin Institute of Technology, Kevin Street, Dublin 8, Republic of Ireland
☎(00 353 1) 402 4894 (general enquiries)
Fax (00 353 1) 402 4651
e-mail: kst.library@dit.ie
Faculty Librarian Ms Mary Helen Davis BSc(Hons) MLIS MCLIP (00 353 1 402 4631;
e-mail: mary.davis@dit.ie)

Library, Dublin Institute of Technology, Cathal Brugha Street, Dublin 1, Republic of Ireland
☎(00 353 1) 402 4423/4 (enquiries and administration)
Fax (00 353 1) 402 4499
e-mail: cbs.library@dit.ie

Faculty Librarian Brian Gillespie BA DipLib (00 353 1 402 4361; e-mail: brian.gillespie@dit.ie)

Library, Dublin Institute of Technology, 40-45 Mountjoy Square, Dublin 1, Republic of Ireland
☎(00 353 1) 402 4108
Fax (00 353 1) 402 4290
e-mail: mjs.library@dit.ie
Faculty Librarian Ms Ann Wrigley BA DLIS (00 353 1 402 4128; e-mail: ann.wrigley@dit.ie)

Library, Dublin Institute of Technology, Aungier Street, Dublin 2, Republic of Ireland
☎(00 353 1) 402 3068/9
Fax (00 353 1) 402 3289
e-mail: ast.library@dit.ie
Faculty Librarian Ms Anne Ambrose BA DLIS (00 353 1 402 3067; e-mail: anne.ambrose@dit.ie)

Library, Dublin Institute of Technology, Learning and Teaching Centre, 14 Upper Mount Street, Dublin 2, Republic of Ireland
☎(00 353 1) 402 7889
Fax (00 353 1) 676 7243
e-mail: ltc.library@dit.ie
Librarian Ms Diana Mitchell BA(Hons)

Music and Drama Library, Dublin Institute of Technology, Lower Rathmines Road, Dublin 6, Republic of Ireland
☎(00 353 1) 402 3461
Fax (00 353 1) 402 7854
e-mail: rmh.library@dit.ie
Faculty Librarian Ms Ann Wrigley BA DLIS (00 353 1 402 4128; e-mail: ann.wrigley@dit.ie)
Librarian Brendan Devlin BA DLIS MLIS (00 353 1 402 3462; e-mail: brendan.devlin@dit.ie)

ECONOMIC AND SOCIAL RESEARCH INSTITUTE

Library, Economic and Social Research Institute, 4 Burlington Road, Dublin 4, Republic of Ireland
☎(00 353 1) 667 1525
Fax (00 353 1) 668 6231
url: www.esri.ie
Chief Librarian Ms Sarah Burns BSocSc (e-mail: sarah.burns@esri.ie)
Assistant Librarian Kevin Dillon BA DipLIS (e-mail: kevin.dillon@esri.ie)

ENTERPRISE IRELAND

Client Knowledge Services, Enterprise Ireland, Glasnevin, Dublin 9, Republic of Ireland

☎(00 353 1) 808 2325
Fax (00 353 1) 837 8854
e-mail: infocentre@enterprise-ireland.com
url: www.enterprise-ireland.com
Head of Department Lorcan O'Sullivan
Librarian in Charge Ms Mary Glennon (00 353 1 808 2389)

INSTITUTO CERVANTES

Library, Instituto Cervantes, 58 Northumberland Road, Ballsbridge, Dublin 4, Republic of
Ireland
☎(00 353 1) 668 2024
Fax (00 353 1) 668 8416
e-mail: bibdub@cervantes.es
url: http://dublin.cervantes.es
Chief Librarian Ms Francisca Segura Pérez

NATIONAL ARCHIVES

National Archives, Bishop Street, Dublin 8, Republic of Ireland
☎(00 353 1) 407 2300
Fax (00 353 1) 407 2333
e-mail: mail@nationalarchives.ie
url: www.nationalarchives.ie
Director Dr David Craig
(Formed by the amalgamation of the Public Record Office of Ireland and the State Paper
Office.)

NATIONAL COLLEGE OF ART AND DESIGN

Library, National College of Art and Design, 100 Thomas Street, Dublin 8, Republic of Ireland
☎(00 353 1) 636 4357
Fax (00 353 1) 636 4387
e-mail: www.ncad.ie/library
url: www.ncad.ie/library
Librarian Edward Murphy BA DipLib MLIS (e-mail: murphye@ncad.ie)

NATIONAL GALLERY OF IRELAND

Library, National Gallery of Ireland, 88–89 Merrion Square West, Dublin 2, Republic of
Ireland
☎(00 353 1) 663 3546 (direct)
Fax (00 353 1) 661 5372
e-mail: library@ngi.ie
url: www.nationalgallery.ie
Librarian Ms Andrea Lydon MA DLIS
(Opening hours 10–5 Mon–Fri.)

NATIONAL LIBRARY OF IRELAND

National Library of Ireland, Kildare Street, Dublin 2, Republic of Ireland
☎(00 353 1) 603 0200
Fax (00 353 1) 676 6690
e-mail: info@nli.ie
url: www.nli.ie
Director Aongus Ó hAonghusa BSc MPA
Keeper (Collections) Dónall Ó Luanaigh MA BComm DipArchiv
Keeper (Systems) Brian McKenna BA
Keeper (Genealogical Office) Fergus Mac Giolla Easpaig MA DipArchiv
Keeper (Manuscripts) Gerard Lyne MA DipLIS HDipEd
Keeper (Administration) Temporary Ms Gráinne Ni Néill DipJourn BA MPA
Keeper (Special Programmes) Ms Catherine Fahy BA DipLIS

National Photographic Archive
National Photographic Archive, Photographic Collection, Meeting House Square, Temple Bar, Dublin 2, Republic of Ireland
☎(00 353 1) 603 0374
Fax (00 353 1) 677 7451
e-mail: photoarchive@nli.ie
url: www.nli.ie
Curator Ms Sara Smyth BA DipLIS

NATIONAL UNIVERSITY OF IRELAND, GALWAY

James Hardiman Library, National University of Ireland, Galway, University Road, Galway, Republic of Ireland
☎(00 353 91) 524411 ext 2540 (enquiries), 524809 (administration)
Fax (00 353 91) 522394; 750528 (interlibrary loans)
e-mail: library@nuigalway.ie
url: www.nuigalway.ie
Chief Librarian Ms Marie Reddan DipLib DipSyAn FLAI MCLIP (00 353 91 524809; e-mail: marie.reddan@nuigalway.ie)
Deputy Librarian John Cox MA DipLib (ext 3712; e-mail: john.cox@nuigalway.ie)
Systems Administrator Peter Corrigan BA DipLIS (ext 2497; e-mail: peter.corrigan@nuigalway.ie)
Reader Services Ms Ann Mitchell BA HDipEd DipLIS (ext 2738; e-mail: ann.mitchell@nuigalway.ie)
Bibliographic Services Ms Monica Crump BA MLIS (ext 3765; e-mail: monica.crump@nuigalway.ie)
Information Services Niall McSweeney BA HDipinEd DipLib

Branch libraries
▶ Medical Library, National University of Ireland, Galway, Clinical Sciences Institute, University Road, Galway, Republic of Ireland
☎(00 353 91) 524411 ext 2791
Fax (00 353 91) 750517

Medical Librarian Timothy Collins BSc HDipEd DipLib DipSyAn FCLIP (ext 2791; e-mail: tim.collins@nuigalway.ie)
▶ Nursing Library, National University of Ireland, Galway, c/o James Hardiman Library, University Road, Galway, Republic of Ireland
☎(00 353 91) 495228/495229
Fax (00 353 91) 495562
Nursing Librarian Ms Maire Ó hAodha BA DipLIS (ext 5228; e-mail: maire.ohaodha@nuigalway.ie), Ms Ann Kelly BA DipLIS (ext 5229; e-mail: ann.p.kelly@nuigalway.ie)

NATIONAL UNIVERSITY OF IRELAND, MAYNOOTH

The Library, National University of Ireland, Maynooth, Co Kildare, Republic of Ireland
☎(00 353 1) 708 3884
Fax (00 353 1) 628 6008
e-mail: library.information@nuim.ie
url: www.nuim.ie/library
Librarian Miss Agnes Neligan BA HDipEd MCLIP ALAI
Deputy Librarian Ms Helen Fallon MA DLIS
Sub-Librarian Ms Valerie Seymour BA(Mod) MCLIP

OIREACHTAS LIBRARY

Oireachtas Library, Oireachtas Library, Leinster House, Kildare Street, Dublin 2, Republic of Ireland
☎(00 353 1) 618 3451
Fax (00 353 1) 618 4109
e-mail: lib@oireachtas.ie
url: www.oireachtas.ie
Librarian Ms Maura Corcoran (00 353 1 618 3412; e-mail: maura.corcoran@oireachtas.ie)

REPRESENTATIVE CHURCH BODY

Library, Representative Church Body, Braemor Park, Churchtown, Dublin 14, Republic of Ireland
☎(00 353 1) 492 3979
Fax (00 353 1) 492 4770
e-mail: library@ireland.anglican.org
url: www.ireland.anglican.org/
Librarian & Archivist Dr Raymond Refaussé BA PhD (e-mail: raymond.refausse@rcbdub.org)

ROYAL COLLEGE OF SURGEONS IN IRELAND

The Mercer Library, Royal College of Surgeons in Ireland, Mercer Street Lower, Dublin 2, Republic of Ireland

☎(00 353 1) 402 2407 (enquiries); 402 2411 (administration)
Fax (00 353 1) 402 2457
e-mail: library@rcsi.ie
url: www.rcsi.ie/library
Librarian Miss Beatrice M Doran BA MBA DipLibr ALAI (e-mail: bdoran@rcsi.ie)

Branch library

RCSI Library, Royal College of Surgeons in Ireland, Beaumont Hospital, Beaumont Road,
Dublin 9, Republic of Ireland
☎(00 353 1) 809 2531
Fax (00 353 1) 836 7396
e-mail: bhlibrary@rcsi.ie
Librarian James Molloy BSc MLIS (e-mail: jmolloy@rcsi.ie)

ROYAL DUBLIN SOCIETY

Library, Royal Dublin Society, Ballsbridge, Dublin 4, Republic of Ireland
☎Direct lines as below
Fax (00 353 1) 660 4014; 240 7274
e-mail: library@rds.ie
url: www.rds.ie
Librarian Ms Mary Kelleher BA(Hons) DipLibInfS (00 353 1 240 7288; e-mail:
mary.kelleher@rds.ie)
Assistant Librarian Gerard Whelan (00 353 1 240 7256; e-mail: gerard.whelan@rds.ie)

ROYAL IRISH ACADEMY

Library, Royal Irish Academy, 19 Dawson Street, Dublin 2, Republic of Ireland
☎(00 353 1) 676 2570/676 4222
Fax (00 353 1) 676 2346
e-mail: library@ria.ie
url: www.ria.ie
Librarian Ms Siobhán Fitzpatrick (e-mail: s.fitzpatrick@ria.ie)
Deputy Librarian Ms Petra Schnabel (e-mail: p.schnabel@ria.ie)

TEAGASC (AGRICULTURE AND FOOD DEVELOPMENT AUTHORITY)

Library, TEAGASC (Agriculture and Food Development Authority), National Food Centre
(food production), Dunsinea, Dublin 15, Republic of Ireland
☎(00 353 1) 805 9500
Fax (00 353 1) 805 9550
url: www.teagasc.ie
Librarian Ms Maire Caffrey BSc DipLIS (e-mail: mcaffrey@nfc.teagasc.ie)

Research libraries

▶ Library, TEAGASC (Agriculture and Food Development Authority), Moorepark

Research Centre (dairy production), Fermoy, Co Cork, Republic of Ireland
☎(00 353 25) 42222
Fax (00 353 25) 42340
Librarian Ms Siobhan Keating (e-mail: skeating@moorepark.teagasc.ie)
▶ Library, TEAGASC (Agriculture and Food Development Authority), Johnstown Castle
Agricultural Research Centre (environment), Wexford, Republic of Ireland
☎(00 353 53) 71200
Fax (00 353 53) 42213
Librarian Ms Eleanor Spillane (e-mail: espillane@johnstown.teagasc.ie)
▶ Library, TEAGASC (Agriculture and Food Development Authority), Oak Park Research
Centre (crops production), Carlow, Republic of Ireland
☎(00 353 59) 917 0200
Fax (00 353 59) 914 2423
Librarian Ms Margaret Collins (e-mail: mcollins@oakpark.teagasc.ie)
▶ Library, TEAGASC (Agriculture and Food Development Authority), Grange Research
Centre (beef production), Dunsany, Co Meath, Republic of Ireland
☎(00 353 46) 902 6700
Fax (00 353 46) 906 1140
Librarian Ms Ann Gilsenan (e-mail: agilsenan@grange.teagasc.ie)

TRINITY COLLEGE DUBLIN

Library, Trinity College Dublin, College Street, Dublin 2, Republic of Ireland
☎(00 353 1) 608 1127 (general enquiries); (00 353 1) 608 1661 (Librarian's office)
Fax (00 353 1) 608 3774
e-mail: library@tcd.ie
url: www.tcd.ie/library/
Librarian and College Archivist Robin Adams MA BA DipLib (e-mail: radams@tcd.ie)

Departmental libraries
▶ John Stearne Medical Library, Trinity College Dublin, St James's Hospital, James's Street,
Dublin 8, Republic of Ireland
☎(00 353 1) 608 2109
Fax (00 353 1) 453 6087
Medical Librarian David Mockler BSc DLIS (e-mail: mocklerd@tcd.ie)
▶ Science and Engineering Library, Trinity College Dublin, College Street, Dublin 2,
Republic of Ireland
☎(00 353 1) 608 1805
Fax (00 353 1) 608 3774
Site Librarian Ms Arlene Healy BA MLIS (e-mail: arlene.healy@tcd.ie)

UNIVERSITY COLLEGE CORK

The Boole Library, University College Cork, College Road, Cork, Republic of Ireland
☎(00 353 21) 490 2794
Fax (00 353 21) 427 3428
e-mail: library@ucc.ie

url: www.booleweb.ucc.ie
Librarian John FitzGerald BA MPhil DLIS (00 351 21 490 2281/2851; fax: 00 353 21 490 3119)

Branch/department library

Medical Library, University College Cork, Cork University Hospital, Wilton, Cork, Republic of Ireland
☎(00 353 21) 490 2976
Fax (00 353 21) 434 5826
e-mail: CUH.Library@ucc.ie
Librarian Ms Una Ni Chonghaile (e-mail: u.nichonghaile@uce.ie)

UNIVERSITY COLLEGE DUBLIN

Library, University College Dublin, Belfield, Dublin 4, Republic of Ireland
☎(00 353 1) 716 7583 (enquiries); (00 353 1) 716 7694 (administration)
Fax (00 353 1) 283 7667
e-mail: library@ucd.ie
url: www.ucd.ie/~library/
Chief Librarian Sean Phillips BA MCLIP ALAI (e-mail: sean.phillips@ucd.ie)
Deputy Librarian Miss Pauline Corrigan BA DipLib ALAI (e-mail: pauline.corrigan@ucd.ie)

Site libraries

▶ Architecture Library, University College Dublin, Richview, Clonskeagh, Dublin 14, Republic of Ireland
  ☎(00 353 1) 716 2741
  Fax (00 353 1) 283 0329
  Librarian i/c Ms Julia Barrett BMus DipLib (e-mail: julia.barrett@ucd.ie)
▶ Library and Business Information Centre, University College Dublin, Michael Smurfit Graduate School of Business, Blackrock, Co Dublin, Republic of Ireland
  ☎(00 353 1) 716 8069
  Fax (00 353 1) 716 8011
  Librarian i/c John Steele BA DipLib MLIS FLAI (e-mail: john.steele@ucd.ie)
▶ Medical Library, University College Dublin, Earlsfort Terrace, Dublin 2, Republic of Ireland
  ☎(00 353 1) 716 7471
  Fax (00 353 1) 475 4568
  Librarian i/c Peter Hickey BA DipLib (e-mail: peter.hickey@ucd.ie)
▶ Veterinary Library, University College Dublin, Belfield, Dublin 4, Republic of Ireland
  ☎(00 353 1) 716 6208
  Fax (00 353 1) 716 6267
  Librarian i/c Ms Gwen Ryan BA MLIS (e-mail: gwen.ryan@ucd.ie)

UNIVERSITY OF LIMERICK

Library and Information Services, University of Limerick, Limerick, Republic of Ireland
☎(00 353 61) 202166 (enquiries); 202156 (administration)

Fax (00 353 61) 213090
e-mail: libinfo@ul.ie
url: www.ul.ie
Director, Library and Information Services Ms Gobnait O'Riordan MA DLIS

Schools and Departments of Information and Library Studies

ABERDEEN BUSINESS SCHOOL

Department of Information Management, Aberdeen Business School, The Robert Gordon University, Garthdee Road, Aberdeen AB10 7QE
☎(01224) 263801 (administration & enquiries)
Fax (01224) 263553
e-mail: sim@rgu.ac.uk
url: www.rgu.ac.uk/abs
Associate Dean, Aberdeen Business School Prof Ian M Johnson BA FCLIP MIMgt
(e-mail: i.m.johnson@rgu.ac.uk)
Associate Head of Department of Information Management Prof Robert Newton
MA PGDip PhD MCLIP (e-mail: r.newton@rgu.ac.uk)

UNIVERSITY OF BRIGHTON

The School of Computing, Mathematical and Information Sciences, University of Brighton, Watts Building, Lewes Road, Moulsecoomb, Brighton BN2 4GJ
☎(01273) 643500
Fax (01273) 642405
url: www.cmis.brighton.ac.uk
Head of School Dr John Taylor BSc PhD CMath FIMA (e-mail:
john.taylor@brighton.ac.uk)
Head of Research Prof Peter G B Enser BA(Econ) MTech PhD MBCS CITP HonFCLIP
(e-mail: p.g.b.enser@brighton.ac.uk)
Head of Division of Information and Communication Dr David S Horner BSc MSc
PhD (e-mail: d.s.horner@brighton.ac.uk)

UNIVERSITY OF CENTRAL ENGLAND IN BIRMINGHAM

School of Computing and Information, University of Central England in Birmingham, The Business School, Franchise Street, Perry Barr, Birmingham B42 2SU
☎0121 331 5600/5626
Fax 0121 331 6281
url: www.cie.uce.ac.uk
Professional Development Co-ordinator for Information and Library Management
William Foster BSc DipLib MCLIP (e-mail: william.foster@uce.ac.uk)
Director of Evidence Base Pete Dalton BA MA (e-mail: pete.dalton@uce.ac.uk)

(See Key Library Agencies section for details of Evidence Base)

CITY UNIVERSITY

School of Information Science, City University, Northampton Square, London EC1V 0HB
☎020 7040 8381
Fax 020 7040 8584
e-mail: dis@soi.city.ac.uk
url: www.soi.city.ac.uk

Head of Department J F Raper BA(Hons) PhD FRGS FGS MCLIP (020 7040 8415;
e-mail: raper@soi.city.ac.uk)
Course Director, Information Science and Technology Ms Pauline Rafferty MA MSc
MCLIP (020 7040 8389; e-mail: lazarza@soi.city.ac.uk)
Course Director, Information Studies Masters Scheme Dr Louise Cooke MA PhD
MCLIP (020 7040 8383; e-mail: louisec@soi.city.ac.uk)

UNIVERSITY COLLEGE DUBLIN

Department of Library and Information Studies, University College Dublin, Belfield, Dublin
4, Republic of Ireland
☎(00 353 1) 716 7055 (administration); (00 353 1) 716 7080 (voice mail)
Fax (00 353 1) 716 1161
e-mail: DepLIS@ucd.ie
url: www.ucd.ie/lis
Head of Department Prof Mary Burke BSc MSc PhD (e-mail: mary.burke@ucd.ie)

LEEDS METROPOLITAN UNIVERSITY

School of Information Management, Leeds Metropolitan University, Priestley Hall, Beckett
Park, Leeds LS6 3QS
☎0113 283 2600 ext 7421 (course enquiries); ext 3242 (school office)
Fax 0113 283 7599
url: www.leedsmet.ac.uk
Head of School John Blake BSc MSc CSTAT MBCS (e-mail: j.blake@leedsmet.ac.uk)

LIVERPOOL JOHN MOORES UNIVERSITY

Information Management, School of Business Information, Liverpool John Moores
University, The John Foster Building, 98 Mount Pleasant, Liverpool L3 5UZ
☎0151 231 3596/3425 (Centre)
Fax 0151 707 0423
url: www.cwis.livjm.ac.uk/faculties/blw/bsn
Subject Group Leader Ms Janet Farrow MA BA MCLIP (0151 231 3596; e-mail:
a.j.farrow@livjm.ac.uk)

LONDON METROPOLITAN UNIVERSITY

School of Information Management, Department of Applied Social Sciences, London
Metropolitan University, London North Campus, Ladbroke House, 62-66 Highbury Grove,
London N5 2AD
☎020 7423 0000 (main switchboard), 020 7133 5129 (postgraduate office)
Fax 020 7133 5203
url: www.londonmet.ac.uk
Head of Department Prof John Gabriel
Academic Leader for Information Management Ms Rosemary McGuinness MSc BA
PGDipLib PGDipHEd (020 7133 5160; e-mail: r.mcguinness@londonmet.ac.uk)

UNIVERSITY COLLEGE LONDON

School of Library, Archive and Information Studies, University College London, Gower Street, London WC1E 6BT
☎020 7679 7204
Fax 020 7383 0557
e-mail: slais-enquiries@ucl.ac.uk
url: www.ucl.ac.uk/SLAIS/
Director Prof David Nicholas MPhil PhD MCLIP

LOUGHBOROUGH UNIVERSITY

Department of Information Science, Loughborough University, Ashby Road, Loughborough, Leics LE11 3TU
☎(01509) 223052
Fax (01509) 223053
e-mail: dis@lboro.ac.uk
url: www.lboro.ac.uk/departments/dis/
Head of Department Prof John Feather MA PhD FCLIP FRSA (e-mail: j.p.feather@lboro.ac.uk)
Director of LISU (Library & Information Statistics Unit) Dr J Eric Davies MA PhD FCLIP MCMI FInstAM FRSA (01509 635680; fax: 01509 635699; e-mail: j.e.davies@lboro.ac.uk)

(See also LISU in Key Library Agencies section)

MANCHESTER METROPOLITAN UNIVERSITY

Department of Information and Communications, Manchester Metropolitan University, Geoffrey Manton Building, Rosamond Street West, off Oxford Road, Manchester M15 6LL
☎0161 247 6144
Fax 0161 247 6351
e-mail: infcomms-hums@mmu.ac.uk
url: www.hlss.mmu.ac.uk/infocomms
Head of Department and Professor of Information Science Prof R J Hartley BSc MLib FCLIP
Professor of Information Management and Director of the Centre for Research in Library and Information Management (CERLIM) Prof Peter Brophy JP BSc FCLIP FRSA

NAPIER UNIVERSITY

School of Computing, Napier University, 10 Colinton Road, Edinburgh EH10 5DT
☎0131 455 2700
Fax: 0131 455 2727
e-mail: info@napier.ac.uk
url: www.soc.napier.ac.uk
Head of School Bob Rankin BSc(Eng) DipCS MBCS ILTM CEng (e-mail: b.rankin@napier.ac.uk)

NORTHUMBRIA UNIVERSITY

Division of Information and Communication Studies, School of Informatics, Engineering and Technology, Northumbria University, Newcastle upon Tyne NE1 8ST
☎0191 227 3702
Fax 0191 227 3662
e-mail: il.admin@northumbria.ac.uk
url: http://northumbria.ac.uk/informatics
Dean Prof Alastair Sambell
Head of Subject Division Ms Shona McTavish BA PGCE MCLIP

THE UNIVERSITY OF SHEFFIELD

Department of Information Studies, The University of Sheffield, Regent Court, 211 Portobello Street, Sheffield S1 4DP
☎0114 222 2630 (dept/administration)
Fax 0114 278 0300
e-mail: dis@sheffield.ac.uk
url: www.shef.ac.uk/is
Head of Department Prof Peter Willett MA MSc PhD DSc FCLIP (0114 222 2633; e-mail: p.willett@sheffield.ac.uk)

STRATHCLYDE UNIVERSITY

Department of Computer and Information Sciences, Graduate School of Informatics, Strathclyde University, Livingstone Tower, 26 Richmond Street, Glasgow G1 1XH
☎0141 548 3700
Fax 0141 548 4523
e-mail: ils_enquiries@cis.strath.ac.uk
url: www.cis.strath.ac.uk
Head of Department Prof Richard Connor
Course Director Paul Burton BA MA MPhil

THAMES VALLEY UNIVERSITY

Information Management, Faculty of Professional Studies, Thames Valley University, St Mary's Road, Ealing, London W5 5RF
☎020 8579 5000 (switchboard); 020 8231 2314 (faculty)
Fax 020 8231 2553
e-mail: management@tvu.ac.uk
url: www.tvu.ac.uk
Programme Leaders, Information Management (Library and Information Services and Business Pathways) Dr Tony Olden (e-mail: tony.olden@tvu.ac.uk), Dr Stephen Roberts (e-mail: stephen.roberts@tvu.ac.uk)

UNIVERSITY OF WALES ABERYSTWYTH

Department of Information Studies, University of Wales Aberystwyth, Llanbadarn Fawr, Aberystwyth, Ceredigion SY23 3AS

470

☎(01970) 622155
Fax (01970) 622190
e-mail: dils@aber.ac.uk
url: www.dis.aber.ac.uk
Head of Department Gwilym Huws BA MCLIP

UNIVERSITY OF THE WEST OF ENGLAND

School of Information Systems, Faculty of Computing, Engineering and Mathematical
Sciences, University of the West of England, Frenchay Campus, Coldharbour Lane, Bristol
BS16 1QY
☎0870 901 0767
Fax 0117 328 3680
e-mail: admissions.cems@uwe.ac.uk
url: www.uwe.ac.uk/cems/
Programme Leader Ian Beeson MA MSc
Co-Programme Leader Ms Jacqueline Chelin BA DipLib MCLIP PGC(HE)

Key Library Agencies and other relevant organizations

Note: Organizations are listed using their full names. If searching for an organization by its acronym, please use the general index

ADVISORY COUNCIL ON LIBRARIES (ACL)

Advisory Council on Libraries (ACL), Department for Culture, Media and Sport (Libraries and Communities Division), Oceanic House, 1A, 2–4 Cockspur Street, London SW1Y 5BG
☎020 7211 6287
Fax 020 7211 6961
url: www.culture.gov.uk/libraries_and_communities/advisory_council_libraries.htm
Secretary Dempster Marples (e-mail: dempster.marples@culture.gsi.gov.uk)
Chair W J Macnaught MA DipLib MCLIP (Head of Cultural Development, Gateshead Metropolitan Borough Council)
ACL is constituted under the Public Libraries and Museums Act 1964. Under the Act, it has a wide ranging remit but, in practice, it concentrates on advising DCMS Ministers, their Chief Library Adviser and the MLA (Museums, Libraries and Archives Council) on public library matters.

AFRICAN CARIBBEAN LIBRARY ASSOCIATION (ACLA)

African Caribbean Library Association (ACLA), c/o Ann Thompson, Waltham Forest Central Library, High Street, London E17 9JN
☎020 8496 1120
e-mail: acla_uk@yahoo.co.uk
url: www.cilip.org/interests/oils2.html
Secretary Ms Ann Thompson BA MA PGDip MCLIP (e-mail: libraryannie@yahoo.co.uk)
Founded in 1981 by Ann Thompson, ACLA is an independent fully constituted organization committed to the full implementation of race equality principles and policies throughout librarianship. It welcomes as members any library or information workers of African or Caribbean origin. ACLA is a founding member of the Diversity Council of CILIP.

AIOPI *see* PIPA

ALM LONDON (ARCHIVES, LIBRARIES AND MUSEUMS LONDON)

ALM London (Archives, Libraries and Museums London), Cloister Court, 22-26 Farringdon Lane, London EC1R 3AJ
☎020 7549 1700
Fax 020 7490 5225
e-mail: info@almlondon.org.uk
url: www.almlondon.org.uk
Chief Executive Graham Fisher (e-mail: graham.fisher@almlondon.org.uk)
Chair Geoffrey Bond
ALM London is the new strategic development agency for London's archives, libraries and museums, established on 1 April 2004. Its mission is to support and promote the sector. The agency works in partnership with a wide range of organizations to ensure that the unique cultural, knowledge and learning resources of the capital's archives, libraries and museums

are made accessible for the benefit of all Londoners and contribute to London's status as a world-class city. ALM London is core-funded by the Museums, Libraries and Archives Council (MLA).

ART LIBRARIES SOCIETY OF THE UK AND IRELAND (ARLIS)

Art Libraries Society of the UK and Ireland (ARLIS), Courtauld Institute of Art, Somerset House, The Strand, London WC2R 0RN
☎020 7848 2703
e-mail: arlis@courtauld.ac.uk
url: www.arlis.org.uk
Administrator Ms Anna Mellows
Chair Dr Sue M Price BSc MA MSc PhD MCLIP
The Society aims to promote all aspects of the librarianship of the visual arts, including architecture and design.

ASIAN LIBRARIANS AND ADVISERS GROUP (ALAG)

Asian Librarians and Advisers Group (ALAG), Croydon Central Library, c/o Croydon Clocktower Complex, Room B4, Katharine Street, Croydon CR9 1ET
☎020 8760 5400 ext 61052
url: www.cilip.org.uk/alag
Ethnic Minorities Information Officer Mrs Krishna Ray (e-mail: krishna.ray@croydon.gov.uk)
Secretary K K Dutt (020 8449 1087)
ALAG was formed in 1982 by a group of Asian librarians to raise awareness and to serve library needs of the diverse Asian communities and, equally importantly, to support library professionals in delivering library services with vision and vigour. ALAG's mission is to promote Asian languages, history, culture and heritage through library and information services to Asians in particular and the population at large. ALAG is an active member of the Diversity Group of CILIP.

ASLIB, THE ASSOCIATION FOR INFORMATION MANAGEMENT

Aslib, The Association for Information Management, Holywell Centre, 1 Phipp Street, London EC2A 4PS
☎020 7613 3031
Fax 020 7613 5080
e-mail: aslib@aslib.com
url: www.aslib.com
Chief Executive Officer Roger Bowes
Aslib is a corporate membership organization promoting best practice in resource management and lobbying on all aspects of management of and legislation concerning information at all levels.

ASSOCIATION OF SENIOR CHILDREN'S AND EDUCATION LIBRARIANS (ASCEL)

Association of Senior Children's and Education Librarians (ASCEL), c/o Claire Styles, Southwark Library and Information Service, 15 Spa Road, London SE16 3QW
☎020 7525 3920
Fax 020 7525 1568
url: www.ascel.org.uk
Secretary Ms Claire Styles BA(Hons) MSc(Econ) MCLIP (e-mail: claire.styles@southwark.gov.uk)
Chair Ms Sue Jones MA MCLIP (e-mail: sue.jones@herts-sls.org.uk)
ASCEL is a pro-active forum comprising heads of children's public and schools library services from across the UK. The Association, through its members, responds to initiatives, stimulates development, establishes best practice and works to support the provision of quality library and education services for children and young people.

ASSOCIATION OF UK MEDIA LIBRARIANS (AUKML)

Association of UK Media Librarians (AUKML), c/o Sara Margetts, PO Box 14254, London SE1 9WL
url: www.aukml.org.uk
Chair Ms Katharine Schopflin (e-mail: katharine.schopflin@bbc.co.uk)
Membership contact Ms Sara Margetts (e-mail: sara.margetts@FT.com)
AUKML is the organization for print and broadcast news librarians, news researchers and information workers in the media industry.

BAILER – THE INFORMATION, EDUCATION AND RESEARCH ASSOCIATION

BAILER – the Information, Education and Research Association, c/o John Feather, Dept of Information Science, Loughborough University, Loughborough, Leicestershire LE11 3TU
☎(01509) 223050
Fax (01509) 223053
url: www.bailer.ac.uk
Chair Prof John Feather MA PhD FCLIP FRSA (e-mail: j.p.feather@lboro.ac.uk)
BAILER includes all teaching and research staff in the 18 Information and Library Schools in the UK and Ireland and aims to reflect and help focus the evolution of the field of information and library studies through the development and encouragement of members. It acts as a forum within the UK for matters relating to information and library studies education and research, and maintains contact with organizations outside the UK concerned with education for information work.

BOOK INDUSTRY COMMUNICATION (BIC)

Book Industry Communication (BIC), 39/41 North Road, London N7 9DP

☎020 7607 0021
Fax 020 7607 0415
url: www.bic.org.uk
Managing Agent Brian Green (e-mail: brian@bic.org.uk)
Chairman Michael Holdsworth
Book Industry Communication was set up and sponsored by the Booksellers Association, the Publishers Association, The Library Association (now CILIP) and the British Library to develop and promote standards for electronic communication and supply chain efficiency in the book and serials industries.

BOOKTRUST

Booktrust, Book House, 45 East Hill, London SW18 2QZ
☎020 8516 2977
Fax 020 8516 2978
e-mail: bookinfo@booktrust.org.uk
url: www.booktrust.org.uk; www.booktrusted.co.uk
Executive Director Chris Meade (e-mail: chris@booktrust.org.uk))
Booktrust is the national charity for books and reading in the UK. It works with readers of all ages, helping people to discover books through projects such as the national Bookstart programme, through prizes and promotions such as the Orange Prize for Fiction, and by providing a wide range of information about books and writers through its websites.

BRITISH AND IRISH ASSOCIATION OF LAW LIBRARIANS (BIALL)

British and Irish Association of Law Librarians (BIALL), 26 Myton Crescent, Warwick CV34 6QA
☎(01926) 491717 (tel/fax)
url: www.biall.org.uk
BIALL Administrator Ms Susan Frost BA MCLIP (e-mail: susanfrost5@hotmail.com)
Chair Ms Hazel Hewison
BIALL was formed in 1969 with the objectives of pursuing policies to bring benefits to its members, enhancing the status of the legal information profession and promoting better administration and exploitation of law libraries and legal information units nationwide.

BRITISH ASSOCIATION OF PICTURE LIBRARIES AND AGENCIES (BAPLA)

British Association of Picture Libraries and Agencies (BAPLA), 18 Vine Hill, London EC1R 5DZ
☎020 7713 1780
Fax 020 7713 1211
e-mail: enquiries@bapla.org.uk
url: www.bapla.org
Chief Executive Officer Ms Linda Royles

BAPLA represents over 450 member picture libraries and agencies. All members sign a code of conduct. The website provides details about BAPLA services and benefits to picture researchers, to photographers and of membership. The site also has a useful search engine facility.

BRITISH COMPUTER SOCIETY – INFORMATION RETRIEVAL SPECIALIST GROUP (BCS IRSG)

British Computer Society – Information Retrieval Specialist Group (BCS IRSG), c/o Andrew MacFarlane, Dept of Information Science, City University, Northampton Square, London EC1V 0HB
☎020 7040 8386
Fax 020 7040 8584
url: http://irsg.bcs.org
Secretary Andrew MacFarlane PhD MSc (e-mail: andym@soi.city.ac.uk)
Chair Ayse S Goker-Arslan
The BCS IRSG provides a forum for academic and industrial researchers and practitioners to discuss core issues involved in the representation, management, searching, retrieval and presentation of multimedia electronic information.

CAPP (COUNCIL OF ACADEMIC AND PROFESSIONAL PUBLISHERS) *see* PUBLISHERS ASSOCIATION

CENTRE FOR DIGITAL LIBRARY RESEARCH (CDLR)

(BUBL, CAIRNS, Glasgow Digital Library, HaIRST, HILT, SAPIENS, SCONE, SPEIR, Victorian Times)

Centre for Digital Library Research (CDLR), Department of Computer and Information Sciences, Strathclyde University, Livingstone Tower, 26 Richmond Street, Glasgow G1 1XH
☎0141 548 4752
Fax 0141 552 5330
e-mail: cdlr@strath.ac.uk
url: http://cdlr.strath.ac.uk
Director Dennis Nicholson BSc MCLIP (e-mail: d.m.nicholson@strath.ac.uk)
Depute Director Gordon Dunsire BSc MCLIP (e-mail: g.dunsire@strath.ac.uk)
Research Co-ordinator Ms Emma McCulloch BA(Hons) (e-mail: e.mcculloch@strath.ac.uk)
CDLR seeks to combine theory with practice in innovative ways with the aim of being a centre of excellence on digital libraries issues ranging from information policy and information retrieval to document storage technologies and standards.

CENTRE FOR RESEARCH IN LIBRARY AND INFORMATION MANAGEMENT (CERLIM)

Centre for Research in Library and Information Management (CERLIM), Department of Information and Communications, Manchester Metropolitan University, Geoffrey Manton Building, Rosamond Street West, Manchester M15 6LL
☎0161 247 6142
Fax 0161 247 6979
e-mail: cerlim@mmu.ac.uk
url: www.cerlim.ac.uk
Director Prof Peter Brophy BSc HonFCLIP FCLIP FRSA ILTM
CERLIM undertakes research and consultancy in the library and information management field.

CHARTERED INSTITUTE OF LIBRARY AND INFORMATION PROFESSIONALS (CILIP)

Chartered Institute of Library and Information Professionals (CILIP), 7 Ridgmount Street, London WC1E 7AE
☎020 7255 0500
Fax 020 7255 0501
e-mail: info@cilip.org.uk
url: www.cilip.org.uk
Textphone 020 7255 0505
Chief Executive Bob McKee PhD MCLIP FRSA
CILIP (The Chartered Institute of Library and Information Professionals) is the leading professional body for librarians and information professionals in the UK, with members in all sectors, including business and industry, further and higher education, schools, central government departments and agencies, the health service, the voluntary sector and national and public libraries. CILIP is committed to enabling its members to achieve and maintain the highest professional standards, and encouraging them in the promotion of high-quality library and information services responsive to the needs of users.

CHARTERED INSTITUTE OF LIBRARY AND INFORMATION PROFESSIONALS IN SCOTLAND (CILIPS)

Chartered Institute of Library and Information Professionals in Scotland (CILIPS), First Floor, Building C, Brandon Gate, Leechlee Road, Hamilton, Lanarkshire ML3 6AU
☎(01698) 458888
Fax (01698) 283170
e-mail: cilips@slainte.org.uk
url: www.slainte.org
Director Ms Elaine Fulton BA MCLIP (e-mail: e.fulton@slainte.org.uk)
Assistant Directors Ms Rhona Arthur BA FCLIP, Ms Catherine Kearney BA MEd DipLib DipEdTech MCLIP

CILIPS is the professional body for librarians and information personnel, and represents personal members from all sectors – public, school, FE/HE libraries, and libraries/information services from both the voluntary and private sectors.

CHARTERED INSTITUTE OF LIBRARY AND INFORMATION PROFESSIONALS IRELAND (CILIP IRELAND)

Chartered Institute of Library and Information Professionals Ireland (CILIP Ireland), c/o Belfast Education and Library Board, 40 Academy Street, Belfast BT1 2NQ
☎028 9056 4011
url: www.cilip.org.uk/ireland
Executive Secretary Ms Elga Logue (e-mail: elgal@belb.co.uk)
The function of CILIP Ireland is to represent the interests of library staff across the sectors. It supports staff by providing access to expert advice on qualifications and continuing professional development. It identifies issues of concern to the profession, and where necessary provides intervention in the form of both advice and advocacy. CILIP Ireland works with relevant bodies such as LISC(NI) and the relevant departments of the Northern Ireland Assembly.

CHARTERED INSTITUTE OF LIBRARY AND INFORMATION PROFESSIONALS WALES (CILIP WALES)/SEFYDLIAD SIARTREDIG LLYFRGELLWYR A GWEITHWYR GWYBODAETH CYMRU (CILIP CYMRU)

Chartered Institute of Library and Information Professionals Wales (CILIP Wales)/Sefydliad Siartredig Llyfrgellwyr a Gweithwyr Gwybodaeth Cymru (CILIP Cymru), c/o Department of Information Studies, University of Wales Aberystwyth, Llanbadarn Fawr, Aberystwyth, Ceredigion SY23 3AS
☎(01970) 622174
Fax (01970) 622190
e-mail: scm@aber.ac.uk
url: www.dis.aber.ac.uk/cilip_w.index.htm
President Andrew Green MA DipLib MCLIP
Executive Officer Ms Sue Mace BA(Hons) DMS MCLIP MCMI
CILIP Wales promotes the professional development of individual members; seeks to influence the development of policies on the provision of information and library services at a local and national level; provides and disseminates information about/promoting library and information services in Wales.

AN CHOMHAIRLE LEABHARLANNA (THE LIBRARY COUNCIL)

An Chomhairle Leabharlanna (The Library Council), 53-54 Upper Mount Street, Dublin 2, Republic of Ireland

☎(00 353 1) 676 1167/676 1963
Fax (00 353 1) 676 6721
e-mail: info@librarycouncil.ie
url: www.librarycouncil.ie
Director Ms Norma McDermott
An Chomhairle Leabharlanna/The Library Council is the statutory agency that advises the Minister for the Environment, Heritage and Local Government and public library authorities in Ireland on public library development. An Chomhairle also promotes policies, strategies and activities that foster co-operation and partnership between library and information services and other relevant agencies in Ireland, with the United Kingdom and within Europe.

CIRCLE OF OFFICERS OF NATIONAL AND REGIONAL LIBRARY SYSTEMS *see* CONARLS

CITY INFORMATION GROUP (CIG)

City Information Group (CiG), PO Box 13297, London SW19 8GH
☎020 8543 7339
Fax 020 8543 7639
e-mail: admin@cityinformation.org.uk
url: www.cityinformation.org.uk
Chair 2004/5 Nick Collison
Administrator Ms Phillipa Mills
The aim of the City Information Group is to promote, develop and advance the practice of collecting, collating, evaluating and disseminating financial and business information and to foster and promote education and training in these matters. The effective management of business information is seen as a critical function within a wide range of organizations, both public and private, and CiG aims to help its members to work together to share ideas and promote the ethical and effective use of information and knowledge. CiG carries this out by offering a regular programme of seminars, debates and networking events. Anyone with an interest in business information can join the Group. Information is also distributed through a website and a quarterly newsletter.

CONARLS

(formerly Circle of Officers of National and Regional Library Systems)

CONARLS, c/o Kate Holliday, Library HQ, Yorkshire Libraries and Information, Balne Lane, Wakefield, Yorkshire WF2 0DQ
☎(01924) 302210
Fax (01924) 302245
url: www.thenortheast.com/conarls
Officer Ms Kate Holliday (e-mail: kholliday@wakefield.gov.uk)
CONARLS is a library sector co-operative concerned with the co-operation of strategic and operational affairs relating to the resource discovery and delivery of library and information collections in the UK and Ireland. Its website and e-list act as a conduit for dialogue on resource discovery.

CONSORTIUM OF RESEARCH LIBRARIES IN THE BRITISH ISLES (CURL)

Consortium of Research Libraries in the British Isles (CURL), Room 1211, 12th Floor, Muirhead Tower, University of Birmingham, Edgbaston, Birmingham B15 2TT
☎0121 415 8106
Fax 0121 415 8109
url: www.curl.ac.uk
Executive Director Robin Green
CURL's mission is to increase the ability of research libraries to share resources for the benefit of the local, national and international research community.

CONSTRUCTION INDUSTRY INFORMATION GROUP (CIIG)

CIIG (Construction Industry Information Group), (no postal address; please see website for contact details)
url: www.ciig.org.uk
Chair Mike Waring (e-mail: m.waring@maxfordham.com)
Vice-Chair Ms Vivienne Tregenza (e-mail: vivienne.tregenza@avup.com)
Secretary Clive Lacey (e-mail: clacey@estate.fco.gov.uk)
CIIG is an organization for professionals concerned with the provision, dissemination and use of information in the construction industry.

CONVENTION OF SCOTTISH LOCAL AUTHORITIES (COSLA)

Convention of Scottish Local Authorities (COSLA), Rosebery House, 9 Haymarket Terrace, Edinburgh EH12 5XZ
☎0131 474 9200
Fax 0131 474 9292
e-mail: enquiries@cosla.gov.uk
Chief Executive Rory Mair
President Pat Watters
COSLA is the representative voice of Scotland's unitary local authorities. Its main objectives are to promote the interests of its member councils and of local government; to liaise with the Scottish Parliament, Scottish Executive, UK Government, European institutions and appropriate partner organizations on issues of mutual interest; and to provide support for member councils in strengthening local democracy and raising awareness of and support for local government.

COUNCIL FOR LEARNING RESOURCES IN COLLEGES (COLRIC)

Council for Learning Resources in Colleges (CoLRiC), 122 Preston New Road, Blackburn, Lancashire BB2 6BU

☎(01254) 662923
Fax (01254) 610979
e-mail: colric@colric.org.uk
url: www.colric.org.uk
Executive Director Jeff Cooper MA FCLIP
CoLRiC is an independent organization dedicated to enhancing and maintaining the quality
of learning resources services in further education colleges throughout the United Kingdom
and Ireland.

CYMAL: MUSEUMS ARCHIVES AND LIBRARIES WALES

CyMAL: Museums Archives and Libraries Wales, Unit 10, The Science Park, Aberystwyth,
Ceredigion SY23 3AH
☎(01970) 610224
Fax (01970) 610223
e-mail: cymal@wales.gsi.gov.uk
url: www.cymal.wales.gov.uk
Director Ms Linda Tomos
CyMAL is a policy division of the Welsh Assembly Government established on 1 April 2004
to develop and implement policies for local museums, libraries and archives in Wales, and
to provide advice and support to the sector. An Advisory Council, chaired by the Minister
for Culture, Welsh Language and Sport, has also been established.

DEPARTMENT FOR CULTURE, MEDIA AND SPORT (LIBRARIES AND COMMUNITIES DIVISION) (DCMS)

Department for Culture, Media and Sport (Libraries and Communities Division) (DCMS),
2-4 Cockspur Street, London SW1Y 5DH
☎020 7211 6368
Fax 020 7211 6382
e-mail: libraries@culture.gov.uk
url: www.culture.gov.uk
Head of Libraries and Communities Ms Vanessa Brand (020 7211 6367; e-mail:
vanessa.brand@culture.gov.uk)
Acting Head of Libraries and Local Government Roger Stratton-Smith (020 7211
6481; e-mail: roger.stratton-smith@culture.gov.uk)
The Department for Culture, Media and Sport is the government department with overall
policy responsibility for the public library sector in England.

DEPARTMENT OF CULTURE, ARTS AND LEISURE (DCAL)

Interpoint, Department of Culture, Arts and Leisure (DCAL), 20-24 York Street, Belfast
BT15 1AQ

☎028 9025 8843
Fax 028 9025 8987
e-mail: dcalni@nics.gov.uk
url: www.dcalni.gov.uk
Director of Culture Division Colin Jack (e-mail: colin.jack@dcalni.gov.uk)
DCAL is responsible for the central administration of arts and culture, museums, libraries, sport and leisure visitor amenities, inland waterways and inland fisheries. It also has responsibility for Ordnance Survey, the Public Record Office, language policy, matters relating to National Lottery distribution, Millennium events and the Northern Ireland Events Company.

EAST MIDLANDS MUSEUMS, LIBRARIES AND ARCHIVES COUNCIL (EMMLAC)

East Midlands Museums, Libraries and Archives Council (EMMLAC), 56 King Street, Leicester LE1 6RL
☎0116 285 1350
Fax 0116 285 1351
e-mail: admin@emmlac.org.uk
url: www.emmlac.org.uk
Chief Executive Dr Tim Hobbs MA PhD DipLib MCLIP
Chair Ms Helen Forde DAA PhD FSA RMSA
EMMLAC's mission is to provide strategic leadership for museums, archives and libraries in the East Midlands so that they provide a better service to the public. Its aim, working in partnership with the region's domain-specific bodies, is to ensure that the region's museums, libraries and archives play a full role in the social, educational, cultural and economic life of the region.

EAST MIDLANDS REGIONAL LIBRARY SYSTEM (EMRLS) *see* LIBRARIES AND INFORMATION EAST MIDLANDS (LIEM)

EAST OF ENGLAND MUSEUMS, LIBRARIES AND ARCHIVES COUNCIL (EEMLAC)

East of England Museums, Libraries and Archives Council (EEMLAC), 110 Northgate Street, Northgate Business Park, Bury St Edmunds, Suffolk IP33 1HP
☎(01284) 723100
Fax (01284) 701394
e-mail: info@eemlac.org.uk
url: www.eemlac.org.uk
Chief Executive Terry Turner
Regional Development Officer – Libraries Ms Sue Hughes
EEMLAC is the regional agency for museum, library and archive activity in the East of England.

EDUCATIONAL PUBLISHERS COUNCIL (EPC)

(See also Publishers Association)

Educational Publishers Council (EPC), The Publishers Association, 29B Montague Street, London WCIB 5BW
☎020 7691 9191 (switchboard)
Fax 020 7691 9199
e-mail: mail@publishers.org.uk
url: www.publishers.org.uk
Director Graham Taylor
EPC is a trade association for school publishers.

EVIDENCE BASE

Evidence Base, University of Central England in Birmingham, 84 Aldridge Road, Birmingham B42 2SU
☎0121 331 7670
Fax 0121 331 5286
url: www.ebase.uce.ac.uk
Director Pete Dalton BA MA (e-mail: pete.dalton@uce.ac.uk)
Evidence Base undertakes research, consultancy and evaluation in the library and information management field.

ISNTO *see* LIFELONG LEARNING (UK) LTD

INTER-LIBRARY SERVICES – NATIONAL LIBRARY OF SCOTLAND (NLS-ILS)

Inter-Library Services – National Library of Scotland (NLS-ILS), Causewayside Building, 33 Salisbury Place, Edinburgh EH9 ISL
☎0131 466 3815 (direct), 0131 226 4531 ext 3329 (switchboard)
Fax 0131 466 3814
e-mail: ils@nls.uk
url: www.nls.uk; www.nls.uk/professional/interlibraryservices/index.html
Manager, Inter-Library Services Miss Patricia M A McKenzie BA MCLIP
The Inter-Library Services (ILS) Division of the National Library of Scotland operates as the Scottish centre for interlibrary loans and represents Scotland in the interlending community. It provides bibliographic verification and location search services, is responsible for the Scottish Union Catalogue and is, therefore, heavily involved with the UnityWeb database. Additionally, ILS has its own collection of c.150,000 titles which are available via interlibrary loan to libraries anywhere in the world. Electronic or postal document delivery is also available.

JIBS USER GROUP

JIBS User Group, c/o Systems & Electronic Resources Service, SERS Building, Oxford University Library Services, Osney Mead, Oxford OX2 0ES

☎(01865) 280033
Fax (01865) 204937
Chair Ms Frances Boyle (e-mail: fb@sers.ox.ac.uk)
The JIBS User Group is one of the major means of feedback for end-users of the UK's networked resources. It encompasses users and librarians in both the higher education (HE) and further education (FE) sector. JIBS originated as the user group for 'JIsc (assisted) Bibliographic dataserviceS' but now sees its remit as extending beyond bibliographic material to all electronic content of interest to HE and FE institutions available either via JISC's Information Environment (IE), or delivered independently by other sources.

JOINT INFORMATION SYSTEMS COMMITTEE (JISC)

Joint Information Systems Committee (JISC), Northavon House, Coldharbour Lane, Bristol BS16 1QD
☎0117 931 7256
Fax 0117 931 7255
url: www.jisc.ac.uk
Secretary Dr Malcolm Read (e-mail: m.read@jisc.ac.uk)
The Joint Information Systems Committee (JISC) promotes the innovative application and use of information systems and information technology in higher and further education across the UK.

THE LASER FOUNDATION

The Laser Foundation, c/o Martin House Farm, Hilltop Lane, Whittle-le-Woods, near Chorley, Lancs PR6 7QR
☎(01257) 274833
Fax (01257) 266488
url: www.bl.uk/concord/laser-about.html
Company Secretary Ms Frances Hendrix (e-mail: frances@laserfoundation.org.uk)
The Laser Foundation was created from the transfer of the LASER (London and Southeastern Library Region) into a grant making trust, continuing the ethos and focus of LASER in its grant making policies. The Foundation awards grants primarily for project proposals that take a focused, planned approach at making a real difference to the public library landscape. The overall objective in funding is to assist end users of public libraries in co-operative ways.

LIBRARIES AND INFORMATION EAST MIDLANDS (LIEM)

(formerly East Midlands Regional Library System (EMRLS))

Libraries and Information East Midlands (LIEM), c/o Lynn Hodgkins, Alfreton Library, Severn Square, Alfreton, Derbyshire DE55 7BQ
☎(01773) 835064
Fax (01773) 831359

e-mail: liem@derbyshire.gov.uk
url: www.liem.org.uk
Regional Librarian Ms Lynn Hodgkins BA(Hons) MCLIP (e-mail:
lynn.hodgkins@derbyshire.gov.uk)
Acting Chair Roy Knight BA MCLIP
Libraries and Information East Midlands is the strategic body for libraries across all sectors
in the region. LIEM is funded entirely by membership subscriptions and its members
include all the public and university libraries together with many of the further education
and special libraries in the East Midlands. LIEM acts as an advocate for libraries on policy
and strategic issues, and promotes awareness of libraries' role in the educational, cultural,
social and economic vitality of the region. It continues to encourage and support regional
co-operation and partnership working related to resource sharing.

LIBRARIES NORTH WEST (LNW)

Libraries North West (LNW), University College Chester, Parkgate Road, Chester CH1 4BJ
☎(01244) 220362 (direct line)
Fax (01244) 370927
e-mail: lnw.contactus@chester.ac.uk (Chester Office); lnw@lancscc.gov.uk (Interlibrary
Loans Business Unit)
url: www.lnw.org.uk
Executive Officer Ms Sue Valentine BA(Hons) MCLIP FRSA
LNW represents the interests of all libraries based in the North West of England. We work
closely with a range of organizations to provide a strategic voice at regional and national
level. Our vision is "to bring together all groups within the library domain in the North
West to provide a strategic lead through the formulation of plans, policies, representations
and expressions of view". Our members enjoy the benefits of an organization specifically
created to meet their needs through a range of activities such as advocacy, resource
sharing, interlending and other services.

LIBRARY AND INFORMATION SERVICES COUNCIL (LISC(NI))

Library and Information Services Council (LISC(NI)), PO Box 1231, Belfast BT8 6AL
☎028 9070 5441
Fax 028 9040 1180
url: www.liscni.co.uk
Executive Officer Ms Mairead Gilheany (e-mail: mairead@liscni.co.uk)
LISC(NI)'s mission is to enhance the standard of library and information services by
providing advice to the Department of Culture, Arts and Leisure (NI) and other
government departments, providing a voice for the sector and acting as a catalyst for
progress and development in all areas of provison.

LIBRARY ASSOCIATION OF IRELAND (CUMANN LEABHARLANN NA HÉIREANN)

Library Association of Ireland (Cumann Leabharlann na hÉireann), 53 Upper Mount Street,

Dublin 2, Republic of Ireland
☎(00 353 21) 454 6499
url: www.libraryassociation.ie
President Ms Ruth Flanagan BA DipLib ALAI (e-mail: president@libraryassociation.ie)
Hon. Secretary Denis Murphy BA DLIS (e-mail: honsec@libraryassociation.ie)
The Library Association of Ireland is the professional body in Ireland for those engaged in
librarianship and information management. It encourages professional training for library
staff and acts as an educational and examining body whose fellowship diploma is a
recognized qualification in librarianship.

THE LIBRARY CAMPAIGN

The Library Campaign, 22 Upper Woburn Place, London WC1H 0TB
☎0870 770 7946
Fax 0870 770 7947
e-mail: librarycam@aol.com
url: www.librarycampaign.com
Director Vacant
National Secretary Andrew Coburn (01245 356210)
The Library Campaign is a registered charity (no. 1102634) and is the UK organization
representing and co-ordinating friends and user support groups for libraries of all kinds.

LIFELONG LEARNING (UK) LTD

(formerly ISNTO)

Lifelong Learning (UK) Ltd, Suite 303, Parkgate House, Parkgate, Bradford BD1 5BS
☎(01274) 391773
Fax (01274) 391828
url: www.lifelonglearninguk.org
Regional and Constituency Support and Development Officer Ms Alix Craven
(e-mail: alix@isnto.org.uk)
The Sector Skills Council for Community Learning and Development, Further Education,
Higher Education, Libraries, Archives and Information Services and Work-based Learning.

LISU

LISU, Research School of Informatics, Holywell Park, Loughborough University,
Loughborough, Leics LE11 3TU
☎(01509) 635680
Fax (01509) 635699
e-mail: lisu@lboro.ac.uk
url: www.lboro.ac.uk/departments/dis/lisu
Director Dr J Eric Davies MA PhD FCLIP MCMI FRSA (e-mail: j.e.davies@lboro.ac.uk)
LISU is a national research and information centre focusing on the analysis, interpretation,
development and dissemination of statistics performance assessment measures and related
management data to contribute to good management practice in the information economy
and cultural services.

LOCAL GOVERNMENT ASSOCIATION (LGA)

Local Government Association (LGA), Local Government House, Smith Square,
Westminster, London SW1P 3HZ
☎020 7664 3131
Fax 020 7664 3030 (switchboard); 020 7664 3131 (information helpline)
url: www.lga.gov.uk
Team Leader, Information Services Nick Georgiou (e-mail: nick.georgiou@lga.gov.uk)
The LGA's mission is to promote better local government. It works with and for its
member authorities to realize a shared vision of local government that enables local people
to shape a distinctive and better future for their locality and its communities.

LONDON LIBRARIES DEVELOPMENT AGENCY (LLDA)

London Libraries Development Agency (LLDA), 35 St Martin's Street, London WC2H 7HP
☎020 7641 5266 (tel/fax)
url: www.llda.org.uk
Director Michael Clarke (e-mail: michael.clarke@llda.org.uk)
Office Administrator Vacant
Development Manager Ms Fiona O'Brien (e-mail: fiona.o'brien@llda.org.uk)
The LLDA has been created to develop and realise a co-ordinated strategic vision for all
library and information services across London.

MLA WEST MIDLANDS: THE REGIONAL COUNCIL FOR MUSEUMS, LIBRARIES AND ARCHIVES

MLA West Midlands: the Regional Council for Museums, Libraries and Archives, 2nd Floor,
Grosvenor House, 14 Bennetts Hill, Birmingham B2 5RS
☎0121 631 5800
Fax 0121 631 5825
e-mail: info@mlawestmidlands.org.uk
url: www.mlawestmidlands.org.uk
Chief Executive Kathryn O P Gee

MUSEUMS ASSOCIATION (MA)

Museums Association (MA), 24 Calvin Street, London E1 6NW
☎020 7426 6970
Fax 020 7426 6961
e-mail: info@museumsassociation.org
url: www.museumsassociation.org
Director Mark Taylor

The Museums Association is the professional membership body for anyone involved in museums, galleries and related organizations.

MUSEUMS, LIBRARIES AND ARCHIVES COUNCIL (MLA)

Museums, Libraries and Archives Council (MLA), 16 Queen Anne's Gate, London SW1H 9AA
☎020 7273 1444
Fax 020 7273 1404
e-mail: info@mla.gov.uk
url: www.mla.gov.uk
Chief Executive Chris Batt OBE HonFCLIP BA FCLIP
Media & Events Manager Ms Emma Wright (e-mail: emma.wright@mla.gov.uk)
The Museums, Libraries and Archives Council is a strategic agency working with and on behalf of museums, archives and libraries. It replaced the Museums and Galleries Commission and the Library and Information Commission in April 2000. MLA has three main objectives: to provide strategy, advocacy and advice. The organization undertakes work in all three of these areas to improve the context in which museums, archives and libraries operate and to improve services for users and potential users.

MUSEUMS, LIBRARIES AND ARCHIVES NORTH WEST (MLA NORTH WEST)

(formerly North West Museums, Libraries and Archives Council (NWMLAC))

Museums, Libraries and Archives North West (MLA North West), Ground Floor, The Malt Building, Wilderspool Park, Greenalls Avenue, Warrington, Cheshire WA4 6HL
☎(01925) 625050
Fax (01925) 243453
e-mail: info@mlanorthwest.org.uk
url: www.mlanorthwest.org.uk
Chief Executive Ms Clare Connor BA PGDipLIS MCLIP MILT
MLA North West is the regional strategic development agency for the museums, libraries and archives sector in the North West of England, working to promote and develop the social, cultural and economic potential of the sector, and its contribution to learning, inclusion and social cohesion.

NATIONAL ACQUISITIONS GROUP (NAG)

National Acquisitions Group (NAG), 12 Holm Oak Drive, Madeley, Crewe, Cheshire CW3 9HR
☎(01782) 750462 (tel/fax)
e-mail: nag@btconnect.com
url: www.nag.org.uk
Administrator Ms Diane Roberts BA(Hons) MRes
Chair Ms Jo Grocott BA MCLIP

NAG's mission is to recruit and unite members in common discussion of acquisitions policies and practices, and to promote knowledge and understanding of technological developments in publishing, bookselling and library and information work, and their use in acquisitions.

NATIONAL FORUM FOR INFORMATION PLANNING (NFIP)

National Forum for Information Planning (NFIP), School of Information Systems, Kingston University, Kingston upon Thames, Surrey KT1 2EE
☎020 8547 2000
url: www.bl.uk/concord/linc/nfip.html
Chair John Lindsay (e-mail: lindsay@kingston.ac.uk)
The National Forum for Information Planning (NFIP) is a forum for organizations involved in the practical implementation of information planning in the United Kingdom and Republic of Ireland. It promotes the Library and Information Plan (LIP) concept: intra-sectoral, cross-sectoral and cross-domain library and information planning on a geographical or subject basis at local, regional and national levels. It provides exchange of experience, advice and support, and is an active contributor to the policy debate on the development of a national information plan.

NATIONAL LITERACY TRUST

National Literacy Trust, Swire House, 59 Buckingham Gate, London SW1E 6AJ
☎020 7828 2435
Fax 020 7931 9986
e-mail: contact@literacytrust.org.uk
url: www.literacytrust.org.uk; www.rif.org.uk; www.readon.org.uk
Director Neil McClelland
The National Literacy Trust aims to make an independent, strategic contribution to the creation of a society in which all enjoy the skills, confidence and pleasures of literacy to support their educational, economical, social and cultural goals. The Trust incorporates Reading is Fundamental, UK and runs the National Reading Campaign.

NORTH EAST MUSEUMS, LIBRARIES AND ARCHIVES COUNCIL (NEMLAC)

North East Museums, Libraries and Archives Council (NEMLAC), House of Recovery, Bath Lane, Newcastle upon Tyne NE4 5SQ
☎0191 222 1661
Fax 0191 261 4725
e-mail: nemlac@nemlac.co.uk
url: www.nemlac.co.uk
Chief Executive Ms Sue Underwood MA FMA

The North East Museums, Libraries and Archives Council (NEMLAC) is the regional development agency for museums, libraries and archives in North East England. NEMLAC will facilitate the sector's development across the region through strategic leadership, advocacy, advice, exemplar projects and service delivery.

NORTH WEST MUSEUMS, LIBRARIES AND ARCHIVES COUNCIL (NWMLAC) *see* MUSEUMS, LIBRARIES AND ARCHIVES NORTH WEST (MLA NORTH WEST)

PIPA (PHARMACEUTICAL INFORMATION & PHARMACOVIGILANCE ASSOCIATION)

PIPA (Pharmaceutical Information & Pharmacovigilance Association), PO Box 254, Haslemere, Surrey GU27 9AF
e-mail: pipa@pipaonline.org
URL: www.pipaonline.org
Administrator Mrs Sharon Braithwaite (administrator@pipaonline.org)
President: president@pipaonline.org
PIPA is the professional organization for individuals in the pharmaceutical industry involved in the provision and management of information and those involved in the fulfillment of regulatory requirements relating to drug safety. The Association was formed in 1974 and was previously known as AIOPI (Association of Information Officers in the Pharmaceutical Industry). PIPA exists to support and assist its members in the development of their professional skills and responsibilities.

PUBLIC LENDING RIGHT (PLR)

Public Lending Right (PLR), PLR Office, Richard House, Sorbonne Close, Stockton-on-Tees TS17 6DA
☎(01642) 604699
Fax (01642) 615641
url: www.plr.uk.com
Registrar Dr Jim Parker (e-mail: jim.parker@plr.uk.com)
PLR is a statutory scheme which makes payments to authors for the free lending of their books by public libraries in the UK.

THE PUBLISHERS ASSOCIATION
Academic and Professional Division, The Publishers Association, 29B Montague Street, London WC1B 5BW
☎020 7691 9191
Fax 020 7691 9199
e-mail: mail@publishers.org.uk
url: www.publishers.org.uk
Director of Educational, Academic and Professional Publishing Graham Taylor

THE READING AGENCY

The Reading Agency, PO Box 96, St Albans, Hertfordshire AL1 3WP
url: www.readingagency.org.uk
Director Ms Miranda McKearney
Head of Resources Ms Penny Shapland (e-mail: penny.shapland@readingagency.org.uk)
Head of Programme Support Ms Elizabeth Dubber BA MCLIP (e-mail:
liz.dubber@readingagency.org.uk)
The Reading Agency is the development agency for libraries' work with readers, revenue
funded by Arts Council England and CILIP. TRA works in new ways with both adult and
young people's librarians to inspire a reading nation.

READING IS FUNDAMENTAL, UK

Reading Is Fundamental, UK, Swire House, 59 Buckingham Gate, London SW1E 6AJ
☎020 7828 2435
Fax 020 7931 9986
e-mail: rif@literacytrust.org.uk
url: www.rif.org.uk
Director Ms Lis Coulthard
Reading Is Fundamental, UK, is an initiative of the National Literacy Trust that motivates
children and young people aged 0 to 19 to read. Working with volunteers, it delivers
literacy projects that promote the fun of reading, the importance of book choice and the
benefits to families of having books in the home.

RECORDS MANAGEMENT SOCIETY OF GREAT BRITAIN (RMS)

Records Management Society of Great Britain (RMS), Woodside, Coleheath Bottom,
Speen, Princes Risborough, Bucks HP27 0SZ
☎(01494) 488566
Fax (01494) 488590
e-mail: info@rms-gb.org.uk
url: www.rms-gb.org.uk
Administration Secretary Jude Awdry
Chair Dr Paul Duller
Records management is the system(s) by which an organization seeks to control the
creation, distribution, filing, retrieval, storage and disposal of those records, regardless of
media, which are created or received by that organization in the course of its business.
Membership is open to all regardless of status, from students to corporate entities.

THE SCHOOL LIBRARY ASSOCIATION (SLA)

The School Library Association (SLA), Unit 2, Lotmead Business Village, Lotmead Farm,
Wanborough, Swindon SN4 0UY
☎(01793) 791787
Fax (01793) 791786

e-mail: info@SLA.org.uk
url: www.SLA.org.uk
Chief Executive Ms Kathy Lemaire BA DipLib MCLIP FRSA
The SLA believes that every student is entitled to effective school library provision. It is
committed to supporting everyone involved in school libraries, promoting high-quality
learning and development opportunities for all, and provides advice, training, publications
and a quarterly journal, *The School Librarian*.

SCOTTISH BOOK TRUST

Scottish Book Trust, Sandeman House, Trunks Close, 55 High Street, Edinburgh EH1 1SR
☎0131 524 0160
Fax 0131 524 0161
e-mail: info@scottishbooktrust.com
url: www.scottishbooktrust.com
Chief Executive Marc Lambert
Scottish Book Trust promotes reading literacy and reading confidence through outreach,
publications and information provision. SBT operates the Live Literature Scotland Scheme.

SCOTTISH EXECUTIVE EDUCATION DEPARTMENT

Scottish Executive Education Department, Victoria Quay, Edinburgh EH6 6QQ
☎0131 244 4011
Fax 0131 244 0353
Head of Arts and Creative Industries Policy Unit Ms Ewa Hibbert
The Scottish Executive Education Department is responsible for sponsorship of the
National Library of Scotland and development of policy on libraries in Scotland.

SCOTTISH LIBRARY AND INFORMATION COUNCIL (SLIC)

Scottish Library and Information Council (SLIC), 1st Floor, Building C, Brandon Gate,
Brandon Street, Hamilton, Lanarkshire ML3 6AU
☎(01698) 458888
Fax (01698) 283170
e-mail: slic@slainte.org.uk
url: www.slainte.org.uk
Director Ms Elaine Fulton BA MCLIP (e-mail: e.fulton@slainte.org.uk)
Assistant Directors Ms Rhona Arthur BA FCLIP, Ms Catherine Kearney BA MEd DipLib
DipEdTech MCLIP
SLIC is an independent body that promotes the development of library and information
services in Scotland. It advises Scottish Ministers, the Scottish Parliament and the Executive
on library and information matters, provides support to library and information services
and facilitates the co-ordination of services.

SHARE THE VISION (STV)

c/o National Library for the Blind, Share the Vision (STV), Far Cromwell Road, Bredbury,
Stockport SK6 2SG
☎0161 355 2079
Fax 0161 355 2098
e-mail: sharethevision@nlbuk.org
url: www.nlb-online.org
Executive Director David Owen OBE BA DipLib MCLIP
Established in 1989, STV is a partnership of the main voluntary sector and publicly-funded
library bodies which aims to enhance lis for visually impaired people via greater
co-operation and co-ordination of service delivery and campaigning services.

SINTO (THE INFORMATION PARTNERSHIP FOR SOUTH YORKSHIRE AND NORTH DERBYSHIRE)

SINTO (the Information Partnership for South Yorkshire and North Derbyshire), Learning
Centre, Sheffield Hallam University, Collegiate Crescent, Sheffield S10 2BP
☎0114 225 5739/40
Fax 0114 225 2476
e-mail: sinto@shu.ac.uk
url: www.sinto.org.uk
Director Carl Clayton BA MCLIP DMS
Assistant Ms Gilly Pearce
SINTO's mission is to promote library and information services in South Yorkshire and
North Derbyshire through co-operation and partnership.

SOCIETY OF ARCHIVISTS

Society of Archivists, Prioryfield House, 20 Canon Street, Taunton, Somerset TA1 1SW
☎(01823) 327030
Fax (01823) 271719
e-mail: societyofarchivists@archives.org.uk
url: www.archives.org.uk
Executive Secretary Patrick Cleary
The principal aims of the Society are achieved both through the work of the Society's
Council and its various committees, groups and regions, and by its position as spokesman
for the profession, submitting evidence and comment on matters of professional concern
to any official body which seeks advice or whose activities affect archives.

SOCIETY OF CHIEF LIBRARIANS (SCL)

Society of Chief Librarians (SCL), c/o Mrs Alison Bramley, Shade House, Fradley Junction,
Alrewas, Burton-on-Trent, Staffs DE13 7DN
url: www.goscl.com
SCL Development Officer Mrs Alison Bramley (e-mail: alison.bramley@virgin.net)
SCL aims to take a leading role in the development of public libraries by influencing

statutory, financial and other decisions. The association represents the views of its member to the Department of Culture, Media and Sport (DCMS), the Welsh Assembly Government, Members of Parliament, MLA (the Museums, Libraries and Archives Council), the Advisory Council on Libraries (ACL), CILIP (the Chartered Institute of Library and Information Professionals), the Local Government Association, the Audit Commission and other government departments and bodies.

SOCIETY OF COLLEGE, NATIONAL AND UNIVERSITY LIBRARIES (SCONUL)

Society of College, National and University Libraries (SCONUL), 102 Euston Street, London NW1 2HA
☎020 7387 0317
Fax 020 7383 3197
url: www.sconul.ac.uk
Secretary A J C Bainton
SCONUL works to improve the quality and extend the influence of UK higher education libraries, of Irish university libraries, and of the national libraries of the UK and Ireland. Through its expert groups, SCONUL seeks to develop and promote policy at a national and international level. SCONUL's advisory groups also disseminate good practice and shared knowledge to strengthen the roles of senior library management.

SOCIETY OF INDEXERS

Society of Indexers, Blades Enterprise Centre, John Street, Sheffield S2 4SU
☎0114 292 2350
Fax 0114 292 2351
e-mail: admin@indexers.org.uk
url: www.indexers.org.uk
Administrator Ms Wendy Burrow
Secretary Ms Ann Kingdom
The Society of Indexers is a non-profit organization, membership of which is open to any person who is, or intends to be, directly involved in indexing. Its formal objectives include promotion of standards and instruction on techniques for all forms of indexing, the training and continuing education of indexers, and publishing guidance, information and ideas about indexing.

SOUTH EAST MUSEUM, LIBRARY AND ARCHIVE COUNCIL (SEMLAC)

South East Museum, Library and Archive Council (SEMLAC), 15 City Business Centre, Hyde Street, Winchester, Hants SO23 7TA
☎(01962) 858844
Fax (01962) 878439
e-mail: info@semlac.org.uk
url: www.semlac.org.uk
Chief Executive Helen Jackson

SEMLAC is the regional development agency for museum, library and archive activity in the South East of England.

SOUTH WEST MUSEUMS, LIBRARIES AND ARCHIVES COUNCIL (SWMLAC)

South West Museums, Libraries and Archives Council (SWMLAC), Creech Castle, Bathpool, Taunton, Somerset TA1 2DX
☎(01823) 259696
Fax (01823) 270933
e-mail: general@swmlac.org.uk
url: www.swmlac.org.uk
Chief Executive Bob Sharpe
Library and Information Development Officer Ms Angela D Haynes BA DipLib PGDip
(e-mail: angelahaynes@swmlac.org.uk)
SWMLAC aims to maximize the value that museums, libraries and archives add to the social, cultural, educational and economic well-being of the South West.

SOUTH WESTERN REGIONAL LIBRARY SYSTEM (SWRLS)

South Western Regional Library System (SWRLS), Operational Interlending Business Unit, Central Library, College Green, Bristol BS1 5TL
☎0117 927 3962
Fax 0117 923 0216
e-mail: swrls@swrls.org.uk
url: www.swrls.org.uk
SWRLS Librarian Alex Ball (e-mail: librarian@swrls.org.uk)
SWRLS Chair Rob N Froud BLib DMS MIMgt FCLIP (e-mail: rnfroud@somerset.gov.uk)
(Head of Cultural Services, Somerset County Council: refer to for strategic issues)
SWRLS is a co-operative of member libraries set up to promote co-operation and facilitate interlending.

SPRIG – PROMOTING INFORMATION IN LEISURE, TOURISM AND SPORT

SPRIG – Promoting Information in Leisure, Tourism and Sport, c/o Central Library, Chamberlain Square, Birmingham B3 3HQ
☎0121 303 4220
url: www.sprig.org.uk
Secretary Peter Drake (e-mail: secretary@sprig.org.uk)
Publicity Officer Vacant
Chair Martin Scarrott BA DipLib MCLIP ILTM
SPRIG promotes information sources in leisure, tourism, sport, recreation and hospitality management. It aims to: act as a special interest group for information managers; disseminate information to users; lobby information providers – such as government

organizations – for better provision; and improve awareness of information sources to those outside the library and information profession.

THEATRE INFORMATION GROUP (TIG)

Theatre Information Group (TIG), c/o Claire Hudson, Theatre Museum, 1E Tavistock Street, London WC2E 7PR
☎020 7943 4720
Secretary John Collis (e-mail: john@bruford.ac.uk)
The Theatre Information Group is a support organization for libraries, archives, museums and other bodies dealing with performing arts information and collections.

UK LIBRARIES PLUS

UK Libraries Plus, c/o Information Services, Learning Resources Centre, Roehampton University, Roehampton Lane, London SW15 5SZ
☎020 8392 3454
Fax 020 8392 3026
url: www.uklibrariesplus.ac.uk
Convenor Adam Edwards BA MSc MCLIP (e-mail: adam.edwards@roehampton.ac.uk)
UK Libraries Plus is a reciprocal access and borrowing scheme linking the majority of UK higher education libraries. Borrowing membership is open to all part-time, distance learning and full-time placement students and offers reference access to all other users of the member libraries.

UK SERIALS GROUP (UKSG)

UK Serials Group (UKSG), Hilltop, Heath End, Newbury, Berks RG20 0AP
☎(01635) 254292
Fax (01635) 253826
url: www.uksg.org
Chair Keith Courtney
Business Manager Ms Alison Whitehorn (e-mail: alison@uksg.org)
The UKSG exists to encourage the exchange and promotion of ideas on printed and electronic serials and the process of scholarly communication. The organization aims to increase professional awareness, to stimulate research and to provide a training and education programme, bringing together all parties in the serials information chain.

UKOLN

UKOLN, Library, University of Bath, Bath BA2 7AY
☎(01225) 386250
Fax (01225) 386838
e-mail: ukoln@ukoln.ac.uk
url: www.ukoln.ac.uk
Director Dr Elizabeth Lyon
A centre of expertise in digital information management, providing advice and services to the library, information, education and cultural heritage communities.

YORKSHIRE LIBRARIES AND INFORMATION (YLI)

Yorkshire Libraries and Information (YLI), Library HQ, Balne Lane, Wakefield, West Yorks WF2 0DQ
☎(01924) 302210
Fax (01924) 302245
e-mail: lib.admin@wakefield.gov.uk
url: www.yli.org.uk
Manager Ms Kate Holliday (e-mail: kholliday@wakefield.gov.uk)
YLI is the regional library system for Yorkshire and Humber.

YORKSHIRE MUSEUMS, LIBRARIES AND ARCHIVES COUNCIL (YMLAC)

Yorkshire Museums, Libraries and Archives Council (YMLAC), Farnley Hall, Hall Lane, Leeds LS12 5HA
☎0113 263 8909
Fax 0113 279 1479
e-mail: info@ymlac.org.uk
url: www.ymlac.org.uk
Chief Executive Ms Annie Mauger MCLIP MBA
Regional Libraries Adviser Ms Liz Roberts MA BA
Director (Learning, Access & Skills) Ms Jane Walton MEd MCLIP FCIPD
YMLAC is the regional agency for museum, library and archive activity in Yorkshire.

The Regions of England

The nine Regional Agencies of the Museums, Libraries and Archives Council (MLA) are listed in the Key Agencies section under the headings:

- East of England Museums, Libraries and Archives Council (EEMLAC)
- East Midlands Museums, Libraries and Archives Council (EMMLAC)
- ALM London (Archives, Libraries and Museums London)
- North East Museums, Libraries and Archives Council (NEMLAC)
- Museums, Libraries and Archives North West (MLA North West)
- South East Museum, Library and Archive Council (SEMLAC)
- South West Museums, Libraries and Archives Council (SWMLAC)
- MLA West Midlands: the Regional Council for Museums, Libraries and Archives
- Yorkshire Museums, Libraries and Archives Council (YMLAC)

Public library authorities are arranged within the nine Government regions in England. (Upper Norwood Joint Library is included. This is not a public library authority but a service jointly managed by the London Boroughs of Croydon and Lambeth. However it has a separate entry). Full entries for these public library authorities will be found in the English sections of both the Public Libraries and Children's, Youth and Schools Library Services categories.

East
Bedfordshire
Cambridgeshire
Essex
Hertfordshire
Luton
Norfolk
Peterborough
Southend on Sea
Suffolk
Thurrock

East Midlands
Derby
Derbyshire
Leicester
Leicestershire
Lincolnshire
Northamptonshire
Nottingham
Nottinghamshire
Rutland

London
Barking and Dagenham
Barnet
Bexley
Brent
Bromley
Camden
City of London
Croydon
Ealing
Enfield
Greenwich
Hackney
Hammersmith and Fulham
Haringey
Harrow
Havering
Hillingdon
Hounslow

Islington
Kensington and Chelsea
Kingston upon Thames
Lambeth
Lewisham
Merton
Newham
Redbridge
Richmond upon Thames
Southwark
Sutton
Tower Hamlets
Upper Norwood Joint Library
Waltham Forest
Wandsworth
Westminster

North East
Darlington
Durham
Gateshead
Hartlepool
Middlesbrough
Newcastle upon Tyne
North Tyneside
Northumberland
Redcar and Cleveland
South Tyneside
Stockton-on-Tees
Sunderland

North West and Merseyside
Blackburn with Darwen
Blackpool
Bolton
Bury
Cheshire
Cumbria
Halton
Knowsley
Lancashire
Liverpool
Manchester

Oldham
Rochdale
St Helens
Salford
Sefton
Stockport
Tameside
Trafford
Warrington
Wigan
Wirral

South East

Bracknell Forest
Brighton and Hove
Buckinghamshire
East Sussex
Hampshire
Isle of Wight
Kent
Medway
Milton Keynes
Oxfordshire
Portsmouth
Reading
Slough
Southampton
Surrey
West Berkshire
West Sussex
Windsor and Maidenhead
Wokingham

South West

Bath and North East Somerset
Bournemouth
Bristol
Cornwall
Devon
Dorset
Gloucestershire
North Somerset

Plymouth
Poole
Somerset
South Gloucestershire
Swindon
Torbay
Wiltshire

West Midlands

Birmingham
Coventry
Dudley
Herefordshire
Sandwell
Shropshire
Solihull
Staffordshire
Stoke-on-Trent
Telford and Wrekin
Walsall
Warwickshire
Wolverhampton
Worcestershire

Yorkshire and The Humber

Barnsley
Bradford
Calderdale
Doncaster
East Riding of Yorkshire
Kingston upon Hull
Kirklees
Leeds
North East Lincolnshire
North Lincolnshire
North Yorkshire
Rotherham
Sheffield
Wakefield
York

Name and place index

All page numbers from 3 to 202 refer to public libraries or public library authorities; page numbers from 275 to 471 refer to academic institutions and special libraries. Pages 475 to 500 refer to key library agencies. Numbers in italic relate to the Children's, Youth and Schools Library Services sections (pages 205–272)